# Supply Chain Management

## TEXT AND CASES

SECOND EDITION

# Supply Chain Management

## TEXT AND CASES

### SECOND EDITION

**Janat Shah**

*Indian Institute of Management Udaipur*

*Associate Editor—Acquisitions*: Varun Goenka
*Senior Editor—Production*: C. Purushothaman



ISBN 978-93-325-4820-6

First Impression, 2016

Eighth Impression, 2022

**Ninth Impression, 2023**

Published by Pearson India Education Services Pvt. Ltd, CIN: U72200TN2005PTC057128

**Head Office:** 1st Floor, Berger Tower, Plot No. C-001A/2, Sector 16B,
Noida – 201 301,Uttar Pradesh, India.
**Registered Office:** 7th Floor, SDB2, ODC 7, 8 & 9, Survey No.01 ELCOT IT/ ITES SEZ,
Sholinganallur, Chennai – 600119, Tamil Nadu, India.
Website: in.pearson.com, Email: companysecretary.india@pearson.com

*Compositor*: Cameo Corporate Services, Coimbatore.
*Printed in India* at Saurabh Printers Pvt. Ltd.

*To*
*my parents,*
*Ghanshyambhai and Padmaben,*
*my wife,*
*Seema,*
*my daughter,*
*Riddhi,*
*and*
*her cousins,*
*Medha, Stuti, Niket, Rishwa and Yashwi*

# ABOUT THE AUTHOR

Janat Shah, a mechanical engineer from the Indian Institute of Technology Mumbai, held several middle- and senior-management positions before returning to academia in 1989. A Fellow in Management from the Indian Institute of Management Ahmedabad, Professor Shah has worked for a short duration at the Institute of Rural Management, Anand, before moving to the Indian Institute of Management Bangalore as Assistant Professor in 1991. As visiting scholar at the Sloan School of Management, MIT, in 1997, he has worked on areas related to supply chain management. He was also a visiting faculty at the Logistics Institute, National University of Singapore in 2001.

Currently, Janat Shah is a professor of operations management at the Indian Institute of Management Udaipur, and holds the position of Honorary Professor at the Nottingham University Business School in the operations management division.

Professor Shah conducts management education programmes for executives in a number of companies, and offers consultancy services in the area of design and development of decision-support systems for supply chain management. He is a consultant to companies such as Tata Chemicals Limited, Mahindra & Mahindra, Infosys, Marico, Tata Teleservices, IBM, Aditya Birla Group, Yokogawa Blue Star Limited, and Ingersoll Rand. He has edited two volumes, *Logistics and Global Outsourcing* (2004) and *Operational Research in the Indian Steel Industry* (1993), besides contributing chapters to numerous books on supply chain management. In addition, he is also on the editorial board of international journals such as *International Journal of Procurement Management*, *International Journal of Product Lifecycle Management* and *International Journal of Logistics: Research and Applications*, and has refereed diverse journal articles and proceedings.

Professor Shah, voted the best teacher by the MBA class of 1999, has won numerous teaching awards. Significant among them is the IBM faculty award that was awarded to Professor Shah and his team for two successive years, 2005 and 2006, for their work on human resource supply chain management.

His research interests lie in the fields of supply chain management, and design of manufacturing systems.

# CONTENTS

# PREFACE

I have benefited from many suggestions from students, colleagues, and senior supply chain executives from industry on my first edition. Based on the received comments as well as from my experience in using my text, I have made several changes in this edition.

The most significant change from the previous edition is the addition of two chapters. Chapter 11 is about supply chain contracts. Supply chain contract is emerging as a valuable instrument to coordinate various supply chains. Few popular contracts such as buyback contracts and revenue sharing contracts are discussed in depth. The other new chapter is Chapter 14. It deals with emerging field of sustainable supply chain management. Sustainable supply chain encompasses economic development, environment performance, and social betterment. Apart from focusing on managing relevant trade-offs, the chapter also deals with issues related to reverse supply chains.

Significant changes have been made in Chapter 1 while dealing supply chain evolution. Discussion about third revolution has been strengthened using recent examples from Apple and Airtel. Chapter 4 has been reorganized and discussion on periodic review model has been moved from appendix to main chapter. Section on e-retailing has been focussed in detail in Chapter 6. Chapter 8 dealing with IT has been updated with recent advances in technologies.

A few new cases have been added in Part V, and for two cases Kurlon and Subhiksha, recent updates have been captured as Case (b).

## PREFACE FOR 1ST EDITION

Supply Chain Management: Text and Cases presents a comprehensive, yet structured, view of logistics and supply chain management, with a focus on supply chain innovations for firms operating in competitive markets.

This book evolved from a supply chain management course that I have been teaching at the Indian Institute of Management Bangalore since 1998. When I first offered this course, the discipline of supply chain management was still in its infancy, leaving me to draw on my experiences with various Indian industries. Between then and now, however, many good books on supply chain management have been published, which brings us to an important question.

### Why Another Book on Supply Chain Management?

As globalization and technological innovation continue to etch new contours on the landscape of business, supply chain management continues to evolve. In such a dynamic scenario, this book places equal weight on state-of-the-art know-how in supply chain management as it does on the fundamentals.

Moreover, while it is important for Indian companies to learn from the West, even tried-and-tested solutions may not always be applicable to Indian firms. Issues such as poor infrastructure, large numbers of customers at the base of the economic pyramid and complex distribution and taxation structures require solutions specific to the Indian context. This book addresses these issues by blending the best global supply chain practices with an in-depth knowledge of the Indian environment, encouraging practitioners and readers to innovate. Numerous real-life examples of firms that have successfully evolved their supply chain management strategies help the reader relate to the theory presented and make learning easier.

Throughout the book, while presenting mathematical models, every possible attempt has been made to foster in the reader an intuitive feel for the concepts described. This approach is intended to benefit those students who are intimidated by the use of mathematics. The final material presented in the book has been thoroughly tested at executive MBA programmes as well as several in-company programmes.

## The Structure of the Book

The book is divided into five parts. The first four parts of the book equip readers with the necessary concepts, frameworks, tools and techniques for understanding, analysing and enhancing supply chain performance. In Part V, the focus is on applying these concepts to real-life business situations.

### *Part I: Introduction and a Strategic View of Supply Chains*

Part I lays the foundation for understanding and analysing supply chains from a strategic perspective. For this, the framework for aligning the supply chain strategy with the business strategy is presented. The key strategic supply chain decisions regarding the boundary of the firm, reflected in the make versus buy decisions faced by a firm, are extensively discussed. Part I also establishes several leads for the three remaining parts of the book.

### *Part II: Managing Material Flow in Supply Chains*

Part II focuses on issues related to material flow: network design, transportation and inventory. Furthermore, the idea of supply chain optimization is introduced here. Using analytical models based on this approach, a firm can design and operate material flow in an efficient and effective manner.

### *Part III: Managing Information Flow in Supply Chains*

For several key decisions related to material flow discussed in Part II, access to real-time, undistorted data is essential. This information, rather than customer orders, is the basis of demand forecasting in most global supply chains. This part examines the various methods of demand forecasting and the related implementation issues. The contribution of information technology in facilitating the availability of these data is also discussed.

### *Part IV: Supply Chain Innovations*

In Part IV, innovative supply chain strategies that enhance supply chain performance are highlighted. The three strategies discussed are integration, reconfiguration and optimization of supply chains. Within supply chain design and operations decisions, specific issues, decisions and models involved in network design, inventory and transportation are scrutinized.

## Part V: Supply Chain Cases

Ten case studies, designed to bring real-life supply chain environments within the classroom, are presented in this part. Collectively, these 10 cases cover all aspects of the rich landscape of issues that managers confront in the Indian supply chain context. Some of these cases are sharply focused on specific dimensions of supply chains whereas others are quite comprehensive, dealing with the whole gamut of supply chain issues that affect a business. Under the skilful guidance of a faculty member, the readers are expected to analyse and synthesize conflicting data and points of view to define and prioritize goals, to persuade and inspire others who think differently and to make tough decisions with uncertain information.

# Features

### The Role of Supply Chain Management in Economy and Organization

**Learning Objectives**

After reading this chapter, you will be able to answer the following questions:

> Why is a supply chain important?
> What are the key supply chain decisions made by a firm?
> How has the supply chain evolved over the past century?
> What are the unique challenges of managing a supply chain in India?

**The learning objectives** define the salient points in each chapter that the student needs to focus on while reading the chapter. Their purpose is to minimize the need for repeatedly reading the chapter.

Picture this scenario: A father–daughter duo walks into a three-storey outlet that houses every imaginable brand of jeans. The daughter wants to buy a new pair of jeans for college. The father, a busy man, is aware that his only role is to flash his credit card at the appropriate time. He impresses on the salesman that he needs to be back in his office within an hour and follows his daughter in a bemused manner from one display to another, as she flits around, turning the place inside out in her hunt for the perfect pair. Meanwhile, the salesman plies the father with offers of food and drink, all of which are impatiently refused. The father cannot imagine why his daughter, surrounded by a veritable sea of denim, cannot find what she wants. Gnawing at his nails, he remembers how, when he was a boy, all it took was 15 minutes to walk into a store, look at everything that was available, and walk out with two pairs of trousers and two shirts. The daughter breaks into his reverie with a casual "Not a thing here, Dad! You can go to your office. I saw some interesting online offers on my mobile. I will order 4–5 jeans on cash on delivery. I will keep one which I like and return rest of them. Sounds familiar? In this era of hypertechnology and globalized markets, customers have become very demanding. They know what they want and will not settle for anything else. To keep up with the demands of such fastidious and fickle customers, it is essential for a company that its supply chain functions efficiently. Supply chain management is not a new concept for businesses. However, companies are just realizing that a wide product variety is not going to give them an edge over their competitors unless it is backed up by an equally efficient supply chain, ensuring that the entire product range is made accessible to a potential customer.

The purpose of this book is to explore ways and means of improving performance on this dimension.

**Opening vignettes** capture incidents from the real world. These lay the foundation for the theory covered in the chapter and exemplify the consequences of the application of theory to real-world situations.

Each chapter carries an **interview** of a senior management executive/CEO of a firm that is a supply chain leader within the industry. The interviews highlight the supply chain challenges that real companies face and the innovative supply chain practices that companies have adopted to establish themselves as the market leaders.

INTERVIEW WITH

SABYASACHI PATNAIK

*Asian Paints is India's largest paint company and the third-largest paint company in Asia today, with a turnover of Rs 36.7 billion. Sabyasachi Patnaik is the General Manager, Manufacturing, for the Decorative Paint Business Unit (DBU) at Asian Paints.*

*What is the level of complexity of the supply chain at Asian Paints?*

**Sabyasachi Patnaik:** At DBU, we manage around 500-odd vendors, 5 main manufacturing plants, 13 processing centres, 7 regional distribution centres and 76 depots. We serve about 19,000 dealers who are spread all over the country. On the variety front, we have to manage 750 raw materials and packing materials and 1,500-odd inventoried SKUs at the FG level.

*What are the supply chain challenges that you face?*

**Sabyasachi Patnaik:** Increasingly our customers have become more demanding and as a result we are constantly expected to improve service levels. Further, we add 80–100 new SKUs every year. These new SKUs are more complex products requiring new materials and complex manufacturing processes but usually have lower volumes compared to our existing product lines. It is expected that our business should not only service a larger number of SKUs at higher service levels but also reduce costs related to the supply chain. So, unlike most other businesses, where chains have to be either efficient or responsive, we are expected to be responsive as well as efficient. How to manage this stretch is the most important challenge for supply chain managers at Asian Paints.

we could offer a large variety to customers without increasing the number of SKUs at the factory. Way back in 1998 we restructured ourselves and created different business units. In the business of decorative paints, we created a position of Vice President supply chain that is responsible for the end-to-end supply chain. We have been early users of information technology in India and we make sure that our information technology initiatives are driven by our business people. Our early investments in information technology has helped us in reducing forecast errors, reduced safety stocks and lowered the freight costs. In past few years, we have focused on improving our capabilities in manufacturing. We have implemented Six Sigma and other lean methodologies to improve quality, reduce cycle times and reduce rework.

To reduce our material costs we have focused on sourcing efficiency as well as on improving formulation efficiency. Hence, our material costs are probably the lowest in the industry. We also have reduced our working capital requirement by exploring ways in which we can get higher credit from suppliers and by reducing the FG and RM inventory levels. Optimal balancing has been done between higher creditors and material costs. I guess our main strength is quality of our execution.

*What are the future supply chain initiatives that the firm is working on?*

**Sabyasachi Patnaik:** With increased variety, we realize that holding stocks close to customers may not be the best option. We are exploring the idea of keeping stocks at central distribution centres (CDC) located close to the plant so that

## LAUNCH OF THE SEVENTH HARRY POTTER BOOK

*Harry Potter and the Deathly Hallows,* the much-awaited seventh and final book in the Harry Potter series of novels, was released in 93 countries simultaneously on 21 July 2007. Managing a launch of this magnitude is a supply chain nightmare. Ensuring that the book is available in sufficient quantity at tens of thousands of outlets across 93 countries across the globe poses substantial challenges to supply chain managers, who have also to ensure that the content of books is not leaked out before the launch date. The books had to reach the stores just in time for the launch, neither too early nor too late. Penguin India, the distributor of Harry Potter books in India, had to manage the seemingly impossible task of delivering the books simultaneously to 300 destinations just a few hours prior to the launch time of 6:30 a.m.

The **caselets** are snippets that present actual industrial practices or unique solutions adopted by companies.

A **summary** at the end of the chapter recapitulates the important concepts and definitions from the chapter. It allows the students to concentrate on the salient points in the chapter.

## Summary

- Supply chain restructuring focuses on questioning the existing processes and architecture of the chain.
- Supply chains can be characterized using the following three dimensions: shape of the value-addition curve, point of differentiation and customer entry point. Restructuring of the supply chain process involves altering the supply chain process on at least one of the three dimensions.
- Supply chain restructuring involves supply chain innovations involving either product redesign or process redesign or value offering to customers so as to improve customer service and reduce cost. Using supply chain restructuring firms like Dell Computers and National Panasonic have managed to move from the MTS to the CTO business model.
- Restructuring supply chain architecture involves either altering the way in which material flow takes play in a chain or alteration in inventory placement in a chain.
- Unlike supply chain integration and supply chain optimization, supply chain restructuring goes beyond supply chain function and will require integrating product and process engineering with supply chain function. Similarly, it may also involve closer integration between marketing and supply chain function.
- Business benefits of supply chain restructuring can be quantified with the help of analytical inventory models.

## Discussion Questions

1. What are the key dimensions in a supply chain process?
2. What are the ways in which a firm can move from an MTS model to a CTO Model?
3. Identify industry and technology characteristics that make postponement strategy viable.
4. How do other business functions like product design, process technology and marketing contribute to supply chain restructuring decisions?
5. Why will one want to design different material flow systems for fast- and slow-moving items?
6. Identify variables that affect the inventory placement decisions within a chain?
7. HUL has 100 plants (geographically spread throughout India) where a number of different product lines are manufactured and supplied to 50 odd depots that are geographically spread throughout India. To improve responsiveness and simultaneously to reduce costs, HUL has come up with the concept of regional depots. The company has four regional depots (one in each zone of the country) and all slow-moving items are first brought to regional depots from which the entire basket of slow-moving goods is shipped to 50 odd depots. All fast-moving items are shipped directly from the plants to depots. One of the management trainees has suggested that HUL should redesign its supply chain (for slow-moving items). He has come with the following two options:
   - Have only one central depot at Nagpur (centre of India) and serve the entire 50 depots from one central depot for all slow-moving items.
   - Have four regional depots but each depot should specialize and stock only selected items that gets produced from the plants that are located in that zone. So all depots will get served from four regional depots for slow-moving items (instead of the current arrangement where each depot is served from the closest regional depot for all slow-moving items). Each of the slow-moving items will get stocked at only one of the four regional depots.

   Critically analyse the above two options.

Each chapter includes **discussion questions** at the end of the chapter. These questions are designed to facilitate a review of the concepts presented in the chapter.

**Mini projects** are activity- and/or analysis-oriented assignments that give the student a clear view of the problems that a supply chain manager faces in the real world. These are designed to help the reader correlate theory with reality.

## Mini Project

How will your analysis of the problem discussed in section "Restructure Placement of Inventory in Chain" change if we bring product variety in the analysis: Let us say the company offered three variants and weekly demand for each of the variants in each of the market follows normal distribution with a mean equal to 100 with a standard deviation of 50. The manufacturing company had two sub-stages: manufacturing component and assembly. The manufacturing component accounted for 80 per cent of value addition and lead time.

1. Where should company hold stocks in the system?
2. Determine the optimal level of safety stocks, given the above decision.

**Exercises** are included at the end of selected chapters where key supply chain issues are discussed. These numerical problems are designed to help a student/reader to apply the concepts presented in the chapter to analyse and interpret data.

# The Teaching and Learning Package

## *For Students*

**Study Card:** The study card is a six-page pullout that captures the essential learning from the book. It is designed to enable the reader to rapidly recapitulate the important concepts and equations from each chapter.

## *For Instructors*

**Instructors' Manual:** This book is designed to offer considerable flexibility to instructors in course design. Suggested alternative course outlines have been included in the instructors' manual, available at www.pearsoned.co.in/janatshah. Using these alternative outlines, the instructor can customize the course to meet the needs of the students, keeping their aptitude/background and the number of contact hours in mind.

Apart from this, each chapter is summarized from the instructor's point of view. Teaching tips to make learning more interesting and relevant to student groups are provided. To help the instructor, detailed solutions for numerical exercises have been provided, wherever relevant.

The instructors' manual also features detailed case teaching notes for all the cases in Part V. It is designed to help the instructors in structuring their classroom discussions in an effective manner. These can also be used by the instructor to integrate the theory/models/concepts discussed in the course with the managerial problems presented in the case.

**Lecture Slides (PowerPoint Presentations):** PowerPoint slides for each chapter are available along with the instructors' manual. These provide lecture outlines, important diagrams and additional material that can be used by the instructor to deliver lectures and make presentations in an effective and engaging manner.

## Acknowledgements

This book is the outcome of my journey into the world of supply chain management spanning the last two decades. This journey has been influenced by four sets of people: teachers, colleagues, students and industry practitioners.

My teachers from IIM Ahmedabad, specifically Arabinda Tripathy, Jahar Saha, N. Ravichandran and Priyadarshini Shukla, have influenced the way I look at and perceive the world of management.

My colleagues and co-researchers have contributed significantly to various ideas and frameworks that I have developed in the field of supply chain management. From IIM Bangalore, I would like to acknowledge L. S. Murty, Jishnu Hazra, B. Mahadevan, D. Krishna Sundar, Harith Saranga, R. Srinivasan, D. N. Suresh and Rahul Patil. A special thanks to L. S. Murty, a friend and a colleague for the last 17 years, who despite being subjected to all my half-baked ideas, has always found time to offer constructive feedback. I would also like to acknowledge Kulwant Pawar of the University of Nottingham; Chandra Lalwani of Hull University; G. Raghuram of IIM Ahmedabad; N. Viswanadham from the Indian School of Business, Hyderabad; Mark Goh from the National University of Singapore; and Jeremy Shapiro from MIT.

I am grateful to the postgraduate management students, doctoral students and participants of executive programmes for their patience and support with the early versions of this manuscript. They identified errors and suggested ideas for new examples. The outcome of my interactions with these students and industry participants has found a place in the discussion on agile supply chains. A special thanks to Ashish Dhongde for contributing a section on supply chain disruptions. I would specifically like to acknowledge several doctoral students who have helped polish my ideas: Balram Avittathur, Nitin Singh, Ashish Tewary, Divya Tiwari and Punit Mathur. Ashish Tewary has also contributed Chapter 8—'IT and Supply Chain Management'. Balram and Nitin Singh have co-authored the Kurlon and *Tendupatta* case studies, respectively.

I have learnt a lot from several industry colleagues, of whom I would specifically like to mention Vinod Kamat of Marico Industries, H. G. Raghunath of Titan, John S. Dischinger of IBM, S. Ravichandran of TVS Logistics, S. S. Varma of Tata Chemicals, B. K. Dutta of BPCL, and Suprakash Mukherjee of John Deere.

Several ideas in the book have been supported with data from the Indian manufacturing industry. I wish to credit the CMIE database, Prowess, for the data used for the analysis in the book.

The contribution of the team at Pearson India Education Services Pvt. Ltd deserves a special mention.

Finally, this book would not have been possible without the constant encouragement and moral support from my wife Seema and daughter Riddhi.

**Janat Shah**

# REVIEWERS

## Consultant Board

The consultant board provided us with a detailed and critical analysis of each chapter and worked with us throughout the development of the book. We would like to thank the following for their time and commitment:

A. K. Dey
*Birla Institute of Management Technology, Greater NOIDA*

R. Dorai
*Indian Institute of Planning and Management, Bangalore*

Sunil Sharma
*Faculty of Management Studies, University of Delhi*

## Reviewers

The guidance and thoughtful recommendations of many helped us improve this book. We are grateful for the comments and helpful suggestions received from the following reviewers:

Balram Avittathur
*Indian Institute of Management Calcutta*

N. Chandrasekaran
*Loyola Institute of Business Administration, Chennai*

Debadyuti Das
*Faculty of Management Studies, University of Delhi*

Robert De Souza
*Executive Director, The Logistics Institute–Asia Pacific, National University of Singapore*

S. G. Deshmukh
*Indian Institute of Technology Delhi*

John Dischinger
*Supply Chain Program Director, IBM*

Subroto Guha
*Patna Women s College, Patna*

Rahul Gupta
*Invertis Institute of Management Studies, Bareilly*

V. K. Gupta
*Institute of Management Technology Ghaziabad*

Ananth V. Iyer
*Krannert School of Management, Purdue University*

Jayanth Jacob
*Anna University, Chennai*

Govindan Kannan
*University of Southern Denmark*

K. V. Krishnankutty
*College of Engineering, Thiruvananthapuram*

L. S. Murty
*Indian Institute of Management Bangalore*

Bodhibrata Nag
*Indian Institute of Management Calcutta*

S. S. Pal
*Amity Business School, NOIDA*

Rahul Patil
*Indian Institute of Technology Mumbai*

Chandrasekharan Rajendran
*Indian Institute of Technology Madras, Chennai*

Jyoti Prakash Rath
*International School of Business and Media, Pune*

R. Raghavendra Ravi
*Technology Associates, Chennai*

Narayan Rangaraj
*Institute of Technology Bombay, Mumbai*

A. Vidyadhar Reddy
*Osmania University, Hyderabad*

Srikanta Routroy
*Birla Institute of Technology and Science, Pilani*

Santanu Roy
*Indian Institute of Technology Kharagpur*

Sadananda Sahu
*Indian Institute of Technology Kharagpur*

Ajay Sholkey
*Kurukshetra University*

G. Srinivasan
*Indian Institute of Technology Madras, Chennai*

Viplava Thakur
*Xavier Institute of Social Sciences, Ranchi*

Pramod Kumar Tiwari
*L. N. Mishra Institute of Economic Development and Social Change, Patna*

Ranjan Upadhyaya
*WISDOM, Banasthali*

N. S. Uppal
*Bharatiya Vidya Bhawan, Delhi*

Asif Zameer
*FORE School of Management, New Delhi*

# PART I

## Introduction and a Strategic View of Supply Chains



Thanks to the liberalization of economies, firms have discovered that the globe is their playing field. The emergence of global markets has significantly altered the way businesses work. In a globalized economy, efficiency and speed of response becomes even more critical, and supply chains become the new competitive weapon. Firms operating in the Indian scenario face many supply chain challenges that are unique to the Indian context. This book deals with the concepts of supply chain management and dwells on the problems that are unique to the Indian scenario

Chapter 1 defines supply chain management, traces its evolution over the past century and identifies major trends that have made performance critical for business success. The chapter also discusses the implications of the unique challenges that are presented by the complex supply chains of Indian firms for practising managers.

Chapter 2 focuses on supply chain strategy and supply chain performance measures. The framework for integrating business and supply chain strategies is presented with a specific focus on the inherent cost and customer service trade-offs. This chapter also presents the framework for prioritizing supply chain initiatives so as to enhance business performance on an ongoing basis.

Chapter 3 deals with key strategic supply chain decisions regarding the boundary of the firm within the supply chain, including critical issues such as outsourcing versus inhouse operations. In this chapter, several perspectives on outsourcing have been analysed. The chapter also presents the classification approach for various sourcing strategies that may be adopted for different categories of products.

The goal of the three chapters in Part I is to provide a foundation for understanding and analysing supply chains from a strategic perspective. This framework helps in identifying supply chain initiatives that improve business performance. Part I also establishes several leads for the remaining three parts of the book, which focus on supply chain flow and innovations.

# The Role of Supply Chain Management in Economy and Organization

## Learning Objectives

After reading this chapter, you will be able to answer the following questions:

> Why is a supply chain important?
> What are the key supply chain decisions made by a firm?
> How has the supply chain evolved over the past century?
> What are the unique challenges of managing a supply chain in India?

Picture this scenario: A father–daughter duo walks into a three-storey outlet that houses every imaginable brand of jeans. The daughter wants to buy a new pair of jeans for college. The father, a busy man, is aware that his only role is to flash his credit card at the appropriate time. He impresses on the salesman that he needs to be back in his office within an hour and follows his daughter in a bemused manner from one display to another, as she flits around, turning the place inside out in her hunt for the perfect pair. Meanwhile, the salesman plies the father with offers of food and drink, all of which are impatiently refused. The father cannot imagine why his daughter, surrounded by a veritable sea of denim, cannot find what she wants. Gnawing at his nails, he remembers how, when he was a boy, all it took was 15 minutes to walk into a store, look at everything that was available, and walk out with two pairs of trousers and two shirts. The daughter breaks into his reverie with a casual "Not a thing here, Dad! You can go to your office. I saw some interesting online offers on my mobile. I will order 4–5 jeans on cash on delivery. I will keep one which I like and return rest of them. Sounds familiar? In this era of hypertechnology and globalized markets, customers have become very demanding. They know what they want and will not settle for anything else. To keep up with the demands of such fastidious and fickle customers, it is essential for a company that its supply chain functions efficiently. Supply chain management is not a new concept for businesses. However, companies are just realizing that a wide product variety is not going to give them an edge over their competitors unless it is backed up by an equally efficient supply chain, ensuring that the entire product range is made accessible to a potential customer.

The purpose of this book is to explore ways and means of improving performance on this dimension.

## Introduction

A quick research carried out in a local grocery store will reveal that, on an average, it takes 3–4 months for goods to reach the end customer. Sometimes, it takes as much as a year for goods to reach the end customer in the chain. It is indeed an amazing realization that there is a very complicated chain in place to ensure that one can buy the denims of one's choice at a retail store.

Companies have managed supply chains for decades, but never in history did they have the variety of the kind they handle now, or the kind of competitive pressures that they face now. Companies all over the world have realized that the difference between good and bad supply chain management can affect their profitability significantly. Firms like Apple and Wal-Mart have demonstrated the impact of supply chain management on business performance. Due to its superior supply chain systems, Apple managed a significantly higher return of assets at 20 per cent, compared to other players in same business. Similarly, Wal-Mart has emerged as the largest American corporation with return of assets close to 8 per cent, which is considerably higher than that of its competitors in the retailing business. Within India, firms like Asian Paints and Marico Industries have maintained significantly higher levels of profitability and growth compared to competitors in their respective industries because of their superior supply chain capabilities.

The aim of this chapter is to introduce the concept of supply chain management, trace the evolution of supply chain concepts over the past century and identify major trends that have made supply chain performance critical to success. We briefly look at the performance of the Indian economy and firms across various sectors, focusing on the supply chain dimension. We also identify key supply chain challenges for Indian firms. As the Indian economy is growing at 8 per cent annually, despite the infrastructure bottlenecks, we have to look at the challenges in supply chain management that are unique to the Indian scenario. The goal is not only to understand and apply the concepts that have already evolved but also to continue to look for innovations and solutions customized to meet the requirements of companies operating in the Indian scenario. It is obvious that significant improvements will come only from innovative solutions that can resolve supply chain problems that are specific to the Indian context.

## What Is Supply Chain Management?

The supply chain encompasses all activities involved in the transformation of goods from the raw material stage to the final stage, when the goods and services reach the end customer. Supply chain management involves planning, design and control of flow of material, information and finance along the supply chain to deliver superior value to the end customer in an effective and efficient manner. A typical supply chain is represented in Figure 1.1.

As can be seen from the definition, the supply chain not only includes manufacturers, suppliers and distributors but also transporters, warehouses and customers themselves. Of late, firms have realized that it is not the firms themselves but their supply chains that vie with each other in the marketplace. Thus, it is not Hindustan Unilever (HUL) versus Procter & Gamble (P&G). Rather, the supply chains of both these firms compete against each other. The customer is interested only in the price, availability and quality of the product at the neighbourhood retail outlet, where they actually come into contact with products supplied by HUL and P&G. If customers observe inefficiency on account of non-availability, damaged packaging, etc. at the retail end with regard to HUL's products, they attribute inefficiency to HUL and not to its chain partners. The customer is only interested in getting the desired product at the right place, at the right time and at the right price. For a simple product like soap, the HUL supply chain involves ingredient suppliers, transporters, the company's manufacturing plants, carrying

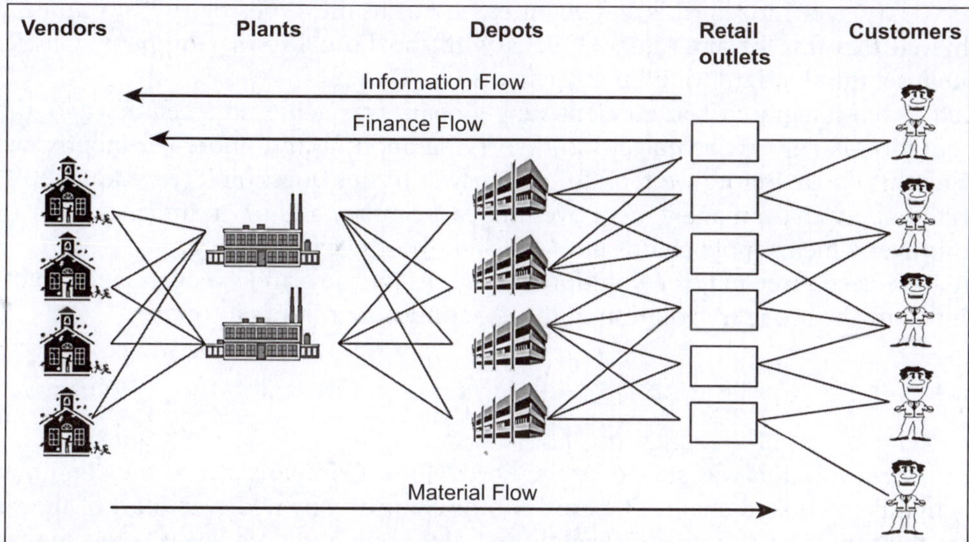


**Figure 1.1**
A supply chain network.

and forwarding agents, wholesalers, distributors and retailers. Obviously, HUL does not own all these entities, but the HUL brand name is at stake and it has to be ensured that the entire chain delivers value to the end customer. HUL cannot afford to focus only on those parts of the chain that are owned by it and ignore the other parts of chain. Firms need to realize that the performance of the chain is determined by its weakest link.

The supply chains of automobile companies (Maruti, Tata Motors and TVS) and other companies like BPL, LG and Whirlpool, dealing in consumer durables, will be very similar to the one depicted in Figure 1.1. On the other hand, companies in the consumer non-durables business—for example, HUL, P&G, Godrej Soaps and Nestlé—have to work with supply chains that are likely to be much longer and more complex. The term *chain* is a little misleading because it gives the impression that there is only one entity at each stage of the supply chain. In reality, as seen in Figure 1.1, multiple entities are involved at each stage: a manufacturer receives material from several suppliers and, in turn, distributes the products through multiple distributors. The more appropriate term probably will be either *supply networks* or *supply web*. However, the term *supply chain* has been widely accepted by both practitioners and academicians; hence, we will continue to use the same throughout the book.

## Evolution of Supply Chain Management

The evolution of supply chain management has been a gradual process. Over the last century, there have been three major revolutions in the field of supply chain management and we examine each of them in the context of the broader evolution in the economic and technological environment. Consider the following statement made by the chief executive of an automobile firm:

> Our aim is always to arrange the material and machinery and to simplify the operations so that practically no orders are necessary. Our finished inventory is in transit. So is most of our raw material inventory. Our production cycle is about eighty-one hours from the mine to the finished machine (automobile) in the freight car.[1]

It is clear from this statement that this firm had a well-integrated supply chain in place that allowed it to minimize cost and maximize asset productivity. Most people, including students and business executives, are surprised to learn that the company that achieved this, did so almost a century ago. Indeed, this statement came not in the 1960s or 1970s. Rather, Henry Ford achieved this fine balance in the 1910s with the Ford Motor Company. Clearly, this achievement set the standard for all managers the world over.

If such a well-integrated and efficient supply chain was achieved a century ago, then the obvious question is why are managers still worrying about it and, more pertinently, why are you reading this book? Before we look for the answer to this question let us take a look at the evolution of supply chain management over the past century and try to understand of the key dimensions over which supply chains have evolved over the past century.

There have been three major revolutions along this journey, and we examine each of them in the context of the broader evolution in the economic environment.

## The First Revolution (1910–1920): Vertical Integrated Firms Offering Low Variety of Products

The first major revolution was staged by the Ford Motor Company where they had managed to build a tightly integrated chain. The Ford Motor Company owned every part of the chain—right from the timber to the rails. Through its tightly integrated chain, it could manage the journey from the iron ore mine to the finished automobile in 81 hours. However, as the famous saying goes, the Ford supply chain would offer any colour, as long as it was black; and any model, as long as it was Model T. Ford innovated and managed to build a highly efficient, but inflexible supply chain that could not handle a wide product variety and was not sustainable in the long run. General Motors, on the other hand, understood the demands of the market place and offered a wider variety in terms of automobile models and colours. Ford's supply chain required a long time for set-up changes and, consequently, it had to work with a very high inventory in the chain.

Till the second supply chain revolution, all the automobile firms in Detroit were integrated firms. Even traditional firms in India, like Hindustan Motors, were highly integrated firms where the bulk of the manufacturing was done in-house.

## The Second Revolution (1960–1970): Tightly Integrated Supply Chains Offering Wide Variety of Products

Towards the end of the first revolution, the manufacturing industry saw many changes, including a trend towards a wide product variety. To deal with these changes, firms had to restructure their supply chains to be flexible and efficient. The supply chains were required to deal with a wider product variety without holding too much inventory. The Toyota Motor Company successfully addressed all these concerns, thereby ushering in the second revolution.

The Toyota Motor Company came up with ideas that allowed the final assembly and manufacturing of key components to be done in-house. The bulk of the components was sourced from a large number of suppliers who were part of the keiretsu system. Keiretsu refers to a set of companies with interlocking business relationships and shareholdings. The Toyota Motor Company had long-term relationships with all the suppliers. These suppliers were located very close to the Toyota assembly plants. Consequently, set-up times, which traditionally used to take a couple of hours, were reduced to a couple of minutes. This combination of low set-up times and long-term relationships with suppliers was the key feature that propelled the second revolution—and it was a long journey from the rigidly integrated Ford supply chain. The principles followed by Toyota are more popularly known as lean production systems.

The Toyota system, involving tight linkages, did get into some problems in the later part of the century. Gradually, when Toyota and other Japanese firms tried to set up assembly plants in different parts of the world, they realized that they would have to take their suppliers also along with them. Further, they found that some of the suppliers in keiretsu had become complacent and were no longer cost competitive. With the advent of electronic data interchange (EDI), which facilitated electronic exchange of information between firms, it was possible for a firm to integrate with the suppliers without forcing them to locate their plants close to the manufacturers' plant.

In actual practice, the Toyota supply chain also had certain rigidities, such as a permanent relation with suppliers, which could become a liability over a period of time. This, in turn, led to the third revolution spearheaded by couple of progressive companies like Dell Computers, Apple Inc., and Bharti Airtel, which offered, its customers the luxury of customization with loosely held supplier networks.

## The Third Revolution (1995–2020): Virtually Integrated Global Supply Networks Offering Customized Products and Services

Technology, especially information technology, which is evolving faster than enterprises can find applications for some of the innovations, is the fuel for the third revolution in supply chain. It will probably take at least couple of years before we can fully understand the IT-enabled model that has emerged and begin to apply it to all industries. However, we have enough information to get a reasonably good understanding of the contours of the third revolution. We will illustrate key characteristics of the third revolution using the example of Dell computers, Apple Inc., and Bharti Airtel. The first is a product company, the second combines product and service, and third is a pure service organization. In each of these organisations, we will see different aspects of the third revolution.

Dell computers allows customers to configure their own laptops (in terms of processors, video cards, screen sizes, memory, etc.) and track the same in their production and distribution systems. Apple offers personal digital devices to its customers and iPod is a classic example. However, it is not just about the product. Apple allows the consumer to have a personalized user experience through the features and services. Users can personalize the music and other media content on their device through the various features available on iPod. Similarly, Bharti Airtel allows services like My Airtel through which customer can have unique personalized experience.

As one can see we have moved to the stage where firms offer a bundle of goods that leads to personalized experiences, which would be of great value to individual customer. Value is unique to each customer, and therefore, each customer would wish a customized experience to be fully satisfied with the value delivered to him or her. In summary, we have moved from single product (Model T black colour) to wide variety as offered by Toyota to customization as offered by companies such as Dell computers, Apple, and Bharti Airtel. Businesses can no longer be content in providing select product variety to customers.

Organizations have moved from offering products to offering user experiences, which are a bundle of goods and services selected by the user. This has changed the way supply chains are configured to deliver value.

Let us begin with Dell. To make sure its customers get the completely customized product, Dell has built a strong network of vendors who are cost and technology leaders. These medium term relationships are based on the understanding that the vendors will adhere to a high benchmark on cost and technology leadership which in turn will reflect in Dell's products.

Apple Inc. brings together a product and a user experience in a revolutionary new way. Similar to Dell, Apple has global partners with which it maintains medium term relationships based on cost and technology benchmarking to fulfil its product manufacturing requirements. However, for creating a better user experience, it has gone a step further by creating a platform that enables anyone to contribute to the Apple user experience. Take the example of Apple iTunes and App Store. At the first level, iTunes made it possible for Apple to provide all the music in the world to its users through a seamless and tightly integrated platform. While this was only about entertainment, the App Store took it to the next level. It created a global community of small and medium sized application development teams who could become partners with Apple, use its App Store platform, and offer a rich bouquet of utilities and applications which would all help create a one-of-its-kind user experience. So now, in addition to its strategic global manufacturing partners, using this platform, Apple also built a global network of partners in a few core areas like app development who had very low engagement with the company itself. Practically, anyone could become a partner to Apple on this platform. A key thing to note here is that the primary driver that enabled Apple to build this platform was information technology and the use of Internet.

In Bharti Airtel, we have a company that has broken several stereotypes. For a telecom company, the core activities like network management and IT being handled in-house was considered a given. However, Bharti Airtel chose to go with strategic outsourcing and partnerships with global partners for these core activities. Although the relationships were still medium term similar to Dell, the companies were thoroughly aligned and worked like a single entity because of common goals and revenue sharing arrangements. This ensured that Bharti Airtel was free to focus on the user experience which was the ultimate service it provided to the consumer.

To summarize, organizations are moving from an era where the central theme was the satisfaction of a customer need with a product to an age where the need is satisfied with a user experience that combines products and services. It is the age of virtual integration where all information regarding the customer is harnessed to provide a personalized customer experience. There are three key characteristics of these global networks that are enabling companies to deliver this experience seamlessly. The first involves high degree of engagement in the medium term with strategic partners based on cost and technology leadership for the core offerings. This is obvious in the way Dell, Apple, and Bharti Airtel create and engage in strategic partnerships with a close group of technology vendors with clear alignment. For example, Bharti Airtel is a telecom major that outsources the core activity of network management to a strategic partner with a clear revenue sharing arrangement, which ensures both are aligned completely. Similarly, Apple, which is known for its amazingly designed products, does none of the manufacturing itself but completely outsources it to its strategic manufacturing partners. The second is the way global resources of varying kinds, which are crucial to delivering the unified customer experience, are harnessed with the help of information technology and a highly evolved and efficient transportation infrastructure world over. Physical proximity of the strategic partner is no longer an important factor in making the choice of partners. Whether it is Dell using specialized chip manufacturers, Apple sourcing apps from the far flung corners of the world, or Bharti outsourcing core telecom activities to global technology leaders, this trend of utilizing global resources from near or far-flung corners of the world is evident in the operations of all leading companies. The third characteristic involves leveraging IT in the creation of a platform using which multiple partners each having very low engagement contribute to non-core activities, which enable the enhancement of the user experience while keeping individual transaction costs very low. Apple's app development platform is an example of this characteristic.

An organization which exhibits these three characteristics—ability to carry out strategic outsourcing by building strong medium term relationships based on cost and technology leadership, ability to harness global resources, and the creation of an easy to use platform to diversify global supply base—are able to create the virtual integration necessary to provide the user experience.

Our discussion of the three major revolutions in supply chain has given us an understanding of how the dynamic markets and rapidly evolving technologies force us to continuously improve our understanding of supply chain concepts. To be able to apply the key concepts of supply chain management, we must be able to observe how they are used in the context of the business and market scenario. With this backdrop in mind, let us look at some of the key supply chain concepts and understand why it has become such a critical success factor in most industries and how firms find better and more efficient ways of managing this crucial aspect of business in today's world.

## Key Concepts in Supply Chain Management

Traditionally, firms have focused their energies on three main functions: purchasing, manufacturing and distribution. Transport and storage activities within individual functions and across functions have not received adequate attention, and have usually been handled by the department managing the logistical aspects of the company. Initially, supply chain management focused on the internal integration of activities in these three functional areas with the logistics function. Gradually, firms realized that these activities have to be coordinated, not just within a firm, but across the entire supply chain, keeping in mind the material/product flow, right from the vendor to the end customer.

To integrate material flow across the chain, information and financial flow across the chain also have to be integrated. As shown in Figure 1.1, a typical supply chain involves managing all the three flows in the chain. In firms like Asian Paints and Marico Industries, material, information and finance flow seamlessly across department and organization boundaries. Customer pull, and not any internal compulsion, governs all the three flows in well-managed chains. In most chains, there exist many blocks, both at the departmental and the organizational boundaries. Individual departments and firms are more interested in performance at the local level rather than the performance at the chain level. Thus, numerous bottlenecks occur at the boundaries and the flow gets badly distorted. As observed earlier, often, material and products seem to spend a significant amount of time at the departmental and organizational boundaries. Since most of the inefficiencies seem to creep in at the boundaries, while studying supply chains, our focus will be on linkages rather than on individual operations. Though a typical supply chain will have a large number of firms, the standard practice is to analyse supply chains from the perspective of a focal firm like HUL, Asian Paints or Marico Industries. The concept of focal firms is discussed in Box 1.1.

In certain situations, apart from the forward flow of material and products, firms are also interested in the reverse flow of material as many companies also have to manage product returns, warranty claims, etc. As per the European Union regulations, firms that manufacture and sell consumer products are also expected to take the responsibility for product disposal at the end of the life of the product. Tougher regulations and increasingly liberal product take backs are forcing firms to focus their attention on reverse material flow as well. There is a growing realization that we need to develop a special field to deal with the reverse flow of material/product from the customer to the manufacturer and it is known as reverse supply chain management. Refer Chapter 14 on Green Supply Chain for details on reverse supply chain management. In this book, by and large, we will focus our attention on the forward flow of materials/products.

**BOX 1.1** Focal Firms

The firm that provides identity to the products in terms of brand has higher stakes in the chain, and such a firm is identified as the main entity in the chain. By virtue of being the main entity, the firm concerned also has the necessary clout and resources and usually takes on the responsibility of designing the incentive systems for the various entities in the supply chain. For example, Nike might not manufacture the product, or may not own the retail outlets, but since the end customers identify the product with Nike, we will identify Nike as the main entity in the supply chain. In general, we will refer to this entity as the focal firm or central node or the main entity in the chain. While studying supply chains, we analyse them from the perspective of this main entity, also known as the focal firm or the nodal firm, which is at the strategic centre of the supply chain. In marketing literature, the focal firm is known as a steward firm that provides leadership to the entire value chain and ensures that the chain simultaneously addresses customers' best interest and drives profit for all chain partners.

## Decisions in a Supply Chain

Successful supply chain management involves several decisions with varying time frames. We can broadly classify them as design decisions and supply chain operations decisions.

### Design Decisions

Supply chain design (network design) or strategic decisions involve the following critical issues:

- What activities should be carried out by the nodal firm and what should be outsourced?
- How to select entities/partners to perform outsourced activities and what should be the nature of the relationship with those entities? Should the relationship be transactional in nature or should it be a long-term partnership?
- Decisions pertaining to the capacity and location of the various facilities.

The decisions pertaining to location and capacity are for those facilities that are owned by the nodal firm. In addition to manufacturing locations and capacities, the firm has also to worry about locations and capacities for warehouses (depots). Supply chain design decisions are made for the long term (usually a couple of years) and are very expensive to alter at short notice.

### Operations Decisions

Once supply chain design decisions are in place, the firm has to take decisions regarding the management of supply chain operations for shorter horizons. This involves tactical decisions, which have a horizon of about three months to a year; and operations decisions, which usually have a horizon ranging from a day to a month. Both tactical and operations decisions involve the following areas:

- Demand forecasting
- Procurement planning and control
- Production planning and control
- Distribution planning and control
- Inventory management
- Transportation management
- Customer order processing
- Relationship management with partners in the chain

Given the demand forecast and the business strategy of the firm, decisions related to procurement, production, planning, distribution and transportation have to be integrated with customer order processing and inventory management decisions. Relationship management essentially involves the alignment of incentives to the various entities in the chain so that the overall supply chain performance meets customer requirements at the lowest cost. Though not so obvious, the supply chain has also to be integrated with other important functions of the firm, for example, customer relationship management and new product development. Since customer relationship creates demand, the supply chain must ensure that it is in a position to fulfil the demand created by customer relationship management in a profitable way. Well-managed firms integrate their customer relationship and supply chain activities. Similarly, while designing new products, well-managed firms ensure that supply chain issues are kept in mind at the design stage. Firms have to find a way in which the new products can use the existing product platforms and components, so as to minimize the supply chain costs for the product family as a whole.

Traditionally, terms like *integrated logistics* or *business logistics* have been used synonymously with the term *supply chain management*. In some firms, traditional logistics professionals have taken up the responsibility of integrating supply chain activities within the firm under the banner of integrated logistics. In some other firms where this integration is quite weak, the top management has taken on the responsibility of developing the supply chain culture within the organization. Since both these approaches are prevalent in the industry, a lot of practitioners and academicians refer to this body of knowledge as logistics and supply chain management.

### LAUNCH OF THE SEVENTH HARRY POTTER BOOK

*Harry Potter and the Deathly Hallows,* the much-awaited seventh and final book in the Harry Potter series of novels, was released in 93 countries simultaneously on 21 July 2007. Managing a launch of this magnitude is a supply chain nightmare. Ensuring that the book is available in sufficient quantity at tens of thousands of outlets across 93 countries across the globe poses substantial challenges to supply chain managers, who have also to ensure that the content of books is not leaked out before the launch date. The books had to reach the stores just in time for the launch, neither too early nor too late. Penguin India, the distributor of Harry Potter books in India, had to manage the seemingly impossible task of delivering the books simultaneously to 300 destinations just a few hours prior to the launch time of 6:30 a.m.

## The Importance of the Supply Chain

In the past, customers were not very demanding and competition was not really intense. As a result, firms could afford to ignore issues pertaining to the supply chain. Today, firms that do not manage their supply chain will incur huge inventory costs and eventually end up losing a lot of customers because the right products are not available at the right place and time. The following are the five major trends that have emerged to make supply chain management a critical success factor in most industries.

- *Proliferation in product lines.* Companies have realized that more and more product variety is needed to satisfy the growing range of customer tastes and requirements. This is evident from the fact that every time a customer walks into a neighbourhood store, he or she is bound to discover a couple of items on the shelf that he or she had not seen during his or her last visit and that he or she has more varieties to choose from now. Every time you walk into a neighbourhood store, do not be surprised to find that even a simple product like toilet soap has 50-odd varieties.

  We define stock-keeping unit (SKU) as a unit of variety. For example, the same brand of soap may be offered in varying colours and sizes. Each variety is treated as a separate SKU. Companies like HUL, in their personal care products, manage, on an average, 1,200 SKUs. Chains like Foodworld manage about 6,000 SKUs. With increasing product variety, it becomes rather difficult to forecast accurately. Hence, retailers and other organizations involved in the business are forced to either maintain greater amount of inventories or lose customers.

- *Shorter product life cycles.* With increased competition, product life cycles across all industries are becoming shorter. For example, technology leaders like Apple works with a life cycle as short as 6 months. So a firm like Apple , which has, on an average, just

5 days of inventory, as compared to the industry average of 35 days, does not have to worry about product and component obsolescence. Its competitors with higher inventories end up writing off huge amounts of stocks every year as obsolete. In the past, in developing countries where inflation was a way of life, higher inventories used to be a major source of profits for the firm. With inflation in control and shorter product life cycles, firms have had to change the way they manage their inventories. Also, with shorter product life cycles, there is not much data available for demand forecasting. Most of the technology firms find that 50 per cent of their revenue comes from products that were introduced in the last three years.

- *Higher level of outsourcing.* As discussed in the section on "Evolution of Supply Chain Management", firms increasingly focus on their core activities and outsource non-core activities to other competent players. Michael Dell, the CEO of Dell Computers, had mentioned that if his company was vertically integrated, it would need five times as many employees and would suffer from a drag effect. Apart from primary activities in the value chain, even support activities that were usually done in-house are outsourced in a big way now. Bharti Tele-Ventures, India's number one private telecom service provider, has outsourced network-management services, IT services and call centre operations. This trend towards outsourcing is irreversible but a higher level of outsourcing makes supply chains more vulnerable, thereby forcing firms to develop different types of supply chain capabilities within the organization.
- *Shift in power structure in the chain.* In every industry, the entities closer to customers are becoming more powerful. With increasing competition, a steadily rising number of products are chasing the same retail shelf space. Retail shelf space has not increased at the pace at which product variety has increased. So there have been cases of retailers asking for slotting allowance when manufacturers introduce new products in the market place. Savvy firms have started talking about trade marketing and treating dealers and retailers as their customers while simultaneously trying to woo the retailers aggressively. There is a clear shift in the power structure. Retailers have realized that they are powerful entities in the chain and hence expect the manufacturers to be more responsive to their needs and demands. Discount retailers like Wal-Mart have been asking their suppliers to replenish the supplies on a daily basis based on actual sales data from their point-of-sales systems. In general, manufacturers are forced to respond more quickly to the customers' demands, because of changes in the power structure within the chain.
- *Globalization of manufacturing.* Over the past decade, tariff levels have come down significantly. Many companies are restructuring their production facilities to be at par with global standards. Unlike in the past, when firms use to source components, produce goods and sell them locally, now firms are integrating their supply chain for the entire world market. For example, companies like ABB have developed some global centres of excellence for each of their product lines that take care of the global market. General Motors is talking about a world car and has been designing a few cars for global markets. In the telecommunications and electronics industry, companies usually get their chips from Taiwan, test them in Europe and finally integrate them with other products in the United States of America to sell in the international market. This has made managing supply chains extremely complicated. Unlike information and finance flow, which can be managed electronically, materials and products have to move physically, and as this movement can even be across continents, managing supply chains is now an extremely complex issue.

**INTERVIEW WITH**

**ELLEN MARTIN**

*VF Corporation (Major brands: Wrangler and Lee) is the largest apparel manufacturer in the world with sales of $6.5 billion. Ellen Martin is the vice president of supply chain systems at VF Corp.*

*What are your volumes?*

**Ellen Martin:** VF has 850,000 SKUs of style, colour and size. And our business is getting more and more seasonal, so that 850,000 is not the same 850,000 every year. As much as 60 per cent of it could change. And it could change twice a year.

*How has that (supply chain) changed today?*

**Ellen Martin:** This outsourcing (to Asia) puts a huge challenge on the supply chain. The challenges in the last 10 years have changed substantially. We still need to have very accurate plans of what needs to be made, but factors such as inventory policies, safety stocks and risk management—not to mention relationship management (we have hundreds of contract manufacturers)—have become much higher priorities than they were before. The product had better be on the shelf when the order comes in, or you'll miss the sale because, with a 6-month lead time, you won't have time to produce it fast enough to order. You would miss the season altogether. So we went from a 1-week lead time to a 4-week lead time when we moved down south, and to a 6-month lead time for Asia.

*What are VF's biggest supply chain challenges now?*

**Ellen Martin:** We have to shorten the 6-month lead time. I've asked everyone why it has to take so long. They say the product is 40 days on the water. But where is it the rest of the time? The sewing takes the same time, wherever it's done, as do some of the other operations, like cutting and laundering. The answer is in acquiring the raw material. This is one of the longest lead-time factors. So what we're working on is increasing that verticality between the mill and the manufacturer and the wholesaler by creating partnerships.

*Source:* Victoria Cooper (2006), "Planning at a Global Scale", *Supply Chain Leader*, 4–8 October.

## Enablers of Supply Chain Performance

As mentioned in the previous section, managing supply chains is becoming increasingly complex. Despite this, firms have actually managed to reduce their logistics costs. For example, in a country like the United States of America, logistics costs used to account for 15 per cent of the gross domestic product (GDP) in the 1980s. Today, because of innovations in technology and management practices, logistics costs account for about 8.5 per cent of their GDP. Three major enablers that have helped firms and nations in reducing supply chain costs are briefly discussed below.

### *Improvement in Communication and IT*

Computing power has become cheaper and communication costs too have come down. This has helped firms in coordinating global supply chains in a cost-effective manner. Advances in enterprise resource planning (ERP) systems have helped firms in automating several business processes resulting in seamless information flow throughout the company across different functions. The way ERP systems have changed the nature of information flow within organization, Internet technology is likely to change the nature of information flow in interfirm transactions. In the past, only large companies could integrate with partner firms using expensive EDI technologies. Now, even small firms can communicate with their chain partners using the worldwide web at a fraction of the earlier cost. Companies are realizing that they can replace physical inventory by information. To really exploit their IT investments, companies need to re-engineer their supply chain and other supporting organizational processes and try to replace physical inventory with information. Unfortunately, many Indian companies have invested in information systems but have not made the corresponding changes in their supply chain systems and processes, which has resulted in the company failing to exploit the information system to its full potential. For example, a company with multiple plants can work with a common pool of safety stock of raw materials and does not need to have safety stocks for each individual plant. Similarly, on the order-processing side, companies can offer greater customization as compared to the past because their order-processing system can be designed to handle customized orders and their manufacturing and distribution system would allow them to track these customized products in the system. In the absence of an information system, this would not have been possible at all. But unfortunately a significant number of companies have used IT to just automate the existing supply chain systems and processes. Companies that have successfully exploited IT have made major changes in their supply chain structure, systems, processes and strategy.

## Emergence of Third-party Logistics Providers

Traditionally, many firms have been managing their logistics activities internally. Lately, companies have realized that they need to focus their energies on managing core business activities, and hence have been exploring the possibility of outsourcing logistics activities to third-party logistics (3PL) service providers. In developed countries, almost 90 per cent of the logistics activities are outsourced and are managed by 3PL companies. Apart from bringing in the much needed professionalism to the field, 3PL companies have economies of scale as they are able to pool demand across customers. In developed markets, global firms would like leading 3PL companies to go beyond the traditional role and play the role of a fourth-party logistics (4PL) company that can integrate the capabilities, resources and technology so as to provide comprehensive supply chain solutions to its customers.

Currently, the 3PL industry in India is still evolving. Two sets of companies have emerged in this field. One set of companies involves traditional transporters, shippers, warehouse service providers and freight forwarders, who want to offer value-added services and would like to see if they can develop competencies and become a 3PL company. The second set of service providers comprises international 3PL companies that have come to India along with their global MNC customer. For example, when Toyota wanted to set up a manufacturing plant in India, it asked its logistics service provider Mitsui and Co. to come to India to take care of its logistics requirements.

Currently, not many companies in India employ the services of other 3PL companies. However, with the evolution of the Indian market, new MNCs and progressive Indian companies operating in the mid-volume, mid-variety segment have started using the services of 3PL companies. Over a period of time, the 3PL companies would not only develop the competence required to function smoothly in the Indian context but also take care of the logistics requirements of the bulk of the industries in India as well.

## Enhanced Inter-firm Coordination Capabilities

Successful coordination across a global network of companies has been a comparatively new phenomenon in the corporate world. It has been realized that for a network to function meaningfully one needs a firm to play the role of the strategic centre. Many companies, like Apple, Nike, Benetton, Nintendo, Sun and Toyota, have successfully managed complex networks, played the part of the strategic centre and, hence, have emerged as role models to other companies. While each company in the network focuses on its core competencies, the strategic centres function as a leading and orchestrating system. Consequently, supply chains become more efficient and responsive. However, there have been a large number of failures also, where firms within the chain could not align their interests, and as a result the network could not function effectively. The industry is still on the learning curve in this matter, but better understanding and coordination of issues would greatly help in diffusing the third supply chain revolution across all industries.

## Supply Chain Performance in India

Supply chain performance measures involve multiple dimensions and they are discussed in detail in the subsequent chapters. In this section, the focus is on performance, both in terms of inventory turnover ratio at the organizational level and logistics costs at the economy level. Logistics costs include inventory-carrying costs, transportation costs and logistics administration costs.

As can be seen in Table 1.1, logistics costs in India are quite high when compared with other countries. Of course, one could argue that since customer service expectations are not the same across countries, logistics costs may not be strictly comparable. However, as tariff levels have been coming down with globalization, logistics costs do become comparable to a significant extent.

Higher logistics costs definitely affect the competitiveness of the Indian industry. Firms often argue that inefficiency in the transport and warehousing sector makes it difficult for them to compete in the global market. For example, the cost of sending an export cargo to Mumbai from Punjab and that of shipping it further to London from Mumbai are the same. Further, variable transit time and in-transit damages make transportation in India a very expensive affair

We now analyse the performance of the supply chains of Indian firms using inventory turnover ratio as a measure of performance. When we look at the performance of the Indian manufacturing sector in last decade (Figure 1.2), we find that performance has gradually improved in the time period between 2003 and 2008. After 2008, the inventory turn has dropped significantly and subsequently improving gradually. Impact of global financial crisis had deep impact on Indian manufacturing, and even after five years, Indian manufacturing has not reached level of performance achieved in 2008. Over a decade, Indian manufacturing industry has more or less maintained the performance and has shown only marginal improve-

***Table 1.1:* Ratio of logistics cost with GDP for few selected countries.**

| Country | Japan | United States | Korea | India |
|---|---|---|---|---|
| Ratio of logistics cost with GDP (in %) | 8.7 | 8.5 | 16.5 | 12.3 |

*Source:* G. Raghuram and J. Shah, "Roadmap for Logistics Excellence: Need to Break the Unholy Equilibrium," Working Paper, Indian Institute of Management Ahmedabad, No. 2004-08-02.

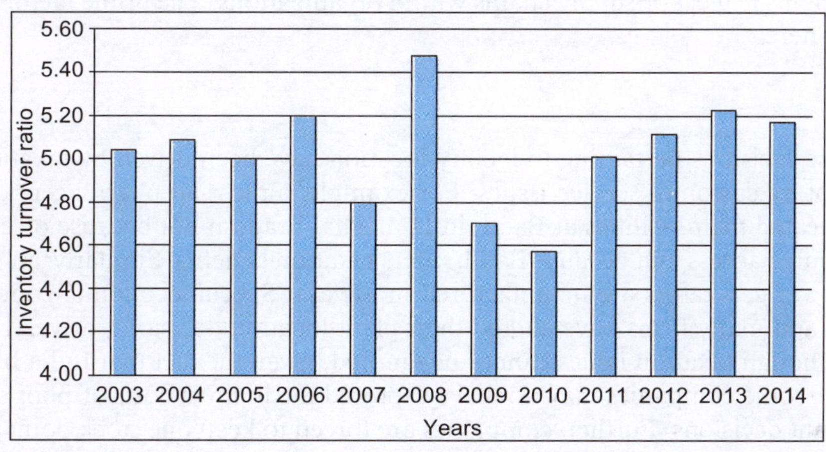


**Figure 1.2**

Performance of the Indian manufacturing industry [*Source:* Prowess (CMIE)].

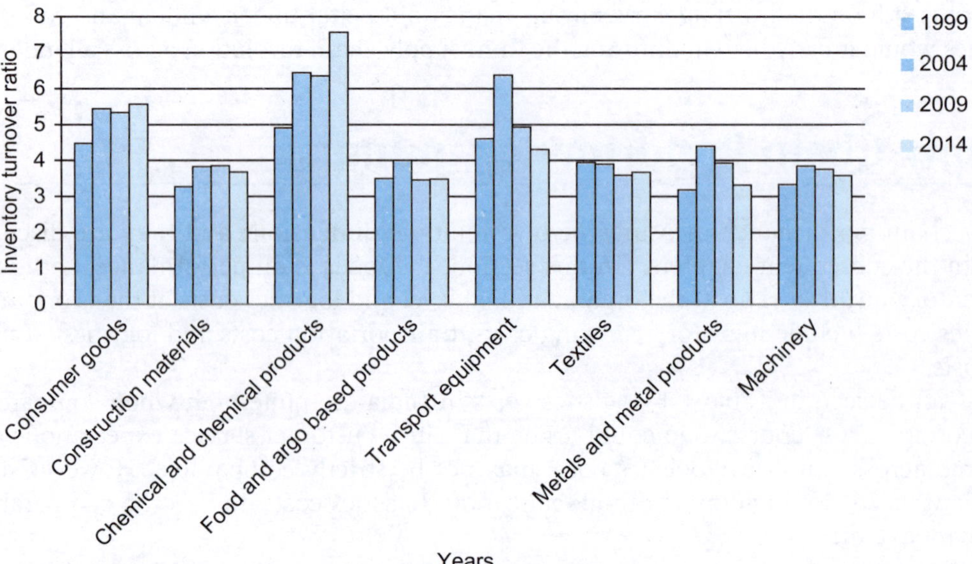


**Figure 1.3**

Sector-wise inventory performance of Indian firms [*Source:* Prowess (CMIE)].

ment. Though there is evidence of moderate improvement, this rate of improvement has to be sustained. On the other hand, the best international firms have improved at much faster rates in the past decade when compared to the best Indian firms. The sector-wise performance of Indian firms is shown in Figure 1.3.

We find that most sectors show performance trend similar to the overall manufacturing sector except consumer goods, construction, and chemicals. Unlike other sectors, consumer goods and construction sector have maintained inventory levels in last decade, whereas chemical industry had shown significant improvements in the last few years. To compete successfully in the global market the Indian firms need to improve their performance in managing their inventory and keep their logistics costs low. Let us now look at the challenges that Indian firms face when it comes to supply chain management. Many of these challenges—which arise due to the economic environment, taxation structures and also the geography of India—are unique to the Indian scenario.

## Challenges in Maintaining a Supply Chain in India

Most Indian firms traditionally have focused on the production and sales aspects of the business. Logistics was a neglected area. Until recently, not many firms made a concerted effort to improve the performance of their respective supply chains. There are many reasons that have contributed to this neglect of supply chains within organizations. The prime factors responsible are discussed here.

### Taxation Structure Drives Location Decisions

In India, most decisions pertaining to facility location have been driven by taxation considerations and not by customer service issues. For example, almost all pharmaceutical manufacturers have located their facilities at Baddi in Himachal Pradesh not because of either market access or resource access, but because Baddi offers taxation benefits. Similarly, air conditioners and diesel power generators are manufactured in Silvasa. Special economic zones offer taxation benefits, and many firms have altered their plant location decisions, driven by these considerations. Though taxation issues cannot be ignored, given the fact that India has poor road infrastructure, some companies may not have captured the indirect costs of poor service while making relevant decisions. Further, companies are forced to keep one stock point in each state to avoid taxes on inter-state sales. Currently, all inter-state sales attract a central sales tax (CST).

There have been lots of discussions in industrial and political circles regarding this issue, and it is most likely that CST will be scrapped under the new modified tax regime. This will have a significant impact on the supply chain structure of most companies. A plethora of state taxes affect supply chain operations. Currently, firms have to grapple with various state-level taxes, like local sales tax, entry tax, octroi and turnover tax. So, at each state border, one has to negotiate through numerous checkpoints leading to increased transportation lead time. In states like Bihar, Uttar Pradesh and West Bengal, a special road permit is to be obtained before one can send a truck to these states. Further, the necessity to pay taxes at various levels has forced firms to carry out more activities in-house rather than focusing only on core activities. There are ample data to show that a firm needs to be part of a network comprising multiple firms, with each firm focusing on its competencies. But in the current structure, supply chains comprising multiple firms will have to pay sales tax for every inter-firm material transaction, resulting in a cascading effect. The proposed concept of unified GST (goods and service tax) will remove this anomaly. The likely impact of GST on design and operations of supply chains is discussed in Box 1.2

### Poor State of Logistics Infrastructure

Both the transportation and the warehousing industry are in the unorganized sector. About 90 per cent of the trucks in the country belong to owners who have less than five trucks. An unorganized trucking industry, such as this, results in unreliable lead times and high in-transit damages. With lots of old trucks on the road, breakdowns are quite frequent, further adding to unreliability. Modernizing warehouse management is an idea that is yet to see the light of the day in India.

Logistics, being a neglected area in traditional organizations, did not attract the best talent in the industry. It is only since the last couple of years that firms have realized the importance of this function and have started inducting qualified people to handle supply chain management.

### BOX 1.2 Effect of GST on Supply Chain Design and Operations

The Government of India has indicated that it would like to move to a better tax structure, one which simplifies and rationalizes the present taxes at centre and state levels. The Goods and Services Tax (GST) aims to subsume taxes at the central level viz. central excise duty, service Tax, additional customs duty, surcharge, and cesses as well as the taxes at the state level viz. VAT/sales tax, entertainment tax, entry tax (not in lieu of Octroi), other taxes, and duties (including luxury tax, taxes on lottery, betting and gambling, and all cesses and surcharges by states). Under the GST regime, the goods will be levied a value added tax at every point in the supply chain. Further, manufacturers will also be able to avail credit for taxes paid earlier in the supply chain. The tax structure will also remain common across all the states. Taxes will be redistributed across all categories resulting in lower taxes. Further, the interstate transfer of goods will become tax neutral as CST (Central Sales Tax) is reduced to 0%. In other words, manufacturers can look at India as one unified market rather than markets divided between many states.

The GST regime will also help to bring in efficiencies in supply chain design and rationalizing the number of distribution centres based on factors relevant to business rather than on tax avoidance. Companies would also be able to leverage benefits accrued due to economies of scale because of lesser number of larger distribution centres, reduce inventory carrying costs, and reduce the working capital employed in supply chains. More importantly, decisions related to choice and number of suppliers, number of products manufactured, manufacturing locations, expansion of manufacturing facilities, or distribution centres will be based on supply chain efficiencies and cost efficiencies. Studies show that the number of distribution centres can be reduced by 30 to 50 percent with the new GST regime. The move to GST would definitely benefit the manufacturers because of lower number of distribution centers as well as reduced costs due to inventory, transport, and documentation. With the design of lean supply chains, manufacturers can then dedicate their attention to improve operational efficiencies, cost efficiencies, reduce cost, and improve product variety to meet the changing consumer preferences.

With the induction of new blood and greater re-organization at the boardroom level, we are likely to see many innovations on this front.

Indian firms obviously need to learn from the progressive companies operating in developed economies. However, a country like India has its own unique problems and challenges. Thus, ready-made solutions that have been tried and tested in the developed economies may not work. For example, complex distribution structures, large numbers of customers at the bottom of the economic pyramid, poor infrastructure and complex taxation structures are issues unique to India that require innovative solutions. Amul, the Shakti project of HUL and the *dabbawalas* of Mumbai are cases in point where Indian firms have come up with unique solutions to supply chain challenges in India.

To discuss these issues in their specific context, we focus on the fast-moving consumer goods (FMCG) sector and identify a couple of challenges unique to the Indian context.

## Supply Chain Challenges for the Indian FMCG Sector

The fast-moving consumer goods (FMCG) sector is the fourth-largest sector of the economy with a size of about Rs 500 billion. The FMCG sector generally includes a wide range of frequently purchased consumer products such as soaps, dairy produces, confectionery, soft drinks, fruits and vegetables and batteries. FMCG products usually have a low unit cost but large volumes. The top 10 FMCG companies in India consist of both global players, such as HUL, Nestlé, Cadbury, P&G, and home-grown Indian companies, such as Amul, Asian Paints, Dabur and Marico Industries. The FMCG sector is also known as the consumer packaged goods sector.

In the FMCG sector, the performance of the supply chain is a key factor. The FMCG industry is characterized by a complex distribution network and intense competition forcing firms to constantly work on supply chain innovation. Over a period of time, supply chain innovations from the FMCG sector will be adopted by other industries as well. Companies with better supply chain practices will perform well, whereas those with poorly managed supply chains will find it tough to even survive in the competitive market. There are numerous supply chain challenges that an organization in the FMCG sector faces in India. Some of the major challenges are briefly discussed in this section.

### HUL'S SHAKTI INITIATIVE

A significant part of India lives in rural areas not well connected by road. Hence, most FMCG companies have not been able to penetrate these rural areas. HUL has launched a new initiative called project Shakti to increase its penetration in rural areas in a cost-effective manner. HUL has partnered with self-help groups (SHGs) to extend its reach to rural areas, particularly those areas where there are no established HUL distribution networks because of lack of connectivity. A Shakti dealer is a member of an SHG, who works as a direct-to-consumer HUL distributor, selling primarily to villages in her neighbourhood. The business objectives of this initiative are to extend HUL's reach into untapped markets and to develop its brand through local influences. In the process, HUL also provides sustainable livelihood opportunities to underprivileged rural woman.

### Managing Availability in the Complex Distribution Set Up

The Indian FMCG sector has to work with a very complex distribution system, comprising multiple layers of numerous small retailers, between company and end customer. For example, a company like Marico has to ensure reach to 1.6 million retailers spread geographically throughout the country (see Box 1.3 for details on Marico's supply chain structure). As the numbers of SKUs have been increasing exponentially, just ensuring availability at the last stage of distribution has become a nightmare for companies. Standard solutions applicable

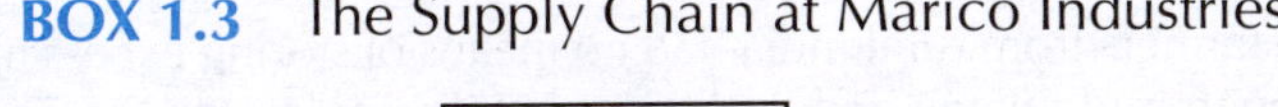

**BOX 1.3** The Supply Chain at Marico Industries

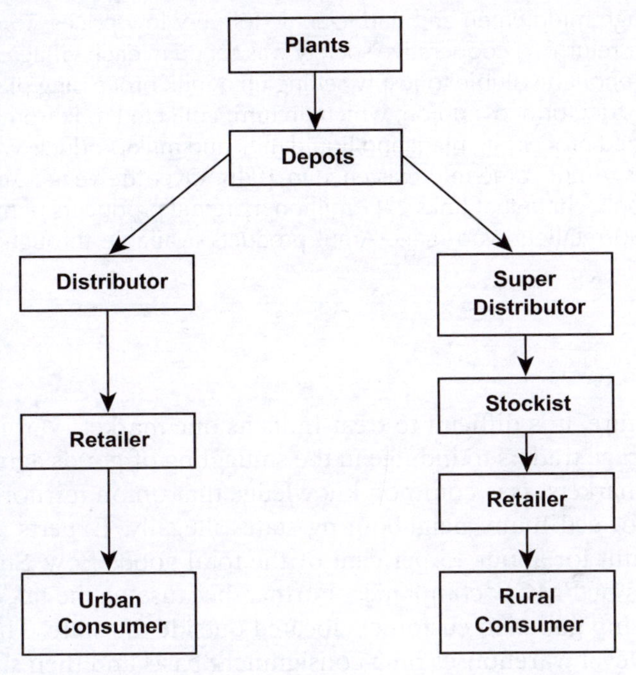


The retail trade for the company consists of 1.6 million retailers, of which less than 2 per cent represent organized retailers. More than 95 per cent of the retailers are grocery stores, each occupying less than 300 square meters.

To reach all areas of the nation, the company's products (35 million consumer packs per month), bought by 18 million Indian households monthly, are sold to approximately 1,000 distributors. These intermediaries, in turn, store, sell and deliver the company's products directly to those 1.6 million retailers or indirectly through 2,500 stockists. See the accompanying schematic figure for details of the company's distribution network. A part of the company's business strategy is to expand continuously into ever-smaller locales until its brands are available to most Indian households. Currently, the company's distribution network covers every Indian community with a population of 20,000 or more, and the plan is to penetrate more of the rural areas, where 70 per cent of India's people live. Currently, its rural sales and distribution network ranks among the top three in the industry and contributes 24 per cent to the company's sales.

in developed countries are not always suitable for a country like India. A large-scale study showed that at the SKU level, availability in the organized retail is as low as 65 per cent.[3] As the availability levels at an organized retail player are so low, one can imagine the situation for a typical retailer.

## Working with Smaller Pack Sizes

Unlike in developed countries, where companies have been trying to work with large pack sizes (reduction in transportation, handling and packaging costs for large pack sizes can be passed on as price cuts to price-sensitive customers), in India the trend is in the opposite direction. To increase market penetration, Indian companies have realized that they need to reach out to consumers present at the lower end of the economic pyramid. This consumer base can be tapped into only by offering smaller pack sizes. However, smaller pack sizes mean higher packaging and transportation costs for the companies. Eventually, companies will have to find innovative ways of balancing market penetration and logistics costs.

## Entry of National Players in the Traditional Fresh Products Sector

National players want to market "fresh" products that have been traditionally handled by local players in each region. For example, ITC wants to make inroads in the market for *atta* (wheat flour) and Nestlé for yoghurt. In these items, the freshness of the product is an important requirement from the consumers' point of view. Traditionally, national companies have worked with centralized plants, where they can manage quality and also enjoy big economies of scale. As freshness is one of the most important criteria from the customers' point of view, national players will have to work with decentralized manufacturing plants. Balancing quality, freshness and cost is a major issue for national players. Amul is an interesting case where a local firm has successfully managed the complex trade-offs by building superior supply chain capabilities.

### AMUL

Milk is a perishable commodity and poor farmers from rural India had no means of storing excess milk. The farmers were forced to sell milk through middlemen and had to settle for very low prices. To circumvent the middlemen and improve their returns, a cooperative society was set up in each village. As each village-level society would not have enough volume to justify setting up a milk processing plant, all the village cooperative societies in a district formed a union, which, in turn, collected milk from all the societies and processed it in a centralized processing plant and liquid milk and milk products were marketed to customers all over India. Thus, Amul came into existence in 1946. Over the years, Amul has set up a very efficient and effective supply chain that links 2.41 million marginal producers of milk from the rural areas of Gujarat to 500,000 retailers who make Amul products available throughout India.

## Dealing with Complex Taxation Structures

Because of the complex taxation structure, it is difficult to treat India as one market. Varying local-tax structures across states encourage traders to indulge in the smuggling of goods across states, leading to the creation of grey markets. It is common knowledge that union territories with lower state-level taxes are used to feed many neighbouring states illegally. Experts are of the view that smuggled goods account for about 15 per cent of the total goods flow. Such activities distort the plans and activities of FMCG companies. Further, because of the tax on inter-state sales, companies can never ship goods to customers located outside the state. They first have to transfer goods to the state-level warehouses on a consignment basis and then supply the goods to the customers. With the introduction of value added tax, harmonization of taxes across states and the possible removal of tax on inter-state sales, FMCG companies will see lots of changes in the way they have been managing their supply chains. FMCG companies need to prepare themselves for this transition, which will affect them significantly.

## Dealing with Counterfeit Goods

According to a recent study conducted by Assocham,[4] counterfeits accounted for loss of sale worth Rs 300 billion for the FMCG sector every year. P&G found that various counterfeit products of Vicks Vaporub raked in sales equivalent to 54 per cent of the original. To prevent such losses, FMCG companies in India have to ensure that they exercise greater control over their distribution channel and not just leave it to the market forces.

## Opportunistic Games Played by the Distribution Channel

It is a common notion in distribution that only 50 per cent of the promotion actually reaches the final customer. This is due to the fact that many distributors work unscrupulously. Rather than playing the role of the facilitator, they try to grab a significant part of the promotion budget for themselves. One FMCG company found that it ended up paying significant amounts as rebate to its trade channel because of illegal printing of coupons by some wholesalers and distributors. Some of these distributors also indulge in the illegal movement of goods from one market to another during local promotions, due to which companies lose control of the sales of their products (the company may want to target a specific market but the distributors might divert the goods to a different region). Thus, FMCG companies end up wasting a significant part of their resources on these issues, which do not really add any value to their customers.

## Infrastructure

Poor roads and unreliable transport systems have an adverse impact on costs and uncertainties. Non-availability of infrastructure, like cold chains, affects certain product categories significantly. Even if the cold chain is available, power problems add to the uncertainty. For example, in the ice-cream business, if the ice cream melts even once because of the non-availability of power, the quality in general, and the taste in particular, of the ice cream are adversely affected. Most Indian cities face power problems in summer and ice-cream manufactures have to live with these problems in their distribution network. In general, FMCG companies have to take these issues into account while planning their supply chain activities. The *dabbawalas* of Mumbai present an innovative supply chain approach that uses the existing infrastructure to deliver high-quality service at low cost.

### *THE DABBAWALAS OF MUMBAI*

The *dabbawalas* of Mumbai deliver home-prepared food to the middle-class office workers. On every working day, they collect 175,000 lunchboxes (*dabbas*) from the customers' houses between 7:00 and 9:00 a.m. and deliver the same to the respective offices by 12:30 p.m. The empty lunchboxes are picked up by 3:30 p.m. and returned to the homes of the respective customers by 6:00 p.m. To ensure that no more than one in 6,000,000 deliveries (six-sigma quality) goes astray, the *dabbawalas* have developed ingenious systems that use a very simple but effective coding system to sort the lunchboxes, on both the forward and the reverse journeys. The extensive use of public infrastructure in Mumbai (local trains) helps keep the operation costs low. The use of local trains and an ingenious coding system allows them to manage their supply chain remarkably well, which translates into high-quality service, at an affordable cost, for the customer.

## Emergence of Third-party Logistics Provider

Traditionally, most companies have been managing all logistics activities themselves. So far, the logistics sector in India has lacked professionalism. Of late, many 3PL providers, who claim to have the requisite expertise, have entered the market. These new players are still to learn a lot about Indian conditions and also are not in a position to offer economies of scale. Hence, they will be of value only to new MNCs and FMCG players who operate in the mid-volume, high-variety segment of the market. Established FMCG companies like Nestlé and HUL are unlikely to use their services as logistics solution providers, as they are not likely to be cost effective. The problem gets compounded further because most Indian FMCG companies have skewed sales patterns that place huge demands on service providers in the last week of the month. Thus, service providers are not in a position to manage their resources effectively. Over a period of time, these 3PL companies will develop an understanding of the Indian market and also the relevant capabilities necessary to handle these markets, which will enable them to bring down their costs and to provide cost-effective services to even large-volume players like HUL.

## Reservation for the Small-scale Sector

There are many items that have been traditionally reserved for the small-scale sectors. So FMCG companies had to source material/products from various small players. With liberalization likely on this front, companies will have to rework their sourcing strategies.

## Emergence of Organized (Modern ) Retail

In the West, large departmental/discount chains have managed to grab huge market shares and have clout with FMCG companies. On account of their bargaining power, they are able to demand huge discounts from FMCG companies.

In India, the nascent organized retailing sector accounts for less than 8 per cent of the total retail business. Like in developed markets, modern retailers in India have been trying to extract higher margins from FMCG companies so as to offer better deals to their customers. Unlike in the West, margins in distribution are traditionally quite low in India. Hence, in India, the FMCG sector finds it difficult to offer the kind of deep discounts that the modern retailers have been demanding. The FMCG companies are in a dilemma. On one hand, FMCG companies will have to bypass their existing stockists and distributors, so there is a likelihood of channel conflict. On the other hand, they also have to examine the impact of higher discounts to modern retailing on the overall distribution system. Further, modern retail chains are also likely to introduce private-label brands, which will pose a considerable threat to the existing manufacturers.

As the use of Internet and online applications gather pace, customers are increasingly making use of web-based transactions to purchase FMCG products. The story of online retail industry in India is similar to the one in the US in the 1990s when online retailers such as eBay and Amazon grew rapidly to challenge the competitive position of traditional retailers. Online retail in India has grown swiftly and has been growing at CAGR (Compounded annual growth rate) of close to 50% during 2012–2015. Led by factors such as increase in the Internet penetration and broadband services, the online retail industry is poised for exponential growth in the future in India, as more and more rural areas are included within its domain.

## Summary

- The supply chain encompasses all activities associated with the transformation of goods from the raw-material stage to the final stage, when the goods and services reach the end customer.
- Supply chain management involves planning, design and control of flow of material, information and finance along the supply chain to deliver superior value to the end customer in an effective and efficient manner. In well-managed chains, material, information and finance flow seamlessly across department and organization boundaries.
- On account of globalization and increased competition, firms have to manage a larger number of product lines with shorter product life cycles under the situation of changed power equations within a chain.
- Most supply chains the world over are slow, costly and do not deliver good value to the end customer. However, technological and managerial innovations, along with the development of logistics specialists, have helped progressive firms to improve supply chain performance under trying times.
- The Indian economy as a whole, and the manufacturing sector in particular, need to improve supply chain performance considerably if Indian firms are to compete globally.
- Indian firms need to learn from progressive firms in developed economies, which have managed to improve supply chain performance considerably. However, at the same time emerging economies like India and China have their own unique supply chain problems and challenges. Obviously, different geographies and their economies have their own unique set of problems and we need to look for specific solutions to these problems.

## Discussion Questions

1. Describe the supply chain involved in making the bar of Lux soap that you have just picked up from your neighbourhood retail store.
2. A customer planning to buy a book can either order the book on the Internet from Flipkart.com or go to the nearby Landmark outlet. How are the supply chains different for these two companies? Are customers looking for the same kind of service from both the companies? How can these factors affect the strategies of both these companies?
3. Though supply chain principles are universal in nature, application of these depends on the context of the country, which is why India has to find its own unique solutions. Explain why you agree or disagree with the above statement.
4. Compare and contrast the supply chains followed by the two food product firms mentioned below:

   (i) A firm offering a food product targeted at the lower end of the economic pyramid (e.g., Tiger biscuit offered by Britannia).

(ii) A firm offering a premium food product (e.g., Lays offered by Pepsi).

5. Indian companies complain that high logistics costs make their products less competitive in international markets. Identify products that are likely to be significantly affected by the poor logistics infrastructure in India.
6. Most Indian firms have increased their product variety by about 50 per cent in the past five years. What are the implications of these increased varieties on supply chain management practices in these firms?
7. HUL has decided to increase its reach in rural areas. What are the implications of this decision for the department that manages the supply chain for HUL products?
8. With the emergence of organized retailing, power structure in the supply chain is likely to shift over a period of time. What do you think are the implications of this for manufacturing firms?
9. Can ideas of supply chain management be applied to firms like Wipro and Infosys, which offer software services?

## Mini Project

**Field Study: Estimating the Length of a Supply Chain for an FMCG Company**

The objective of the study is to estimate the length of the supply chain for packed goods. This field study will help you in understanding supply chain opportunities in distribution in India.

**Methodology**

- Pick up two competing companies from the FMCG sector. Identify the different product lines offered by these companies.
- Select four retailers (two from organized sector and two from the unorganized sector) for the study.
- From each retail store, collect the following data for each of the selected product lines:
    - Packing/manufacturing date on stock held at retailer (as per the law, all packaged goods companies are expected to print manufacturing date/month data on each package)
    - Estimate of average sales rate (How many units are sold per month?)
    - Stock available with the retailer
- Estimate length of chain

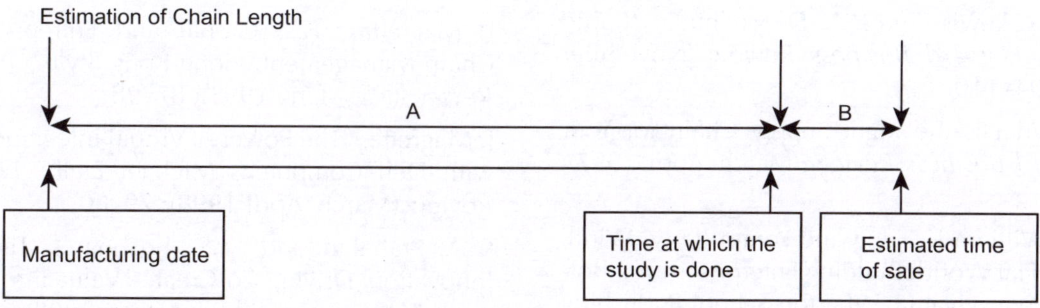


| Item | Data collected from retailer | | | A | B[a] | A + B |
|---|---|---|---|---|---|---|
| | Stock (units) | Sales (units) /Month | Date of manufacture on stocks held[b] | (in months) | (in months) | (in months) |
| Product line X | 20 | 40 | October 2014 | 2.5 | 0.25 | 2.75 |
| Product line Y | 40 | 20 | September 2014 | 3.5 | 1 | 4.5 |
| Product line Z | 30 | 10 | August 2014 | 4.5 | 1.5 | 6.0 |

[a]Average time stock would spend at retailer from the time of study = (stock/sales)/2.
[b]If the date of manufacture is August 2014, we can assume that the actual date of manufacture is 15 August 2014.

- Let us suppose that three products X, Y and Z have been chosen for the study and the study was carried out at the end of December 2014. Data (stocks, sales rate, manufacturing date on stocks on the shelf) and estimation of the length of the chain for the three product lines is as shown in the table above.
- The same analysis can be carried out for multiple retailers for the same company. Use the above methodology to carry out the following analysis:
    - Compare the time taken by a large firm (say Colgate) and small firm (say Anchor).
    - Compare and contrast the time taken in chain for a fast-moving product (Colgate toothpaste) vis-à-vis a slow-moving product (Colgate-Palmolive shaving cream).
    - Compare the time taken by a chain for the organized retailer (Subhiksha, Foodworld) vis-à-vis a neighbourhood kirana (the unorganized retailer, also known as mom-and-pop stores) store.

## Notes

1. Henry Ford, *Today and Tomorrow* (Cambridge, MA: Productivity Press, 1988).
2. B. Avittathur and J. Shah, "Tapping Product Returns Through Efficient Reverse Supply Chains: Opportunities and Issues," *IIMB Management Review* 16 (2004): 84–93; V. D. R. Guide, T. P. Harrison, and L. V. Wassenhove, "The Challenge of Closed-Loop Supply Chains," *Interfaces* (2003): 3–6; V. D. R. Guide, L. Muyldermans, and L. V. Wassenhove, "Hewlett-Packard Comny Unlocks the Value Potential from Time-Sensitive Returns," *Interfaces* (2007): 281–293.
3. M. Anand, "Operations Streamline," *Business World* (18 February 2002).
4. K. K. Shankar, "India Inc Raises Voice against Rs 30,000 Cr Counterfeit Trade," *The Indian Express* (4 January 2007).

## Further Reading


R. D. Blackwell and Kristina Blackwell, "The Century of the Consumer: Converting Supply Chains into Demand Chains," *Supply Chain Management Review* (Fall 1999): 22–32.

K. Ferdows, M. A. Lewis, and J. A. D. Machuca, "Rapid Fire Fulfilment," *Harvard Business Review* (November 2004, Vol 82): 104–110.

M. L. Fisher, "What is the Right Supply Chain for Your Product?" *Harvard Business Review* (March–April 1997): 83–93.

Victor K. Fung, William K. Fung and Yoram (Jerry) Wind, "Competing in a Flat World: Building Enterprises for a Borderless World", Pennsylvania: Wharton School Publishing (First Impression, 2008).

C. Gianpaolo, D. M. Xavier, S. Regine, V. Wassenhove, and W. Linda, "Inventory-Driven Costs," *Harvard Business Review* (March 2005, Vol 83): 135–141.

Çağrı Haksöz, Sridhar Seshadri, and Ananth V. Iyer, "Managing Supply Chains on the Silk Road: Strategy, Performance and Risk", CRC Press (January 2012): 105-120.

R. Henkoff, "Delivering the Goods," *Fortune* (November 1994): 64–78.

Larry Lapide, "Demand – Shaping with Supply in Mind", *Supply Chain Management Review* (November 2013).

Hau L. Lee, "The Triple – A Supply Chain", *Harvard Business Review* (October 2004).

Hau L. Lee, "Don't Tweak Your Supply Chain – Rethink it End to End", *Harvard Business Review* (October 2010).

J. Magretta, "Fast Global and Entrepreneurial: Supply Chain Management, Hong Kong Style," *Harvard Business Review* (May–June 1993): 87–98.

J. Magretta, "The Power of Virtual Integration: An Interview with Dell Computer's Michael Dell," *Harvard Business Review* (March–April 1998): 79–80.

C.K. Prahalad and M.S. Krishnan, "The New Age of Innovation: Driving Co-Created Value through Global Networks", Mc Graw Hill Education (2008).

F. J. Quinn, "Re-engineering the Supply Chain: An Interview with Michael Hammer," *Supply Chain Management Review* (Spring 1999): 20–26.

Y. Sheffi and J. B. Rice, "A Supply Chain View of the Resilient Enterprise," *MIT Sloan Management Review* (Fall 2005): 41–48.

R. E. Slone, "Leading a Supply Chain Turnaround," *Harvard Business Review* (October 2004): 114–121.

# Supply Chain Strategy and Performance Measures

## Learning Objectives

After reading this chapter, you will be able to answer the following questions:

> What are the key supply chain performance measures?

> How does supply chain performance affect financial performance?

> Why is it necessary to ensure a good fit of the business strategy with the supply chain strategy?

> What are the different dimensions of customer service?

> What are the ways in which a firm can simultaneously reduce supply chain costs and improve customer service?

Three management students are poring over data that they have recently acquired and want to incorporate it into their presentation for the next morning. They have been at it for quite some time, when one of them calls Domino's and orders pizzas for the whole group. The pizzas arrive in exactly 25 minutes. While they take a break and devour the pizzas, they wonder how Domino's manages to deliver pizzas within 30 minutes to almost any location in Bangalore even with the traffic snarls in Bangalore and the unpredictability of the timing and quantity of the pizza that might be ordered by customers.

Domino's, in its efforts to deal with such unpredictable variables, has set up outlets at 50 strategic locations across Bangalore. It plans its resources (raw material, equipment and human resource) in such a manner that it can deliver on time to any location in Bangalore. Domino's business strategy to deliver delicious pizzas in 30 minutes is a reflection of its commitment to bring fun and excitement into the lives of its customers. It designs and operates its supply chain so that it can support this business strategy.

In this chapter, the focus is on supply chain strategy and supply chain performance measures. We discuss customer service and cost trade-offs and suggest ways by which a firm can integrate business and supply chain strategies. We also look at the various dimensions of customer service and use two of these, namely, order delivery time and responsiveness, to characterize various types of supply chains. A framework to analyse the impact of supply chain initiative on business performance has been provided. Finally, an approach that can help firms in enhancing their supply chain performance on an ongoing basis has been suggested.

# Introduction

A firm's supply chain strategy should ensure that its supply chain provides superior value to the end customer in an efficient manner. Value offering (bundling of goods and services) to a customer should be available at a reasonable price. In almost all product categories, customers want more variety and quicker services at lower prices. Firms must recognize the nature of trade-offs between customer service and costs and arrive at an optimal decision on this front. If various processes and decisions within the chain are not aligned to suit a company's business strategy, it obviously cannot remain competitive in the long run. The firm has to understand the relationship between business strategy and supply chain decisions and how different business environments pose different kinds of challenges to the supply chain.

Although at any given point managers need to understand customer service and cost trade-offs, in the long run firms will have to find a way of improving performance on both cost and service fronts. Because of the nature of competition, customers will demand better services at lower prices over a period of time. Progressive firms resolve this paradox through various supply chain innovations. To enhance supply chain performance, firms have to identify the right kind of initiatives to help improve both costs and customer service simultaneously on an ongoing basis.

# Customer Service and Cost Trade-offs

A firm must ensure a smooth fit between its business strategy and supply chain strategy. As a part of its business strategy, the firm decides the market segment in which it wants to operate and the level of customer service it wants to offer. The supply chain strategy includes issues of cost that the firm has to incur to provide the targeted level of customer service.

Well-managed firms identify and develop external market opportunities and internal supply chain capabilities until the two are mutually consistent.

To understand the relationship between the supply chain strategy and the business strategy, we need to understand cost versus service trade-offs in business. As discussed earlier, the supply chain must provide superior value to the end customer in an effective and efficient manner. For a given supply chain design, firms generally have an efficient frontier, which defines the nature of trade-offs between supply chain costs and customer service. Ideally, firms prefer to provide a very high level of customer service (high variety, short delivery time, etc.) at very low cost. However, as illustrated in Figure 2.1, firms must recognize the nature of trade-offs between the supply chain cost (marginal cost) and customer service. If a firm wants to improve its performance on the customer service front, it must accept deterioration

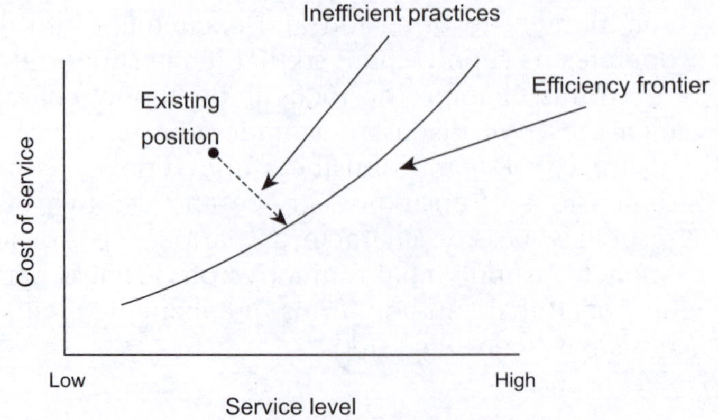


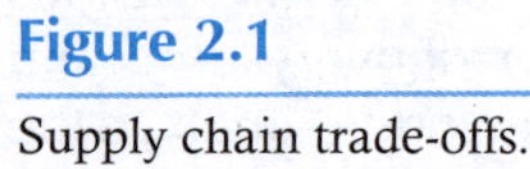
**Figure 2.1**

Supply chain trade-offs.

in performance on the cost front and vice versa. For example, if a pizza company delivering pizzas in 40 minutes wants to deliver in 20 minutes, its costs would increase. An efficient frontier, shown in Figure 2.1, provides a lower envelope, below which a firm cannot choose to operate. Efficient firms can choose to operate on any point of the efficiency frontier. For example, a firm may choose to provide lower service levels at lower costs or higher service levels at higher costs, but it cannot hope to provide higher levels of customer service at low cost. In other words, if a firm is on the efficiency frontier, it represents the best attainable compromise between the two dimensions at any given point in time. The efficiency frontier is an upper ceiling on performance and is an outcome of the supply chain structure and processes of the firm.

If the supply chain operations of a typical firm are to be mapped, the firm will lie somewhere above the efficiency frontier curve, as shown in Figure 2.1. This is because most firms do not operate their supply chains efficiently. Inefficient executions of supply chain processes result in gaps between existing and potential performance, as defined by the efficiency frontier. Of course, by implementing several innovative ideas a firm can shift its overall supply chain efficiency frontier. These issues are discussed later in this chapter.

The business strategy of a firm helps in choosing an appropriate position on the efficiency frontier. The demand and price that a company commands in the market are a function of customer service. So a company works to optimize its performance based on the interaction between the revenue curve (price × demand) and the total cost curve (cumulative cost incurred to produce the relevant quantity that is required at the given level of service). As shown in Figure 2.2(a), the revenue response to customer service level is usually found to be an S-shaped curve. First, there is a minimum threshold level of service, below which a firm is not able to attract many customers. Similarly, there is a point beyond which any improvement in service will not produce a significant increase in demand, resulting in service overkill. For example, a cement company found that dealers were willing to wait up to a day for delivery, and improvement in delivery time to less than a day did not have any appreciable changes in demand. On the other hand, if the company worked with a 2-day delivery time, it lost about 20 per cent of the potential demand. Similarly, in the case of the pizza company, if delivery takes two hours, there is not likely to be any demand. Of course, the shape of the revenue curve is a function of the customer's genuine need and what competitors have on offer. Total costs increase exponentially with increase in service, while revenue follows an S-shaped curve. Therefore, it will be optimal for a firm to operate at a specific level of customer service, as shown in Figure 2.2(b). This level, however, is not always static but changes with customer taste and competitive offerings, affecting the shape of the revenue curve, while supply chain innovations affect the cost curve.

A company will need to conduct market research to determine the revenue and contribution potential of increased customer service. Further, customer profitability analysis

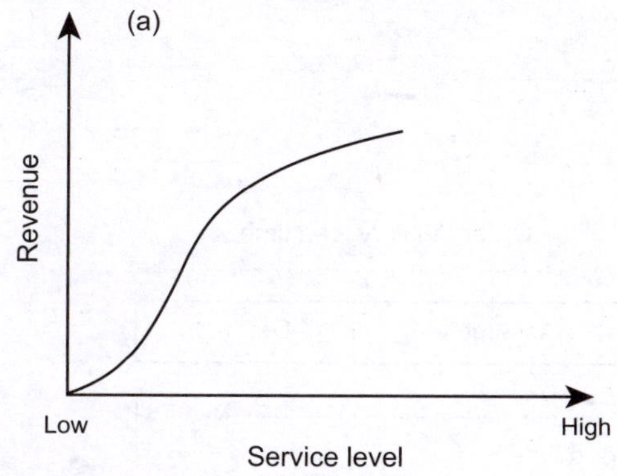


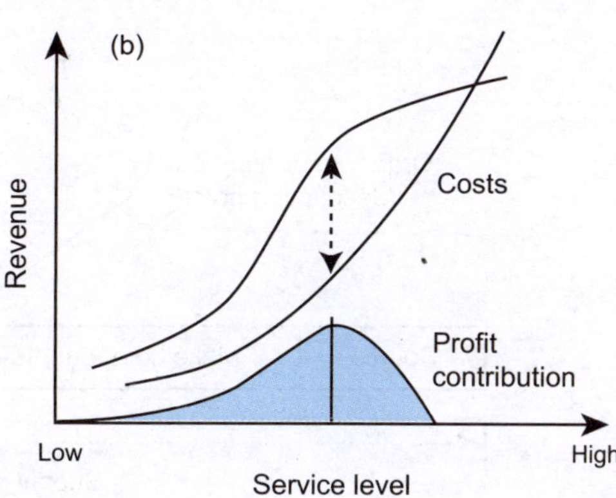


**Figure 2.2**

(a) Revenue impact of service level; (b) Profit impact of service level.

must be carried out to identify the right market segments. Similarly, while planning sales promotions, marketing and supply chain strategists should work together to ensure that the supply chain is well equipped to handle any additional demand in a profitable way. Thus, well-managed firms always consider marketing and supply chain decisions in tandem, and not independently.

In order to keep things simple, the discussions so far have dealt with only two dimensions—cost and customer service. However, customer service in itself has multiple dimensions. From a supply chain perspective, customer service consists of the following four dimensions:

- Order delivery lead time
- Responsiveness
- Delivery reliability
- Product variety

Shorter lead time, higher responsiveness, higher reliability and higher product variety lead to better customer service. Improvement in performance on any of these four fronts will result in higher costs. Depending on customer expectations and product characteristics, different dimensions of the supply chain have varying levels of impact on the overall value of customer service.

## Order Delivery Lead Time

Order delivery time is the time taken by the supply chain to complete all the activities from order to delivery. This dimension of customer service has a significant impact on the way a supply chain is designed and operated. Customer expectations on order delivery time could be practically zero, as in the case of most of FMCG goods, or could be 1 week for certain consumer durables. For example, a typical customer might expect pizzas to be served in 15 minutes at any pizza outlet, or expect delivery in 40 minutes if the order has been placed for home delivery. E-retailers like Fabmart promise to deliver goods within 48 hours at the doorstep of customers located in major cities. Caterpillar pledges its commitment to customers: service within 48 hours at any place on earth. For each of these firms, promised order delivery lead time has tremendous implications on supply chain design and operations.

As shown in Figure 2.3, a typical firm sources material, manufactures components, assembles the product and delivers the finished product to the end customer, with each of these activities having a certain lead time. If we aggregate all the four lead times, we get the supply chain lead time, which is the total time required for the supply chain to carry out all activities from the beginning to the end. Unfortunately, for many firms, supply chain lead times and order delivery lead times usually do not match. Ideally, a firm will prefer to work with a delivery lead time that is larger than the supply chain lead time. In a competitive market, however,

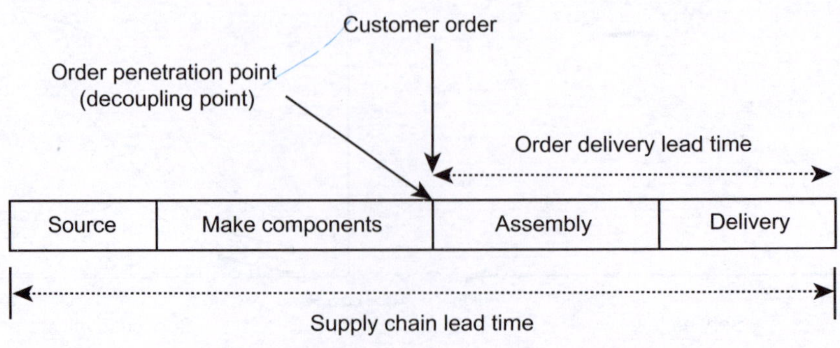


**Figure 2.3**

Interaction between supply chain lead time and delivery lead time.

the order delivery lead time is dictated by competitive offerings and customer needs and the supply chain lead time is usually much longer than the order delivery lead time. The point at which the customer enters the supply chain (Figure 2.3) is called the order penetration point. After the order penetration point, all activities do not face any uncertainties because they are against specific customer orders. All the activities prior to the customer order must be carried out against forecast and not on actual orders. For example, one wants pizzas to be delivered within 40 minutes. Obviously the firm cannot procure the material, make the dough and bake a base in those 40 minutes. A firm in the pizza home delivery business has to forecast likely demand and execute most of the activities like procurement, preparing the pizza base and making all the other ingredients ready before the order so that they can satisfy customer demand within 40 minutes. As all activities after the penetration point are carried out against an order, and all activities prior to the penetration point are carried out against forecast, this point is also known as the decoupling point. Essentially, the firm has to keep a decoupling stock ready at the customer penetration point and manage both sides, that is, before and after order penetration point, differently.

A critical characteristic of the supply chain is the customer order penetration point or decoupling point. There are essentially three types of supply chains characterized by the customer order penetration point: make to stock (MTS), make to order (MTO) and configure to order (CTO). Figure 2.4 is a conceptual representation of these three types of supply chains. If customers expect their order (an order can either be a formal document or even an informal instruction, e.g., a customer asking a retailer for a tube of tooth paste is treated as an order) to be fulfilled instantaneously, then the supply chain is in the MTS business. If the supplier gives enough time to the firm to assemble the product before delivery, it is in the CTO business. If the customer gives enough time to the manufacturer to carry out the complete set of operations (source, make, assemble and deliver) after placing the order, it is in the MTO business. Typically, firms in the consumer products business operate on an MTS basis where the customer expects the products to be on the shelf at the retailer's outlet. Equipment manufacturers typically operate with an MTO supply chain where all the activities are started after getting the order. A firm in the pizza home delivery business is in the CTO business, because your pizza is configured the way you want, with the toppings of your choice, using ingredients kept in readiness, prior to an order. CTO is also known as assemble to order (ATO) or build to order (BTO) business model.

For a firm operating with a wide variety of products, forecasting is a very difficult exercise. For such a firm, if the variety explosion takes place during the assembly stage, it can improve its business performance by moving from the MTS model to the CTO model. By doing so, the firm has to forecast only at the component level rather than at the end-product level. If the firm

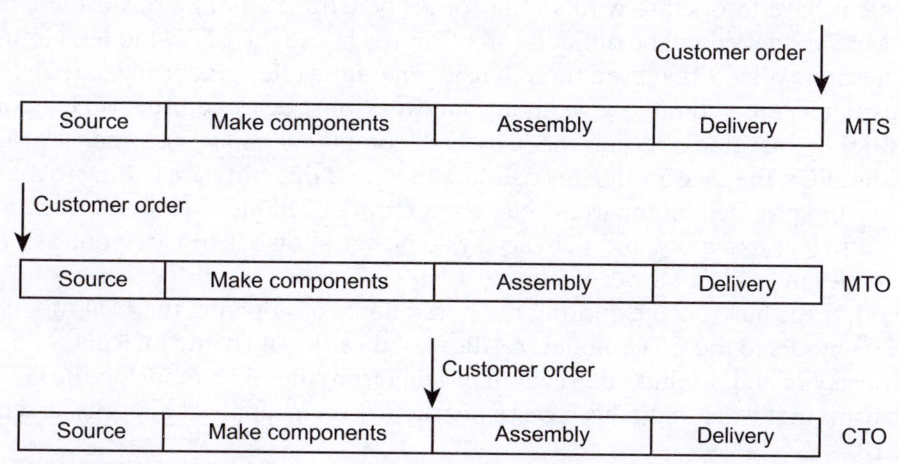


**Figure 2.4**
Order penetration point based supply chain typology.

## INTERVIEW WITH MICHAEL DELL

*Dell, a $55 billion company, is famous for its build-to-order supply chain model. Michael Dell founded the company in 1984 with a simple business insight: he would bypass the dealer channels to sell directly to the customers and build products to order. The formula became known as the direct business model, and it gave Dell Computer Corporation a substantial cost advantage.*

*What is the build-to-order model?*

**Michael Dell:** We build to our customers' order, typically, with just 5 or 6 days of lead time. We only maintain a few days—in some cases a few hours—of raw materials on hand. We communicate inventory levels and replenishment needs regularly—with some vendors, hourly. We tell our suppliers exactly what our daily production requirements are, "Tomorrow morning we need 8,562, and deliver them to door number seven by 7 a.m.".

The direct model has allowed us to leverage our relationships with both suppliers and customers to such an extent that I believe it's fair to think of our companies as being virtually integrated.

*What are the key performance measures?*

**Michael Dell:** Inventory velocity is one of a handful of key performance measures we watch very closely. It focuses us on working with our suppliers to keep reducing inventory and increasing speed. With a supplier like Sony, which makes very good, reliable monitors, we figure there's no need for us to have any inventory at all.

**Michael Dell:** In our industry, if you can get people to think about how fast inventory is moving then you create real value. Why? Because if I've got 11 days of inventory and my competitor has 80, and Intel comes out with a new 450-MHz chip, that means I'm going to get to market 69 days sooner.

*What is the current industrial practice?*

**Michael Dell:** In our industry, there's a lot of what I call bad hygiene. Companies stuff the channel to get rid of old inventory and to meet short-term financial objectives. We think our approach is better. We substitute information for inventory and ship only when we have real demand from real end customers.

*What is the benefit of the direct model to the suppliers?*

**Michael Dell:** We can go to Sony and say, "We're going to be pulling monitors from you in a very consistent, predictable way because the distance between the demand and the source of supply is totally shrunk". The longer that distance, the more intermediary channels you add, the less likely it is you will have good information about demand—so you will end up with more variability, more inventory, higher costs and more risk.

*Source:* J. Magretta, "The Power of Virtual Integration: An Interview with Dell Computer's Michael Dell," *Harvard Business Review* (March–April 1998): 72–84.

belongs to an industry where, because of modular design, there is an explosion in variety at the assembly stage, it can significantly improve business performance by carrying out assembly, based on orders rather than against forecast.

In the PC industry, where most players operate on an MTS basis, Dell Computers has managed to operate on a CTO basis. This has helped Dell in reducing inventories and operating with larger margins, as compared to its competitors. Generally, firms operating in a similar market segment have to operate with similar order penetration points. If all the competitors choose the MTS model, it will be difficult for a firm to choose the MTO model. Naturally, this raises the question: Why is that even though its competitors offer practically zero delivery lead time, the customers are willing to give about one week of order lead time to Dell computers? The answer lies in the value offerings made by Dell computers: Since customers are allowed to customize their PCs, they see a value in customization and therefore are willing to allow longer order delivery time to Dell, compared to its competitors. Dell also has invested in building a flexible and efficient assembly and delivery system that allows it to carry out assembly and delivery activities in less than a week's time.

In general, firms have been exploring the possibilities of applying the Dell model to move from the MTS model to the CTO model. As discussed earlier, it is only logical that firms offering a wide variety in end products be keen on moving from the MTS model to the CTO model. Essentially, firms that want to do this have to restructure their supply chains, discussed in detail in Chapter 10.

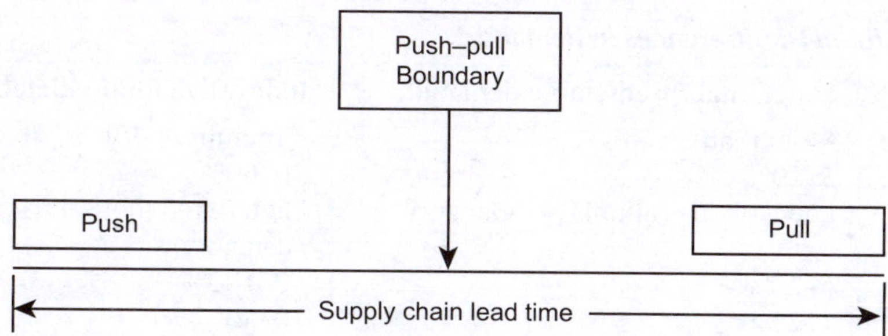


**Figure 2.5**

Push–pull boundary of supply chains.

### Push–Pull Boundary of the Supply Chain

Order delivery lead time also can be used for drawing a push–pull boundary of the supply chain. All the processes in the supply chain are divided into two categories based on their position in a supply chain with respect to the customer order point. As shown in Figure 2.5, all the processes carried out before the customer order point are managed through the push approach, and all the processes carried out after the customer order are managed through the pull approach. The interface between the push-based processes and the pull-based strategy is known as the push–pull boundary. All the processes managed by pull approaches do not face any uncertainty because they are carried out against specific orders. As they are executed against specific customer orders, they operate on customer pull and, hence, are known as pull-based processes. On the other hand, processes prior to the customer order are executed based on forecast, and as there is no known customer pull in this case, these activities are pushed within the chain; thus, they are known as push-based processes.

The inventory at the push–pull boundary is used to decouple the push and the pull processes. Firms like Asian Paints and Dell Computers are able to assemble and deliver a wide variety of finished goods demanded by the end customer from relatively few components stocked at the push–pull boundary. In MTS supply chains, the push–pull boundary is at the end of chain and all processes are managed using the push approach. In MTO supply chains, all processes are managed using the pull approach and the push–pull boundary is located at the beginning of the chain. In CTO supply chains, the push–pull boundary is usually positioned after component manufacturing.

## Supply Chain Responsiveness

Responsiveness captures the firm's ability to handle the uncertainty of market demand. In addition to delivery lead time, supply chains have also been characterized on the basis of the nature of demand uncertainty faced by products in the market place. Based on the nature of demand uncertainty, products can be classified as functional products or innovative products.

Functional products (grocery) are those that satisfy the basic needs of a customer and therefore have low variety, stable and predictable demand, long life cycles and low profit margins. Innovative products (fashion and technology products) are those that try to satisfy a broad range of customers' wants and have the following features: high variety, unstable and very-hard-to-predict demand, short life cycles, high profit margins and frequent stock-outs and markdowns. See Table 2.1 for details on the differences of various aspects of demand for different product categories.

Conceptually, the main functions of a supply chain are physical transformation of raw material into the end product and market mediation. *Physical function* is the process of converting materials into parts, then to finished products and then transporting them across the various stages of the chain. Relevant costs incurred are due to production, transportation and inventory storage. The *market mediation function* ensures that the variety of products reaching

*Table 2.1:* ***Functional versus innovative products: differences in demand.***

| Aspects of demand | Functional (predictable demand) | Innovative (unpredictable demand) |
|---|---|---|
| Product life cycle | More than 2 years | 3 months to 1 year |
| Contribution margin (% of sales price) | 5–20% | 20–60% |
| Product variety | Low (10–20 variants per category) | High (often thousands of variants per category) |
| Likely forecast error | 5–20% | 40–100% |
| Average stock-out rate | 1–2% | 10–40% |
| End-of-season markdown | 0% | 10–30% |

*Source:* Adapted from M. L. Fisher, "What Is the Right Supply Chain for Your Product?" *Harvard Business Review* (March–April 1997): 83–93. 

the market matches the needs of the customers. Relevant costs incurred are due to demand–supply mismatch, resulting in either obsolescence or lost sales and dissatisfied customers. In the case of functional products, the focus is on meeting predictable demand cost effectively, while for innovative products, the focus is on meeting unpredictable demand cost effectively.

For functional products, low stock-out rate and low margins suggest that the physical function is crucial for the supply chain of these products. Hence, for the supply chain of functional products, achieving physical efficiency is a critical success factor. High stock-out rates and high margins for innovative products suggest that the market mediation function is a crucial factor in the supply chain. Thus, it is evident that functional products need efficient supply chains, while innovative products need responsive chains.

### INVENTORY WRITE-OFF BY CISCO[1]

Cisco, the global market leader in networking equipments like routers and switches, had seen more than 50 per cent growth rate in 1999 and 2000. A similar growth trend had been forecast for 2001. Unfortunately, there was a downturn in the economy and Cisco took a long time to respond to the change in the economic environment. During the economic downturn, other networking companies cut back on inventory while Cisco decided to build inventory. Cisco had entered into long-term commitments with its manufacturing partners and certain key component makers. Cisco took sometime to recognize the downturn and by the time Cisco started putting brakes on its supply chain, it was quite late. Cisco ended up writing off inventory worth $2.2 billion. Its stock price plunged from $83 to $13.

Most firms often fail to take this into account when they introduce changes in their product lines/offerings. For example, firms operating in the innovative products space would have usually started their business with functional products and therefore would have focused on logistics efficiencies. As they grew, they would have introduced innovative products to compete effectively in the market but may not have changed their supply chain structure and processes. This would naturally result in a mismatch between the product characteristics and the supply chain. As shown in Figure 2.6, firms must ensure an appropriate match between the type of supply chain and the nature of product characteristics. Demand unpredictability could occur either on the volume side or on the product-mix side. In some instances, it is difficult to estimate the overall volume of demand itself, resulting in volume uncertainty, while in others, the overall volume is predictable but predicting demand at the individual variant level is extremely difficult, leading to product-mix uncertainty. For example, when it comes to new technology products, firms face volume uncertainty. While in the case of some innovative products, where the overall category is at a mature stage (garments, jewellery), firms usually face product-mix uncertainty. Within the life cycle of products, they are likely to face high volume uncertainty

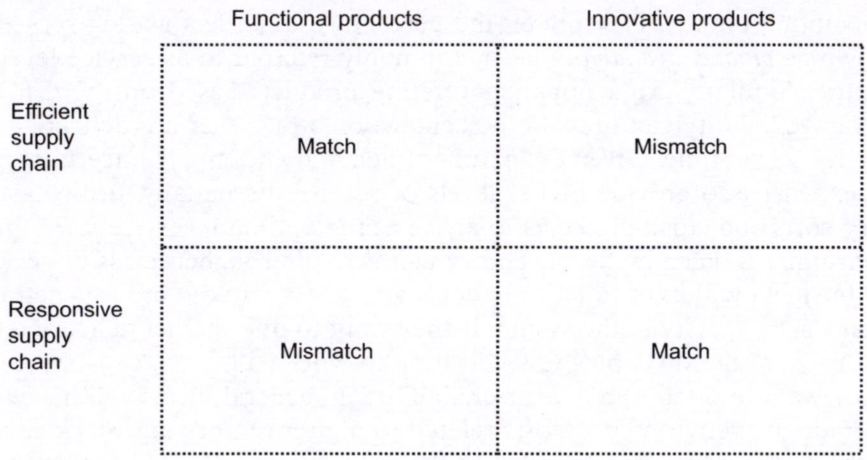

| | Functional products | Innovative products |
|---|---|---|
| Efficient supply chain | Match | Mismatch |
| Responsive supply chain | Mismatch | Match |

**Figure 2.6**

Matching supply chain design with nature of products.

*Source:* M. L. Fisher, "What Is the Right Supply Chain for Your Product?" *Harvard Business Review* (March–April 1997): 83–93. Reprinted with permission. © 1997 by the Harvard Business School Publishing Corporation. All rights reserved.

at the growth stage. Thus, during the growth stage firms need to work with a responsive chain, and over a period of time, at the mature stage, firms require an efficient chain.

For innovative products, like fashion products, demand is inherently unpredictable at the final customer end. Risk mitigation strategies involve buy back contracts, postponements or innovations in a supply chain design that enhance flexibility. These issues are discussed extensively in Part IV.

Although, in theory, functional products ought not to face much demand uncertainty, in real life manufacturers of functional products such as food products do see a large variability. In a typical supply chain, it has been observed that for functional products, as we move down from retailers to wholesalers and on to manufacturers, each stage in the chain distorts demand and the variability in demand keeps increasing as we move down the chain. Thus, though variability can be quite low at the end (final customer), a manufacturer usually sees high demand variability at his end. In Chapter 9 (Supply Chain Integration), the ways through which supply chains can avoid these distortions in the chain are discussed.

So far we have focused our attention on demand uncertainty. However, a firm could also face uncertainty on account of supply in the chain. Unlike demand uncertainty, supply uncertainty has not received enough attention in supply chain literature. Unlike demand, a firm can exercise greater control on supply and the popular view was that uncertainty in supply can be handled by choosing appropriate partners in a chain. Thus, traditionally, the focus has been on supplier selection and supplier development rather than on the management of supply uncertainty. The terrorist attack in September 2001 forced firms to look at their supply chain vulnerabilities, and firms have realized that they need to focus on both demand uncertainty and supply chain disruptions. Managing supply chain disruptions involves managing certain events that have a low probability of occurrence but have a high impact on supply chain performance. We discuss the relevant concepts and challenges in managing supply chain disruptions in Part IV.

Firms that have configured their supply chain design and operations to handle high levels of demand uncertainty and supply chain disruptions effectively are known as firms with agile supply chains.

## Delivery Reliability

As discussed in the earlier section, delivery lead time is an important dimension of customer service, and delivery reliability essentially captures the degree to which a firm is able to service its customers within the promised delivery time. *Delivery reliability* measures the fraction of customer demand that is satisfied within the promised delivery lead time.

For firms operating on an MTS model, the percentage of orders getting served from the stock is known as *product availability*, also commonly referred to as service level in supply chain literature. Similarly, for companies offering products based on the CTO or MTO model, delivery reliability captures the percentage of orders that are delivered within the promised delivery lead time. Given the nature of demand and supply uncertainty, it is obviously more expensive to provide higher levels of service. Essentially, firms have to trade-off inventory costs and stock-out costs to arrive at the optimum service level. In the MTS business, a firm has to keep higher inventory if it is to offer higher levels of service. Firms in the CTO business will have to hold higher inventory before the order penetration point and after that slack capacity in the system if they want to offer higher delivery reliability to customers. Firms in the MTO business will have to work with slack capacity in the entire system if they want to offer high delivery reliability. In general, firms will have to arrive at an optimal trade-off between cost (costs related to high inventory and slack capacity) and service level while deciding on this issue. In the industrial products category, performance on the delivery reliability front is monitored and the supplier is usually chosen based on performance on this front.

### SAFEXPRESS: OFFERING TIME-DEFINITE SERVICE FOR EXPRESS DISTRIBUTION[2]

Safexpress wanted to start a *time-definite* service for express distribution in the mid-1990s. Aware of the poor infrastructure and the multiplicity of check points at state borders, Safexpress knew that time-definite delivery across India would prove to be a Herculean task. Therefore, before they started the service, they mapped all the routes and identified all the check points and potential areas where trucks may get delayed. They have identified 88 delivery gateways, including 44 strategically located hubs so that they can manage time-definite service at an all-India level. Its entire fleet is equipped with GPS units so that any vehicle can be tracked with a precision of 50 meters. To ensure that they offer the lowest transit times, they operate 24/7, 365 days a year. Safexpress has identified its key strength as "knowledge and understanding of India" and has focused only on domestic business.

## Product Variety

The quantum of variety offered by a firm is an important dimension of customer service. In the past couple of years, a "variety explosion" has taken place in most product categories. Higher product variety offers greater choices to the customer who is likely to get a product that fits closest to his or her actual requirements. Some firms like Dell Computers and National Panasonic go to the extent of allowing their customers to design their own products. Obviously, higher

### 99-COLOUR CAMPAIGN BY TVS MOTORS[3]

TVS Motors, a two-wheeler manufacturing company, has been offering the Scooty range of two wheelers for the young generation. TVS, in its market research, found that colour is the prominent way of self-expression among women consumers. Based on this finding, TVS recently introduced the 99-colour campaign in select cities with the intention of attracting young women. The customer can choose from a range of 99 shades, available for a premium of Rs 1,000–1,900. Offering 99 shades can be a supply chain nightmare. TVS has come up with an innovative way of managing such a wide variety of offering. TVS stocks unpainted panels at the retail outlet. These unpainted panels are sent to Asian Paints who return the panel, painted in the colour chosen by a customer, to the retail outlet within 24 hours. So TVS can manage product delivery in 48 hours without worrying about the large amount of finished stock at the retail outlets.

variety would lead to greater complexity, resulting in higher supply chain costs. Some firms have found that variety explosion has affected firm profitability in an adverse way. Firms like P&G have worked on product rationalizations and have reduced overall product variety. While deciding the optimum level of product variety, a firm has to manage trade-offs with other dimensions of customer service like order lead time. For example, if you go to a fast food outlet, you know there is less variety but expect food to be served in a few minutes; in a restaurant, you are ready to wait for 15–20 minutes but do expect a greater variety.

Firms have realized that, while deciding product strategy, they must balance customer satisfaction and supply chain capabilities. While offering larger variety, progressive firms have tried to work with ideas such as platform products and modular design, among others. This has helped the firms to offer a large variety without increasing the complexity of the supply chain. In general, while designing new products, firms need to keep supply chain issues in mind so that they can offer high variety at a reasonable price.

## Supply Chain Performance Measures

In this section, we look at an exhaustive list of supply chain performance measures and demonstrate the significant impact of supply chain performance on business performance using benchmarking data and also show the methodology for linking the two.

Among various sets of supply chain performance measures discussed in the literature, we focus on a set of performance measures that have been most widely accepted in the industry. The Supply-Chain Council is an independent, non-profit, global corporation interested in getting the industry to standardize supply chain terms so that meaningful supply chain benchmarking can be carried out. It has developed the Supply Chain Operations Reference (SCOR) model as the industry standard for supply chain management. Several supply chain software vendors have adopted the SCOR performance measures in their performance management module. SCOR recognizes six major processes: Plan, Source, Make, Delivery, Return, and Enable. As per the SCOR model, supply chain performance measures fall under the following five broad categories:

- Cost
- Assets (Asset Management Efficiency)
- Reliability
- Responsiveness
- Agility

Further, the SCOR model develops 10 performance measures as shown in Figure 2.7. The Supply-Chain Council refers to measures related to costs and assets as internal-facing measures, while reliability, responsiveness, and agility are termed as customer-facing measures. Typically, a firm offers a bundle consisting of price, delivery and flexibility to its customers. Price, in competitive markets, is dictated by the market place. Thus, only delivery- and response-related measures are termed as customer-facing measures. The performance measures related to assets and costs affect the profitability of the firm and are, thus, termed as internal-facing measures. The use of standard measures allows firms to carry out meaningful benchmarking studies.

Benchmarking studies carried out by the Supply-Chain Council have shown that there are significant differences in performance across firms in various industries. Figure 2.8 shows the performance of supply chain costs as a percentage of revenue for various industries. The best in the class firms seem to work with substantially lower supply chain costs (difference of about 5–6 per cent of revenue) across industries. These firms also seem to have substantial differences in performance measures of reliability, assets and flexibility, as shown in Figure 2.9.

**Figure 2.7**

SCOR supply chain performance metrics.

*Source*: www.supply-chain.org. Reproduced with permission.

| SCOR Model Supply chain metrics | Customer facing | | Internal facing | | |
|---|---|---|---|---|---|
| | Reliability | Responsiveness | Agility | Cost | Assets |
| Perfect order fulfillment | * | | | | |
| Order fulfillment cycle time | | * | | | |
| Upside flexibility | | | * | | |
| Upside adaptability | | | * | | |
| Downside adaptability | | | * | | |
| Overall value-at-risk | | | * | | |
| Total cost to serve | | | | * | |
| Cash-to-cash cycle time | | | | | * |
| Return on fixed assets | | | | | * |
| Return on working capital | | | | | * |

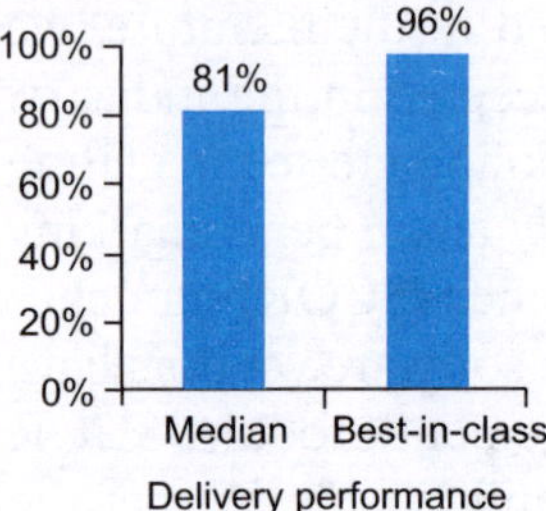


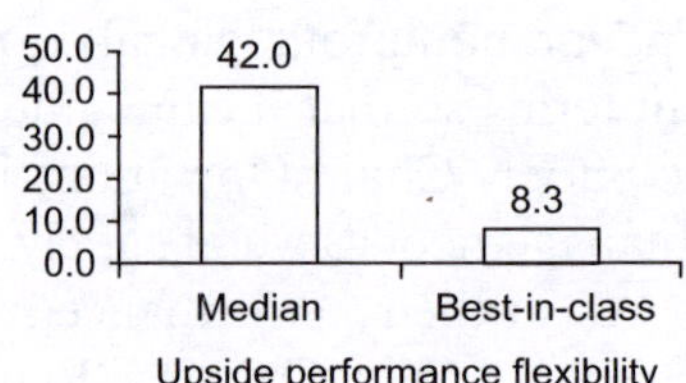


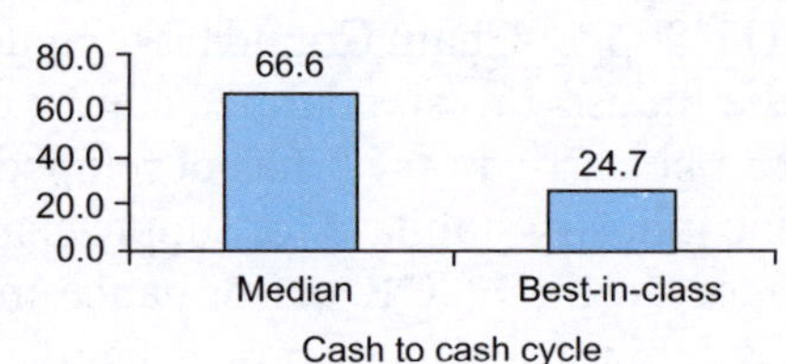


**Figure 2.8**

Superior performers spend less on supply chain management.

*Source*: www.supply-chain.org. Reproduced with permission.

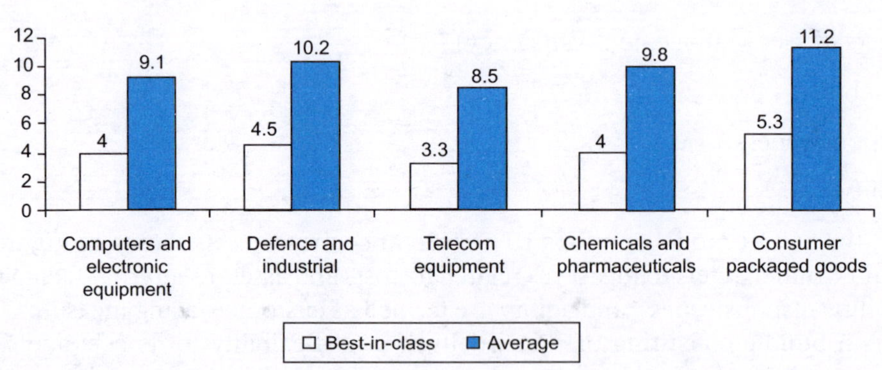


**Figure 2.9**

Comparative performances for consumer package goods.

*Source*: www.supply-chain.org. Reproduced with permission.

Such significant differences in performance also mean that firms seem to follow a wide variety of processes and systems.

SCOR measures, however, do not capture measures related to product variety. So, to that extent, performance measures under the SCOR model do not seem to be comprehensive. While relating the SCOR model to the cost versus customer service trade-off framework, we combine costs- and assets-related measures.

Supply chain benchmarking using frameworks like SCOR is difficult to implement in countries in Asia where data availability is a big problem. Alternatively, one may like to focus on

fewer but important metrics like cost and assets utilization data, for which data are available in financial statements of listed companies.

## Benchmarking Supply Chain Performance Using Financial Data

Though supply chain benchmarking has received much attention, we have found that firms face multiple sets of problems while carrying out this exercise. Unlike Western countries, most countries in Asia suffer from the problem of data availability. Even if the relevant data are available, one is not sure of the validity and reliability of the data. In this section, we present a set of supply chain performance measures that can be collected from financial statements of listed companies. In most countries, it is not difficult to get financial databases that are reliable. All the listed companies maintain their data on their Web sites and most countries have an agency that compiles these data and makes it available to interested parties at a nominal price. For example, India has the "Prowess" databases, maintained by the Centre for Monitoring Indian Economy (CMIE), compiled using publicly disclosed financial performance data.

The relevant expressions (data for which are usually available in databases like Prowess) that are used in this section are shown in Table 2.2.

Using the data presented in Table 2.2, one can calculate the following three performance measures:

- *Total length of the chain.* The total length of the chain is arrived at by adding up the days of inventory for raw materials, work in progress and finished goods. The firm that has the minimum total length of the chain is said to have the best performance.
- *Supply chain inefficiency ratio.* This ratio measures the relative efficiency of internal supply chain management. The ratio will be low for the firms with better performance.
- *Supply chain working capital productivity.* The analysis of firms on this metric will also be based on the levels of inventory, accounts receivable and accounts payable. Firms with efficient supply chains will usually have high supply chain working capital productivity.

### Calculating the Length of Various Stages of the Chain

The following formulae (terms defined in Table 2.2) are used to calculate the length of the various stages in the supply chain:

$DRM$, $DWIP$, $DFG$ = Days of raw material, work in process and finished goods, respectively

$$DRM = RM \times 365/CRM,$$

**Table 2.2: Terms directly obtained from the financial statements.**

| Terms from the income and expenditure statement | Symbol | Terms from the balance sheet | Symbol |
|---|---|---|---|
| Cost of raw materials* | *CRM* | Inventories (inclusive of raw materials, semi-finished goods and finished goods) | *INV* |
| Cost of production* | *CP* | Raw materials inventory | *RM* |
| Cost of distribution* | *DC* | Semi-finished goods inventory | *SFG* |
| Cost of sales* | *CS* | Finished goods inventory | *FG* |
| Net sales* | *NS* | Account receivables (excluding loans and advances) | *AR* |
| | | Account payables | *AP* |

* Data for one financial year.

$$DWIP = SFG \times 365/CP,$$
$$DFG = FG \times 365/CS$$

Total length of chain in days = $DRM + DWIP + DFG$

The duration of time taken by the material flow is captured by this measure. Firms like Dell Computers perform very well on this dimension.

## Evaluating the Efficiency of Supply Chain Management

The internal supply chain inefficiency ratio is a measure of the efficiency of internal supply chain management. To calculate this ratio, we consider total inventory carrying costs and the distribution costs to be components of the internal supply chain management costs. We calculate the internal supply chain inefficiency ratio as follows:

$$SCC = DC + INV \times ICC \quad \text{and} \quad SCI = SCC/NS$$

where $SCC$ is the supply chain management costs, $ICC$ is the inventory carrying cost and $SCI$ is the supply chain inefficiency ratio.

The inventory carrying cost for most firms is estimated to be in the range of 0.15–0.25. The methodology for estimating inventory carrying costs is presented in Chapter 4. In the absence of any data, one can work with an inventory carrying cost of 0.2.

The supply chain inefficiency ratio (the lower the better) provides an insight into the internal supply chain management efficiency of the firm. This measure is termed the supply chain inefficiency ratio since the supply chain cost will be higher if there are inefficiencies in the system. Firms with efficient supply chain systems will have relatively lower scores on this performance measure.

## Supply Chain Working Capital Productivity

The supply chain working capital productivity is calculated using the following formula:

$$SWC = INV + AR - AP$$

where $SWC$ is the supply chain working capital.

$$SWCP = NS/SWC$$

where $SWCP$ is the supply chain working capital productivity.

A firm can compare its own performance with that of its competitors and the industry aggregate in order to ascertain where it stands in terms of supply chain performance. Using benchmarking data, a firm can also map a supply chain profile that allows it to effectively capture both the dimensions of time and cost in one diagram. Further, a firm can also compare its own profile with that of its competitors in order to ascertain where it stands in terms of costs and length of time in the chain. Benchmarking is a useful tool for comparing the performance of competing firms so as to identify areas of improvement for further detailed investigation, which may lead to process improvements. In this section, we have focused on financial benchmarking, which can help a firm in comparing its supply chain performance with competitors using financial data. Once a firm has identified performance gaps, it should try and carry out a process benchmarking exercise. Process benchmarking focuses on the investigation of business processes of leading firms with the objective of identifying and observing the best practices from one or more benchmark firms.

Rather than re-inventing ideas, process benchmarking focuses on borrowing ideas from best practice firms.

## Linking Supply Chain and Business Performance

Not all supply chain measures, however, are of equal importance. Any supply chain initiative that results in an improvement in some aspect of supply chain performance must ultimately get translated into improved business performance. In the final analysis, each firm is primarily interested in improving its return on assets (ROA).

The impact of various supply chain initiatives can be estimated in terms of costs and benefits using the following broad groupings:

- Cost reduction is achieved by
  - Reducing inventory
  - Reducing logistics expenses
  - Reducing direct material expenses
  - Reducing indirect material expenses
- Improving revenue and profitability by
  - Selling higher margin products
  - Achieving higher market share
  - Reducing backorder and lost sales
  - Attacking new markets
  - Decreasing supply time to market
- Improving operational efficiency by
  - Reducing procurement expenses
  - Increasing assets utilization
  - Delaying capital expenditure
- Reducing working capital by
  - Reducing inventory
  - Reducing accounts receivables

Finally, what we need is a single framework to integrate various related costs and benefits. The strategic profit model, also known as the Dupont model (Figure 2.10), is a popular and comprehensive model that captures the benefits of supply chain initiatives on business performance. Competing supply chain initiatives can be compared and prioritized using this model.

## Enhancing Supply Chain Performance

As discussed above, most firms are under pressure to improve on cost as well as customer service dimensions simultaneously. Assume we locate the current performance of a firm on

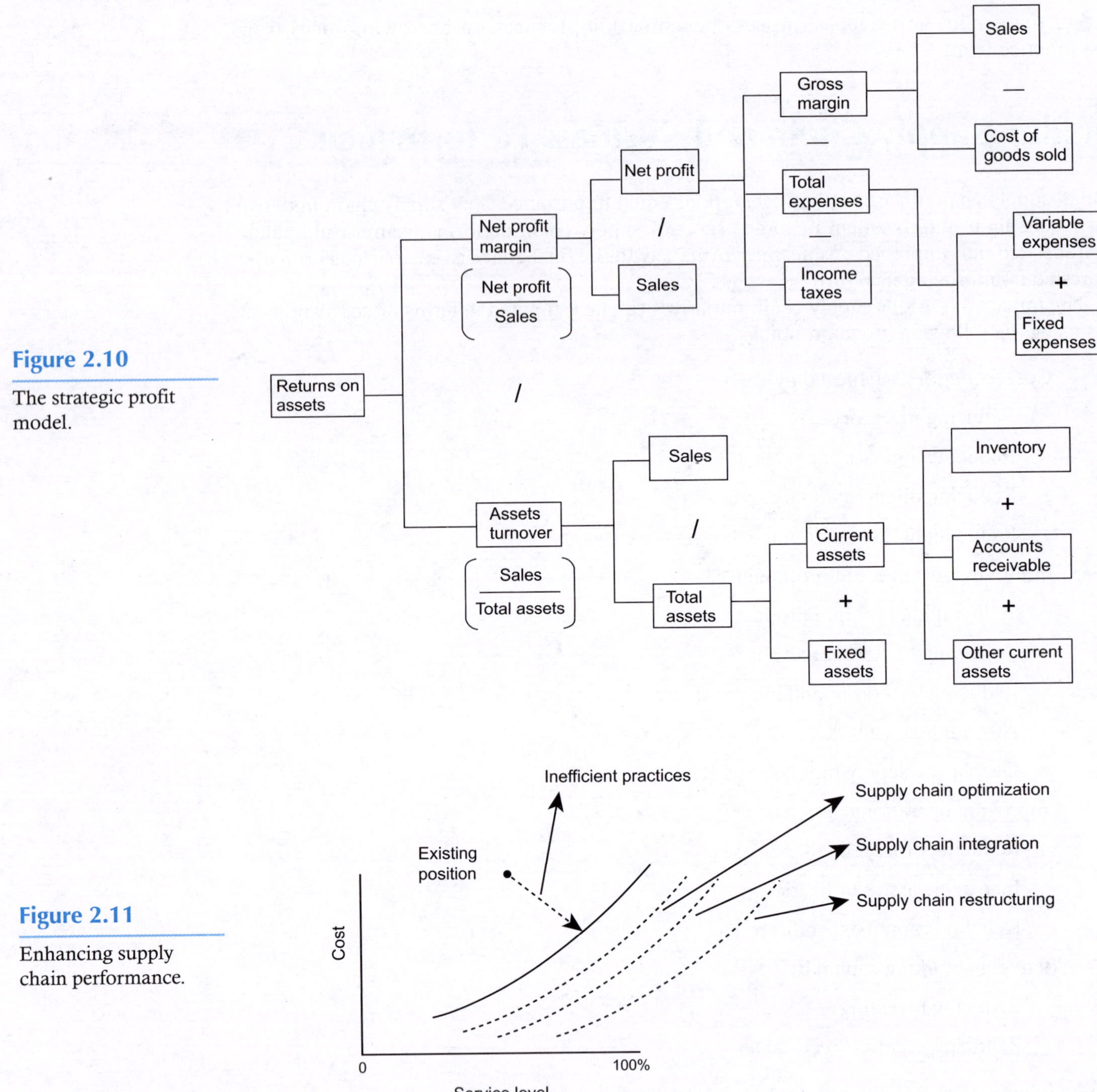


**Figure 2.10**

The strategic profit model.

**Figure 2.11**

Enhancing supply chain performance.

a cost–service map and that the firm is operating at a point shown in Figure 2.11. Since most firms typically do not manage their supply chain processes efficiently, for a typical firm, the current position on the cost–service map is likely to be at some distance from its efficiency frontier. So, it is in a position to improve on both the cost and the customer service fronts. By ensuring that activities are done right the first time and by ensuring proper monitoring of current processes and practices, the firm can reach a particular point on the efficiency frontier without any change in the supply chain structure, processes or technology. Of course, it is quite likely for a firm to notice a degradation in performance wherein it would move away from an efficient frontier. Chrysler USA is one such example.

Once a firm is on the efficiency frontier, any attempt at improvement on one particular dimension will force the firm to sacrifice performance on the other dimension. At this stage, the only way for a firm to improve performance, on both fronts simultaneously, is by moving the entire efficiency frontier curve in a downward direction. There are three different ways in which a firm can shift its efficiency frontier downward: integration, optimization and restructuring.

### HIGH INVENTORY AT CHRYSLER[4]

Constant monitoring of processes and practices is essential for a firm to excel on both cost and customer service fronts. Chrysler, the American automobile company, forgot the lessons it learnt in 1979. In 1979, Chrysler was floundering as it insisted on producing vehicles that were not in demand simply so that the capacity of the manufacturing unit could be completely utilized. Lee Iacocca engineered a turnaround in the company's fortunes by streamlining the processes and working with a market-focused approach. However, Chrysler failed to keep up with this strategy. In 2006, it was sitting on 83 days of unsold finished goods inventory comprising low fuel efficiency automobiles like SUVs and pickups. Chrysler's dealers were reluctant to lift any more cars because they also had a high inventory of about 100 days.

## Supply Chain Optimization

By improving on the forecasting, location, transportation and inventory management decisions, a firm is in a position to improve on the cost and the service fronts and hence push the efficiency frontier downward. Initiatives involving improvement in the above practices can be achieved by using optimization tools—these set of initiatives are known as supply chain optimization. These issues are discussed in detail in Part II.

## Supply Chain Integration

It has been found that there are significant wastages at all departmental and organizational interfaces. However, better intra- and inter-firm integration of supply chains helps reduce waste in the system and improve the overall efficiency, which results in the downward movement of the efficiency frontier. To make this possible, organizations will have to make corresponding changes in the organization structure processes and performance measures. These issues are discussed in detail in the Part IV.

## Supply Chain Restructuring

Restructuring of supply chains helps a firm in moving the entire efficiency frontier in the downward direction. Supply chain restructuring involves significant changes in the supply chain structure in terms of the way material and information flows are managed in the chain. Some ways in which supply chains can be restructured include the following:

- Moving from the MTS model to the CTO model
- Reducing the number of stock points in distribution

- Differentiating fast-moving and slow-moving items in terms of material flow in chain
- Product and process redesign

By restructuring its supply chain, a company can either change the slope of the efficiency frontier curve so as to make it flatter or shift the entire frontier downward.

In the case of functional products, the focus is on supply chain integration; in the case of innovative products, the focus is on supply chain restructuring. For example, functional products require smooth flow of material in the system and do not need much inventory within the chain, while innovative products require more flexibility in the chain, which can be achieved by keeping a high inventory of material at appropriate locations in the chain. These issues are discussed at greater length in the chapter on Supply Chain Restructuring (Chapter 10).

In the above section, a specific sequence in which supply chain innovation should take place was discussed. Yet a firm may decide to change the sequence in which it wants to work on enhancing the supply chain performance. Alternatively, a firm may also decide to work on all the three approaches: supply chain optimization, supply chain integration and supply chain reconfiguration simultaneously. Though the focus is on the supply chain process, issues relating to organization structure and processes have also be dealt with as they have a significant impact on supply chain operations and supply chain performance outcomes.

## Summary

- A firm must ensure a smooth fit between business strategy and supply chain strategy. As a part of the business strategy, a firm decides the market segment in which it wants to operate and the level of customer service it wants to offer.
- Supply chain strategy results in costs that firms have to incur to provide the targeted level of customer service. Firms must recognize the nature of trade-offs between customer service and costs and arrive at an optimal decision.
- Firms will have to decide on the optimum level of customer service by targeting performance levels across four dimensions of customer service: order delivery lead time, responsiveness, delivery reliability and product variety.
- Two of these customer service dimensions, namely, order delivery time and responsiveness, help in characterizing supply chains. Depending on the order delivery time or order penetration point, supply chains can be characterized as MTS, MTO or CTO. Similarly, based on product characteristics, one can label a supply chain as either an efficient chain or a responsive chain.
- Firms must monitor their supply chain performance and benchmark the same against competitors. Firms must also realize that not all supply chain measures are of equal importance.
- Any supply chain initiative planned by a firm must get translated into business performance, since a firm is ultimately interested in improving its ROA. To this end, firms can use the strategic profit model framework to prioritize various supply chain initiatives.
- Though at any given point in time managers have to understand customer service versus cost trade-offs, in the long run firms have to find a way of increasing performance on both the costs and the services fronts.
- By working on supply chain innovations involving optimization, integration and restructuring, firms can improve performance on these fronts on a sustained basis.

## Discussion Questions

1. Why do some firms keep stocks close to the market while others keep stocks in the component form at their plants? How do these decisions affect their performance?
2. Identify two products each in the functional and innovative categories. Identify similarities and differences in the way supply chains for these products are managed by their respective firms.
3. Within the same industry, one finds significant differences in the supply chain performance measures across firms. What could possibly explain these differences in performances across firms in the same industry?
4. What are the advantages of moving from an MTS model to a CTO model?
5. Over a period of time, a product is likely to move from the introduction stage to the growth stage and from the growth stage to the maturity stage. Would this movement across different stages of the product life cycle affect supply strategy and practices of the firm?
6. Titan offers two brands of watches—Sonata and Fastrack. Sonata is targeted for a mass market while Fastrack is targeted at a premium segment. Should Titan manage both brands with the same supply chains? Should they share warehouses, transportation, supply chain software and other assets or should Titan handle them separately in all areas of business?
7. A firm has been complaining of facing very high demand uncertainty, but it has a very poor contribution margin. Consequently, it is not able to apply ideas suggested in the literature for innovative products? What is your advice on this issue?

## Mini Project

**Supply Chain Benchmarking Study**

The objective of the study is to carry out a supply chain benchmarking study for a selected industry.

### Methodology

Identify at least three listed (public limited) firms from the industry selected for the benchmarking study. For example, for the paints industry you could select the following top four firms: Asian Paints (India) Ltd., Goodlass Nerolac Paints Ltd., Berger Paints and Jenson & Nicholson Ltd.

Collect the relevant financial data (see Table 2.1 for details) for last three financial years for the companies in the set. The electronic database Prowess managed by CMIE can be used to collect the relevant data. Alternatively, visit the company Web site and download the annual reports of the respective companies.

Calculate following three performance measures for last three financial years for all the companies in the set:

- Total length of the chain (days of raw material inventory + days of work in process inventory + days of finished goods inventory)
- Supply chain inefficiency ratio
- Supply chain working capital productivity

Compare the performance across companies over the last three years.

A longitudinal analysis allows you to see how individual firms have improved on these supply chain performance measures over the years.

## Notes

1. Refer www.news.com/2100-1033-257278.html.
2. Refer www.safexpress.com.
3. Refer www.tvsmotor.in.
4. Sharon Silke Carty, "Chrysler Wrestles With High Levels of Inventory as Unsold Vehicles Sit On Lots," *USA Today*, 11/2/2006. Refer www.usatoday.com/money/autos/2006-11-02-chrysler-high-inventory_x.htm.

## Further Reading


APICS Supply-Chain Council (2014), "Supply-Chain Operations Reference-model. Overview of SCOR Version 11".

M. L. Fisher, "What Is the Right Supply Chain for Your Product?" *Harvard Business Review* (March–April 1997): 83–93.

L. R. Kopczar and M. E. Johnson, "The Supply Chain Management Effect," S*loan Management Review (*Spring 2003): 27–34.

H. L. Lee, "Aligning Supply Chain Strategies with Product Uncertainties," *California Management Review* (Spring 2002): 105–119.

H. L. Lee, "The Triple-A Supply Chain," *Harvard Business Review* (October 2004): 102–112.

J. Magretta, "*The* Power of Virtual Integration: An Interview with Dell Computer's Michael Dell," *Harvard Business Review* (March–April 1998): 79–80.

F. J. Quinn, "Reengineering the Supply Chain: An Interview with Michael Hammer," *Supply Chain Management Review* (Spring 1999): 20–26.

J. Shah and N. Singh, "Benchmarking Internal Supply Chain Performance: Development of a Framework," *The Journal of Supply Chain Management* (2001): 37–47.

R. E. Slone, "Leading a Supply Chain Turnaround," *Harvard Business Review* (October 2004): 114–121.

# Outsourcing: Make Versus Buy

## Learning Objectives

After reading this chapter, you will be able to answer the following questions:

> How do firms take make-versus-buy decisions?
> What is the underlying theoretical logic for make versus buy decisions?
> What are the costs and benefits of outsourcing?
> What should be the nature of the relationship with vendor firms?
> How can a firm design its sourcing strategy based on a purchase portfolio matrix?
> How has the Internet affected the sourcing decisions of firms?

A boisterous group of young adults walks into a Nike outlet. The life-sized poster of a prominent cricketer has drawn these people to the store. Ecstatic over India's win in the recently concluded Twenty20 World Cup, they admire the poster and browse around the store. They are looking for the perfect pair of shoes that they can flaunt anywhere and everywhere.

What they are not aware of is the fact that Nike is a virtual corporation. The actual manufacturing is done by Nike sub-contractors working out of Taiwan, Hong Kong and South Korea. The actual manufacturing plants are located in Indonesia, China and Vietnam. The logistics, which involves transportation and storage, is handled by third-party companies. And the stores that sell the final products are franchisee outlets. Nike is a virtual corporation that has outsourced almost all activities. It has retained only two processes in-house—designing and brand management. In other words, Nike, with a global presence, offers a truly global product to its customers.

In this chapter, we look at this strategic supply decision from various perspectives. We start with the strategic perspective, where the focus is on identifying core competence whereby a firm can handle core activities internally and outsource all non-core activities to independent firms. Subsequently, the institutional economics perspective is discussed, wherein economists have looked at this issue from a market versus hierarchy perspective. When an activity is outsourced, the supply chain is coordinated using market mechanisms, whereas if the activities are managed internally, the chain is coordinated using the hierarchical processes within the firm. Of course, make versus buy represents two extremes along a continuum of possibilities, explored in the subsequent section. Once a firm has decided to buy a certain set of activities/items, not all items are sourced using the same approach. One specific classification approach is discussed where, based on importance and availability, items are classified into four categories, and a different sourcing approach is suggested for each category. The chapter ends with an analysis of the impact of the Internet on the sourcing approach.

## Introduction

The decision of a firm to perform its activities internally or get those activities done from an independent firm is known as the make versus buy decision. This make versus buy issue is strategic in nature and involves the following key decisions: What activities should be carried out by the firm and what activities should be outsourced? How to select the entities/partners to carry out outsourced activities and what should be the nature of the relationship with those entities? Should the relationship be transactional in nature or should it be a long-term partnership?

When Bharti Airtel, India's number one private telecom service provider, announced its decision to outsource key network management activities, it sent shockwaves in the Indian industry. In addition to outsourcing network management services, it decided to outsource IT services and call centre operations also. This bold decision by Bharti generated a huge debate, not only among the telecom players but also among the Indian industries in general. One view is that by outsourcing these key activities, Bharti might lose its edge in the long run to end up as a hollow company, while the other view is that by outsourcing these activities to more competent external firms, Bharti can focus its energies on designing innovative offerings, customer relationships and brand building.

## Make Versus Buy: The Strategic Approach

The supply chain involves a number of firms and encompasses all activities associated with the transformation of goods from the raw material stage to the final stage, wherein the goods and services reach the end customer. While studying make versus buy decisions, we analyse from the point of view of the focal firm or the nodal firm, which is at the strategic centre of the supply chain. The firm that provides an identity to the product in terms of brand (Bharti, HUL, Nike, etc.) has higher stakes in the chain and has been identified as the main entity of the chain, as discussed in Chapter 1.

The make versus buy decision evaluates the contribution of each activity. Using the value chain framework developed by Michael Porter, we classify all supply chain activities as primary activities and support activities. Primary activities consist of inbound logistics, operations, outbound logistics, sales and service. Secondary activities involve procurement, technology development, human resource management and firm infrastructure management. The make versus buy decisions look at each of these activities critically and ask the question: Should this activity be done internally or can it be outsourced to an external party? Once the decision to outsource has been taken, the firm has to choose among competing suppliers and also decide on the nature of the relationship it would like to establish with the supplier firm.

Traditionally, firms believed that everything should be done internally unless there is a compelling logic in favour of outsourcing. Thus, all outsourcing-related decisions had to be justified. We have come a long way from the days of the Ford Motor Company, where vertical integration was the norm. Now, perhaps, we are on the other extreme with our discussion of virtual corporations, where a firm starts with the assumption that all activities must be outsourced unless there is a compelling logic to justify keeping activities in-house. Michael Dell, the CEO of Dell Computers, has stated that if his company was vertically integrated, it would need five times as many employees and would suffer from a drag effect. Apart from primary activities in the value chain, even support activities that were usually done in-house are outsourced in big way now. Rather than taking extreme positions, we need to build up managerial logic to understand these issues. Hence, we first look at a few cases where firms have made these decisions in recent years and then bring out a conceptual framework that can help firms in their make versus buy decisions.

### BHARTI AIRTEL: OUTSOURCING OF NETWORK OPERATIONS[1]

Bharti Airtel Limited, formerly known as Bharti Tele-Ventures, is one of India's leading private sector providers of telecommunications services with a market capitalization of Rs 936 billion, revenue of Rs 185 billion and customer base of 27 million. Bharti Airtel has been rated as one of the top 10 best-performing companies in the world in the *BusinessWeek* IT 100 list. For the last couple of years, its subscriber base has been growing steadily at 60 per cent per annum.

In 2004, Bharti decided to outsource the following three areas of operations:

- *Network management to Ericsson, Nokia and Siemens.* These outsourcing partners manage the existing network and deploy and operate new base stations in the future. About 800 people from Bharti were transferred to the outsourcing partners. The value of the 3-year contract was $725 million. Bharti uses the pay-per-use model (dollar per Erlang; Erlang is a measure of traffic), and the outsourcing partner gets paid for the capacity used by Bharti and not on the capacity installed by the outsourcing partner. Bharti has a network management team to manage the interface with the outsourcing partner.
- *IT management to IBM.* IBM manages all IT services (billing, customer relations management), operates data centres, help desk for IT support and application development. About 200 people from Bharti were transferred to IBM. The $750 million contract was signed for a 10-year period. Bharti uses a revenue-sharing model with IBM. As revenues grow, Bharti shares a smaller percentage of revenue with IBM. Bharti has a seven-member architecture review board, which ensures that IBM decisions are aligned to the long-term goals of Bharti.
- *Customer service call centres to Hinduja TMT, Mphasis, IBM Daksh and Teletech India.* These outsourcing partners set up about 6,000 seats and have been managing customer service call centres for all customers except corporate clients and high-value clients. Bharti has about 1,500 seats in-house to maintain customer service for these high-end customers. This $350 million contract was signed for a 3-year period.

Bharti prepared a very comprehensive set of detailed service-level agreements (SLAs) with each outsourcing partner. These SLAs take care of almost all contingencies. Bonuses and penalties for the partners are linked to performance on crucial SLA measures. The partners committed 99.99 per cent availability of service. Bharti put up extensive mechanisms for managing its relationship with the outsourcing partners.

In India, Bharti has decided to focus on customer delight and brand building and leave network management and a host of other services to its outsourcing partners.

When Reliance put up its refinery in Jamnagar, it realized that the volume of logistics had increased significantly and therefore decided to build internal competence. Thus, Reliance Logistics came into being, and today, not only does it manage its own logistics activities but also provides services to the food division of ITC.

## Identifying Core Processes

As exemplified by Bharti Airtel, the decision to identify selected processes as core processes and focus on improving those can have a significant impact on the performance of a firm. The identification of core processes is a crucial decision. If this is driven by short-term benefits such as re-engineering of balance sheets and improved return on investments, then the long-term business sustainability is endangered. Instead of becoming the best in the chosen category (represented by core processes), the firm runs the risk of ending up as a mere hollow corporation.

The mere decision to focus the resources on core activities to match capabilities with the best-in-class performance is not enough; firms must strive to be the best in the world in that specific area.

In these areas they can invest in people, equipments and R&D. Such a focus will also help the firm in attracting the best talent from that field. Many corporations have realized that they can never hope to attract the best talent in IT; hence, they have decided to depend on their outside partners for the IT support required for business application.

Thus, the first step for a firm is to develop the capability to distinguish between core activities and commodity activities. Even among core activities, it has to keep certain activities in-house, and for all outsourced critical activities, it has to maintain some knowledge so that it can manage an effective relationship with its outsourcing partner. The two ways through which one can identify a firm's core processes are the business process route and the product architecture route.

### *MICROSOFT'S ENTRY INTO VIDEO GAME BUSINESS*[2]

When Microsoft decided to get into the business of video games in the mid-1990s, it decided that it would not carry out manufacturing and distribution activities in-house. Microsoft wanted to ensure that the Xbox was on the retailers' shelves in October 2001 and was sold for $400. Microsoft was very clear that it would focus only on the software part of the Xbox and leave the hardware design and manufacturing to Flextronics, a large electronics manufacturing service provider. While Sony keeps both design and manufacturing functions in-house, because it has competence in these areas, Microsoft decided to outsource these activities. Michael Marks, CEO and Chairman, Flextronics, commented: "Without Flextronics, there would be no Xbox—only the idea of it. Microsoft has a ton of money, but if they had to build factories, they wouldn't have done this project. If guys like us didn't exist, guys like Microsoft wouldn't do a hardware product. The risk would be too high."

## *The Business Process Route*

For any firm, three core and high-level business processes include customer relationship, product innovation and supply chain management. Customer relationship focuses on acquiring new customers and building relationships with existing customers. Product innovation focuses on developing new products and services, while supply chain management focuses on fulfilment of customer orders. It is possible to un-bundle the three business processes and a firm can afford to outsource two of these business processes. Some researchers have argued that a firm must identify and ensure that it builds core capabilities in-house in at least one of these areas. Firms like HP and high-end pharmaceutical firms focus on product innovations. Firms like Nike and Benetton focus on brand building and customer relationships. Firms like Wal-Mart and Dell Computers focus on supply chain management capabilities. Of course, within the identified core business process, firms can examine each of the activity and probably outsource those activities that are of the commodity type. For example, within supply chain management, firms might outsource the warehousing or transportation functions.

In the case of Microsoft, it decided that customer relationship management and software design are its core processes, while design and manufacturing is not core to its business. Bharti decided that customer relationship was core and network management was not.

Core processes retained within the company must be strategic from the business point of view. Firms must realize that value within the chain gets distributed to the chain partners on the basis of the unique capabilities that they bring to the table. A firm has to ensure that it has a relatively higher bargaining power within the chain. A firm has to make sure that in-house business processes give it enough strategic power in the chain and do not allow other chain partners to dictate the terms of value exchange in the chain. In the PC business, the power within the chain went to Intel and Microsoft. So, even though IBM was at a strategic point in product development, it lost its power and became a peripheral player in the chain.

## The Product Architecture Route

In the product architecture approach, the focus is on sub-systems and components and the make or buy decisions are made at that level. A product like a car can be divided into sub-systems such as engine, chassis and transmission. The engine sub-system can be divided into components such as power cylinder, fuel system and engine electronics. In a product, first the sub-systems are classified as strategic and non-strategic. A sub-system is strategic if it involves technologies that change rapidly, if it requires specialized skills and technologies and if it can significantly impact the performance of the product on attributes that are considered important by the customer.

By keeping theses strategic sub-systems internal, a firm can ensure that it can offer differentiated products and can avoid being commoditized. Further, within a sub-system, the same kind of analysis has to be done for all major components. All those components where the firm is technologically ahead of potential suppliers or can hope to achieve a leadership position with some investments are kept internal to the firm. In case the suppliers have a huge technological lead, which will be impossible to bridge in the foreseeable future, or if the time and investments required for catching up may not be worth the effort, then the component should be outsourced and the supplier should be treated as a strategic partner (see Figure 3.1 for a diagrammatic view of the overall framework). Of course, if a firm finds that for all the components the suppliers have a lead and it has no hope of catching up in the near future,

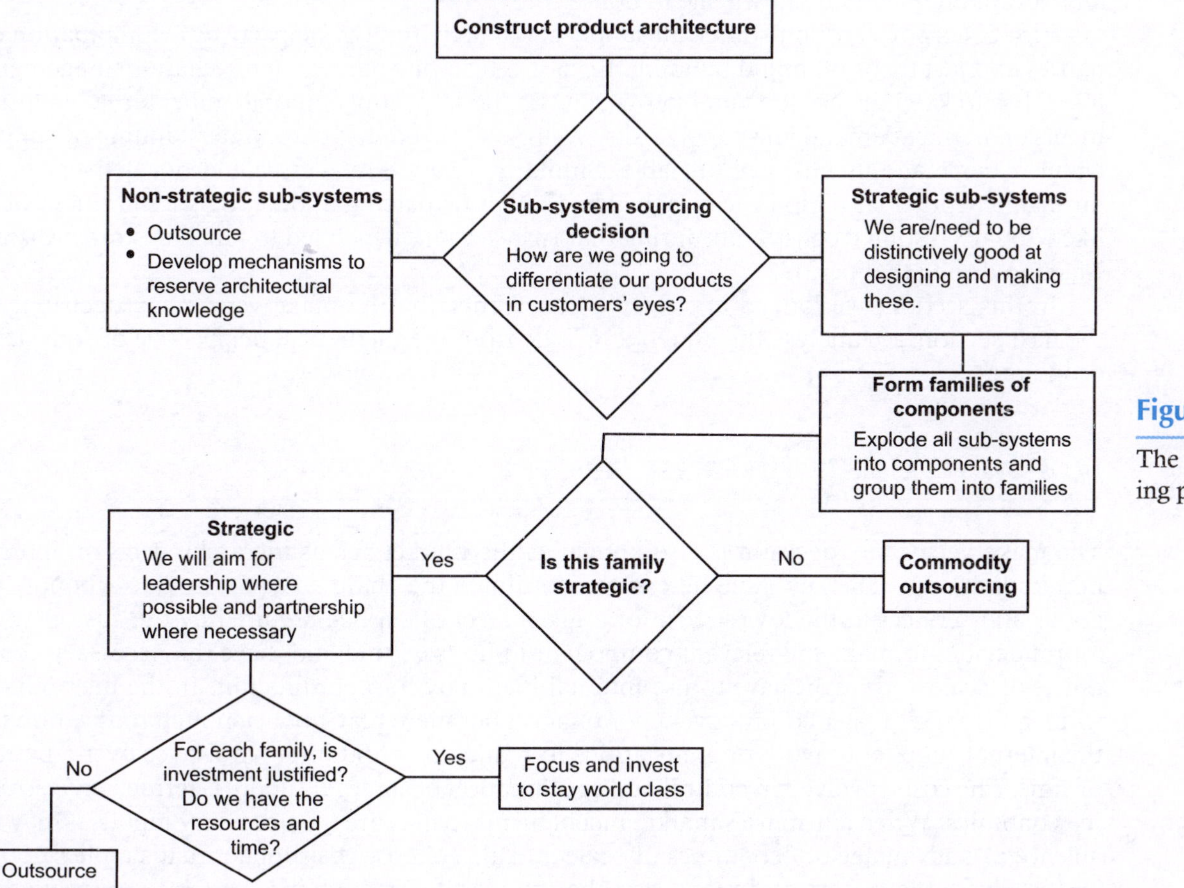


**Figure 3.1**

The strategic outsourcing process.

then the firm has become a hollow corporation and will see a decline in its fortunes over a period of time. Tata Motors realized that in diesel engine technology it was far behind its suppliers and will never be in a position to catch up with them. So it decided to buy diesel engines from Fiat and treat Fiat as a strategic partner. Cummins discovered that pistons were part of a strategic sub-system but that its suppliers were far ahead in the relevant technologies and therefore decided to buy pistons rather than make them internally. Honda might treat engine technology a strategic sub-system, while Nissan might treat transmission as a strategic sub-system. Of course, once Tata Motors decided to source the design of diesel engine sub-systems from the supplier, it ensured that in the other systems kept in-house, it maintained the position of a leader.

Even when one outsources a strategic sub-system or component, one should retain the knowledge of its architecture in-house. Ravi Venkatesan, Chairman, Microsoft Corporation (India) Pvt Ltd, defines architecture knowledge as follows:

> Architecture knowledge is the intimately detailed and specialized power of translation required to capture customer requirements and reproduce them in the language of sub-system performance specification. It is based on many detailed understandings of the linkages between user requirements, system parameters and component specifications; it is unique to each company, intuitively developed in countless conversations by a team of strategists, designers and marketing people.[3]

A firm might not produce the engine, but it may control its design and manufacturing by remaining the expert in architectural knowledge. Cummins realized that it must keep architectural knowledge, that is, the ability to develop good piston specifications, to meet engine power requirements. In the case of Bharti, its network engagement team of 50 people allows it to keep all relevant architectural knowledge in-house.

Virtual corporations outsource all supply chain activities to one party or a combination of parties and just focus on brand building. Even if a firm outsources supply chain management, it still has to keep the architectural knowledge of the impact of internal and external environments on market demand and supply risks. Webvan realized that poor understanding of supply chain issues made its business unviable. Similarly, many e-retailers could not deliver goods during the Christmas period because they had not anticipated that their logistics partners were likely to face resource constraints during that rush season, which led to much customer dissatisfaction during that period.

In this section, we looked at strategic issues affecting the make versus buy decision. In the next section, we analyse the underlying logic from the theoretical perspective of industrial economics.

## Market Versus Hierarchy

The make versus buy decision is also known as the market versus hierarchy decision in economics literature. The key issue here is to coordinate the chain so as to provide a bundle of goods and services at the lowest cost for a given level of service required by the customer. If a firm decides to make the relevant component in-house, it may not have the necessary economies of scale and might have to use internal hierarchy for coordination. In the hierarchical form, a firm has greater control over coordination but there may not be enough motivation for the internal supplier to work on innovations to reduce cost and improve service over a period of time. The costs involved in control and coordination of internal supply is termed *agency costs* in economics. When a firm uses market mechanisms to procure the necessary inputs, it may be able to take advantage of economies of scale and also choose the supplier that supplies goods and services at lower prices. In this case, the supplier has enough motivation to innovate and the firm, as a buyer, has the flexibility of changing the supplier, which is not an option available to the firm that chooses to make inputs internally. However, there are costs incurred in the control and coordination of the external supplier and are termed as *transaction costs* in economics. Costs related to economies of scale are tangible in nature but the bulk of agency and transaction costs are intangible in nature. We first look at each of the three issues, economies of scale, agency costs and transaction costs, in detail and finally study the overall framework of the decision-making process.

Initially, the focus will be purely on the make versus buy decision, where we assume that the firm has an arm's-length relationship with the firm from where it is buying and that it is managing coordination and relationship with the supplier firm only through a formal contract. At a later stage, we will look at the entire continuum, where several intermediate types of relationships are possible between the pure make versus buy situations.

## Economies of Scale

Firms that specialize in production of input can usually achieve higher economies of scale vis-à-vis vertically integrated firms. A vertically integrated firm produces only for its internal needs, while an external supplier firm can aggregate demands of many potential buyers and, thereby, enjoy huge economies of scale. Economies of scale can be achieved in manufacturing or logistics activities. There are four major sources of economies of scale, which are briefly discussed here.

- *Higher volume allows a firm to spread its fixed cost over a larger volume of operations.* Any manufacturing or logistics process will involve investments in fixed costs. A firm with higher volume is able to spread its fixed costs over a higher output and thus has lower cost of operations. For example, the cost of a truck trip from Mumbai to Bangalore is more or less fixed because major costs like driver cost, bulk of fuel cost and administrative cost are independent of the load carried by the truck. Similarly, when a firm sets up its manufacturing unit, the set-up cost is the same, irrespective of the volume of production. So a firm with bigger batch sizes will have lower costs of operation.

- *Higher volume allows a firm to choose more efficient technologies.* Higher volume allows a firm to invest in technologies that are capital intensive but result in lower fixed and variable costs per unit of output. In the semiconductor industry, capital-intensive technologies capable of handling wafers of diameter 300 millimetres allow firms to obtain twice as many chips per wafer compared to older technologies, which could handle wafers only with diameters up to 200 millimetres. This allows a semiconductor manufacturing firm, willing to invest in more capital-intensive technologies, to bring down the cost per chip. Increasingly, firms manufacturing semiconductors are using foundries from Taiwan, providing advantages of lower costs because of their higher scale of operations. Recently, Motorola decided to outsource the manufacturing of chips to third parties. Similarly, a transport firm that can transport 40 tons per trip in a Volvo truck will have lower costs per ton of material compared to a transport firm that requires four trucks of 10-ton capacity each to transport the same volume of goods. The same will be true in warehousing also, where larger warehouses can invest in IT, which will reduce its costs per unit of operations, while small warehousing firms will not find such investments viable.

- *Pooling of buffer capacities and inventories.* If firms keep their activities in-house, they have to keep buffer capacities and inventories to take care of the uncertainties in demand. A supplier, on the other hand, is able to pool uncertainties over a larger number of customers and as a result needs much lower levels of buffer capacity and safety inventory. A supplier can also ensure utilization of high capacity by pooling demand across customers who have different demand profiles. For example, a logistics firm that transports Maruti cars from Gurgaon to Bangalore carries Kurlon's mattresses to their Delhi warehouse on the return trip. Consequently, it is able to offer lower transport costs to Maruti as well as to Kurlon. Similarly, a contract manufacturer can improve capacity utilization if it can work with two different companies having seasonal demands in different seasons: one with seasonal demand in the winter and the other with seasonal demand in the summer.

- *Learning curve effect*. The learning curve captures the impact of cumulative production on the average cost of production. The management and the workers are able to improve their performance based on experience gained through the cumulative production of a firm. In several industries, it is found that with doubling of cumulative production the average cost declines by 10 to 20 per cent.

The pressure faced by firms due to steadily rising costs is forcing them to review their earlier decisions, and increasingly, firms are availing the advantages of third-party companies that provide manufacturing and logistics services. A supplier who is providing services to a larger set of customers will always have lower costs. Firms are turning to contract manufacturers whenever they think that the manufacturing process does not provide sources of competitive advantage. Within the electronics industry, a bulk of manufacturing has shifted to electronics manufacturing service providers like Flextronics, Solectron and Celestica. Similarly, very few firms own transportation- and warehousing-related asset, and depend on transport and warehousing firms for their logistics operations. Many firms are outsourcing their IT operations to firms like IBM and Wipro, which have strong economies of scale. Then there is also the case of Indo Nissin Foods Ltd, the manufacturer of Top Ramen noodles, which has outsourced its distribution operations to Marico.

However, if a firm has large volumes and a reasonably stable demand, internal manufacturing is likely to offer more or less similar costs of production. Hence, almost all automobile companies assemble vehicles internally, unlike the electronic goods manufacturers or white goods manufacturers. Wal-Mart has huge volumes and finds it more economical to own a fleet of vehicles. In general, the marginal benefit of a "buy" decision starts coming down if a firm has large volumes of operation. So a multi-product firm may benefit from vertically integrated operations.

Third parties will offer services at a lower cost, provided there is enough competition in the supply market. If there are not enough suppliers, then the supplier may use its monopolistic power and may not pass on the benefits of scale to the customers.

## Agency Cost

Bharti used to manage customer billing operations through its internal IT department. The important question here is, "How does one ensure that the interest of the IT department and that of the marketing departments are aligned, and how does one make sure that the IT department is putting its best effort and is not slackening?" This issue is known as the *agency problem* in economics literature. The IT department is known as the agent and the marketing department as the principal. A firm with its own fleet of trucks faces a similar problem of motivating the transport department, where the internal transport department is the agent and the marketing department is the principal. In a hierarchical firm, there is greater control over coordination, but there may not be enough motivation for the internal supplier to work on innovations to reduce costs and improve service over a period of time. The cost involved in control and coordination of internal supply is termed *agency cost* in economics.

There is significant time and effort involved in the control and coordination of internal activities. If one decides to manufacture the necessary inputs within the firm, then the firm has to worry about agency issues. It is quite common that managers and workers of internal supply units sometimes knowingly do not act in the best interests of the firms. Thus, the top management incurs agency costs associated with in-house supply. In-house divisions within a firm are usually treated as cost centres and are usually insulated from competitive pressures as they have captive internal markets. Further, most large firms have common overheads and joint costs, which are allocated to different units, so it is usually difficult to measure individual divisions' contributions to overall profitability. The absence of market competition along with problems involved in measuring divisional performance make it difficult for the top management to evaluate the current performance of input supply operations with respect to its best achievable performance.

## Transaction Cost

There are costs involved in using market mechanisms, which can be avoided if those relevant activities are brought inside the firm. These costs are known as transaction costs. The transaction costs comprise the following:

- *Search and information costs.* Costs involved in locating and evaluating the right supplier.
- *Bargaining and contracting costs.* A firm has to first negotiate the terms of exchange and finally prepare the contract so that it is assured that the supplier will provide the required goods and services as per the agreed terms and conditions.
- *Policing and enforcement costs.* A firm has to constantly monitor the supplier so as to ensure that the supplier sticks to the terms and conditions of the contract. Firms might also have to legally enforce the contract if the supplier does not follow the contract. Bharti has put in elaborate mechanisms for monitoring the SLAs with IBM and Ericsson.
- *Cost incurred because of loss of control.* The use of market mechanisms may result in underinvestment in relationship-specific assets, which, in turn, increase the cost for buyers. Further, there may be additional costs that firms may have to incur because of poor coordination. There is also the risk of leakage of strategic information that will hurt the buyer firm in long run.

The cost incurred because of loss of control is a major component of transaction costs in several situations of market exchange. If it were possible to write a perfect contract and enforce it, one may not have to worry about costs incurred because of loss of control. Unfortunately, we live in a world of incomplete contracts and hence discuss the reasons and the implications of the same in the following section.

## Incomplete Contracts

In theory, it is possible to write a complete contract that stipulates each party's responsibilities and rights for each and every contingency that could conceivably arise during the transactions. Unfortunately, in practice, it is impossible to write a complete contract. The reasons why contracts are not complete are as follows:

- *Bounded rationality.* Managers have a limited capacity to process information; hence, when dealing with complex situations, they are unlikely to seek and process all the information available. For example, it will be difficult for managers of Bharti and IBM to think through all possible scenarios related to regulatory change, technology and market conditions. Therefore, both parties will, at best, identify major scenarios and include the relevant conditions in the contract, but will find it difficult to think through all possible scenarios.
- *Difficulties in specifying or measuring performance.* Even if managers are willing to seek and process comprehensive sets of information, it will still not be possible to write a complete contract if one cannot specify and measure performance. For example, when buying an advertising service or consultancy service, service performance is not easy to specify at the

time of writing the contract. Even if the quality requirements are specified in the contract, certain aspects of quality cannot be measured easily. In several situations, quality is ensured through process controls and cannot be easily checked at the delivery stage. In the pharmaceutical industry, the temperature maintained during the transit stage affects the effectiveness of drugs, and this aspect of quality cannot be checked at the receipt stage. When hiring a management graduate, companies accord a higher importance to the reputation of the college because it is difficult to judge a candidate, straight out of college, for a managerial job. Firms assume that reputed management colleges have process controls in place to ensure quality in the graduate. Several attributes in a physical product can be measured only through destructive testing. So there is a possibility of opportunistic behaviour by the external supplier, which will have an adverse impact on the long-term performance of the firm.

- *Asymmetry of information.* There may be asymmetry of information at the time of writing of the contract. For example, certain information about future changes, either in technology or the supply market, may result in lower costs, but the supplier may not provide the relevant information and may take advantage of it while fixing either the price or other conditions in the contract. For example, Bharti has better information about future markets and IBM has better information about future technologies, and each may hide this information from the other so as to ensure more favourable terms.

Even if it is possible to write a complete contract, in some emerging economies like India, where legal infrastructure is weak, it takes an enormous amount of time to get a legal remedy. In some countries like China, the contract may not be enforceable. So, in effect, we have to work with incomplete contracts.

With the unfeasibility of a complete contract that specifies the consequences of every possible contingency, the reputation of the supplier plays an important role. Since the supplier firm has to maintain its reputation, it might resist from behaving opportunistically in an unforeseen contingency. Of course, reputed firms will usually charge a premium, and this premium, charged by a reputed supplier firm, can be included in transaction costs.

The inability to write a complete contract results in a significant increase in the cost of transacting business through market exchange and includes the following situations:

- Presence of relationship-specific assets
- Poor coordination affecting supply chain performance
- Leakage of strategic information resulting in adverse supply chain performance

## Relationship-specific Assets

A relationship-specific asset is an investment made to support a given transaction. In several situations, a firm will be able to improve the efficiency of transactions and reduce costs in the process if the supplier can invest in specialized assets. These specialized assets are known as relationship-specific assets, as they cannot be redeployed for other customers without any significant costs. These specialized assets could involve either physical assets or human capital.

We illustrate the idea of a relationship with several examples from different contexts:

- Maruti Suzuki has asked several of its suppliers to locate either finishing operations or stock points close to its Gurgaon plant.
- FMCG players typically ask the packaging material suppliers to locate their facilities close to the buyer's plant.
- Mahindra & Mahindra, while developing Scorpio, decided that they will ask vendors to invest in the necessary tools and moulds. Earlier, Mahindra use to develop the tools and moulds or pay for the same at the product-development stage.

- Another automobile manufacturer (Toyota Kirloskar) has asked its supplier to modify its equipment so as to produce a narrow range of grade of output so as to suit the buyer's requirements.
- Microsoft expects its recent introduction of Xbox 360 to be a huge success and has asked its contract manufacturers to build additional capacity for the same.
- Bharti wants Ericsson to build network capacity on the basis of its demand projections.
- Wal-Mart has made radiofrequency identification (RFID) mandatory for its top 100 suppliers. All supply from 2005 onwards is supposed to be RFID tagged.
- Marico prefers all its dealers to work with MIDAS (distributor application software developed by Marico).

In all these cases, a firm wants its supplier to invest in physical or human capital assets (relation-specific assets) so that it can improve its supply chain performance. In most of the above cases, the supplier will not be able to use these specialized assets if the firm decides to change its supplier. Once the supplier invests in any of the above-mentioned assets, the supplier becomes vulnerable. Since these investments do not have alternative use, the supplier will be rightfully worried that after the investments are made the customer might behave opportunistically and change the terms of exchange at a later stage. This is known as the *hold-up* problem. And because of the possibility of hold-up, suppliers prefer to make as little investments as possible in relationship-specific assets. Additional costs incurred by the firm because of the lack of investments in relationship-specific assets by the supplier are captured in transaction costs of market exchange.

## Poor Coordination

In several supply chain situations, coordinating decisions between both parties is essential for overall performance. Because of differences in objectives and priorities, coordination on all occasions is not guaranteed between buyers and suppliers. The problems of coordination are illustrated with several examples:

- Soft drink firms spend enormous amounts of money on advertising campaigns, and to ensure that the campaigns have the desired impact, they need the cooperation of the local bottlers at the implementation stage. Coke and Pepsi have realized that they need to coordinate retailing activities, traditionally handled by the local bottlers. So they have decided to take greater control over bottling plants, and in some markets they have decided to even own the bottling plants.
- Marico has invested in a computerized supply chain planning system and will not benefit if the dealers do not implement the same system. Marico had to put in lot of effort to get a buy-in from all the dealers for participation in its system. Several FMCG majors are not able to get any advantage from the integrated information system because their dealers have refused to implement the system proposed by the firm.

In mid-2004, all telecom operators in India were racing against each other to launch EDGE (enhanced data rate for global evolution) services in the market. Bharti was the established market leader in innovations but this time it could not launch this service ahead of its competitors. A possible reason could be that outsourcing network operations may have slowed down Bharti's speed of response. In general, it is held that outsourcing slows down the speed of response because of coordination problems in non-routine situations between the buyer and the supplier firm.

Additional costs incurred by a firm because of poor coordination contribute to the transaction costs of market exchange.

**INTERVIEW WITH**

**SUNIL MITTAL**

*Bharti Airtel is the largest telecom player in India with an annual income of Rs 185 billion. Sunil Mittal, chairman of the company, spoke to Business World on why he outsourced the network and IT functions.*

*What is the extent of outsourcing?*

**Sunil Mittal:** The areas where we have touched upon and which have a major impact on the industry are IT and network. There have been cases of IT outsourcing in the past, except that it was only in verticals. We have gone in a more comprehensive way right from my own desktop to the most complex piece of IT architecture—all is with IBM.

Similarly, on the infrastructure side, it is the first of its kind outsourcing in the world. We were wondering why do we buy these boxes, we do not understand the technology inside these, and how they perform, so why are we doing it all in-house?

*How do you monitor vendors?*

**Sunil Mittal:** Every month, a dashboard comes out with orange, red and green signs. The dashboard shows the key parameters—call drops, blockages, network efficiency, coverage, capacity, everything. There are about 100 parameters that we look at. If the dashboard remains green, they get a bonus on top of the rates that we have. Red or orange leads to a penalty. It is in their interest to keep it green.

*What are the costs and benefits of outsourcing?*

**Sunil Mittal:** We will save lot of time (managerial) now. We feel we have mitigated risk by going with the best in the world. It was not only cost saving which we have achieved. It was provoked more by our concern about delivering quality to the customer. We are now really managing our core competency, which is customer relations.

*Will this mean a change of religion for the telecom industry?*

**Sunil Mittal:** The main opposition comes from very well entrenched departments in these areas. Let me tell you about a very large telecom operator. Tell him we want to outsource the network. How many people are impacted? 9,000 people in network, another 7,000 people in IT. People who run those departments are not going to let it go.

*Will you become an IBM shop at the end of contract?*

**Sunil Mittal:** That will not happen. We have an architecture review board. The architecture design is in our hands. We tell them (IBM) what we need.

*Source*: Shelley Singh and Rajeev Dubey, "The Man Who Gave Away His Network," *Business World* (4 October 2004).

### Leakage of Strategic Information

If one is buying from a firm that is also supplying similar inputs to competitors, a lot of strategic and sensitive information is likely to get leaked to the competitors. It may relate to product design or customer information or future plans. In such a case, this problem can be avoided by making the input internally. For example, the selection of dyes and designs for new products is regarded as critical information, so Benetton keeps dyeing operations within the firm.

In a world of complete contracts, all the three issues discussed above can be taken care of. But in a world of incomplete contracts, all these issues contribute to transactions costs of market exchange. If the transactions costs are substantially high, the firm is better off by bringing the activity in-house.

## *Integrative Framework of Market Versus Hierarchy*

To resolve the make versus buy issue, a firm has to look at the benefits as well as the costs involved. Costs should not be viewed from a narrow perspective; instead, the costs and risks associated with loss of control should also be captured in the transaction costs involved in market exchange.

Costs related to economies of scale, agency costs and transactions costs have been integrated in the framework provided in Figure 3.2. If additional costs due to poor economies of scale plus agency costs of internal control and coordination are less than transaction costs of

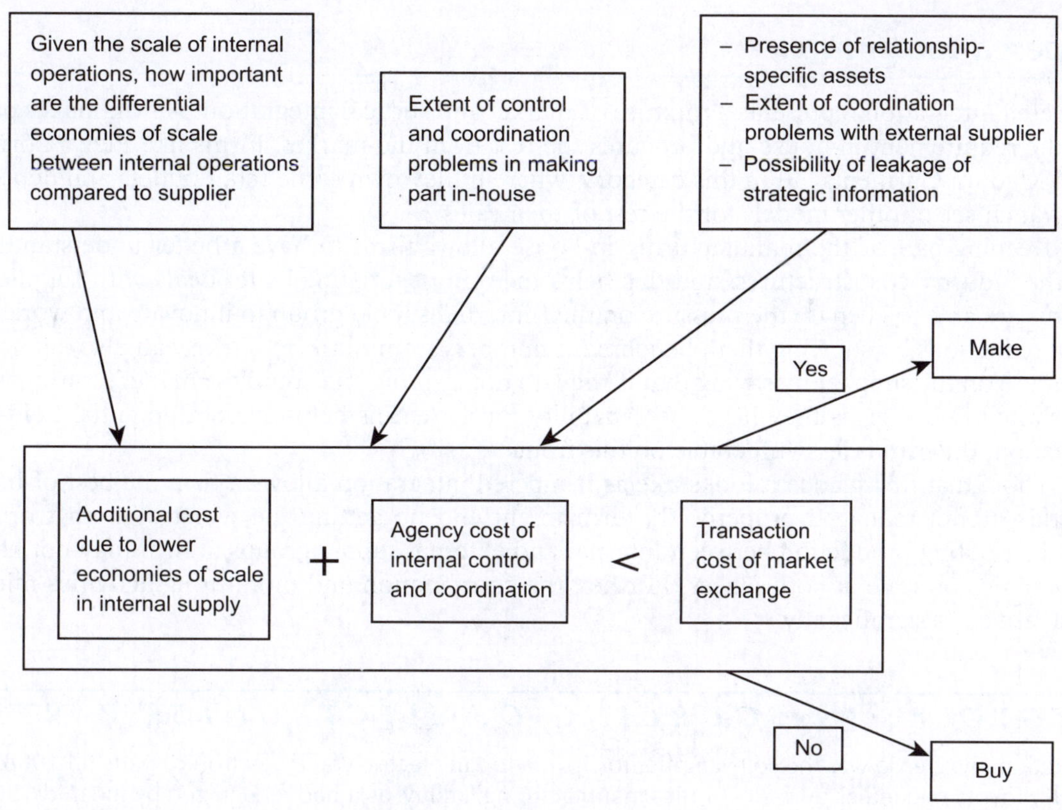


**Figure 3.2** The integrative framework of make versus buy.

market exchange, the firm should settle for the *make* option, else the firm should opt for market exchange.

Capturing the true value of agency and transaction costs requires a deep understanding of business. Though most garment firms outsource manufacturing operations, Zara Corporation, a leading European garment company, has decided to keep the bulk of its manufacturing facilities within the firm. In the past few years, Benetton has also decided to increase internal manufacturing capacities. Both these firms value responsiveness and want tighter control over their operations, so they prefer internal manufacturing capacities for a quick response to market trends.

So far, we have only looked at simple and clear make versus buy decisions. Independent suppliers are well coordinated with market mechanisms and there is an arm's-length relation between buyers and suppliers in market mechanisms. Though, in reality, pure *make* and pure *buy* are two extreme ends of the make-versus-buy continuum.

## The Make-Versus-Buy Continuum

We started out by exploring two extreme positions: (a) *make* an input or *buy* an input using the market and (b) vertical integration versus market, where the buyer has an arm's-length relationship with the suppliers. There are several alternative ways in which the exchange can be organized. In this section, we discuss two important alternatives:

(a) Tapered integration, where a firm both makes and buys a given input.

(b) Collaborative relationship, which could be a formal contractual relation or a long-term informal relationship, based on trust. In some cases, it can lead to alliances or joint ventures.

## Tapered Integration

Tapered integration represents a mixture of market and vertical integration. A firm makes part of the requirement in-house and procures the rest from the market. Firms like Pizza Corner and Madura Garments fall in this category, wherein they own some retail outlets and depend on franchisee or other models for the rest of their sales.

Keeping part of the manufacturing in-house allows firms to have a better understanding of the industry cost structures, and this helps them in negotiating better deals with suppliers. Firms are able to keep up the pressure on their internal supply group to innovate and work on cost reductions by showing them benchmark numbers from markets. Firms can also keep the pressure on the supplier by saying that if they do not improve the complete manufacturing will be shifted in-house, as they have the capability for it. As this helps avoid a potential hold-up situation, the firm is less vulnerable on this front.

Though at first glance it looks like as if tapered integration allows a firm the best of both worlds, if not managed properly, the firm might end up getting the worst of both worlds. By distributing production between internal and external supply groups, a firm may not have economies of scale at both places. Further, the coordination and monitoring activities might increase costs significantly.

### TOYOTA: IN-SOURCING OF ELECTRONICS PARTS

Traditionally, Denso was the sole supplier for Toyota for all electrical and electronics parts till 1988. In 1988, Toyota opened its own electronics manufacturing facility, as it had recognized by the mid-1980s that electronics was going to play an important part in automobile manufacturing. It is estimated that, today, about 30 per cent of the total vehicle content is related to electronics. As the share of electronics in cars is increasing and as these technologies change at a pace faster than those of traditional automobile technologies, Toyota identified electronics as a core and strategic function and decided to master it so that it can manage its suppliers effectively. They still depend a lot on Denso for supply, but they have consciously built design and manufacturing capability within the firm.

Airtel has decided to shift the bulk of its call centres to external firms, but has retained support centres for strategic customers internally so that it does not to face coordination or communication issues with its important patrons.

## Collaborative Relationship

In a collaborative relationship, the supplier is an extension of the firm. The firm treats its suppliers as strategic partners and usually a supplier is assured of business for a reasonably long period of time. The firm does not indulge in competitive bidding every year and does not change its supplier to get the small price reduction offered by a competing supplier. Information is shared freely across firms, and the supplier is willing to invest in relationship-specific assets. Usually, the supplier gets involved early at the product design stage and the price paid to the supplier is based on the actual costs incurred. One major concern in collaborative relationships is ensuring that the supplier keeps working on innovations. Just like the internal supplier, the partner in a collaborative relationship is assured of business, and this may result in complacency on the part of the supplier. Firms should periodically benchmark the partner's costs with the market so as to ensure that the supplier remains competitive. Dell Computers benchmarks all its partners on cost and technology leadership. Only if the supplier maintains leadership on both these fronts does Dell continue with the same partner.

Firms like Toyota buy 80 per cent of the required components from the market. But Toyota and other Japanese firms do not keep their suppliers at an arm's length and do not work with contractual relationships. Japanese manufacturers work with a network of suppliers with whom they maintain close long-term relationships. Japanese companies have subcontractor networks called *keiretsu*. This network involves vendors, bankers and distributors. Firms within a *keiretsu* are linked by informal personal relationships. As they share long-term relationships, they avoid most of the problems associated with market exchange relationships and are willing to invest in higher relationship-specific assets and do not worry about information asymmetry and hold-up problems. This allows each firm within the *keiretsu* to focus on its core competence and all get the necessary economies of scale. However, since they are assured of a market they may also suffer from agency problems discussed in vertical integration.

American and European automakers have realized the importance of collaborative relationships and have been progressing in that direction over the past two decades without creating *keiretsu*-like structures. To get similar benefits out of collaborative partnerships, Western firms have explored strategic alliances and joint ventures.

## Sourcing Strategy: Portfolio Approach

Firms buy a large number of components and services and, of course, not all of them should be handled in same way. The popular *portfolio approach* developed by Kraljic (see Figure 3.3) classifies items based on the importance of the item in terms of value of purchase (high versus low) and associated supply risk in the supply market. Supply risk captures two dimensions: number of suppliers in the market and the demand–supply gap in the supply market. If an item has very few suppliers who have monopoly in the market and supply is less than the demand, the buyer faces a significant supply risk. In supply markets where there are large numbers of players and there is surplus capacity in the market, the items bought will be classified as low-supply-risk category items. Packaging material and transport service markets come in this category and represent low-risk items. Diesel engines, diesel fuel systems and proprietary technology items have few suppliers, so they represent the high-risk-supply category. For example, Bosch has a market share of 81 per cent in the fuel-injection equipment market, so obviously it comes under the high-risk category. Similarly, oil and steel in the early part of the 21st century represented the high-risk category because demand outstripped supply. There was a strong demand for steel and fuel in India and China and, as a result, demand outstripped supply. Because of the supply uncertainty created by the disturbances in Iraq, the supply risk for oil increased significantly after the interventions by the United States of America in Iraq. Classifying items on their purchasing value is a straightforward issue because it just needs internal data and growth projections at the firm level. Supply risk, on the other hand, represents a more sophisticated

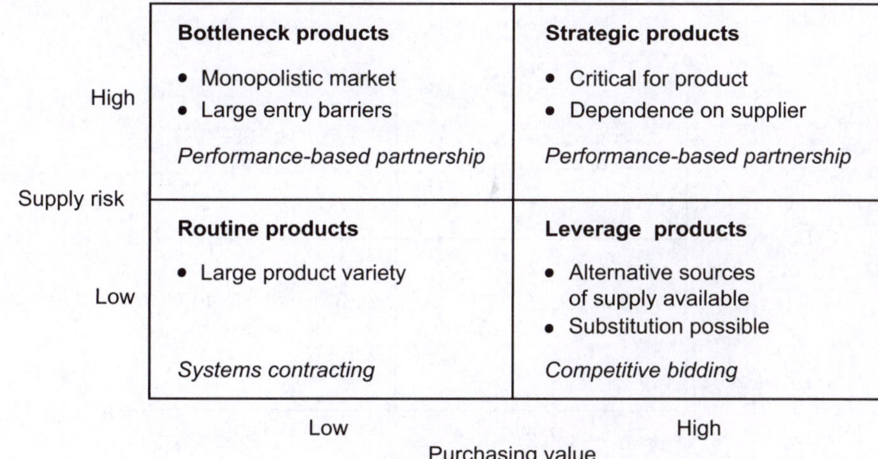


**Figure 3.3**

Purchasing portfolio analysis.

*Source:* Adapted from C. J. Gelderman and A. J. van Weele, "Purchasing Portfolio Models: A Critique and Update," *The Journal of Supply Chain Management* (2005, Vol 41): 41.

analysis because the focus is on the supply markets, and in the case of many commodities, the supply markets are global in nature. So firms should either develop adequate capability in this area or should take help from experts for carrying out this exercise.

Like everything else, purchasing expenditure per item also follows the 80–20 rule, that is, 20 per cent of the items represent about 80 per cent of the value of purchase. Similarly, the bargaining power of buyers and suppliers depends on the demand–supply conditions in the supply markets and hence are different for different items. Typically, managers end up spending equal amounts of time and effort on all items and all suppliers. Because each supplier has to go through supplier certification, if there are large numbers of items and distinct components the purchasing manager may not be focusing on items where opportunities may be high or supply risks are significant.

To understand this issue better, see Figure 3.4, which has aggregate data from the portfolio analysis carried out by a couple of Indian firms. As can be seen in Figure 3.4, 4–10 per cent of parts accounted for about 70–80 per cent of the purchase value. On supply-risk dimensions, 82–90 per cent of the items represent low-supply-risk situations. What is most striking is the low-value, low-risk quadrant. Items in this quadrant account for 80–85 per cent of the items and 15–25 per cent of the purchase value. The explicit data on purchase orders are not presented in the study, but it is very likely that the low-value, low-risk quadrant will account for the largest number of purchase orders and, therefore, will take up the bulk of the purchasing manager's time. We obviously need a different sourcing strategy for each quadrant.

As shown in Figure 3.3, the four quadrants are named as follows: routine products, leverage products, strategic products and bottleneck products. We take each category and discuss the sourcing strategy.

- *Routine products.* This quadrant represents significant opportunity. The focus is on reducing the number of parts and the number of suppliers. The aim is to reduce administrative and logistics complexity. The time saved here is used to focus on strategic suppliers and bottleneck suppliers. The focus is on moving to system buying rather than component buying. A large number of items and suppliers come in this quarter, which represents a non-critical, low-valued supply. Unfortunately, managers end up spending much energy in this quarter. Ideally, the purchasing department should not waste its energy on small items. Rather, it should aggregate components into systems and start sourcing the systems. This issue is discussed in greater detail in the section titled "Reconfiguration of the Supply Base".
- *Leverage products.* This quadrant consists of high-value, standard products. These items provide an opportunity for leveraging buying power in low-supply-risk situations. In these supply markets, there are a large number of suppliers and switching costs are low. So firms should be aggressive in their attempts to encourage competitive bidding in order to leverage their position. Most of the benefits obtained by firms in reverse auctions have been in this category.

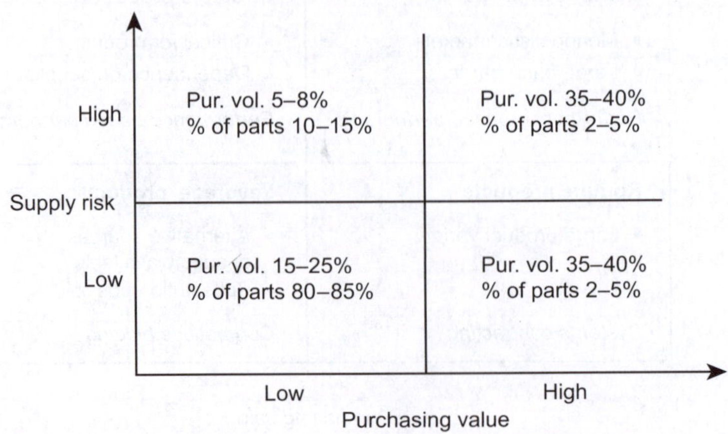


**Figure 3.4**

Representative data in the purchase portfolio matrix.

A firm can reduce the number of suppliers and focus on operational-level integration so that apart from purchasing costs inventory and administrative efforts can also be reduced.

- *Strategic products.* This quadrant represents high-value products with high supply risks. As shown in Figure 3.4, this quadrant usually accounts for less than 5 per cent of the items and for almost 40 per cent of purchase value. Items in this quadrant are treated as strategic items, and a firm must work towards establishing collaborative, long-term relationships with suppliers in this quadrant. Firms must create opportunities for mutual cost reduction by working together on all aspects, including product design. Because fewer parts and suppliers are involved, firms can invest in building collaborative relationships. The top management of firms should get actively involved in devising a strategy for this category of items.

- *Bottleneck products.* These items represent relatively low value, but a firm is vulnerable on this front because of the supply risk inherent in this market. Since a firm is likely to be buying relatively smaller value, it is also unlikely to have much clout with suppliers. Here, the focus is on securing supply, and a firm should actively keep looking at alternative sources of supply. If possible, the firm should also look at substitutes that are from low-risk supply markets. For example, in the diesel fuel system, there may not be too many suppliers of the required capability and competence. A firm might try and develop a better understanding of supplier priorities and their planning systems so that it can align its buying plan with the suppliers' operating plans. For example, some steel producers produce certain grades of steel only once in a year. If an interested firm knew of their internal processes, it might be in a better position to obtain reliable supply. If required, the firm should also be willing to pay a premium for a reliable source of supply.

In doing the above-mentioned analysis, firms seem to focus on items involved in direct purchases or those that affect the cost of goods sold. But firms buy a huge quantity of indirect goods and services, such as travel, advertising, IT and human-resources-related purchases, which have rarely come under the radar of sourcing executives. In the United States of America, direct purchases account for 47 per cent of the firm's expenses and indirect purchases account for 24 per cent of its expenses. Firms like American Express and Chase Manhattan Bank have managed to reduce costs by 10–15 per cent in their purchase of indirect goods and services. Ideas of portfolio analysis are equally applicable for indirect purchases. Typically, they are handled by the marketing, human resources and IT departments, who do not have the necessary skills of sourcing and end up paying premium prices without getting anything substantial in return in terms of higher services.

## Reconfiguration of the Supply Base

Most Indian companies work with a large number of vendors. In the past, a number of items were reserved for the small-scale sector and this forced Indian corporations to source material from many small players. Most of these small firms had very little motivation to innovate. Further, purchasing managers preferred to work with a large number of suppliers so that as a buyer the firm could play one supplier against another at the bidding stage. If we take the example of freight, typically, Indian firms work with a large number of transporters. Toyota Kirloskar has just one strategic supplier of logistics services with whom it has a collaborative relationship. Other firms may not want to go all the way to single sourcing, but they have to work on reconfiguring their supply base so as to reduce the number of suppliers. Reconfiguration involves the following two ideas:

- Move to system buying
- Reduce the number of suppliers per item/system

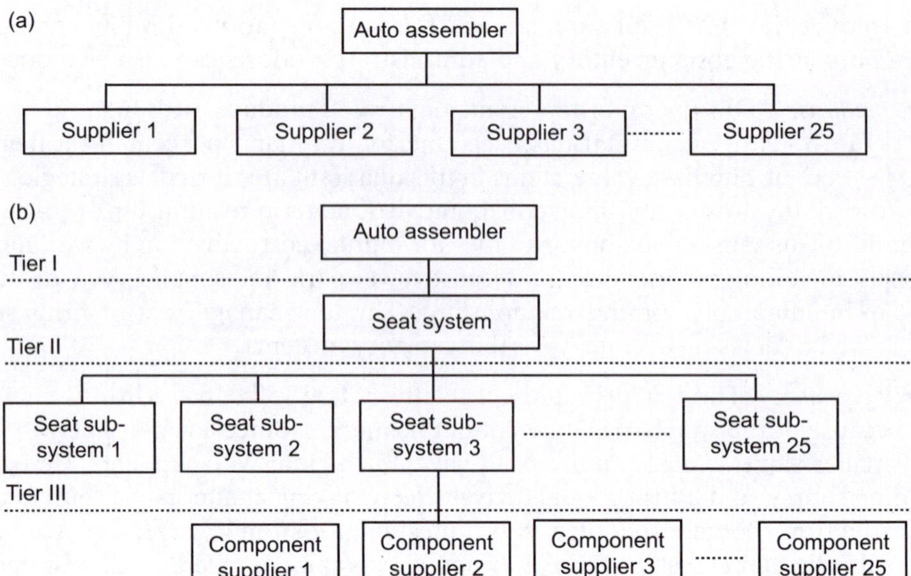


**Figure 3.5** An example of a three-tier system: (a) traditional structure; (b) tiering in suppliers.

As discussed earlier, purchase portfolio analysis reveals that 80 per cent of the items constitute 20 per cent of the value. Rather than buying individual components, firms should buy systems and modules. This is illustrated with an example from the automobile industry. Typically, a firm like GM used to buy seat parts from 25-odd suppliers, while Japanese firms like Nissan buy the complete seat from a supplier. This does not mean that the supplier manufactured all the 25 components of the seat; it just means that the supplier is a first-tier supplier who in turn buys sub-systems from second-tier companies, who in turn depend on third-tier companies. The difference between GM's and Nissan's approach is illustrated in Figure 3.5. It is not difficult to appreciate the difference between the coordination costs involved in procuring car seats at GM and at Nissan. Auto assemblers, globally, have minimized their coordination costs by moving to system/module buying, which requires a pyramid-shaped supply structure. Auto assemblers work closely with tier I suppliers who are responsible for the design and delivery of complete modules like seats, doors, and dashboards. These system suppliers buy their own sub-systems from tier II suppliers, who in turn buy individual items from tier III suppliers. By working only with tier I suppliers, a firm can not only reduce coordination costs but also work on various initiatives to improve material and information flow across the chain.

### VENDOR RATIONALIZATION BY MARUTI UDYOG LIMITED

Maruti Udyog Limited (MUL) has been the leader of the Indian automobile industry for about two decades. In the face of increased competition, MUL is under increased pressure to bring down costs. To improve its efficiency, MUL started the vendor rationalization programme in 2002. By 2004, it had managed to slash the number of vendors from 350 to 220. Maruti found that by lowering the time and the cost involved in dealing with more vendors, it has successfully been able to increase the efficiency of the supply chain. Maruti plans to build a set of technically capable and financially sound vendors who can match up to its standards on a priority basis. In India, Toyota works with less than 100 suppliers while Mahindra & Mahindra has more than 1,000 suppliers.

Once a firm has moved to system buying, it can try and reduce the number of suppliers for each system. Reducing the number of suppliers does not necessarily mean sole sourcing, that is, having only one supplier. Sole sourcing is valid for large complex systems that require massive investments in tools. Usually, Japanese firms like to have dual suppliers for every system and they motivate suppliers by shifting a fraction of their business from one supplier to another, based on supplier performance. They also encourage suppliers to compare performances with each other.

With fewer suppliers, a firm can move to electronic information flow and then to process qualification rather than having inspections at the receipt stage. Firms can also work with the idea of a green channel where a supplier's material goes directly to the assembly line and thus the firm can reduce many non-value-added activities in the chain.

## Impact of the Internet on Sourcing Strategy

Some years back there was the view that the Internet will fundamentally alter the sourcing strategy of firms. A large number of researchers and practitioners argued that with the advent of the Internet firms can source from anywhere in the world and that old ideas of sourcing will not be valid in the virtually connected world. During the days of the dotcom bubble, some analysts expected the three big auto companies GM, Ford and Chryster to save to the tune of $2,500 per $19,000 vehicle, using Covisint, the electronic collaborative exchange. In the post-dotcom-bubble era, firms have realized that the fundamentals of sourcing strategy remain valid in the post-Internet era also. In this section, we critically analyse the impact of Internet technology on sourcing strategy.

Ideally, firms prefer to evaluate a large number of potential suppliers, as a broadening range of suppliers will definitely help the firm in lowering the price at which it will buy the item. Also, a larger number of potential suppliers will reduce the risk of opportunistic behaviour, inherent in situations involving bargaining among a few parties that are highly dependent upon each other. Unfortunately, the costs involved in locating and evaluating the right supplier and the interactions are strictly the function of the number of suppliers included in the search process. Consequently, a firm determines the optimal number of suppliers by trading off the cost of further searches against the expected benefit from identifying a better supplier. Since search and evaluation costs are lower for suppliers in the geographical neighbourhood, most of the firms traditionally work with a limited number of suppliers located in their geographical proximity. Internet technology has changed the nature and extent of costs involved in the search and evaluation process.

Because of advances in IT in general and the Internet in particular, costs related to computer-aided information search and coordination have declined, averaging 25 per cent per year. It was argued that the optimal number of suppliers in the consideration set is bound to increase as the Internet lowers search and evaluation costs. Further, suppliers in the consideration set will be globally distributed and not limited to the geographical neighbourhood of the firm. Also, the Internet fuelled a lot of electronic public market exchanges and industry-sponsored exchanges where information about suppliers can be obtained without much effort. Further, electronic reverse auction (see Box 3.1) became a popular technology, which allowed the buyer to organize auctions where potential suppliers all over the world could bid via the Internet and the firm could select the most suitable supplier.

These developments raised serious discussions among scholars and practitioners about the direction of evolution of the buyer–supplier relationship. There was also concern about whether we are going back to an era in purchasing where the only thing that mattered was the price. Over the past few years, after a detailed study of reverse auctions, it has been found that reverse auctions work best for items such as plastic resin, transport services and personal computers, where there are a large number of suppliers and there is excess capacity in the system. It was observed that reverse auctions and market exchanges worked reasonably well for items

**BOX 3.1** Reverse Auction

Unlike a typical auction, the roles of buyers and sellers are reversed in reverse auction. Firms use this approach to identify suppliers willing to supply specific items like steel or service like freight at the lowest bid price. Suppliers bid electronically for a contract over a window of about 30–60 minutes. At the bidding stage, all suppliers have access to information about the lowest bid in real time, and since the amount in an auction is usually large, the supplier is under tremendous pressure to reduce the bid and usually ends up bidding a lower amount than would be bid during normal circumstances. Tata Motors saved Rs 160 million on purchase worth approximately Rs 2.5 billion in 2001, when it first tried out the reverse auction model for a few commodities like tyres, bearings, forgings, springs and fasteners. Several companies have reported gains of about 10 per cent by using reverse auctions, though not all companies have been happy with reverse auctions. Some firms have found that the initial so-called reported savings are a mirage because of large-scale supply disruptions that forces them to go back to old suppliers. In the process, the total cost of ownership had not come down, and they also ended up with poor relationships and a bad reputation among the supply base. The lessons learnt by some firms over the last few years are summarized here.

Reverse auction must be used for items under the low-supply-risk market category in the purchase portfolio matrix, because for these items there are a large number of suppliers and there is surplus capacity in the market; hence, there is enough incentive for suppliers to reduce their bids during reverse auctions.

Specifications must be clearly stated in the request for quotation (RFQ) document: RFQs must be detailed and they must take care of all the issues including delivery lead times, treatment of urgent orders, warranty and so on. There have been cases where a supplier assumes that the buyer would want uniform delivery throughout the month, while in actual practice the buyer would want bulk of the delivery in the last week of the month. Most of the reported conflicts at the post-auction stage involve refusal by suppliers to provide some services not stated in the RFQ. Existing suppliers may have knowledge of implicit requirements not stated in the RFQ, but new suppliers will not be willing to offer services not stated in the RFQ.

Firms must have a robust supplier qualification process: An incapable supplier is likely to bid an arbitrary price to get a contract that the supplier will not honour finally. Existing suppliers are likely to perceive reverse auctions as a negotiation ploy when unqualified suppliers are included in the bidding. This creates credibility problems about the sourcing process from the point of view of suppliers. However, it is the inclusion of new suppliers that allows the firms to reduce costs significantly. Thus, firms must be careful and put all potential suppliers through a rigorous selection process.

Firms must ensure that the purchase lots in a reverse auction are large enough to motivate suppliers. To achieve aggressive price reductions, firms must motivate suppliers by ensuring that the volume of purchase at stake is large enough. A firm must pool its requirements across locations and business units. It may even involve a pooling family of parts like gaskets and bushes as rubber parts so as to ensure that the purchase lot has significant volume.

in the low-supply-risk category in the purchase portfolio matrix. As per the industry estimate, an average of 4 per cent of total corporate expenditure is sourced using reverse auctions, indicating that the goods and services to which reverse auctions can be successfully applied to are limited. Similarly, the popularity of public market places underwent a substantial decline after the dotcom bubble burst.

Even when IT provides the capability to connect to more potential suppliers inexpensively, managers cannot ignore the supplier power and the incentive effect such a move will have. For low-strategic items, firms deal with high-supply-risk market situations where the supplier has a higher bargaining power and so will not be interested in participating in reverse auctions. Further, strategic items, firms prefer to provide incentives to suppliers to invest in relationship-specific assets, and for such firms, working closely with a small number of supplier partners will always remain optimal, regardless of how low search and coordination costs become. As discussed earlier, if a firm wants its suppliers to invest in relationship-specific assets, it must guarantee them a fair share of the benefits, and this can only be assured by working with a collaborative model. So instead of increasing the number of suppliers for strategic items, the

Internet is helping firms in changing the nature and extent of coordination and interaction with their existing partners.

Many companies, in the past, had asked their strategic suppliers to be part of electronic data integration (EDI), as EDI helps in better coordination with strategic partners. Building EDI linkage required suppliers to make larger fixed technological and organizational investments. Further, if investments in electronic integration are specific to a particular buyer and thus not transferable to new relationships, they create switching costs, and not all partners in the strategic category will be willing to make the necessary investments. Because of the Internet, technology investments in electronic integrations are less likely to be relationship specific, so suppliers will be willing to make those investments, thereby increasing the nature and extent of collaboration between partner firms for strategic items in the purchase portfolio matrix.

### *E-SOURCING AT MARICO*

Marico is a market leader in the hair care business. For its Parachute brand, it procures copra (raw material) worth Rs 3 billion in money value and equivalent to 600 million coconuts in quantity terms annually. Copra supply has traditionally been in the unorganized market and most of the producers are illiterate. Buying copra on this scale required lot of time and effort on the part of Marico. In 2004, Marico launched an e-sourcing initiative (implemented in stages), which transformed the buying process gradually from manual to an automated electronic process. Potential vendors send their quote through SMS and get an electronic confirmation within half an hour. The payment is also made electronically. Apart from making the process more efficient, e-sourcing has given Marico much greater control over the buying process.

To summarize, the basic logic underlying the sourcing strategy using the purchase portfolio matrix is not going to change because of the Internet. In fact, the Internet is an enabler in implementing the sourcing strategy based on the purchase portfolio matrix. Ideas like electronic reverse auctions help firms in reducing efforts and total costs of ownership for low-risk-supply items like routine items and leverage items. For strategic items, the Internet will reduce the cost of coordination and will help firms in bringing in more strategic items under collaborative relationships.

## Summary

- Traditionally, firms started with the assumption that everything should be done internally unless there is a compelling logic for outsourcing an activity. Now, a large number of firms want to be virtual corporations where they start with the assumption that activity must be outsourced unless there is a compelling logic that justifies keeping activities in-house.
- Since outsourcing is a strategic decision that cannot be altered in the short run, firms must look not at the immediate costs but at the long-term supply chain costs and risks in making this decision.
- Firms can identify core activities from a strategic perspective either through the business process route or by the product architecture route. When a firm decides to outsource some core process/sub-systems, it must keep the necessary architecture knowledge in-house.
- A firm has to look at the benefits as well as the costs involved in their make versus buy decisions. If additional costs due to poor economies of scale plus agency costs of internal control and coordination are less than transaction costs of market exchange, the firm should opt for *make*.
- Pure *make* and pure *buy* are two extreme ends of the make versus buy continuum. There are many ways of managing outsourced activities—tapered integration and collaborative partnerships are two among several

hybrid ways in which outsourced relationships can be managed.

- Not all items are sourced using same the approach. Purchase portfolio matrix is one popular approach for classifying items into four categories: routine items, leverage items, strategic items and bottleneck items. Purchase portfolio classifies items based on the importance of the item in terms value of purchase and the supply risk associated with the item in the supply market.
- Firms should try and reconfigure their supply base and use new technologies like the Internet and e-commerce in implementing sourcing strategies based on the purchase portfolio matrix.

## Discussion Questions

1. Bharti has entered into a 10-year contract with IBM for IT services while its network management contract with Ericsson is of 3 years duration only. What factors determine such differences in contract lengths?
2. Why do you think Wal-Mart owns a fleet of trucks, though most retailers do not?
3. You supply steering wheels to Mahindra & Mahindra for their existing products. Mahindra approaches you to develop and supply steering wheels for its new product, the Logan. It wants you to invest in the necessary tools required for the same and this will involve substantial investment. What can Mahindra do to reduce transaction costs in this arrangement?
4. Are there economies of scale in purchasing? Should a firm with multi-plants operation centralize its purchasing?
5. A firm is planning to outsource its supply chain planning operations to i2 technologies. What is the architecture knowledge that the firm needs to keep in-house?
6. Indo Nissin Food Ltd has outsourced its distribution to Marico. How is this decision likely to be affected in the following situations?
   - Indo Nissin increases its size of operations.
   - Indo Nissin enters the premium products market.
   - Indo Nissin wants to enter rural markets.
7. IIM Bangalore has not used audio-visual training material in the past. It wants to explore the distance education market and develop relevant training material using the audio-visual medium. Should this activity of developing audio-visual material be carried out internally or should it be outsourced to an external party?
8. Indian IT firms have been hiring engineering students who are not trained software specialists. IT firms spend enormous resources on training these young graduates. Should they outsource software training to colleges from which these students are hired?
9. How important is coordination between cola companies and their bottling plants? Is it necessary to own bottling plants if the cola companies want to achieve a better degree of coordination at the local level of operations?
10. The purchase portfolio matrix in Figure 3.4 showed some distribution in terms of percentage of items located in each quadrant. Can one see a similar distribution for most of the manufacturing firms?
11. Why do you think reverse auction does not work for all items? Should Tata Motors use reverse auctions for procuring crank shafts?
12. HP has outsourced its manufacturing activities to third-party electronic manufacturing service (EMS) companies like Flextronics but has kept sourcing activities in-house. Firms like Flextronics argue that since they buy inputs for a large number of clients, they have better economies of scale compared to HP, and HP may be better off by outsourcing sourcing activities to EMS companies. Why do you think HP wants to keep its control on sourcing?
13. A firm can increase its ROI by selling its plant and machinery. So should firms sell their plants and machineries and outsource all manufacturing operations. Is there any fallacy in the above logic?

## Mini Project

**Analysis: Outsourcing Trends in the Indian Industry**

The objective of the study is to understand the trends in outsourcing in Indian industries.

The study consists of two parts:

- Analysing the outsourcing trends from financial data of companies
- Carrying out a field study to understand the outsourcing practices in Indian industries

**Analysing the outsourcing trends from the financial data of companies**

**Methodology**

Identify an industry (e.g., the automobile industry) and select at least three listed (public limited) firms (Tata Motors, Mahindra & Mahindra Ltd, Maruti Udyog Ltd, Hindustan Motors, etc.) from the selected industry. Collect data on the following two parameters for the last 10 financial years for all the companies in the study:

- Raw material consumed: RM
- Cost of sales: CS
- Outsourcing ratio = RM/CS

The electronic database Prowess maintained by CMIE can be used to collect the relevant data. Alternatively, visit the Websites of the companies for downloading the annual reports of the respective companies.

Observe the trend in outsourcing ratio for different firms in the same industry. One expects that, with the present trend in outsourcing, the outsourcing ratio should increase over a period of time.

**Field study to understand the outsourcing practices in the Indian industry**

**Methodology**

Identify a company in your neighbourhood and interview a senior manager about the outsourcing practices for the company. Identify activities that are outsourced and find out the activities that are likely to be outsourced in the future.

Using the framework provided in this chapter, identify core and non-core activities for the firm and see whether practices followed by the firm matches with the insights derived from the chapter.

## Notes

1. Shelley Singh and Rajeev Dubey, "The Man Who Gave Away His Network," *Business World* (4 October 2004).
2. www.wired.com/wired/archive/9.11/flex.html.
3. R. Venkatesan,"Strategic Sourcing: To Make or Not to Make," *Harvard Business Review* (November-December 1992): 98–107.

## Further Reading


M. Bensaou, "Portfolio of Buyer–Supplier Relationships," *MIT Sloan Management Review* (Summer 1999, Vol 40): 35–44.

D. Besanko, D. Deanove, M. Shanley, and S. Schaefer, *Economics of Strategy* (Singapore: John Wiley, 2004).

H. Chesbrough and D. Teece, "When Is Virtual Virtuous: Organising for Innovation," *Harvard Business Review* (1996, Vol 74): 65–74.

Susan Cramm, "Outsource the Work, not the Leadership", *Harvard Business Review*, July 19, 2010.

L. M. Douglas and K. A. Michael, "We're in This Together," *Harvard Business Review* (December 2004, Vol 82): 114–122.

C. H. Fine, R. Vardan, R. Pethick, and J. Ei-Hout, "Rapid-Response Capability in Value-Chain," *MIT Sloan Management Review* (Winter 2002, Vol 43): 69–75.

C. J. Gelderman and A. J. van Weele, "Purchasing Portfolio Models: A Critique and Update," *The Journal of Supply Chain Management* (2005, Vol 41): 19–28.

Ben Gomes-Cassseres, "Outsourcing: Where will you Draw the Line?", August 31, 2009.

Ranjay Gulati, "How to do away with the Dangers of Outsourcing", *Harvard Business School*, June 06, 2013.

Paul Guttry, "Learning Curve: Making the Most of Outsourcing", *Harvard Business School*, April 10, 2013.

R. B. Handfield, D. R. Krause, T. V. Scannell, and R. M. Monczka, "Avoid the Pitfalls in Supplier Development," *Sloan Management Review* (Winter 2000, Vol 41): 37.

P. F. Johnson and R. D. Klassen, "E-Procurement," *MIT Sloan Management Review* (Winter 2005, Vol 46): 7.

P. Kraljic, "Purchasing Must Become Supply Management," *Harvard Business Review* (September–October 1983, Vol 61): 109–117.

Mary C. Lacity and Leslie P. Willcocks, "Outsourcing Business Processes for Innovation", Spring 2013.

J. K. Liker and Y. Yu, "Japanese Automakers, U.S. Suppliers and Supply-Chain Superiority," *MIT Sloan Management Review* (Fall 2000, Vol 42): 81.

J. P. MacDuffie and S. Helper, "Creating Lean Suppliers: Diffusing Lean Production Through the Supply Chain," *California Management Review* (1997, Vol 39): 118–151.

R. Monczka, R. Handfield, and R. J. Trent, *Purchasing and Supply Chain Management* (New Delhi: Thomson Learning Asia, 2001).

T. Nishiguchi and J. Bookfield, "The Evolution of Japanese Subcontracting," *MIT Sloan Management Review* (Fall 1997, Vol 39): 89–101.

D. Smagalla, "Supply-Chain Culture Clash," *MIT Sloan Management Review* (Fall 2004, Vol 46): 6.

I. Stuart, P. Deckert, D. McCutcheon, and R. Kunst, "Case Study: A Leveraged Learning Network," *MIT Sloan Management Review* (Summer 1998, Vol 39): 81–93.

A. J. van Weele, *Purchasing and Supply Chain Management* (London: Business Press, Thomson Learning, 2000), 2nd edition.

J. P. Womack, D. L. Jones, and D. Roos, *The Machine that Changed the World* (New York: Macmillan, 1990).

PART

# II

# Managing Material Flow in Supply Chains



In Part II, the focus is on issues relating to the management of material flow in supply chains. Apart from focusing on the drivers of cost and service, we extensively discuss the supply chain optimization approach wherein, using analytical models, firms can make improvements on the cost as well as customer service fronts simultaneously.

Indian firms find that a significant amount of working capital is locked up in the inventory. Chapter 4 presents not only the basic factors affecting inventory but also a few inventory models that can help firms in improving their performance on this front. This chapter summarizes key analytical methods that are useful to managers in working out an optimal level of inventory.

Transportation-related decisions significantly affect cost as well as the responsiveness of the supply chain. With increasing globalization and offshore sourcing, transportation issues have become vital for supply chain managers. Chapter 5 presents the options and cost structures for the available modes of transport. It also examines the impact of product and demand characteristics on the transportation strategy and the issues involved in choosing the optimal transportation mode.

Chapter 6 discusses concepts related to network design and operations. The supply chain is essentially a network consisting of nodes and linkages. Nodes represent conversion or storage/demand points, and linkages represent transportation activities enabling material flow in the chain. For firms with multiple plants and markets, the allocation of resources and volumes to each node is a crucial tactical decision that hinges on a complex interplay of various factors such as location, demand and supply characteristics and product characteristics. This chapter also deals with relevant optimization models.

The concepts discussed here are critical for the understanding of the drivers of supply chain innovations, discussed in Part IV of the book.

# Inventory Management

## Learning Objectives

After reading this chapter, you will be able to answer the following questions:

> Why do firms carry inventory? What are the various types of inventory carried by an organization?

> What are the components of cost that are affected by inventory decisions?

> How can a firm reduce inventory in the organization?

> How do firms determine the optimum level of cycle stock in chain?

> How do firms decide on the required level of safety stock in chain?

It is not easy to deal with customer dissatisfaction, especially if the customer in question is a 4-year-old boy. Picture this: A petulant toddler demanding the Spider-Man costume for an upcoming party. If he cannot be transformed into Spider-Man, he cannot attend the party. It is imperative that he find it. He is trying his best to convince his mother by crying his lungs out and flailing his arms wildly. The mother looks at her son and turns to glare at the apologetic sales executive. In the face of such blatant blackmail, she has no option but to hop across to the next mall. The store has lost another customer.

To keep pace with such demands, retail chain outlets like Shoppers' Stop manage a staggering 300,000 SKUs at each outlet. Ensuring the availability of each SKU across 21 stores in the country is a supply chain challenge. To accomplish this, Shoppers' Stop has four regional distribution centres at Delhi, Mumbai, Bangalore and Kolkata. These four centres service the entire network. Over 400 vendors supply the regional distribution centres.

Shoppers' Stop has to decide how much inventory the regional distribution centres shall carry and how much inventory stores shall maintain. They cannot risk non-availability of a product as it will adversely affect their reputation. On the other hand, carrying too much inventory at either the distribution centres or the stores increases the inventory-carrying cost and brings on the problem of obsolescence.

When asked how it manages the supply chain, Sanjay Badhe,[1] the Director of Operations replied, "There is no one in India that offers logistics, so we had to develop our own logistics department. We have linked every office in the country via leased lines and V-SATs".

A typical supply chain consists of multiple items and stock points where each stock point has a customer and a supplier. Given the supply and demand characteristics of suppliers and customers, a decision maker at a stock point makes essentially two decisions: how much to order and when to order. In this chapter we address this issue.

## Introduction

Every participant in a supply chain, whether retailer, wholesaler, manufacturer or vendor, prefers to reduce inventories and yet maintain customer service so as not to lose customers because of non-availability of goods. Huge inventories are a drain on resources, as it blocks money and increases cost of operations. So it is no surprise that all firms want to reduce inventory in the supply chain. In the past, the zero-inventory slogan had attracted a lot of attention from financial controllers of firms for some time because it gave them the illusion that it was possible to work with a zero inventory and improve financial performance. Zero inventory was a very popular term in business literature, but as we shall see zero inventory translates into zero business. The chapter brings out the logic of why a business needs inventory and suggests possible ways of improving performance in this area.

Figure 4.1 captures the inventory turnover ratio of the 10 largest Indian manufacturing firms for the years 2003 and 2013. It is interesting to note that the performance of all firms in petroleum sector have shown improvement, whereas all firms in steel industry have shown decline over the last decade. In automobile sector, we have mixed results; while the performance of Tata Motors has declined, Mahindra & Mahindra has shown considerable improvement. Even though the sales of most of these companies have substantially increased (almost 5 to 15 times), there does not seem to be significant improvement in inventory performance. It might be argued that such a comparison is not fair as these companies are not from the same industry. The data for various firms within an industry listed in CMIE were analysed to arrive at a more reasonable comparison. The results are presented in Table 4.1. A comparison of the worst performer, the best performer and the average performer from all the sectors of Indian economy on inventory turnover ratio throws up interesting results.

As is evident from the data, the best performers in each industry segment seem to be working with 10 to 20 times higher inventory turnover ratios compared to the worst performers. Essentially, this shows that within Indian firms there is a significant potential for reduction in inventory across industries. Of course, each of these firms works with multiple SKUs and has multiple levels in supply chains. Firms like IndianOil work with thousands of SKUs and have to keep material at the RM, WIP and FG levels. Further, it has to carry RM and WIP at multiple plant locations and carry FG inventory at various levels within the distribution channel. Given this complexity, it is tempting to take the view that these firms perhaps work with the optimal level of inventory, and since these firms seem to have their own complexities, they should not be compared. We then come back to the basic question: How much inventory is good enough?

We had the opportunity to study one pulp-making firm, APR Ltd, in great detail, and we found that this firm used to carry about 4 months of wood inventory. One extreme view is to say that the

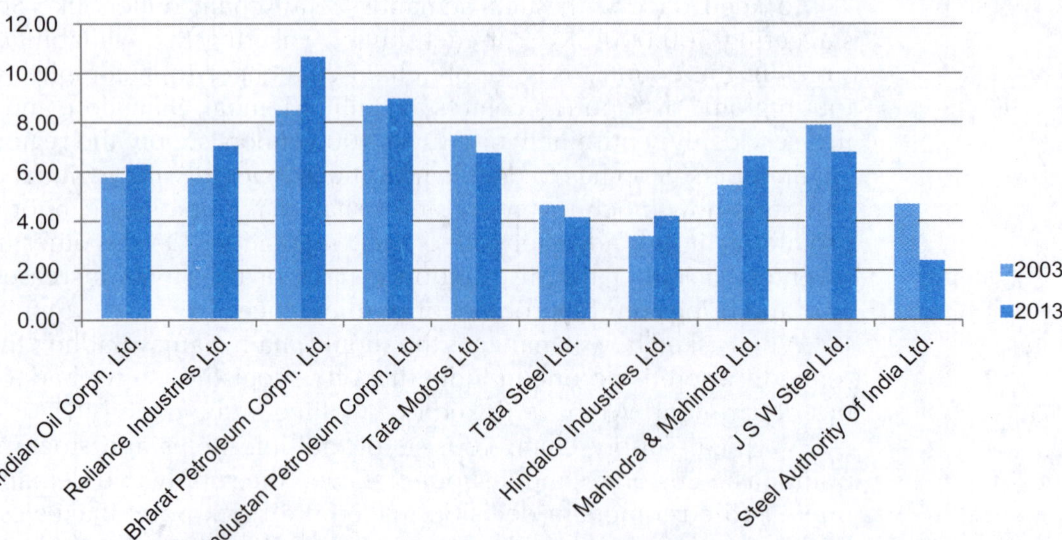


**Figure 4.1**

Performance of the top 10 Indian manufacturing companies [*Source:* Prowess (CMIE)].

*Table 4.1:* **Performance on inventory turnover ratio of Indian industry for year 2013: sector-wise***

| | Food- and agro-based products | Textiles | Chemicals and chemical products | Consumer goods | Construction materials | Metals and metal products | Machinery | Transport equipment |
|---|---|---|---|---|---|---|---|---|
| Worst | 0.9 | 1.3 | 1.8 | 1.6 | 1.8 | 1.5 | 0.9 | 1.2 |
| Average | 5.5 | 6.3 | 5.6 | 6.9 | 4 | 13.7 | 6 | 7.9 |
| Best | 21.2 | 25.9 | 17.1 | 27.6 | 8.5 | 93.7 | 26.5 | 22.9 |

*Bottom 10% and top 10% of the firms have been removed as outliers.
*Source*: Prowess, CMIE.

huge inventory carried by APR Ltd is unnecessary and, therefore, carrying inventory at all is a waste. The other view might be that since APR has always carried 4 months of inventory, and on an average every firm in that industry carries the same, APR should continue carrying the same inventory. Either extreme does not serve any purpose. When APR carried out a detailed analytical exercise, it came to the conclusion that it should be able to manage its affairs with just 18 days of inventory.

In this chapter, a new approach termed the zero-based inventory budgeting approach is proposed. Zero-based inventory budgeting is essentially a bottoms-up approach to inventory management. It starts with zero level of inventory, and for all the identified drivers of inventory, a firm carries out an analytical exercise to determine the appropriate level of inventory required for each of the identified drivers. To identify all the drivers, zero-based inventory budgeting classifies inventory into various categories based on the reasons why the organization needs to carry inventory. Further, managerial decisions regarding inventories must ultimately be made at the product level. The decision maker controls inventory through two critical decisions: how much to order and when to order. Though a detailed analysis of this kind is carried out for only a few critical items/products, the exercise helps the firm in setting broad targets for the inventory turnover ratio. More importantly, this exercise helps managers to understand the various drivers that force firms to maintain the current level of inventory. This in-depth analysis helps firms to explore ideas to improve both the turnover ratio and the service. In a supply chain environment, there are many possible options for firms to improve on both these fronts. However, the key questions are where to target the improvement effort and what are the anticipated benefits. The analytical approach discussed in this chapter equips you with the necessary tools in this regard.

A typical supply chain consists of multiple items and stock points, where each stock point has a customer and a supplier. Keeping in mind the demand and supply characteristics of customers and suppliers, a decision maker at stock points decides how much to order and when to order. In this chapter, we assume that to arrive at the decision the decision maker follows a policy of continuous review. There are two popular review policies: continuous review and periodic review. The firm following a periodic review policy does not track inventory position on a continuous basis. Inventory position is reviewed after a fixed period of time, and based on a pre-specified order up to level the firm decides the size of the order. Since most firms have real-time inventory information systems in place, we focus only on the continuous review systems in the main chapter. The relevant issues for periodic review policy are discussed in Appendix A. While discussing various inventory models, we assume that there is only one item at a stock point. At the end of the chapter, we discuss how to apply these ideas for multiple item situations.

# Types of Inventory

Inventory may be divided into various categories. This categorization helps managers to view inventories as being controllable rather than as an evil to be avoided. In general, there are six main categories of inventories: cycle stock, safety stock, pipeline stock, seasonal stock, decoupling stock, anticipation inventory and dead stock.

## Cycle Inventory

Because of the economies of scale involved in production and transportation, it makes sense to produce and transport goods in batches. The inventory resulting from the production or purchase in batches is called cycle stock, since the lots are produced or purchased in cyclical lots. Companies have a choice of ordering frequently and incurring large ordering costs or ordering less frequently and incurring significant inventory cost. Companies that attempt to follow the just-in-time philosophy found ways and means of reducing cycle inventory in recent times. Apart from economic considerations, sometimes quality considerations may force firms to produce in large batches. Analytical models for deciding optimal cycle stock are discussed at a later stage.

## Safety Stock

Safety stocks, as the name suggests, are maintained as a safeguard against uncertainties of demand and supply. In case of an assured supply and predictable customer demand, safety stocks will be unnecessary. Since the loss of customers due to non-availability of products is likely to result in significant costs, firms end up carrying a large quantity of safety stocks. Customer demand is difficult to control but firms may work on supply uncertainty to bring it down gradually. In a country like India where transportation and supply uncertainties are large, safety stock constitutes a significant portion of a firm's inventory. Analytical models for deciding optimal safety stock are discussed later.

## Decoupling Stocks

Since it is not possible to carry out supply chain operations with just one decision maker, the entire supply chain is usually divided into various decision-making units. Usually, the demarcation of decision-making units takes place both at organizational and departmental boundaries. It is not uncommon for organizations to hold large inventories at organizational as well as departmental boundaries. This decoupling inventory provides the flexibility needed by each decision-making unit to manage its operations independently and to optimize its performance (in the respective spheres of operations in the supply chain). Improving co-ordination across various decision-making units within the supply chain can reduce decoupling inventory significantly. This issue is discussed in greater detail in Chapter 9 (Supply Chain Integration). In most organizations, internal supply chain is divided into three decision units, materials, manufacturing and distribution, which take care of the buy, make and deliver functions, respectively.

## Anticipation Inventory

Anticipation inventory consists of stock accumulated in advance of expected peak in sales or that which takes care of some special event that does not occur on a regular basis. Anticipation stock may further fall into two categories, seasonal stock and speculation stock.

### Seasonal Stock

When the requirements of an item varies with time (e.g., paints and consumer durables exhibit high demand during festival seasons; refrigerators and air conditioners exhibit peak demand during the summer season), it may be economical for the firm to build inventory during the low-demand season to take care of peak-season demand. Of course, the firm can build enough capacity so as to produce and supply the goods during the peak season, but this means surplus capacity for the firm during the lean season. Though the firm may have enough physical capacity in terms of plants and equipments, it may not like to work with varying production rates because of certain adverse implications for labour and supplier relationships. So for such predictable seasonal variability in demand, firms prefer to plan in advance.

### Speculation Stock

If certain events like labour or transport strike, which can result in a temporary price or supply shock, are anticipated, a firm may carry certain stocks to take care of the eventuality. For example, due to some disturbance in the Middle East, an oil price increase may be expected. Therefore, an excess quantity of diesel oil may be carried to take care of this eventuality. Similarly, a high finished goods inventory may be held if a supply problem with some of the major competitors is anticipated. As the name suggests, this inventory is meant to be a preventive measure against an event that may never happen. Many firms hold high inventory in anticipation of price increase. Instead of holding higher physical inventory, firms may like to use ideas like hedging and forward contracts rather than holding physical inventory. Of course, speculation inventory or hedging has certain risk-related implication for the firm also. Even if firm decides to hold speculation inventory, as speculation is for a specific eventuality, after the temporary phase one should not hold any inventory on this account.

## *Pipeline Inventory*

Since production and transportation activities take certain finite time, firms need to carry pipeline or in-transit stock. Pipeline inventory consists of materials actually being worked on (work-in-process inventory) or being moved from one location to another in the chain (in-transit inventory). The pipeline inventory of an item between two adjacent locations is the product of the process time or transport time and the usage rate of the item. Thus, the pipeline inventory may be affected by choosing alternative modes of production or transportation. For example, pipeline inventory may be reduced by transporting goods by air rather than the sea. Similarly, by reducing manufacturing lead time, work-in-process inventory in the system can be reduced.

## *Dead Stock*

Dead stock refers to that part of the non-moving inventory that is unlikely to be of any further use in supply chain operations or markets. Dead stock essentially includes items that have become obsolete because of changes in customer taste, design or production processes. Unfortunately, in many firms, dead stock is allowed to accumulate. Ideally, firms should dispose off dead stock on a periodic basis, even if it means incurring a loss in the disposal process. However, firms refrain from disposing off the dead stock as its disposal shows up in the account books as a financial loss. Instead, they choose to show these items as assets in their balance sheet, despite the fact that these items have very little market value. Currently, many companies need inventory write-off decisions be approved at the board level. This makes it almost impossible to dispose off dead stock because the board has too many things to deal with and consequently dead stock keeps accumulating. The higher the accumulation of dead stock, the tougher it is to dispose it off, as this will have an adverse impact on the financial results of the firm in that specific year. A company may monitor all finished goods inventory, and for items that have not moved for more than six months, the marketing department may be asked to identify customers for that item on a priority basis. Some companies with multiple units share information about non-moving items with other units to see if they can be used meaningfully by another unit within the company. In the developed world, in the fashion goods business, obsolescence is quite a common phenomenon. To take care of this, firms in the business identify slow-moving items and offer huge discounts so as to dispose them off by the end of the season. The important thing is to put a process in place where periodically non-moving items are analysed and those that are unlikely to be used or demanded are classified as dead stock and disposed off.

## Inventory-related Costs

Three general classes of costs are important for inventory-related decisions: ordering costs, carrying cost and stockout costs. These three types of costs are in conflict with each other; therefore, while making inventory decisions to minimize the total inventory cost of the system, the formula used is one that minimizes ordering cost plus inventory cost plus stockout cost. In situations where the value of items gets affected by ordering or inventory policies (e.g., when a supplier offers quantity discounts), the item cost should be taken into account while evaluating various options.

### Ordering Costs

The ordering cost includes all fixed costs (components of costs that do not vary with the size of the order) associated with placing an order. The main components of the ordering cost include the following:

- *Administration costs involved in placing the order.* Preparing the purchase order will involve documentation, getting the necessary approval and other formalities. Electronic ordering can reduce the time required by the buyer and thus reduce this component of cost.
- *Transportation cost.* A fixed transportation cost is often incurred regardless of the size of the order.
- *Receiving cost.* This refers to the cost incurred on account of the administrative work that has to be undertaken on receiving the order. For example, at the time of receipt, the receiver will have to prepare the goods receipt note, update inventory records, and make necessary checks against the respective purchase order.

All fixed costs (components of cost that do not vary with order quantity) that are associated with ordering should be included in ordering costs, and all those costs that vary with order size should be included in the cost of the item. A significant part of the ordering cost in a purchase situation is information intensive. By using electronic ordering one will be in a position to reduce ordering cost substantially. In a production environment, the ordering cost is the fixed cost of the set-up. Unlike the ordering cost in a purchase situation, set-up costs are less information intensive and a significant component of cost is the time lost in set-up activity. So in a production environment, the focus is on set-up time reduction.

Ordering costs are difficult to compute because they are not captured at one place in the accounting books. If a company follows activity-based costing, then it will be in a position to find appropriate cost drivers and come up with meaningful numbers. In large firms, where a lot of administrative procedures have to be followed for placing an order, the ordering cost can be any number from ₹1,000 to ₹10,000 per order. In a manufacturing setup, since each facility has a machine-hour rate based on time spent on the setup, one can calculate ordering cost without too much difficulty.

### Inventory-carrying Costs

Carrying cost tries to capture all the actual and opportunity costs that are incurred because of holding inventory. The main components of carrying cost include the following:

- *Financing cost.* The inventory represents the assets and the working capital of a firm. Usually, this represents a major and possibly an important part of cost of carrying and some firms estimate this to be cost of borrowing. Ideally, this should represent cost of opportunity as the funds can be deployed for alternative use. The best estimate of this is the weighted average cost of the capital that is used in capital budgeting. This component of cost is directly proportional to the value of the item.

- *Storage and handling cost.* Space costs are charges that the company incurs because of storage of inventory, and it will be a function of the size of the item and not the value. Of course, space costs are not relevant while calculating pipeline inventory.

- *Inventory risk.* Cost associated with deterioration, obsolescence, shrinkage, theft or damage. This will depend on the nature of the item, for example, fashion goods, perishable goods and high-technology products are likely to have much higher risks.

Now, it is not necessary that all items have similar spoilage or obsolescence rate. Similarly, storage cost is a function of size and not value. Inventory-carrying cost is calculated at the firm level in terms of rupees per rupee of inventory per year. If the company has two different types of components with varying risk or difference in size/value ratio, it may be worthwhile to have different inventory-carrying costs for different category of items. But the usual practice is to come with one value of inventory-carrying cost. For any item, the inventory-carrying cost per unit per year is calculated by multiplying the inventory-carrying cost by the value of item.

In India, the inventory-carrying cost varies from 15–30 per cent in different firms based on their cost of funds, nature of industry, and details of costs that get included in this exercise. If there is any difficulty in estimating cost of carrying, it is best to start with a conservative estimate of 20 or 25 per cent depending on whether the firm deals in mature products or in high-technology or fashion products.

## Stockout Costs

Stockout cost captures the economical consequences of running out of stock. Stockout costs are incurred when the customer places an order but it cannot be filled from the inventory. There are two possible scenarios—in one case, the customer is willing to wait and items are back-ordered (firm incurs backorder cost), and in the other, customer is not willing to wait and with a result, order is lost (firm incurs lost sales cost). In a situation, when a company loses potential sales because of the non-availability of finished goods, it is treated as a lost sales case, and the cost incurred is the opportunity of making profit on that transaction. Apart from being a lost opportunity, it may affect the goodwill of the firm, and hence, the future sales. Backorder cost is incurred in a situation where the customer is willing to wait for his or her order to be fulfilled. Backorder results in additional administrative costs and may involve an additional transportation and handling cost when the material is rushed through to meet this situation.

Stockout costs are never captured in profit and loss accounts (company's books) but represent opportunity cost including loss of goodwill. Some of these costs are tangible, but it also includes other intangible costs such as firm goodwill and future sales. These costs are intangible, and therefore, difficult to measure. With the result, most decision makers find it difficult to quantify exact values of stockout costs. While they can relatively rank the items in terms of stockout costs, they find it difficult to put an exact number on stockout costs. For items where substitutes are available (different pack sizes in toothpaste), stockout costs are low, but for items where competition is high and the company does not offer substitute products, stockout cost is high. So instead of working with stockout costs, firms find it easier to work with a target service level that the inventory system must meet. Essentially on items for which stockout costs are relatively high, firms work with high customer service level, and for items where stockout costs are relatively low, the company fixes customer service levels at a lower level. A target of 100 per cent service level requires that the inventory system meets all customer demands from inventory. Service level targets ranging from 90 to 99 per cent are the most commonly used service level targets in industry. Therefore, instead of minimizing total system costs, the inventory system is expected to minimize ordering cost plus inventory cost subject to meeting targeted service level.

**INTERVIEW WITH**

**H. RAGHUNATH**

*Titan is India's largest watch company with a market share of 60 per cent in the organized watch market and a turnover of ₹21 billion. H. Raghunath is Vice-President, sourcing and supply chain, at Titan.*

*How complex is the supply chain at Titan Watches?*

**H. Raghunath:** We offer 3,000-odd variants in multiple market segments using a multi-tier distribution system involving 32 depots, 150 re-distribution stockists and 11,000 retail outlets spread across India. We have a complex manufacturing chain, with the final assembly being carried out at four locations: Baddi, Dehardun, Roorkie and Hosur. We are the current market leader, and to maintain this lead, we keep introducing a large number of new models every year.

*What are the inventory management challenges that you face?*

**H. Raghunath:** Balancing availability in the chain, with a tight control on the inventory, has been a tough challenge for us, more so because we are in the fashion retail business. We have kept our inventory in check by focusing on two areas: improved planning capabilities, which allows us to respond to actual market- and supply-related conditions, and we have introduced a production rationalization programme, which allows us to work with an optimal range of products.

*What resources have you invested in to enhance the planning capabilities?*

**H. Raghunath:** We have invested in advanced information technology solution, which has given us better visibility within the chain. It has also allowed us to optimize our inventory in the chain. Over the last few years, we have worked on demand planning, supply network planning and detailed production scheduling. With better forecasts, better production and distribution planning, we have improved service without increasing inventory in the system. We are known to be the leader in the use of information technology in the supply chain space.

*Why did the organization opt for product rationalization?*

**H. Raghunath:** Being in the fashion business, the breadth of our portfolio is a key differentiator in the watch business. However, excessive variety increases complexity in our supply chain exponentially. So, if we are not careful, higher complexity costs would adversely affect our profitability. To take care of this issue, we launched a product mix rationalization initiative as a part of which we systematically examine our portfolio twice a year. This initiative is anchored by the supply chain group and involves all the stakeholders in the firm. It is not an easy decision and we involve product managers, manufacturing people and, of course, field sales people.

*What are the criteria you use for product rationalization?*

**H. Raghunath:** First, we look at the purely economic criterion. We shortlist models based on gross contribution and volume of sales. Then we add models that provide brand image or showcase our technology leadership. And we also keep a few additional models in our portfolio to ensure that our offering covers a reasonable range in each of the important market segments. This has helped us in achieving higher profitability with moderate levels of inventory in the chain.

## Managing Cycle Stock

As discussed earlier, a decision maker who is managing any inventory point has to make two critical decisions—how much to order and when to order. Consider an example of a large retailer who experiences an average daily demand of 100 units for one of the items, and let us assume that he operates for 300 days a year. Let us assume also that there are no uncertainties in demand, which means that every day he sells exactly 100 units. We also assume that the retailer has a very reliable supplier. If he decides to procure 100 units every day from a supplier, so that he does not have to carry any inventory, he has to place 300 such orders in a year, which translates into a huge ordering cost. Or he can decide to go to other extreme and can decide to order once a year for the entire annual demand of 30,000 so that he incurs ordering cost just once but will end up incurring additional cost on account of the huge inventory.

## Cycle Stock Inventory Model

The trade-off between ordering cost and inventory costs can be represented mathematically by using the following notations:

$D$ = annual demand of item, $d$ = daily demand
$A$ = fixed cost of order (cost of set-up in manufacturing environment)
$C$ = cost per unit of item
$i$ = inventory-carrying cost per rupee of inventory per year
$Q$ = order size
$H$ = inventory-carrying costs per unit per year = $C \times i$

We assume that the supplier does not offer any quantity discounts, irrespective of the size of the orders, so the total annual cost of items is not relevant from the inventory management point of view and will be $C \times D$, irrespective of the order size. So the only relevant supply chain costs are cost of carrying and cost of ordering. The inventory in a system will behave as shown in Figure 4.2.

At the beginning of every cycle (just after the replenishment from the supplier), the retailer has stock equal to $Q$ and the same will reduce to zero by end of the cycle (just before the next replenishment). So, on an average, the retailer will carry cycle inventory of $Q/2$ throughout the year. So the retailer will be incurring an annual inventory-carrying cost $Q/2 \times H$. Since the annual demand is $D$, the retailer will have $D/Q$ such cycles in a year and in every cycle the retailer incurs an ordering cost of $A$, thus incurring a total annual ordering cost of amount $A \times D/Q$. As can be seen in Figure 4.3, the inventory-carrying cost increases linearly with order size $Q$, while the annual ordering cost decreases exponentially with order size $Q$.

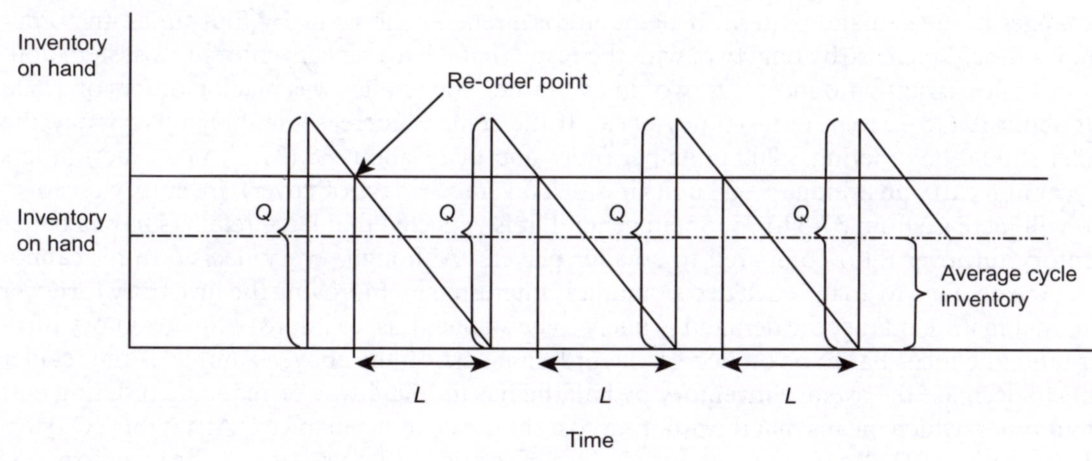


**Figure 4.2** Behaviour of inventory level with time.

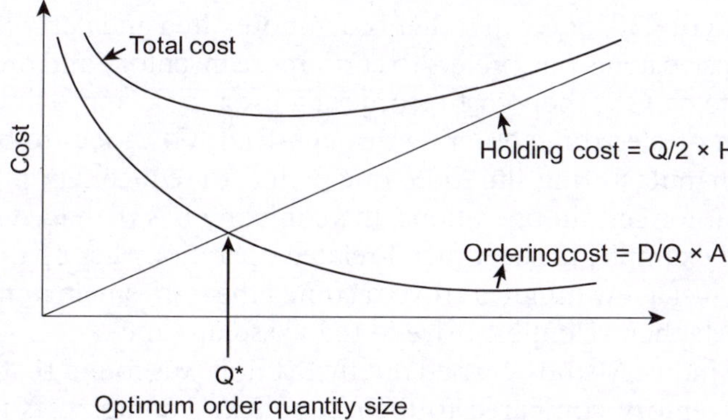


**Figure 4.3** Impact of order size on inventory-related cost.

Optimal order quantity will be at a point where the total inventory-related cost will be lowest at a point given by $Q^*$. This is also known as EOQ, that is, economic order quantity:

$$\text{Optimal order quantity} = Q^* = \sqrt{2AD/H} \tag{4.1}$$

Apart from ordering quantity, we also need to specify when the decision maker should place an order from the supplier. Let us assume that the decision maker gets his material from the supplier who is reliable but has a lead time of $L$ days. During this lead-time period, the quantity of demand faced by the retailer is equal to $L \times d$. So the decision maker should place an order every time his stock reaches the level of $L \times d$ and we will call this point the reorder point $R$. So the retailer has to follow a simple inventory policy and has to continuously monitor the inventory and whenever it reaches the reorder point $R$ the retailer has to place an order for quantity $Q^*$.

Let us go back to the case of the retailer. The product is purchased at ₹30 and the inventory-carrying cost is 20 per cent. The ordering cost for the retailer is estimated to be ₹256 per order. The supplier takes 15 working days to supply the item at the retailer's warehouse.

$$\text{Carrying cost per unit for retailer} = H = 30 \times 0.2 = ₹6 \text{ per unit per year}$$

$$\text{Optimal order quantity} = Q^* = \sqrt{2 \times 256 \times 30000/6}$$

The optimum order quantity is 1,600 and the average inventory is 800 units. So on an average the retailer carries cycle stock of 8 days of demand and has an inventory turnover of 37.5.

## Insights from Cycle Stock Inventory Model

A few key insights can be gained by understanding how the inventory turnover ratio is affected by changes in the demand pattern. If demand for a retailer shoots up by four times, the order quantity should increase by only two, with the result that the average inventory in a system doubles and sales/assets ratio increases two times. Earlier, the retailer was placing orders of 1,600 units about 19 (18.75 to be exact) times a year. If the demand increases to 400 units per day, the retailer should be ordering 3,200 units per order and place about 38 (37.5 to be exact) orders per year and carry an average 1,600 units in stock (average 4 days of cover). Inventory turnover ratio will increase from 37.5 to 75. So, in general, it is expected that large retailers have a better inventory turnover ratio compared to smaller players. Although, every decision unit cannot expect the demand to go up, each decision unit is interested in improving the inventory turnover ratio. In a mature market the demand is likely to be stable; thus, to improve the inventory turnover ratio, the focus has to be on decreasing ordering cost. In the above example, if the retailer wants to decrease the average inventory by half, he has to find a way of reducing ordering cost by four times, which means that the ordering cost should be reduced to ₹64. Again the EOQ formula (Equation 4.1) also provides an insight into managing different items in the inventory system. For example, at the same demand level, if dealing with another more expensive item, say, an item that costs ₹60 instead of ₹30, one will rather order more often and carry less inventory, but if dealing with less expensive items one prefers to carry more inventory and order less often.

According to an estimate by GE, their cost of ordering used to be approximately \$50 per order. With the introduction of electronic ordering through EDI, GE hopes to bring this cost down to \$5 per order. In a manufacturing situation, one prefers to reduce set-up cost or set-up time on machine. At Toyota, for certain operations, the company has managed to reduce the set-up time significantly. For example, in sheet-metal-related operations, set-up time used to be a few hours but now it takes just a few minutes. Toyota coined the term single minute exchange of die (SMED), which reflects their relentless drive to reduce setup time.

In a famous automobile industry study carried out by MIT,[2] it was found that the Japanese carried 1.5 days of parts inventory compared to their American counterparts that carried 8 days of parts inventory. Japanese suppliers required a set-up time of 8 minutes compared to 120 minutes required by American suppliers. A set-up time lower by 15 times on the part of Japanese suppliers (8 minutes vis-à-vis 120 minutes) resulted in reduction of parts inventory by about 5 times (from 8 to 1.5 days).

If there were no economies of scale (i.e., if there was no fixed cost involved), one prefers replenishment to take place on a continuous basis. Japanese companies have managed to work with these principles, and they are able to get their replenishment from suppliers three to four times a day in trips involving multiple deliveries or pickups called milk runs. They do not issue any purchase orders, and the supply from multiple vendors is collected in the same truck using the idea of the milk run. This reduces fixed cost of supply and as a result the firm can reduce the order quantity and thus reduce the average cycle stock inventory in system.

Here we had assumed zero quantity discounts offered, so the cost of the item could be ignored. But if one is considering a situation where quantity discounts are being offered then the cost of the item should also be included in the analysis. Essentially, if orders of a higher size are placed and a higher inventory-carrying cost is incurred, a trade-off between reduction in material cost vis-à-vis high inventory-carrying cost (incurred because of higher order quantity) will be needed.

## Managing Safety Stock

While determining the cycle stock we assumed that the demand was constant, that is, every day the decision unit faced a demand for *d* units consistently. Similarly, we assumed that the supplier was reliable, which means that we get exactly the quantity we ordered in exactly *L* days. Unfortunately, customers do not behave in a predictable way and suppliers also work with production and transportation systems that have some degree of unreliability. As a result, actual demand may be either more or less than 100 per day. Similarly, the actual time taken by the supplier may be either more or less than 15 days. Consequently, all inventory points end up keeping safety stock. In the case of our retailer, when there is no uncertainty, it is optimal to place an order when stock on hand is exactly 1,500 units. At the end of 15 days, stock on hand will be zero because the supplier will take exactly 15 days, and during those 15 days every day customers will demand exactly 100 units per day. If we consider the uncertainty in demand, then, we can only say that the average daily demand is 100 units but it could vary. Similarly, the supplier will take, on an average, 15 days but it could take more time or less. Intuitively, therefore, we can figure that if one works with a reorder point of 1,500 units, 50 per cent of the time one runs out of stock and faces a stockout situation.

In most real-life situations, stockout costs are quite high and such high levels of stockout situations are very costly for the supply chain. So, to take care of this demand and supply uncertainty, we carry safety stock so as to reduce chances of stockout situations. As shown in Figure 4.4,

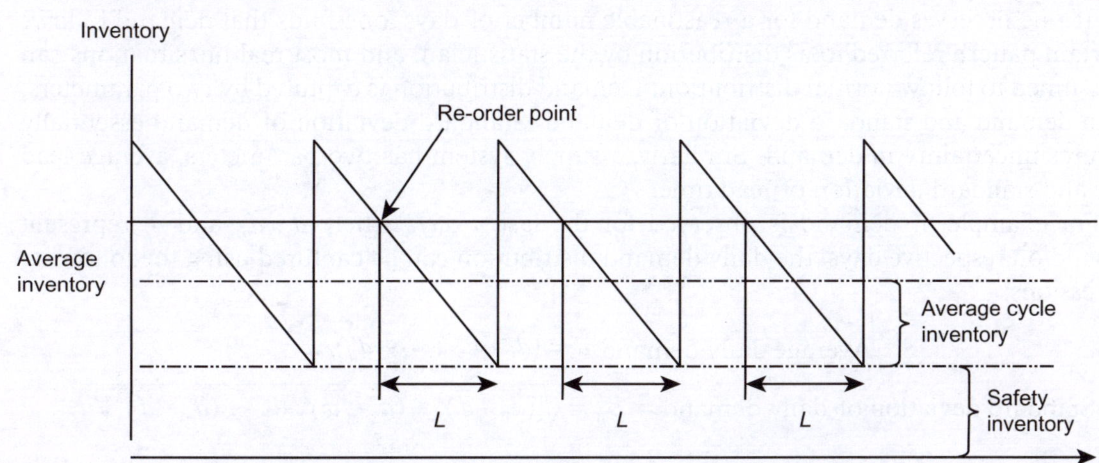


**Figure 4.4**

Inventory level with safety inventory.

one can visualize the system as adding a foundation level of safety stock to take care of this uncertainty. In general, safety stock is the average inventory on hand when the replenishment lot arrives. The average inventory carried by a firm is the average cycle stock plus safety stock.

In this section, we examine the trade-off that the supply chain manager must consider while planning the safety stock inventory. On the one hand, increasing safety stock inventory reduces the chances of stockout situations, but, on the other hand, increasing safety stock increases inventory-carrying cost for the firm. Demand uncertainty in the service sector is managed through safety capacity because unlike product firms they cannot keep finished goods inventory. Safety capacity in terms of human inventory (idle people capacity) is known as people on bench in the software industry. Infosys is very careful with its level of bench and the same is monitored closely by the top management of the firm.

### HUMAN INVENTORY AT INFOSYS[3]

Infosys Technologies Ltd provides consulting and IT services to clients globally and had an employee strength of 80,000 (as on October 2007). Even though wages is a main component of cost for Infosys, it will not like its employee utilization to go beyond the 80 per cent level. Infosys treats this 20 per cent planned idle capacity as a strategic bench (staff waiting to be assigned), which allows the firm to gear up for unexpected new opportunities in the market place. If a new customer opportunity needs 100 Java developers, Infosys can readily staff a new opportunity of this kind from trained staff readily available on the bench. In the absence of a strategic bench, Infosys will miss out on such opportunities. The bench is maintained at offshore locations like India where the cost of maintaining a bench is relatively low.

For firms that are in high-end technology industry these issues are very important because higher safety stock inventory could result in obsolescence. The central question we need to answer is, "How much safety stock should be carried in the supply chain?" This question can be answered by capturing the uncertainty in demand and supply, and evaluating the consequences of a stockout situation. We shall now examine these conditions in detail.

## Capturing Uncertainty

Even though there is bound to be unpredictability both on the part of supplier and the customer, in most supply chain situations this unpredictability can be captured using the distribution of demand and lead time. In general, uncertainty is captured by one of the following measures: range, standard deviation and coefficient of variation. We introduce all the three measures in this section but use standard deviation as the measure of uncertainty in most of the models we use. If one observes demand for a reasonable number of days, one finds that demand follows a certain pattern referred to as distribution by the statistician, and most real-life situations can be assumed to follow normal distribution. Demand distribution is captured by two parameters: mean demand and standard deviation of demand. Standard deviation of demand essentially captures uncertainty in demand. Similarly, a supply system has two parameters, average lead time and standard deviation of lead time.

For example, if demand is observed for the last $n$ days where $d_1$, $d_2$, and $d_n$ represent demand on respective days, the daily demand distribution can be captured using the following expressions:

$$\text{Average daily demand } \bar{d} = (d_1 + d_2 + \cdots + d_n)/n$$

$$\text{Standard deviation of daily demand} = \sigma_d = \sqrt{[(d_1 - \bar{d})^2 + (d_2 - \bar{d})^2 + \cdots + (d_n - \bar{d})^2]/n}$$

*Table 4.2:* ***Demand and lead-time data.***

| **Demand data** | $d_1$ | $d_2$ | $d_3$ | $d_4$ | $d_5$ | $d_6$ | $d_7$ | $d_8$ | $d_9$ | $d_{10}$ |
|---|---|---|---|---|---|---|---|---|---|---|
| Demand | 115 | 95 | 150 | 125 | 28 | 90 | 93 | 115 | 93 | 96 |
| **Lead-time data** | $L_1$ | $L_2$ | $L_3$ | $L_4$ | $L_5$ | $L_6$ | $L_7$ | $L_8$ | $L_9$ | $L_{10}$ |
| Lead time | 12 | 15 | 4 | 21 | 18 | 11 | 12 | 18 | 19 | 20 |

Assume that the demand and lead-time data for the past few observations are as shown in Table 4.2.

From the above data we can calculate $\bar{d} = 100$ units and $\sigma_d = 30$ units. Using lead time data we can find that $\bar{L} = 15$ days and $\sigma_L = 5.0$ days.

If an item X has mean = 100 and standard deviation of 30, and item Y has mean = 50 but standard deviation = 20, item Y has higher uncertainty compared to item X. If two items have the same mean but different standard deviations, then the item that has a higher standard deviation has higher uncertainty. In a more general case, when we want to compare two items with different means, we compare coefficients of variation (CV), where CV = standard deviation/mean.

When comparing two items, the one that has a higher CV has a higher degree of uncertainty. In general, retailers find that fast-moving items have a lower CV and that slow-moving items a have higher CV. At this stage, we introduce a third measure of uncertainty, range. Range is defined as the difference between the two extreme values: largest and smallest value of demand. For instance, in above example, range for demand = 150 – 28, that is, 122, and similarly, range for lead time = 20 – 4, that is, 16 days.

For items or suppliers where one has a past history, one can estimate the mean and the standard deviation from past data. When dealing with a new item or a new supplier, we can subjectively assess the uncertainty. For example, we can get the decision maker's assessment of optimistic (best-case scenario) and pessimistic estimate (worst-case scenario) and use the range value (the difference between optimistic and pessimistic estimate) to estimate the value of standard deviation using the following thumb rule:

$$\text{Standard deviation} = \text{Range}/6$$

In general, the standard deviation is estimated using either past data or subjective assessments. Standard deviation, as a measure, has certain interesting properties, which are quite useful in the analytical models that we discuss in the remaining part of the chapter.

## *Impact of Service Level on Safety Stock*

It is difficult to directly measure stockout costs. So, companies have resorted to specifying target service levels for various categories of items. A service level of 100 per cent means that there will never be a stockout situation and all demands are served from stock. There are two popular ways in which services levels are expressed:

- Service level is the probability that all orders will be filled from stock during the replenishment lead time or during the reorder cycle. This is also known as cycle service level.
- Service level is a percentage of demand filled from stock during a given period of time, for example, a year. This is also known as fill rate.

In the next section, we discuss impact of cycle service level and fill rate on safety stock. In future, we restrict to our discussion to cycle service level. Therefore, if not stated explicitly, we will work with the assumption that whenever we use service level we are referring to cycle service level.

## Safety Stock Inventory Model for a Targeted Cycle Service Level

The safety stock inventory is calculated keeping the target service level and the anticipated uncertainty in demand and supply in mind. For a typical inventory situation depicted in Figure 4.5, it is quite obvious that the stockout is likely to take place only during the reorder cycle. Once the replenishment of items takes place, till one reaches the reorder point there is no possibility of stockout. The firm is exposed to a stockout only before the arrival of order and after the placement of the order. Figure 4.5 shows a typical reorder cycle with various possible scenarios. On the one hand, there could be very little of actual demand before the replenishment, resulting in excess stock at the time of replenishment; on the other hand, demand during a replenishment cycle may be quite high with the result that even a reasonable amount of safety stock may not be enough to avoid the stockout situation. This uncertainty of demand during lead time is because of uncertainty in actual demand (demand may be higher or lower than average) or uncertainty in supply (the actual lead time being lower or higher than the average lead time) or a combination of both. If there was no uncertainty in demand or supply, one prefers the reorder level to be at a value such that the inventory at the time of replenishment is exactly zero (as discussed in the Cycle Stock section). To take care of this uncertainty, we need to retain the safety stock, and the value of the safety stock can be determined by using expressions shown below:

$$\text{Safety stock} = K\sigma_{LTD}$$

$$\text{Reorder point } R = LTD + \text{Safety stock} = LTD + K\sigma_{LTD}$$

where $LTD$ is the mean demand during replenishment cycle, $\sigma_{LTD}$ is the standard deviation of demand during the lead time and $K$ is the safety factor.

Demand during the lead time can be captured using a distribution with the mean equal to $LTD$ and standard deviation equal to $\sigma_{LTD}$. We can capture these by capturing data using the last couple of replenishment periods in the same way that we captured demand distribution. Or we can capture demand and lead-time distribution independently using following formulas to find values of lead time demand distribution:

$$LTD = \bar{L}\bar{d}$$

$$\sigma_{LTD} = \sqrt{\bar{L}\sigma_d^2 + \bar{d}\sigma_L^2}$$

where $\bar{L}$ and $\sigma_L$ are the mean and the standard deviation of the lead time and $\bar{d}$ and $\sigma_d$ are the mean and the standard deviation of the demand. Or by calculating the mean and the standard deviation of the lead-time demand in the case of a retailer.

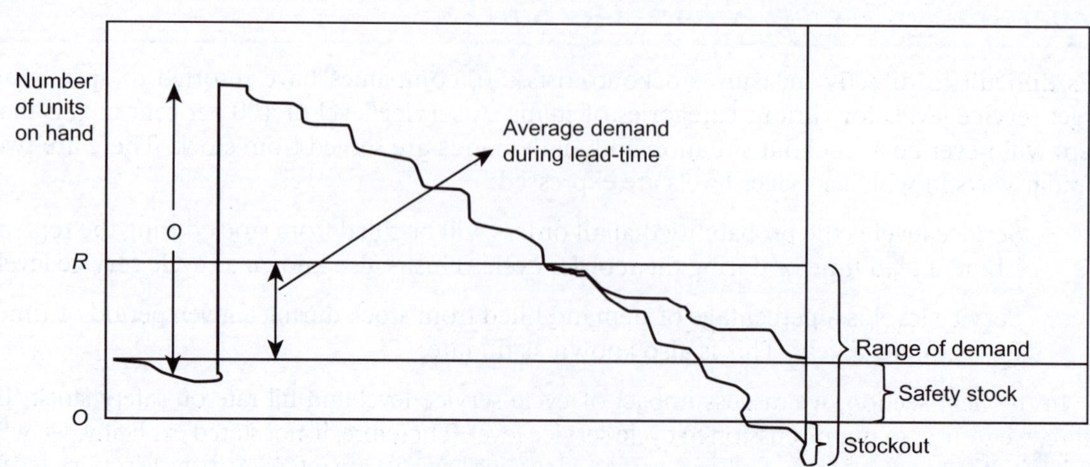


**Figure 4.5**

Inventory level during re-order cycle under a situation of uncertainty.

In the case of the above retailer who faces uncertainty in demand as well as supplier uncertainly, based on past data, the relevant calculations are as follows.

Average daily demand = 100 units, standard deviation of daily demand = 30 units

Average lead time = 15 days, standard deviation of lead time = 5 days.

$$LTD = 100 \times 15 = 1500$$

$$\sigma_{LTD} = \sqrt{15(30^2)+(100^2 \times 5^2)} = \sqrt{13500+25000} = 513.3 \approx 513$$

Given the desired service level, one can determine the value of *k* from Table 4.3, because in most real-life systems, demand during lead time follows a normal distribution. Similarly if one has knowledge about the quantity of safety stock held by a firm, one can determine the value of the safety factor (*K*) from the safety stock formula and estimate the service level using the data in Table 4.3. For example, if we hold safety stock equal to one standard deviation ($K = 1$), we could provide a service level equal to 84.1 per cent, so chances of a stockout in a cycle is equal to 15.9 per cent. As can be seen, the relationship between *K* and the service level is not linear. For example, when the value of *K* is increased from 0 to 1, the service level improves by 34.1 per cent, and further improvement of *K* by 1 unit will increase the service level by 13.6 per cent and further improvement in *K* will increase the service level by 2.2 per cent. Managers need to keep this in mind while fixing service levels. At some point in time, however, increasing the safety stock does not result in a corresponding level of improvement in service level.

Let us say that the retailer has specified a service level of 97.7 per cent, which means that during 100 such reorder cycles, we can expect stockout situations in about two cycles, which will result in *K* being equal to 2.

Similarly, suppose the retailer is working with seven days of inventory as safety stock, that is, an inventory of 700 units.

So value of the service factor *K* is equal to $700/513 = 1.36 \cong 1.4$. From Table 4.3, the value of the service level effective level for $K = 1.4$ is 91.6 per cent.

***Table 4.3:* Service factors and service levels*.**

| *K* | Service level (%) | *K* | Service level (%) | *K* | Service level (%) | *K* | Service level (%) |
|---|---|---|---|---|---|---|---|
| −3.0 | 0.13 | −1.4 | 8.1 | 0.1 | 54 | 1.6 | 94.5 |
| −2.9 | 0.19 | −1.3 | 9.7 | 0.2 | 57.9 | 1.7 | 95.5 |
| −2.8 | 0.26 | −1.2 | 11.5 | 0.3 | 61.8 | 1.8 | 96.4 |
| −2.7 | 0.35 | −1.1 | 13.6 | 0.4 | 65.5 | 1.9 | 97.1 |
| −2.6 | 0.47 | −1.0 | 15.9 | 0.5 | 69.2 | 2.0 | 97.7 |
| −2.5 | 0.62 | −0.9 | 18.4 | 0.6 | 72.5 | 2.1 | 98.2 |
| −2.4 | 0.8 | −0.8 | 21.2 | 0.7 | 75.5 | 2.2 | 98.6 |
| −2.2 | 1.1 | −0.7 | 24.5 | 0.8 | 78.8 | 2.3 | 98.9 |
| −2.2 | 1.4 | −0.6 | 27.5 | 0.9 | 81.6 | 2.4 | 99.2 |
| −2.1 | 1.8 | −0.5 | 30.8 | 1.0 | 84.1 | 2.5 | 99.38 |
| −2.0 | 2.3 | −0.4 | 34.5 | 1.1 | 86.4 | 2.6 | 99.53 |
| −1.9 | 2.9 | −0.3 | 38.2 | 1.2 | 88.5 | 2.7 | 99.65 |
| −1.8 | 3.6 | −0.2 | 42.1 | 1.3 | 90.3 | 2.8 | 99.75 |
| −1.7 | 4.5 | −0.1 | 46 | 1.4 | 91.9 | 2.9 | 99.81 |
| −1.6 | 5.5 | 0.0 | 0 | 1.5 | 93.3 | 3.0 | 99.87 |
| −1.5 | 6.7 | | | | | | |

*For a given value of *K*, the Excel function NORMDIST(*K*, 0, 1, 1) can be used to get the value of service level in fraction terms. For example, NORMALDIST(2, 0, 1, 1) = 0.97725. Similarly, for a given service level s in percentage terms, the excel function NORMINV(*s*/100, 0, 1) can be used to get a value of *K*. For example, NORMINV(97.725/100, 0, 1) = 2.

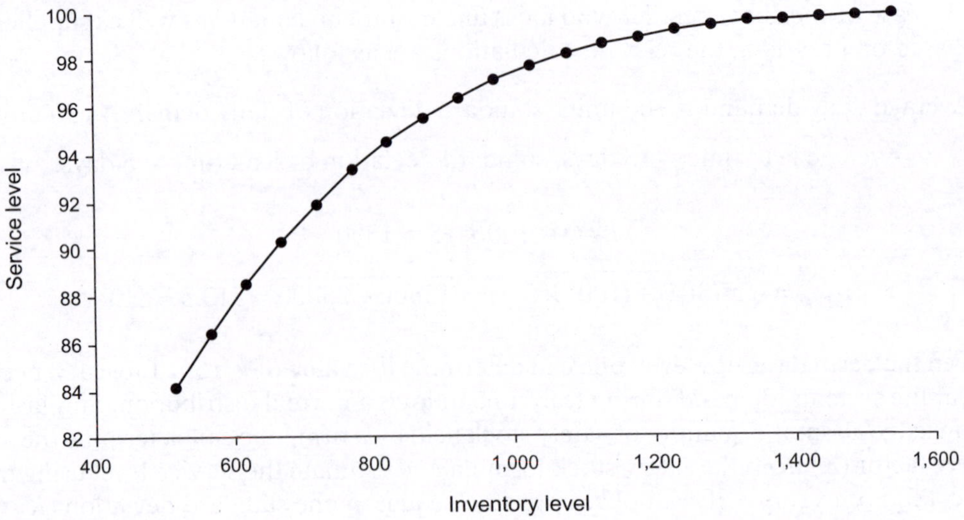

**Figure 4.6**

Impact of service level on safety stock.

In Figure 4.6, we plot how the safety stock required by a retailer will vary with changes in service levels. As can be seen, the marginal increase in safety stock increases as the service levels rise. For example, when the retailer increases the safety stock from 600 to 800, there is a significant increase in the service level. But when retailer increases the safety stock from 1,200 to 1,400, one observes very little improvement in service levels. This phenomenon highlights the importance of selecting suitable service levels.

## Safety Stock Inventory Model for a Targeted Fill Rate

Unlike the cycle service level discussed in the previous section, fill rate helps one to calculate the average quantity that is short in any cycle. Therefore, it allows one to calculate the percentage of orders in a year that could not be executed from stock. Cycle service-level measure discussed in the previous section merely captures whether there was an instance of stockout or not during the re-order cycle but do not capture the magnitude of shortage. Further, if you know the stockout costs per unit, you can calculate the annual stockout costs using the fill rate. The relationship between the fill rate and the safety stock is as follows:

$$\text{FR} = 1 - [\sigma_{LTD} \times E(K)/Q]$$
$$\text{Safety stock} = K \times \sigma_{LTD}$$

where FR is the fill rate, $Q$ is the order quantity per replenishment cycle (economic order quantity), $\sigma_{LTD}$ is the standard deviation of demand during the lead time, and $K$ is the service factor. $E(K)$ is the standard loss function, that is, the expected number of lost sales when demand comes from standard normal distribution(mean = 0 and standard deviation = 1 and safety stock = $k$) for a given value of $K$; $E(K)$ can be determined from the following Table 4.4.

Suppose, we take the case of a retailer whose average daily demand is 100 units and $Q$ = 1,600 and $\sigma_{LTD} = 513$.

If the retailer keeps a safety stock equal to two days of demand (100 × 2 = 200 units), we can determine the fill rate value as follows:

$$K = \text{safety stock}/\sigma_{LTD} = 200/513 = 0.389 \cong 0.4$$

Given the value of $K = 0.4$, we can determine the value of $E(k) = 0.23$ from the Table 4.4:

$$FR = 1 - (513 \times 0.23/1600) = 0.926$$

**Table 4.4: Relationship between K and E(K)*.**

| E(K) | K | E(K) | K | E(K) | K | E(K) | K |
|---|---|---|---|---|---|---|---|
| 4.500 | −4.50 | 2.205 | −2.20 | 0.399 | 0.00 | 0.004 | 2.30 |
| 4.400 | −4.40 | 2.106 | −2.10 | 0.351 | 0.10 | 0.003 | 2.40 |
| 4.300 | −4.30 | 2.008 | −2.00 | 0.307 | 0.20 | 0.002 | 2.50 |
| 4.200 | −4.20 | 1.911 | −1.90 | 0.267 | 0.30 | 0.001 | 2.60 |
| 4.100 | −4.10 | 1.814 | −1.80 | 0.230 | 0.40 | 0.001 | 2.70 |
| 4.000 | −4.00 | 1.718 | −1.70 | 0.198 | 0.50 | 0.001 | 2.80 |
| 3.900 | −3.90 | 1.623 | −1.60 | 0.169 | 0.60 | 0.001 | 2.90 |
| 3.800 | −3.80 | 1.529 | −1.50 | 0.143 | 0.70 | 0.000 | 3.00 |
| 3.700 | −3.70 | 1.437 | −1.40 | 0.123 | 0.80 | 0.000 | 3.10 |
| 3.600 | −3.60 | 1.346 | −1.30 | 0.100 | 0.90 | 0.000 | 3.20 |
| 3.500 | −3.50 | 1.256 | −1.20 | 0.083 | 1.00 | 0.000 | 3.30 |
| 3.400 | −3.40 | 1.169 | −1.10 | 0.069 | 1.10 | 0.000 | 3.40 |
| 3.300 | −3.30 | 1.083 | −1.00 | 0.056 | 1.20 | 0.000 | 3.50 |
| 3.200 | −3.20 | 1.000 | −0.90 | 0.046 | 1.30 | 0.000 | 3.60 |
| 3.100 | −3.10 | 0.920 | −0.80 | 0.037 | 1.40 | 0.000 | 3.70 |
| 3.000 | −3.00 | 0.843 | −0.70 | 0.029 | 1.50 | 0.000 | 3.80 |
| 2.901 | −2.90 | 0.769 | −0.60 | 0.023 | 1.60 | 0.000 | 3.90 |
| 2.801 | −2.80 | 0.698 | −0.50 | 0.018 | 1.70 | 0.000 | 4.00 |
| 2.701 | −2.70 | 0.630 | −0.40 | 0.014 | 1.80 | 0.000 | 4.10 |
| 2.601 | −2.60 | 0.567 | −0.30 | 0.011 | 1.90 | 0.000 | 4.20 |
| 2.502 | −2.50 | 0.507 | −0.20 | 0.008 | 2.00 | 0.000 | 4.30 |
| 2.403 | −2.40 | 0.451 | −0.10 | 0.006 | 2.10 | 0.000 | 4.40 |
| 2.303 | −2.30 | 0.399 | 0.00 | 0.005 | 2.20 | 0.000 | 4.50 |

*For a given value of $K$, the Excel functions NORMDIST ($K$, 0, 1, 1) and NORMDIST ($K$, 0, 1, 0) can be used to get the value of standard normal loss quantity as follows: $E(K) = -K*(1 - \text{NORMDIST}(K, 0, 1, 1) + \text{NORMDIST}(K, 0, 1, 0)$.
$E(K)$ is the standard loss function, that is, the expected number of lost sales when demand comes from standard normal (mean = 0 and standard deviation = 1 and safety stock = $K$).

This means that if the company keeps a safety stock equal to two days demand, on an average it can expect 92.6 per cent fill rate, which means that in every cycle, the retailer is likely to lose demand for 118 units [1,600 × (1 – 0.926)].

If the retailer wants to provide 98 per cent fill rate, he or she will have to maintain a certain service factor (value of $K$ that will provide the required value of $E(K)$, which results in 98 per cent fill rate), that is, $0.98 = 1 - (513 \times E(K)/1{,}600)$.

From the table, we can determine the corresponding value of $K$ (=1.15) given that $E(K) = 0.0624$. Therefore, the required safety stock = $1.15 \times 513 = 590$.

If the retailer maintains a safety stock of 590 units, the retailer can ensure that 98 per cent of orders are serviced from stock and in an average cycle will face a stockout of 32 units.

In case, the retailer faced a stockout cost of ₹15 per unit, the total annual stockout costs for 98 per cent can be determined as follows:

Annual quantity short = Quantity short per cycle × number of cycles per year
= (1 – 0.98) × 1,600) × (300 × 100/1,600)
= 600 units

Annual stockout costs = 600 × 15 = ₹9,000

Unlike the service-level method, where one cannot determine the annual stockout costs, the fill rate measures allow firms to compute stockout costs.

## Managerial Levers for Reducing Safety Stock

Given the consequences of carrying safety stock, firms are under tremendous pressure to reduce cost and prefer to find ways and means of reducing the safety stock. The management can work on the following factors to reduce investment in safety stock:

- *Reduction in demand uncertainty.* In the case of the retailer discussed in the preceding section, the standard deviation of demand captures the forecast error. This error can be mitigated either by better forecasting or by entering to contracts with some customers for assured stable demand.
- *Reduction in supplier lead time.* The retailer can work with the supplier and find ways and means of reducing supplier lead time. The retailer may also reduce the internal processing time or use a faster mode of transport.
- *Reduction in supply uncertainty.* Again the retailer can work with the supplier for reducing uncertainty in supplier lead time, which may involve the use of more reliable modes of transport. This will mean that the retailer may have to track the supplier on the reliability of delivery. So when choosing a supplier this criterion should get top priority.

In Table 4.5, these various scenarios are shown and the required safety stock level that the retailer will have to maintain to work with 97.8 per cent service level is determined.

Interestingly, in this particular case, reduction in supplier uncertainty will provide the highest payoffs. Surprisingly, improvement in forecast accuracy and reduction in average lead time do not seem to have much impact on the required safety stock level. This kind of analysis has important implications in terms of prioritization of efforts on the part of the retailer. In our experience, we have found that many firms waste energy on improvement initiatives, which do not provide any substantial benefits. In this case, it is predominantly supplier unreliability that is hurting the retailer. The retailer may be willing to pay an incentive to the supplier to reduce uncertainty or may have to give more importance to this attribute while selecting a supplier in the future. Sometimes, a retailer may have to invest in technology and analysis of this kind as it helps to arrive at desirable trade-offs involved in various relevant options.

We may need to make some modifications in the way we use safety stock models in case of periodic review situations where inventories are not tracked continuously but only periodically, may be once a week or once a month. For instance, a firm could run its material planning system only once a week or a retailer could place an order only at the time of the salesman's visit,

*Table 4.5:* **Impact of demand and supply characteristics on safety stock.**

| Average demand | Standard deviation of demand | Average lead time | Standard deviation of lead time | Safety stock units | Safety stock in days of inventory | Remark |
|---|---|---|---|---|---|---|
| 100 | 30 | 15 | 5 | 1,026 | 10.3 | Base case |
| 100 | 30 | 15 | 0 | 232 | 2.3 | No supply uncertainty, |
| 100 | 0 | 15 | 5 | 1,000 | 10 | No demand uncertainty |
| 100 | 15 | 15 | 5 | 1,006 | 10 | Reduce demand uncertainty |
| 100 | 30 | 15 | 2.5 | 526 | 5.3 | Reduce supply uncertainty |
| 100 | 30 | 7.5 | 5 | 1,003 | 10 | Reduction in lead time |

which may happen only once a week. Effective lead time in our calculations will be supply lead time plus review period and not just supply lead time. Obviously, under periodic review situations where the order can be placed only at specific periods, one will have more safety stock compared to the situation of continuous review where the order could be placed at any point in time.

## Managing Seasonal Stock

In this section, we discuss situations where demand varies significantly across seasons. When requirements of items vary with time, it may be economical for the firm to build seasonal stock of inventory during the low-demand season to take care of peak-season demand. Of course, the firm can build enough capacity so that it is in a position to produce and supply the goods during peak season, but then it will land up with lots of surplus capacity during the lean season. A surprisingly large number of industries face this kind of seasonal demand. Seasonal demand can happen because of weather conditions or because of certain cultural practices. For example, in tropical countries like India, refrigerators and air conditioners follow seasonal demand because of weather and climate conditions. The toy industry in the United States and Europe finds that a substantial demand takes place around Christmas time because of cultural practices like gifting. In India, home appliances and paints face a seasonal demand, because people do not buy home appliances during a certain season or prefer to paint their houses during the festival season or weddings may take place only during certain seasons. Similarly, in the plant equipment and office appliance sector, since companies can claim depreciation benefits if they postpone their purchases till end-September or end-March, capital goods demand follows a seasonal pattern with two peaks, one in September and the other in March. In the agricultural goods sector, supply could be seasonal in nature and demand could be more stable, for example, in the case of edible oil and tobacco. So firms in these sectors will have to buy raw material during the season (tea, tobacco, oilseed or wheat buying) and manufacture and supply the finished goods at a constant rate throughout the year.

In the section "Managing Cycle Stock", while working out the cycle stock we had assumed that demand was constant, that is, 100 units per day. But actual demand may be seasonal, for example, during summer 200 units may be sold per day and during rest of the year the sale may be just 50 units per day. Now for a manufacturer there may be choices in terms of the way production is handled in order to take care of this issue. One may want to build a capacity that can handle more than 200 units per day and decide not to carry seasonal inventory at all. Or maybe produce at level production throughout the year and carry seasonal inventory to take care of the summer demand. Another option is to keep the plants and equipment capacity at a level that is more than 200 units per day but change effective capacity by changing the level of labour during different seasons. For example, in the fertilizer industry, where demand is seasonal, and since capital constitutes the main part of the cost, a firm may prefer to produce at the same rate throughout the year. But in the case of labour-intensive operations such as assembly line one may increase capacity by hiring temporary workers whose work can be terminated at the end of the season or alternatively multiple shifts may be run or overtime wages may be paid to the existing workers during the peak period.

These seasonal demands are quite predictable and can be estimated with reasonable accuracy. For example, Kurlon, the largest mattress manufacturer in India, has observed that the demand shoots up during the Diwali month and is usually twice that of the usual demand. For purposes of our discussion in this section, we will assume that the size of peak demand is predictable in nature. In case there is uncertainty about the likely size of peak demand, certain amount of safety stock may be held to handle the uncertainty.

A company that faces seasonal demand can follow either of two basic approaches:

- *Chase option.* Produce as per demand in each season and carry no seasonal inventory. Here capacity can be procured by either hiring more people or by running overtime or by running a second shift or by outsourcing excess requirement during the peak season.

- *Level option.* Produce at the same level throughout the year and build inventory during lean season and use that inventory to take care of excess demand during the peak season.

Using one of the two options, one may minimize the total cost involved and decide how much seasonal inventory to carry, if any. The approach discussed in this section is also popularly described as *aggregate planning* or *sales and operations planning* by industry practitioners and supply chain academicians. The suitability of each option is discussed with the help of an example in the following section.

## Planning for Seasonal Demand

We will illustrate the issues involved by taking the case of a toy manufacturer who faces this kind of demand. The toy manufacturer expects that the last quarter (Q4) is going to have a peak demand and the other three quarters will have a lean demand. Inventory-carrying cost per unit per quarter is ₹3. Each worker can produce 500 units of toys per quarter. Each temporary worker who is hired just for one quarter will result in an additional cost of ₹6,000. This cost is mainly due to poor productivity, training time involved and cost incurred by HR in hiring and managing necessary documentation and other additional activities that are mandatory to satisfy labour laws.

| | **Quarter 1 (Q1)** | **Quarter 2 (Q2)** | **Quarter 3 (Q3)** | **Quarter 4 (Q4)** |
|---|---|---|---|---|
| Expected demand in units | 8,000 | 8,000 | 8,000 | 12,000 |

The company can decide either to work with level production, which is to produce at the same level throughout the year, that is, of the total requirement of 36,000 toys, it can produce 9,000 every quarter or produce the quantity exactly equal to demand in each quarter.

Relevant cost will be the inventory cost in the case of level production choice, while it would be the incremental cost associated with hiring of temporary workers in the case of chase choice.

- *Level option.* There will be an inventory of 1,000 at the end of period 1, 2,000 at the end of period 2 and 3,000 at the end of period 3.

Inventory carried for one quarter 1,000 × 3 = ₹3,000
Inventory carried for two quarters 2,000 × 3 = ₹6,000
Inventory carried for three quarters 3,000 × 3 = ₹9,000
Total costs of level option = 3,000 + 6,000 + 9,000 = ₹18,000

- *Chase option.* In the case of chase demand eight temporary workers will have to be hired for one quarter at the beginning of period 4, resulting in a total cost of ₹48,000.

Because of this cost structure it will make sense for the toy manufacturer to work with level production and build inventory in the lean period so as to take care of demand during the peak period. The company could also explore the possibility of providing discounts in the lean season so as to shift the demand from the peak period to the lean period. So either pricing or promotion could be used to shift demand or the manufacturer could find alternatives for creating capacity during the peak period, such as use of overtime or use of subcontracting. Finally, the optimal solution may not be pure chase or pure level production. This exercise is usually done annually and is also called aggregate production planning. At this level, the company does a broad level of resource and demand matching and does not work with individual SKUs. For example a paint company will work with tons of paints or a toy manufacturing company will convert demand of different types of toys into some standard toys.

In case a firm has a large number of SKUs, it will be important for the firm to decide on which specific variety of products are needed to be carried as seasonal inventory. One will rather carry SKUs that have comparatively stable demand (so as to avoid a situation where one may land up with idle inventory at the end of season) and have low inventory-carrying cost and keep this seasonal stock at a central place rather than holding it at all the regional points. Actual shipment to respective regions can be made just before the start of the season. Closer to the season one will have better demand estimates and be able to avoid unnecessary movement of materials from low-demand regions to high-demand regions.

## Analysing Impact of Supply Chain Redesign on the Inventory

Any supply chain redesign has a significant impact on the inventory and other components of supply chain costs. Since any major change of this kind has long-term implications, supply chain managers have to justify the same with a rigorous cost–benefit analysis. The models and issues discussed in this chapter provide the necessary tools in this regard. This is illustrated using two specific examples in this section on centralization versus decentralization and choice of mode of transport. These examples, apart from analysing the impact on inventory, also illustrate the trade-offs between inventory and transportation cost. The centralization versus decentralization example also illustrates the concept of *risk pooling.*

### *Centralization Versus Decentralization*

Let us take the case of a company that currently has 16 regional stock points and has been serving its dealers from the stock point that is closest. This firm wants to explore the possibility of centralizing its stock holding. This will mean that stocks will be held only at one central point and all the dealers will be served from this central point. Obviously, this is going to increase the time that the firm will take to service dealers or customers. As this will result in higher inventory at the dealer's end, the firm will have to use a faster mode of transport so as to provide more or less the same delivery time as in the decentralization case. Since the firm cannot force dealers to hold higher inventory, it will have to work with a faster and more expensive mode of transport to maintain the same service level. As a result, the company will reduce inventory-related costs but will have to pay higher transport cost. For simplicity, we assume that each region has similar demand distribution with mean daily demand as 100 and standard deviation of demand being 30. Each of the stock points (in both centralization and decentralization cases) gets served from the plant and that takes a lead time of exactly 15 days. In the decentralization case, the average transport cost was Re 1 per unit, and in centralization case, the transport cost will increase by 10 per cent to ₹1.10 per unit. Let us assume that all other relevant data will be similar to the case of retailer (ordering cost, ₹256; inventory-carrying cost per unit, ₹6; required service level, 97.7 per cent). So in the decentralized case, each stock point will be carrying cycle stock inventory of 800 units and safety stock of 232 units. Let $d_1, d_2, \ldots, d_n$, represent the daily demand faced by individual regional stock points and let $\sigma_{d1}, \sigma_{d2}, \ldots, \sigma_{dn}$ represent the standard deviation of demand at the respective stock points. The daily demand ($d_c$) and the standard deviation of demand ($\sigma_{dc}$) at the central stock point will be as shown below:

$$d_c = d_1 + d_1 + ... + d_n$$
$$\sigma_{dc} = \sqrt{\sigma_{d_1}^2 + \sigma_{d_2}^2 + \cdots + \sigma_{d_n}^2}$$

The average demand faced by the centralized stock point is the sum of the average demand faced by the existing 16 stock points. However, the standard deviation of demand in the centralized case will not be simply additive. In general, whenever we pool demand across locations, the phenomenon called risk pooling may be observed. Risk pooling suggests that demand uncertainty is reduced when one pools demand across demand locations. This happens because higher demand at one regional market will get offset by lower demand at another regional market. Lower uncertainty results in lower safety stock in the centralization case.

Details of cycle stock, safety stock and transportation cost implications have been worked out in Table 4.6. As can be seen in Table 4.6, cycle stock in centralization gets the benefit of economies of scale and the cycle stock in the system reduces to 25 per cent of the current level. The safety stock reduces because of lower uncertainty faced by the centralized system compared to the decentralized system. But transport costs go up because a firm will like to maintain the same level of customer service (delivery lead time in this case). As we can see in this case, moving to centralization will reduce the cost by ₹26,304. Of course, apart from inventory costs, the company will also make savings in terms of facility and establishment costs as it has to manage fewer establishments.

In general, the higher the demand uncertainty, the higher the savings in safety stocks. Similarly, the higher the number of stock points involved in risk pooling, the higher the savings in cycle stock because of economies of scale. However, to provide the same level of service, if the organization has to increase transportation costs substantially, the firm may want to work with a decentralized system. For example, in the current case, if transportation costs increased by 25 per cent decentralization may be a better option. So for goods (products like salt, wheat flour, etc.), which are fast moving, that have low demand variability and have high transportation costs, centralization will not make sense. But where transportation is not a significant part of the cost and demand variability is high (slow-moving items, service items), it will be better to centralize. Many firms have used this approach while redesigning their supply chains. IBM (in the service industry) and Reliance (in the manufacturing sector) have redesigned their operations and moved to centralization of resources to achieve the benefits of risk pooling.

***Table 4.6:* Analysis of centralization versus decentralization example.**

| | Decentralized system | Centralized system | Remark |
|---|---|---|---|
| Number of Stock points | 16 | 1 | |
| Cycle stock/stock point = $Q^*/2$ | 800 | 3,200 | 16 times higher value of demand at centralized stock point, increased cycle stock by 4 times |
| Safety stock per stock point | 232 | 928 | 4 times increase in value of standard deviation of demand at centralized stock point, increased safety stock by 4 times |
| Total Inventory in number of units for the system (overall stock points) | (232 + 800) × 16 = 16,512 | 928+3,200 = 4,128 | |
| Total inventory-carrying cost | 16,512 × 6 = 99,072 | 4,128 × 6 = 24,768 | Centralized system will reduce inventory carrying cost by ₹74,304 |
| Incremental transportation cost | | 300 × 100 × 16 × 0.1 = 48,000 | Centralized system will increase transportation cost by ₹48,000 |

### OPTIMIZATION OF GLOBAL HUMAN SUPPLY CHAIN AT IBM[4]

Traditionally, IBM used to operate in a decentralized manner. Each line of business in each geographical area planned independently for their resources and maintained their own bench. Because of the cost pressure in the industry and the fact that the opportunity cost of idle resource is high, IBM decided to share resources across different lines of businesses and across geographies. In 2004, it began a workforce optimization initiative to achieve this objective. First IBM developed a skill database of all 320,000 employees using standard skill taxonomy. Like in physical supply where each part has an identity, IBM classified all the people using the same taxonomy across the firm. This allowed them to treat all the 320,000 people resources as a global pool to be tapped by all businesses within IBM. As a consequence of this initiative, IBM saved approximately $1 million. The staff utilization went up to 7 per cent on account of centralization of resources, thereby enabling IBM to work with a lower bench level within the organization.

### OPTIMIZATION OF SPARES INVENTORY AT RELIANCE LTD[5]

For firms in the process industry, like Reliance, maintaining high uptime of equipment is of great importance. To ensure a high uptime of equipments, process industries typically maintain a high level of spares inventory. Reliance Industries has manufacturing facilities at three locations (Patalganga, Hazira and Jamnagar). Each location has a number of plants within a facility. Till the mid-1990s, each plant at each location used to maintain its own spares inventory. In 1997, Reliance used to maintain spares inventory worth ₹3.48 billion (4 per cent of the value of annual sales). In the last decade, Reliance has centralized its spares operations and works with a common pool of spares across the three manufacturing locations. With the centralization initiative, Reliance is able to work with a much lower level of spares inventory. Over the last decade, its sales have increased 10-fold while spare inventory has increased 3-fold only. Hence, over the last decade, the value of spares inventory has dropped to 1 per cent of the annual sales value.

## Choice of Mode of Transport

The choice of mode of transport can significantly alter the performance of the supply chain. As discussed earlier in this section, many firms, while redesigning the supply chain, have to change the mode of transport for optimum efficiency within the chain.

Consider a computer marketing firm that serves its market from one central depot and the demand observed is 100 PCs per day, with the standard deviation of demand being 30. The company has a policy of maintaining a service level of 97.8 per cent. Currently, it sources its PCs from Europe and has to allow six weeks (36 days) of lead time: 1 week to manufacture at its Europe plant and five weeks for shipping. The company is exploring the possibility of airlifting the material, which will reduce the lead time to two weeks (12 days). This will result in increase in transportation cost from ₹100 to ₹400 per unit of PC. Inventory-carrying cost for PC is ₹6,000 per unit per year.

Since there is no change in demand structure and ordering costs, the cycle stock will not change but this decision will affect the safety stock and the pipeline cost. Details of inventory cost and transportation costs have been worked out in Table 4.7.

As can be seen in Table 4.7, shipping PCs by air will lower the overall annual cost by ₹7.3 million. As can be seen, most of these savings are achieved because of reduction in pipeline inventory costs in the above case. Normally, one will lift high-value items by air and low-value items by sea.

To sum up, different categories of inventories, which get affected by supply chain decisions, should be identified, and appropriate models for quantifying the costs and benefits of the proposed supply chain redesign initiative should be used.

**Table 4.7: Analysis of choice of mode of transport example.**

| | Transportation via sea | Transportation via air | Impact on cost by shifting from sea to air |
|---|---|---|---|
| Annual inventory-carrying cost for safety stock = safety stock × $H$ | $2 \times 30 \times \sqrt{36} \times 6{,}000$ = 216,000 | $2 \times 30 \times \sqrt{9} \times 6{,}000$ = 108,000 | |
| Annual inventory-carrying cost for pipeline stock = $D \times L$ (in year) × $H$ | [(100 × 300) × 36/300] × 6,000 = 21,600,000 | [(100 × 300) × 9/300] × 6,000 = 5,400,000 | |
| Annual inventory-carrying cost | 216,000 + 21,600,000 = 21,816,000 | 108,000 + 5,400,000 = 5,508,000 | Reduction in inventory cost by ₹16,308,000 |
| Transportation cost | 100 × 300 × 100 = 3,000,000 | 100 × 300 × 400 = 12,000,000 | Increase in transportation cost by ₹9,000,000 |

## Managing Inventory for Short Life Cycle Products: Newsvendor Model

In this section, we look at inventory models for a special category of products that have short life cycles. Short life cycle products is a special category of items where demand takes place during a short period of time; hereafter, referred to as the selling season, and goods are kept ready in stock to take care of demand during that short cycle. If there is not enough stock, you will not be in a position to produce or replenish goods during the selling season, and the price at which these short life cycle goods can be sold reduces drastically at the end of the season. Two kinds of products fall into this category—style goods and perishable goods. Perishable products like bread, or a meal prepared before the rush hour in a restaurant or fruit, suffer reduction in prices because they physically deteriorate by the end of the selling season. In the case of style goods like fashion products or newspaper, physical deterioration in the product does not take place, but the perceived value of the product as seen by the customer drops drastically by the end of the selling season, since fashion-conscious customers will not buy a fashion garment at the end of the season; similarly, yesterday's newspaper cannot be sold. Further, as the season is quite short, one does not have an opportunity of replenishment during the season. Therefore, likely sales should be anticipated before the selling season and the requisite stock carried. Carrying less stock (in the case of understocking) than the actual demand results in loss of opportunity of cashing in on the demand, and carrying excess stock ( case of overstocking) will incur huge losses due to goods having very little value at the end of season. For example, in the case of fashion garments, huge discounts are offered to dispose off goods that are left at the end of the selling season. Normally, the inventory of unsold goods can be carried forward since it can be stored from one period to the next so that all replenishment decisions can be done for multiple periods. While in the case of style goods, inventory decisions have to be made for a single period—the selling season. The model discussed in this section is also known as the newsvendor model or single-period inventory model in supply chain literature. In a newsvendor situation, selling season is a day and newsvendor has to make decision before the start of the day before he has observed the demand, and at the end of a day, leftover stock has very little value.

Consider the case of a music retailer who has to book in advance the number of CDs that need to be purchased before the release of the movie. Based on past experience, the retailer is aware that the bulk of the demand takes place during the first two weeks of a movie release. During this period, the retailer will not be able to get replenishment from the manufacturer in case the demand turns out to be more than the estimate. However, at the end of two weeks all the unsold CDs will have hardly any demand and CDs will have to be sold at throwaway prices.

For simplicity we would assume that Retailer destroys all the CDs at the end of season. It is very easy to incorporate disposal value in the calculations, but jut for ease of discussion we make this assumption.

For example, the retailer buys CDs at ₹80 each and sells them at ₹100 during the first two weeks. After two weeks the retailer will destroy all the unsold stock. Based on experience, the retailer expects that demand for this kind of CD has a mean demand of 100 and a standard deviation of demand of 30. To arrive at the optimum order level, the following notations may be used (concept of service level and service factor being exactly same as in the Safety Stock section):

$C_U$ = cost of understocking
$C_O$ = cost of overstocking
Optimal service level = $(C_U \times 100)/(C_U + C_O)$
Optimum order size = Mean demand + $K \times$ standard deviation of the demand
$K$ = service factor

The cost of understocking is an opportunity loss by a firm for each unit of lost sales. The cost of overstocking is the loss incurred by a firm for each unsold unit at the end of the selling season.

In the music retailer's case, $C_U$ = Price – cost = 100 – 80 = 20 and $C_O$ = Cost – disposal value = 80 – 0 = 80.

So the optimum service level or critical fractile = $(20 \times 100)/(20 + 80) = 20$ per cent.

(Optimal service level in this kind of situation is also popularly known as critical fractile.)

From Table 4.3, the service level of 20 per cent means $K = -0.84$.

Therefore, the optimum order size = $100 - 0.84 \times 30 = 74.75 \approx 75$.

Now, if the CD supplier was offering a buy-back option wherein the retailer could return all the leftover stock of the CDs to the manufacturer. At the end of season, the cost of overstocking for retailer would reduce drastically and this would influence retailers' stocking decision. We discuss several innovative supply chain contracts of this kind in Part IV of this book.

So far, we have assumed that all these decisions have to be made before the start of season; thus, all the decisions made by the retailer and the manufacturer are speculative in nature. Once the season starts, the retailer will be in a much better position to estimate the overall demand for the season and this is called reactive assessment. Progressive firms in the fashion goods industry have been trying to be more responsive so that they can supply a part of a retailer's requirement during the actual selling season. The first lot is supplied before the start of the selling season to take care of the demand during the early part of the season and this supply is based on the speculative assessment made by the retailer. The second lot is supplied by the manufacturer during the season based on the retailer's reactive assessment done on the basis of observation of actual demand. Profitability of supply chain improves considerably because of reduction in the cost increased by overstocking as well as understocking by the various members of the supply chain. In the case of fashion goods, the concept of designing and operating a responsive supply chain has received considerable attention. We do not discuss these complex models, but the relevant managerial issues have been discussed in several chapters in Part IV & Part V of the book.

## Multiple-item, Multiple-location Inventory Management

In this chapter, we have considered managing the inventory for a single item. However, in actuality, managing the inventory in a supply chain involves dealing with a large number of items, often stocked at multiple stock points at various stages in the supply chain. So far we have only looked at the problem of managing inventory for a single item at a single stock point. As discussed earlier, the supply chain can rarely be managed by a single decision maker. Complex supply chains are decomposed into multiple decision-making units managing individual stock points, which in turn connect various production and transportation activities within a chain. For each stock point, one can identify relevant supply and demand processes. However, the optimal way of dividing the supply chain into decoupled stock points is by no means a trivial exercise. Similarly, parameters for the supply and demand processes do not remain static at all times. These get affected by various supply chain integration initiatives taken by the firm. But once the supply chain design is completed, for a given level of supply chain integration, the performance at each stock point can be improved using the concepts discussed in this chapter. Finally, supply chain improvement involves working on structure (optimal number of stock points), improving supply chain integration (altering parameters of supply and demand processes) and simultaneously optimizing performance of individual stock points.

For multiple items, theoretically, supply chain analysis can be carried out for each and every item using the approach outlined in this chapter. But the supply chain manager cannot be expected to focus on all items with the same energy and time because he or she has limited resources and the energy spent all on all the items do not result in the same kind of benefits. For this purpose, we discuss selective inventory control techniques that help managers in dividing items into multiple categories and handle different categories of items in different ways.

## Selective Inventory Control Techniques

When dealing with a large number of items, the management may not be in a position to focus attention on all items. For example, a large company like IndianOil will have lakhs of SKUs to handle; similarly, a grocery chain like Foodworld has to manage thousands of SKUs. Obviously, not all items are likely to be of equal importance. So it makes sense for a company to classify items so that managers can pay suitable attention to different categories of items. There are several classification schemes for categorizing SKUs:

- *ABC classification.* Items are classified into three categories based on the value of the consumption. A-category items contribute significantly to the value of inventory and consumption and are controlled tightly and get more managerial attention. ABC classification is discussed in greater detail at a later stage.

- *FSN classification.* Items are classified based on volume of usage: fast moving (F), slow moving (S) and non-moving (N). Fast-moving items are usually stocked in a decentralized fashion while slow-moving items are stocked centrally. Non-moving items are candidates for disposal and the firm will like to make sure that non-moving items do not take up a significant share of inventory investment. This classification is quite popular in the retail industry.

- *VED classification.* Items are based on criticality: vital (V), essential (E) and desirable (D). This classification is quite popular in maintenance management. Based on the VED classification, one can fix different service levels for different items. Of course, a firm prefers to work with a very high service level for V category of spare items. For example, Reliance industry maintains a 99.995 per cent service level for V category of spares. While deciding the inventory level for a D category product, one will fix relatively lower levels of service requirements.

Cummins India is a classic example of a firm that has applied ideas of selective inventory control techniques in managing its spares inventory.

### ABC Classification

One of the most popular methods of classification of items is the ABC classification. It is a common practice to use three ratings: A (very important), B (moderate importance) and C (little importance). SKUs in A categories can be given higher priority in terms of allocation of

*Table 4.8:* **Sample list of SKUs in descending order of sales quantity.**

| Item ID | Item ranked by sales value | Annual sales in quantity | Cumulative percentage of total sales | Cumulative percentage of total items |
|---|---|---|---|---|
| SDL72*35*4 | 1 | 11,032 | 36.81 | 0.8 |
| SDL75*35*4 | 2 | 4,563 | 51.39 | 1.6 |
| Apsara72*35*4 | 3 | 2,438 | 59.69 | 2.4 |
| Romantique75*35*4 | 126 | 0 | 100.00 | 100.00 |

management time. To carry out the ABC analysis, all the items are rank-ordered based on the sales in value terms. Cumulative percentages of the total sales (in rupee) and the total number of items are computed and these percentages are plotted. We illustrate the concept with an example of ABC analysis carried out by a mattress manufacturing firm for its sales office at Delhi. In this particular case, since all the items had more or less the same price, ABC analysis was done on quantity, but typically it should be done on rupee value.

The company has 126 SKUs, but the top three SKUs (2.4 per cent of items) accounted for about 60 per cent of the sales volume. The format of the ABC analysis is illustrated in Table 4.8.

The same data have been plotted in Figure 4.7. As can be seen, 75 per cent of the items constitute less than 5 per cent of value, so the firm has to find a method for the Delhi sales manager to prioritize his time. That is, he should have very simple systems for these 75 per cent of items and spend most of his time and attention on A-category items.

ABC categorization has been used with success in following areas:

- *Allocation of managerial time.* An A-category item should receive the bulk of managerial attention and C category items should receive very little.
- *Improvement efforts.* The improvement effort should be directed at A-category items only. For example, supplier relationships, lead time reduction, reduction in uncertainty in lead time, etc.

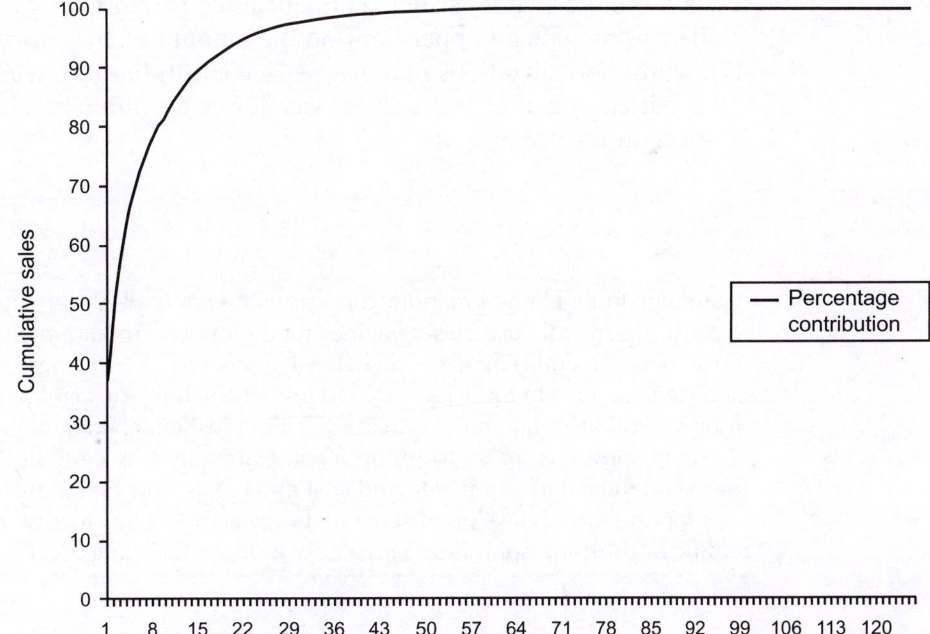


**Figure 4.7**

ABC diagram.

- *Setting up of service levels.* According to one philosophy, the A category should receive 99 per cent service level, the B category should receive 95 per cent and the C category should receive 90 per cent service level so that the overall weighted service level for the company will be around 97 per cent. Some firms do exactly the opposite. They provide 99 per cent of service level to C-category items, 95 per cent to B-category items and 90 per cent to A-category items. It is not that the firm actually allows 10 per cent of stock-outs in A-category items, but during the replenishment cycle, the firm monitors closely all the A-category items in terms of actual demand as well as the status of supply. If the manager anticipates the possibility of a stockout situation, even before the actual stockout takes place he or she start working on contingency plans so that he or she can avoid the stockout situation. So although actual safety stock is kept at a low level, the effective service level is very high. Obviously, this kind of close monitoring cannot be handled for all items but can be carried out for a few A-category items. We suggest that the firm work with this approach of low safety stock but have contingency plans in place for A-category items.
- *Stocking decision in the distribution system.* A-category items are kept at all regional distribution points, but C-category items are kept at a central warehouse only. B-category items are kept only at a few regional hubs but not at all regional stock points.

ABC analysis can be done on sales data as well as on inventory data, on supplier data and on purchase orders data. One will find a similar relationship. Although the exact distributions among the three categories vary according to industry, based on our field experience, we find that the range within which distribution is likely to vary could be as follows:

| Class | Percentage of items | Percentage of total sales value |
|---|---|---|
| A | 5–15 | 55–75 |
| B | 20–30 | 20–30 |
| C | 55–75 | 5–15 |

Some firms use a similar concept, called the 80–20 rule, that is, 80 per cent of the sales is taken care of by 20 per cent of the items. In this system, items are classified in just two categories.

So far we have focused on constraints related to managerial time. The company may have certain other constraints such as financial constraints. It is not uncommon for financial controllers to provide an upper limit on the amount of inventory that the company should keep. Sometimes organizations may have space constraint too, which may force the firm to look at all the items together and vary service levels for different category of items to meet the constraints on finance or space.

### IMPROVING SERVICE LEVELS FOR SPARES PARTS AT CUMMINS INDIA[6]

Cummins India Limited manufactures a wide variety of diesel engines ranging from 60 to 2,700 hp. Many firms in India use diesel engines for their power requirements. To ensure low downtime for their customers, Cummins manages an extensive service network consisting of 200 engineers and about 100 service locations. In the 1990s, due to poor availability of spare parts at Cummins, its customers faced long downtime of equipment. In 2000, Cummins launched a major supply chain initiative to improve its service levels from 35 to 98 per cent. Cummins classified all the spare parts into four categories, based on the nature of the demand (fast moving vs slow moving) and the nature of the part (staple part vs support part). It developed separate policies for each category of spares and also worked out a scientific basis (using appropriate inventory models) for fixing inventory norms.

## Summary

- Indian firms find that a significant amount of money is locked up in the inventory. Organizations should use the concept of zero-based inventory planning to improve their performance on the inventory front.
- The decision maker controls inventory by deciding two critical questions: how much to order and when to order.
- Based on the demand characteristics, supply characteristics, cost structure and the desired service level, firms can decide the optimum level of inventory.
- In the long run, a firm should try and influence some relevant parameters so that it can reduce inventory-related costs, improve inventory turnover ratio and simultaneously improve customer service.
- A company can carry out an ABC analysis and target its effort on A-category items to improve supply chain performance.

## Discussion Questions

1. What is the relationship between service levels and inventory levels?
2. Why does the inventory in a system increase with an increase in stock points in the system?
3. What factors should a manager consider while deciding service levels?
4. The sales turnover for Subhiksha retail in Bangalore has doubled in last 2 years. What is the impact of this on the inventory turn for the firm?
5. While computing the ordering cost, one is supposed to consider only the fixed component of the ordering cost. Why?
6. What is the impact of inventory centralization on various supply chain performance measures?
7. A global software service firm operating in seven geographical locations, has five lines of business (LOB) and employs 100,000 people. The firm traditionally has been managing human resources independently, that is, each LOB in each geographic region manages its resources independently. Now it wants to explore the possibility of using a common pool of resources across geographical regions for all LOBs. The firm wants to quantify benefits of this idea of this common resource pool. Suggest a methodology for quantifying these benefits.

## Exercises

1) A regional warehouse purchases hand tools from various suppliers and then distributes them on demand to retailers in the region. The warehouse operates 5 days per week, 52 weeks per year. The following data are estimated for one product, namely the 1-inch drill:

Average daily demand = 100 drills

Standard deviation of daily demand = 30 drills

Supplier lead time = 3 days

Holding cost = ₹9.40 per unit per year

Ordering cost = ₹35 per order

Service level = 98 per cent

Design an inventory system for this product

The finance department has instructed the warehouse to reduce the investment in average inventory by half. What are the options available to the manager of the warehouse.

2) Akaga Corporation distributes video game terminals throughout India. The marketing manager estimates the demand for next year to be 500 units per month. The base price of the video game terminal is ₹500 and the cost of placing an order is ₹5,000. The estimated holding cost is 20 per cent of the base price per unit per year. The video game terminals are imported from suppliers in Japan and the delivery lead time is 1 month.

Design an inventory policy for Akaga Corporation.

If the supplier insisted on a minimum batch size of 1,200 for any order, what should the inventory system be. What is the implication of this minimum batch size to Akaga Corporation?

Akaga realized that monthly demand is not going to be constant and is likely to have mean demand of 500, with standard deviation of 100 units. And the marketing manager wants to ensure a 98 per cent service level. Work out the system requirement under both situations (both with and without the batch size constraint).

The marketing manager had some difficulty in explaining the concept of 98 per cent service level to his top management team, so he decided to work with the following promise to the top management. He promised the top management that the inventory policy would work towards a target level of two instances of stockouts in a year.

Design an inventory policy for the following two situations:

(a) No minimum batch size constriant.

(b) Minimum batch size of 1200.

3) Egrowth Software Services is doing a manpower planning exercise for the first two quarters of the next financial year. HRD requires 6 months to get software professionals. The company incurs a cost of $5,000 for every software engineer employed with the organization. The company usually charges $20,000 per software employee for all the projects that are taken up by organization. The marketing team is of the view that the actual demand for software engineers in the next 6 months is likely to be uncertain. Most probably the requirement will be for 500 engineers but the actual demand may be quite off the mark. The worst-case scenario will involve the actual demand being as low as 60 per cent of the projected numbers, while the best-case scenario will involve actual demand being as high as 140 per cent of the projected numbers.

How many software engineers should the organization plan for? Discuss the limitations of your approach.

4) You are in charge of Anusmaran (reunion event for your college) at Chennai. Although large attendance is expected, you will not know until the evening of the event exactly how many people will attend. Your understanding with the caterer is that you will have to communicate to him, 1 week before the event, the number of dinners that will have to be served at the event. The price for these dinners will be ₹400 each. If fewer people than the committed number show up, you are still required to pay for the committed number. If more people attend, the additional number will be served at a cost of ₹600 each. Your judgement about the number attending can be described by normal distribution with a mean of 200 people and a standard deviation of 80.

(a) Suppose that the cost of the entire dinner is being borne by the alumni association. What kind of number will you commit to the caterer.

(b) Suppose the event is organized by your college and the college wants to use this event for raising funds and each person attending the event is charged ₹500. What kind of number will you commit to the caterer. You can assume that the likely number of people attending the event does not change based on this pricing policy.

How will your answer change (for parts a and b) if the caterer does not provide any flexibility. The caterer will serve exactly the committed number of dinners, so in case more people attend than your committed number, some people will have to go hungry (may be you will prioritize participants based on batch (older batches will get dinner first) or you will give tokens to people on first cum first served basis.

5) Foodworld, a grocery store, carries a particular brand of tea that has a daily demand of 20 units and a standard deviation of 5 units. Its current supplier sells tea to Foodworld at ₹50 per unit but requires two weeks lead time. Foodworld has an alternative supplier who is willing to supply at ₹49.50 per unit but requires three weeks of lead time and insists on a minimum order size of 500 units per order. The company has an ordering cost of ₹200 per order and an inventory-carrying cost of 25 per cent. The management at Foodworld is of the view that a target level of one stockout in two years is acceptable for grocery items. Which supplier should the company choose?

6) Bangalore Hospital orders its antibiotics every 4 weeks when a sales person from a pharmaceutical company visits it. Zombacycline, which costs ₹25 per capsule, is one of its most prescribed antibiotics, with an average daily demand of 50 capsules. The standard deviation of daily demand, derived from examining prescriptions filled over the past 6 months, was found to be 15 capsules. It takes two weeks for the order to arrive. Bangalore Hospital will like 99 per cent of all demand from prescriptions to be satisfied from stock. The cost to place an order is ₹1000 and the holding costs are 20 per cent of the purchase price. The sales person has just arrived and there are currently 1,000 capsules in stock.

How many capsules should be ordered? (Hint: see Appendix A)

Bangalore Hospital has just hired a consultant who has suggested that instead of ordering at the time of a sales person's visit, the company should monitor its stocks regularly and place an order whenever they feel appropriate. Devise an optimal ordering policy based on the consultant's suggestion. What will be the cost savings if Bangalore Hospital follows the policy suggested by the consultant?

## Notes

1. Retrieved online from www.exchange4media.com/Brandspeak/brandspeak.asp?brand_id=42#1.
2. See James P. Womack, Daniel T. Jones, and Daniel Ross, *The Machine that Changed the World* (New York: Harper, 1990).
3. See www.infosys.com.
4. Kotrill Ken, "Can Your Supply Chain Move People," *Supply Chain Strategy* (2005, Vol 1): 1–3.
5. Data on spares inventory collected from Prowess, Centre for Monitoring Indian Economy.
6. A. V. Nerlikar, K. S. Bheda, and N. Patil, "Cummins India: Implementation of Spares Supply Chain." In Malini Gupta, ed. *Supply Chain Excellence* (Mumbai: SP Jain Institute of Management and Research).

## Further Reading

R. H. Ballou, *Business Logistics Management* (Upper Saddle River, NJ: Prentice Hall, 1999).

M. L Fisher, Janice H. Hammond, Walter R. Obermeyer, and Anant Raman, "Making Supply Meet Demand in an Uncertain World," *Harvard Business Review* (May–June 1994): 83–93.

H. L. Lee and Corey Billington, "Managing Supply Chain Inventories: Pitfalls and Opportunities," *Sloan Management Review* (Spring 1992): 65–73.

H. L. Lee, Corey Billington, and Brent Carter, "Hewlett-Packard Gains Control of Inventory and Service Through Design for Localization," *Interfaces* (July–August 1993): 1–11.

E. A. Silver, David Pyke, and Rein Peterson, *Inventory Management and Production Planning and Scheduling* (New York: Wiley,1998).

J. Verity, "Clearing the Cobwebs from the Stockroom," *Business Week* (21 October 1996).

P. H. Zipkin, *Foundations of Inventory Management* (Boston, MA: McGraw Hill, 2000).

## Appendix A: Periodic Review Policies

Given the supply and demand characteristics of suppliers and customers, a decision maker at stock points makes essentially two decisions: how much to order and when to order. Firms following periodic review polices do not track their inventory positions on a continuous basis. The inventory position is reviewed after a fixed period of time and based on a pre-specified order up to level a firm will decide the size of the order. The review period $T$ is the time between two successive orders. Review period policy is also known as the fixed time period model. Periodic review periods are simpler to manage because a continuous review policy will require continuous updating of records. In a periodic review policy, one just has to take stock of inventory once in a week or month based on the review period selected by the concerned manager. For example, firms running their MRP (material requirement planning) system once a week essentially follow the periodic review system. Similarly, if a retailer places an order at the time of a salesman's visit, the periodic review system is being followed.

We will first develop the safety stock model for a periodic review policy and then get into issues related to order quantity decisions. While reviewing the inventory position, we know that the next opportunity for ordering will come only after the review period $T$ and subsequently replenishment will take place after the lead time $L$. That is, the safety stock in the system must protect us against demand uncertainty for the vulnerable time period, that is, the review period plus the lead time. Unlike a continuous review case where the vulnerable period was only the lead time, in periodic review it is the review period plus the lead time. So our safety stock formula should be modified as follows:

$$\text{Safety stock} = K \times \sigma_{d(L+T)}$$

where $L$ is the supply lead time, $T$ is the review period, $\sigma_{d(L+T)}$ is the standard deviation of demand over the review period and the lead time, and $K$ is the safety factor.

Let us take a case of a retailer whose daily demand follows normal distribution, with mean equal to 100 and standard deviation equal to 30. We start with a case where the lead time of supply is constant and equal to 15 days and the review period is 30 days. The retailer will like to work with a cycle service level of 98 per cent, that is, $K = 2$.

$$\sigma_{d(L+T)} = \sqrt{15+30} \times 30 = 201.2$$

$$\text{Safety stock} = 2 \times 201.2 = 402.4$$

$$\text{Safety stock in the continuous review case} = 2 \times \sqrt{15} \times 30 = 232.4$$

The simplicity of the periodic review system over the continuous review system comes at the cost of higher safety stock.

Now while placing an order we will have to ensure that the existing inventory + order quantity should take care of the demand in the vulnerable period.

$$\text{Order up to level} = d(L + T) + K \times \sigma_{d(L+T)}$$

$$\text{Order quantity} = \text{Order up to level} - \text{Inventory on hand}$$

$$\text{Order quantity} = d(L + T) + K \times \sigma_{d(L+T)} - I$$

where $I$ is the existing inventory that includes physical inventory plus all the pending orders that are still to be delivered.

Unlike a continuous review case where order quantity is constant, the order quantity will vary in every review cycle in a periodic review case.

If at review stage the retailer found that there are 1,600 units on hand:

$$\text{Order quantity} = 100 \times (15 + 30) + 402.4 - 1{,}600 = 3302.4$$

$$\text{On the average the order quantity} = T \times d = 30 \times 100 = 3{,}000$$

$$\text{Average inventory in the system} = (T \times d)/2 + SS = 3{,}000 \times 0.5 + 402.4 = 1902.4$$

If the retailer faced uncertainty on the supply side with the mean lead time being $L$ and the standard deviation of the lead time being $\sigma_L$, the relevant formula for $\sigma_{d(L+T)}$ is as follows:

$$\sigma_{d(L+T)} = \sqrt{(\bar{L} + T)\sigma_d^2 + \bar{d}^2\sigma_L^2}$$

If the mean lead time is 15 days and the standard deviation of the lead time is 5 days, the quantity of safety stock required by retailer should be as follows:

$$\text{safety stock} = 2 \times \sqrt{(15+30) \times 30^2 + 100^2 \times 5^2} = 1{,}078 \text{ units}$$

In summary, while a periodic review has fixed ordering time but variable order quantity, a continuous review results in fixed order quantity but variable ordering time. Periodic review systems are simpler to manage but result in higher safety stock in the system.

# Transportation

## Learning Objectives

After reading this chapter, you will be able to answer the following questions:

> What are the key transportation-related decisions made by a firm?
> What are the main drivers of transportation decisions within a firm?
> How do firms choose the optimum transportation mode mix?
> What are main transportation strategies used by firms? How to choose the optimum transportation strategy?
> How important are transportation-related decisions for e-retailers?

Karthik is a dynamic professional who has just made his way through the hallowed portals of the boardroom and relocated to Chicago, USA. He works long hours and rarely finds either the time or the energy to go out shopping despite the 24X7 outlets that have mushroomed all over the city. Karthik does most of his shopping online. Amazon.com is one of his favourite sites as it offers flexibility in terms of product and pricing.

Amazon.com opened its first online store in 1995. From being just an online bookstore, Amazon.com has now become one of the biggest online stores. From books to music to jewellery, amazon.com offers it all. The process is simple. The user has to choose the items to be purchased, key-in the payment details and choose the mode of transportation of the items. Amazon.com offers its users three choices in transportation. The choice of the mode of transport not only affects the delivery time but also the cost. Amazon.com usually offers subsidized shipping schemes to its regular users.

In keeping with its business strategy, Amazon.com tries to ensure quick delivery of the product at minimal cost to the customer. However, Amazon.com has discovered that transporting items quickly and cheaply to customers is an expensive option. In fact, Amazon.com does not completely recover shipping charges from the customers. It is very important for Amazon.com to work out an optimal mode of transportation of products so that they can serve customers at minimal cost. Ideally, Amazon.com prefers to ship all the items ordered as one bundle so that it can have economies of scale in transportation, but since it stocks different categories of items at different fulfilment centres located at different cities in the United States of America, it is be forced to ship them separately and incur higher transportation cost. Shipping and delivery is a significant component of cost for e-retailers like Amazon.

In the last decade, global manufacturing trade has doubled and is expected to grow at a similar rate in the coming future. With increasing globalization and offshore sourcing, transportation issues have become vital for supply chain managers.

# Introduction

Transportation provides a significant link between the various stages in the supply chain. Transportation-related decisions significantly affect cost as well as responsiveness of the supply chain. The key transportation decisions made by a firm are

- *Selection of transportation strategy.* The transportation strategy involves designing the most effective way of reaching products to geographically dispersed markets from plants in a cost-effective way.
- *Choice of transportation mode.* Choosing the most effective mode of transport from among several feasible options.

Firms like Toyota Kirloskar and Amul Dairy have worked with several innovations like cross-docking and use of milk runs to align their transportation strategy with the overall supply chain strategy. Progressive firms have realized that one cannot make transportation decisions in isolation. Facility, location, transportation and inventory management are interrelated decisions, so a firm has to evaluate the impact of transportation decisions on the total cost of the supply chain.

We start by first understanding the drivers of transport decisions. The knowledge of transport-cost structures and understanding the impact of product and demand characteristics on the total cost of the supply chain is vital for all transportation-related decisions. With this conceptual foundation in place, we look at the transportation strategy and issues involved in choosing the optimal transportation mode in the subsequent sections. As vehicle scheduling plays an important role, both in inbound as well as in outbound transportation, we look at one popular algorithm that can help firms in designing near optimal routes. Finally, we look at the role of transportation in the emerging business of e-retailing.

# Drivers of Transportation Decisions

Transportation cost is a significant component of the supply chain cost for most manufacturing firms. A thorough understanding of the cost structures in transportation allows a firm to make relevant trade-offs when taking relevant decisions. Apart from economies of scale, transportation cost is also influenced by the demand–supply gap between the points of origin and destination. Further, the nature of the product and its demand characteristics also affect supply chain costs in a significant way. In this section, we examine the major drivers of transportation decisions.

## *Transportation Cost Structures*

The transportation cost for a given mode of transport is a function of the distance and the quantity of the goods shipped. In general, transport rates (rupees per ton) taper with increasing distance. This implies that with increasing distance the rate of increase of transportation costs will go down. For longer distances travelled, the related fixed costs at the points of origin and destination are distributed over more kilometres. Further, longer the distances travelled, the overall utilization of the vehicle is likely to be higher. This is known as the economies of distance in transportation. Similarly, there are strong economies of scale in transportation; thus, transportation rates decrease with increase in shipment weight. Driver- and crew-related costs and the bulk of the fuel-related costs are a function of distance and do not depend on load. Thus, truck operators always prefer a full-truck load (FTL) shipment. With a less than full-truck load (LTL) shipment, the transport operator will have to run the vehicle at low capacity utilization or will

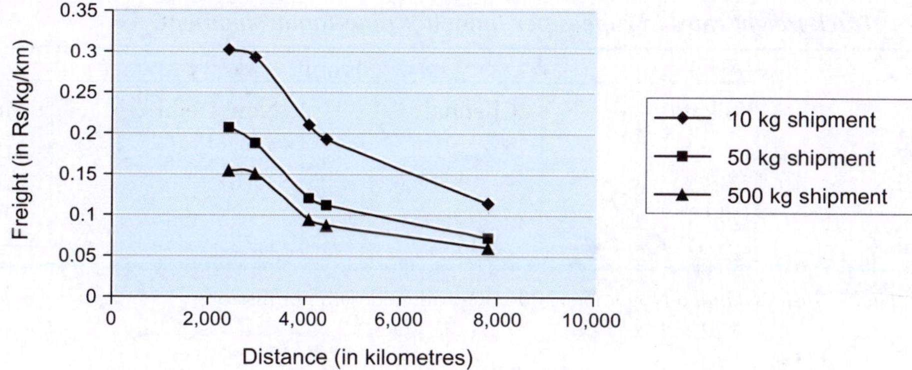


**Figure 5.1**

Impact of distance and load on air freight.

have to aggregate a number of small shipments in one trip, which will increase transaction costs for the operator. In either situation, the operator will have higher costs and as a result higher rates will be charged to shippers for lower shipment sizes. Further, a higher load will allow the transport operator to use a bigger vehicle, which results in the reduction of costs per ton of shipment. Of course, as demonstrated by the Indian Railways, it is always possible to reduce the cost of transportation by better use of existing assets.

Air freight data from Mumbai to Singapore, Beijing, Frankfurt, London and New York for shipment sizes of 10, 50 and 500 kg have been collected and plotted in Figure 5.1. The rate per kilometre per kilogram plotted for the above-mentioned three shipment sizes shows the effect of distance and shipment size on transport rates. With increasing distance and shipment size, costs start coming down, but at a decreasing rate. This clearly shows that there are economies of distance and economies of scale in the transport industry.

In addition to distance and shipment size, transport rates also depend on the point of origin and the destination of the freight. This is because demand and supply at origin and destination will have an impact on freight rates. To illustrate this point, we present the to and fro freight costs for four metros in India in Table 5.1. As can be seen in the table, the rate for the Mumbai–Kolkata trip is not same as the Kolkata–Mumbai trip for the same size of shipment. As there is a huge volume of freight to Kolkata but not enough volume of freight originating at Kolkata, one ends up with asymmetrical rate structures in transportation cost.

The rate from any other metro to Kolkata is about 20 per cent higher than the freight rate from Kolkata to any other metro. In general, transport rates are usually quoted for origin–destination pairs. Further, FTL and LTL shipments carry different rates in all modes of transport.

### TURNAROUND AT INDIAN RAILWAYS[1]

Indian Railways managed to earn a surplus of Rs 215 billion in the year 2006–2007, while just 6 years earlier, a World Bank report had predicted that Indian Railways was on the verge of a financial crisis. Indian Railways managed to reduce cost by using its assets (wagons and locomotives) in more productive ways. It started carrying extra load to the extent of 8 tons per wagon. It redesigned its operations so that it could run freight trains over longer distances without changing locomotives. It increased the effective availability of wagons by reducing the frequency of inspections for wagons and tracks. By ensuring that the loading operations are carried out throughout the day, Indian Railways managed to bring down the turnaround time of goods trains from 7 to 5 days. Higher load per wagon and lower turnaround time of wagons allowed Indian Railways to take advantage of the booming Indian economy. Higher asset utilization has allowed Indian Railways to reduce costs and compete with other modes of transport, not only in the freight business but also in the passenger business.

Pricing schemes used by courier firms are different as they work with much simpler rate structures when compared with other companies in the transport business. Courier companies work

*Table 5.1: Truck freight rates in rupees per tonne for nine-tonne shipment.*

| To | From | | | |
|---|---|---|---|---|
| | **Kolkata** | **Chennai** | **New Delhi** | **Mumbai** |
| Kolkata | — | 2,777 | 2,278 | 3,166 |
| Chennai | 2,330 | — | 3,167 | 2,444 |
| Delhi | 1,830 | 3,333 | — | 2,222 |
| Mumbai | 2,670 | 2,111 | 1,722 | — |

*Source: The Hindu BusinessLine,* 6 November 2006. Reproduced with permission.

with lower shipment sizes and the bulk of their costs are the fixed cost of setting up a network and the fixed cost involved in handling the shipment both at the origin and at the destination. FedEx in the United States charges uniform rates throughout the country for a given shipment weight. UPS works with zonal rates, whereby a country is divided into four zones and the rates are the same within a zone. XPS, a courier express cargo company in India, has divided the entire country into six zones, and pricing within a region is uniform.

Of course, while making transportation-related decisions, shippers cannot look at transportation cost alone because it also affects the inventory carried by the chain. For example, lower shipment sizes increases transportation costs but reduces the cycle-stock in the chain. Similarly, use of a faster mode of transport increases transportation cost but reduces the safety and pipeline stock in the supply chain. So while making transportation decisions a firm has to focus on the total cost that includes transportation as well as inventory-carrying costs.

To understand the nature of inventory and transportation cost trade-off, we need to understand the impact of product and demand characteristics on the total cost.

## Impact of Product and Demand Characteristics on System Cost

As discussed in the previous chapter, the demand for the product is a key factor that determines the inventory of the product. Since the choice of a mode of transportation involves a trade-off between the inventory and the transportation costs, the demand for the product plays a critical role in transportation-related decisions. The nature of the product is also a major consideration. The nature of the product characteristics is captured by a concept called value-density.

### Value-Density

Value-density captures the ratio of rupee value of the product to its weight. It shows the importance of transportation costs in the overall product cost. It also allows the firm to examine the trade-off between inventory and transportation cost. For products with higher value-density, firms can afford to work with faster and more expensive modes of transport as transportation cost is a relatively small fraction of the total product cost, while for low-value-density products, firms have to use slower modes of transport because a small increase in transportation-related cost can affect the profitability of the product in a significant way. Further, several transportation decisions have an impact on the amount of inventory carried within the supply chain. Value-density is able to capture the nature of the transportation inventory trade-off, as the inventory-carrying cost is a function of the value of the product and the transportation cost is a function of the weight of the product. In high-value-density products, such as electronics products and high-technology products, the transportation cost is relatively less important, while in low-value-density products, such as cement, coal and other commodity products, transportation is going to play a relatively more important role. So far we have assumed that the transportation cost is related to the weight of the product, but in a few bulky products, such as cycles and water storage tanks, the transportation cost is captured by the physical volume rather than by the weight. In the air freight industry, volumetric weight is measured using a standard formula

(1 m$^3$ = 166 kg of volumetric weight) and the freight rate is charged based on the physical weight or the volumetric weight, whichever is higher. While using value-density, one might use either weight or volume depending on the attribute that is relevant to the product concerned. Sabare International understands theses issues very well and has come up with a counterintuitive idea of setting up of manufacturing facilities in the United States for some of its products.

### SETTING UP OF PILLOW MANUFACTURING FACILITY IN THE UNITED STATES BY SABARE INTERNATIONAL[2]

Sabare International, with a turnover of 3.75 billion dollars (as on 2006–2007), is a major manufacturer and exporter of home furnishings textiles and has been serving major retailers like Wal-Mart, JC Penny and Kmart in the United States. It realized that for pillows the transportation cost is a dominant component of the cost because of the bulky nature of the product. So rather than manufacturing pillows in India, it has set up a state-of-the-art manufacturing facility in Atlanta for pillow filling and bedding. Despite the higher cost of labour in the United States, Sabare is able to save substantial transportation costs in serving the US markets.

### Demand Characteristics

The demand characteristics for a product capture the volume of demand for the product and the nature of uncertainty associated with the product demand. Cycle-stock and safety stock are associated with volume and demand uncertainty, respectively. Higher volumes of demand allow firms to work with bigger batch sizes while moving goods from the plant to the market, thereby affecting the volume of the cycle-stock carried in the chain. Lower volumes of demand may not allow firms to benefit from the economies of scale in transportation as higher shipment sizes results in significantly high cycle-stocks. Thus, they may be forced to work with LTL shipments. Higher demand uncertainty affects the amount of safety stock carried by a firm. If a product takes a longer lead time because of a slower mode of transport, firms end up with high amounts of safety stocks for products with high demand uncertainty. So for high uncertainty products, firms should use faster modes of transport and use slower modes of transport for products that have a stable demand.

# Modes of Transportation: Choices and Their Performance Measures

In this section, we analyse various transport modes and study the impact of transport modes on supply chain performance measures. We start out by looking at the available choices and then go on to evaluate the performance of each.

## *Choices Available*

A supply chain typically uses a combination of the following five modes of transportation:

- Rail
- Road
- Water
- Air
- Pipeline

### Rail

Rail transport is the ideal mode of transport for low-value-density products, which are not sensitive to time. Though freight cost is lower, it suffers from long and unreliable lead times. In India, private rail companies are not allowed and the railways are completely under government ownership. The share of railways in freight has been gradually declining over the last 30 years. Indian Railways today accounts for about 30 per cent of freight movement in India. A total of 95 per cent of the freight carried by the railways is in bulk goods and within that coal accounts for 50 per cent of the traffic. Traditionally, railways in India have not been run on commercial lines. For example, freight is charged on a distance basis irrespective of the demand and supply of freight at the point of origin or destination. Lately, Indian Railways has been working on freight rationalization and making railways responsive to products other than bulk goods.

### Road

Trucks are the dominant mode of transport in India, accounting for about 65 per cent of freight movement. Though trucking is more expensive than rail transport, it offers the advantage of door-to-door shipment and shorter delivery time. India has the largest road network of 3.32 million kilometres, but the national highways, which carry about 40 per cent of freight, account for only 2 per cent of the length of roads in India. Most highways are highly congested and the average truck speed is only 30–40 km/h. India's trucking industry is deregulated and is highly fragmented. More than 90 per cent of the vehicles are owned by entrepreneurs who own less than 5 trucks. It is estimated that truck-freight rates in India are among the lowest in the world. Though direct freight rates are low, the quality of service is very poor, with long and unreliable transit times and high in-transit damages. The trucking industry in India has been caught in a low-cost low-service equilibrium, which is termed as the unholy equilibrium. All the players—shippers, trucking companies and the government—will have to work together to break this unholy equilibrium in the Indian trucking industry. It means substantial investments by all parties and significant change in practices on the part of both the shippers and the trucking companies.

### Water

Water transport is one of the cheapest modes of transport and is used extensively for international cargo, but it is also the slowest among all the modes of transport. Further, there are often considerable delays at ports. On an average, the turnaround time for a ship is about 4 days in India, which is significantly higher than in most other countries. Though India has an extensive coast line of 7,517 km, none of its ports figures in the top 10 ports of the world. Its largest container port, the Jawaharlal Nehru Port at New Mumbai, handles only 37 million tons of cargo against 4,000 million tons handled by the Shanghai port.

### Air

Air carriers are fairly fast but expensive. So transportation by air is an effective option only for time-sensitive, high-value-density goods. Currently, air transport accounts for a very small percentage of freight but is likely to play an important role in the future. Airports are currently managed by the Airports Authority of India, a Government of India undertaking. Infrastructural facilities at most Indian airports need to be upgraded.

### Pipelines

Pipelines are generally used for bulk transportation of predictable volumes of specialized products like petroleum products and natural gas. This mode is not used in most situations discussed here; hence, it will not be considered hereafter.

**BOX 5.1** Multimodal Transport

Multimodal transport is generally considered as the most efficient way of handling an international door-to-door transport operation. Among the choices of transportation available, each transportation mode has its own advantages and disadvantages. Multimodal transport allows service providers to combine in one voyage the advantages of each mode, such as the flexibility of road and the cost advantage of rail and water, in the best possible fashion. Therefore, the shipper does not have to deal with multiple transport companies that traditionally have focused on a single mode of transport.

The major requirement for efficient multimodal transport is that one should be able to transfer goods and information effortlessly from one service provider to another in a situation where each one of them may be specializing in one mode of transport. Developments like EDI have made it possible to transfer information seamlessly across service providers. The emergence of container technology (containers of standard size) has made it possible to transfer goods across different modes of transport in an effortless manner. There is a view that containerization in particular, and development in multimodal transport in general, have been the primary drivers of globalization.

In the last couple of years, several logistics companies in India have invested in container freight stations and inland container depots to facilitate multimodal transport of goods, mainly for international trade.

In this section, we have discussed each mode of transport independently. But increasingly the shipper wants to use multimodal transport where more than one transport mode is used in one voyage. See Box 5.1 for a brief discussion on multimodal transport.

## Comparison of Modes of Transportation on Supply Chain Performance Measures

The performance of the four major modes of transport can be compared on the following performance measures related to the supply chain:

- *Freight cost.* Water is the least expensive mode of transport while air is the most expensive mode.
- *Lot size.* Shipment size is least in air and a typical shipment will be of a few kilograms in size, while shipping through water requires at least a container equivalent load of about 20–40 tons. Bigger lot size results in bigger cycle-stock-inventory. Differences in required shipment sizes translate to differences in cycle-stock-related inventory.
- *Delivery time.* Shipment through water has the longest delivery time and air shipment offers the shortest delivery time. As pipeline inventory and safety stock carried in a supply chain is a function of the lead time in transport, differences in delivery time get translated in differential pipeline- and safety-stock-inventory.
- *Delivery time variability.* Like delivery lead time, variability in lead time is also the highest for water and the least for air. As the safety stock carried in a supply chain is also a function of the variability in lead time in transport, firms can capture the impact of the differences in variability in delivery time by calculating the corresponding differences in safety-stock inventory-carrying costs.
- *Losses and damages.* Empirical data show that losses and damages are highest for rail and least for water. Losses and damages can be converted to costs in a straightforward manner.

See Table 5.2 for a relative comparison of the four modes of transport.

**Table 5.2: Relative ranking* of transportation mode by performance measures.**

| Mode of transportation | Cost (1 = least) | Lot size (1 = smallest) | Delivery time (1 = fastest) | Delivery time variability† (1 = least) | Loss and damage (1 = least) |
|---|---|---|---|---|---|
| Rail | 2 | 3 | 3 | 3 | 4 |
| Road | 3 | 2 | 2 | 2 | 3 |
| Water | 1 | 4 | 4 | 4 | 1 |
| Air | 4 | 1 | 1 | 1 | 2 |

*1 is most favourable and 4 is least favourable from the shipper's point of view.
†Delivery time variability in absolute terms.
*Source:* R. H. Ballou, *Business Logistics Management* (Upper Saddle River, NJ: Prentice Hall, 1999).

## Total Cost Approach to Performance Measures

As expected, the four modes of transport perform differently on different performance measures, which are important from the perspective of supply chain managers. So we need a methodology that enables us to convert and compare differing performances on various performance measures in terms of cost. We have to convert the differences in other performance measures into cost. Once the total costs for all the relevant modes of transport have been worked out, firms can choose the mode that has the least cost for the service desired by the shipper.

$$\begin{aligned}\text{Total cost} = {} & \text{Transportation cost} + \text{Cycle-stock inventory-carrying cost} \\ & + \text{Pipeline inventory-carrying cost} + \text{Safety-stock inventory costs} \\ & + \text{Cost of losses and damages}\end{aligned}$$

If different modes of transport result in different number of handlings, handling costs also should be incorporated in the total cost equation presented above. For example, if the rail terminal is located far from the plant and depot, firms have to hire trucks to shift the goods from the plant to the rail terminal and additional handling costs will be incurred in transferring goods from road to rail and again from rail to road. Even though rail is cheaper in terms of freight cost, several firms find that from a total cost perspective road is the least expensive mode of transport.

## Impact of Speed of Delivery

The speed of delivery is a major area of concern for specific products. For example, in the spares business, if a firm is offering 24-hour delivery time, but stocks spares only in a few places in India, transportation by air may be the only option available.

Let us take the case of a global company that has decided to use India as its manufacturing base for the supply of printers to the European markets. The company offers three types of printers: high-end, standard and low-end. All three types of printers offered by the firm are similar in size and shape. The only differences are in the software and the chip used in the printers. The three models of the printers cost Rs 20,000, 15,000 and 10,000 per unit, respectively. If the firm decides to use air as the mode of transport, it can fly the goods in smaller lots of 100 units, while shipping via sea requires a minimum shipment size of 400 units. The demand in Europe is stable at 100 units per week for each of the three types of printers. Transportation and customs clearance take one week if air is used as the mode of transport; the same will take four weeks if sea is used as the medium of transport. Freight by air will be Rs 360 per unit while freight by sea will be Rs 90 per unit. The annual inventory-carrying cost for the firm is 20 per cent of the cost of the item. The firm wants to decide on the optimum mode of transport.

The relevant calculations for high-end products are shown below.

*Table 5.3:* ***Cost comparisons for different modes of transport under stable demand.***

| Product | Mode of transport | Cycle-stock (units) | Pipeline inventory (units) | Average inventory | Inventory-carrying cost (thousand rupees) | Transportation costs (thousand rupees) | Total cost per annum (thousand rupees) |
|---|---|---|---|---|---|---|---|
| High end | Sea | 200 | 400 | 600 | 2,400 | 468 | 2,868 |
| | Air | 50 | 100 | 150 | 600 | 1,872 | 2,472 |
| Standard | Sea | 200 | 400 | 600 | 1,800 | 468 | 2,268 |
| | Air | 50 | 100 | 150 | 450 | 1,872 | 2,322 |
| Low end | Sea | 200 | 400 | 600 | 1,200 | 468 | 1,668 |
| | Air | 50 | 100 | 150 | 300 | 1,872 | 2,172 |

For sea as the mode of transport:

Cycle-stock = 0.5 × Lot size of shipment = 0.5 × 400 = 200 units

Pipeline inventory = Lead time × Demand rate = 4 × 100 = 400 units

Total inventory = Cycle-stock + Pipeline inventory = 200 + 400 = 600 units

Annual inventory-carrying cost = 600 × 20,000 × 0.2 = 2,400,000 rupees

Annual transportation cost = Annual demand × Transport rate per unit
= 100 × 52 × 90 = Rs 468,000

Similarly, we can work out the cost for air as a mode transport and also carry out similar calculations for standard and low-end products. Cost comparisons for both the modes of transport for all the three types of printers are presented in Table 5.3. For high-value-density products like the high-end product, air is a much better option, while for low-density products, sea is the preferred mode of transport. So the firm should use air as the mode of transport for high-end printers and use sea for standard and low-end printers.

## Impact of Demand Uncertainty

The choice of mode of transport for a particular product also depends on demand uncertainty. This demand uncertainty is reflected in the safety stocks that a firm has to maintain. For a given service level, the quantity of safety stocks changes with changes in the mode of transport on account of the variation in the delivery lead time in each case. Let us examine the impact of demand uncertainty on the three products discussed in the previous example.

Let us say that for European countries the firm targets a service level of 98 per cent. Each of the three products faces similar demand uncertainty and has standard deviation of demand equal to 30 units.

$$\text{Safety stock} = \text{Service factor} \times \text{Standard deviation of demand} \times \sqrt{\text{lead time}}$$

A service level of 98 per cent means that the service factor is equal to 2.

$$\text{Safety stock for sea transport} = 2 \times 30 \times \sqrt{4} = 120 \text{ units}$$

$$\text{Safety stock for air transport} = 2 \times 30 \times \sqrt{1} = 60 \text{ units}$$

All other calculations remain the same; we just add the inventory-carrying cost for the safety stock. As can be seen in Table 5.4, even for the standard printer, air is the preferred mode of transport.

It is interesting to note that the optimal mode of transport may change with either change in volume of demand or demand uncertainty or value-density. For example, change in product design alters the value-density of the firm. Competition may reduce prices, because of

**Table 5.4: Cost comparisons in situations of high demand uncertainty.**

| Product | Mode of transport | Total cost per annum for stable demand (thousand rupees) | Safety stock inventory-carrying cost (thousand rupees) | Total cost (thousand rupees) |
|---|---|---|---|---|
| High-end | Sea | 2,868 | 480 | 3,348 |
| | Air | 2,472 | 240 | 2,712 |
| Standard | Sea | 2,268 | 360 | 2,628 |
| | Air | 2,322 | 180 | 2,502 |
| Low-end | Sea | 1,668 | 240 | 1,908 |
| | Air | 2,172 | 120 | 2,292 |

which the value-density of the product changes. Competition can also change the nature of the demand uncertainty in the market place. Similarly, at different stages in the product life cycle, demand characteristics are likely to change. Thus, one may have to periodically re-examine optimal choices in this area, even though transport rates may not have changed over a period of time.

**INTERVIEW WITH**

**S. S. VARMA**

*Tata Chemicals Limited (TCL) is India's leading manufacturer of inorganic chemicals with an annual turnover of over Rs 58 billion. Effective and efficient transportation management for their largest plant at Mithapur is the biggest challenge for the logistics group at TCL. Mr S. S. Varma is General Manager, Logistics, heading the corporate logistics at TCL.*

*How complex are the logistics operations at the Mithapur plant?*

**S. S. Varma:** The Mithapur plant in Gujarat is the largest inorganic chemicals complex in India. Soda ash and salt are the two main products of this complex. We produce 2,400 tons per day of soda ash and 1,500 tons per day of vacuum-evaporated salt at Mithapur. The customers for soda ash are spread all over India. However, the salt is transported in 50-kg bags to 15 packaging units located all over India, from where it is packed in to 1-kg bags and sold to retail market all over India through complex distribution channels. Such large volumes of material flow pose enormous challenges on both inbound and outbound logistics fronts.

*What are the major challenges in logistics management at TCL?*

**S. S. Varma:** We are trying to cater to the pan-India market for both soda ash and salt from Mithapur. Managing large-scale inbound and outbound logistics has always been a challenge. The transportation cost is a significant part of the cost in both products. Therefore, the logistics has to be handled in an efficient yet cost-effective manner. Moreover, our customers have become very demanding. Flat glass and detergent industries are the major customers for soda ash. They do not want to hold too much of inventory and demand just-in-time supply from us. The entry of organized players has increased the competition manifold especially in the case of salt. The logistics problem is compounded by poor transport infrastructure in the region and erratic supply of rakes and trucks. We try and work with all the three modes of transport so that we can handle uncertainty.

*What are the logistics innovations that have been developed to deal with these problems?*

**S. S. Varma:** We have developed an optimization model (Optimizer) that helps us in preparing an optimal movement plan for dispatch of all the products in a cost-effective manner, considering the various constraints. Optimizer is an Excel-solver-based tool, which uses linear programming to provide an optimal movement plan for the different products by different transportation modes (rake, road, coastal, mix-mode). Our model can handle rake availability constraints as well as capacity-related constraints.

We also have come up with idea of a jumbo bag where we can transport soda ash in large-sized flexible containers. Transporting in a jumbo bag helps in reducing handling costs, both for us and our customers. We have also been working closely with Indian Railways to reduce uncertainty on the rake-supply front. We have been exploring ideas of owning wagons under the "Own Your Wagon Scheme". We also have created a corporate logistics group so that we can transfer the best practices across businesses across plants.

# Devising a Strategy for Transportation

Now that it is clear that the choice of the mode of transportation affects not only the cost but also other supply chain performance measures, let us now understand how to design a transportation strategy for a given product. The idea is to find the most effective way of despatching products from plants to geographically dispersed markets in a cost-effective way. To do so, we first identify the major options in the distribution network design and go on to compare the various options.

## *Distribution Network Design Options*

To design and set up the distribution network, a firm has to consider issues of how many depots would be needed and where to locate them. This aspect is dealt with in greater detail in the next chapter. In this section, we focus on issues involved in designing a logistics strategy to transport products from plants to depots.

The issues involved in designing transportation strategies are illustrated through the example of a manufacturing firm that has three plants (A, B and C), each manufacturing a different product line and serving a stable market through three depots (X, Y and Z). Plant A is manufacturing menswear, plant B is manufacturing ladies wear and plant C is manufacturing children's wear. The firm is in the premium garment business. Each of the plants will be supplying to all the three depots: X, Y and Z. This is different from a situation where all the plants are manufacturing the same range of products and the firm has to decide on optimal plant depot linkages. We look at this problem in Chapter 6. Here, all the depots have to be served from all the plants. There are three main strategies the firm can explore.

### Ship Directly from Each Plant to Each Market

As can be seen in Figure 5.2, this involves nine trips. This will work very well if each product line has high volumes and low degree of demand uncertainty. To get economies of scale in transport, each trip involves FTL shipments, resulting in high cycle-stock at each depot for each product line.

### Aggregate Demand Across Depots and Using a Milk Run from Each Plant

As can be seen in Figure 5.3, this involves aggregating product-wise demand across all three depots. Each truck trip starts from a plant and visits depots X, Y and Z in that sequence and comes back to the plant after serving the last depot in the trip. Instead of nine trips, there will only be three trips, but the depots get served more often. This increases transportation costs because the truck has to travel between depots. But this results in lower cycle-stock inven-

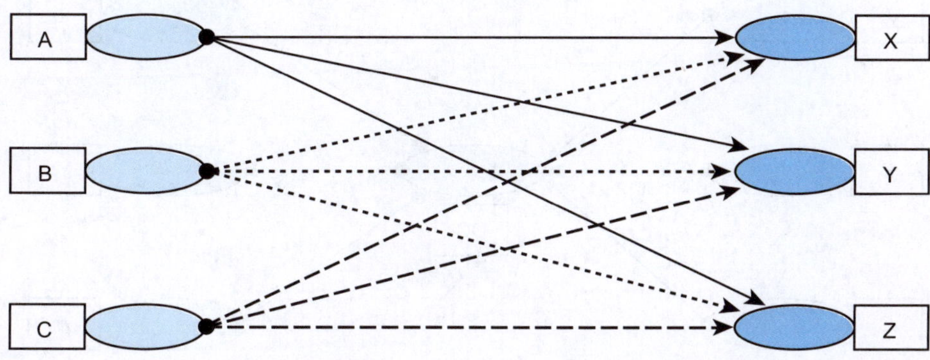


**Figure 5.2**

Direct shipping.

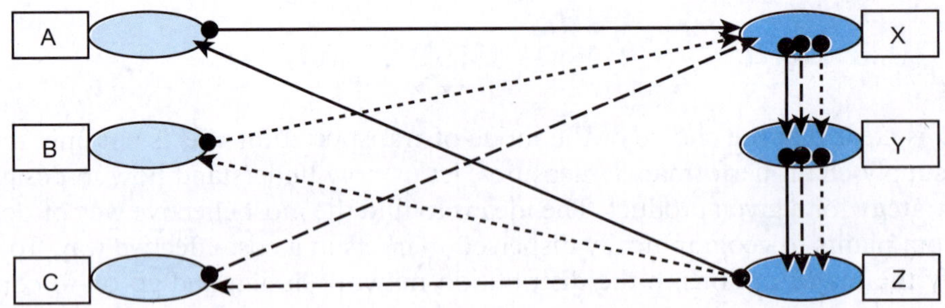


Figure 5.3

Shipping using milk run.

tory because each market gets served more often and in each trip they get smaller volumes of supply. This approach works well if all the depots are relatively in close proximity.

### Ship via Distribution Centre

As can be seen in Figure 5.4, we have six linkages: three linkages from the plants to the distribution centre (DC) and three linkages from the DC to the three depots. As far as the plants are concerned, the DC is the customer, so in each trip from the plant, the firm is able to aggregate demand across depots. Similarly, for a depot, instead of dealing with three suppliers it has to deal with only one supplier, that is, the DC. This option results in cycle-stocks at depots that are of similar value to the milk run option and will have transportation cost that is higher than direct shipping, but lower than the milk run option. But this involves putting additional facility, additional inventory at the DC and additional loading and unloading costs at the DC.

All the transportation strategies except for the direct shipment strategy involve aggregation of demand over products or markets to accommodate frequent shipments without loss of economies of scale. The major players in the package carriers industry (FedEx and UPS in the United States) have come up with the hub-and-spoke model to handle transportation of a large number of time-sensitive small-size shipments that originate from geographically dispersed areas and also have to be distributed over large geographical areas. See Box 5.2 for details of the hub-and-spoke model.

## Comparison of Distribution Network Design Options

To evaluate the performance of each transportation strategy, let us re-examine these three options for a garment company involving three plants (each plant specializing in one product-line) and three depots. We look at the sum total of the transportation cost and the inventory-carrying cost to arrive at the best-suited strategy for the firm. Weekly demand at each of the three depots is 100 units for each of the three types of garments. A truck can carry 300 units of

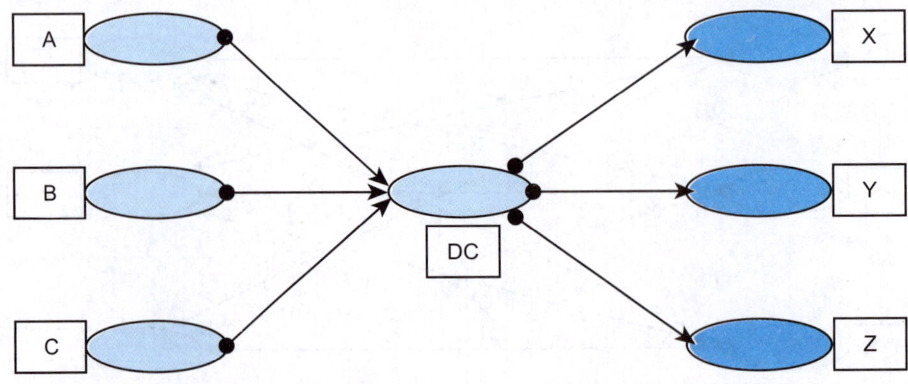


Figure 5.4

Shipping via a central distribution centre.

**BOX 5.2** Hub-and-spoke Model

In the hub-and-spoke model followed in the transportation industry, all the destinations (cities and towns) in the region are inter-connected through a central hub. Like in a bicycle wheel, routes are similar to spokes and the centre in the wheel acts as the hub. The other contrasting model is a point-to-point model, where all the cities are directly connected with each other.

Fred Smith, the founder of FedEx, pioneered the idea of the hub-and-spoke model for overnight package delivery in the 1970s. FedEx established its hub at Memphis airport, which allowed it to create a low-cost centre through which all the major cities in the United States were connected. Later on, all its competitors like UPS and Airborne Express also decided to follow the hub-and-spoke model for its overnight delivery system.

In the hub-and-spoke model, all the operations like sorting are centralized at the hub, thereby permitting economies of scale in operations. This model also helps add new cities to the network easily compared to the point-to-point model. In the hub-and-spoke model, $n$ cities are connected through $n - 1$ routes only and every city is connected directly to the hub city. However, in a point-to-point model there will be $n(n - 1)/2$ routes. Suppose you want to connect the top 50 cities in India, the point-to-point model will require 1,225 routes whereas the hub-and-spoke model will require only 49 routes. This simplicity in route network in the hub-and-spoke model comes at some cost. For example, let us take a case of a courier company with a hub at Nagpur. Even though two cities like Bangalore and Chennai are just 331 km apart, all the parcels between theses two cities will be routed through Nagpur, resulting in the packets travelling 2,132 km instead of 331 km.

Pricing in the hub-and-spoke model follows a very different approach and all packets are charged at the same rate irrespective of the distance involved. For example, a packet originating from Chennai and going to Bangalore or Delhi will be charged the same amount even though the distances involved are considerably different. But any problem at the hub (e.g., bad weather at the hub) can result in delays across the entire network.

In practice, firms modify hub-and-spoke model by creating regional hubs instead of one central hub. For example, instead of one hub at Nagpur, firms may have four regional hubs where each city within the region is connected to the regional hub. This helps in avoiding movement across long distances for nodes that are geographically close to each other. Of course, firms need to create adequate infrastructure at each regional hub.

garments and the transportation cost is Rs 2 per km for FTL shipments. To obtain economies of scale, the firm has decided to work with FTL shipments and all the trips will carry 300 units of garments. The firm can bundle menswear, ladies wear and children's wear in one trip but all together it can carry only 300 units in one trip. The inventory-carrying cost is at 20 per cent per annum. All the products cost Rs 200 per unit, so the inventory-carrying cost is Rs 40 per unit per year. The facility cost of maintaining a DC is Rs 12,000 per year.

In the direct shipping option, as truck's capacity is 300 units, three weeks' worth of demand will be supplied in every trip, and this cycle will be repeated every three weeks. In the milk run and in the shipping via the DC option, as they can aggregate demand across depots, each trip will have one week's worth of supply and this cycle will be repeated every week.

## Computing Transportation Costs

The spatial arrangement of the plants and the depots are shown in the grid in Figure 5.5. Plants A, B and C and depots X, Y, and Z are located on the grid with their respective coordinates. For the third option, the DC is located at point O on the grid. Coordinates for all the relevant points on the grid allow us to calculate the distances for the different parts of the trip used in transportation, and the same data are tabulated in Table 5.5. From the data on coordinates, one can compute all the relevant distances. The distance between point $i$ with coordinates $(x_i, y_i)$ and point $j$ with coordinates $(x_j, y_j)$ can be computed as follows:

$$\text{Distance}(i, j) = \sqrt{(x_i - x_j)^2 + (y_i - y_j)^2}$$

The distance calculated above is a radial distance, which is the shortest distance between points $i$ and $j$, and this may not be valid in all circumstances. For example, in cities you may have

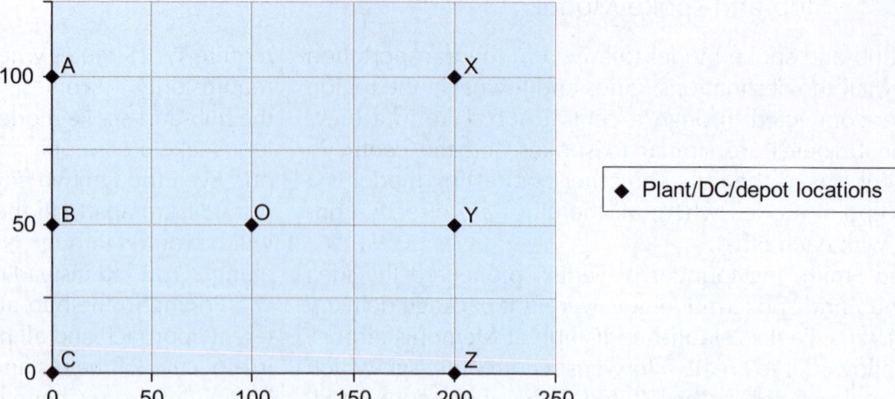


**Figure 5.5**

Spatial data representation.

*Table 5.5:* **Computation of distances.**

| | **(x, y) Coordinate** | **Trip** | **Distance** |
|---|---|---|---|
| A | (0, 100) | AX, BY, CZ | 200 |
| B | (0, 50) | AZ, CX | 223.6 |
| C | (0, 0) | AY, BX, BZ, CY | 206.15 |
| X | (200, 100) | XY, YZ | 50 |
| Y | (200, 50) | AO, CO, OX, OZ | 111.8 |
| Z | (200, 0) | BO, OY | 100 |
| O | (100, 50) | | |

perpendicular roads that are essentially laid from north to south and east to west. In such a situation, rectilinear distances may be more appropriate.

Since demand is stable for all the products we ignore the inventory-carrying cost on account of safety stock in this case. Since distances are short we also ignore pipeline inventory in this case. Relevant costs are cycle-stock inventory-carrying cost and transportation cost.

To calculate the annual transport costs for each option, we first need to calculate the distance travelled in each cycle for each of the options.

For direct shipping option:

Distance travelled per cycle = 2XA + 2XB + 2XC + 2YA + 2YB + 2YC + 2ZA + 2ZB + 2ZC
= 3,744 km

Travel cost per cycle = 3,744 × 2 = Rs 7,488

Number of cycles per year = 52/3

Annual transport cost = 7,488 × 52/3 = Rs 129,781

Using the same approach one can calculate the annual transport costs for the other two options, which is shown in Table 5.6.

## Computing Relevant Inventory-carrying Cost

To calculate the inventory-carrying cost, we need to estimate the cycle-stock inventory under each option. In the direct shipment option, each depot receives a shipment of 300 units of each of the products, so the average cycle-stock at each depot will be 150 units for each product line. This results in an average of 450 garments of cycle-stock at each of the depots. So the total average cycle-stock across the three depots equals 1,350 units in the direct shipping option.

Thus, the inventory-carrying cost in the direct-shipping option at three depots
= 1,350 × 40 = Rs 54,000.

*Table 5.6:* ***Comparison of the three shipping strategies.***

| Option | Distance travelled in one cycle | Frequency of transportation cycle | Annual transportation cost in rupees | Annual facility cost | Premium garment (Average garment cost = Rs 200) | | Low-end garment (Average garment cost = Rs 75) | |
|---|---|---|---|---|---|---|---|---|
| | | | | | Annual inventory-carrying cost | Annual total cost | Annual inventory-carrying cost | Annual total cost |
| Direct shipping | 3,744 | Once in 3 weeks | 129,781 | 0 | 54,000 | 183,781 | 20,250 | 150,031 |
| Milk run | 1,560 | Once a week | 162,191 | 0 | 18,000 | 180,191 | 6,750 | 168,941 |
| Shipping via DC | 1,294 | Once a week | 134,620 | 12,000 | 18,000 | 164,620 | 6,750 | 153,370 |

In the other two options, each depot receives a shipment of 100 units for each of the products, so the average cycle-stock will be 50 units for each of the product line at each depot. This results in an average of 150 units of garments of cycle-stock at each depot in the milk run and the shipping via the DC options. So the total average cycle-stock across all three depots will be equal to 450 units.

Thus, the inventory carrying cost for the other two options = $450 \times 40$ = Rs 18,000.

As can be seen in Table 5.6, shipping via the DC is the best option for the firm. Direct shipping is the most expensive option for the firm. It will be interesting to see the result for a garment company that is in the low-end garment business, where the average cost of a garment is Rs 75 per unit. Now transportation and facility costs at the DC are not a function of the value of the product, so those costs will remain the same for a low-end garment manufacturing firm, but then the inventory costs will be much lower. As can be seen in Table 5.6, for a low-end garment company, direct shipping is a much better option, as reduced inventory in the shipping via the DC option is of much lower value. So value-density plays an important role in the selection of an appropriate transportation strategy.

In shipping via the DC, one can question the value added by the DC facility. Wal-Mart has worked on the idea of cross-docking, where one does not need a physical DC at point O.

## Cross-docking

Cross-docking involves coordinating the six trips shown in Figure 5.4 in such a way that goods unloaded from incoming vehicles at the DC are straightaway loaded on to trucks that originate from the DC. A major advantage here is that a firm need not have inventory at the warehouse and the warehouse is essentially *a flow through warehouse.* This will result in transit of full truck loads of goods and frequent delivery of supply, without there being any investment in a physical DC. This is possible only if a firm is working in an environment of predictable volumes and lower uncertainty in transit times. For example, all six trucks have to be available at the cross-dock point at the same point in time; otherwise, the firm will need a physical DC where the goods can be stored in readiness for such an eventuality. In the shipping via the DC option, a firm does not have to tightly coordinate the six trips. In cross-docking, it has to ensure that schedules of all the six trucks are tightly coupled and therefore needs a lot more control over the vehicles. That is one reason why Wal-Mart prefers to own the vehicles and likes greater control over logistics in its business. Wal-Mart has been using cross-docking extensively so as to cut costs in the inbound part of the supply chain.

### Cross-docking Practices Followed by the Indian Trucking Industry

In India, cross-docking has been used quite extensively by the trucking industry, with cross-docking taking place at all the major transportation hubs in the country. For example, a trucking company like TCI has its trucks that aggregate LTL shipments requiring delivery at any place in India from smaller towns like Hubli, Mangalore and Bellary. All the trucks plying from the smaller towns of Karnataka will arrive at the Bangalore hub and the goods from theses trucks will be cross-docked into four trucks leaving for Mumbai, Chennai, Delhi and Kolkata. All the shipments that are booked for the eastern part of India will be loaded into trucks leaving for the Kolkata hub. Well-managed transport companies are able to manage these complex movements without stocking at intermediate points. But since the bulk of the trucking industry is in the unorganized sector, truck movements are not well coordinated and transit times are uncertain, resulting in goods being usually stocked in open places at the intermediate points. This might result in lower transportation costs but then it leads to higher damages and long, unreliable lead times for the LTL shipments.

### Cross-docking Practices in the Indian Automobile industry

Auto assembler companies like Maruti, Toyota Kirloskar and Tata Motors have started using the concept of cross-docking.

#### CROSS-DOCKING AT TOYOTA KIRLOSKAR

Toyota Kirloskar works with a fine-tuned transportation strategy for its inbound logistics. At Toyota Kirloskar, the supply received through milk runs from Gurgaon is cross-docked to trucks going to the Bidadi plant in Karnataka. Since 2004, Toyota practises double cross-docking, wherein the first cross-docking is done at Gurgaon and the second cross-docking is done at Pune, where a vehicle coming from Gurgaon and another from Jabalpur are cross-docked so that one big vehicle moves from Pune to Bidadi. Apart from maintaining lower inventory at the plant, cross-docking also helps Toyota in protecting itself from transportation reliability problems. In the traditional system (receipt of FTL shipment directly from each supplier), if the truck in transit is involved in an accident, the entire assembly line will close down for at least a couple of days because of non-availability of material of one supplier. In the current system, because all the parts from all the suppliers from the north and the west come in on a daily basis, failure of one truck will disrupt supply for a maximum of one day.

This system requires a lot of coordination and discipline on the part of all suppliers. Each supplier will have to make the supply ready on a daily basis. If the shipment is not ready at the appointed time, the vehicle doing a milk run will not wait, and it will be the responsibility of the supplier to ensure that the supply reaches the auto assembler on time. If required, the supplier has to air lift those materials to the auto assembler's plant. It took a lot of time and effort from all the parties involved, but over a period of time auto suppliers have got used to the discipline required in the whole system.

## *Transportation Strategies Followed by Retail Firms*

Retailers like Wal-Mart and Tesco have paid a lot of attention to their transportation strategies and they use a mix and match of all the transportation strategies discussed in this section. Earlier, transport decisions were left to individual vendors, but of late, these firms have decided to work with factory-gate pricing where goods will be picked up by the retailer from the manufacturer's factory. The retailers are able to pool shipments across vendors and have managed to use transportation assets more effectively. Home Depot, the third largest retailer in the world, realized that a large number of suppliers delivered them with LTL shipments because Home Depot wanted frequent replenishment from suppliers. Now with better coordination and using the concept of milk runs and cross-docking, Home Depot has saved significant transportation costs in inbound operations.

Earlier, the focus used to be on efficiency, so all supply used to be in the FTL shipment mode. As a result, firms had transportation efficiency but also had to manage with higher inventories. Once the firms realized that inventory costs are high and it is difficult to predict customer demand accurately, they started insisting on frequent deliveries of small lots from suppliers. This resulted in lean inventories but high transportation costs because each vendor was asked to supply in LTL shipments. Now, the concepts of milk run and cross-docking are helping firms in managing frequent delivery from suppliers without sacrificing transportation efficiencies. This has in fact become a serious issue in the last few years because fuel prices have shot up considerably and LTL supplies can add significant costs to firms.

The actual transportation strategy adopted by a firm is a combination of various modes of transport that are chosen keeping in mind the kind of product to be transported, the demand and supply uncertainties, and the cost-efficiency of the final strategy. Players in the retail sector find the concept of the milk run most attractive. However, designing an optimal milk run requires a good conceptual understanding of vehicle-scheduling concepts. In the next section, we discuss relevant issues in vehicle-scheduling.

## Vehicle Scheduling

Consumer-durable and non-durable firms like HUL and BPL serve all the dealers within a geographical region once a week. Milk dairies like Amul collect milk from framers who are geographically dispersed and bring the milk to a central dairy for processing, twice every day. Courier companies distribute and collect parcels from customers every day. In each of the above-mentioned situations, the respective firms are dealing with the problem of visiting $n$ nodes from a central depot using $k$ number of vehicles. The firm has to assign all customers to one of the $k$ vehicles and has to form a sequence within a route. Sequencing $n$ customers/suppliers on a single vehicle is not a trivial problem and involves exploring $n!$ alternatives. The problem becomes more complicated, once we bring in the dimension of multiple vehicles. Further, final routes must observe vehicle capacity constraints and time window constraints (customer/supplier can be visited only during a specific time window). Instead of solving the problem optimally, most of the real-life vehicle-scheduling problems are solved using heuristics and we discuss one such heuristic approach called saving algorithm, which seems to provide reasonably good solutions.

### *Saving Algorithm for Vehicle Scheduling*

The savings algorithm involves the following steps:

- *Step 1.* Calculation of a saving matrix. To start with, the algorithm requires a cost matrix that contains information about the cost involved in travelling from node $i$ to node $j$ and for links involving all pairs of nodes $i$ and $j$. For 10 nodes, we have 45 possible links. From the cost matrix, calculate saving matrix for all the links.

$$\text{Savings } S_{ij} = C_{0j} - C_{ij} + C_{i0}$$

where $C_{ij}$ and $S_{ij}$ represents costs and savings, respectively, associated for links $i$ to $j$. The savings matrix represents the saving that is realized when two nodes are consolidated in one route. As can be seen in Figure 5.6(a) and (b), savings methods starts with routes where each route serves just one node. Let us say we have two nodes that are served currently by two different routes. The cost for these two routes will be $2C_{0i} + 2C_{0j}$. If these two nodes are served by one route where the vehicle will go to customer $i$ from the depot and visit node $j$ from node $i$ and finally return to depot 0, one cuts down the trip from the centre point to node $j$ as

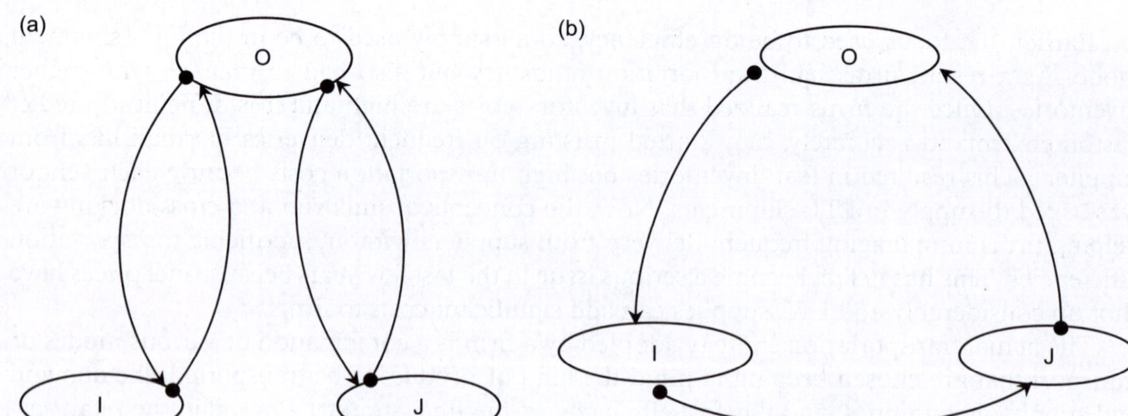


**Figure 5.6**

(a) Two independent routes. (b) Merged route.

well as the trip from node *i* to the centre point, but will make an additional trip from point *i* to *j*. As we know that in a triangle the sum of two sides is always grater than the third side, the resulting savings will always be non-negative.

- *Step 2.* Start the new route (0–*i*–*j*–0) with link (*i*, *j*), which has the highest savings amongst all unassigned nodes. At the beginning of the algorithm all the nodes are in the list of unassigned nodes.
- *Step 3.* Find the first feasible link with highest savings, which can be used to extend one of the two ends of the existing route. If the current route is (0–*p*–*q*–0), then check for all the links involving unassigned nodes, and nodes *p* or *q*. If the current route is (0–*p*–*q*–*r*–*s*–0), then check for all the links involving unassigned nodes, and nodes *p* or *s*.
- *Step 4.* Go back to step 3 and continue till the route cannot be extended because of feasibility constraints or because no unassigned nodes are left in the list.
- *Step 5.* Go back to step 2 until all nodes are assigned.

## Applying the Saving Algorithm

Let us assume the problem of a consumer goods company, which has to serve 10 dealers from a depot located at point 0. The spatial location of the dealers and the depot is shown in the grid in Figure 5.7. The data of average dealer demand and distance between depot and dealer

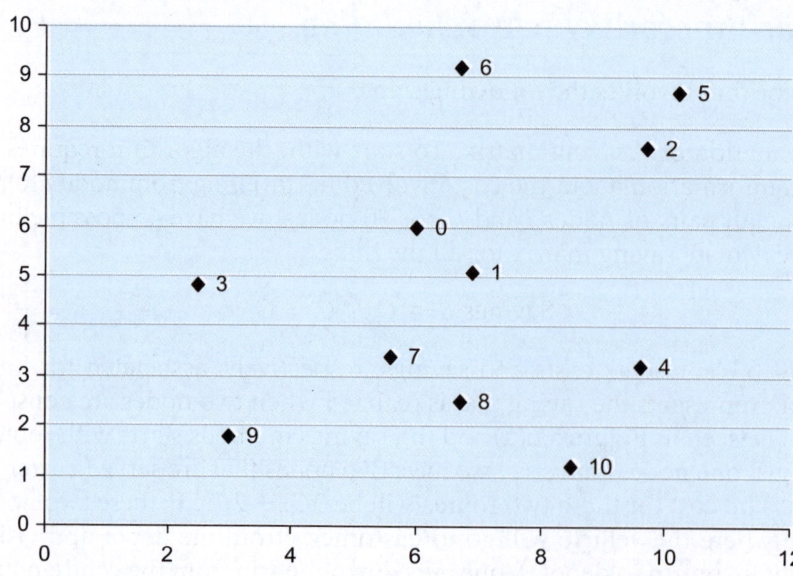


**Figure 5.7**

Spatial representation of the depot and the dealers.

*Table 5.7:* **Distance and load-related data for the consumer goods company.**

| Dealer | 1 | 2 | 3 | 4 | 5 | 6 | 7 | 8 | 9 | 10 |
|---|---|---|---|---|---|---|---|---|---|---|
| Distance from depot | 8 | 24 | 22 | 27 | 30 | 20 | 16 | 21 | 31 | 32 |
| Average demand (tons) | 2 | 4 | 3 | 4 | 2 | 3 | 4 | 3 | 4 | 2 |

are presented in Table 5.7. Each vehicle can handle up to 12 tons of load. The firm wants to design optimal schedules.

We use the savings algorithm to the problem of designing routes for the 10 nodes. Before we start the algorithm, we need a cost matrix. Ideally, one should work with cost data, but distance can act as a proxy for cost and it is easy to generate a distance matrix as cost data may not be easily available. Distances can be computed from the grid shown in Figure 5.7, where we have coordinates of all the relevant nodes. As discussed earlier, distance between node $i$ with coordinates $(x_i, y_i)$ and node $j$ with coordinates $(x_j, y_j)$ can be calculated as follows:

$$\text{Distance}(i, j) = \sqrt{(x_i - x_j)^2 + (y_i - y_j)^2}$$

Using the above formula from the coordinates of all 10 customers, we can calculate the distance matrix shown in Table 5.8. Here, we assume that the distance involved in travelling from node $i$ to $j$ is the same as the distance involved in travelling from node $j$ to node $i$. This assumption does not hold good for travel in a city where there are many one-way roads and the volume of traffic is heavy; thus, time and cost of travelling may be different in different directions.

From the distance matrix, we can calculate the saving matrix using the formula $S_{ij} = C_{0j} - C_{ij} + C_{i0}$. Distance data from the depot to the customers are shown in Table 5.7, and distances between all pairs of customers are shown in Table 5.8.

The saving matrix is as calculated and presented in Table 5.9.

In the first step, the highest saving of 47 is obtained on link (5–2), and this route will have load equal to 2 + 5 = 7 units. So our first route is (0–5–2–0). Now the only possible links that we can explore are links involving nodes 5 and 2. Among all the unassigned nodes that are linked to node 5, the highest saving is obtained with the link (6–5), and is equal to 29. Among all the unassigned nodes that are linked to node 2, the highest saving is obtained with the link (2–4), being equal to 24. So we choose link (6–5), as it has the highest savings and check if route (0–6–5–2–0) is feasible or not. This route will have a load equal to 7 + 2 =9 units. Since our vehicle capacity is 12 units, this is a feasible route. So far we have three nodes in the route and we can go on adding nodes to the route till we reach the capacity limit. Now we can explore the links involving end-point nodes, that is, nodes 6 and 2. The link with the highest saving is

*Table 5.8:* **Distance matrix.**

| | 1 | 2 | 3 | 4 | 5 | 6 | 7 | 8 | 9 | 10 |
|---|---|---|---|---|---|---|---|---|---|---|
| 1 | 0 | | | | | | | | | |
| 2 | 23 | 0 | | | | | | | | |
| 3 | 26 | 46 | 0 | | | | | | | |
| 4 | 20 | 26 | 44 | 0 | | | | | | |
| 5 | 29 | 7 | 52 | 33 | 0 | | | | | |
| 6 | 25 | 20 | 36 | 40 | 21 | 0 | | | | |
| 7 | 13 | 35 | 20 | 24 | 42 | 35 | 0 | | | |
| 8 | 16 | 36 | 29 | 18 | 43 | 40 | 9 | 0 | | |
| 9 | 31 | 53 | 18 | 40 | 60 | 50 | 18 | 23 | 0 | |
| 10 | 25 | 39 | 42 | 14 | 46 | 49 | 22 | 13 | 33 | 0 |

*Table 5.9:* **Saving matrix.**

| | 1 | 2 | 3 | 4 | 5 | 6 | 7 | 8 | 9 | 10 |
|---|---|---|---|---|---|---|---|---|---|---|
| 1 | 0 | | | | | | | | | |
| 2 | 9 | 0 | | | | | | | | |
| 3 | 4 | 0 | 0 | | | | | | | |
| 4 | 15 | 25 | 5 | 0 | | | | | | |
| 5 | 9 | 47 | 0 | 24 | 0 | | | | | |
| 6 | 3 | 24 | 6 | 7 | 29 | 0 | | | | |
| 7 | 11 | 5 | 18 | 19 | 4 | 1 | 0 | | | |
| 8 | 13 | 9 | 14 | 30 | 8 | 1 | 28 | 0 | | |
| 9 | 8 | 2 | 35 | 18 | 1 | 1 | 29 | 29 | 0 | |
| 10 | 15 | 17 | 12 | 45 | 16 | 3 | 26 | 40 | 30 | 0 |

(4–2), savings equal to 25. If we add node 4 to the route, the load on the route will be 9 + 4 = 13, which violates the capacity constraint; thus, we cannot add node 4 to the route. Next, the highest savings is with link (10–2), with savings equal to 17, and the route will have load = 9 + 2 = 11 units. So we have a feasible route (0–6–5–2–10–0) with four nodes and a load of 11 units. Since no unassigned node has a volume of less than 2 units, we cannot add any other node to this route. So now we start the second route with the link (9–3), with savings equal to 35. If we continue with this process, we will finally have the following three routes:

Route 1 = (0–6–5–2–10–0) with load = 11 units

Route 2 = (0–3–9–7–0) with load = 11 units

Route 3 = (0–4–1–8–0) with load = 9 units

The final routes are as shown in Figure 5.8.

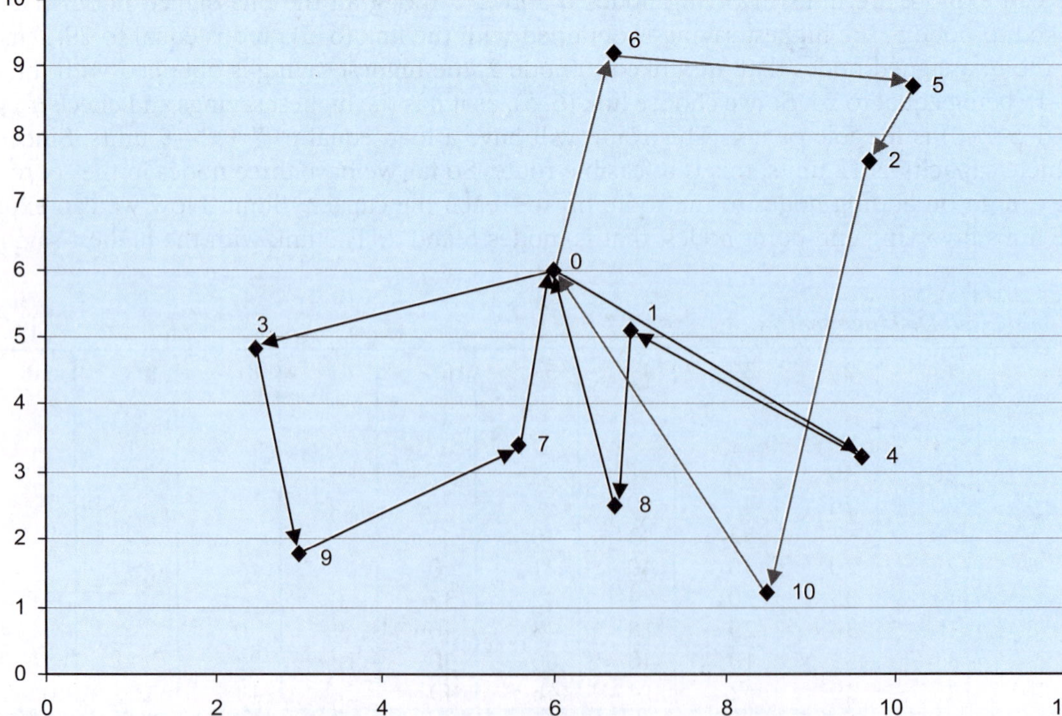


**Figure 5.8**

Vehicle routes.

### Managing Other Constraints

While forming the routes we assumed that there are no other constraints, apart from capacity constraints. In general, while extending routes one has to check for all the relevant constraints. In practice, it has been found that constraints related to the time window are the most difficult to handle. Time-window constraints reduce the flexibility available to the scheduler and can potentially increase transport costs significantly.

Firms that deal with a known set of customers/vendors have a choice of offering static routes that are fixed in advance and do not change over a period of time. The pros and cons of using static routes versus dynamic routes are discussed in the next section.

## *Static-Versus-Dynamic Scheduling*

Once the vehicle route has been worked out by the firm, the frequency of collection and dispatch depends not only on the demand and supply but also on other constraints as discussed in the preceding section. Keeping these in mind, a firm has the option to choose between two possible strategies for optimal utilization of resources.

Take the case of Amul Dairy. Here, schedules are announced well in advance and farmers know at what point in time the vehicle will visit their village for milk collection. In other words, it works with static schedules (see Box 5.3) for its milk collection. Automobile companies also work with static schedules for part collection from their vendors. Some firms work with similar static routes for serving dealers. Firms like HUL cluster all dealers into six groups and each group gets served on one of the working days, and even within that day, the route followed by the vehicle is announced well in advance. Static schedules results in a by-and-large uniform load on the depot and the transport system, and helps a dealer in planning the work ahead because the dealer knows the exact slot within a week when delivery can be expected. For

**BOX 5.3** Vehicle Routing for Milk Procurement at Amul Dairy[3]

Amul Co-operative Dairy collects milk from 800 points. Typically, village co-operative dairies collect milk from farmers and this is picked up by Amul Dairy twice a day. The vehicle routes are decided keeping in mind the expected collection at the nodes during the coming year. Transportation cost for milk procurement accounts for 17 per cent of the operating cost and hence gets much attention from co-operative managers.

**Milk procurement has the following special problems:**

- *Impact of route length on the quality.* As milk is a perishable commodity, it must reach the dairy within five hours of collection so as to avoid curdling. There is no constraint on the overall route length but the time taken for a vehicle from the first pick-up point to the dairy should be less than five hours.
- *Data preparation for scheduling.* One of the main inputs to the vehicle-routing problem is the distance matrix giving shortest distance between all the pairs of pick-up points. Normally, we calculate radial distances using co-ordinates of all the pick-up points from the map of the region. But because of the sparse road network available in rural areas, radial distances will grossly underestimate the actual distances.
- *Difficulty in changing route-pattern.* Most of the farmers have worked out their work schedules and lifestyles based on the existing routes because the milking time has to be co-ordinated with the time at which the vehicle is going to pick-up the milk. Any change in route will result in a change in the time at which the vehicle will visit village co-operative society, and for this farmers will have to change their lifestyles. As the framers are the owners of the co-operative, it is difficult to change routes because of resistance from the framers.

Application of the savings algorithm for preparing a vehicle schedule for Baroda Dairy, a small unit that had 131 nodes, demonstrated savings to the extent of 15–20 per cent. The solution obtained by applying the savings algorithm reduced the distance travelled by 20 per cent and required only nine vehicles for milk collection, while traditional routes designed manually worked with 12 vehicles. Implementing new routes entails confronting several problems and farmers have to be involved so as to get their approval for the new routes.

example, if the schedule is for a Wednesday delivery, the dealer is expected to place the order by lunch time on Tuesday. Static methods are easy to work with and work very well when demand is uniform and stable. So in the cases of Amul Dairy and auto companies, supply is expected to be uniform and stable, so static schedules work very well.

On the distribution side, several firms face demands that are skewed towards the month-end. In such a situation, vehicles will be running empty during the first three weeks and in the last week the firms will have to hire extra vehicles. In a dynamic system, schedules are formed on the basis of actual orders placed by dealers. Since the order-arrival pattern will vary from time to time, schedules will also keep changing from time to time. Generating manual dynamic schedules may be difficult, but with computerized vehicle-scheduling packages, we can generate dynamic schedules without too much effort. Usually, a vehicle is scheduled only when the aggregated order is enough to take care of the vehicle capacity. But this will result in variability in order-delivery time and a dealer will not be sure when exactly the service will be obtained. To get around this problem, some firms offer a time limit within which the service will be provided. A firm might say that service will be provided within four working days so that it can balance customer service and transport efficiencies. In general, while deciding on vehicle scheduling strategy, a firm has to arrive at a trade-off between simplicity of operations and efficiency of vehicle utilization. Of course, larger firms with high volume of operations will be in a better position to ensure quick and reliable service without compromising on transportation efficiencies.

## Transportation Costs in E-Retailing

The Internet has given rise to a new set of retailers called the e-retailers, who provide the convenience of shopping from home. Customers do not have to travel and spend time in searching for goods in the neighbourhood stores. Instead of the customer coming to your store, if you can deliver products at the customers' doorstep, you do not have to invest in costly real estate and expensive sales people. Further, as discussed in the chapter on inventory management, an e-retailer will be able to hold inventory at a central location and as a result will get the advantage of pooling and will also be in a position to work with relatively lower inventory, as compared to a brick-and-mortar store. However, delivering small shipments at the customer's doorstep increases transportation costs significantly. Last-mile transportation involved in door delivery is quite expensive in general, and it can play a decisive role in the profitability of e-retailing if transportation costs are a significant part of product costs.

In this section, we examine the shipping charges of e-retailers. We analyse the consequences of the kind of product and cost of shipping on the performance of the e-retailer. We end with a brief discussion of prominent success stories and failures in this sector.

### *Shipping Charges by E-Retailers*

Let us first look at how shipping services are being charged by e-retailers. E-retailers have experimented with various options, and to understand the issues involved, see Table 5.10 for data on charges used by Amazon.com for shipping fees charged by Amazon when buying items from a seller on the Amazon.com. As one can expect, shipping charges consist of a fixed component and a variable component. For items such as books, DVDs and clothing, which are reasonably homogenous in terms of physical characteristics, there are no fixed charges and the shipping charges are based on the number of items ordered, whereas for computers, electronic items, and office products, where physical characteristics like volume and weight vary across items, the shipping charges depend on the weight of the items. Both the fixed component and the variable component increase steeply if the customer wants faster service.

*Table 5.10:* **Shipment charges (in $) at Amazon.com for products to be delivered within the United States of America.**

| Type of product | Standard shipping (4–14 days) | | Expedited shipping (2–6 days) | | Two-day shipping | | One-day shipping | |
|---|---|---|---|---|---|---|---|---|
| | Per shipment | Per Item | Per shipment | Per Item | Per shipment | Per Item | Per shipment | Per item |
| Books | — | 3.99 | — | 6.99 | — | 14.99 | — | 19.99 |
| CDs and DVDs | — | 3.99 | — | 6.99 | — | 14.99 | — | 19.99 |
| Computers and electronics | 4.49 | 0.50/lb | 6.49 | 0.99/lb | Not Available | | Not Available | |
| Office products | 4.49 | 0.590/lb | 8.99 | 0.99/lb | Not Available | | Not Available | |

*Source:* http://www.amazon.com/gp/help/customer/display.html?nodeId=537734 as on 16/05/2015

Interestingly, e-retailers in India currently have been working with relatively simpler structure of shipping charges. As can be seen in Table 5.11, delivery charges vary based on delivery time and shipping is free for any order value which exceeds Rs. 500. In the past, several retailers used to charge shipping charge based on value. For example, Firstandsecond.com, an Indian e-retailer of books, used to charge 7 per cent of the order value or Rs. 30, whichever was higher, for standard shipping of order value of less than Rs. 5,000 and for order value above Rs. 5,000, incremental shipping rates were charged at 3 per cent of the order value. At rediff.com, the shipping charges were Rs. 30.00 or 10 per cent of the order value, whichever was higher, with the maximum shipping charge not exceeding Rs. 50.

*Table 5.11:* **Shipment charges (in Rs.) at Amazon.com in India.**

| Delivery time | Charges per order |
|---|---|
| **Guaranteed** Same-Day Delivery | 149 |
| **Guaranteed** One-Day Delivery | 99 |
| **Guaranteed** Two-Day Delivery | 79 |
| **2–4, 4–7**, and **7–10** Business days | 49 FREE for orders above 499 |

## Impact of Transport Cost on Business Performance of E-Retailers

To understand the importance of transportation cost for e-retailers, we will look at three different product categories from diverse industries, which have received a lot of attention from researchers as well as practitioners who have been studying successes and failures in e-retailing. We look at electronics (Dell Computers sells computers through the Internet);books (Amazon.com, started its business in US with books, similarly Flipkart in India started its business with book category); and Grocery (Internationally Tesco has been successfully selling grocery via net Several corporates including Tata group are planning to start selling grocery on net from 2015).

### Impact of Value-density on Transport Cost of E-Retailers

To understand the importance of transportation cost for different industries, we look at shipping charge as a proxy for transportation cost. We look at one typical shipment from for each of the three product categories that we want to analyse. For electronics we look at the shipment of one laptop, for book category we look at the shipment of three books and for grocery we

*Table 5.12:* ***Importance of transportation cost for different companies in e-retailing.***

| | Average price (in Rs./unit) | Average weight (in kg./unit) | Value density (in Rs./kg) | Shipment (in units) | Shipment in value (Rs.) | Transport cost* per shipment | Shipping cost as percentage of price |
|---|---|---|---|---|---|---|---|
| Laptop | 30,000 | 3.0 | 10,000 | 1 laptop | 30,000 | 150 | 0.5 |
| Book | 400 | 0.5 | 800 | 3 books | 1,200 | 96 | 8.0 |
| Grocery | 100** | 1.0 | 100 | 10 kg | 1,000 | 422 | 42.2 |

*Transportation cost is calculated using data taken from Indian post website for parcel services for a neighbourhood state. http://www.indiapost.gov.in/expressparcel.aspx

**For grocery units 1 kg.

look at the shipment of ten kilograms of groceries. See Table 5.12 to see the importance of transportation cost likely to be incurred by e-retailers for the three typical shipments. In Table 5.12, we also compare the value-density of the three products.

As can be inferred from Table 5.12, the value-density for a laptop is quite high, so the transportation cost is an almost insignificant component for Dell Computers. But the transportation cost accounts for 8 per cent of the order value for book category for Amazon.com/Flipkart and 42.2 per cent for Webvan for grocery category. Of course, with bigger shipment sizes, shipping cost decreases because of the fixed shipping charges charged by e-retailers. In general, e-retailers prefer shoppers to place larger orders so that they can take advantage of economies of scale in transportation. E-retailers have been offering incentives of reduced shipping charges for high-value orders. For example, Flipkart Webvan used to offer free shipping for all orders above $50 and similarly Flipkart offers free shipping for order size above Rs. 500.

Let us compare the advantages obtained through inventory centralization against the increased costs involved in transportation for the three above-mentioned product categories. The advantages of centralization are significantly high for products like laptops where the demand-uncertainty is high and moderate for companies like book where the demand-uncertainty is of a moderate kind. Since the demand uncertainty is quite low for grocery, the benefit of centralization is quite low for e-retailers like Tesco So retailing on the Web is likely to be extremely beneficial only for firms that have high product-variety, high value-density and high demand-uncertainty. For firms in grocery retailing, where value-density is low and demand-uncertainty is low, e-retailing is going to be a difficult business. The largest e-retailer in the grocery industry Webvan had to declare bankruptcy in 2001.

In our discussion, we have not looked at issues of product return. Managing product return is more difficult in the e-retailing business, and as per available empirical data, the extent of product return is much higher for e-retailers as compared to the brick-and-mortar stores. For Indian retailers there is additional cost of offering cash on delivery (COD) which incrses cost further.

To summarize, transportation-related decisions play an extremely important role for e-retailers and because of the high cost involved in last-mile transportation to customers' homes, retailing on the Web is likely to be extremely beneficial only for firms that have high product variety, high value-density and high demand-uncertainty.

## Importance of Transport Costs for Amazon.com

If one looks at the history of Amazon.com, one understands the importance of transportation costs for such a firm. Amazon.com started with one warehouse and over a period time has invested in many warehouses spread across the United States of America so that they can reduce their transportation costs. By 2015, Amazon had 68 warehouses with about 50 million square foot space in the United States of America and 61 warehouses with 35 million square foot space in other parts of the world. Because of the highly competitive environment, Amazon.com is not able to fully recover shipping costs from their customers. In the 2013 financial year, the shipping revenue alone accounted for about $3.1 billion against the outbound

*Table 5.13:* **Trend in Net Shipping cost at Amazon.**

| | 2013 | 2012 | 2011 | 2010 | 2009 | 2008 | 2007 | 2006 |
|---|---|---|---|---|---|---|---|---|
| Net Sales | 74,452 | 61,093 | 48,077 | 34,204 | 24,509 | 19,166 | 14,835 | 10,711 |
| Income from Ops | 745 | 676 | 862 | 1406 | 1129 | 842 | 655 | 389 |
| Shipping Revenue | 3097 | 2280 | 1552 | 1193 | 924 | 835 | 740 | 567 |
| Shipping Cost | 6635 | 5134 | 3989 | 2579 | 1773 | 1500 | 1200 | 884 |
| Net shipping cost/Net Sales | 4.8% | 4.7% | 5.1% | 4.1% | 3.5% | 3.5% | 3.1% | 3.0% |

shipping cost of $6.6 billion incurred by the firm. Given that the net profit earned by Amazon. com was $745 million on net sales of $ 75 billion in the same year, managing transportation costs is extremely crucial for the firm. Refer table 5.13 for trend in % net shipping cost over last several years. Interesting net shipping cost as percentage of net sales increased from 3.0% in 2006 to 5.1% in 2011 since than Amazon has managed to reduce that number to 4.8%.

## Grocery on the Internet: Experience of Webvan and Tesco

Webvan was launched in June 1999. It wanted to revolutionize the supermarket industry by taking customers' orders online and delivering groceries to their doorsteps—a concept that helped the company raise about $800 million from venture capitalists. Webvan started with the notion that it will have to create a new type of logistics operations to achieve its objectives. Hence, it decided to build highly automated, state-of-the-art, 330,000 square foot warehouses or hubs at the cost of $30 million each. It was planning to build 26 such warehouses at the cost of $1 billion over a period of time. The company implemented a hub-and-spoke system of distribution. Containers with customer orders used to be transferred from a hub to 10 stations located within 50 miles of the distribution hub. At each station, containers with orders were transferred to smaller temperature-controlled vans and delivered to consumers' homes within a 30-minute window of their choosing.

The Webvan management believed that this process will be extremely efficient and hoped that they will be able to offer lower prices. The firm was expected to show an operating margin of 12 per cent when run at the designed capacity, compared to the grocery industry's norm of four per cent. Unfortunately for Webvan, most of its assumptions went wrong. After just two years of its launch, its hub was operating at less than 20 per cent of its designed capacity of 8,000 orders per day. The company made huge losses and declared bankruptcy in July 2001. During the initial days it had created a major hype and at one point in time it had a market capitalization of $16 billion. Now, Webvan is known as one of the most spectacular failures of the dotcom economy.

Unlike Webvan, supermarket giant Tesco decided to put small bets on the Internet for its grocery business. At the initial stage of its e-business experiment, Tesco decided that it will not invest in dedicated warehouses for e-business till it had a better sense of the online consumer demand. It decided to supply customer orders from its existing infrastructure at the initial stages. Thus, in the beginning, the company did not offer home delivery and customers were expected to pick-up their packaged orders from the nearby stores. Based on orders received on the Web, Tesco pre-packaged the orders so that customers did not waste any time when they come for pickup. The company kept experimenting with the sales and delivery process over a period of time. After two years of operations on the Web, Tesco started offering home-delivery for Web orders in areas that were located geographically close to its physical stores. From the beginning the company imposed a delivery charge for home delivery service. This approach helped Tesco in recovering part of its delivery costs and also ensured that the customers did not place small orders that are not likely to be economical for Tesco Over a period of time Tesco has complemented its in-store picking model by a small number of specialised dotcom-only stores. Tesco.com is the largest and most profitable grocery retailer on the Internet.

## Summary

- There are strong economies of distance and economies of scale in the transport industry.
- Value-density and demand characteristics of the product strongly influence transportation decisions and therefore, are vital for supply chain managers. A poor understanding of transportation cost drivers can have serious business implications for firms.
- Firms insisting on FTL shipments may get transportation efficiencies but might end with an overall increase in cost because of increased level of inventories. Transportation decisions should not be looked at in isolation.
- Innovative ideas like milk run and cross-docking help firms in managing frequent delivery from suppliers without sacrificing transportation efficiencies.
- Transportation cost has become quite a serious issue in the last few years because fuel prices have shot up considerably and LTL supplies can add significant costs to firms.
- Transportation decisions play an extremely important role for e-retailers. Because of the high costs involved in last-mile transportation to customers' homes, retailing on the Web is likely to be extremely beneficial only for firms that have high product-variety, high value-density and high demand uncertainty.
- Progressive firms like Wal-Mart and Tesco have paid a lot of attention to their transportation strategy and use a mix and match of all the transportation strategies discussed in this section.

## Discussion Questions

1. What transportation challenges do e-retailers like Amazon.com (www.amazon.in/) face? Visit Websites of the following e-retailers: eBay (www.ebay.in/), Flipkart.com (www.flipkart.com/) and Snapdeal.com (www.snapdeal.com/). Compare and contrast the shipping rates policy employed by various Indian e-retailers.
2. What are the main drivers of trucking rate structures?
3. A firm wants to design incentive systems for its transport contractor so as to improve transport lead-time reliability. To design this system they want to quantify the benefits of transport lead-time reliability. Suggest a suitable approach for this quantification exercise.
4. Compare and contrast issues involved in vehicle routing in the following four applications:
    - Milk collection for a dairy co-operative
    - Courier company
    - Employee pick-up for a software service company
    - Product delivery to retailers by a soft-drink company (the van is also expected to pick-up the empty glass bottles)
5. How do transport companies benefit from a technology like global positioning system (GPS)? With the help of GPS, can transport companies track their trucks on a real-time basis?
6. What are the benefits of cross-docking? What are the difficulties in implementing cross-docking?
7. There is a concern that crude prices might touch 150$ per barrel and high transport costs for the US market might drive away some of the manufacturing industry located in China and India to Mexico. For what category of products will this have the greatest impact?
8. Indian Railways has a common pool of marketing officers who service all its clients, and it wants to explore the idea of creating a few industry verticals within marketing. It wants to create specific industry verticals only for those industries that will have significant business potential.
    - Identifying a few strategic industries where Indian Railways has high business potential, suggest a methodology that can help the railways in identifying the right industry verticals.
    - Will a firm like FedEx target similar verticals or should they look for a different set of verticals? Suggest two industries that will be good from FedEx's point of view.

## Exercises

1. Tata Motors procures components from three suppliers located in Chennai. Components purchased from supplier A are priced at Rs 250 each and used at the rate of 20,000 units per month. Components purchased from supplier B are priced at Rs 500 each and used at the rate of 2,500 units per month. Components purchased from supplier C are priced at Rs 1,000 each and used at the rate of 1,000 units per month. Currently, Tata Motors purchases the components separately (transport them separately in individual trucks). As part of their just-in-time (JIT) drive, Tata Motors wants to get more frequent supplies from these suppliers and has decided to share a truck for the three suppliers from Chennai. The trucking company charges a fixed cost of Rs 15,000 for each truck trip with an additional charge of Rs 3,000 per stop. So, if Tata asks the trucking company to pick material from one supplier, the trucking company will charge Rs 18,000 per trip and charge Rs 21,000 if asked to pick material from two suppliers in each trip and so on.
   - Compare the two policies (sharing truck and not sharing truck). Assume that Tata Motors incurs a holding cost of 20 per cent per year and that there are no capacity constraints on the truck trips.
   - Tata Motors has decided to implement JIT manufacturing in its true spirit and prefers to get one truck every day with just the required number of components. What are the additional costs of JIT implementation? What should be the cost of each trip to make the daily trip an optimal decision? Assume that Tata Motors operates for 25 days a month.

2. A company is examining two choices for moving its goods from the plant to its depot in eastern India: truck and rail. The relevant information are as follows:

| Transport mode | Transport lead time (days) | Rate (Rs/unit) | Shipment size (units) |
|---|---|---|---|
| Rail | 12 | 20 | 5,000 |
| Road | 4 | 30 | 500 |

   The company is planning to ship 20,000 units per year. The cost of the product is Rs 500 per unit. Assume the inventory-carrying cost to be 20 per cent.
   - Which mode of transport should the company choose?
   - Will your answer change if you realize that the time shown above are average times and that actually time will follow a normal distribution with a standard deviation of 4 days.

3. Design the vehicle route for a consumer goods company that has 10 dealers. The capacity of the vehicle is 25 units and other relevant data are as follows:

***Distance- and load-related data for a consumer goods company.***

| Dealer | 1 | 2 | 3 | 4 | 5 | 6 | 7 | 8 | 9 | 10 |
|---|---|---|---|---|---|---|---|---|---|---|
| Distance from depot | 16 | 18 | 10 | 17 | 26 | 18 | 7 | 12 | 15 | 21 |
| Average demand (tons) | 8 | 4 | 6 | 6 | 4 | 8 | 8 | 6 | 8 | 4 |

***Distance matrix in kilometres.***

| | 1 | 2 | 3 | 4 | 5 | 6 | 7 | 8 | 9 | 10 |
|---|---|---|---|---|---|---|---|---|---|---|
| 1 | | | | | | | | | | |
| 2 | 34 | | | | | | | | | |
| 3 | 7 | 27 | | | | | | | | |
| 4 | 33 | 12 | 27 | | | | | | | |
| 5 | 41 | 8 | 35 | 19 | | | | | | |
| 6 | 31 | 13 | 24 | 23 | 14 | | | | | |
| 7 | 19 | 20 | 14 | 15 | 28 | 24 | | | | |
| 8 | 24 | 20 | 19 | 12 | 28 | 27 | 6 | | | |
| 9 | 12 | 32 | 12 | 26 | 40 | 33 | 12 | 15 | | |
| 10 | 32 | 23 | 28 | 12 | 31 | 33 | 15 | 9 | 22 | |

   - Apart from capacity constraints, how will your answer change if we put an additional constraint saying that route length should not exceed 45 km?

4. A company is examining two alternative choices for moving goods from its plant in Thane to its depot in Chennai. It has been traditionally shipping goods in the FTL mode so as to save transportation costs. Its finance department has been complaining about high inventories at Chennai. A full truck load results in a shipment size of 160 units, while LTL shipments allow the firm to get lots of 40 units each. The average demand at the Chennai depot is 80 units per month. The cost of the product is Rs 500 per unit and the firm works with an inventory-carrying cost of 20 per cent. Shipping through the FTL mode results in a transport cost of Rs 40 per unit, while the LTL mode shipment results in a transport cost of Rs 50 per unit.
   - Should the company shift to LTL shipments?
   - The firm realizes that LTL shipments result in damages of 1 per cent of the goods shipped. How will this information affect the decision?
   - Currently, the firm is going through serious working capital problems and the finance department has informed marketing that inventory will be charged at an inventory-carrying cost of 30 per cent. How will this affect the transportation mode decision?

## Notes


1. G. Raghuram, "Turnaround of Indian Railways: A Critical Appraisal," Working Paper, IIM Ahmedabad, 2007.
2. M. Allirajan, "Textile: Cushion and Comfort," *Business World* (June 2007).
3. J. Shah, "Vehicle Routing for Milk Procurement," *IIMB Management Review* (December 2000): 72–74.


## Further Reading


D. O. Bausch, G. G. Brown, and D. Ronen, "Consolidation and Dispatching Truck Shipments of Mobil Heavy Petroleum Products," *Interfaces* (1995, Vol 25): 1–17.

J. B. Fuller, J. O'Connor, and R. Rawlinson, "Tailored Logistics: The Next Advantage," *Harvard Business Review* (May–June 1993): 87–98.

J. F. Robeson and W. C. Copacino, eds. *The Logistics Handbook* (New York: Free Press, 1994).

J. Shah, "Vehicle Routing for Milk Procurement," *IIMB Management Review* (December 2000, Vol 12): 72–74.

Lovell Antony, Richard Saw, and Jennifer Stimson, "Product Value-Density: Managing Diversity Through Supply Chain Segmentation," *The International Journal of Logistics Management* (2005, Vol 16): 142–158.

R. H. Ballou, *Business Logistics Management* (Upper Saddle River, NJ: Prentice Hall, 1999).

R. Henkoff, "Delivering the Goods," *Fortune* (November 1994): 64–78.

Roy D. Shapiro, "Get leverage from Logistics," *Harvard Business Review* (May–June 1984): 119–127.

# Network Design and Operations: Facility Location

## Learning Objectives

After reading this chapter, you will be able to answer the following questions:

> What is role of network design and operations in supply chain management?

> What are the key factors that drive network design decisions? How do firms make optimal network design decisions?

> How do firms make optimum supply chain operations planning decisions?

> What are the different types of roles that a facility can play within a supply chain network?

> In what way do network design decisions for the service sector differ from those of product businesses?

Reliance Retail,[1] the retail mega vision of Mukesh Ambani, started operations in the third quarter of 2006. When the first store was launched, Arvind Singhal, head of retail consultancy Technopak, remarked, "Nowhere in the world has a project started on such a grand scale—it has taken just 15 months from planning to execution." However, before the retail operations were executed, a detailed blueprint for the entire operation was drawn up. Reliance Retail invested approximately Rs 300 billion in all, of which Rs 80 billion was earmarked for the supply chain network only. Fully aware of the fact that the success of a retail chain hinges on the efficiency of the supply chain network, Reliance Retail planned out its supply chain network meticulously.

Reliance plans to set up an integrated supply chain infrastructure, including a cold chain for frozen food. Currently, seven large wholesale terminals serve the entire retail chain. Eventually, RIL plans to set up over 150 distribution centres across the country to supply the retail chain. Reliance is also working on an exclusive contract-farming project in a few states, whereby it will procure the farm produce directly from the farmer. Reliance hopes that this system will enable it to offer products at low prices to the end customer and reduce wastage, which currently ranges from 30 to 40 per cent within the chain.

Reliance hopes that the supply chain network will become a key differentiator for the firm in the coming years. Reliance has taken into consideration the fact that network design decisions are strategic decisions that have long-term implications which are not easy to reverse.

Where to locate the plants and warehouses is an important strategic network design decision. A supply chain is essentially a network consisting of nodes and linkages, and in this chapter, we focus on strategic and tactical decisions regarding network design and operations. Network design focuses on the location of nodes for plants and storage points, for given customer nodes and network operations focus on identifying the optimal linkages between plants and markets.

## Introduction

Network design consists of decisions regarding the location of plants, suppliers and distribution centres so as to serve customers in a cost-effective way. Among the several elements of supply chain decisions, network design plays a crucial role and has significant implications on supply chain performance. Most global firms work with multiple plants and operate in multiple markets. The most important tactical issues that firms have to resolve include allocation of volumes to plants and allocation of plants to markets. Where to locate the plants is an important strategic network design decision. A supply chain is essentially a network consisting of nodes and linkages. Nodes represent conversion or storage points or demand points, and linkages represent transportation activities through which material flow takes place in the chain. Network design focuses on the location of nodes for plants and storage points for given customer nodes, and network operations focus on identifying the optimal linkages between plants and markets.

Sometimes, firms end up making long-term decisions on the basis of short-run considerations. Firms tend to focus on near-term issues and sometimes forget that the selected action is bound to have long-term strategic implications. When Tata decides to locate its small car factory in West Bengal, it has to live with that decision for a considerable point in time. Unlike other decisions, a network design decision is strategic in nature and has long-term implications and is not easy to reverse.

We start our discussion by focusing on network operations planning and subsequently look at network design decisions. Any change in the external or internal environment may force a firm to question the existing network, and redesigning may include the closure of some existing facilities or the starting of new facilities at a new site.

## Network Operations Planning

Decisions pertaining to operations planning are tactical in nature. When taking a decision on operations planning, the firm not only has to ensure establishing appropriate links between the various entities in the chain, but also has to consider many other related issues. A firm with a multi-plant network has to decide which suppliers should be linked to which plants, which plants should be linked to which warehouses, and which warehouses should be linked to which markets. The firm also has to decide the appropriate activity levels at each plant—that is, how much to produce at each of the plants.

Let us take the example of a global firm like Dell Computers, which manufactures its computer systems in seven locations around the world: Austin, Texas; Nashville, Tennessee; Winston-Salem, North Carolina; Eldorado do Sul, Brazil; Limerick, Ireland; Penang, Malaysia and Xiamen, China. Computer markets are dynamic in nature; demand across the globe keeps fluctuating. Hence, optimal service of the global market, using its seven facilities, is a complex planning operations decision that Dell has to make every quarter. Grasim, an Aditya Birla Group company, manages its cement business with seven facilities and faces similar problems.

We start by examining the relevant costs for network decisions. We proceed to scrutinize the two available approaches for the optimization of network operations.

### *Relevant Costs for Network Decisions*

Three types of costs are important for network design and operations-related decisions: fixed facility costs, variable production costs and transportation costs. Facility costs are fixed in nature and do not depend on the volume of production and storage. So, for tactical decisions like network operations planning, fixed facility costs will be incurred irrespective of the allocation

**Figure 6.1**

Location of plants and markets.

decision and hence are not relevant for decision making. If the supply chain production consists of multiple stages, then production costs will include costs involved in conversion as well as in transportation from a downstream stage to the upstream stage.

Let us look at the case of a hypothetical company called Indian Paints, a paint manufacturing firm, which has four manufacturing plants located at Ahmedabad, Hubli, Nagpur and Vishakapatnam. The firm has recently added one more plant at Baddi in Himachal Pradesh because of the attractive tax concessions available there. The firm primarily operates in six major markets. The geographical positioning of all the plants and markets is presented in Figure 6.1. The marketing group prepares market estimates every quarter and expects the supply chain to plan its operations so that the firm can deliver its products to all six markets at the lowest possible cost. Keeping in view the capacity constraints of each plant and the existing cost structure, the supply chain group has to decide the volume of produce at each plant and allocate market demands to plants. Table 6.1 presents the relevant data.

From Table 6.1, we can calculate that the firm faces a total demand of 1,060 units and has a capacity of 1,500 units; now with one more plant at Baddi, its capacity has gone up to 1,900 units.

***Table 6.1(a): Plant data.***

| Plant | Capacity | Fixed facility cost | Unit variable production cost |
|---|---|---|---|
| Ahmedabad | 350 | 78,000 | 675 |
| Baddi | 400 | 42,000 | 525 |
| Hubli | 450 | 36,000 | 650 |
| Nagpur | 300 | 38,000 | 625 |
| Vishakapatnam | 400 | 34,000 | 675 |

***Table 6.1(b): Market data.***

| Market | Bangalore | Chennai | Delhi | Mumbai | Lucknow | Kolkata |
|---|---|---|---|---|---|---|
| Quarterly demand | 165 | 135 | 280 | 200 | 125 | 155 |
| Price per unit | 1,030 | 950 | 1,000 | 975 | 900 | 850 |

*Table 6.1(c):* ***Transportation cost matrix.***

| | Bangalore | Chennai | Delhi | Mumbai | Lucknow | Kolkata |
|---|---|---|---|---|---|---|
| Ahmedabad | 235 | 278 | 100 | 65 | 189 | 261 |
| Baddi | 511 | 558 | 97 | 328 | 216 | 305 |
| Hubli | 77 | 138 | 327 | 105 | 372 | 326 |
| Nagpur | 165 | 160 | 183 | 117 | 148 | 235 |
| Vishakapatnam | 163 | 107 | 328 | 217 | 303 | 203 |

## Network Operations Optimization: Cost Minimization Model

Given a fixed network design, it is possible to plan and execute network operations in such a manner so as to minimize the cost. This is achieved primarily by solving the demand allocation problem.

The demand allocation problem can be modelled as a linear programming problem and solved using standard linear programming packages. The general network operations planning problem can be formulated as follows:

$M$ = Number of plants; let $i = 1, \ldots, m$ describe $m$ respective manufacturing plants
$N$ = Number of markets; let $j = 1, \ldots, n$ describe $n$ respective markets
$Dem_j$ = quarterly demand at market $j$
$Cap_i$ = quarterly production capacity at plant $i$
$Cost_{ij}$ = Cost of producing and transporting one unit from plant $i$ to market $j$
$Fcost_i$ = Fixed cost of facility $i$

From the production and transportation data in Table 6.1, one can calculate the per unit production and transportation cost, shown in Table 6.2.

Given this cost structure, the firm has to allocate the demand from different markets to various plants. Let $Quant_{ij}$ = Quantity shipped from plant $i$ to market $j$ every quarter.

Since the firm likes to minimize the total cost, its objective function will be

$$\text{Minimize } \sum_{i=1}^{m}\sum_{j=1}^{n} Cost_{ij} \times Quant_{ij}$$

Subject to following constraints:

$$\sum_{i=1}^{m} Quant_{ij} = Dem_j \quad \text{for } j = 1, \ldots, n \tag{6.1}$$

$$\sum_{j=1}^{n} Quant_{ij} \le Cap_i \quad \text{for } j = 1, \ldots, m \tag{6.2}$$

$$Quant_{ij} \ge 0 \quad \text{for } j = 1, \ldots, m,\ j = 1, \ldots, n. \tag{6.3}$$

The constraints in Equation 6.1 ensure that demand at each of the market place is satisfied. Constraints in Equation 6.2 ensure that production at each factory does not violate the capacity constraint at the plants. Constraints in Equation 6.3 ensure that supply will always be non-negative.

*Table 6.2:* ***Production plus transportation cost per unit.***

| | Bangalore | Chennai | Delhi | Mumbai | Lucknow | Kolkata |
|---|---|---|---|---|---|---|
| Ahmedabad | 910 | 953 | 775 | 740 | 864 | 936 |
| Baddi | 1,036 | 1,083 | 622 | 853 | 741 | 830 |
| Hubli | 727 | 788 | 977 | 755 | 1,022 | 976 |
| Nagpur | 790 | 785 | 808 | 742 | 773 | 860 |
| Vishakapatnam | 838 | 782 | 1,003 | 892 | 978 | 878 |

Of course, it is assumed that the aggregate capacity of the plants is more than the aggregate demand at all markets—otherwise the above constraints cannot be satisfied. This is a linear programming problem with the number of variables, $n \times m$, and the number of constraints equal to $n + m$ (not counting the non-negativity constraints in Equation 6.3). A simple linear programming software called Solver is available in MS Excel where linear programming problems can be modelled and solved easily from data kept in the Excel form. We have to define one cell for objective function, one cell for the right-hand side and another cell for the left-hand side of the constraint. (See Appendix A for details on how the above linear programming model can be formulated and solved in Excel.) In the Indian Paints example, we have five plants and six markets, so we have a linear programming problem with 30 variables and 11 constraints. Solver or any other linear programming software can handle problems of much larger size without any difficulty. Optimal allocation for Indian Paints from Excel Solver is shown in Table 6.3.

The allocation in Table 6.3 will result in the following financial performance for Indian Paints:

Revenue = 1,017,450
Variable cost = 773,770
Gross profit (revenue – variable cost) = 1,017,450 – 773,770 = 243,680
Net profit = Gross profit – Fixed cost = 243,680 – 228,000 = 15,680

While planning network operations, it is assumed that all the markets must be served, so we have worked with the constraint that supply is equal to demand (see Equation 6.1). It assumes that the marketing department has made necessary plans and that the supply chain is expected to fulfil the demand at each of the markets as specified by the marketing function. Now it is possible that some of the markets may not be profitable. Even in firms where the marketing department focuses on profits and not just revenues, they usually work with average cost of supply number and not specific cost of supply to individual markets and customers. Indian Paints incurs a cost of Rs 773,770 to deliver 1,060 units, so the average cost per unit of supply works out to be Rs 739.4, which is lower than the price realized in each of the markets. Even if marketing function had access to all the cost data, and not just average cost data, there is not going to be much concern because even a market like Kolkata, which has the lowest price realization per unit, can be served profitably from the Baddi plant, against a price realization of Rs 850. The cost of serving Kolkata market from Baddi is Rs 830. So the marketing department will make plans believing that it is worthwhile serving all markets. Unfortunately, this way of looking at each market and plant individually is not correct. In a complex network, it is not easy to figure out the cost of supply to any specific customer or market because each source of supply may have multiple opportunities and hence it is not the actual cost of supply but the opportunity cost of supply that is more important.

Progressive firms try and understand the inter-connectedness of relevant decisions. Instead of operating in silo, where marketing executives make their plans looking at the revenue target and ask the supply chain people to execute the plan with the least cost, a firm can make integrated plans so as to optimize performance. If marketing and supply chain departments decide

***Table 6.3:* Network operations: optimal allocation with minimum cost as objective.**

| | Bangalore | Chennai | Delhi | Mumbai | Lucknow | Kolkata | Supply |
|---|---|---|---|---|---|---|---|
| Ahmedabad | 0 | 0 | 0 | 200 | 0 | 0 | 200 |
| Baddi | 0 | 0 | 280 | 0 | 120 | 0 | 400 |
| Hubli | 165 | 0 | 0 | 0 | 0 | 0 | 165 |
| Nagpur | 0 | 0 | 0 | 0 | 5 | 155 | 160 |
| Vishakapatnam | 0 | 135 | 0 | 0 | 0 | 0 | 135 |
| Demand met | 165 | 135 | 280 | 200 | 125 | 155 | 1,060 |

Objective function value = Total variable costs = 773,770.

to work jointly, it will be more sensible to solve the joint problem as a profit maximization issue; rather than serving all markets, the decision maker should be given the flexibility to serve only those markets that are profitable.

## Network Operations Optimization: Profit Maximization Model

So instead of cost minimization, a firm might solve the profit maximization problem, where the objective function includes a term for revenue, which is obtained by multiplying the volume of shipment to markets with their respective price. As fixed costs are not relevant for the decision, profit maximization is equivalent to the gross profit (revenue – variable cost) maximization problem.

The objective function is

$$\text{Maximize} \sum_{i=1}^{m}\sum_{j=1}^{n} Price_j \times Quant_{ij} - \sum_{i=1}^{m}\sum_{j=1}^{n} Cost_{ij} \times Quant_{ij}$$

$$\sum_{i=1}^{m} Quant_{ij} \leq Dem_j \text{ for } j = 1,\ldots,n \tag{6.4}$$

$$\sum_{j=1}^{n} Quant_{ij} \leq Cap_i \text{ for } i = 1,\ldots,m \tag{6.5}$$

$$Quant_{ij} \geq 0 \text{ for } i = 1,\ldots,m,\ j = 1,\ldots,n \tag{6.6}$$

The demand specified by the marketing department becomes the upper bound; that is, you cannot supply more than the volume specified by marketing group. If the market is not profitable or if the company has supply problems, company may decide not to serve that market. Constraint 6.1 will therefore be modified and the equality constraint will be changed to less than the equal constraint as shown in Equation 6.4.

The optimal allocation for Indian Paints from Excel Solver is shown in Table 6.4.

The allocation in Table 6.4 will result in following financial performance for Indian Paints:

Revenue = 885,700; Variable cost = 640,470
Gross profit (revenue – variable cost) = 885,700 – 640,470 = 245,230
Net profit = Gross profit – Fixed cost = 245,230 – 228,000 = 17,230

As we can see from the Solver output shown in Table 6.4, it is not profitable for Indian Paints to serve the Kolkata market. So even though the firm has a lower top line, it has higher profits and the profit has increased by almost 10 per cent. At first glance this will be counterintuitive. As one can see, it is more profitable for Baddi to supply to other markets, and forcing Baddi to supply to Kolkata will lower the profitability for the firm. In general, it is not straightforward to understand the profitability of individual markets. In Appendix A, we discuss the concept of shadow price, which can help firms in understanding the profitability of various markets.

**Table 6.4: Network operations: optimal allocation with maximum profit as objective.**

| | Bangalore | Chennai | Delhi | Mumbai | Lucknow | Kolkata | Supply |
|---|---|---|---|---|---|---|---|
| Ahmedabad | 0 | 0 | 0 | 200 | 0 | 0 | 200 |
| Baddi | 0 | 0 | 280 | 0 | 120 | 0 | 400 |
| Hubli | 165 | 0 | 0 | 0 | 0 | 0 | 165 |
| Nagpur | 0 | 0 | 0 | 0 | 5 | 0 | 5 |
| Vishakapatnam | 0 | 135 | 0 | 0 | 0 | 0 | 135 |
| Demand net | 165 | 135 | 280 | 200 | 125 | 0 | 905 |

Objective function = maximize total gross profit = 245,230.

For optimization of network operations, the firm has to ensure that all decisions made are in line with the firm's long-term strategy. Therefore, firms have to take into account other factors that may not appear to be immediately relevant. Some factors that firms take into consideration are discussed herewith.

### Handling New Markets

Often, a firm may like to serve a market even if it is not profitable, because it has been identified as a strategic market. Many global companies do not make profit in new markets in the initial years, but make a strategic decision to serve those markets for some years, willing to sustain losses. For example, Kelloggs, a cereal manufacturer, identified Japan as a strategic market and incurred losses during the first 10 years of operations. Similarly, it is incurring losses in the Indian market at present, but is continuing operations from a long-term strategic perspective. Thus, a company's structure and business strategy makes a difference in the way it models and handles network operations planning issues.

### Impact of Allocation Decision on Individual Plant Performance

In the above example, the assumption was that we are only interested in optimizing overall network performance and are not worried about its impact on the individual plant's performance. First, how does one determine the performance of each of these five plants? Each plant can be treated as a profit centre by allocating a transfer price to the plant, based on the price realized in the market that has been allocated to the plant. To understand the impact of such a scheme on different plants in the network, let us take the example of the Nagpur plant. If such a scheme is implemented, Nagpur will prefer to get an allocation from Mumbai because Mumbai has better price, and no plant manager likes to get allocated markets like Lucknow and Kolkata, which have lower price realizations. To avoid this problem, the firm may decide to work with transfer price, which is nothing but the weighted average price realized by the network. The unit transfer price will be determined by first deducting the total transport cost from the total revenue and subsequently the same will be divided by the total volume. This means that all plants will have the same unit transfer price, which will not be based on specific markets allocated to individual plants. Even with uniform transfer price, a plant like the one in Nagpur will show huge losses because it will not be able to cover its fixed cost due to the relatively lower volume of allocation made to it. Since the Nagpur plant is allocated only five units, it will show losses as far as financial performance is concerned. So even though Nagpur has the second lowest production cost (Baddi has the lowest production cost), it gets very low volume, which results in poor performance; hence, it is quite likely that the Nagpur plant manager will get a lower bonus compared to other plant managers. The only solution is to treat plants as cost centres rather than as profit centres. In that case, firms will try to optimize the overall network performance and each plant will take responsibility for its fixed and variable costs. Of course, this does not solve the problem completely because under this scheme each plant is measured on cost alone and will not have the motivation to come up with any value-added service. In case some customers require higher-quality service or want to work on collaborative product development, the plant will not be willing to provide the service unless it gets specific credit for same.

### Managing Allocation Decisions in a Multi-plant Global Firm

So far we have assumed that the entire network was under a centralized control and a firm could align the activities of individual plants through an appropriate performance measurement scheme. As discussed, creating alignment is not easy even in a firm that has complete control over its units, but issues get really complicated when dealing with a global multinational firm having a separate legal entity in each country of operation. Conflict will set in because the local unit manager will naturally be more interested in the performance of the local legal entity, as his or her performance in the local community will be determined by the local unit's performance. Most of the multinationals ensure that they do not judge the unit manager by the performance of the local legal entity. Usually, the important yardstick is the extent to which the individual entity manager is able to align his or her unit with the interest of the global network. This is possible only if the global firm has 100 per cent stake in the local legal entity. Unfortunately, in several countries, multinationals are forced to have local partners, either because the law does not permit 100 per cent foreign equity or at the market-entry stage the global firm may prefer to have a local partner so as to understand local issues. Suzuki, for example, entered India with the Government of India as partner. Similarly, Ford Motor Company entered India with Mahindras as partner. As long as local companies are taking care of only the local market and are not treated as part of the network, such arrangements work without too many difficulties. But the moment multinationals want to treat the local unit as part of a network, the local alliance partner objects if the local unit gets hurt in the process. Like the case of the Nagpur plant in the Indian Paints example, an Indian venture may get lower allocation in the network in the interest of the global network, and the allocation may have nothing to do with the productivity of the local unit. Let us take an example of a global firm that has two manufacturing facilities in South Asia, one in Colombo and one in Faridabad. In the past all customers in Chennai will to be assigned to the Faridabad plant managed by the Indian venture. Now with the reduction in custom tariff the global firm may decide to allocate the Chennai customer to the Colombo plant, which is geographically closer to the customer. So what may be good for a network is not necessarily good for individual units. It is a serious problem when each unit is a separate legal entity and may have local partners. This is the reason why multinational firms prefer 100 per cent control so that they can work with a network strategy and do not have to worry about individual units' profit performance.

In general, planning decisions of supply chain operations must be integrated with the strategic interest of the firm (Should Kolkata be treated as strategic market?) and management control systems and performance measures of individual units and managers managing various entities in the chain must be aligned with the overall business strategy. Otherwise it can create dysfunctional behaviour on the part of the various managers and they may sabotage the network planning operations system. Finally, the organization may end up with locally optimal but globally suboptimal decisions.

## Network Design Problem

So far we have looked at tactical problems of optimal demand allocation across plants for a given network. This problem is usually solved on a monthly or a quarterly basis. However, over a period of time market structures might change. For example, market demand in South India may increase at a faster place or the cost structures may change significantly. A differential rate of change in wages, utilities or transport cost alters the competitiveness of different plants. A firm

### NETWORK RESTRUCTURING AT UNILEVER[2]

Unilever is a European multinational with a turnover of 40 billion Euros. It is the market leader in home and personal care products, and foods and beverages in several global markets. The company has recently announced that it wants to streamline its manufacturing and supply chain operations. It plans to close about 50 of its 300 factories and to reduce its regional centres from about 100 to 25, as part of a bid to save 1.5 billion euro a year by 2010. The majority of restructuring is to be carried out in Europe, where structural costs are highest and where regional supply chain management offers the greatest opportunity. Network restructuring is an ongoing exercise in Unilever. After the European integration in the 1990s, Unilever Europe, carried out an analysis for three product lines for which they had 35 plants in Europe. Based on the analysis they had changed their network design, and the new network had only nine plants, resulting in substantial savings in costs.

may find new locations more attractive and might like to add capacities in these new emerging areas. In general, a firm should periodically question the existing network design and come up with a design that is optimal for the future demand projections and cost structures. Global firms like Unilever go through the exercise of major network restructuring every few years.

This is a common phenomenon in global firms, where they may want to add new capacities in Asia and shut down some facilities in Europe or America. Usually, fixed cost is not a function of volume, so if some plants are not getting enough volume because they are less productive and if there is excess capacity in the system, a firm may want to shut down certain facilities so that it can reduce total system costs. For example, Special Economic Zones in Mexico found that in 2002 about 200 firms had shut down their facilities because they had invested in facilities in China, which have much lower costs of production. With restructuring of the taxation system, India is likely to become one market and this is going to change the way distribution centres are located within the Indian market. In the pharmaceutical and the packaged-goods industries, mergers and acquisitions result in excess capacity for the system as a whole. Oil companies in Europe went through a major rationalization in the 1980s because of mergers and acquisitions. Several case studies have shown that firms use network design models for rationalizing facilities after a merger.

In the case of Indian Paints, let us assume that the firm decides to rationalize network design because it has surplus capacity in the network. As the firm has excess capacity and fixed costs account for a significant part of costs, the firm may explore the idea of closing some facilities so as to save some fixed costs in the process. Now the firm has to first decide whether to keep the plants open or closed, supply being possible only from plants that are open. Of course, if a plant is closed, the firm does not incur any fixed cost on that plant. So we make a modification in the model and introduce binary variables, which can take values of either 0 or 1. Apart from *nm* linear variables, the network design formulation will have *m* binary variables.

## Network Design Model: Cost Minimization Model

If a firm wants to work with an objective of cost minimization for the network, the revised objective function will be as follows:

$$\text{Minimize } \sum Fac-open_i \times Fcost_i + \sum_{i=1}^{m}\sum_{j=1}^{n} Cost_{ij} \times Quant_{ij}$$

$$\sum_{i=1}^{m} Quant_{ij} = Dem_j \quad \text{for } j = 1,\ldots,n \tag{6.7}$$

$$\sum_{j=1}^{n} Quant_{ij} \leq Fac\text{-}open_i \times Cap_i \quad \text{for } i = 1,\ldots,m \tag{6.8}$$

$$Quant_{ij} \geq 0 \quad \text{for } i = 1,\ldots,m \quad \text{for } j = 1,\ldots,n \tag{6.9}$$

$$Fac-open_i = 0 \text{ or } 1 \text{ binary variable for } i = 1,\ldots,m \tag{6.10}$$

Unlike a network operation planning case, fixed costs are the relevant costs of decision making and have been included in the objective function. Only if the binary variable $Fac\text{-}open_i$ takes the value of 1 does the fixed cost for that plant get added to the total cost in the objective function. Similarly, the right-hand side of Equation 6.8 ensures that the effective capacity of a plant is 0 if the relevant binary variable takes the value of 0 and that the effective capacity is equal to the plant capacity if the binary variable takes the value of 1.

For solving the above problem, we need a software that can handle binary decision variables also. Pure linear programming software will not be able to handle binary variables. Excel Solver

**Table 6.5: Network design: optimal allocation with minimum cost as objective.**

| | Bangalore | Chennai | Delhi | Mumbai | Lucknow | Kolkata | Supply | Plant (open/close) |
|---|---|---|---|---|---|---|---|---|
| Ahmedabad | 0 | 0 | 0 | 0 | 0 | 0 | 0 | Close |
| Baddi | 0 | 0 | 280 | 0 | 120 | 0 | 400 | Open |
| Hubli | 165 | 135 | 0 | 60 | 0 | 0 | 360 | Open |
| Nagpur | 0 | 0 | 0 | 140 | 5 | 155 | 300 | Open |
| Vishakapatnam | 0 | 0 | 0 | 0 | 0 | 0 | 0 | Close |
| Demand met | 165 | 135 | 280 | 200 | 125 | 155 | 0 | |

Objective function = Total costs = 891,760.

can handle binary decision variables and the relevant details are discussed in Appendix A. Optimal allocation for Indian Paints from Excel Solver is as shown in Table 6.5.

The allocation shown in Table 6.5 will result in the following financial performance for Indian Paints:

Revenue = 1,017,450
Variable cost = 775,760
Gross profit (Revenue – Variable cost) = 1,017,450 – 775,760 = 241,690
Net profit = Gross profit – Fixed cost = 241,690 – 116,000 = 125,690

This suggests that the Ahmedabad and Vishakapatnam plants should be closed. Ahmedabad has significantly high fixed cost and Vishakapatnam has relatively lower volume of allocation, so they are ideal candidates for closure, given the excess capacity in the system. Comparison with Table 6.3 shows that these changes lead to an increase in the net profit, despite the increase in the total variable cost in the system. Since fixed costs have come down because of the closure of the two plants, the overall profit has increased significantly.

## Network Design Model: Profit Maximization Model

If the network design problem is solved as a profit maximization problem (all markets need not be served), the objective function will be as follows:

$$\sum\sum Price_j \times Quant_{ij} - \sum Fac\text{-}open_i \times F\cos t_i - \sum_{i=1}^{m}\sum_{j=1}^{n} Cost_{ij} \times Quant_{ij}$$

$$\sum_{i=1}^{m} Quant_{ij} \le Dem_j \quad \text{for } j = 1,\ldots,n \tag{6.11}$$

$$\sum_{j=1}^{n} Quant_{ij} \le Fac\text{-}open_i \times Cap_i \quad \text{for } i = 1,\ldots,m \tag{6.12}$$

$$Quant_{ij} \ge 0 \quad \text{for } i = 1,\ldots,m,\ j = 1,\ldots,n \tag{6.13}$$

$$Fac\text{-}open_i = 0 \text{ or } 1 \text{ binary variable} \quad \text{for } i = 1,\ldots,n \tag{6.14}$$

The optimal allocation for Indian Paints from Excel Solver is as shown in Table 6.6.

The allocation in Table 6.6 will result in the following financial performance for Indian Paints:

Revenue = 833,700
Variable cost = 601,015
Gross profit (Revenue – Variable cost) = 833,700 – 601,015 = 232,685
Net profit = Gross profit –Fixed cost = 232,685 – 78,000 = 154,685

*Table 6.6:* **Network design: optimal allocation with maximum profit as objective.**

| | Bangalore | Chennai | Delhi | Mumbai | Lucknow | Kolkata | Supply | Plant (open/close) |
|---|---|---|---|---|---|---|---|---|
| Ahmedabad | 0 | 0 | 0 | 0 | 0 | 0 | 0 | Close |
| Baddi | 0 | 0 | 280 | 0 | 120 | 0 | 400 | Open |
| Hubli | 165 | 85 | 0 | 200 | 0 | 0 | 450 | Open |
| Nagpur | 0 | 0 | 0 | 0 | 0 | 0 | 0 | Close |
| Vishakapatnam | 0 | 0 | 0 | 0 | 0 | 0 | 0 | Close |
| Demand met | 165 | 85 | 280 | 200 | 120 | 0 | | |

Objective function= Total net profit = 154,685.

This suggests that the Ahmedabad, Vishakapatnam and Nagpur plants should be closed. The Ahmedabad plant has significantly high fixed cost and the Vishakapatnam plant has relatively lower volume of allocation, so they are ideal candidates for closure given the excess capacity in the system. Further, if it is not necessary to serve the Kolkata market, the Nagpur facility can also be closed to save the relevant fixed cost. Comparison of Table 6.6 with Table 6.4 shows that the net profit has increased and thus the overall profit has increased significantly.

As presented in Table 6.7, we can compare all the four approaches discussed above in terms of profitability. As we can see, network redesign significantly improves the profitability of a firm. Further, integrated problem solving has greater profitability when compared to a situation when marketing and supply chain decisions are made independently. Of course, following the profit maximization model for both network design and operations will lead to higher profitability at the cost of the top-line. Sometimes firms may have some top-line objectives and may be willing to sacrifice their bottom-line objectives in the process.

Though network design decisions help bring down overall costs and improve profitability, the firm has to consider all related issues and take into account the possible consequences of the decision on such issues. For example, network design decisions have a tremendous impact on the performance of individual plants. We briefly discuss such issues here.

## Political Dimensions of Network Design Decisions

Network design decisions definitely improve the performance of the network, but such measures also put much pressure on individual plants. It is possible that a plant might be closed because of issues that are not under the control of the plant manager. For example, the Nagpur plant, which was the lowest cost producer before Indian Paints decided to put up the Baddi plant, is now on the chopping block. This issue is quite tricky in multi-product situations. Different ways of cost allocation across products result in different costs and this, in turn, results in different decisions. Usually, plant managers try and play around with numbers so that they can retain more products in their portfolio and they can spread their fixed cost over a larger number of products. Also, within a firm, the plant with a bigger portfolio will have more political clout in the system. So if one is not careful, network design decisions can become

*Table 6.7:* **Performance comparison of different decisions.**

| Decision problem | Type of decision | Objective | Revenue | Net profit | % Net profit/ sales |
|---|---|---|---|---|---|
| I | Network operations | Cost minimization | 1,017,450 | 15,680 | 1.54 |
| II | Network operations | Profit maximization | 885,700 | 17,230 | 1.95 |
| III | Network design | Cost minimization | 1,017,450 | 125,690 | 12.35 |
| IV | Network design | Profit maximization | 833,700 | 154,685 | 18.55 |

highly political in nature. Further, some plants have a historical legacy—older plants have higher energy cost, older labour force and high labour cost. Will it be fair to compare plants that are not comparable in the first place? Again, if a global firm has local alliance partners, they are not going to be comfortable with extreme decisions of this kind. In general, frequent network redesign decisions will give a clear signal to plant managers that they are competing against each other. If plant managers are rewarded on how well they perform relative to other plant managers, there will be no incentives for knowledge sharing. Minimizing cost on a short-run basis may result in loss of opportunity for long-term cost reduction through the sharing of best practices. BMW, a global automobile major, has designed a strategic planning model that provides decision support to the firm whenever it has to make these allocation-related decisions.

### STRATEGIC PLANNING MODEL AT BMW[3]

The BMW group manufactures and sells three premium car brands, BMW, MINI and Rolls Royce, globally. It sold about 1.25 million cars in 2006. BMW has eight full-fledged manufacturing plants and seven complete knockdown manufacturing plants located in different parts of the world. Allocating global volumes to these different units used to be a tough and challenging problem for the group. To optimize its volume-allocation decision, BMW has developed a strategic planning model. This model includes supply of raw material as well as the distribution of finished goods and works with a planning horizon of 12 years. Apart from allocation decisions, it also helps the firm in making optimal investment decisions in major departments like body assembly, paint shop and final assembly. This strategic model allows BMW to understand the impact of investment decisions on cost drivers of the supply chain.

The crucial issue here will be to insulate plant managers' performance measures from the plant closure decision. As mentioned earlier, many plants in Mexico were closed as firms had put up new facilities in China. Even if one attempts to insulate the plant manager of a Mexico plant from the closure decision, he or she may not be willing to move to China if the opportunity is provided, and even if he or she is willing to move, the firm may not be interested in shifting the manager because of cultural differences.

Even if firms may not use the solution suggested by optimization models, the recommendation of the models can help the firms in establishing right benchmarks in evaluating alternative solutions. It is possible that a model does not capture all the intangibles and the firm may choose locations other than the ones suggested by the model. It is necessary to remember that a firm will have to live with the facility decision for a long time to come. Thus, it is important that the firm generates several scenarios based on the world view of likely developments in the future. Asian Paints is trying to move away from country-focused manufacturing to a network approach but is aware of the sensitivities involved and wants to gradually move to the idea of regional hubs before moving to a full-fledged global network.

### ASIAN PAINTS' INTERNATIONAL OPERATIONS[4]

Asian Paints is India's largest paint company, with a turnover of Rs 36.7 billion. Over a period of time, it has increased its international operations with a strong focus on developing countries. It operates in 21 countries and has a manufacturing facility in each of these countries. With reduction in import duties, Asian Paints wants to explore the idea of redesigning its plant network and work with the idea of regional manufacturing units rather than country-specific units. Asian Paints has divided its global market into five regions, viz, South Asia, South-East Asia, South Pacific, the Middle East and the Caribbean.

Setting up regional manufacturing units in place of country-specific units will allow the company to get better economies of scale in manufacturing. They have already invested in the necessary IT infrastructure and other processes that will allow them to successfully achieve the complex integration of manufacturing and distribution under the new setup.

In general, plant closures are extremely painful for a firm and this issue also has political dimensions as local governments are extremely concerned about facility closures and job cuts. Thus, progressive multinationals do not look at facility location decisions as short-term decisions because they are aware of the difficulties involved in closing facilities. It also creates an image of bad management and may have certain implications for the kind of people the firm is likely to attract. One of the ways in which firms try and avoid extreme decisions like closure is by assigning a higher strategic role to each facility, thereby avoiding chances of extreme decisions like closure. At a later stage in this chapter we discuss how firms can assign different strategic roles to different units so that each unit brings more value to the network than just being a node in the network.

# Network Design and Operations Models: Extensions

In this section, we discuss the network design and operations models that may be applicable in situations with increased limitation on account of factors like seasonality of supply and short life cycle of the product. As discussed earlier, the ability of a plant to deal with complex network designs or operations planning problems puts it at a strategic point in the supply chain, thereby enabling it to avoid consequences like closure.

## *Seasonal Products: Tactical Planning Problems*

In normal tactical situations, it is assumed that opening inventory is the same as closing inventory; hence, inventory is removed from the model. But in seasonal products, inventory does not remain the same throughout the year. So depending on the period of the year, the opening inventory will be expected to be different from the closing inventory. At the relevant stock point, Equation 6.15 will ensure that planned increase or decrease in inventory takes place in the relevant period.

$$\text{Opening inventory} + \text{Inflow} - \text{Outflow} = \text{Closing inventory} \tag{6.15}$$

## *Multiple Capacity: Deciding on the Best Option*

Let us assume that Indian Paints is exploring two options while putting up a new facility at Baddi, to put up either a facility with a moderate capacity of 400 units or a high-capacity one with 600 units. The firm expects economies of scale; therefore, the higher-capacity option will have lower variable cost as well as fixed cost per unit of capacity. But if the plant is not going to get enough volume, then excess investments will be a wasteful expenditure. To handle this case, the model will have six possible plants in its network design instead of five plants. The Baddi site will be represented by two rows: Baddi-moderate and Baddi-high. One additional constraint (6.16) will be added to ensure that at most one plant (either moderate or high capacity) should be kept open at Baddi:

$$\textit{Fac-Open}_{\text{Baddi-Moderate}} + \textit{Fac-Open}_{\text{Baddi-High}} \leq 1 \tag{6.16}$$

Similar logic can be used in case the firm has options of three or more types of facilities, using binary variable for each facility type for each site, and by introducing a constraint like 6.16, one can ensure that at most one type of facility is opened at each site.

So far we have only studied plants and markets. It is possible that to ensure better response time to markets, intermediate warehouses will be needed; and the optimal mix of warehouses in a network design problem need to be identified. Similar to plant variables, we will introduce binary variables at each potential warehouse location. Additional data will be needed on the plant-to-warehouse transport cost matrix, warehouse-to-market transportation cost matrix and fixed cost of opening a warehouse. We will have to introduce a constraint to ensure that the inflow to the warehouse is the same as the outflow from the warehouse.

## Short Life Cycle Products: A Suitable Network Design

For firms dealing with products that have a short life cycle, cost considerations do not form the only important factor in the network. Changing fashion trends and rapid technological advances force the firms to align themselves quickly to reflect the changes. In such an environment, a firm has to be prepared for either volume variability or mix variability or a combination of both, and this cannot be handled by holding a high safety stock of finished goods. The entire network must have a short lead time so that it can respond fast to market or technology shocks. So the network design for short life cycle products must balance the cost and time involved in the sourcing, production, storage and transportation activities in the supply chain. Two different ways can be used to capture time in the network: cycle time and weighted activity time.

Cycle time is the time taken on the longest path of the network. Weighted activity time is sum of the processing/transporting times for each individual segment of the network multiplied by the number of units processed by the node or shipped through the link. This includes all the paths and not just the longest path in network. Digital Equipment Corporation had developed an elaborate decision support system for global supply chain analysis, where it minimized cost or weighted activity time or a combination of both. As shown below, the objective function is a composite of time and cost:

$$\alpha \times \text{Cost} + (1 - \alpha) \times \text{Time}, \quad 0 \le \alpha \le 1$$

The difference between the two different concepts of time (weighted activity time and cycle time) are illustrated with an example.

Consider the case of a simplified version of the PC supply chain described in Figure 6.2. The supply chain involves manufacturing disks and motherboards, assembling PCs and shipping them to the North American market. The firm is trying to make location decisions for each of the three manufacturing centres. As shown in Figure 6.2, the firm has two choices for each of the manufacturing locations. Relevant data for the problem are presented in Table 6.8.

We want to measure the time element in the chain using both the concepts of weighted time and cycle time.

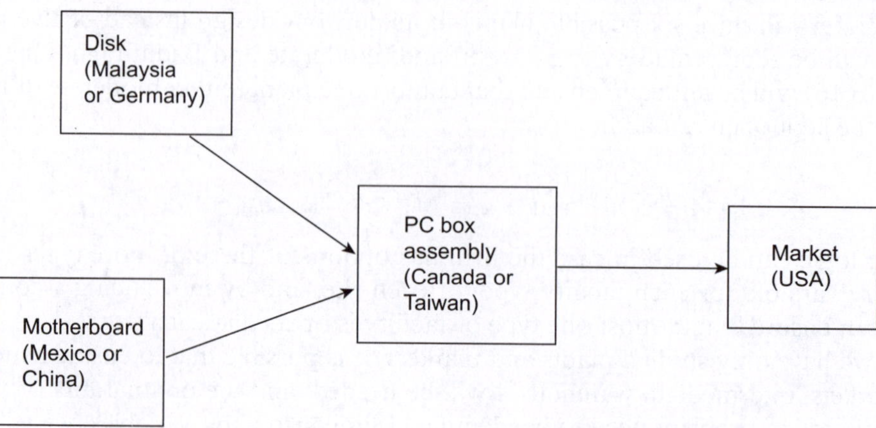


**Figure 6.2**

PC supply chain.

*Table 6.8(a):* ***Production cost (value added) and lead time data.***

| Product/component | Location | Production lead time (PLT) (in weeks) | Value added (VA) (US$) |
|---|---|---|---|
| PC box | Canada | 2 | 50 |
| PC box | Taiwan | 1 | 35 |
| Disk | Malaysia | 3 | 50 |
| Disk | Germany | 2 | 68 |
| Mother board | Mexico | 3 | 150 |
| Mother board | China | 2 | 130 |

*Table 6.8(b):* ***Transportation time and transportation cost.***

| Component/ subassembly | | Transportation time (TLT) (weeks) | Transportation cost (TCST) (US$) |
|---|---|---|---|
| PC box (PB) | Canada–USA | 1 | 8 |
| PC box | Taiwan–USA | 3 | 20 |
| Disk (DK) | Malaysia–Canada | 2 | 7 |
| Disk | Malaysia–Taiwan | 1 | 4 |
| Disk | Germany–Canada | 2 | 5 |
| Disk | Germany–Taiwan | 1 | 3 |
| Mother board (MB) | Mexico–Canada | 1 | 5 |
| Mother board | Mexico–Taiwan | 2 | 10 |
| Mother board | China–Canada | 3 | 13 |
| Mother board | China–Taiwan | 1 | 5 |

## Comparing Supply Chain Configurations

There are eight supply chain configurations possible. But we examine just the two configurations described below:

Configuration 1: Disk—Germany; Motherboard—Mexico; PC Box—Canada

Configuration 2: Disk—Malaysia; Motherboard—China; PC Box—Taiwan

For the two configurations described above we work out cost, cycle time and weighted activity time using following formulas:

$$\text{Cost (Configuration)} = VA(DK) + TCST(DK - PC) + VA(MB) + TCST(MB - PC) + VA(PC) + TCST(PC - USA)$$

$$\text{Cycle time (Configuration)} = \text{Max}\{[PLT(DK) + TLT(DK - PC)], [PLT(MB) + TLT(MB - PC)]\} + PLT(PC) + TLT(PC - USA)$$

Weighted activity time (Configuration) =

$$VA(DK) \times PLT(DK) + [(VA(DK) + TCST(DK - PC)]TRLT(DK - PC) + VA(MB)PLT(MB) + [(VA(MB) + TCST(MB - PB)]TRLT(DK - PB) + [VA(DK) + TCST(DK - PB) + VA(MB) + TCST(MB - PB) + VA(PB)] \times PLT(PB) + [VA(DK) + TCST(DK - PB) + VA(MB) + TCST(MB - PB) + VA(PB) + TCST(PB - USA)] \times PLT(PB)$$

Cost (Configuration 1) = 68 + 5 + 150 + 5 + 50 + 8 = 286

Cost (Configuration 2) = 50 + 4 + 130 + 5 + 35 + 20 = 244

Cycle time (Configuration 1) = Max[(2 + 2), (3 + 1)] + 2 + 1 = 7 weeks

Cycle time (Configuration 2) = Max[(3 + 1), (2 + 1)] + 1 + 3 = 8 weeks

$$\text{Weighted activity time (Configuration 1)} = 68 \times 2 + (68 + 5) \times 2 + 150 \times 3 + (150 + 5) \times 1 + (68 + 5 + 150 + 5 + 50) \times 2 + (68 + 5 + 150 + 5 + 50 + 8) \times 1 = 1{,}729$$

$$\text{Weighted activity time (Configuration 2)} = 50 \times 3 + (50 + 4) \times 1 + 130 \times 2 + (130 + 5) \times 1 + (50 + 4 + 130 + 5 + 35) \times 1 + (50 + 4 + 130 + 5 + 35 + 20) \times 3 = 1{,}555$$

Thus, depending on the importance of cost versus time (value of $\alpha$ in the objective function), a firm can make appropriate choices. Of course, Configuration 2 provides better performance on the cost front, while performance on the time front will depend on the choice of performance measures. If one uses weighted activity time as a measure of time, Configuration 2 will perform better; but if cycle time is used as a measure of time, Configuration 1 will perform better. Cycle time as a measure of time will capture responsiveness of the chain while weighted activity time will capture the pipeline inventory in the chain. Though Digital Corporation had used weighted activity time in its decision support system because it is easier to compute, cycle time may be more appropriate for capturing measures related to the responsiveness of a chain.

## Impact of Lead Time on Supply Chain Performance

As discussed in the chapter on inventory, lead time in production and transportation has implications for pipeline and safety stock inventory. Pipeline inventory is a direct function of the lead time of the process, while safety stock is a function of the square root of the lead time. But

**INTERVIEW WITH**

**SUPRAKASH MUKHERJEE**

*Deere & Company (usually known by its brand name John Deere) is an American corporation with a presence in 27 countries and a revenue of $22.148 billion (2006). Mr Suprakash Mukherjee is the Senior General Manager, Global Sourcing, Enterprise Supply Management, at John Deere India.*

*What are the issues related to specifically global supply chain networks?*

**Suprakash Mukherjee**: Unlike local supply chains, global supply chain networks function under multiple sources of uncertainty and different types of risk, including raw material prices, product prices, product demand, and foreign exchange rates amongst others, which vary across countries. This makes managing a global supply chain a very dynamic and resource-intensive process. For example, the India plants manufacture 5,000 series tractors of which only 50 per cent are for the domestic market. The remaining 50 per cent are exported to more than 50 countries. Similar tractors are manufactured at six other locations in the world. Hence, we need to ensure that we meet the demand in each of the markets while ensuring minimum costs and adequate utilization at each of the facilities.

*How do you manage the uncertainties you mentioned above?*

**Suprakash Mukherjee:** Along with its challenges, global supply chain also throws open the opportunities of lowering costs by allowing access to low-cost suppliers. For example, the cost advantages of India sourcing are significant and the Regional Supply Management Centre at the John Deere Technology Centre leverages those sources. The supply base in India supports factories globally as India's steel and plastics go into products for sale worldwide.

Recently, we also compiled a model to ascertain the impact of foreign exchange fluctuations on revenues across different markets. The model helped us to reassess our allocation across different plants in order to ensure minimal fluctuation in the revenue because of exchange rate fluctuations in different markets.

*How important do you think is it for an organization to optimize on its supply chain network?*

**Suprakash Mukherjee:** The growth in globalization has led to supply chain management being a key focus area for management of top multinational enterprises. A lot of companies fail in the present context because of the inability to configure global manufacturing plants and markets. Hence, I believe global supply chain management, based on enhanced integration of suppliers and customers, not only makes better business sense but is also a source of competitive advantage.

a shorter lead time allows a firm to respond to changes in an environment that cannot be predicated. Further, in the fashion industry, maintaining large safety stock is not the optimal way of dealing with a highly uncertain demand situation. As discussed later, "sense and respond" is the most effective strategy in the fashion industry, and a short lead time is the most important characteristic of such a strategy. Sony, to its horror, found that it had landed with an unresponsive supplier who could not deliver a few minor components at short notice, and this resulted in huge losses of sales for its PlayStation II during Christmas in 2000.

# Data for Network Design

Network design will require cost- and demand-related data. Though an organization may have relevant transactions data, converting the same into meaningful data is an important task and requires some considerations. A discussion of this issue is presented in this section.

## *Demand Data*

A firm may have numerous SKUs in its product portfolio, but it will be counter-productive to include all of them in its network design models. For example, an auto company could offer 200 product variants consisting of various combinations. However, these variants may also be aggregated into three families: large, medium and small. We should keep in mind the supply chain related characteristics like transportation cost, inventory cost and demand placed on capacity. For example, if two different models are manufactured at two different types of facilities, then one cannot aggregate them, and both have to maintain separate identities for the sake of network design. The problem of aggregation is likely to be more serious for retailers like Food World or Pantaloon, where one may work with thousands of SKUs in the product portfolio.

Like they do with products, a firm will have to aggregate its customers and markets also. A firm may be dealing with thousands of customers, and those in close proximity of one another are good candidates for aggregation. Few large A-category customers can be treated individually while all the B-category and C-category customers can be aggregated on a geographical basis. There is a trade-off involved in the aggregation process. Whenever data are aggregated, there is loss of some information, but for any meaningful analysis there should not be too many binary variables. Also with too large a model, a firm will be unable to communicate with the decision makers in a meaningful way. There may also be problems in getting the required data.

## *Supply Side Cost Data*

Relevant data from the supply perspective is necessary to capture production- and transportation-related costs. The production cost is incurred at nodes (facilities) and transportation cost is incurred at arcs (between facilities) in the network

### Production Cost: Comparable Costs Across Facilities

Different plants may have different accounting systems and may use different methodologies while allocating common cost (e.g., overhead allocation) across product categories. In many instances where firms have been merged, these problems are more serious and unless costs are used in a comparable way, the results will not be meaningful and will also create problems of credibility. Since the results of the network design can have serious implications like plant closure, it is important that production costs are comparable across plants. If firms are using activity based costing, they can identify cost drivers for each product category and allocate costs on a reasonably fair and accurate basis.

### Transportation Costs

Allocation of transportation costs is relatively easy because for most of the links data will be available from the logistics provider. But in the case of a new network, firms can use distance as proxy for cost. When dealing with rural and semi-urban areas where the details of distance may not be available, then firms can calculate Euclidian distances from the coordinates of the nodes of the network.

## Strategic Role of Units in the Network

So far in our discussion we assumed that a network is optimized only to minimize costs. This is a very narrow and short-term view of plant capability. In this section, we introduce a framework to examine the role of a unit from a broader perspective.

### *Strategic Role Framework*

Ferdows has suggested that we should look at the role of a plant from a long-term perspective and it is possible that each unit within the network may play a different role. As shown in Figure 6.3, individual plants can play a lower strategic role where it is primarily located for accessing either market or low-cost resources or knowledge or a plant can play higher strategic role and make multiple contributions to the overall network. As shown in Figure 6.3, a plant can play six possible roles in a network and each of them is described below.

#### Offshore Plant

An offshore facility is established to take advantage of low-cost labour or material in the region. It produces products/services for export markets. Global multinationals have been establishing low-cost manufacturing plants in Asia. China accounts for 70 per cent of the world's toys, 60 per cent of its bicycles, 50 per cent of shoes and 33 per cent of luggage. Global software companies have been setting up offshore facilities for backend services in India. Many countries in Asia have established free trade zones where labour costs are low, infrastructure is good, facilities are close to a port and all the import tariffs are waived provided the goods are exported and are not used for the domestic market. Offshore plants play a limited strategic role and investments in technical and managerial resources are usually quite low.

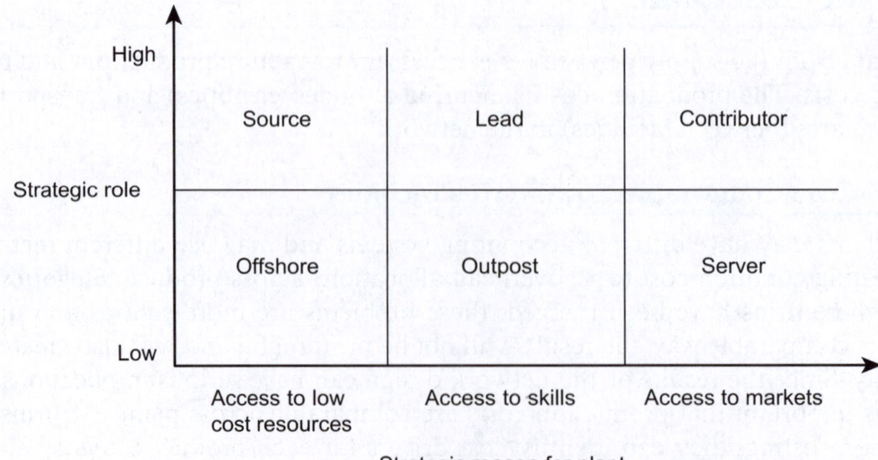


**Figure 6.3**

Role of plant in network.

### Server Facility

Server facility is established with an objective of supplying products/services to specific national or regional markets. It provides relatively lower-cost market access. A server facility is useful in a situation of tariff barriers, local content requirements or high logistics cost to supply to that region. Many multinationals established plants in India in the 1980s to serve local market because of high import tariffs prevalent in India. A server facility has a higher strategic role than an offshore plant because it may be allowed to make some changes in the products to cater to local tastes; similarly, it may be allowed to make changes in some processes to take advantage of the differential capital and labour costs. But it is not expected to play any role beyond that region, so in that sense it plays a limited strategic role.

### Outpost Plant

An outpost is established to tap into the local knowledge available in that region. There are advanced clusters in any industry where advanced suppliers, competitors, research laboratories and customers are located. Being present in that region allows a firm access to tacit information and knowledge, which is difficult to access from other places. For example, many companies dealing with cutting edge technology and hi-tech items are located in Silicon valley, the United States, and in Bangalore, India. Similarly, many pharmaceutical companies like Glenmark Pharma have set up labs in Switzerland, which though being a high cost economy is most likely to provide state-of-the-art information and knowledge to the organization.

### Source Plant

The main objective of establishing a source facility is low-cost production. But it plays a broader and more strategic role in a network than an offshore facility. A source plant might be the primary source of a product for the global network. A source facility will usually start as an offshore facility and will then gradually start playing a bigger and more strategic role in the network. Offshore facilities that show technical and managerial capability are usually upgraded to source status. ABB has centres of excellence for each product category. Source factories are located in regions where not only are the production costs low but adequate number of people with technical and managerial skills are available and the necessary infrastructure is in place.

### Contributor Plant

The main objective of establishing a source facility is low-cost market access. But it plays a strategic role in the network, which is broader than that of the server facility. Apart from serving specific regional or national markets, its responsibility extends to product and process engineering as well as supplier development. Over a period of time a server plant that develops those capabilities and takes necessary responsibilities becomes a contributor plant. For example, multinationals in India, like Unilever, have stared playing the role of contributor where they have made necessary investments in the relevant research and development labs.

### Lead Facility

A lead facility creates new processes, products and technologies for the entire network. It not only collects data for the headquarters, but also taps into local resources and becomes a hub, performing critical value-added activities.

## Role Evolution Within a Network

Typically, any new plant will start with a rather low strategic role and will provide market access, resource access or knowledge access. Whatever may be the rationale behind establishing a manufacturing facility at a specific location, the strategic role of the plant is likely to change over a period of time. Many multinationals had established offshore facilities in East Asia and Mexico to manufacture electronic parts, because of the low labour cost in that region. But over a period of time, labour cost went up and only those plants that had anticipated theses changes and managed to change the strategic role of facilities survived. Otherwise, over a period of time, firms have moved to China where labour costs are still relatively low. HP Singapore is an interesting case of a facility that has managed the transition very well.

### EVOLUTION OF THE SINGAPORE FACILITY AT HP[5]

HP Singapore started with manufacturing basic electronic components, and over a period of time demonstrated its capability to handle the entire product and not just the components. When the Singapore plant was asked to find ways of reducing the manufacturing costs for hand-held computers, they argued that since the bulk of manufacturing costs get decided at the design stage, they had to get the mandate to design the product to be in a position to reduce the manufacturing costs. Once they got the broader role, they managed to reduce the manufacturing costs by 50 per cent, as a consequence of which they got the additional responsibility of design and manufacturing. Over a period of time, through a series of capability building projects, the HP Singapore facility has established itself as a leader plant in the HP network.

Many software facilities in India are concerned with similar issues. They know that multinationals have located their facility here because of the low cost of skilled labour. But given the increasing cost (about 15 per cent per annum), there is concern that eventually these multinational might move to either Eastern Europe or to some other part of world. Local managers of these facilities are trying to ensure that these facilities are justified by their quality of work and innovations so that in the future they are not justified by labour cost alone. The chief of Dell India[6] recently said, “We came to India for quality and stayed back because of innovations”.

LG had identified India as big potential market and decided in 1995 to set up manufacturing facilities here. The Indian facility started as a server, but over a period of time it has started playing the role of a contributor. In 2005, LG India spent about 1 billion rupees on research alone. LG India still imports the basic technology from South Korea, but 90 per cent of the required R&D work for new products is done locally.

Countries like Singapore have invested heavily in the education sector to ensure that local units in Singapore start playing a more strategic role in their respective networks. They have invited world-class institutes from around the globe to set up campuses in Singapore so that they can offer skilled labour in the IT and finance sectors, which can absorb the high cost of labour.

## Location of Service Systems

The discussion thus far on network design and operations has focused on ways of maximizing profits, minimizing costs, locating plants, handling complexities within the network and extracting the relevant data. We have not considered the location of service systems within the scope of our discussions. Such decisions are important strategic and tactical decisions that are of paramount importance in the retail and other similar sectors. In this section, we look at various issues associated with the location of service systems.

Deciding optimal locations for services where the facility will be visited by customers involves considerations that are very different from decisions related to plant networks for product businesses. Since the services sector consists of diverse sets of services, we focus our discussion on retail, public system services and aftermarket services.

Customer convenience is one of the key considerations in the retail network design. Unlike Dell Computers, which manages its global operations with just seven plants, Wal-Mart works with 3,900 stores in the United States alone and 2,700 stores in the rest of the world. Currently,

Wal-Mart operates in 15 countries other than the United States, and the number of international stores is bound to go up significantly if Wal-Mart wants to have a global reach like Dell Computers. Within India, Food World, the market leader in organized retailing with a turnover of Rs 3 billion, owns more than 80 stores across 12 metros in southern India and has 29 stores in Bangalore.

## Locating Retail Outlets

The technique of locating retail outlets has been studied extensively, and the most popular model is the spatial interaction model developed by Huff. Huff's model groups population within a geographical region in clusters and the probability of a customer from one cluster visiting a store located in some other cluster is as shown below:

$$P_{ij} = \frac{S_j/(D_{ij})^2}{\Sigma_j S_j/(D_{ij})^2}$$

where $P_{ij}$ is the probability of customer from cluster $i$ travelling to retail location $j$, $S_j$ is the size of retail location $j$ and $D_{ij}$ is the distance from population cluster $i$ to retail location $j$.

The probability of attracting a customer to a store is directly proportionate to the size of the retail outlet and inversely proportionate to the distance travelled by the customer. Finally, a retailer is in a competitive market, and the probability that a customer will visit the store is a function of the relative attractiveness of the store. Let us assume that a firm wants to design a retail network for Bangalore city. Bangalore's population of 6.52 million is located over an area of about 700 km$^2$. So Bangalore can be divided into 70 clusters of 10 km$^2$ each. It is assumed that the entire population within a cluster is located at the centre of that cluster. Once the clustering is done, a firm can capture relevant data like customer population and distances from the GIS of the relevant region. Given the locations of competitors and the cost economics involved in locating a facility, a firm can use the above model in designing an appropriate network structure.

### Impact of a New Outlet on the Existing Network

Adding a new unit at a different location in the existing network will definitely attract a whole lot of new customers, but at the same time it might eat into the customer base of the existing units. Some customers of the existing units, finding the new unit more conveniently located, might switch to the new unit and in the process hurt the business and financial prospects of some of the existing units. On the positive side, the new unit will add to the system-wide revenue but might hurt some of the existing individual units in the network. Issues of conflict in service networks design are very similar to the one discussed earlier in the case of a global multinational's manufacturing business. In services, this issue is even more relevant because a lot of services operate with the franchise model. In franchise service operations, increasing one more outlet with a new franchisee in same city will hurt the franchisees of existing outlets. For its retail oil business, Reliance Industries Ltd is planning to build a network of about 2,000 retail outlets. Out of these 2,000 outlets, about 75 per cent will be run by franchisee partners and the balance will be company-owned outlets. As Reliance goes on increasing the number of outlets in the same geographical area like a city, we are sure to see issues of conflicting interest on the part of Reliance and its different franchisee partners. Any additional outlet in the network will add to business for the network but it will also eat into the business of existing units and franchisees.

While designing customer retail outlets where there will be interaction with customers, firms have to ensure that the backend network is able to serve these retail outlets, placed close to customers, in an efficient manner. Wal-Mart designed clusters of stores near distribution centres to facilitate frequent replenishments at the lowest cost. This was extremely important because Wal-Mart competed primarily on cost, and its overall network design and business practices were designed and operated so that it can offer products at the lowest possible prices in the retail outlets.

## Locating Public Service Systems

The model discussed above will not be applicable while designing networks for emergency and public service systems. In an emergency service system, instead of the average distance, one has to minimize the maximum distance for all the users who are likely to use the emergency system. See Box 6.1 for a discussion on the issue of designing a comprehensive trauma system at Bangalore. Similarly, while designing health care systems and deciding primary school locations in rural areas, the focus will have to be on equity and not just efficiency issues. While designing a network of schools it may be important that no child will have to walk more than three kilometres to reach school. In designing public systems, apart from efficiency considerations we will have to worry about equity issues also.

## Designing Aftermarket Service System Network

Designing aftermarket service systems involves issues similar to those discussed in designing of retail network systems. The design of an aftermarket service network is likely to receive much attention from manufacturers once they realize its importance from a business perspective. In developed markets, businesses earn 45 per cent of gross profit from aftermarket services, although it accounts for only 24 per cent of the revenue. Unlike in the case of retail outlets where the customer travels to a retail outlet for aftermarket services, a service provider will have to travel to the customers' premises (along with necessary parts). Since a customer is usually promised guaranteed service delivery time, decisions regarding location of after-service facilities with necessary resources (people and parts) are of vital importance. Unlike in retail services, an after-market service firm can work with geographical hierarchy of facilities. Firms like Tata Motors work with three-tier stocking centres and different categories of parts are located at different tiers. Tata Motors has one central distribution facility, where expensive parts required at low frequency are stocked. It maintains four regional service centres, where moderately expensive parts with moderate frequency requirements are stocked; and fast-moving,

**BOX 6.1** Comprehensive Trauma Consortium at Bangalore: Operation Sanjeevani[7]

Every year about 7,000 to 8,000 accidents take place in Bangalore and about 800 of them are fatal. Unfortunately, like in any other city, it used to take a couple of hours before medical help could be made available to victims after the accident. It is a well-known fact that when accident victims receive treatment within an hour of being injured, life can be saved in most of the cases and the extent of damage to organs also can be controlled significantly. To provide this service, the Comprehensive Trauma Consortium (CTC), a voluntary organization, was formed.

This initiative provides paramedical help to all medial emergencies and accidents and liaises with 22 hospitals to ensure that the best help is available to the victim within the "golden hour" of the accident/emergency. CTC has 25 ambulances and these are stationed at different locations around the city and are always on call, complete with preliminary medical equipment and a paramedic. On receiving a call, the CTC call centre directs the nearest ambulance to the accident spot. Through a global positioning system and wireless facility (installed in all CTC ambulances and partner hospitals), the control room directs the ambulance to the accident spot.

As per CTC estimates, after CTC came into being, the rate of patients being declared "dead on arrival" has gone down drastically from a high of 32 per cent (including 10 per cent in transit) to just 3 per cent.

CTC is working towards its mission of reaching its victims to the nearest hospital within 10 minutes.

low-valued parts are stocked in decentralized stock points located in every state. Of course, the firm may not offer the same service to all customers. Firms offer differentiated services like the platinum service, where a customer is assured of response in less than 24 hours, while customers of normal service are responded to within 72 hours. Different service offerings result in different service network designs.

Service network design issues are, however, not relevant for pure information-based services like travel, hotel booking and banking services, which do not require physical cash. Unlike software and music, pizza and service parts cannot be delivered through the Internet. So any service system that requires the delivery of some form of physical product will definitely face service network design issues discussed in this section.

## Incorporating Uncertainty in Network Design

Facility design decisions are strategic in nature and a firm will have to live with facility location and capacity decisions for several years. Most of the data used in the network design model are likely to change over a period of time. Projections of cost, price and demand over a longer horizon usually have a lot of uncertainties associated with those numbers. For example, in international network design, foreign exchange rates affect relative cost structures significantly and predicting the same is extremely difficult, if not impossible. Firms like Birla Cement or Asian Paints do not face this problem because they design multi-plant networks within a country. Though cost of living, inflation and other factors are likely to vary in different regions even within a country, the extent of variations is likely to be of much lower in magnitude because migration within a country is much easier compared to migration across countries. So, in general, design decisions about multi-plant networks within a country are easier compared to global networks. There are several ways in which firms handle these issues. Firms try and use scenario building through which they try and generate large numbers of likely future scenarios and select an option that performs reasonably well across the projected scenarios. So the focus shifts to selecting a robust solution rather than on picking a solution that is optimal for one scenario.

Over a period of time, Toyota has introduced greater flexibility in its plants worldwide. That is, a plant should be able to produce models that are required in the domestic market but must also be able to produce models for a few export markets. On the whole, the network will have excess capacity, so based on the exchange rates movement, volume will be allocated to the respective plants in the network. For example, Toyota might look at its Indian and Thai plants as the supply source for the South Asian market and keep excess capacity at both places. If baht is cheaper, it can allocate more volume to the Thailand facility, and if rupee is cheaper, it can allocate a higher share of the export market to India. This excess capacity in network provides the luxury of options to the Toyota network. This is known as real option because it provides a firm flexibility similar to financial options in financial markets. But unlike financial options, real options are difficult to trade. Firms that have excessively focused on their global manufacturing facilities have realized that any significant change in Yuan rate can change the cost structures in a significant way. There is a lot of pressure on China to devalue Yuan. Currently, LG uses its China facility as an export base and exports 70 per cent of its production from China. Given the uncertainty on the Yuan front, LG has decided to build excess capacity in India so that there is another hub available as an option for export.

The idea of excess capacity in global networks may go against the current logic of a lean supply chain design. In the lean philosophy, firms are not encouraged to keep this excess capacity, which has associated costs. Because of the pressures faced by global firms, it is quite tempting to avoid any excess capacity that may not have short-term payoffs. However, by doing so, the process firms will lose their flexibility.

## Summary

- The decision to allocate volumes and markets to plants is an important tactical decision for a global firm. The decision to locate these plants is an important strategic network design decision and has significant implications on the supply chain performance.
- Firms can use linear programming models to decide on optimal networks design and operations.
- A company's organization structure, performance measurement schemes and business strategy are key factors that affect the way network operations planning issues and design problems are modelled and solved.
- Network designing requires a large amount of data, and converting transactions data into meaningful data that can be used in the model is not a trivial task.
- Deciding optimal locations for services where the facility will be visited by customers involves considerations very different from decisions related to plant networks for product businesses.
- A firm has to live with a facility decision for a long time to come, so it should generate several scenarios based on the world view of likely developments in the future before taking a final decision.
- Global firms disperse their manufacturing plants to different locations and keep excess capacity in network as a hedge against uncertainties in markets and prices of finished products and raw material.

## Discussion Questions

1. How is managing a multi-plant international network different from managing a domestic multi-plant network?
2. A global company has put up a captive facility in India to manage a couple of internal backend processes. The CEO of the local unit is worried about the long-term competitiveness of the Indian unit. Labour cost has been increasing at the rate of 15 per cent in the last few years, and the CEO is worried that in the near future these processes may get shifted to Eastern Europe or some other part of the world. What should the CEO do so that the local unit can survive in the long run?
3. Reliance is trying design a network for its retail operations from the scratch. Suggest a suitable approach.
4. The central government has given several tax concessions for plants located in Baddi, and hence a large number of pharmaceutical and consumer non-durable firms have located their plants there. Why do you think auto component companies and garment companies have not moved to Baddi?
5. While Hyundai India Limited has only one manufacturing plant in India, Asian Paints has 18 processing centres. Why do firms in different industries work with different numbers of plants for serving the same market? List the pros and cons of having a large number of facilities?
6. Why should global firms question their network design decisions every few years?
7. Over a period of time Amazon.com has built new warehouses located at geographically different parts of the United States of America. Why should an e-retailer need multiple warehouses located at different parts of the country?

## Exercises

1) Take the example of Indian Paints. If the company is expecting that demand in each of the six markets will grow by 50 per cent in the next 2 years, should the firm close down any facilities? How much should each plant produce?
2) If Indian Paints decides to produce an extra 500 units in the second quarter to take care of the peak demand in the third quarter, what should the production and distribution plan be? Assume that 500 units will be shipped to all six regions in proportion of their normal demand and stocked in warehouses located close to the market.
3) Magic Mattress, a mattress manufacturing company in Bangalore, is trying to finalize its distribution network for northern India. The company has a manufacturing facility and a central inventory depot in Bangalore

attached to it. In the northern region, the firm presently markets its product through six demand points—Delhi, Kanpur, Jalandhar, Jaipur, Faridabad and Dehra Dun. Each of these demand points belongs to different states and union territories. If the firm serves retailers within the region from distribution centres (DCs) located in the same region (state/union territories) then it does not have to pay central sales tax (CST). CST is an inter-state sales tax and is levied on goods that are sourced from outside the region. If the firm locates DCs in all six regions it can avoid paying CST completely. The fixed cost per period of installing (apportioned) and operating a DC is Rs 2,500 per week. Transportation cost is Rs 0.2 per kilometre per unit, and the unit cost of a mattress is Rs 1,000. The firm has decided to locate at least one DC in the northern region so that the lead time for the retailer is less than 48 hours. The firm will try to serve a market in any region from a DC located closest to the market.

***Demand point specific data.***

| | Delhi | Kanpur | Jalandhar | Jaipur | Faridabad | Dehra Dun |
|---|---|---|---|---|---|---|
| Distance from central warehouse | 2,050 | 1,855 | 2,415 | 2,000 | 2,020 | 2,240 |
| Weekly demand | 40 | 16 | 16 | 16 | 8 | 4 |

***Distances matrix (in km).***

| Warehouse/ market | Delhi | Kanpur | Jalandhar | Jaipur | Faridabad | Dehra Dun |
|---|---|---|---|---|---|---|
| Delhi | 0 | 480 | 375 | 260 | 30 | 235 |
| Kanpur | 480 | 0 | 855 | 520 | 450 | 575 |
| Jalandhar | 375 | 855 | 0 | 635 | 405 | 365 |
| Jaipur | 260 | 520 | 635 | 0 | 290 | 495 |
| Faridabad | 30 | 450 | 405 | 290 | 0 | 260 |
| Dehra Dun | 235 | 575 | 365 | 495 | 260 | 0 |

The firm wants to decide the optimal location of its DCs so as to minimize the total cost. The total cost will include transport cost, fixed facility cost and CST-related cost.

(a) Where should the company locate its warehouses? Current CST rate is 4 per cent.

(b) The Indian government is planning to reduce CST over a period of time. How will your decision change if CST is brought down to 2 per cent.

4) Applichem (this exercise is based on "Applichem (A)", a case published by Harvard Business School), a manufacturer of release-ease, a speciality chemical, markets its product in six countries and has six plants in each of the six countries. Relevant data on plant capacity, production cost, market demand data, exchange rate and duty structure are as shown in the table below:

| | Mexico | Canada | Venezuela | Germany | USA | Japan |
|---|---|---|---|---|---|---|
| Unit production cost* | 9,167 | 119.3 | 498.8 | 183 | 103 | 35,955 |
| Capacity | 22 | 3.7 | 4.5 | 47 | 18.5 | 5.0 |
| Demand | 3 | 2.6 | 16 | 20 | 26.4 | 11.9 |
| Duty** | 60% | 0% | 50% | 9.5% | 4.5% | 6% |
| Exchange rate (currency/ $US 1) | 96.5 Pesos/ $US 1 | 1.23 Canadian dollar/ $US 1 | 4.3 Bolivareas/ $US 1 | 2.38 Deutsche Mark/ $US 1 | 1.0 | 235.0 Yen/ $US 1 |
| Currency used | Pesos | Canadian dollar | Bolivareas | Deutsche Mark | US dollar | Yen |

* Cost per unit in local currency.

**Percentage duty in each country was imposed on the value of the release-ease imported.

Transportation cost matrix from the plant to markets is as shown below:

***Transport costs ($/unit)***

| From/to | Mexico | Canada | Venezuela | Germany | USA | Japan |
|---|---|---|---|---|---|---|
| Mexico | 0.0 | 11.4 | 7.0 | 11.0 | 11.0 | 14.0 |
| Canada | 11.0 | 0.0 | 9.0 | 11.5 | 6.0 | 13.0 |
| Venezuela | 7.0 | 10.0 | 0.0 | 13.0 | 10.4 | 14.3 |
| Germany | 10.0 | 11.5 | 12.5 | 0.0 | 11.2 | 13.3 |
| USA | 10.0 | 6.0 | 11.0 | 10.0 | 0.0 | 12.5 |
| Japan | 14.0 | 13.0 | 12.5 | 14.2 | 13.0 | 0.0 |

What is the optimal production and the market allocation plan?

(Hint: Convert all costs in US$)

How will the decision change if there is a change in exchange rate; the new exchange rate structure is as follows:

| | Mexico | Canada | Venezuela | Germany | USA | Japan |
|---|---|---|---|---|---|---|
| Exchange rate (currency/$US 1) | 22.7 | 1.09 | 4.3 | 2.10 | 1.0 | 240.0 |

(a) How will the decision change if as a part of GATT agreement Mexico and Venezuela bring down the import duty on imported release to 10 per cent?

## Notes

1. See www.imagesretail.com/cover_story2_apr06.htm and www.thehindubusinessline.com/catalyst/2006/11/09/stories/2006110900010100.htm.
2. See www.unilever.com and Geoffrey Jones and Peter Miskell, "European Integration and Corporate Restructuring: The Strategy of Unilever, c. 1957-c. 1990," *European History Reviews* (2005, Vol LVIII): 113–119.
3. B. Fleischmann, S. Ferber, and P. Henrich, "Strategic Planning of BMW's Global Production Network," *Interfaces* (2006).
4. See www.asianpaints.com and interview of Ashwin Dani, VC & MD, Asian Paints, at www.cio.in/topview/viewArticle/ARTICLEID=1237.
5. Kasra Ferdows, "Making the Most of Foreign Factories," *Harvard Business Review* (March–April 1997): 73–88.
6. Romi Malhotra in interview with Mckinsey, see www.mckinsey.com/clientservice/bto/pointofview/pdf/MoIT8_Dell_F.pdf.
7. Based on personal discussion with Dr N. K. Venkatramana, Director for Neurological Disorders, Manipal Hospital.

## Further Reading

B. C. Arnzten, G. B. Brown, T. P. Harrison, and L. L. Trafton, "Global Supply Chain Management at Digital Equipment Corporation," *Interfaces* (1995, Vol 25): 69–93.

R. H. Ballou, *Business Logistics Management* (Upper Saddle River, NJ: Prentice Hall, 1999).

J. D Camm, T. E. Chorman, F. A. Dill, J. R. Evans, D. J. Sweeney, and G. W. Wegryn, "Blending OR/MS, Judgement, and GIS: Reconstructing P&G's Supply Chain," *Interfaces* (1997, Vol 27): 128–142.

Kasra Ferdows, "Making the Most of Foreign Factories," *Harvard Business Review* (March–April 1997): 73–88.

B. Kogut, "Designing Global Strategies: Profiting from Operational Flexibility," *Sloan Management Review* (1985, Vol 27): 27–38.

D. Lessard and J. Lightstone, "Volatile Exchange Rates Put an Operation at Risk," *Harvard Business Review* (1986, Vol 64): 107–114.

C. Markides and N. Berg, "Manufacturing Offshore Is Bad Business," *Harvard Business Review* (1998, Vol 66): 113–120.

## Appendix A: Solving Network Design and Operations Problem Using Excel Solver

Network operations planning and design problems can be formulated as linear programming problems and solved using Excel Solver. In this appendix, we describe the use of Excel Solver for formulating and solving network planning and design problems.

We illustrate the use of Excel Solver through the example of Indian Paints. We will work with cost minimization for both network operations planning and design formulations. The whole exercise involves three steps:

Step 1: Preparing base data in Excel

Step 2: Formulating the model in Solver

Step 3: Solving the problem and carrying out sensitivity analysis of the solution using Solver

### *Step 1: Preparing Base Data*

As can be seen in Figure A6.1, cells B3:G7 contain production and transportation cost data ($Cost_{ij}$) for supply of product from plant to market, cells H3:H7 and I3:I7 contain capacity

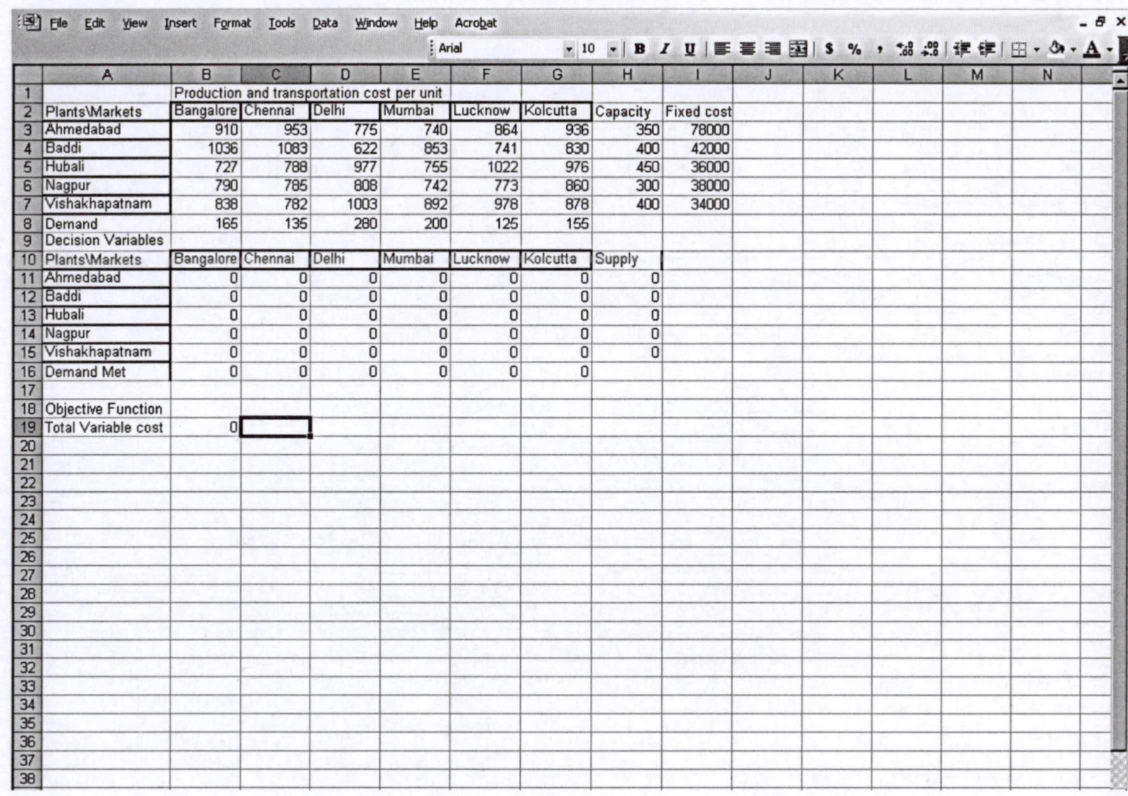

| | A | B | C | D | E | F | G | H | I |
|---|---|---|---|---|---|---|---|---|---|
| 1 | | Production and transportation cost per unit | | | | | | | |
| 2 | Plants\Markets | Bangalore | Chennai | Delhi | Mumbai | Lucknow | Kolcutta | Capacity | Fixed cost |
| 3 | Ahmedabad | 910 | 953 | 775 | 740 | 864 | 936 | 350 | 78000 |
| 4 | Baddi | 1036 | 1083 | 622 | 853 | 741 | 830 | 400 | 42000 |
| 5 | Hubali | 727 | 788 | 977 | 755 | 1022 | 976 | 450 | 36000 |
| 6 | Nagpur | 790 | 785 | 808 | 742 | 773 | 860 | 300 | 38000 |
| 7 | Vishakhapatnam | 838 | 782 | 1003 | 892 | 978 | 878 | 400 | 34000 |
| 8 | Demand | 165 | 135 | 280 | 200 | 125 | 155 | | |
| 9 | Decision Variables | | | | | | | | |
| 10 | Plants\Markets | Bangalore | Chennai | Delhi | Mumbai | Lucknow | Kolcutta | Supply | |
| 11 | Ahmedabad | 0 | 0 | 0 | 0 | 0 | 0 | 0 | |
| 12 | Baddi | 0 | 0 | 0 | 0 | 0 | 0 | 0 | |
| 13 | Hubali | 0 | 0 | 0 | 0 | 0 | 0 | 0 | |
| 14 | Nagpur | 0 | 0 | 0 | 0 | 0 | 0 | 0 | |
| 15 | Vishakhapatnam | 0 | 0 | 0 | 0 | 0 | 0 | 0 | |
| 16 | Demand Met | 0 | 0 | 0 | 0 | 0 | 0 | | |
| 17 | | | | | | | | | |
| 18 | Objective Function | | | | | | | | |
| 19 | Total Variable cost | 0 | | | | | | | |

**Figure A6.1**

Spreadsheet for the data.

($Cap_i$) and fixed cost ($Fcost_i$) data for each of the five plants, and B8:G8 contains demand ($Dem_j$) data for each of the market.

Objective function and the respective left-hand sides of demand (Equation 6.1) and supply (Equation 6.2) are prepared using the formula shown in Table A6.1.

Decision variable supplies from plant to market ($Quant_{ij}$) are represented by Cells B11:G15. Objective function is represented by cell B19. The left- and right-hand sides of Equation 6.1 are represented by cells B16:G16 and B8:G8. Similarly, the cells H11:H15 and H3:H7 represent the left- and right-hand sides of Equation 6.2. The left-hand side of Equation 6.3 is represented by cells B11:G15. Now we are ready to set up the Solver in Excel.

## Step 2: Formulating Model in Solver

Choosing Solver from the tool menu displays the Solver parameter box, as can be seen in Figure A6.2. This parameter box allows us to set up the model in the Solver. The objective function cell (B19) is treated as the target cell in Solver, and as we are working on a minimization problem, we choose the minimization option. Decision variables (B11:G15) are entered in the box indicated "Guess".

***Table A6.1:* Relevant spread formulae.**

| Cell | Cell formula | Equation | Copied to | Remark |
|---|---|---|---|---|
| B19 | = SUMPRODUCT(B3:G7,B11:G15) | Objective function | | |
| B16 | = SUM(B11:B15) | Demand constraint (Equation 6.1) | C16:G16 | Six demand constraints |
| H11 | = SUM(B11:G11) | Supply constraint (Equation 6.2) | H12:H15 | Five supply constraints |

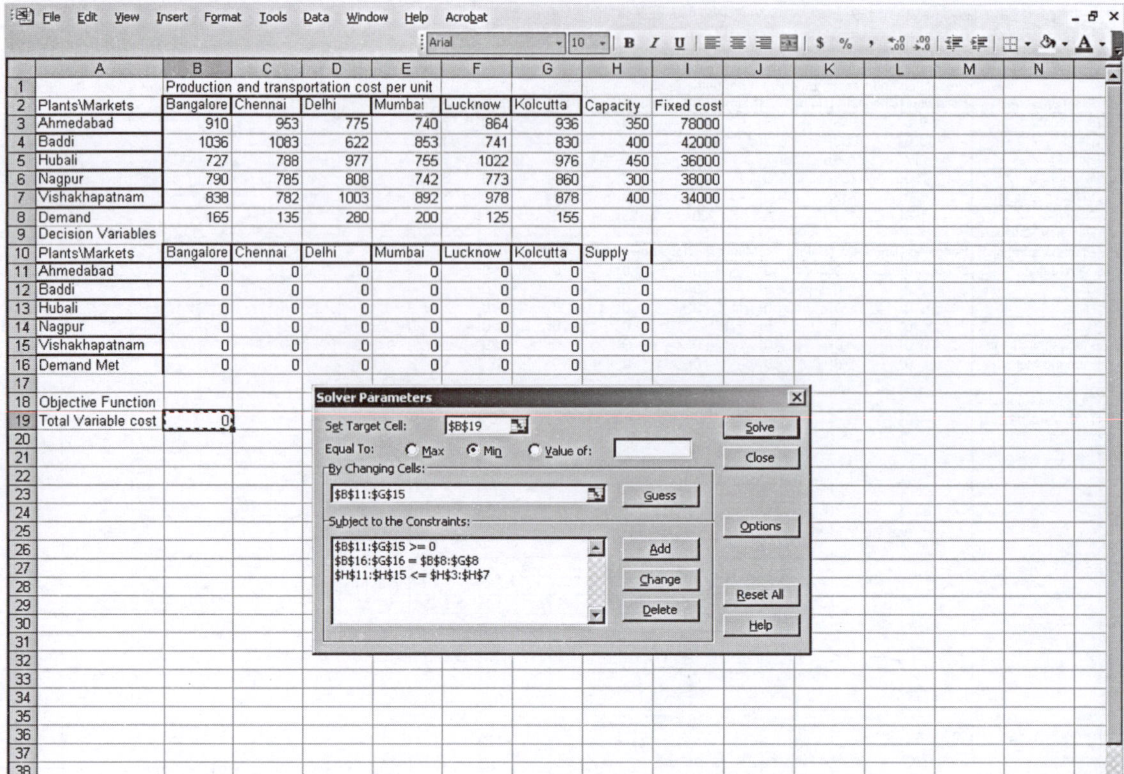

| | A | B | C | D | E | F | G | H | I |
|---|---|---|---|---|---|---|---|---|---|
| 1 | | Production and transportation cost per unit | | | | | | | |
| 2 | Plants\Markets | Bangalore | Chennai | Delhi | Mumbai | Lucknow | Kolcutta | Capacity | Fixed cost |
| 3 | Ahmedabad | 910 | 953 | 775 | 740 | 864 | 936 | 350 | 78000 |
| 4 | Baddi | 1036 | 1083 | 622 | 853 | 741 | 830 | 400 | 42000 |
| 5 | Hubali | 727 | 788 | 977 | 755 | 1022 | 976 | 450 | 36000 |
| 6 | Nagpur | 790 | 785 | 808 | 742 | 773 | 860 | 300 | 38000 |
| 7 | Vishakhapatnam | 838 | 782 | 1003 | 892 | 978 | 878 | 400 | 34000 |
| 8 | Demand | 165 | 135 | 280 | 200 | 125 | 155 | | |
| 9 | Decision Variables | | | | | | | | |
| 10 | Plants\Markets | Bangalore | Chennai | Delhi | Mumbai | Lucknow | Kolcutta | Supply | |
| 11 | Ahmedabad | 0 | 0 | 0 | 0 | 0 | 0 | 0 | |
| 12 | Baddi | 0 | 0 | 0 | 0 | 0 | 0 | 0 | |
| 13 | Hubali | 0 | 0 | 0 | 0 | 0 | 0 | 0 | |
| 14 | Nagpur | 0 | 0 | 0 | 0 | 0 | 0 | 0 | |
| 15 | Vishakhapatnam | 0 | 0 | 0 | 0 | 0 | 0 | 0 | |
| 16 | Demand Met | 0 | 0 | 0 | 0 | 0 | 0 | | |
| 17 | | | | | | | | | |
| 18 | Objective Function | | | | | | | | |
| 19 | Total Variable cost | 0 | | | | | | | |



**Figure A6.2**

Solver parameter box.

As can be seen in Figure A6.2, Equations 6.3, 6.1 and 6.2 are entered in that order in the constraint box.

## *Step 3: Solving Problem and Carrying Out Sensitivity Analysis of the Solution Using Solver*

Clicking solve within the Solver parameter box will result in an optimal solution as shown in Figure A6.3. The details of the solution are reported in Table 6.3.

While clicking solve on Solver parameter box, one can choose to obtain data on sensitivity analysis as one of the outputs of Solver. The sensitivity analysis output contains two outputs: (a) sensitivity analysis on constraints (see Figure A6.4(a)) and (b) sensitivity analysis on parameters of objective function (see Figure A6.4(b) for a partial extract of the output).

For each demand and supply constraint, the shadow price is also reported in the above table. The shadow price of the constraint equation measures the marginal value of this resource. If we look at supply constraints, the shadow price is –32 for Baddi and zero for all other plants. So, if the capacity of the Baddi plant is increased by one unit, the objective function (total variable cost) will increase by –32. For all other plants change in capacity will have no impact on objective function. This is quite intuitive because all other plants are operating at less than full capacity in the final solution, so a change in the capacity value will have no impact on network planning decisions. The shadow price of –32 for Baddi will be valid from the capacity range of 280 (400 – 120) to 405 (400 + 5). Beyond this range of capacity, one will have to run Solver again to understand the impact of change in the capacity on the objective function. Similarly, if demand from Delhi increases by one unit, the objective function will increase by 654, while any increase in unit demand at Kolkata will increase cost by 860. This information will help the marketing department in making appropriate plans for different markets.

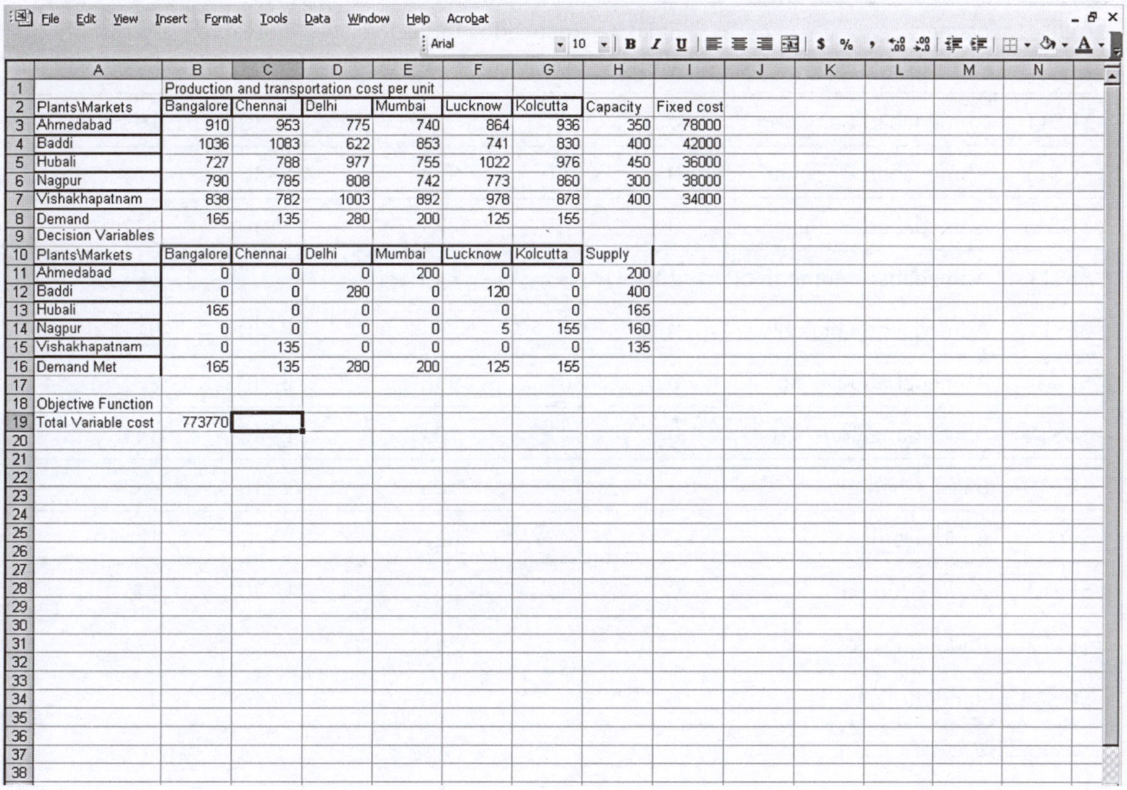

| | A | B | C | D | E | F | G | H | I |
|---|---|---|---|---|---|---|---|---|---|
| 1 | | Production and transportation cost per unit | | | | | | | |
| 2 | Plants\Markets | Bangalore | Chennai | Delhi | Mumbai | Lucknow | Kolcutta | Capacity | Fixed cost |
| 3 | Ahmedabad | 910 | 953 | 775 | 740 | 864 | 936 | 350 | 78000 |
| 4 | Baddi | 1036 | 1083 | 622 | 853 | 741 | 830 | 400 | 42000 |
| 5 | Hubali | 727 | 788 | 977 | 755 | 1022 | 976 | 450 | 36000 |
| 6 | Nagpur | 790 | 785 | 808 | 742 | 773 | 860 | 300 | 38000 |
| 7 | Vishakhapatnam | 838 | 782 | 1003 | 892 | 978 | 878 | 400 | 34000 |
| 8 | Demand | 165 | 135 | 280 | 200 | 125 | 155 | | |
| 9 | Decision Variables | | | | | | | | |
| 10 | Plants\Markets | Bangalore | Chennai | Delhi | Mumbai | Lucknow | Kolcutta | Supply | |
| 11 | Ahmedabad | 0 | 0 | 0 | 200 | 0 | 0 | 200 | |
| 12 | Baddi | 0 | 0 | 280 | 0 | 120 | 0 | 400 | |
| 13 | Hubali | 165 | 0 | 0 | 0 | 0 | 0 | 165 | |
| 14 | Nagpur | 0 | 0 | 0 | 0 | 5 | 155 | 160 | |
| 15 | Vishakhapatnam | 0 | 135 | 0 | 0 | 0 | 0 | 135 | |
| 16 | Demand Met | 165 | 135 | 280 | 200 | 125 | 155 | | |
| 17 | | | | | | | | | |
| 18 | Objective Function | | | | | | | | |
| 19 | Total Variable cost | 773770 | | | | | | | |

**Figure A6.3**

Optimal Solver solution.

| Cell | Name | Final Value | Shadow Price | Constraint R.H. Side | Allowable Increase | Allowable Decrease |
|---|---|---|---|---|---|---|
| \$B\$16 | Demand Met Bangalore | 165 | 727 | 165 | 285 | 165 |
| \$C\$16 | Demand Met Chennai | 135 | 782 | 135 | 265 | 135 |
| \$D\$16 | Demand Met Delhi | 280 | 654 | 280 | 120 | 5 |
| \$E\$16 | Demand Met Mumbai | 200 | 740 | 200 | 150 | 200 |
| \$F\$16 | Demand Met Lucknow | 125 | 773 | 125 | 140 | 5 |
| \$G\$16 | Demand Met Kolkata | 155 | 860 | 155 | 140 | 155 |
| \$H\$11 | Ahmedabad Supply | 200 | 0 | 350 | 1E+30 | 150 |
| \$H\$12 | Baddi Supply | 400 | -32 | 400 | 5 | 120 |
| \$H\$13 | Hubli Supply | 165 | 0 | 450 | 1E+30 | 285 |
| \$H\$14 | Nagpur Supply | 160 | 0 | 300 | 1E+30 | 140 |
| \$H\$15 | Vishakapatnam Supply | 135 | 0 | 400 | 1E+30 | 265 |

**Figure A6.4(a)**

Sensitivity analysis on constraints.

| Cell | Name | Final Value | Reduced Cost | Objective Coefficient | Allowable Increase | Allowable Decrease |
|---|---|---|---|---|---|---|
| $B$11 | Ahmedabad Bangalore | 0 | 183 | 910 | 1E+30 | 183 |
| $C$11 | Ahmedabad Chennai | 0 | 171 | 953 | 1E+30 | 171 |
| $D$11 | Ahmedabad Delhi | 0 | 121 | 775 | 1E+30 | 121 |
| $E$11 | Ahmedabad Mumbai | 200 | 0 | 740 | 2 | 1E+30 |
| $F$11 | Ahmedabad Lucknow | 0 | 91 | 864 | 1E+30 | 91 |
| $G$11 | Ahmedabad Kolkata | 0 | 76 | 936 | 1E+30 | 76 |
| $B$12 | Baddi Bangalore | 0 | 341 | 1036 | 1E+30 | 341 |
| $C$12 | Baddi Chennai | 0 | 333 | 1083 | 1E+30 | 333 |
| $D$12 | Baddi Delhi | 280 | 0 | 622 | 121 | 1E+30 |
| $E$12 | Baddi Mumbai | 0 | 145 | 853 | 1E+30 | 145 |
| $F$12 | Baddi Lucknow | 120 | 0 | 741 | 2 | 121 |
| $G$12 | Baddi Kolkata | 0 | 2 | 830 | 1E+30 | 2 |

**Figure A6.4(b)**

Sensitivity analysis on parameters of objective function.

Using the parameter of objective function, sensitivity is captured by reduced cost. If the relevant decision variable ($Quant_{ij}$) is positive, the reduced cost will be zero. But wherever $Quant_{ij}$ is zero, the reduced cost will tell us by what amount the cost parameter should change so that the corresponding decision variable will get a non-zero value in the optimal solution. For example, Baddi does not supply to Mumbai and the corresponding cell E12 has reduced cost to 145. Hence, only if the cost of production plus transportation from Baddi to Mumbai drops by 145 will Baddi start supplying to Mumbai. Similarly, Delhi gets it supply from Baddi and will keep getting supply from Baddi as long as the per unit cost increase is not more than 121. So it allows one to understand the impact of change in value of objective function parameters on optimal solution.

## Network Design Decision

We work with cost minimization for network design formulations. In network design problems, we need to introduce binary variables. As can be seen in Figure A6.5, apart from $Quant_{ij}$

***Table A6.2:* Relevant spreadsheet formulae.**

| Cell | Cell formula | Equation | Copied to | Remark |
|---|---|---|---|---|
| B19 | = SUMPRODUCT (I3:I7,H11:H15) + SUMPRODUCT(B3:G7,B11:G15) | Objective function | | |
| B16 | = SUM(B11:B15) | Left side of Demand constraint (Equation 6.7) | C16:G16 | Six demand constraints |
| I11 | = SUM(B11:G11) | Left side of Supply Constraint (Equation 6.8) | I12:I15 | Five supply constraints |
| J11 | = H3*H11 | Right side of Supply Constraint (Equation 6.8) | J12:J15 | Five supply constraints |

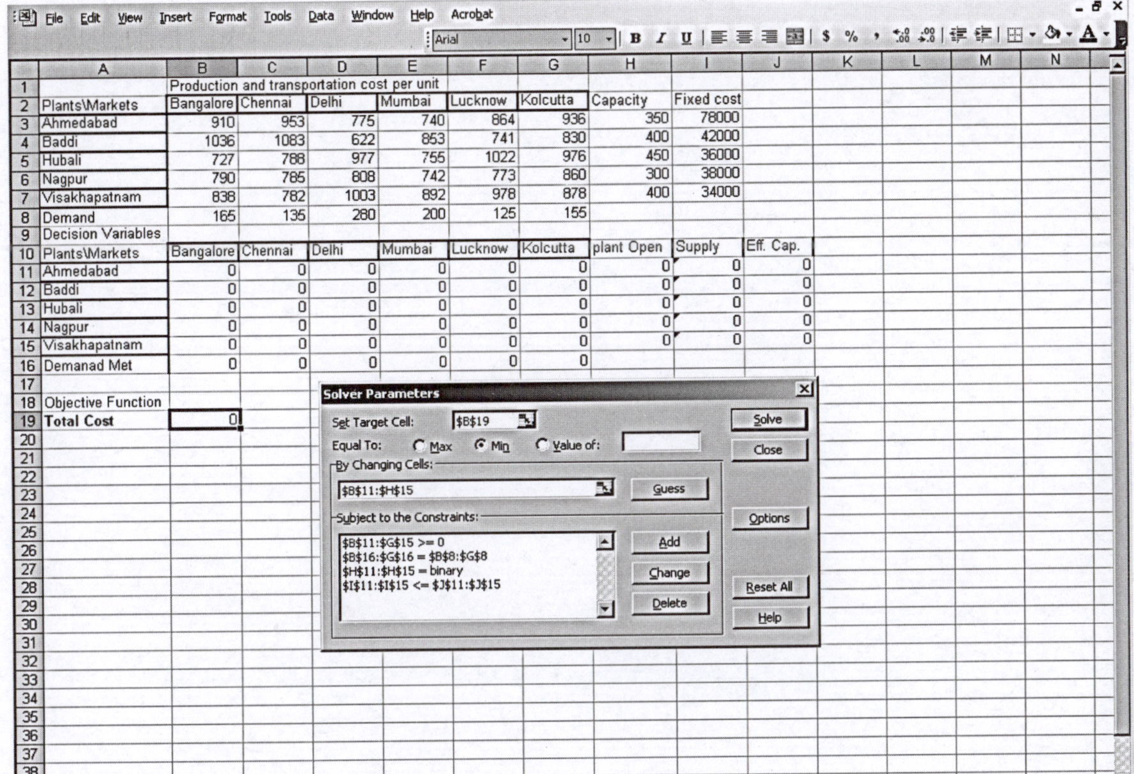

| | A | B | C | D | E | F | G | H | I | J |
|---|---|---|---|---|---|---|---|---|---|---|
| 1 | | Production and transportation cost per unit | | | | | | | | |
| 2 | Plants\Markets | Bangalore | Chennai | Delhi | Mumbai | Lucknow | Kolcutta | Capacity | Fixed cost | |
| 3 | Ahmedabad | 910 | 953 | 775 | 740 | 864 | 936 | 350 | 78000 | |
| 4 | Baddi | 1036 | 1083 | 622 | 853 | 741 | 830 | 400 | 42000 | |
| 5 | Hubali | 727 | 788 | 977 | 755 | 1022 | 976 | 450 | 36000 | |
| 6 | Nagpur | 790 | 785 | 808 | 742 | 773 | 860 | 300 | 38000 | |
| 7 | Visakhapatnam | 838 | 782 | 1003 | 892 | 978 | 878 | 400 | 34000 | |
| 8 | Demand | 165 | 135 | 280 | 200 | 125 | 155 | | | |
| 9 | Decision Variables | | | | | | | | | |
| 10 | Plants\Markets | Bangalore | Chennai | Delhi | Mumbai | Lucknow | Kolcutta | plant Open | Supply | Eff. Cap. |
| 11 | Ahmedabad | 0 | 0 | 0 | 0 | 0 | 0 | 0 | 0 | 0 |
| 12 | Baddi | 0 | 0 | 0 | 0 | 0 | 0 | 0 | 0 | 0 |
| 13 | Hubali | 0 | 0 | 0 | 0 | 0 | 0 | 0 | 0 | 0 |
| 14 | Nagpur | 0 | 0 | 0 | 0 | 0 | 0 | 0 | 0 | 0 |
| 15 | Visakhapatnam | 0 | 0 | 0 | 0 | 0 | 0 | 0 | 0 | 0 |
| 16 | Demanad Met | 0 | 0 | 0 | 0 | 0 | 0 | | | |
| 17 | | | | | | | | | | |
| 18 | Objective Function | | | | | | | | | |
| 19 | **Total Cost** | 0 | | | | | | | | |



**Figure A6.5**

Solver parameter box for network design problem.

variables, additional variables *Fac-open*$_i$ have been introduced in cell H11:H15. The relevant spreadsheet formulae are presented in Table A6.2.

As can be seen in Figure A6.5, in the constraint box Equations 6.9, 6.7, 6.10 and 6.8 are entered in that order. Solver solves binary linear programming problems using the branch and bound solution methodology.

# PART III

# Managing Information Flow in Supply Chains



Supply chain management involves planning, design and control of flow of material, information and finance along the supply chain in order to deliver superior value to the end customer in an effective and efficient manner. In Part III, we focus on issues on managing information flow in supply chains. For several key decisions pertaining to material flow, real-time undistorted information about demand and supply is critical. Recent advances in information and communication technologies have helped firms in improving information flow not only within the firm but also across organizations within the chain.

In complex global supply chains, firms have to dynamically change their activity mix based on demand as well as supply information within the chain. Demand forecasts rather than actual orders become the basis for demand information in MTS and CTO supply chains. In Chapter 7, we discuss different types of forecasting methods and present various models that are useful in qualitative and quantitative forecasting. We also discuss important characteristics of forecasts that help in developing the right perspective and in the process help us in applying forecasting ideas in practice.

Supply chain managers can make effective decisions if they have access to timely information about the activities of all the other entities in the supply chain. IT can link all activities in a supply chain into an integrated and coordinated system that is fast and flexible so that supply chain managers get the needed information. In Chapter 8, we present the four major functional roles played by IT in supply chain management: transaction execution, collaboration and coordination, decision support and measurement and reporting. We also present a strategic framework for adoption of IT in supply chains. The chapter concludes with a brief discussion on the recent advances in technology and their possible consequences on innovative supply chain solutions.

# Demand Forecasting

## Learning Objectives

After reading this chapter, you will be able to answer the following questions:

> What is the role of forecasting in supply chain management?

> What are the different methods of forecasting? How do firms choose the most appropriate model for a given context?

> How do firms use historical demand data in forecasting?

> What are the significant behavioural issues that need to be considered while designing a forecasting system in the organization?

Mr and Mrs Ahluwalia have come to Ambala to see off their son. While waiting for the train, Mr Ahluwalia picks up a local newspaper and a huge, four-colour supplement catches his eye. Browsing through it he realizes that it is an advertisement. Big Bazaar has floated a scheme called "Sabse Sasta Teen Din" offer wherein it is offering products at rock-bottom prices. Tempted by the attractive prices, the couple decide to stop over at the Big Bazaar outlet before driving back home. When they finally emerge from Big Bazaar a few hours later, they realize, to their dismay, that now they have more stuff to carry than they possibly can! Who could have predicted that this will happen? Even Mr and Mrs Ahluwalia had not known that this will happen.

When Big Bazaar, launched this scheme, "Sabse Sasta Din" (as it was known then) in 2006, they sold goods worth Rs 260 million. Encouraged by the response, they ran the scheme for three days in 2007. During this 3-day period, approximately six million people visited their stores. The 43 outlets of Big Bazaar sold goods worth Rs 1.25 billion. A total of 108 thousand bed sheets, 30,000 cell phones and 11,000 pieces of apparel were sold. There were reports that the company had to shut down many of the outlets as they had not anticipated the customer response and the stocks of several popular items had been exhausted. Predicting the demand for such schemes is always a tricky job.

Forecasting in the supply chain context is the art and science of predicting future demand. It is a combination of intuitive judgement, observation and analysis of past trends. Forecasts can be made using either the qualitative approach or the quantitative approach. In this chapter, we discuss the important characteristics of forecasts that help in understanding the role of forecasting from the perspective of the decision maker. We also present different types of forecasting models including the time-series model.

## Introduction

Forecasting in the supply chain context is the art and science of predicting future demand. From time immemorial, mankind has attempted this crystal gazing exercise. Many managers treat forecasting as purely an art form and assume that the best forecasts are made by experienced managers using their intuition. We take the view that in most situations managers can improve their forecasts by using structured approaches. Of course, forecasts made even with the most sophisticated tools will never be precise. This does not mean that forecasting is a futile exercise, but it is important to recognize that forecasts will never be perfect and therefore firms should find ways and means of reducing the error involved in the exercise. In certain situations, future demand can be estimated accurately using structured analysis, while in others it will be very difficult to forecast demand, and an organization has to learn to live with the uncertainty. So, apart from forecasting future demand, firms should also estimate the likely errors in the forecasts so as to be prepared for the eventuality that demand is bound to be different from that forecasted.

We first discuss a few important characteristics of forecasts that help in understanding the role of forecasting from the perspective of the decision maker. In the subsequent sections, different types of forecasting are discussed and various models that are useful in time series forecasting are also presented. Finally, we discuss issues related to implementing the various forecasting techniques.

## The Role of Forecasting

Whatever the industry, forecasting is unavoidable. See Box 7.1 for some famous quotations that indicate people's perception of forecasting and forecasters. Demand forecasting has been the weakest link in most supply chain planning. Most organizations prefer to live in a world where they do not have to carry out the exercise of demand forecasting. As we have argued earlier, in most firms, the customer order delivery time is shorter than the supply chain lead time required by the firm. Hence, a significant part of activities have to be carried out on the basis of forecasts. Even though firms in the made-to-order business like Dell Computers assemble PCs only on a made-to-order basis, it still has to carry out forecasting to ensure that it has sufficient capacity in place to assemble the PCs for the coming period.

Further, in many businesses we need to forecast beyond the time horizon of the supply chain lead time. In case of products with high seasonal demands (e.g., paints and consumer durables exhibit high demand during festival seasons; refrigerators and air conditioners exhibit

**BOX 7.1** Forecasting—Famous Quotations[1]

I think there is a world market for maybe five computers.
Thomas Watson, IBM, 1943

640K ought to be enough for anybody.
Bill Gates, 1981

Everything that can be invented has been invented.
Commissioner, US Office of Patents, 1899

Prediction is very difficult, especially if it's about the future.
Niels Bohr

I always avoid prophesying beforehand because it is much better to prophesy after the event has already taken place.
Winston Churchill

An economist is an expert who will know tomorrow why the things he predicted yesterday didn't happen today.
Evan Esar

peak demand during the summer), if the respective firms do not have sufficient capacity during the peak period of demand, then they have to carry out forecasting for a longer horizon and build inventory during the lean season so as to meet the demand during peak periods.

## Characteristics of Forecasts

Before we discuss forecasting methods, we first need to understand a few characteristics of forecasting that have serious implications on the design of the forecasting system for a firm. Some important characteristics and their implications are listed below.

### The Forecast Is Always Wrong

Whatever level of sophistication one introduces in the forecasting methodology, the actual demand will never match the forecast. This does not mean that an organization should not carry out forecasting, but it implies that it should be prepared for the eventuality that actual demand is likely to be different from the forecast. So apart from the forecast a firm should also estimate the forecast error, because that will help the firm in preparing contingency measures in terms of safety stocks and safety capacity required to handle various scenarios that are likely to develop in the future. Of course, this way of handling forecasting error is not cost free, so firms prefer to come up with forecasting methods that have lower forecasting errors. Further, most forecasting methods are based on certain inherent assumptions, which may not hold for a radically changed environment, and the firm might be faced with a disastrous situation where the actual demand is way off from the forecast. During the economic downturn of 2001, Cisco paid a huge price by ignoring signals from the environment and by relying too heavily on its forecasting software. So it is important that forecast accuracy is monitored, and in case of significant deviations, the forecast model needs to be re-examined.

### OVERRELIANCE ON FORECASTING SOFTWARE LEADING TO BUSINESS PROBLEM AT CISCO[2]

During the economic downturn in 2001, Cisco found that its sales plunged by 30 per cent and it was stuck with huge inventory. Cisco decided to write off an inventory of $2.2 billion, and Cisco's stock price dropped to a record low at $13.63 (stock price was quoted at $82 in 2000). Though all networking companies were adversely affected by the downturn, the losses suffered by Cisco surprised everyone. Cisco relied very heavily on its state of the art *virtual close* software and expected that demand will rise when other companies in the industry expected demand to decline. Cisco's software had built-in growth bias and was not designed to capture the impact of change in economy. Experts believe that this over reliance on the forecasting technology led people to undervalue human judgment and intuition, and inhibited frank conversations among (supply chain) partners". The CEO John Chambers admitted in an interview that "We never built models to anticipate something of this magnitude".

### The Longer the Forecast Horizon, the Worse the Forecast

Forecast for a longer time horizon is likely to be less accurate than forecast for a shorter time horizon. It stands to reason that forecasting the weekly demand for the next week will be more accurate than a forecast for weekly demand for a time period that is a few months down the line. This has an important implication for firms and it reinforces the importance of lead time reduction programmes within a firm. If an organization is able to reduce the lead time of various processes, it will have to forecast for a shorter horizon. Japanese firms have focused on reducing the lead time and making processes more reliable. Thus, they do not have to keep too much safety stocks in the system. In general, firms that do not have to carry out short-term forecasting because lead times are shorter than customer lead times are likely to have a superior supply chain performance. So while focusing on building better forecasting models so as to reduce forecast errors, firms have to simultaneously find a way of reducing the lead time so that the forecasting horizon is reduced and flexibility is also built into the supply chain, enabling them to respond better to actual demand, which may be different from the forecast value.

### Aggregate Forecasts Are More Accurate

A forecast of aggregate demand (all Maruti 800-cc cars, tons of paint for Asian paints, tons of toothpaste for Colgate, etc.) is more accurate than forecast for individual end items (red 800-cc Maruti car, 1-litre pack of yellow paint, 50-g pack of Colgate Gel, etc.). This has important implications because depending on the point of differentiation, firms may have to forecast at different levels of aggregation. Aggregation can be on product variants (demand for 800-cc cars vis-à-vis demand for red 800-cc cars), it can be along time (demand for week vis-à-vis demand for day) or it can be along geography (demand for Karnataka vis-à-vis demand for Bangalore). Recognizing that different decisions at various stages in the supply chain may require different levels of aggregation, firms should ensure that disaggregated forecasts are not used unless they are required for a particular decision at that stage.

### Forecasts Are an Integral Part of Decision Making

As discussed earlier, forecasting involves two important decisions: (a) determining the appropriate level of aggregation and (b) determining the appropriate forecast horizon. To judge the appropriateness of level of aggregation and length of horizon, we must understand how this forecast is used by the relevant decision maker in the decision-making process. The level of aggregation required by different decision makers will change from one context to another. For example, the sales manager of a firm may be interested in geographically disaggregated demand, while the production manager will be interested in aggregated demand; similarly, while the production manager may be interested in the disaggregated model-wise demand, the commodity buyer who is in charge of procuring steel may only be interested in an aggregated demand for all models for the coming month. Similarly, the marketing manager may be interested in forecasting for the next month, while the purchase manager may be interested in a 6-month horizon because he or she has to work with supplier lead time that may be really long. Within the forecasting horizon, a firm will have to decide on the appropriate unit of forecasting period, which is the basic unit of time for which forecasts are made. For example, the forecast horizon can be one quarter, and within that, the forecasting unit could be one month. Forecasting horizon is the number of time periods in the future covered by the forecast.

## *Time Horizons for Forecasting*

The key factor in choosing a proper forecasting approach is the time horizon for the decision requiring forecasts. Forecasts can be made for various timeframes: short, medium and long terms. Of course, *time* is a term that depends on the product-market context and is used in a relative sense. For instance, high-technology and fashion products have a very short life cycle, and a product like the new model of an automobile will have a life cycle of at least 4–6 years. Similarly, the horizon in consideration will be of a different magnitude for a new model of a cell phone or a laptop, which will have life cycles of about 4–6 months.

In this section, for the purpose of discussion we focus on a consumer durable or an automobile having a product life cycle ranging from 3 to 6 years. While discussing forecasting methods, the focus will be on methodology that is equally valid for short, medium and long terms. In the long run, as the trend itself changes, quantitative data become irrelevant, and economists are usually worried about the business cycles issue, which has not been included in our discussion.

### Short-term Forecasting

In the short term (1 day to 3 months), managers are interested in forecasts for disaggregated demand (for specific product, for specific geography, etc.). There is very little time to react to errors in demand forecasts, so the forecasts need to be as accurate as possible. Time-series analysis is used most often for short-term forecasting. When historical data are not available, managers use judgement methods for short-term forecasts during the product launch stage. Decisions regarding production, transportation scheduling, procurement and inventory management involve short-term forecasting.

### Medium-term Forecasting

The time horizon for a medium term is 3 months to 24 months. The need for medium term relates to aggregate planning (sales and operations planning, as popularly called in practice). To handle seasonality in demand across a time period from 6 months to 1 year, medium-term forecast is used to build up seasonal inventory, budgeting and work force planning. It allows a firm to have a horizon of 6–12 months for managing resource planning and budgeting. Forecast is carried out at aggregate levels (across product variants at category level). Both time-series models as well as causal models are used for medium-term forecasting. For products with long life cycles, time-series models are used extensively. But for products with shorter life cycles (about 1–3 years), causal models are preferred as they can handle the turning points (growth to maturity, maturity to decline) in the life cycle better.

### Long-term Forecasting

For time horizons exceeding two years, forecasts are usually made in aggregate measures (rupee value, sales across product categories, etc.). Long-term forecasts are used for process selection, capacity planning and location decisions. Judgement models and causal models are primarily used for long-term forecasts. Even when causal models are used, managers apply their judgements on the number generated from the quantitative models.

With this background information on forecasting, we move on to examine the various forecasting methods available. Forecast methods are classified as follows: qualitative forecasting and quantitative forecasting. We start the discussion with qualitative forecasting methods.

## Qualitative Forecasting Methods

Qualitative forecasting methods are primarily subjective and they rely on human expertise and judgement. These methods are most appropriate when little historical data are available, like in the case of demand forecasts for new products or the estimation of sales from a newly developed Internet-based electronic channel. Similarly, long-term forecasts involving forecast beyond a couple of years may involve an understanding of the changes taking place in technology and markets, and historical data may not provide any relevant data in this regard. In the early part of the product life cycle, that is, when the product is either at the introductory stage or in the early part of the growth stage, there are not enough data to do any meaningful quantitative forecasting.

In this section, we discuss four popular qualitative forecasting methods: Delphi, market research, life cycle analogy and judgemental methods.

### *The Delphi Approach*

The Delphi method employs a panel of experts in arriving at the forecast and proceeds through a series of rounds. It is an iterative method wherein each expert is asked to make individual predictions based on available data. The first step in this approach is to identify the experts who will constitute the panel. Usually, one will try and form a panel consisting of experts from both the technology and the marketing fields. For example, one may use the Delphi method to forecast penetration of the RFID technology in tracking consumer products or to forecast demand for the battery-powered car segment. In both cases, an insight into how technology might evolve and how the potential customers are likely to view these new products and ideas in the market place is essential. The exact mix depends on the extent of uncertainties in technology and markets, as well as the nature of the product or the idea for which forecasting is being done. In the first round, each individual expert is asked to give his or her forecast individually, on the basis of his or her judgement At the end of first round, responses are tabulated and fed back to the panel along with the overall statistics of the responses, but all individual response are treated anonymously.

Each member is asked to reconsider his or her judgement based on the data available about the aggregate responses from other experts. The responses in the second round are again tabulated and fed back to the group and individuals are asked to revise their responses, if necessary. This process is repeated till no significant changes are observed or sufficient convergence is achieved within the group. Usually, it takes anything from three to six rounds for completing the study. This methodology eliminates the influence that authority usually has over groups. Further, since it collects data individually it avoids the herd effect, where people prefer to follow the group and get biased by the bandwagon effect, which is what happens in the face to face panels. Delphi is an expensive and time-consuming method.

## Market Research

Market research involves estimation of the market size based on testing new products or ideas with a few selected potential customers. Market testing is used when a prototype of the new product is available, and based on the reaction from the sample market survey, the overall demand for market is projected. Market surveys are useful when a new product or service idea is at the conception stage and firms attempt to capture attitudinal and purchase intention data from the survey carried out among potential representative buyers. It is a relatively expensive method of forecasting and is useful when a firm is working with stable technology (no major technological breakthroughs are expected in the future) and is planning moderate changes on product innovation (products involving new features), or when a firm is market testing one of its new offerings.

## Life Cycle Analogy

Typically, all products go through a life cycle of introduction, growth, maturity and decline. Based on the experiences of similar products in the past, one can make use of the diffusion model, where given the proportion of innovators, imitators and the overall market size, one can estimate demand distribution over a product's life cycle. Relevant parameters can be estimated form the life cycle demand data available for products of similar characteristics introduced in past. For example, if one wants to forecast demand for a new product in India, then one might look at the experience of the same product in a different market or the experience of a similar product in India before. Demand for flat screen TV can be estimated using parameters from the demand history of cathode ray TV introduced in the country in the mid-nineties. Or, one can look at the diffusion of flat screen TV in Korea and try and estimate relevant parameters for India and plug it in the relevant diffusion models.

## Informed Judgement

The forecast is made by an individual or a group based on experience and understanding of the situation. For example, many companies use sales force estimates to arrive at the demand for the next year. As the sales force is supposed to be close to the customer and has a better understanding of the ground reality, sales force estimates could be good for short-term forecasting. Firms also use a group of experienced executives to make estimates about forecasts. A group of experienced executives are good at estimating new product demand or estimating demand during technological changes or when a product is likely to move from one phase of life cycle to another. Informed judgement methodology is also used for medium-term forecasting.

Empirical evidence suggests that a vast majority of people are overoptimistic and they underestimate future uncertainty significantly. Similarly, most executives have a "recency bias", which means that they are greatly influenced by recent events. So, firms have to be careful in using judgemental forecasting.

## INTERVIEW WITH

## B. K. DUTTA

*Bharat Petroleum Corporation Limited (BPCL), a Fortune 500 Company with a sales turnover of Rs 1,000 billion, is a leading player in the petroleum sector in the country. BPCL is involved in refining and marketing of a whole range of oil products in the country. Mr B. K. Dutta is an executive director of the supply chain optimization group at BPCL.*

*Given the scale of operations of BPCL, what is the level of complexity of the supply chain?*

**B. K. Dutta:** BPCL currently has refineries at Mumbai and Kochi with a capacity of 12 million metric ton (MMT) and 7.5 MMT per annum, respectively, for refining crude oil. On the retail front, BPCL is engaged in the retailing of petrol, diesel and kerosene through its vast network of 6,553 retail outlets and 1,007 kerosene dealers. We also cater to the requirements of fuel and other petroleum products of about 8,000 industrial customers spread across the country Since the principal products like MS, diesel and LPG are sensitive in nature, we have to ensure that we provide the highest level of product availability and achieving the same has been a major challenge.

To add to this, we are under constant pressure to reduce cost in all areas of business because of additional burdens faced such as upward oil price movements. The risks associated with the volatile price movements of crude oil and finished products in the international market are expected to continue. However, it is not possible to pass on the increases in the prices of sensitive petroleum products to the consumers because of Indian government restrictions. As such, companies that market oil and oil-based products will continue to grapple with the challenge of managing their finances in the midst of this uncertainty without compromising on their future plans and programmes.

*What are the forecasting practices that BPCL has adopted?*

**B. K. Dutta:** Given the nature of products we are in, we are expected to provide very high level service. So, it is important that we increase forecast accuracy at depot level so that we can place our products in a way that we can work with moderate level of inventory even while operating at high level of service. We ensure that we never face a stock-out situation.

We do short-term forecasting for every market. Based on past data and inputs from the marketing department we come up with a forecast at the market level. We take care of growth in our short-term forecasting models. For example, for products like diesel, a significant consumer base is from the agriculture sector and hence our demand depends on the monsoon. Of course, sometimes, we get into difficulty when there are rumours of price change and people forward their buying requirements.

We also have developed long-term forecasting models where we capture the impact of macroeconomic factors and its implications for the products we serve. This enables scenario planning for our long-term capacity.

We also have been working on price forecasting. We try and procure crude oil in the spot market as well as in the term market. We try to find a correlation between spot and forward markets. We also try to analyse how price trends vary over a period of time. This helps us in planning our strategy in crude procurement.

*What are the future initiatives to optimize the supply chain at BPCL?*

**B. K. Dutta:** Recently, we have instituted a supply chain optimization group that provides support to all SBUs. In the area of forecasting, we are able to transfer our learning across all businesses in which we operate. We find that over the last few years we have reduced our forecast errors by refining our forecasting processes. We also want to develop more complex price forecasting models which will allow us to improve our procurement decisions by minimizing the risk.

A company may find that it is difficult to select one model that is most appropriate for forecasting. Several companies use multiple forecasting methods, and some studies have shown that a combination of forecasts, arrived at using different approaches, is very effective. We now discuss the quantitative methods of forecasting.

# Quantitative Methods

Within quantitative models, the following two types are commonly used in forecasting applications: time series and causal.

## *Time-series Method*

The time-series method of forecasting uses historical data to make forecasts. It is assumed that the future is going to be very similar to the past. As shown in Figure 7.1, we are trying to forecast $n$ future periods at the end of the $t$ period using information about demand up to the $t$ period.

We use decomposition methods that break a time series into its major components. Rather than trying to predict an overall pattern, an attempt has been made to predict each major component separately.

### Decomposition of Time-series Data

Demand is decomposed following a systematic part that can be predicted and a random part that cannot be predicted. It is assumed that the random component comes from distribution, which has a mean equal to 0 and standard deviation that can be estimated from the past data. So the forecasting model attempts to predict the systematic component and estimates standard deviation of forecast error using past data.

$$\text{Demand} = \text{Systematic part} + \text{Random part}$$

While breaking time series into components, the three most common patterns observed are trend form, seasonal form and level form. If data of seasonality and trend effect are removed, one essentially sees the level form where data move around a horizontal line. As shown in Figure 7.2, demand data can be decomposed into the three forms. Time-series methods attempt to estimate parameters of these three forms and the magnitude of forecasting error. It is not unusual to find mention of business cycle while discussing systematic components of the demand data. The business cycle involves shifts over time between periods of relatively rapid growth of output and periods of relative stagnation or decline. Though termed cycles, these fluctuations in economic growth and decline do not follow a predictable periodic pattern. So we do not include business-cycle-related patterns in our discussion of the systematic component of data.

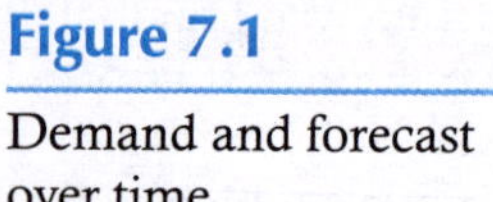

**Figure 7.1**

Demand and forecast over time.

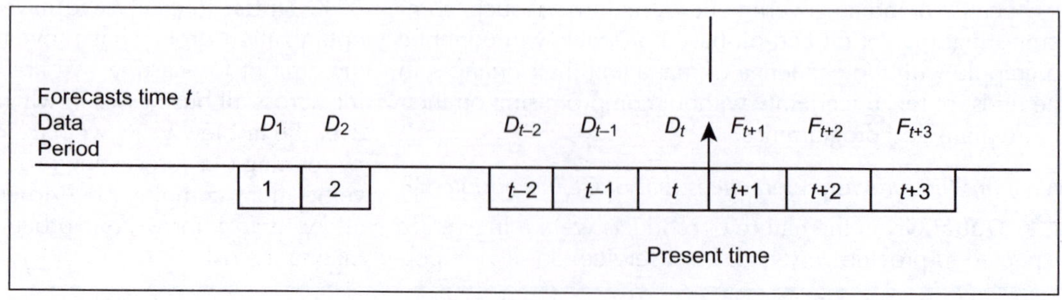

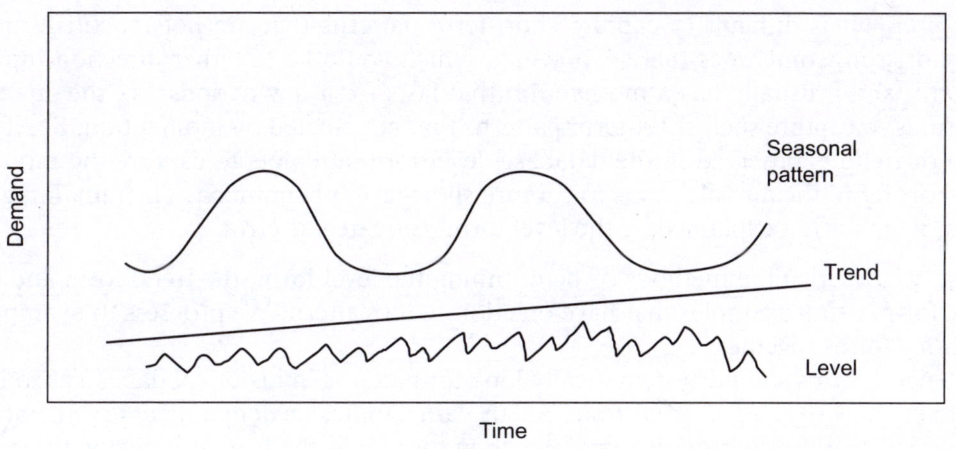


**Figure 7.2**

Decomposition of time-series data.

Demand is decomposed as follows:

Demand ($t$) = (Level ($t$) + Trend parameter × $t$) × Seasonality parameter ($t$) + Random

Level, trend and seasonality are captured as systematic components and the balance is treated as a forecast error. Decomposition of time-series data is depicted in Figure 7.2. As the figure shows, unlike seasonality and trend forms it is difficult to separate the random part from the level form.

Our attempt in the time-series forecast is to first find the linear trend and seasonality, which are simple and recognizable patterns. There may be some other kinds of patterns that are difficult to detect because of the smallness of the sample size. After the effect of linear trend and seasonality are removed, it is assumed that data has only level form and random effect.

Before we discuss the model in detail, we will first look at each form more closely.

- *Seasonality*. A seasonal pattern (e.g., quarter of the year, moth of the year, week of the month, day of the week) exists when demand is influenced by seasonal factors. For example, sales of air conditioners shoot up every summer and dip during the winter. So, if we plot data for several years, we will find this pattern repeating every year. Similarly, we can see higher levels of withdrawals at ATMs on Fridays and higher levels of demand in movie halls on weekends. The relevant parameter here is the periodicity $p$, which is the number of time periods after which the seasonal cycle repeats itself. Seasonal variations can be attributed to weather (e.g., demand for air conditioners in the summer), to festivals (e.g., demand for paint during festivals such as Diwali, Dussera and Sankaranti) or to organization policy (e.g., sales during last week, sales during last quarter of financial year). If we plot scatter data, we can usually see this repetitive pattern and identify periodicity, which is the length of each repetitive cycle. De-seasonalized demand represents the demand that is observed in the absence of any seasonal pattern. After estimating seasonal pattern, data are usually de-seasonalized so as to identify the parameters of other forms and patterns in the data.

- *Trend*. As discussed earlier, during the growth and decline stages of the product life cycle, a consistent trend pattern in terms of demand growth or demand decline can be observed, as shown in Figure 7.2. By looking at the scatter diagram of past data it is not difficult to infer the existence or non-existence of a trend pattern in the data. Statistical analysis reveals whether the visual trend observed in the data pattern of the scatter diagram is statistically significant or not. Here, we will restrict ourselves to analysing the patterns in the linear trend only. De-trended data represent the demand that is observed in the absence of a trend component. After estimating the trend parameters, data are usually de-trended to identify the relevant level parameters in the demand data.

- *Level form.* It is difficult to capture short-term patterns that are not repetitive in nature. In the short run, sometimes there is a swing, which could be in either direction, upward or downward, and it usually has a momentum that lasts for a few periods. So, the attempt in a level form is to capture such short-term patterns that are created by momentum. So, if no seasonality or trend is observed in the database, level form attempts to capture the momentum. In the short term, the aim always is to capture short-term phenomena. The remaining part of demand, which is not explained by the level form, is treated as error.

First, we describe the methods of determining the level form, the trend form and the seasonality form, using examples that have one dominant pattern. We progress to examples with all the three forms together.

In general, firms should systematically look for patterns in historical data so as to improve forecast accuracy over a period of time. Asian Paints mines its demand data systematically to identify micro-patterns within the data, which in turn helps the firm in reducing forecast error over a period of time.

### DEMAND FORECASTING AT ASIAN PAINTS[3]

Asian Paints found that in certain districts of Maharashtra there is spike in demand for 50–100-mL packs of deep orange shade during a specific period of the year. Further investigations revealed that a few districts of Maharashtra observe a local festival called Pola, and during that festival, farmers paint the horns of bullocks with deep orange shade. Asian Paints is aware of the fact that the paint-buying decision in India is linked to festivals, and India being a diverse country with different regions celebrating various festivals at different times of the year, it is important for Asian Paints to capture the same in its forecasting models. Detailed analysis of past data allows Asian Paints to include this aspect in their forecasting process so as to arrive at an accurate demand forecast that enables them to develop a relevant manufacturing and distribution plan so as to meet the demands of the market place. Poor forecast can mean either lost opportunity in the market place or excess but imbalanced inventory in the supply chain.

## Causal Models

Causal forecasting models show the cause for demand and its relation to other variables. Usually, regression is used for modelling the cause-and-effect behaviour. Demand for soft drinks can be related to the average summer temperature. Similarly, rainfall can give us an estimate of crop and in turn an estimate of the demand for consumer durables in the rural areas. Demand for auto spares is a function of current demand. Similarly, growth of BPO investment will lead to growth in catering and transport businesses. So if one can predict the likely number of people employed in the BPO sector, then one can estimate the growth in the catering sector also. Long-term demand of consumer durables can be linked to the population growth and the economic growth of a region.

In many cases, the cause is a leading variable and the effect is a lagging variable, so by observing the actual value of the leading variable, one can predict future demand. In some other cases, causal variables are easier to estimate, so using the estimate of causal variables and using regression analysis one can estimate the demand forecast for the product that the firm is interested in. In the earlier section, we discussed methods of trend analysis. In trend analysis, we treat time as an independent variable, while in causal methods, instead of time, summer temperature or income level or BPO investments can be dependent variables. In case there are multiple causal variables, one will use multiple regression methodology wherein using past data one can estimate the relevant parameters of causal models. Causal models are good for medium- to long-term forecasting. Apart from regression, econometric models, input–output models and simulation models are also used.

## Forecast Error

As discussed earlier, future demand has a component that is systemic in nature, which forecasting attempts to predict. Even with the best forecasting methodology, one will still not be able to predict some part of demand, which is known as "random" demand since it is unpredictable in nature. The forecasting method is judged by estimating the degree to which it can predict future demand. The forecast error for one particular period, period *t*, is quantified as follows:

$$\text{Forecast error } (t) = \text{Demand } (t) - \text{Forecast } (t)$$

That is, the forecast error for the time period *t* is the difference between the actual demand and the forecast for that time period. Since we usually need to forecast over a longer horizon, we also need an aggregate measure of forecast error over the forecast horizon. In the later part of this section, we present four different aggregate measures that are used. In general, the error estimate helps us in following ways:

- *Selecting the forecasting model.* An organization may be exploring different forecasting models. An estimate of the forecasting error helps the organization in narrowing down choices and ultimately selecting a forecasting model that may be used in the future.
- *Monitoring forecasting process.* At the time of choosing a forecasting method, a firm endeavours to choose the most suitable method with the lowest forecast error. However, it is possible that either because of a change in the environment or because of a change in the policies followed by the firm, factors that affect the systematic component of forecast has changed and as a result the forecasting model currently used by firm may need modification. Tracking forecasting error over a period of time helps the firm in checking the validity and appropriateness of the model in use.
- *Making optimal decisions about safety stock and safety capacity.* As actual demand may turn out to be higher than the forecast, a firm may like to keep buffer capacity or buffer stocks in the system. An accurate estimate of the forecast error helps a firm in making the optimal choice in this regard.

### Estimating Forecast Error

For calculating aggregate measures of the forecast error we use the following notations: $e(t)$, $D(t)$ and $F(t)$, which denote forecast error, actual demand and forecast, respectively, for a time period $t$. We use $|e(t)|$ to denote the absolute value of the forecast error. This term just captures the absolute deviation from demand and ignores the positive or negative sign associated with the forecast error. For a time horizon consisting of $n$ periods, four popular methods of capturing aggregate measures are as follows:

Mean error (ME) = $(\Sigma e(t))/n$
Mean absolute deviation (MAD) = $(\Sigma|e(t)|)/n$
Mean square error (MSE) = $(\Sigma e(t)^2)/n$
Mean absolute percentage error (MAPE) = $(\Sigma|e(t)/D(t)|) \times 100/n$

ME just calculates the average error over $n$ time periods. It is most likely that we will have a positive error during certain time periods and a negative error during certain time periods, which means that the error may have a value that is close to 0. So ME will not capture the magnitude of error associated with individual time periods. To avoid this problem, we can either work with the square of error or with the absolute values of error. MSE averages the square of the error over $n$ time periods, while MAD averages absolute deviations over the time period. The MSE method of aggregation assumes that the cost associated with the forecast error does not increase linearly and that a higher value of error should attract significantly

*Table 7.1: Different estimates of forecast error.*

| Month | Sales | Forecast | Error | Absolute deviation | Square error | Absolute % error |
|---|---|---|---|---|---|---|
| 1 | 328 | 326 | 2 | 2 | 4 | 0.6 |
| 2 | 310 | 337 | –27 | 27 | 729 | 8.7 |
| 3 | 355 | 348 | 7 | 7 | 49 | 2.0 |
| 4 | 362 | 359 | 3 | 3 | 9 | 0.8 |
| 5 | 375 | 369 | 6 | 6 | 36 | 1.6 |
| 6 | 380 | 380 | 0 | 0 | 0 | 0.0 |
| 7 | 408 | 391 | 17 | 17 | 289 | 4.2 |
| 8 | 415 | 401 | 14 | 14 | 196 | 3.4 |
| 9 | 417 | 412 | 5 | 5 | 25 | 1.2 |
| 10 | 412 | 423 | –11 | 11 | 121 | 2.7 |
| 11 | 429 | 434 | –5 | 5 | 25 | 1.2 |
| 12 | 434 | 444 | –10 | 10 | 100 | 2.3 |
| 13 | 449 | 455 | –6 | 6 | 36 | 1.3 |
| 14 | 471 | 466 | 5 | 5 | 25 | 1.1 |
| 15 | 475 | 476 | –1 | 1 | 1 | 0.2 |
| 16 | 489 | 487 | 2 | 2 | 4 | 0.4 |
| Mean | | | 0.06 (ME) | 7.56 (MAD) | 103.06 (MSE) | 1.98 (MAPE) |

higher penalties compared to lower values of forecasting error. So depending on the context a firm chooses either MAD or MSE as the appropriate measure of forecasting error.

MAPE also works with absolute errors but provides only a relative measure of error unlike MAD, which provides the absolute measure of forecasting error. MAPE works with a ratio of absolute error to demand and calculates the average over *n* time periods and converts the same into percentages. This helps managers in comparing forecasting errors across product categories (for which products we are able to predict well and for which products we are not able to predict well). Items with a higher value of MAPE have higher degree of errors compared to those items that have low values of MAPE. This helps managers in comparing and evaluating various forecasting processes used in different parts of the firm.

Four methods of estimating forecast error are shown in the illustration presented in Table 7.1. From past data we have 16 data points and forecast has been generated using time-series analysis. The last row in the table gives all the four measures of forecast errors.

MAD and MAPE are the most popular measures of forecasting errors, and we will be using these in the remaining part of the chapter. MAD is also a statistically useful measure, as standard deviation of forecasting error can be approximated to 1.25 times the value of MAD. This measure of standard deviation error is useful in determining the safety stocks required in inventory situations.

Of course, while tracking the validity of a forecasting model, firms should use both ME and MAD. MAD gives the absolute measure of error and ME can help a firm in tracking the bias in the forecast. As discussed earlier, ME should ideally be close to 0. But during implementation if we consistently get a positive or negative value of MEA, it means that the forecasting method is giving forecasts that are systematically biased on the higher or lower side. This may require a recalibration of the parameters used in forecasting methods. Similarly, if the MAD value is significantly higher or lower, it is again a signal that we need to calibrate the model.

## Time-series Forecasting Models

So far in the chapter, we have looked at various ways of forecasting demand. All these methods require past demand data and forecast so as to forecast the demand for the next time period.

Qualitative forecasting relies on the judgement of an expert, which is based on the knowledge of past data and experience. Time-series analysis is one of the most widely used quantitative methods of forecasting. This process involves the following steps:

- Drawing a scatter diagram of past data. Examining data for visual patterns of trend and/or seasonality.
- Using an appropriate forecasting model based on the forms and patterns observed in the data.
- Estimating relevant parameters for the patterns observed in past data.
- Estimating forecasting error.

To illustrate the time-series forecasting methodology, we use the following four cases consisting of one or more patterns of data:

- *Case 1.* Data with level pattern only (no trend or seasonality)
- *Case 2.* Data with trend and level patterns (no seasonality)
- *Case 3.* Data with seasonality and level patterns (no trend)
- *Case 4.* Data with seasonality, trend and level patterns

## Case 1: Forecasting Level Form

Most of the methods of forecasting level patterns attempt to try and smoothen out the errors involved. We discuss four popular methods of forecasting for level pattern demand data. Since most forecasting methods used for level form forecasting assign significant weight to the last observation of demand, it is usually used for forecasting only one period ahead. So every time the actual demand is observed, the information is used to forecast the next demand period. In case we have to forecast for more than one period, most of the forecasting methods show future demand beyond the next period as being identical to the next period of forecast. We first discuss moving average and exponential smoothening methods, which are the most widely used methods for level form forecasting. Later on we introduce naive forecast and simple average methods, which are also used in practice. We take one dataset (see Table 7.2 for the dataset of demand for 16 time periods) of demand for illustration purposes; the scatter diagram for this is presented in Figure 7.3. The data do not seem to exhibit any patterns of seasonality or trend, so we will just attempt to capture the level form in the data series.

### Moving Average

In the moving average methodology, the forecast for the next period is obtained by the average demand over the last $k$ periods. The forecaster chooses the appropriate value of $k$:

$$F(t+1) = [D(t) + D(t-1) + \cdots + D(t-k+1)]/k$$

In this methodology, it is assumed that the entire past information is captured in the last $k$ period demand and that all the $k$ period demands have equal value and so all are given equal weights. Once information for $t + 1$st period is available, $D(t + 1)$ is used and information about $D(t - k + 1)$ is discarded from the system.

The forecaster will have to select an appropriate value of $k$ and then take one dataset and compare the value of forecasting error for three values of $k$, that is, 3, 4 and 5. As can be seen in Table 7.2, we have 16 data points from the past, but to make fair comparisons we look at average forecasting errors for the last 10 data points for which all the three forecasts are available. As can

**Table 7.2: Forecasting using the moving average*.**

| t | Demand | k = 3 | | k = 4 | | k = 5 | |
|---|---|---|---|---|---|---|---|
| | | Forecast | Absolute error | Forecast | Absolute error | Forecast | Absolute error |
| 1 | 10 | | | | | | |
| 2 | 18 | | | | | | |
| 3 | 29 | | | | | | |
| 4 | 15 | 19 | | | | | |
| 5 | 30 | 21 | 9 | 18 | 12 | | |
| 6 | 12 | 25 | 13 | 23 | 11 | 20 | 8 |
| 7 | 16 | 19 | 3 | 22 | 6 | 20 | 4 |
| 8 | 8 | 19 | 11 | 18 | 10 | 18 | 10 |
| 9 | 22 | 12 | 10 | 17 | 5 | 17 | 5 |
| 10 | 14 | 15 | 1 | 15 | 1 | 17 | 3 |
| 11 | 15 | 15 | 0 | 15 | 0 | 15 | 0 |
| 12 | 27 | 17 | 10 | 15 | 12 | 17 | 10 |
| 13 | 30 | 19 | 11 | 20 | 10 | 19 | 11 |
| 14 | 23 | 24 | 1 | 22 | 1 | 22 | 1 |
| 15 | 15 | 27 | 12 | 24 | 9 | 21 | 6 |
| 16 | 20 | 23 | 3 | 24 | 4 | 22 | 2 |
| Mean | | | 6.20 = MAD | | 5.80 = MAD | | 5.20 = MAD |

* Mean has been calculated over the last 10 observations ($t = 7, \ldots, 16$). All forecasts have been rounded off to get whole numbers.

be seen in Figure 7.4, a higher value of $k$ leads to greater amount of smoothing. From the data provided, $k = 5$ is most desirable as it gives the lowest MAD value.

Pictorial comparisons of various forecasts (with different values of $k$) are presented in Figure 7.4. As can be observed, a higher value of $k$ results in a greater amount of smoothing. In case we are going to use a five-period moving average, the estimate of the forecasting error is 6.5 (forecast error = 1.25 × MAD). So the demand forecast for the 17th period = [$D(12)$ +

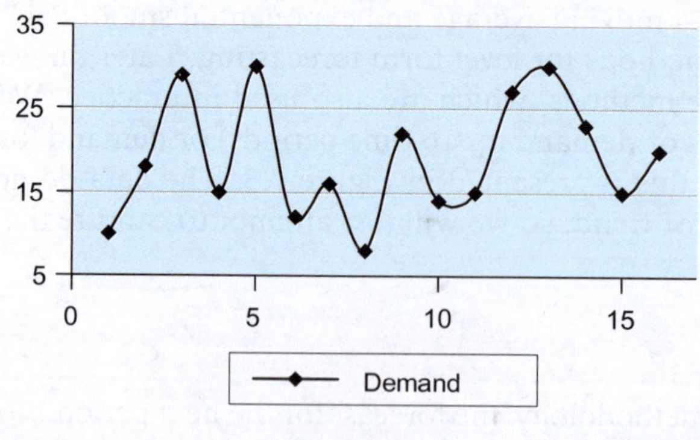


**Figure 7.3**

Demand data: case 1.

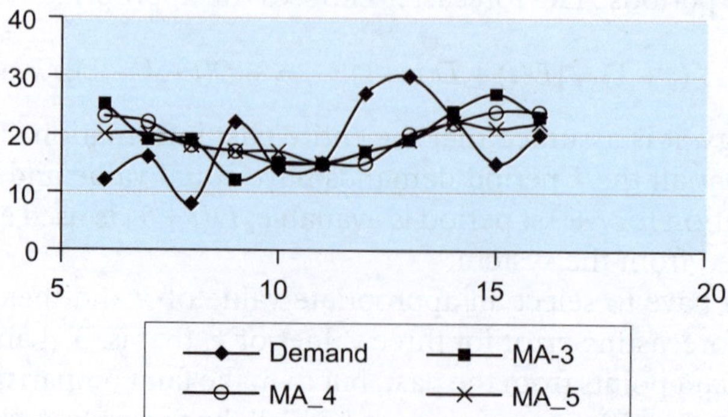


**Figure 7.4**

Moving average forecast: case 1.

$D(13) + D(14) + D(15) + D(16)]/5 = [15 + 27 + 30 + 23 + 15 + 20]/5 = 21.66 \cong 22$, with a forecast error of 6.5.

## Exponential Smoothing

Exponential smoothing estimates are forecast by applying appropriate weights to recently observed demand and using forecasts for the same period that was carried out before the start of the last period:

$$F(t+1) = \alpha D(t) + (1-\alpha)F(t), \quad \text{where } 0 < \alpha < 1.$$

If we substitute $F(t)$ using the same expression we can rewrite the expression for $F(t)$ as follows:

$$F(t+1) = \alpha D(t) + (1-\alpha)[\alpha D(t-1) + (1-\alpha)F(t-1)]$$

which can be rewritten as follows:

$$F(t+1) = \alpha D(t) + \alpha(1-\alpha)D(t-1) + (1-\alpha)^2 F(t-1)$$

If we further substitute $F(t-1)$ and $F(t-2)$, we will get the following expression:

$$F(t+1) = \alpha D(t) + \alpha(1-\alpha)D(t-1) + \alpha(1-\alpha)^2 D(t-2) + \alpha(1-\alpha)^3 D(t-3)$$

So, the last period forecast captures the entire information about past demand. In these days when storage space is at a premium, one of the advantages of exponential smoothing is that firms need not store past data because the last forecast captures all the past information. So the highest weightage is given to the last period demand and lower weightages are given to individual demand points as one goes down in time. So the crucial decision here is selecting the value of $\alpha$. We illustrate exponential smoothing using the same dataset with three values of $\alpha$: 0.1, 0.3 and 0.5. The corresponding forecasts are shown in Table 7.3. For this particular dataset, one can use 0.3 as the value of $\alpha$, as it gives a lower value of MAD. Pictorial comparisons of various forecasts (with different values of $\alpha$) are presented in Figure 7.5. As can be

***Table 7.3:* Forecasting using exponential smoothing*.**

| t | Demand | $\alpha = 0.1$ | | $\alpha = 0.3$ | | $\alpha = 0.5$ | |
|---|---|---|---|---|---|---|---|
| | | Forecast | Absolute error | Forecast | Absolute error | Forecast | Absolute error |
| 1 | 10 | 10 | 0 | 10 | 0 | 10 | 0 |
| 2 | 18 | 10 | 8 | 10 | 8 | 10 | 8 |
| 3 | 29 | 11 | 18 | 12 | 17 | 14 | 15 |
| 4 | 15 | 13 | 2 | 17 | 2 | 22 | 7 |
| 5 | 30 | 13 | 17 | 16 | 14 | 19 | 11 |
| 6 | 12 | 15 | 3 | 20 | 8 | 25 | 13 |
| 7 | 16 | 15 | 1 | 18 | 2 | 19 | 3 |
| 8 | 8 | 15 | 7 | 17 | 9 | 18 | 10 |
| 9 | 22 | 14 | 8 | 14 | 8 | 13 | 9 |
| 10 | 14 | 15 | 1 | 16 | 2 | 18 | 4 |
| 11 | 15 | 15 | 0 | 15 | 0 | 16 | 1 |
| 12 | 27 | 15 | 12 | 15 | 12 | 16 | 11 |
| 13 | 30 | 16 | 14 | 19 | 11 | 22 | 8 |
| 14 | 23 | 17 | 6 | 22 | 1 | 26 | 3 |
| 15 | 15 | 18 | 3 | 22 | 7 | 25 | 10 |
| 16 | 20 | 18 | 2 | 20 | 0 | 20 | 0 |
| Mean | | | 5.40 | | 5.20 | | 5.90 |

* Mean has been calculated over the last 10 observations ($t = 7, \ldots, 16$). All forecasts have been rounded off to get whole numbers.

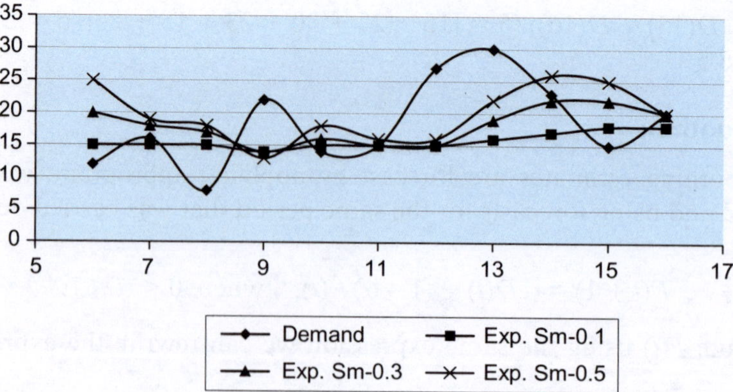


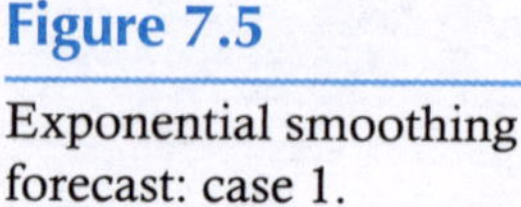

**Figure 7.5**

Exponential smoothing forecast: case 1.

observed, lower values of $\alpha$ result in greater amounts of smoothing. Low values of $\alpha$ attempts to do smoothing, while higher value of $\alpha$ swings along with the swing in observed demand. In general, if the demand is inherently stable, low values of $\alpha$ are suggested; if demand is inherently unstable, high values of $\alpha$ are suggested.

In this specific case, we use exponential smoothing with $\alpha = 0.3$ for future forecasting. The estimated forecasting error is 6.5 (forecast error = 1.25 × MAD). So the demand forecast for the 17th period forecast $= 0.3 \times D(16) + 0.7 \times F(16) = 0.3 \times 20 + 0.7 \times 20 = 20$, with a forecast error of 6.5.

Another way of looking at exponential smoothing is by rearranging the terms as follows:

$$F(t+1) = F(t) + \alpha(D(t) - F(t)) = F(t) + \alpha e(t)$$

So exponential smoothing takes the last period forecast and corrects the same by a correction factor, which is $\alpha$ times the forecast error for a time period $t$.

Since the selection of $\alpha$ is a standard process, that is, one just has to vary the value of $\alpha$ between 0 and 1 and choose the value that results in the lowest value of MAD, it is possible to automate the methodology of finding the appropriate value of $\alpha$.

## Naive Forecast

In the naive forecasting methods, forecast for the next period equals the demand for the current period. This is quite a popular method in practice. This assumes that the past has no relevance and that demand is very dynamic in nature; thus, current demand is the best estimator of future demand:

$$F(t+1) = D(t)$$

Naive forecast can be treated as an extreme case of exponential smoothening where $\alpha$ takes a value equal to 1.

## Simple Average Forecast

In this method, future forecasts are obtained by averaging all demand information available in the system and all the data points are given equal weight:

$$F(t+1) = [D(t) + D(t-1) + \cdots + D(1)]/t$$

This method works very well if one assumes that there are no unrecognized patterns and all that is not captured in the predictable pattern is a part of a random phenomenon. In such a case, mean demand with a large sample size is the best estimator of future demand.

## Case 2: Forecasting the Trend Form

A constant rate of increase or decrease in demand denotes a linear trend. In this discussion, we focus on capturing this linear trend. In the case of a demand series with only trend component, one will work with following: forecast ($t$) = $a + bt$. Essentially, we are interested in estimating the value of $b$, which captures the trend effect.

Given $n$ data points, $\bar{t}$ and $\bar{D}$ represent the average values of $t$ and $D$, respectively:

$$\bar{t} = \sum t \text{ and } \bar{D} = \sum d(t)/n$$

Estimates of $b$ and $a$ can be calculated as follows:

$$b = \sum (t - \bar{t}) \times [d(t) - \bar{D}] / \sum (t - \bar{t})^2$$

$$a = \bar{D} - b\bar{t}$$

We take one dataset (see Table 7.4 for a dataset of demand for 16 time periods) of demand for illustration purposes and the scatter diagram for the same is presented in Figure 7.6. The data do not seem to exhibit any patterns of seasonality but shows a clear trend in terms of steady increase in demand over a period of time.

$$b = \sum (t - \bar{t}) \times [d(t) - \bar{D}] / \sum (t - \bar{t})^2 = 3645.5/340 = 10.72$$

$$a = \bar{D} - b\bar{t} = 406.81 - 10.72 \times 8.5 = 315.67$$

$$d(t) = 315.67 + 10.72t$$

Here, the value of $a$ is nothing but the estimate of level. That is, if there was no trend component, then the forecast of future demand is the average demand for de-trended data. We

**Table 7.4: Forecasting the trend form: case 2.**

| $t$ | $D(t)$ | $t - \bar{t}$ | $D(t) - \bar{D}$ | $(t - \bar{t}) \times (D(t) - \bar{D})$ | $(t - \bar{t})^2$ | Forecast | Absolute error |
|---|---|---|---|---|---|---|---|
| 1 | 328 | −7.5 | −78.81 | 591.09 | 56.25 | 326.42 | 1.58 |
| 2 | 310 | −6.5 | −96.81 | 629.28 | 42.25 | 337.14 | 27.14 |
| 3 | 355 | −5.5 | −51.81 | 284.97 | 30.25 | 347.86 | 7.14 |
| 4 | 362 | −4.5 | −44.81 | 201.66 | 20.25 | 358.58 | 3.42 |
| 5 | 375 | −3.5 | −31.81 | 111.34 | 12.25 | 369.3 | 5.7 |
| 6 | 380 | −2.5 | −26.81 | 67.03 | 6.25 | 380.02 | 0.02 |
| 7 | 408 | −1.5 | 1.19 | −1.78 | 2.25 | 390.74 | 17.26 |
| 8 | 415 | −0.5 | 8.19 | −4.09 | 0.25 | 401.46 | 13.54 |
| 9 | 417 | 0.5 | 10.19 | 5.09 | 0.25 | 412.18 | 4.82 |
| 10 | 412 | 1.5 | 5.19 | 7.78 | 2.25 | 422.9 | 10.9 |
| 11 | 429 | 2.5 | 22.19 | 55.47 | 6.25 | 433.62 | 4.62 |
| 12 | 434 | 3.5 | 27.19 | 95.16 | 12.25 | 444.34 | 10.34 |
| 13 | 449 | 4.5 | 42.19 | 189.84 | 20.25 | 455.06 | 6.06 |
| 14 | 471 | 5.5 | 64.19 | 353.03 | 30.25 | 465.78 | 5.22 |
| 15 | 475 | 6.5 | 68.19 | 443.22 | 42.25 | 476.5 | 1.5 |
| 16 | 489 | 7.5 | 82.19 | 616.41 | 56.25 | 487.22 | 1.78 |
| Mean 8.5 | 406.81 | | | | | | 7.56 |
| Sum | | | | 3645.5 | 340.0 | | 121.04 |

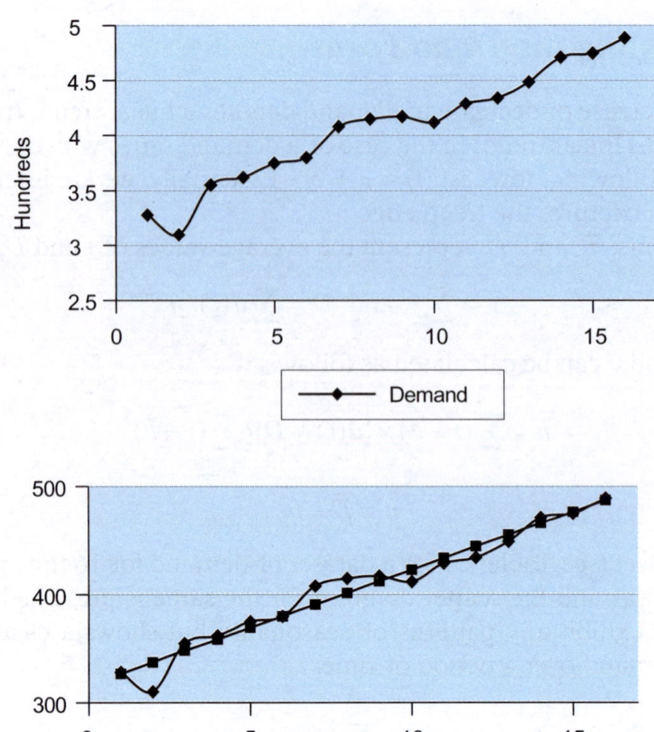


**Figure 7.6**

Demand data: case 2.

**Figure 7.7**

Forecast versus actual demand: case 2.

could have estimated the level pattern using any of the methods described in case 1. We use mean methodology for the sake of simplicity:

$$\text{Forecast } (t) = [\text{Level component } (t) + b \times t]$$

Here, the level component = $a$ = 315.57, and the trend component = $b$ = 10.72.

Using this model, one can obtain a forecast for 16 periods, and the absolute error is reported in Table 7.4. A pictorial comparison of forecast versus actual demand is presented in Figure 7.7. As one can see, there is a good visual fit between the actual and the forecasted data. Apart from a subjective assessment of fit, one can also use the statistical measure $R^2$, which essentially captures the percentage of error explained by the regression. In this specific case, we have regressed demand against time, and using Excel one can determine the value of $R^2$, which is 0.95 in the present case. Given an MAD value of 7.56, the forecast from this model has a forecast error of 9.46.

So the demand forecast for the 17th period = 315.57 + 10.72 × 17 = 497.94, with a forecast error of 9.46.

## *Case 3: Forecasting Seasonality*

The forecast of the seasonal component is illustrated using a data series with 12 data points as shown in Table 7.5 and a scatter plot shown in Figure 7.8.

The relevant parameter is periodicity $p$, which is the number of time periods after which the seasonal cycle repeats itself.

As can be seen in scatter plot, there is a periodicity of 4 periods where the pattern seems to repeat after 4 periods. For example, we observe peak demand in periods 4, 8 and 12, and we see the lowest demand in periods 1, 5 and 9. To obtain the relevant parameters, data are divided into blocks—let us say we have $m$ blocks, with each block having $p$ demand periods. For each

*Table 7.5:* **Forecasting seasonality: case 3.**

| Time | Block | Period within block | Demand | Seasonal index of period | De-seasonalized demand | Forecast | Absolute error |
|---|---|---|---|---|---|---|---|
| 1 | 1 | 1 | 6 | 0.03 | 88 | 14 | 8 |
| 2 | | 2 | 55 | 0.23 | 226 | 52 | 3 |
| 3 | | 3 | 249 | 1.04 | 310 | 171 | 78 |
| 4 | | 4 | 646 | 2.70 | 224 | 614 | 32 |
| 5 | 2 | 1 | 24 | 0.12 | 353 | 14 | 10 |
| 6 | | 2 | 73 | 0.36 | 300 | 52 | 21 |
| 7 | | 3 | 140 | 0.69 | 174 | 171 | 31 |
| 8 | | 4 | 569 | 2.82 | 197 | 614 | 45 |
| 9 | 3 | 1 | 12 | 0.06 | 177 | 14 | 2 |
| 10 | | 2 | 28 | 0.14 | 115 | 52 | 24 |
| 11 | | 3 | 136 | 0.67 | 169 | 171 | 35 |
| 12 | | 4 | 631 | 3.13 | 219 | 614 | 17 |
| Mean | | | | | 213 | | 25.5 |

block *j*, we will calculate the seasonality index for *i*th period and obtain the average seasonality index for period *i* across the blocks by averaging the same over *m* blocks.

$S(i, j)$ captures the seasonal index of period *i* for block *j* and $S(i)$ represents the average seasonality index of period *i* within a block.

$$S(i, j) = (d_i)/[(d_1 + d_2 + d_p)/p] \quad \text{for each period } i \text{ within block } j$$

While calculating the seasonal index, we work with average sales over block *j* so as to simplify the calculations. A more accurate method will involve the use of centred moving average in the denominator rather than using average sales over block *j*.

We find the average seasonality index by taking the average over *m* blocks as presented in Table 7.6.

Now we use this average seasonality index to arrive at the de-seasonalized demand data by dividing each demand by the respective seasonality index

$$\text{De-seasonalized data } (t) = \text{Demand } (t)/S(t)$$

The same has been reported in the fourth column of Table 7.5. That is, if there was no seasonality, we will have observed demand with a mean demand of 213 and with the random error introduced because of the random component. So we assume the level form to be equal to 213, and by applying a corresponding seasonal factor, we arrive at the forecast value

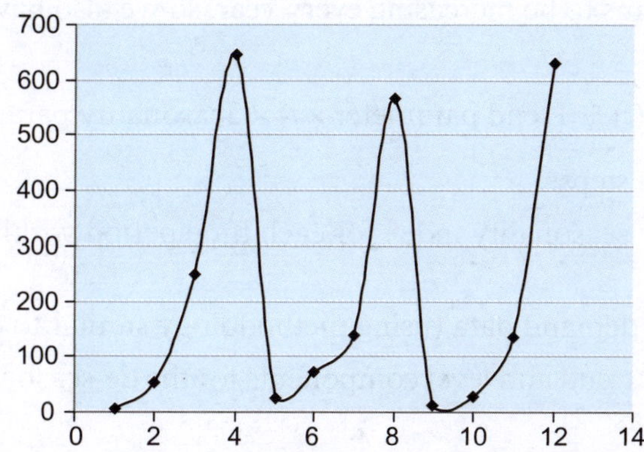


**Figure 7.8**

Demand data: case 3.

*Table 7.6:* **Seasonality index calculations.**

| Period/block | S(i, 1) | S(i, 2) | S(i, 3) | Average seasonality index |
|---|---|---|---|---|
| 1 | 0.03 | 0.12 | 0.06 | 0.07 |
| 2 | 0.23 | 0.36 | 0.14 | 0.24 |
| 3 | 1.04 | 0.69 | 0.67 | 0.80 |
| 4 | 2.70 | 2.82 | 3.13 | 2.88 |

$S(i) = S(i,1) + S(i,2) + \cdots + S(i,m)/m.$

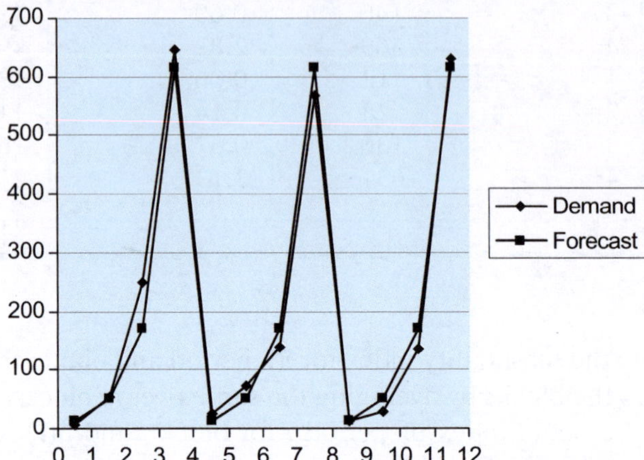


**Figure 7.9**

Demand data versus actual data: case 3.

reported in the second last column of Table 7.5. As the demands have been rounded off, there are no fractional units in the demand:

$$\text{Forecast } (t) = [\text{Level } (t)] \times \text{Seasonal index } (t)$$

In the present case, the level form is 213, and depending on the value of *i* (period within a block), one can use a corresponding value of the seasonality index.

A pictorial comparison of forecast versus actual demand is presented in Figure 7.9. As can be seen, there is a good visual fit between the actual data and the forecast data. Given an MAD value of 25.5, the forecast error works out to be 31.88.

So demand forecast for the 17th period = 213 × 0.07 = 14.91; and the forecast for the 18th period = 213 × 0.24 = 51.12, with a forecast error of 31.88.

## Case 4: Forecasting Combination of Seasonality and Trend

Forecasting involving seasonality and trend component data series with 16 data points is shown in Table 7.7 and the scatter plot for the same is shown in Figure 7.10.

As can be seen from the scatter diagram, there is seasonality with a periodicity of four periods. Further, demand seems to be increasing every year, so we also have a trend component in the data series:

$$\text{Demand } (t) = (\text{Level } (t) + \text{Trend parameter} \times t) \times \text{Seasonality parameter } (t) + \text{Random}$$

We will use following steps:

- *Step 1.* Determine the seasonality index for each time period within a bloc (using methodology similar to case 3).
- *Step 2.* De-seasonlize demand data (using methodology similar to case 3).
- *Step 3.* Determine the trend and level components for the de-seasonalized data series (using methodology similar to case 2).

*Table 7.7:* **Demand data: case 4.**

| Quarter | Sales |
|---|---|
| 1 | 45 |
| 2 | 335 |
| 3 | 520 |
| 4 | 100 |
| 5 | 70 |
| 6 | 370 |
| 7 | 590 |
| 8 | 170 |
| 9 | 100 |
| 10 | 585 |
| 11 | 830 |
| 12 | 285 |
| 13 | 100 |
| 14 | 725 |
| 15 | 1,160 |
| 16 | 310 |

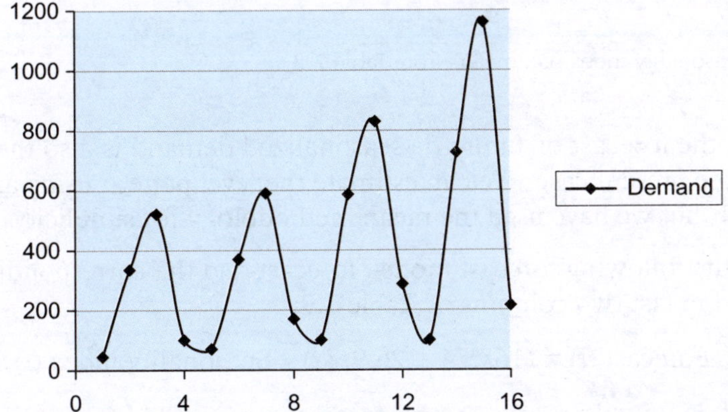


**Figure 7.10**

Demand data: case 4.

- *Step 4.* Finalize the forecast model and use the model for determining the forecast numbers for past data points. Estimate the forecast error.
- *Step 1.* We have data with four blocks with a periodicity of 4. Using methodology similar to case 3, Table 7.8 reports the average seasonality index for each of the four quarters within a year.
- *Step 2.* De-seasonalized data ($t$) = demand ($t$)/$S(t)$. So, in Table 7.9, the fifth column presents de-seasonalized data for 16 data points.
- *Step 3.* We can apply regression as discussed in case 2 to obtain trend and level values for the de-seasonalized data series:

$$D(t) = a + b(t)$$

Regression gives us values of $a = 165.74$ and $b = 26.9$, with $R^2 = 0.88$. This means that the trend is significant. Here, the value of $a$ is nothing but an estimate of level. That is, if there is no

*Table 7.8:* **Computation of seasonality index: case 4.**

| Period/block | 1 | 2 | 3 | 4 | Average seasonality index |
|---|---|---|---|---|---|
| 1 | 0.18 | 0.23 | 0.22 | 0.17 | 0.20 |
| 2 | 1.34 | 1.23 | 1.30 | 1.26 | 1.28 |
| 3 | 2.08 | 1.97 | 1.84 | 2.02 | 1.98 |
| 4 | 0.40 | 0.57 | 0.63 | 0.54 | 0.54 |

*Table 7.9:* **Forecasting using decomposition of time series: case 4.**

| Time | Block | Period within block | Demand | De-seasonalized demand* | Forecast | Absolute error |
|---|---|---|---|---|---|---|
| 1 | 1 | 1 | 45 | 222 | 39 | 6 |
| 2 | | 2 | 335 | 261 | 283 | 52 |
| 3 | | 3 | 520 | 263 | 489 | 31 |
| 4 | | 4 | 100 | 187 | 147 | 47 |
| 5 | 2 | 1 | 70 | 346 | 61 | 9 |
| 6 | | 2 | 370 | 288 | 420 | 50 |
| 7 | | 3 | 590 | 298 | 700 | 110 |
| 8 | | 4 | 170 | 318 | 204 | 34 |
| 9 | 3 | 1 | 100 | 494 | 83 | 17 |
| 10 | | 2 | 585 | 456 | 559 | 26 |
| 11 | | 3 | 830 | 420 | 914 | 84 |
| 12 | | 4 | 285 | 533 | 262 | 23 |
| 13 | 4 | 1 | 100 | 494 | 104 | 4 |
| 14 | | 2 | 725 | 565 | 697 | 28 |
| 15 | | 3 | 1,160 | 586 | 1,128 | 32 |
| 16 | | 4 | 310 | 579 | 319 | 9 |
| Mean | | | | | | 35.25 |

*Using the average seasonality index parameters from Table 7.8.

trend component, the forecast of future de-seasonalized demand is also the average demand, that is, 165.74 in the present case. We can estimate the level pattern using any of the methods described in case 1, but we have used the mean methodology for simplicity.

- *Step 4.* Using the following forecast model, forecast and the corresponding absolute errors have been reported in last two columns of Table 7.9:

$$\text{Forecast }(t) = (165.74 + 26.9 \times t) \times \text{Seasonality index }(t)$$

An MAD value of 35.25 will translate into a forecast error of 44.06.

So we can use the above equation to forecast the demand for the next four periods, which is as follows:

| $t$ | $S(t)$ | Forecast($t$) |
|---|---|---|
| 17 | 0.20 | $(165.74 + 26.9 \times 17) \times 0.20 = 126$ |
| 18 | 1.28 | $(165.74 + 26.9 \times 18) \times 1.28 = 835$ |
| 19 | 1.98 | $(165.74 + 26.9 \times 19) \times 1.98 = 1339$ |
| 20 | 0.54 | $(165.74 + 26.9 \times 20) \times 0.54 = 377$ |

The above forecast will have a forecast error with a standard deviation of 44.06.

In the examples discussed we had only one type of seasonality, but in some complex cases we may have multiple seasonalities superimposed on the data. For example, we might have the last week of the month showing peak sales as well as the last month in a quarter showing higher sales compared to an average month. So we have a seasonality that repeats every month and a seasonality that repeats every quarter. Using the same methodology, one can first capture the quarter effect, then remove the quarter effect from the data and at a later stage capture weekly seasonality.

Of course, in all the four cases, we worked with clean data, so we did not have to remove any point from the sample. But, in general, it is a good idea to check at every stage, visually, whether any point in the data shows unusual characteristics; for example, sales in one particular period showing twice the expected (as per pattern observed) sale. Similarly, one of the generally lean months of the season showing unusually high demand should be checked for possible abnormal events.

## Data Preparation for Building Time-series Models

Usually, past data need to be cleaned up before a dataset is used for building a time-series forecasting model. While analysing past data for identifying appropriate patterns, one has to keep several factors in mind.

### Impact of Local Festivals

Most businesses use the Gregorian calendar, which is a solar calendar. Since most of the festivals are based on the lunar calendar, we might not observe repetitive cycles because festivals like Diwali or the Chinese New Year occur in different weeks or even months during different years. There are some inauspicious periods during which people do not buy consumer durables. So the effect of these festivals and other special periods has to be captured carefully as they do not occur on the same day/month every year. Otherwise, the effect of the festival season will show up as a random phenomenon, which in the final analysis will result in a large and unwanted forecasting error.

### Impact of Promotion and Other Abnormal Events

There are periods during which an organization offers promotions or has a surge in sales because of certain special circumstances (e.g., strike at the competitor's plant). Most organizations do not maintain records of these events. For example, very few organizations keep records of the sales promotions floated; hence, they are not able to remove the effect attributed to these. Of course, iterations involving sales people who may have some memory about these issues might help handle this issue partially. While analysing past data one can identify all the abnormal points (variation in error of more than two times the standard deviation) and work with the relevant managers in identifying data points where abnormality can be assigned to specific causes. Otherwise it may be a good idea to remove all these abnormal points so that we do not end up with a situation where such extremes in variation have a significant effect on the parameters that are used for the time-series forecasting. Data modification should be limited to correction of large anomalies having known causes. Further, these causes should not recur on a regular basis. Data should not be modified just because they appear peculiar with no known cause for the irregularity.

### Sales Is Not the Same as Demand

While analysing time-series data, one works with sales data. Many times sales data underreport demand. There are instances of lost sales because of non-availability of stocks. Even a firm like P&G has 90–93 per cent stock availability on the shelf. This is extremely important in seasonal products where the peak season accounts for a significant part of the annual sales; and non-availability of stocks for even a small time period can result in significant losses in sales, resulting in corresponding underreporting of demand. So to convert sales into demand, a firm has to make an estimate of lost sales. Similarly, a firm may find that certain sales observed during certain periods were actually the result of the substitution effect. Non-availability of a preferred variant was interpreted as a demand for the substitute product. In such a case, sales demand inflates the demand data. Caution has to be exercised to ensure that in company records the sales data should not be treated as the actual demand.

## Behavioural Issues in Forecasting

Forecasting is not just a pure analytical exercise. There are significant behavioural issues involved in forecasting. A few critical issues are discussed below:

- *Involvement of regional sales force in demand forecasting.* It is quite possible to have bottoms up forecasting where sales people from the regions are involved in assessing market demand and this demand gets aggregated at the zonal level and finally at the country level. Most of the sales people in the region may not have the necessary competence to carry out objective forecasting and the head office may be in a better position to prepare demand forecasts. But involving the regional sales force in the process results in ownership by sales people at the local level. So most organizations use a combination wherein both the central office and the regional sales force are involved in demand forecasting. Or the organizations go through iterative processes where numbers given by the regional sales people are matched with the forecast generated by forecasting experts at the central office. Whenever there is a wide deviation between the forecast prepared by the central planner and the one prepared by the regional sales executive, dialogue is initiated and over several iterations the final forecast numbers are arrived at. If regional sales people are not involved in the forecasting process they may not own the final forecast numbers and this may result in motivational problems.
- *Forecast is often confused with goal.* Forecast should reflect what is likely to happen in the market place and not what the company wishes. Many times it is observed that a company with high aspirations may want a growth rate that is higher than the rate at which the market is growing, and internal pressures may result in unduly optimistic forecasts. In such an organization, the management may not be willing to accept lower forecast numbers, and to satisfy the management, the sales force deliberately comes with inflated forecast numbers. Of course, a firm can grow at higher than market share if it has an effective marketing strategy in place and the firm is willing to make the necessary investments in this regard. Unfortunately, many times forecasts are determined more by internal goals and ambitions and do not capture market realities. In such a case, the company ends up with huge inventories of finished goods because it produces goods to match demand as suggested by the internal forecast, which is actually only wishful thinking.
- *Impact of performance measures.* While using judgemental forecasting, one should realize that marketing managers who provide important inputs have a vested interest in lower/higher forecast numbers. They may like their targets to be pegged at a lower level so that they get higher incentive bonuses. If forecast accuracies are not monitored, the marketing department will always provide high forecasts so that they never end up with a stock out situation, which may affect the overall sales. In a situation of lower than expected forecast, the company will end up with surplus stocks and usually the marketing department is not accountable for surplus stocks. So a company needs to maintain a fine balance so that it has checks and balances for the forecasts that are offered. Gillette (India) has managed to improve its forecast accuracy by being sensitive about such issues while designing its forecasting processes. By developing quantitative models of forecast wherever possible, firms can do a reality check on the forecasts offered by the sales department.

### IMPROVING FORECAST ACCURACY AT GILLETTE (INDIA) LTD[4]

Gillette (India) Ltd is the leader in male and female grooming products, alkaline batteries and oral care products. Till the year 2000, nobody was clearly accountable for the accuracy of the forecast at Gillette, and poor forecasting resulted in several supply chain problems including low service levels and high and imbalanced inventory. In 2002, they started formally measuring supply chain accuracy at the SKU level and brand managers were given responsibility and were made accountable for the same. As there were no structured processes, the firm realized that sales managers were more concerned about meeting their targets and were not focusing on forecasting accurate markets demands. In 2003, as a part of a major supply chain restructuring initiative, forecasting activity was moved to the supply chain group and the firm appointed a sales forecasting manager. With the help of structured processes and clear accountability, Gillette has managed to improve the average forecast accuracy across all its business units from an average of 40 to 60 per cent. In one business unit that had a record of poor forecast accuracy, SKU-level forecast accuracy improved from 10 to 50 per cent.

## Summary

- Demand forecasting provides critical information to supply chain planning, both at the design level and at the operations level.
- A key factor in choosing a proper forecasting approach is the time horizon for the decision requiring forecasts. Forecasts can be made for the short-, medium- and long-term horizons.
- Both qualitative and quantitative forecasting approaches are used in practice.
- Qualitative forecasting methods are most appropriate when little historic data are avialbile.
- Demand consists of systematic and random components. The quantitative forecasting model attempts to forecast the systematic component of demand by understanding the underlying patterns in the historical data.
- Quantitative forecasting does not mean blind application of tools to the data available with the firm. A good understanding of business fundamentals is important for choosing the right model and refining the data available in the transaction database.
- Whatever level of sophistication one introduces in the forecasting methodology, actual demand will never be the same as the forecast. So apart from the forecast, firms should also estimate forecast error, because that will help them in preparing contingency measures in terms of safety stocks and safety capacity required to handle various scenarios that are likely to develop in the future.
- Demand forecasting is not just an analytical exercise, there are significant behavioural issues involved in forecasting.

## Discussion Questions

1. Under what circumstances should firms use qualitative forecasting?
2. Why do time-series forecasting methods work well for short-term forecasting but do not work very well in long-term forecasting?
3. What is the need to have multiple measures of forecast errors?
4. What is the role of a manager in the forecasting process using quantitative forecasting techniques?
5. How do organizational structures and performance measures impact the forecasting process in an organization?
6. It is generally said that one needs to clean the past data before one uses them for the purpose of developing forecasting models. What are the various issues to be kept in mind while cleaning the data?
7. What kind of seasonality are you likely to see if you are in any of following fields:
   i Retail chain in metropolitan area
   ii ATM
   iii Restaurant
   iv Consumer durable products
8. As a manager you have observed that for the last 6 months forecast for your division and actual demand matched perfectly. Will you be worried?
9. What role does forecasting play in the following categories of supply chains:
   i Make to stock
   ii Configure to order
   iii Made to order

## Notes

1. See www.met.rdg.ac.uk/cag/forecasting/quotes.html and www.autobox.com/badfore.html.
2. Seer www.cio.com/article/30413/What_Went_Wrong_at_Cisco_in.
3. See www.cio.in/article/viewArticle?ARTICLEID=1237 for interview with Ashwin Dani, VC & MD, Asian Paints.
4. V. Govil, R. Kumar, and Z. Ahmed, "Gillette: An Organizational Initiative to Improve Demand Planning Quality." In Malini Gupta ed. *Supply Chain Excellence* (SP Jain Institute of Management & Research, Mumbai).

## Further Reading

D. M. Georgoff and R. G. Murdick, "Manager's Guide to Forecasting," *Harvard Business Review* (January–February 1986): 2–9.

S. Makridakis, S. C. Wheelwright, and R. J. Hyndman, *Forecasting Methods and Applications*, third edition (Singapore: John Wiley, 1998).

J. Yurkiewicz, "Forecasting Software Survey: Helping to Fine-tune Your Choices," *ORMS Today* (August 2006, Vol 33).

## Exercises

1) Refer to Table 7.3. Compute the forecasting error in case the firm decides to use exponential smoothing with a value of 0.2. Forecast the demand the firm is likely to see during the 17th period.

2) An air conditioner manufacturing company has observed the following demand in the last 3 years in the Bangalore market:

| | 2012 | 2013 | 2014 |
|---|---|---|---|
| Quarter 1 | 210 | 205 | 212 |
| Quarter 2 | 48 | 52 | 54 |
| Quarter 3 | 160 | 142 | 158 |
| Quarter 4 | 96 | 103 | 98 |

(a) Design a forecasting model for the firm for the Bangalore market.

(b) Forecast quarter-wise demand for year 2015. Estimate the forecasting error for the 2015 forecasts.

3) A firm has introduced a new product in January 2013 and sales data for the first 12 months are as follows:

| | Demand | | Demand |
|---|---|---|---|
| January | 63 | July | 204 |
| February | 102 | August | 217 |
| March | 104 | September | 243 |
| April | 137 | October | 233 |
| May | 134 | November | 275 |
| June | 171 | December | 306 |

(a) Design a forecasting model for the firm for the Bangalore market.

(b) Forecast month-wise demand for year 2014. Estimate the forecasting error for the 2014 forecasts.

(c) Actual demand observed during 2014 is as follows:

| | Demand | | Demand |
|---|---|---|---|
| January | 305 | July | 400 |
| February | 331 | August | 400 |
| March | 352 | September | 427 |
| April | 385 | October | 398 |
| May | 385 | November | 395 |
| June | 412 | December | 396 |

Will you recommend a change in the forecasting model for the 2015 projections? Could you possibly explain the large error in the later part of 2014?

4) As a financial analyst you want to project sales for last quarter for year 2014 for Amazon.inc. Data for last few years is as follows (sales in million US$):

| | 2010 | 2011 | 2012 | 2013 | 2014 |
|---|---|---|---|---|---|
| First quarter (March ) | 7,131 | 9,857 | 13,185 | 16,070 | 19,741 |
| Second quarter (June) | 6,566 | 9,913 | 12,834 | 15,704 | 19,340 |
| Third quarter (September) | 7,560 | 10,876 | 13,806 | 17,092 | 20,579 |
| Fourth quarter (December) | 12,948 | 17,431 | 21,268 | 25,587 | |

(a) Forecast the fourth quarter sales.

(b) Amazon generates the bulk of its sales from the following two categories:

(i) Media

(ii) Electronics and other general merchandise

You have noticed that over the last few years the percentage share of electronics has been increasing. Will your forecasting model improve if you forecast sales from each category separately?

(c) Will you like to extend this logic and design a forecasting model for the 500-odd vendors who supply material (i.e., forecasting for each vendor separately)?

*Source*: http://phx.corporate-ir.net/phoenix.zhtml?c=97664&p=irol-reportsHistorical

# Information Technology in Supply Chain Management*

## Learning Objectives

After reading this chapter, you will be able to answer following questions:

> What is the role of IT in supply chain management?
> What are the key challenges in adapting IT to improve the efficiency of the supply chain?
> What are the future trends in terms of the way IT is going to influence supply chain management?

July 10, 2016, 1:30 am: In Jaipur, Ramesh Mehta logs onto the Internet to buy a car. Working with a standard platform, he customizes his automobile with a choice of engine, navigational and entertainment systems, seat configuration and fabric. With a simple click of confirmation, he sends his order directly to the original equipment manufacturer's (OEM's) production schedule, which is shared in real time with a "super integrator" supplier. An online auction/exchange enables the "super integrator" to purchase commodity parts at the lowest cost and then assemble the component systems to be inserted into the OEM's production line just in time. Valued-added, branded components are procured through strategic partnerships with a few suppliers whose business is closely linked to the OEM's.

Everyone in the supply chain collaborates on product development and continuous process improvement. One week later, Ramesh picks up his car from the dealer in his neighbourhood.

If you think this is straight out of a science fiction book, think again. With rapid advances in technology, sharing information in real time is no longer a dream. Many companies have already realized that this is a crucial factor in the performance of the supply chain. The integration and optimization of the three flows in the supply chain—material, information and financial—is important in achieving such a level of business process maturity. In this chapter, we discuss the role of information flow in any supply chain coordination and identify key challenges in IT adaptation of supply chain technologies.

---

* This chapter has been contributed by Ashish Tewary, Industry Principal Consultant, Infosys Tech. Ltd.

## Introduction

Information flow in any supply chain coordinates the physical flows and the interdependencies amongst the organizations in the supply chain and is the focus of this chapter. It allows managers to have access to information on the functions of all the other supply chain entities. For example, to better serve its customers, a retail chain will not only need to know store inventory but will also need information on customer demand, supply lead time and associated variability. Figure 8.1 provides some of the examples of information requirements in different stages of the supply chain.

Supply chain managers use this information to make many important decisions related to key building blocks of the supply chain, that is, inventory, transportation and facility. Setting the inventory level requires information about customers on demand, information about suppliers on availability and information about current inventory levels, costs and margins. Determining transportation policies requires information on delivery and shipping locations, routes, rates, transportation time and quantities to be shipped. Warehouse/store/plant decisions require information on customer and supplier locations, tax implications as well as information on capacities, revenues and material/operating costs.

We start by discussing the role that IT can play in enabling supply chain management. We look at how to develop a suitable strategy for adapting IT to supply chain management. We conclude with a brief discussion on future trends in IT-enabled supply chain management.

## Enabling Supply Chain Management Through Information Technology

IT in an organization has multiple roles: (a) it increases scale efficiencies of the firm's operations; (b) it processes basic business transactions; (c) it collects and provides information relevant to managerial decisions and even makes decisions; (d) it monitors and records the performance of employees and function units; (e) it maintains records of status and change

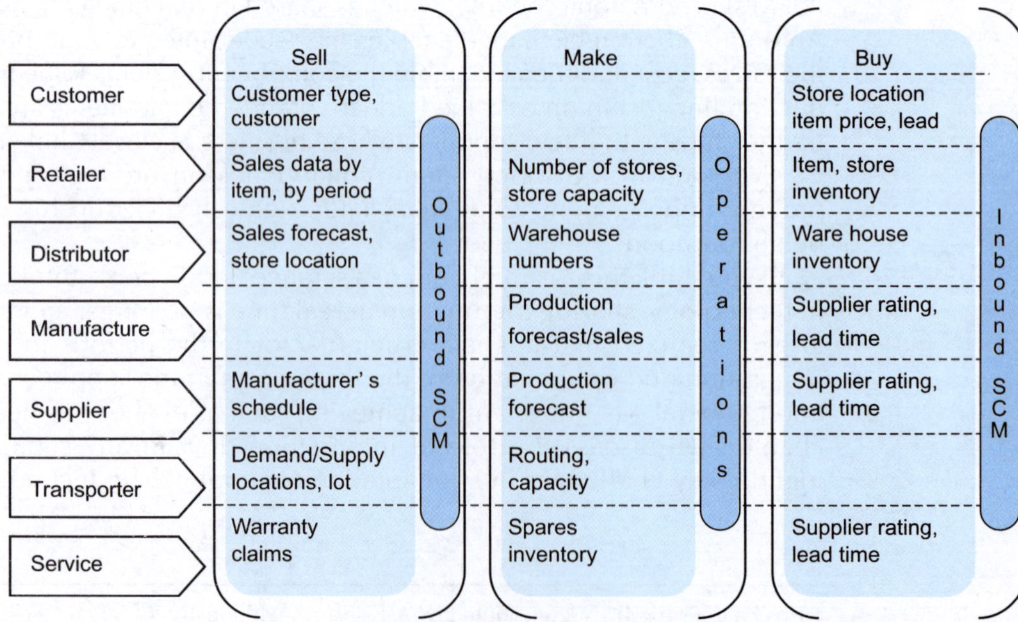


**Figure 8.1**

Use of information across the supply chain (illustrative).

in the fundamental business functions within the organization and maintains communication channels.

Although the above-mentioned roles are in the context of an organization, it is expected that IT will have similar effects also in supply chain. IT can link all activities in a supply chain into an integrated and coordinated system that is fast, responsive, flexible and able to produce a high volume of customized products at low costs. IT plays the following functional roles in supply chain management:

- IT supports frictionless transaction execution through supply chain execution systems. This forms the core of supply chain management. Processes related to the subject of order management, manufacturing execution, inventory management, procurement, transportation execution and warehouse management are mapped.
- IT is a means for enhancing collaboration and coordination in supply chains through supply chain collaboration systems. The collaborative part focuses primarily on cooperation with partners and customers via the Internet.
- IT-based decision support systems (DSS) can be used to aid better decisions through supply chain planning systems. This provides capability to supply chain management to process and evaluate decisions related to supply chain management using different optimization techniques.
- It is important for companies to measure their supply chain performance to know if they are improving. IT-based business intelligence (BI) includes a technology stack with layers for reporting and analysis tools, data warehouse platforms and data integration tools.

All four functional roles are essential for each stage in a supply chain. Each stage should know what is to be done in collaboration with upstream and downstream stages. And it must execute the plan to achieve the performance targets it wants to meet. There are numerous supply chain systems in existence. These can be categorized according to the stages in the supply chain on which they focus and the functional role for which they are used. Figure 8.2 provides a framework to map a particular supply chain management system.

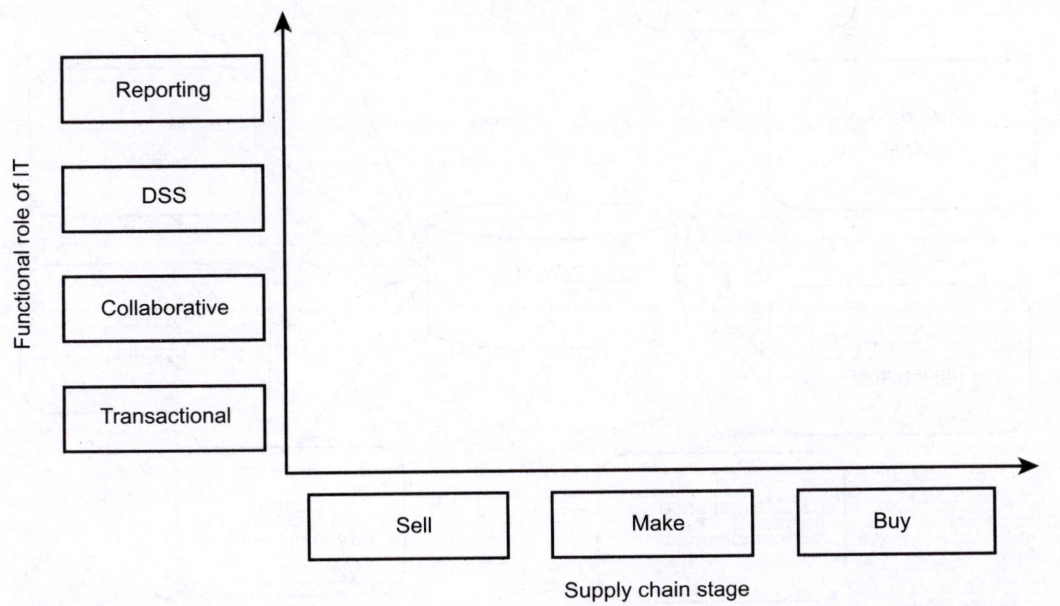


**Figure 8.2**
IT map for a supply chain.

## IT in Supply Chain Transaction Execution

In every company, business functions (i.e., design, manufacture, distribution, service and recycling of products/services) collect, generate and store vast quantities of data. Transaction execution systems automate these activities and enable tracking of data (i.e., material, orders, schedules, etc.) across these business functions. Enterprise resource planning (ERP) systems provided these capabilities to organizations to automate business functions and enable tracking of information throughout the company across different functions. As shown in Figure 8.3, ERP's core is a single comprehensive database. The database collects data from and feeds data into modular applications supporting virtually all of an enterprise's business functions. When new information is entered in one place, related information is automatically updated.

Essentially, ERP is a logical extension of the material requirements planning (MRP) systems of the 1970s and the manufacturing resource planning (MRPII) systems of the 1980s. But ERP systems have limited visibility into upstream and downstream organizations directly interacting with the ERP system. Although ERP systems have the potential to be implemented across organizations, this has not happened successfully in many cases. Supply chain execution systems extend this view to cover neighbouring enterprises as well. Supply chain execution systems not only provide the transaction execution capabilities within any company but also extend this view to cover the supply chain in its entirety. Execution systems convert plans (created with the help from DSS) to specific instructions that can be carried out by operating personnel. As plans are executed, actual results are captured and recorded in the transaction system. In addition to ERP, the following are some of the supply chain execution systems:

Procurement applications enable a streamlined procurement process. The basic purpose is to enable supplier discovery process, purchase order process and keep track of parts, specifications and prices, payments and suppliers performance.

Inventory management systems provide the ability to run the day-to-day detailed management and control of stock for an organization within the supply chain by considering the

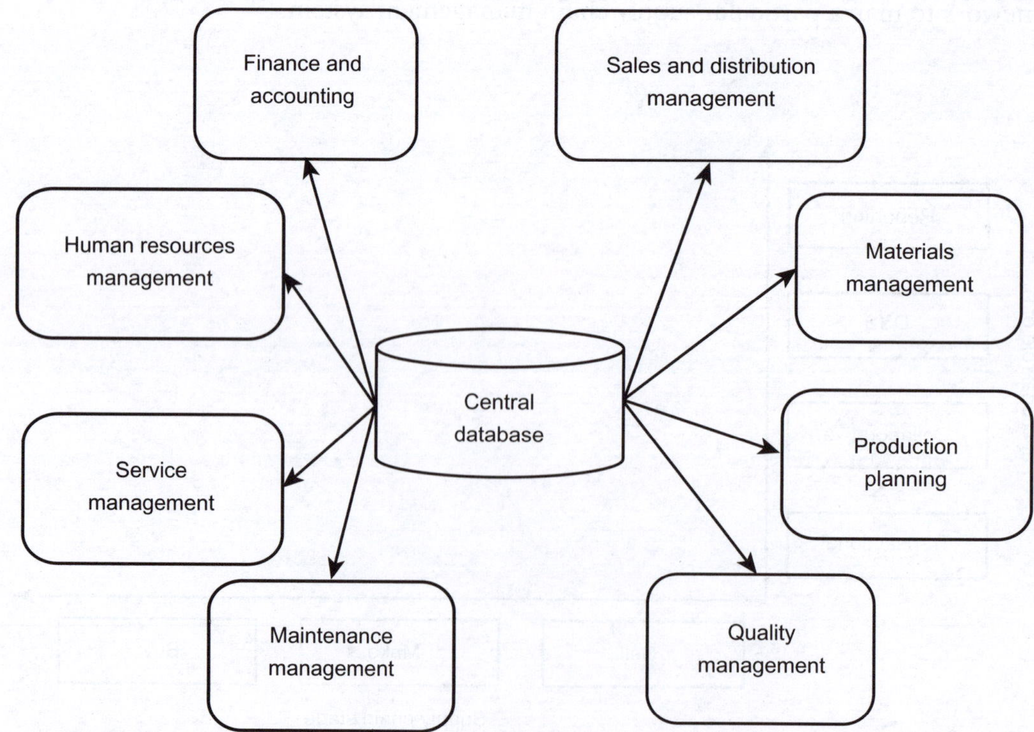


**Figure 8.3**

Application modules map of enterprise systems.

*Source*: Adapted from Thomas H. Davenport, "Putting the Enterprise into the Enterprise System," *Harvard Business Review* (July–August 1998): 121–131. © 1999 Harvard Business School Publishing Corporation. All rights reserved.

upstream and downstream organizations' order, stock and service level data. It controls all the traditional day-to-day activities of materials management operations dealing with stocks: goods receipt, goods inspection, goods issue, etc.

Manufacturing execution systems collect information and keep track of manufacturing data, such as capacity, yield, work-in-process, and machine status.

Transport execution systems assist transport managers in the task of monitoring the effectiveness of their vehicle fleet. Information regarding vehicle details (age, vehicle configuration, etc.) and vehicle activities (miles travelled, tons carried, idle time, fuel used, etc.) is collected.

Warehouse management systems execute inventory planning commands and run the day-to-day operations of a warehouse. Areas covered usually include receipt of goods, allocation of storage locations, inventory replenishment of picking locations, generation of picking list, order picking and issue of goods. These systems also keep track of inventories in warehouses.

Order track and trace allows organizations to have fast, smooth and accurate information about order status. This becomes more important in cases where organizations have multiple tiers of suppliers, subcontractors, plants and inventory locations. Also, by visiting retailers' Web sites customers can find the order status no matter where and in which supply chain partner's possession the order is.

Point of sale (POS) tracking system is a customer-facing IT application. It connects scanning equipment and retailer's inventory management systems. Goods marked with a bar code are scanned by a reader, which in turn recognizes the goods. It notes the item, tallies the price and records the transaction. POS provides an instant record of transactions at the POS. Thus, replenishment of products can be co-ordinated in real time to ensure that stockouts in the retail store are avoided.

Figure 8.4 summarizes the role of IT in transaction execution along the supply chain.

## IT in Supply Chain Collaboration and Coordination

Supply chain management covers all aspects of the business. As a result, it needs IT applications that are integrated beyond the individual company to include the neighbouring enterprises as well. Additionally, the integration should result in data that flow seamlessly throughout the supply chain, enabling all enterprises that are part of the supply chain to work better.

In recent years, collaboration has become the focus of supply chain systems. The ability to link and work effectively with suppliers has produced a new system called supplier relationship

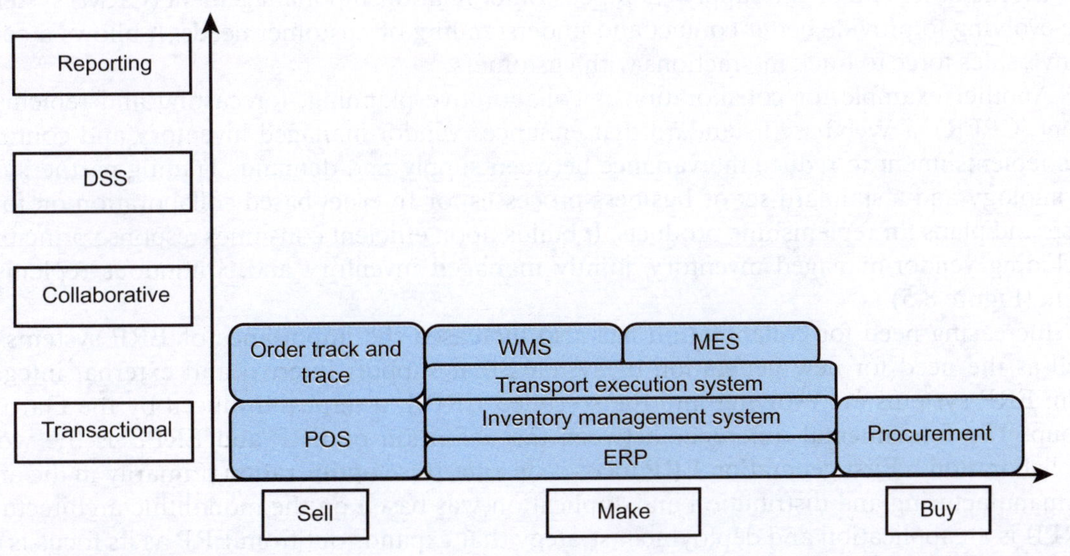


**Figure 8.4**

IT map for a supply chain transaction execution.

## INTERVIEW WITH

**B. S. NAGESH[1]**

*In early 2000, B. S. Nagesh, MD and CEO, Shopper's Stop, faced a very tough decision. The retail software he had staked his name on, to help Shopper's Stop cross over into a pan-Indian chain, was costing the company dearly. Few understood why he would not give up the software worth Rs 45 million and save Shopper's Stop Rs 200 million. As pressure from his suppliers mounted and the media wrote him off, Nagesh stuck to his guns—a decision he does not regret today.*

*When you decided to install the ERP system, it crashed and it took over 6 months to resolve the problem. How did you handle it?*

**B. S. Nagesh:** If I were asked to do things all over again, I'd make sure that human resources were deployed first, followed by financials and then technology. It was one of the key reasons behind the failure of the initial implementation. We bought the car and then looked for the drivers. It was a fundamental mistake. We were a smart organization, though, and had the foresight to spend between Rs 100 and 120 million on technology at a time when our turnover was a mere Rs 280 million. What we lacked, in hindsight, was the ability to tackle change management; getting the right people to drive the technology initiative and supporting it with financials. Personally, the biggest challenge after the crash was to choose between two courses of action. One was to persist with the failing system and see it through and the other was to dump the software in its entirety. At that time, everybody suffered a high level of de-motivation and blamed the software for the organization's woes. Nevertheless, we decided to continue with the technology. I think it is the toughest decision I've had to make. Today, people refer to how great we are technologically, but few know of the time when we questioned our belief in technology.

*What is the return on your investment in technology?*

**B. S. Nagesh:** Everybody says Shopper's Stop's shrinkage (loss of goods due to theft and inventory mismanagement) is the lowest (0.4 per cent) in the retail business. If shrinkage is looked at as a percent of profit, then a mere 3–4 per cent shrinkage seems huge. This is where technology plays a very important role. It identifies areas of shrink.

*What are the benefits of advanced supply chain management systems?*

**B. S. Nagesh**: Our B2S enables the supplier to stay informed of what we've sold and in what quantities. The supplier has evolved into an interested stakeholder as he keeps a close tab of the availability of his products on our shelves. Additionally, they (supply chain management systems) are taking away mundane, repetitive jobs out of the merchandizing process. For example, we have one of the largest dynamic auto-replenishment processes among the Indian retailers. About 26 to 30 per cent of our purchases are automated.

management (SRM). It allows a company to share information with its suppliers in real time over the Internet.

On the other end of the supply chain, customer relationship management (CRM) systems are evolving to provide better contact and understanding of customer needs. It allows a company's sales force to track interactions with customers.

Another example for collaboration is collaborative planning, forecasting and replenishment (CPFR), a Web-based standard that enhances vendor-managed inventory and continuous replenishment to reduce the variance between supply and demand. Trading partners use technology and a standard set of business processes for Internet-based collaboration on forecasts and plans for replenishing products. It builds upon efficient consumer response principles including vendor-managed inventory, jointly managed inventory and continuous replenishment (Figure 8.5).

Increasing need for collaboration has also increased the importance of ERP systems as well as the need for new generation of systems that support internal and external integration. ERP systems are evolving into the so-called ERPII, a term introduced by the Gartner group. The fundamental difference between the definition of ERP and ERPII is the word "collaboration". First-generation ERP focuses on enterprise optimization primarily in the area of manufacturing and distribution and application was based on the monolithic architecture. ERPII is an application and deployment strategy that expands out from ERP as its focus is on

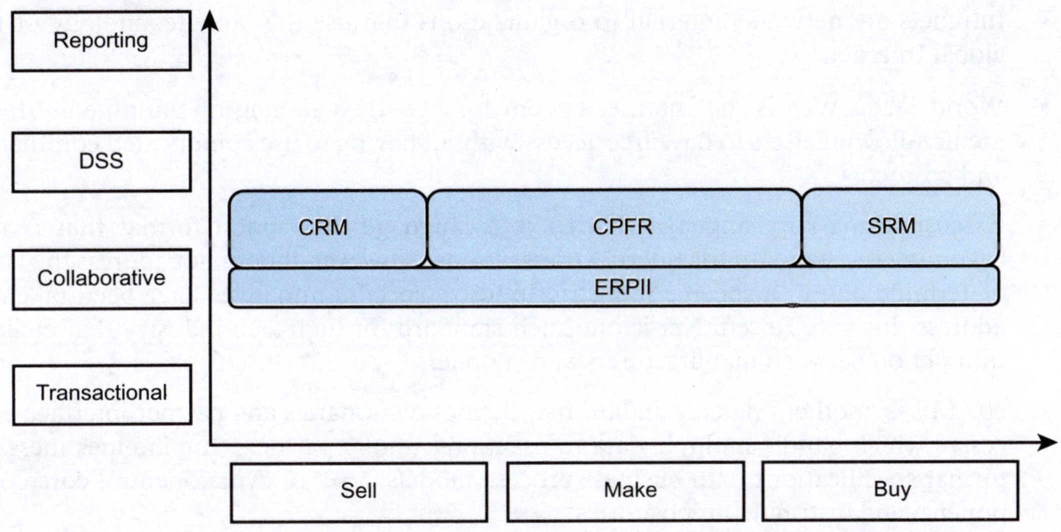


**Figure 8.5**

IT map for supply chain collaboration and coordination systems.

supply chain management including customer facing and supplier facing systems. It is a solution that includes the traditional ERP functionality strengthened by capabilities like CRM, human resources management, document/knowledge management and workflow management. ERPII enables extended portal capabilities that help an organization to also involve its suppliers and customers to participate in the workflow process. This allows ERP to penetrate the entire supply chain and helps the organization achieve greater operational efficiency. Also, ERPII is a Web-based and open system and has a component-based environment. Elements that differentiate between ERP and ERP II are as follows:

- *Optimization.* Traditional ERP was concerned with optimizing an enterprise. ERPII systems are about optimizing the supply chain through collaboration with trading partners.
- *Domain.* ERP systems focused on manufacturing and distribution. ERPII systems cross all sectors and segments of business, including service industries, government and asset-based industries like mining.
- *Process.* In ERP systems, the processes were focused within the four walls of the enterprise. ERPII systems connect with trading partners to take those processes beyond the boundaries of the enterprise.
- *Architecture.* Old ERP systems were monolithic and closed. ERPII systems are Web-based, open to integrate and interoperate with other systems and built around modules or components that allow users to choose just the functionality they need.
- *Data.* Information in ERP systems is generated and consumed within the enterprise. In an ERPII system, the same information will be available across the supply chain to authorized participants.

Specific technologies that may be utilized for an effective supply chain management collaboration and coordination system include the following:

- Electronic data interchange (EDI) refers to a computer-to-computer exchange of business documents in a standard format.
- Internet at the most basic level, a network of networks, provides instant and global access to numerous organizations, individuals and information sources. Through systems like the World Wide Web, Internet users are able to conduct organized searches on specific topics as well as browse various Web sites.

- Intranets are networks internal to organizations that use the same technology of the global Internet.
- World Wide Web is the Internet system for hypertext linking of multimedia documents, allowing users to have free access without having to use complicated commands and protocols.
- Extensible markup language (XML) is a language description format that is fast becoming the standard for Internet transactions. However, it does not address the issue of terminology in a specific industry. Industry-specific initiatives have been taken to address this gap. RosettaNet is one such standard for high-tech industry that enables transaction between manufacturers and suppliers.
- ebXML is another related standard that defines dictionaries and partner interface processes which handle multiple data transactions among partners. It combines message format specifications with business process models, a set of syntax-neutral core components and distributed repositories.

Web services are an emerging set of protocols and standards that reside on the Internet and allow applications to describe their function to each other using standards such as XML, UDDI (universal description, discover and integration) and SOAP (simple object access protocol). Web services will provide self-defined standalone applications that will be offered as components (or functionality) that companies can buy over the Internet. Payment can be on a per-use basis. This will make collaboration easier by deploying a loose-coupling approach to integration since the integration methods are part of the service and do not need to be tailored for every two applications that are being integrated.

Supply chain event management (SCEM) systems form a promising category of new technologies and offer significantly more insight into major changes in the supply chain than the established supply chain solutions. SCEM tracks predefined performance measures for inventory, transportation or other events and alerts users to problems in the supply chain such as stockouts or delays. These alerts can be sent to users through e-mail, over phone or on wireless devices such as personal digital assistants (PDA).

Client/server computing is a form of distributed processing whereby some processes are performed centrally for many users while others are performed locally on a user's PC. The Internet is a form of client/server where the local PC browser processes the HTML (hypertext markup language) pages and Java applets (i.e., small applications) that are retrieved from servers—in this case from all over the world.

Many ERP products use three-tier client/server technology. In this architecture, the presentation logic (user interface programs) resides on the client (first tier), the business logic on the middle tier and other resources such as the database reside on the back end.

Middleware are the applications that reside between the client and the server. Middleware is important in the implementation of supply chain systems as data for these systems exists in a number of locations. Middleware in this case is used to collect the data and format it in a way that can be used by various supply chain tools. When this type of process between companies is applied over the Internet, it is called enterprise application integration.

Product tracking requires a standard way to track products in order to provide participants with the information they need to perform efficiently. Universal product codes are extensively used for scanning and recording information about products using barcodes. Recently, many companies have started RFID tags on their products where a 96-bit code of numbers called electronic product code (EPC) is used on tags. These RFID tags do not have a line-of-sight requirement for them to be detected, and then can be identified within a distance of a few centimetres to a few feet. Also, there are RFID tags that can be detected within a distance of a few meters. This technology combined with wireless communication devices and GPS capabilities enables tracking of tagged containers in shipments. RFID technology is likely to play an important role in supply chain management.

## IT in Supply Chain Decision Support

The transaction system captures data on orders, inventory, shipments, costs, etc., and also keeps it up to date and distributes it to users and other applications. A collaboration and coordination system ensures that the supply chain data are available in a timely manner to all the enterprises in the supply chain. DSS use these data to create feasible and economical plans dealing with different stages of the supply chain (i.e., sell, make and buy). It provides answers to fundamental questions of what should be produced, where, when and for whom. For DSS to create feasible plans, it should not violate any real-world constraints such as lead times, material availability, labour availability, equipment capacity and transport capacity. Advanced DSS uses optimization techniques to ensure that all modelled constraints are respected and that the highest business value is achieved.

### RANBAXY'S ERP AND SCM INITIATIVE[2]

Ranbaxy Laboratories Limited is ranked amongst the top 10 global generic companies (with a sales of US$ 1.3 billion) and hopes to attain a size of US$ 5 billion by 2012. To manage its global operations seamlessly, Ranbaxy decided to invest in ERP systems. The company initially considered this to be a technological project. ERP implementation turned out to be a long torturous exercise. Unfortunately, the organization did not benefit significantly from the ERP implementation. It was at this stage that the top management got involved in the whole process. It decided, after much deliberation, to invest in supply chain management decision support applications to get the maximum benefit out of the recently introduced ERP infrastructure. This strategy worked very well and brought real value to the firm. Ranbaxy also learnt a hard lesson in the process that the implementation of ERP and supply chain management software need a higher level of involvement and attention.

DSS entails various levels of decision making depending on the time frame of the managerial activities and the frequency with which they occur. Mainly, strategic, tactical and operational levels of supply chain management can be distinguished. These levels have different information needs: from operational decisions involving the way to fulfil a customer order, to tactical decisions related to which warehouse to stock with what product or what should be the production plan for the next three months, to strategic decisions about where to locate warehouse and what products to develop and produce. Accordingly, IT applications are grouped under these three categories (Figure 8.6).

- Strategic-level planning involves the supply chain network design, which determines the location, size and optimal numbers of suppliers, the production plants and distributors to be used in the network. This planning phase can be summarized as determining the nodes and arcs of the network and their relationships. Strategic-level planning is long-range planning and is typically performed every few years, when firms need to expand their capabilities. The method most often used is optimization.
- The tactical level of supply chain management covers the planning of supplies, manufacturing schedules and the forecasting of demand. It primarily includes the optimization of flow of goods and services through a given network. Decisions at this level include which products must be produced at what plants in what quantity and which suppliers must source raw materials and sub-components. Tactical-level planning is medium-range planning, which is typically performed on a monthly basis. Advanced planning and scheduling is the key software product for this planning. The method most often used is optimization.
- The operational level of supply chain management focuses on day-to-day operations and enables efficiencies in production, distribution, inventory and transportation

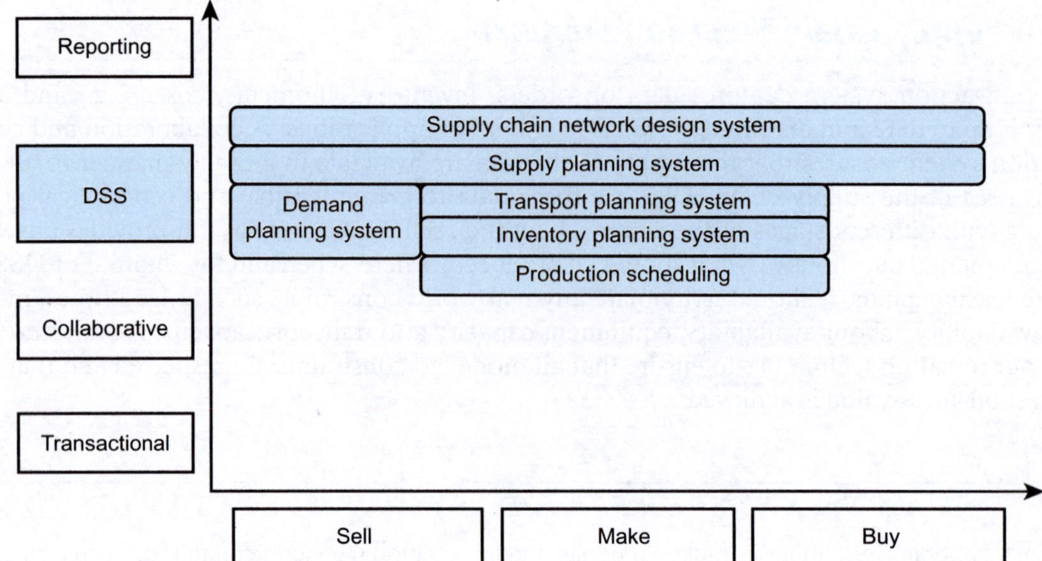


**Figure 8.6**

IT map for supply chain DSS.

for short-term planning. Operation planning systems include the following four factors:

- Demand planning, which generates demand forecast based on various historical and other related information. The method used is mostly statistical analysis.
- Production scheduling at all plants on a day-to-day or hour-to-hour basis based on the tactical plan or demand forecasts. The method used is constraint-based feasibility analysis that satisfies all production constraints.
- Inventory planning generates inventory plans for the various facilities in the supply chain based on average demand, demand variability and source material lead times. The methods used are statistical and computational.
- Transportation planning produces transportation routes and schedules based on availability of transportation on lane, cost and customer delivery schedules. Fleet planning, transportation mode selection, routing and distribution are also part of transportation planning systems. The methods used are mostly heuristic.

Specific technologies that may be utilized for an effective supply chain management DSS include the following:

- *Interface.* DSS must have interfaces to get data from other relational databases.
- *Scheduling algorithms.* Based on the data gathered, a schedule can be generated by running the operations research algorithm for scheduling. DSS should be able to formulate the operations research model. Direct link should be available to commercially available optimizers.
- *Expert system rules.* Once the data have been gathered and a production schedule is produced, expert system rules can capture some of the expertise of the scheduler and can validate the production schedule feasibility.
- *Business warehouse.* To perform pre-defined historical data analysis and status reports, DSS will need a business warehouse where data can be stored after uploading from other systems, and customized queries can be written.
- *Visual composer.* Visual composer is a strong tool to efficiently represent data as graphs. This will be needed to present the results for DSS.

- *Graphical user interface.* A graphical user interface will be needed for display of results, for example, hierarchical drill down, pull down menus and creation of customized result display.

## IT in Supply Chain Measurement and Reporting

The importance of timely supply chain measurement is increasing. As more and more companies seek the promise of a demand-driven supply network (DDSN), companies are using IT to measure and manage all aspects of performance throughout their businesses. Through the 1990s, companies invested primarily on optimization for decision support. However, companies today are more focused on how to measure their supply chain to know if they are improving. DDSN requires an instantaneous sensing of customer demand and an immediate supply chain response to get the product to the customer when the customer wants it. A set of IT applications including BI are used to measure and report supply chain metrics (Figure 8.7). Following are some of the key supply chain metrics:

- *Supply chain planning metrics.* Forecast accuracy, total inventory, plant utilization, warehouse utilization, fleet utilization, dwell time through supply chain, plan versus actual inventory at stores and production plan variance.
- *Supplier relationship management metrics.* Supplier quality, purchase costs, direct material costs, delivery performance and supplier on-time performance.
- *Customer relationship management metrics.* Customer lift, customer retention, customer lifetime value, sales performance, sales offtake versus out of stock at stores, product availability compliance, promotions goal compliance, inquiry handling time and win ratio.
- *Enterprise resource planning metrics.* Perfect order, supply chain costs, accounts payable, accounts receivable, cash-to-cash cycle times, cost detail and order cycle time.

Specific technologies that may be utilized for an effective supply chain management measurement and reporting include the following:

- *Data warehouse.* A data warehouse is a copy of the enterprise transactional data (read only data), suitably modified for decision support and data analysis. However, it is important to note that data warehousing is not just data in the data warehouse but also the architecture

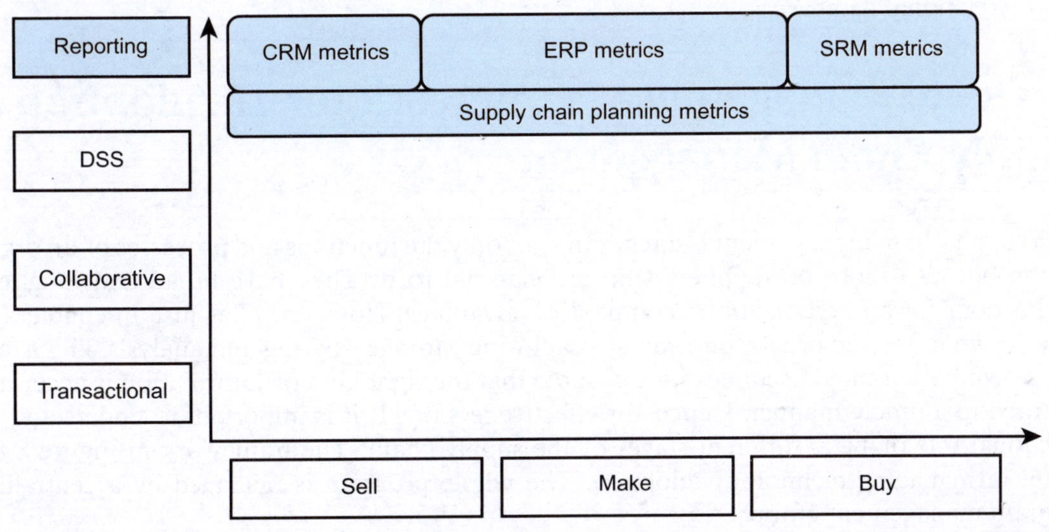


**Figure 8.7** IT map for supply chain reporting.

and software/hardware components to collect query, analyse and present information. It has the following components: before storing data in a consolidated database, organization application data are taken through the process of extracting, integrating, filtering, standardizing, transforming, cleaning and quality checking. Data mining is used for sorting through large amounts of data and picking out relevant information.

- *Online analytical processing.* This is a category of applications and technologies for collecting, managing, processing and presenting multidimensional data for analysis and management purposes. It helps in analysing transaction information at an aggregate level to improve the decision-making process. Reporting tools are used to display and render the data to the user in variety of formats including charts, tables, maps and geographic information systems.

- *Dashboards and scoreboards.* Dashboards provide a unified gateway to access timely and relevant information. It provides alignment, visibility and collaboration across the organization by allowing the business users to define, monitor and analyse business performance via key performance indicators (KPIs). With business dashboards, the data display can include tables, charts, maps and other innovative visual cues such as thermometers, traffic lights, analog speedometers, etc. Such a business dashboard may also contain links to other pertinent information, important summary and highlights and personalized information. A dashboard offers instant snapshots of an organization's designated KPIs and provides real-time trend graphs and ad hoc reports appropriate for each role in the organization's business. Various types of dashboards are given below:
    - *Enterprise performance dashboard.* It consolidates data from various divisions and business segments and provides a holistic view of the enterprise for senior management.
    - *Divisional dashboard.* It displays the performance metrics and numbers specific to divisional and operational managers.
    - *Process/activity monitoring dashboard.* It monitors specific business processes or widespread activities, for example, order-monitoring dashboards may help monitor live order conditions, open orders, overdue orders, perfect orders, etc.
    - *Ad hoc query capability.* Ad hoc query is used to report on data that are not covered by standard reports. By selecting selection fields and output fields, stored data are accessed anywhere within the enterprise system. It does not need any programming skills or pre-defined templates to create reports.
    - *Interface.* Data warehouse and BI tools must have interfaces to get data from other relational databases.

## Strategic Management Framework for IT Adoption in Supply Chain Management

IT in supply chain management is integrating not only the functions and processes of an organization but also those of suppliers who are external to it. They have broad and long-term implications for an organization's competitive advantage. However, IT is just an enabler and provides an infrastructure for information capturing, storage, sharing and analysis. IT systems on its own have limited use unless it is ensured that the right kind of information is accurately captured in a timely manner. Hence, for effectiveness of IT, it is important to understand the functional role of IT at different stages of the supply chain. The framework in Figure 8.8 is useful in managing technology adoption. The whole program is managed by a centralized program management group.

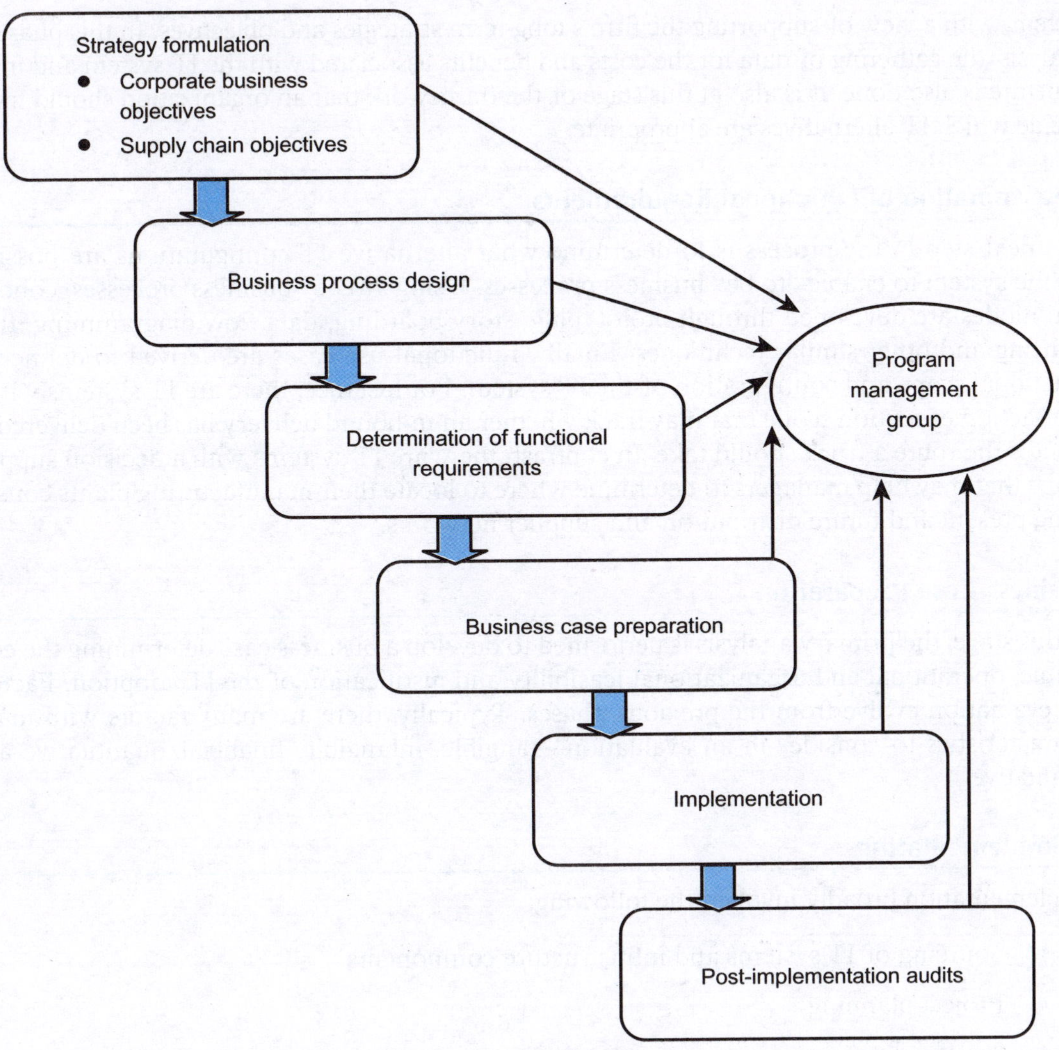


**Figure 8.8**

Strategic management framework.

*Source*: Adapted from Srinivas Talluri, "An IT/IS Acquisition and Justification Model for Supply-Chain Management," *International Journal of Physical Distribution & Logistics Management* (2000, Vol 30): 221–237.

## Strategy Formulation

The decision for the development and implementation of IT begins at the upper levels of management and is closely linked to corporate visions, goals and strategies. Before implementing IT, organizations usually undergo a SWOT-MOSP process in which they assess their strengths, weaknesses, opportunities and threats (SWOT) and then formulate a suitable set of missions, objectives, strategies and policies (MOSP). The result of this process, at the organizational level, is the derivation of a set of business objectives that need to be supported by the specific technology that is chosen. The strategies of supply chain management must be consonant with these business objectives. For example, if the business objective is to control the lost sales then the supply chain management strategy should be to maintain a high service level to prevent stockouts at stores.

## Business Process Design

The next stage of the planning process, known as the "re-engineering" stage consists of two studies named "as is" and "to be". These studies involve a thorough development and determination of the inputs, outputs and business processes of the system that is being evaluated. The "as is" study analyses the current business process, providing baseline measures and factors for later justification. The "to be" study is used to define a rough-cut or preliminary description of the system, with a view of supporting the firm's long-term strategies and objectives. In this phase of analysis, the gathering of data for the costs and benefits associated with the IT system and infrastructure is also done. It is also at this stage of the framework that an organization should try to decide which IT alternatives are appropriate.

## Determination of Functional Requirements

The next step in the process is to determine what alternative IT configurations are possible for the system to enable "to be" business processes. Using "to be" business processes, conceptual modes are developed through prototyping, story boarding, data flow diagramming, flow charting and other similar techniques. Finally, functional use cases are derived to define the functional scope and configuration of the IT system. For instance, there are IT systems with a transaction execution scope that may track whether an in-bound delivery has been delivered or what is the route a truck should take. In contrast, there are IT systems with a decision support scope that may help managers to determine where to locate their manufacturing plants considering present and future distribution and supplier networks.

## Business Case Preparation

In this stage, the primary analysis is performed to develop a business case determining the economic, operational and organizational feasibility and justification of the IT adoption. Factors for evaluation evolve from the previous phases. Typically, there are many factors with many characteristics to consider in an evaluation—tangible, intangible, financial/quantitative and qualitative.

## IT Implementation

Implementation broadly involves the following:

- Sourcing of IT systems and infrastructure components
- Project planning
- Implementation
- Integration
- Testing
- Training and handing over

Systems integration in case of supply chain management systems is one of the more difficult tasks to achieve. The difficulties primarily arise from the use of multiple types of sub-systems, platforms and interfaces, as well as from the dispersion of these sub-systems in terms of their control and physical locations. The task of making sure that future systems can link modularly to the current and past systems is a concern for systems managers.

Depending upon how much time and cost is available and how much risk the company is willing to take, a company can choose the most appropriate implementation method from one of the following ways:

- *Parallel approach.* The existing system and the new system operate simultaneously until there is confidence that the new system is working properly.
- *Big bang or cold turkey approach.* The old system is removed totally and the new system takes over.
- *Phased approach.* Modules of the new system are gradually introduced one at a time using either the big bang approach or the parallel approach.

- *Pilot approach*. The new system is fully implemented on a pilot basis in one segment of the organization.

***FAILED SUPPLY CHAIN INITIATIVE AT KMART*** [3]

In 1990, Kmart, then the largest US discount retailer, found that it had lost its leadership position to Wal-Mart. Throughout the 1990s, the gap between Kmart and Wal-Mart kept widening at a faster pace. In 2000, Chuk Conaway took over as the chief executive of Kmart and identified supply chain weaknesses as a major area of concern. He decided to work with an aggressive goal to make Kmart competitive with Wal-Mart within 2 years. To achieve this objective, in May 2000, the company decided to invest $1.4 billion in supply chain software and services. Tough time pressures forced the firm to start its major supply chain software initiative without working out details of its supply chain strategy. Within 2 years of the announcement, it had to abandon its supply chain software initiative and write off $130 million worth of supply chain hardware and software in the process.

### Post-implementation Audits

This last "feedback" stage helps in "closing the loop" for future development of the system. It is also the primary step required for the inclusion of the concept of continuous improvement. Among the stages discussed earlier there should always be some form of feedback, as shown in Figure 8.8, to minimize the gap between what is required and what is implemented.

## Supply Chain Management Application Marketplace

There are four categories of firms that offer supply chain management applications software:

- ERP vendors offering comprehensive solution for a variety of vertical industries
- Independent vendors offering comprehensive solution for a variety of vertical industries
- Niche players offering solution for specific supply chain functionalities
- Niche players offering solution for specific industries

See Box 8.1 for details on all the four categories.

However, it is important for supply chain managers to understand the interaction between ERP systems and niche functionality provided by supply chain solution vendors. Although they are sometimes viewed as competitors, they also rely on each other. For supply chain solutions to be effective, they will need accurate and timely data from different business functions. ERP systems are most effective in providing these data, and hence managers often combine these two applications to produce the best supply chain management system. Hence, these two streams of solutions will coexist for most of the cases.

## Future Trends

- *Increased polarization of the supply chain management application software market*. ERP vendors, particularly SAP, has added supply chain management functionality to their offerings and succeeded in freezing the market, which makes it difficult for the independent or niche players to sell to ERP vendors' clients. Further, ERP vendors are also developing industry-specific supply chain management solutions. As a result, the share of supply chain

## BOX 8.1 Supply Chain Management Application Marketplace: Relevant Links and Other Sources

**Leading Independent Vendors**
JDA Software, www.jda.com

JDA Software provides JDA Portfolio suite of vertically focused supply and demand chain solutions to retail, manufacturing and wholesale-distribution companies. JDA has acquired Manugistics and i2.

**Niche Vendors**
http://www.kivasystems.com/

Kiva provides next generation automation technology for fulfilment centres. Their solution uses sophisticated control software and hundreds of autonomous mobile robots. It is a wholly owned subsidiary of Amazon

http://www.arkieva.com/

Arkieva provides advanced planning and scheduling (APS) software solutions. It helps companies to profitably plan demand, manage inventories, optimize supply and schedule production to a great extent.

www.insight-mss.com/

For the past 28 years, Insight has focused on using best practices to develop a series of leading-edge software packages for strategic and tactical planning.

http://www.scientific-logistics.com/

Scientific Logistics, Inc. provides proprietary transportation optimization solutions to shippers and carriers as a managed service.

www.logility.com/

Logility is a provider of collaborative solutions to optimize the supply chain. Logility Voyager Solutions enable networks of trading partners, including suppliers, manufacturers, distributors, retailers and carriers to collaborate, integrate and synchronize their planning, production and fulfilment operations.

www.viewlocity.com/

Viewlocity provides visibility and event management solutions for supply chain collaboration and coordination.

www.demandsolutions.com/

Demand solutions provide demand planning solutions predominantly to the small and medium business market space.

www.manh.com/

Manhattan associates with its warehouse management system has diversified into a portfolio of software solutions and technology that leverages its Supply Chain Process Platform to help organizations optimize their supply chains from planning through execution.

www.ortems.com/

Ortems provides advanced planning and scheduling solutions for manufacturers in both discrete and process industries.

**Industry-focused Vendors**
www.aspentech.com/

AspenTech's focus has been on applying process engineering know-how to modelling the manufacturing and supply chain processes that characterize the process industries. It provides solutions in the process industry for process simulation and optimization, advanced process control, advanced planning and scheduling and plant information management.

www.adexa.com/

Adexa provides supply chain solutions predominantly to companies in the high-tech industry. The Adexa "Enterprise Global Planning System" (eGPS) is a comprehensive suite of 13 integrated solutions for manufacturers. It delivers a robust enterprise business planning solution that encompasses supply chain planning, event management, enterprise performance management and intelligent collaboration.

**ERP Vendors**
www.sap.com/

Built on the SAP NetWeaver platform, SAP SCM provides not only planning and execution capabilities to manage enterprise operations but also visibility, collaboration and RFID technology to streamline and extend those operations beyond corporate boundaries.

A key component of the solution, the SAP Advanced Planner and Optimizer (SAP APO) and SAP Integrated Business Planning (IBP), provide the complete toolset needed to plan and optimize supply chain processes at the strategic, tactical and operational planning levels.

www.oracle.com/

The Oracle E-Business Suite Supply Chain Management family of applications integrates and automates all key supply chain activities, from design, planning and procurement to manufacturing and fulfilment. Further, its acquisition of J.D. Edwards and People Soft has further added to its basket of supply chain management solutions.

With the acquisition of Retek, Oracle has a vertically focused supply chain solution for the retail industry.

*(Continued on the next page)*

**BOX 8.1** Supply Chain Management Application Marketplace: Relevant Links and Other Sources (*Continued*)

**Cloud Vendors**

GXS, www.gxs.com

GXS is a B2B e-commerce company providing managed services around the world.

E2Open, www.e2open.com

E2open helps orchestrate critical supply chain processes across multiple tiers of business partners.

management software sales going to the ERP vendors has risen, while the niche and start-up vendors have failed to thrive and the major independent vendors have had drastic reductions in sales.

New technologies will be judged on their business benefits. CPFR and RFID will either prove that they can deliver measurable financial benefit or will fall off the radar screen. Procter & Gamble has prepared the framework for RFID implementation to help its technical people in addressing business issues. See Box 8.2 for a detailed description of RFID technology.

RFID is frequently compared with the bar code. In many organizations, bar codes are commonplace. However, bar codes are not always the perfect solution to address the auto-identification requirements and it is subjected to error and convenience issues. A comparison of some of the attributes of RFID and the bar code is given in Table 8.1.

**BOX 8.2** RFID Technology

Radio frequency identification (RFID) can be used to identify, track, sort or detect a wide variety of objects. It is evolving as a major technology enabler for tracking goods and assets around the world, while taking supply chain and inventory management to a whole new level by making them transparent in real time. An RFID system exchanges information between the tagged object and a reader/writer in the wireless medium. The major components of an RFID system are

- One or more tags or transponders consisting of semiconductor chips and antennae
- Reader/writer devices or interrogators
- Two or more antennae, one on the transponder and another with the interrogator
- A host computer system and the application software

Figure 8.9 can make the scenario more familiar.

An RFID system transmits the identity of a physical item in the form of a unique serial number wirelessly using radio waves. Communication takes place between a reader or interrogator and a transponder or a tag: a silicon chip connected to an antenna. RFID tags are attached on items to

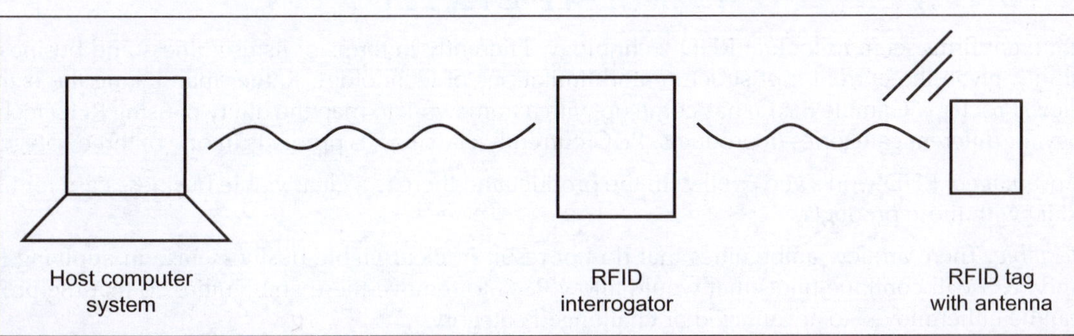


**Figure 8.9**

An RFID system.

(*Continued on the next page*)

## BOX 8.2 RFID Technology (*Continued*)

be tracked, which could be individual items, boxes or even consignments.

Once these tags are read by the RFID readers, information in binary or hexadecimal format is sent to a software system, in this case, the Edgeware system. Edgeware performs multiple roles: integration with auto-identification devices such as RFID readers to collect data, filtering and aggregation of RFID data, device maintenance and configuration and status monitoring. The RFID solution architecture is shown in Figure 8.10.

The business middleware layer comes next. This layer converts the raw RFID data from Edgeware to trigger a business process through the ERP application for automatic transaction posting and stock update. Involvement of each layer also brings its own set of requirements. Any RFID program has to deal with multiple standards related to hardware and software layers.

***RFID standards for tag and reader***

| Tag encoding scheme for parts/tag class | Operating frequency | Air interface protocols | Networking | Power regulations (for readers) |
|---|---|---|---|---|
| SGTIN—64; SGTIN—96; Class 1—write once, read only; Class 2—Gen 2, read write | HF—13.56 MHz; UHF—400–930 MHz | ISO/EPC; ISO 18000 Part 3 for HF; ISO 18000 Part 6 for UHF | TCP/IP; wireless LAN (802.11); ethernet LAN (10base T); RS 485 | 4 Watts in US (frequency hopping); 500 mW in Europe (duty cycle) |

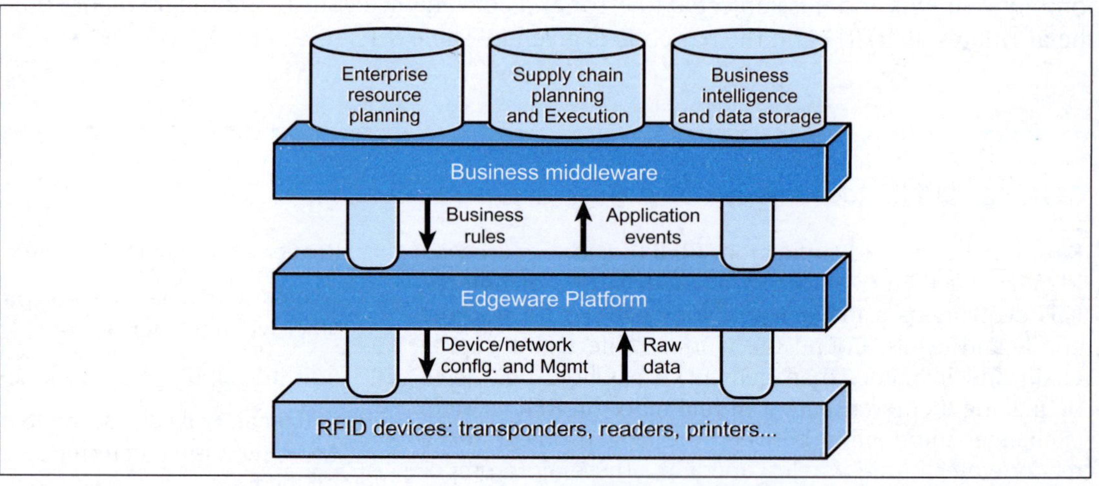


**Figure 8.10**

The RFID solution architecture.

## PROCTER & GAMBLE'S FRAMEWORK FOR RFID IMPLEMENTATION[4]

Different firms seem to look at RFID technology differently in terms of its usefulness and business viability, given the current cost structure and limitations of technology. Rather than taking the extreme view, Procter & Gamble (P&G) has come up with a framework to map the utility of using RFID technology for different categories of products. P&G currently classifies its products in one of three categories:

*Advantaged*: RFID works very well with the product and there is a clear viable business case for use of RFID with those products.

*Testable*: There are few ambiguities that do not result in clear viable business case in applying RFID and P&G will continue pilots that would allow P&G to remove these ambiguities so that the product can be either moved to advantaged or challenged category.

*Challenged*: There is no business case of RFID application for these categories of products.

*Table 8.1:* **A comparison of the attributes of RFID and bar code.**

| Attribute | RFID | Bar code |
|---|---|---|
| Line of sight reads | Support | Counter |
| Range—distance from reader | Support | Counter |
| Read more than one tag simultaneously | Support | Counter |
| Speed of reading | Support | Neutral |
| Harsh environment compatibility | Support | Counter |
| Read/write | Support | Counter |
| Data capacity | Support | Neutral |
| Hands-free reads | Support | Neutral |
| Placement flexibility | Neutral | Neutral |
| Cost | Counter | Support |
| Universally accepted standards | Counter | Support |

*Support*: The attribute supports adoption of the technology. *Neutral*: The attribute neutral. *Counter*: The attribute is an obstacle to the adoption of the technology.

The emergence of SCEM applications, enabled by EDI, Web services and the Internet makes it possible to sense changes in the supply chain environment in near real time. These changes can be increases, decreases or delays to orders, demand, inventory and shipments. The adaptive concept seeks to harness near real-time information and feed it back to planning and execution to enable rapid, highly targeted responses.

- *Agent-based supply chain*. As manufacturers migrate to adaptive supply networks enabled by Web services and SCEM, they will exploit intelligent-agent technology to detect and resolve operational glitches proactively.

Emergence of on-demand-hosted supply chain software (also called SAS—software as service) can solve the supply chain integration problem and the requirement of writing new interfaces as and when supply chain entities are added to the network. Hosted supply chain collaboration applications run on the vendor's computers and companies can access these over the Internet through a Web browser. The hosted front-end of an enterprise's supply chain system has the ability to communicate with the different communication protocols found in today's supply chain. However, vendors providing hosted services will have to address the chief information officer's worry about data security, integrating hosted solution with internal systems, customization requirements and downtime problems. Additionally, these vendors will have to demonstrate that they are long-term players.

- *SOA-based collaboration*. Achieving collaboration among supply chain partners is a big challenge. It requires support for multiple data formats (e.g., EDI, flat file), support for widely adopted standards for business document interchange (e.g., RFC4130, STAR specification), defining common business schema, managing authentication and authorization across multiple business domains and supporting multiple types of end points (e.g., NET, EJB, HTTP). Often organizations handle integration of supply chain in a piecemeal manner using custom development, resulting in point-to-point connections that cannot be reused by other applications requiring the same data.

A service-oriented architecture (SOA) integration platform allows standards-based integration of multiple types of interfaces that communicate using different data formats over different protocols. SOA is not a product or tool. It is an architectural principle that provides a loosely coupled and highly distributed architectural paradigm. The key components of SOA are as follows:

- *Service provider*. One who provides service functionality in the form of Web services that is published by the service broker.

- *Service broker.* One who maintains a registry of services, their interface descriptions, provider information and invocation methods.
- *Service consumer.* One who locates the required service and all information for binding/invoking the service from the service broker.

SOA is based on following key technology standards:

WSDL (Web Services Description Language): An XML document used to describe Web services. It specifies the location of the service and the operations (or methods) the service exposes.

SOAP (Simple Object Access Protocol): A platform and language independent protocol used for communications between applications, specifically Web services.

UDDI (Universal Description, Discovery and Integration): A directory service where businesses can register and search for Web services.

Figure 8.11 depicts the interaction amongst key components of SOA.

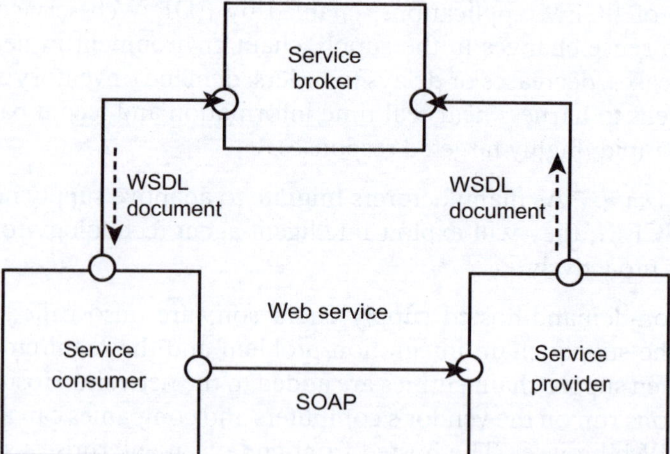


**Figure 8.11**
SOA in action.

With technology evolving at the speed of light, the trends are many and varied, such as Software as a Service (SaaS), Cloud computing, improved demand-sensing tools and usage of mobile devices.

Wireless communications speed has increased dramatically and prices for mobile technology have fallen to allow for many devices that are now deployed to exchange data in real time. This has made mobile technology an efficient solution for the supply chain. Today, in warehouse, a single mobile device can deliver a variety of applications such as imaging at receiving, high bay scanning at put away, voice picking and RFID at the loading dock. The ability of mobile computing to get the right person for the right job at the right time with the right information is a major advantage for improving productivity, accuracy and reducing labour costs.

Key areas for mobile technology applications are as follows:

- the warehouse (inventory management),
- logistics (shipping and delivery),
- fleet operations ( route planning, truck tracking)
- and transactions in sales outlets like inventory taking for reorders,
- automated customer checkout, etc.

**BOX 8.3** Mobile Technology

A mobile system exchanges information between the mobile devices and the application database in the wireless medium. The major components of the mobile system are

- mobile devices
- wireless network connectivity
- secure access to corporate Intranet
- a host computer system, application software and the database

Figure 8.12 explains the scenario very clearly.

Mobile devices uses web browser. Rich client applications are used to capture and send the business data (i.e., order for an item) wirelessly using variety of wireless networks (i.e., GSM/GPRS/EDGE, CDMA as well as 802.11 local-area wireless networks). This data is received in the web server that provides the underlying secure connectivity, thus enabling mobile devices to connect to the corporate intranet. Data received in the web server is sent to a software system; in this case, the application server. Application server performs multiple roles of data encryption, device monitoring, application provisioning as well as database update. The mobile system solution architecture is shown in Figure 8.12.

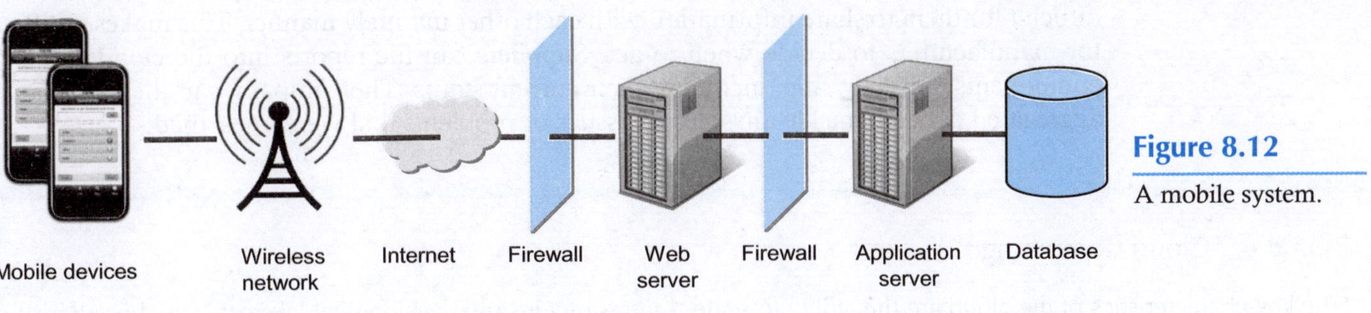


**Figure 8.12**
A mobile system.

Although the adaption of the mobile technology has few challenges for enterprise applications, privacy, security, system integration and multiple standards are the key challenges in wide deployment of mobile technology. However, a great challenge faced by the companies is that gaining the acceptance of employees with mobile supply chain technology, as they perceive this technology as an invasion of their privacy (e.g., tracking both employee and vehicle locations through mobile GPS, video recording of warehouse activities are few such cases). Mobile devices can be lost, and hence, organizations should consider encryption of data on the device, ability to remotely monitor and shutdown the devices. While most of the mobile devices interact with industry-standard interfaces, same is not true for applications and databases. Supply chain applications and databases are required to be ready for mobile technologies for their easy integration with mobile devices to achieve mobile supply chain.

With more companies looking ways to operate efficiently, SaaS (software as a service) or 'on-demand' technology solutions are gaining adaption. Transportation management system has been the pioneering approach, and now, industry analyst expects SaaS adaption in functional areas of the supply chain that demands good visibility, connectivity and collaboration. Another area that has emerged is the IaaS (infrastructure as a service whose focus is to take the back-office burden off the business community and places it with companies whose core competencies are data, hardware, application and security management, as well as disaster recovery). Both the SaaS and cloud computing are modelled on 'Pay for use' concept that can help organizations moving away from software/hardware-related fixed investment and annual maintenance/upgrade charges to transaction-based pricing. Email, Facebook and LinkedIn are examples of this concept where you get different applications to use as well as data storage to store your emails and photographs at very nominal monthly charges.

Cloud-based services can be categorized in the following three areas:

- Infrastructure-as-a-service – services related to accessing storage capacity and raw computing power over internet
- Platform-as-a-service – web-based development environments are made available over internet.
- Software-as-a-service – standardized enterprise applications such as finance and human resources are made available over internet.

First two are more tactical in nature, while SaaS is more strategic decision for organizations and most common way is to start using SaaS for standardized application areas such as finance and human resources that do not provide organizations with competitive advantage.

Supply chain can gain tremendous boost to visibility in those processes where collaboration with and between third parties such as suppliers and partners are key members. For example, in the case of inventory, disjointed processes and spread out partners often make it difficult for them to share information with each other in timely manner. This makes it difficult for manufacturers to decide when to act. Suppliers can file reports into the cloud about the components that they ship, including their current status. The company can then analyse the aggregated data and tackle any specific issues or problems that were unearthed.

**BOX 8.4** Cloud Computing

'The key characteristics of the cloud are the ability to scale and provision computing power dynamically in a cost efficient way and the ability of the consumer (end user, organization or IT staff) to make the most of that power without having to manage the underlying complexity of the technology.

The cloud architecture itself can be private (hosted within an organization's firewall) or public (hosted on the Internet).'

*Source:* www.opencloudmanifesto.org

Figure 8.13 explains the scenario very clearly. Depending upon the type of cloud, it can be one or all the layers related to business process, application, data, infrastructure and development layers that are hosted by the service provider. All the layers that are part of the cloud are managed by service provider. Organizations can subscribe to one or more layers of cloud to access the services. Organizations alone or third-party technology vendors can publish, update and make their components available by subscribing to cloud.

The high-level conceptual architecture of cloud is shown in Figure 8.13.

Visit www.e2open.com and www.gxs.com to find out how these service providers are offering cloud-based services for supply chain.

www.e2open.com/

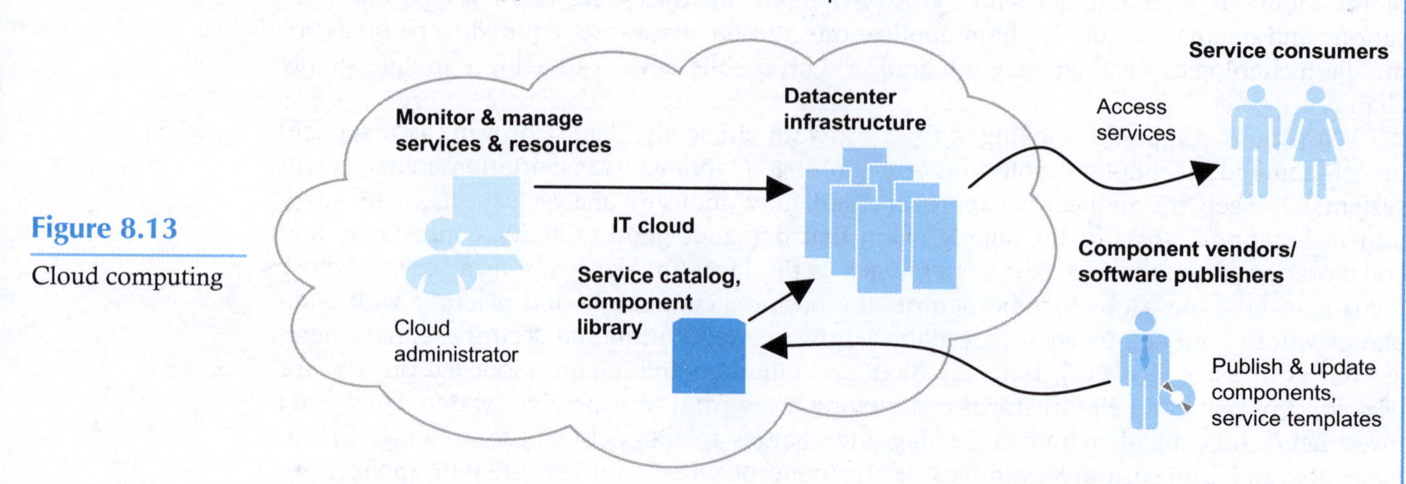


**Figure 8.13**
Cloud computing

The adaption of the cloud computing has few challenges for enterprise applications. The main barriers of cloud is mainly cultural rather than technological; challenges such as becoming part of supply chain network, standardizing on common processes across supply chain and certainty about how much information is to be shared and how early. Further, assurance should be given that such information will not be passed on to rivals and certainty about the supply chain community members that it will not be used against them. Few business-to-business trading hubs are e2Open and GXS.

**BOX 8.5** IoT

Chui et al. (2010) define the 'Internet of Things (IoT)' as ' . . . sensors and actuators embedded in physical objects - from roadways to pacemakers - are linked through wired and wireless networks, often using the same Internet Protocol (IP) that connects the Internet'. The 'Internet of Things' generally refers to the notion that many different 'things' are connected to the internet, and thus, they can be connected to each other. [Reference: Chui M, Loffler M, Roberts R. 2010. The Internet of Things. McKinsey Quarterly (2): 1-9]

- 'Things' can be sensors, databases, other devices or software. Sensors could include pacemakers, location identifiers, such as global positioning system (GPS), and individual identification devices like radio-frequency identification (RFID) tags.
- 'Things' can be intelligent and aware of other 'Things'.
- 'Things' can gather information and knowledge from their interaction with other 'things'.
- 'Things' are potentially autonomous, semi-autonomous or not autonomous.

[Reference: Cluster of European Research Projects (CERP)]

IoT presents endless possibilities in almost every aspect of human life such as healthcare, security and transport. These devices are slowly becoming an integral part of our daily lives through driving assist systems, home security and maintenance systems, payment services, order replenishment and identity establishment. Zebra has a developed an IoT platform called Zatar that connects devices to the cloud and manages them.

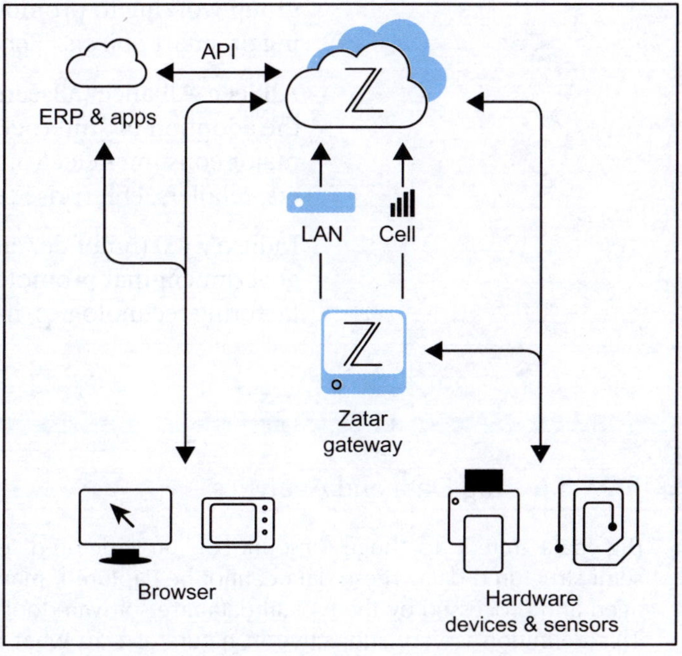


Reference: http://www.zatar.com/

IoT systems are capable of revolutionizing the way in which the industries gather and analyse the information for decision making. It presents opportunities to create smart devices, homes and communities to be run efficiently and automate many routine works.

Examples:

- Kanban - Inventory bins can automatically indicate when they need to be replenished and trigger materials to be retrieved
- Equipment optimization – GE uses IoT capabilities aircraft engines to optimize fuel use.
- Better part traceability – organization can track movement of goods, history of parts on goods and other information captured with RFID. However, corporate IT may have security rules against opening up plant networks to cloud-based remote access.
- Agility – RFID tags and readers can enable materials, locations or tooling to communicate with each other. RFID enabled torque wrench on automobile assembly line can

calibrate itself for the task (e.g., tire assembly, engine mounting) by sensing the sub-assembly that appears in front of it.

**Groups focus on IoT adoption**

Various groups are working to accelerate the IoT. The following are a few IoT-related industry groups:

- Industrial Internet Consortium (IIC) (iiconsortium.org) is an open membership group focused onto support better access to Big Data with improved integration of the physical and digital worlds. The founding members include AT&T, Cisco, GE, IBM and Intel.
- The Internet Protocol for Smart Objects (IPSO) Alliance (ipso-alliance. org) is a group working to promote the value of using Internet Protocol (IP) for the networking of smart objects. The alliance includes many Fortune 500 high-tech companies.
- AllSeen Alliance (allseenalliance.org) is a cross-industry consortium working on the adoption of 'Internet of Everything' in homes and industries. Members include major consumer electronics manufacturers, appliance manufacturers, service providers, retailers, enterprise technology companies and chipset manufacturers.
- Industry 4.0 (bmbf.de/en/19955. php) is an industry project led by the German government that promotes the development and adoption of next generation manufacturing technologies, including the IoT.

**BOX 8.6** Big Data and Analytics

Big data refers to huge amount of un-structured or semi-structured data. These data cannot be captured, managed and processed by the typical database software tools. This definition is very subjective in nature as size what is considered as big data will keep on changing with technology and time. Traditional methods as of now read the data at about 250 Mb/s. With this rate, time taken to read a 3 TB of data would take approximately 30 min. Hence, traditional methods will not be able to solve the problem of analysing Big Data. Apache Hadoop is a framework that solves this problem of analysing and querying the Big Data. Hadoop uses the MapReduce architecture; this uses parallel processing (on a large number of computers called nodes) to accomplish the processing and analysis of Big Data.

**Big data has the characteristics usually defined by the 3 'V's**

1- Variety – data can be in structured (e.g., relations, logs, raw text), unstructured or semi-structured (e.g., logs, video, sound, images) forms.
2- Velocity is about moving data at very high rates (e.g., CERN atomic facility → 40 TB per second).
3- Volume of data scale from Terabytes to Petabytes (1 k TB) to Zettabytes (e.g., 300 billion emails sent per day)

Zettabytes = 1 billion terabytes

**Examples of Big Data**

RFID evets, social networks, photography archives, internet documents, internet search indexing, call detail records, astronomy, genomics, military surveillance, sensor networks, medical records, video archives, atmospheric science and large-scale e-commerce.

**Big Data Analytics**

It offers a solution by providing advanced analytical methods such as data visualization, artificial intelligence, natural language processing and predictive analysis to support the analysis of data. It goes beyond insight (knowing why things happen) to foresight (knowing what is likely to happen in the future) using historical data patterns to identify and quantify probabilities of future opportunities and risks.

1. Data mining: this technology is based on statistical and machine learning methods to extract patterns from large datasets including techniques such as cluster analysis, association rule, classification and regression
2. Modern NLP (Neuro-linguistic Programming): this technology is used for text and speech analysis.

*(Continued on the next page)*

**BOX 8.6** Big Data and Analytics (*Continued*)

3. Spatial analysis: this technology uses Geographic Information Systems (GIS) and analyses the geographic, topological or geometric properties.
4. Google's MapReduce: MapReduce is framework for highly distributed processing among clusters or grid. It is capable of handling unstructured as well as structured data. During the mapping, a master node partitions the input and distributes it among the worker/slave nodes. In the reduce phase, the master node collects the results from the slave nodes, combines and produces output. Hadoop was developed by Yahoo as a clone for Google MapReduce.

**A few users of Big data analytics and how they use it:**
Amazon: suggestions based on previous buys, weather, location, etc.
Facebook: friend suggestions, targeted ads
Google: judge search results, relevant ads
Weather forecasting: weather pattern comes in real-time. Predict path of hurricane in real-time by consolidating data, etc.

Although many enterprises are aware of the benefits that improved data analytics can deliver, only a small number are equipped with the knowledge and technical tools to enable them to make full use of it.

Today's information technology systems gather and store a tremendous amount of supply chain-related data. Supply chain analytics can be used to transform this data into business intelligence. The ultimate goal of the supply chain analytics is to convert the mass of unstructured data into useful information that can help to improve forecasting, service performance and reduce supply chain costs.
Examples:

- Sales and forecasting analysis
  - contextual factors such as weather forecasts, competitive responses and other external factors are combined with the customers' and suppliers' data to determine which factors have a strong correlation with demand.
  - customer demand data are collected and analysed, and then, the product design features are changed to meet the customer's demands.
- Supply chain optimization
  - better inventory optimization in the plants as company gets visibility into which product segment (brand/variant) would have high probability of sale.
  - dynamic rerouting of trucks to meet real-time changes in demand with the real-time truck monitoring and live traffic feeds from telematics devices.
  - simplify distribution networks by factoring in more variables and more scenarios than ever before; for example long-term growth scenarios, plant production configurations for multiple brands, inventory factors across multiple stages and delivery scenarios of full truck loads, direct-to-store delivery, as well as different transport-rate structures per load size and delivery direction.

**BOX 8.7** Social media driven collaborative demand forecasting

Social media typically refers to internet-based applications (e.g., Twitter, Facebook, LinkedIn, Blogging, etc.) that provide platform for users to generate information and interact with each other. It also typically refers to technology-based media that allow users to communicate with each other beyond direct one-to-one relationships.

(*Continued on the next page*)

**BOX 8.7** Social media driven collaborative demand forecasting (*Continued*)

Primary mode of communication within or across organizations is via e-mails, instant messengers, phones and portals that have been created to share the information, etc. The rise of the social media has driven the development of new communication methodologies which is being implemented across organizations now. Microblogs such as Twitter and Yammer have many different usages in the supply chain in terms of providing information about a range of supply chain events such as arrival or departure of a shipment, channel transaction information to multiple communication channels, information about accidents and road closures for rerouting. In addition, companies are using Facebook and other social media for applications that benefit the supply chain.

Social media is being adapted across industries as a tool for collaboration. Social media is being used in the supply chain:

- as a platform to directly communicate with the customer to resolve their grievances. This helps in improving the brand image and creating a loyal customer base.
- to analyse the upcoming trends and take the action accordingly. Trends could be related to negative backlash against certain services, an improvement in the existing product or may be an idea for altogether a new product or idea. In this way, organization will be in a position to produce and deliver what customers actually want
- To broadcast range of supply chain events including supply chain disruption to all the supply chain participants.

The following are couple of examples of usage of social media for B2B collaboration:

- One of the few examples of success stories of implementation of Social Supply Chain is of Kinaxis. Their initiatives such as creating a blog site and developing a video series helped them to connect with their customers and potential customers. Using blog sites, they were able to get leads into the potential requirements of their customers by focusing on the keywords used in the blogs. They also had a set of dedicated engineers to look at LinkedIn website for supply chain groups and use that forum to gain insightful leads.
- Another example is usage of social media by UPS to connect with small business owners. They launched a new initiative 'The new Logistics' (http://thenewlogistics.ups.com) where they have posted case studies on how UPS can help small business owners to grow their business. They have also revamped their presence on social websites to make it a forum for business generating discussions rather than a place to discuss logistics failures.
- Amazon (://www.facebook.com/Amazon) and Best Buy similar to other companies have a presence on Facebook that allows interaction with customers in their online retailing website

The adaption of the social media has few challenges for enterprise applications:

- Image of the word 'Social'
- Trust among key players
- Concerns related to data privacy
- Analysing the vast amount of data
- How to quantify the results of integration of social media with supply chain

**BOX 8.8** Near Field Communication (NFC)

Near Field Communication (NFC) is a technology for contactless communication between electronic devices. It traces and routes via radio frequency identification (RFID) that provides a short communication range for security purposes. NFC chip on the iPhone 6 and 6+ is used for Apple pay contactless payment technology.

*(Continued on the next page)*

### BOX 8.8 Near Field Communication (*Continued*)

**Basic information about NFC:**

- NFC is a short-range wireless communication technology based on radio frequency identification (RFID)
- NFC communication is enabled by bringing 2 NFC compatible devices within very close proximity to one another (typically up to 4 cm)
- Range is intentionally kept small due to security reasons.

**Few applications of NFS:**

- Getting Information: downloading information by bringing your NFC-enabled phone close to a sign with NFC-readable information.
- Paying for goods and services: NFC technology will allow contactless payment at shops.
- Easy to use public transport: contactless tickets for public transport. With NFC-enabled devices like mobile phones, buying tickets and receiving them on your device is possible.
- Sharing of data between devices: connecting your Digicam and MP3 player with computer to download pictures or music by just bringing them close to each other

The mobile telephone industry is evaluating the benefits of near field communications (NFC), which enables consumers to purchase small-valued items directly from their mobile phones. NFC features will soon start appearing in rugged hand-held computers that will enable warehouse operatives to pick stock by location, automatically deducting the items from the location and updating an intelligent, location-based memory device. Using non-volatile storage, this location-based memory would make stock takes automatic, each reporting its physical stock by Wi-Fi or Ethernet connection to the back-office system

**Difference between NFC and Bluetooth:**

NFC and Bluetooth are complementary to each as both provide short-range wireless communication abilities but with following difference.

| **Parameter** | **NFC** | **Bluetooth** |
|---|---|---|
| Network type | Point to point | Point to multipoint |
| Range | 0.2m | 10m |
| Speed | 424 KBPS | 2.1 MBPS |
| Setup Time | 0.1 Sec | 6 Sec |

NOTE: Basic difference between NFC and Bluetooth is their operating range, applications or usage areas.

With 4 cm range, NFC has a shorter range, which provides a degree of security and makes NFC suitable for crowded areas where correlating a signal with its transmitting physical device (and by extension, its user) might otherwise prove impossible.

### BOX 8.9 Location-based tracking

Location-based services (LBS) use positioning technologies to provide individual subjects (e.g., asset, resources) with reachability and accessibility that would otherwise not be available in the conventional commercial realm.

Location-based services (LBS) are the applications that use the geographical information of the subject in order to provide various services. It calculates the location of the subject and resolves the navigating queries in real time.

**Basic Components of LBS are as follows:**

- Devices (Subjects)
- Communication network (e.g., Wireless mobile network)
- Positioning techniques (e.g., network based, GPS based)
- Service providers (e.g., providers of HW/SW, handset/devices, data)

TomTom (www.tomtom.com/) provides LBS platform that can be used by developers to create location-enabled applications for consumers, enterprises and governments markets. It provides capabilities that are very useful for supply chain planning and optimization-route planning, fleet tracking, traffic viewer and geocoding (track locations from a pair of coordinates).

User privacy and interoperability between different service providers are the key challenges in LBS adoption.

### BOX 8.10 Unmanned Aerial Vehicles (e.g., UAV/Drone) driven Supply Chain

Drones also known as unmanned aerial vehicles

There are numerous applications for drones along the supply chain.

- Drones can deliver freight
- Drones carrying freight payloads will significantly reduce air transportation charges, speed up transit times and

*(Continued on the next page)*

### BOX 8.10 Unmanned Aerial Vehicles (e.g., UAV/Drone) driven Supply Chain (*Continued*)

enable cost effective delivery to remote or sparsely populated locations.

Moreover, drones are not adversely affected by certain trucking-specific industry issues such as Hours of Service regulations, or by over-the-road variables affecting timely delivery such as automobile accidents, inclement weather and highway construction.

*Airware (http://www.airware.com/)* provides operating platform for commercial drones that enables the use of a variety of aircraft, sensors and software to address known and future applications.

User privacy, security and affordability (e.g., operations requirements such as runaway and base station) are the key challenges in UAV adoption.

### BOX 8.11 Robotic fulfilment

Robots have been around for a long time. Kiva systems (*http://www.kivasystems.com/*) has put them into use for warehouse fulfilment operations by multiplying not only the fulfilment efficiency manifold but also cut down the utility cost by almost half (as robots do not need air conditioning and lighting).

Robotic fulfilment integrates three technologies to deliver efficient fulfilment solution for warehouse.

- Wi-Fi,
- digital cameras and
- low-cost servers capable of parallel processing

The servers work in real-time; the work involves receiving orders, immediately dispatching robots to bring the required pods to the worker fulfilling the order, and then returning the pods to their storage locations. The robots receive their orders wirelessly, while using cameras to read navigational barcode stickers on the warehouse floor.

Unlike the conveyer belts and 30-ft tall shelves that are bolted down in conventional warehouses, the robotic fulfilment system can easily be moved to a different facility. This allows the ability to shift capacity inexpensively from one centre to another and also expand incrementally as its volumes increase by simply adding robots or pods. Retailers avoid upfront heavy payment to build transitional capital intensive sections of conveyer belts.

### BOX 8.12 3D Printing

3D Printing (a.k.a. additive manufacturing) is a process of making three-dimensional products of virtually any shape from a digital or computer-aided design (CAD) model. The object is created by stacking down successive layers of microscopic thin material until the layers add up to eventually form the product, exactly as depicted in the digital model.

3D Printing can impact the traditional supply chain management processes in multiple ways:

- the reduced need for inventory space for finished goods (as products become made-to-order);
- increased need for inventory space for several types of raw materials and disparate finished products (as 3D printers become multipurpose machines);
- reduced need for inventory space for spare parts (as these can be printed on demand, or perhaps by the end user directly) and
- restructuring the supply chain network and stakeholders (as the new manufacturing mantra would be to 'print at the point of consumption').

However, it remains an extremely complex technology with four key elements for success:

- Continued development of systems and processes. Currently, there are seven additive manufacturing processes based on specific physical principles.
- Materials – the development of material types, such as polymers, metals, ceramics and biomaterials, and the need for industry standards.
- Continued progress in current applications, including aviation, automotive, industry and medical devices.
- The need for peripheral business support, such as preparation, design work, finishing and coatings.

3D printing also likely will have its own set of legal challenges. Companies with extraordinarily complex goods could be at risk of having them scanned and replicated at knock-off print shops. Similar to music downloads, they will need to address how to control unauthorized sharing of their software.

## Summary

- Supply chain managers can take effective decisions if they have access to timely information about the activities of all the other entities in the supply chain. IT can link all activities in a supply chain into an integrated and coordinated system that is fast and flexible so that supply chain managers get the needed information.
- There are four major functional roles of IT in supply chain management: transaction execution, collaboration and coordination, decision support and supply chain measurement and reporting. Each of these functions needs different sets of capabilities to be enabled by IT.
- IT in supply chain management has broad and long-term implications for an organization's competitive advantage as it is integrating not only the functions and processes of an organization, but also those of suppliers who are external to it.
- IT systems on their own have limited use unless they are ensured that the right kind of information is accurately captured in a timely manner.
- At early stages of IT enablement of a supply chain, interest of all the stakeholders involved are properly understood and a realistic expectation is set on what IT can do.
- Advancement in technology is further changing the landscape of supply chain solutions and what it can do.

## Discussion Questions

1. What are the key functional roles of IT in a supply chain?
2. Why is it important to understand the functional role of IT for any supply chain management system implementation project?
3. How is supply chain planning requirements addressed by DSS?
4. What are the technologies used for supply chain measurement and reporting?
5. How can Web services help a company to communicate with its suppliers and customers?
6. Enlist and discuss the limitations of ERP and the new developments taking place for the enhancement of ERP to address supply chain management requirements.
7. Compare the advantages of SCEM systems with that of existing supply chain management systems.
8. Discuss the risks and benefits of SAS models that many software vendors are offering.
9. What are the benefits companies can derive from product tracking technologies such as RFID?
10. How can a supply chain benefit from SOA?
11. What are the major components of the mobile system?
12. Discuss the key challenges to the adaption of the cloud computing.
13. Enlist the supply chain use cases of 'Internet of things'.
14. What is big data and how big data analytics is applicable to supply chain analytics?
15. List down few examples of usage of social media for B2B collaboration.
16. Discuss the challenges in the adaption of the social media for enterprise applications.
17. How is NFC different than Bluetooth technology?
18. What are the key components of location-based tracking?
19. Discuss the potential usage of drones in supply chain.
20. Discuss the robotic fulfilment and the technologies involved.
21. What are the potential business risks involved with the use of 3D Printing?

## Mini Project

The objective of the study is to understand the impact of ERP implementation on supply chain performance. The study consists of two parts:

1) Understanding the impact of ERP implementation using financial data
2) Understanding the impact of ERP implementation through a field study
   (a) Identify a firm that has implemented ERP. Find out the year ERP was implemented. Most of the firms will announce a time when they implemented

ERP (refer company Website). Using financial data, compare and contrast pre-ERP and post-ERP performance on the following dimensions:

Business performance: profitability ratio, ROI

Supply chain performance measures (see Chapter 2)

(b) Field study on ERP/supply chain management software implementation: Identify a company in your neighbourhood that has implemented ERP/supply chain management software and interview a senior IT and supply chain manager on the implementation used by the company. Compare the same with the framework proposed in this chapter.

## Notes

1. See www.ranbaxy.com/ for details on Ranbaxy.
2. See www.carrcommunications.com/clips/kmart-published2001-12.pdf.
3. See www.scdigest.com/assets/NewsViews/06-02-09-1.cfm.

## Further Reading

P. S. Adler, "When Knowledge is the Critical Resource, Knowledge Management is the Critical Task," *IIE Transaction on Engineering Management* (1989, Vol 36): 87–84.

Thomas H. Davenport, "Putting the Enterprise into the Enterprise System," *Harvard Business Review* (July–August 1998): 121–131.

M. Hammer and J. Champy, *Reengineering the Corporations* (New York: Harper Business, 1993).

Srinivas Talluri, "An IT/IS Acquisition and Justification Model for Supply-Chain Management,' *International Journal of Physical Distribution & Logistics Management* (2000, Vol 30): 221–237.

Jessie Scanlon, 'Kiva Robots invade the warehouse', BusinessWeekOnline (16-Apr-2009)

Daniel Edmund O'Leary, 'BIG DATA', THE 'INTERNET OF THINGS' AND THE 'INTERNET OF SIGNS', Intell. Sys. Aee. Fin. Mgmt. (2013, Vol 20): 53-65

Alan L. Milliken, 'Transforming Big Data into Supply Chain Analytics', Journal of Business Forecasting (Winter 2014-2015): 23-27

# PART IV

# Supply Chain Innovations



In Part IV, we focus on supply chain innovations that can help firms in improving the service level and minimizing costs simultaneously. These innovations are meant to steadily improve the performance on both these dimensions.

Chapter 9 focuses on innovation, which will result in better intra-firm and inter-firm integration of supply chains. Through the examples of successful industry-level innovations like VMI, ECR and CPFR relevant implementation issues also have been discussed.

Supply chain restructuring focuses on questioning existing processes and architecture of a chain. Chapter 10 characterizes supply chains using the following three dimensions: shape of value-addition curve, point of differentiation and customer entry point. Through several illustrations it is demonstrated that restructuring of the supply chain process involves altering the supply chain process in at least one of the three dimensions. The chapter also focuses on restructuring supply chain architecture, which involves either altering the way in which material flow takes place in a chain or alteration in inventory placement in a chain.

Among coordination mechanisms, supply chain contract is emerging as a valuable instrument to coordinate various supply chains. The focus of chapter 11 is to present an overview of contracts and discuss few popular contracts like buy back Contract and revenue sharing contract in great details.

Chapter 12 deals with agile supply chains, which are capable of handling uncertainty in both demand and supply. The terrorist attack in September 2001 forced firms to look at their supply chain vulnerabilities, and firms have realized that they need to focus on both demand uncertainty and supply chain disruptions also. While handling high demand uncertainty, the chapter focuses mainly on fashion goods, which have to grapple with high demand uncertainty and short product life cycles.

In Chapter 13, we focus on revenue management and specifically look at pricing decisions by a firm in limited-supply situations. In a situation of limited supply, the bulk of the capacity and supply-related costs have already been incurred and consequently revenue management attempts to make optimal pricing decision so that the firm can generate the highest possible revenue so as to generate the highest possible profit for the firm.

In Chapter 14, we look at what sustainable supply chains encompass and examine factors that drive firms towards green supply chain initiatives. We also look at global firms that have undertaken such initiatives and study the phenomenon of product returns and the associated issues with it. We discuss reverse logistics and other remanufacturing processes and study initiatives of firms towards social betterment. We also suggest ways to design and manage solutions benefiting the firm, environment and people.

# Supply Chain Integration

## Learning Objectives

After reading this chapter, you will be able to answer the following questions:

- What are the different stages of supply chain integration?
- What are the main causes of the bullwhip effect?
- What are the barriers to successful supply chain integration?
- How do firms build successful partnerships in supply chains?
- In what ways do industry initiatives like ECR, VMI and CPFR help firms in achieving supply chain integration?

The retail sector is booming in India and so is pharma retailing. Health care is predicted to record the highest growth rate among all spending categories in the next two decades. This has prompted many retail chain companies to join the fray. Subhiksha, a Chennai-based retail chain, does just this. It sells drugs across all its outlets in the country at a 10 per cent discount. Currently, Subhiksha sells drugs worth Rs 40 million in Mumbai alone.

Recently, there were reports that Subhiksha has sent legal notices to drug wholesalers in Mumbai for withholding supplies. The wholesalers have boycotted Subhiksha on the grounds that it is indulging in an unethical price war by offering a discount. This strategy adopted by Subhiksha has affected the business of standalone retail and wholesale groups. The prevalent fear is that in the days to come Subhiksha will stop dealing with wholesalers completely. Instead, it will deal directly with the companies. Many industry experts feel that this is not justified. The competition should be on value addition and not on the price. How does Subhiksha manage its activities so as to be able to offer this discount to all its customers? Also, if the motive is to serve the end-customer, then what prompts the wholesalers to refuse supplies to Subhiksha, the largest pharma retailer in the country?

We first discuss why supply chain integration is desirable. In this chapter, we argue that most of the inefficiencies in a chain tend to creep in at departmental and organizational boundaries. We present the conceptual basis for supply chain integration in this chapter. The ways to reduce wastages across intra-firm and inter-firm boundaries are also discussed. As seen in the case of Subhiksha, it is difficult to achieve supply chain integration in several contexts. In practice, supply chain integration is an exception rather than a rule. We discuss the difficulties of achieving better integration and coordination within the chain. We also suggest an approach to help firms in working towards achieving better coordination across chains.[1]

# Introduction

In well-managed chains, material, information and finance flow seamlessly across departmental and organizational boundaries and it is the end customer pull and not internal compulsions that govern these. However, in the case of inefficient chains, there are blocks at departmental as well as organizational boundaries. For example, individual departments and firms may be more interested in performance at the local level rather than performance at the chain level, resulting in material and products waiting for a considerable period of time at both boundaries. Since most of the inefficiencies tend to creep in at the boundaries, this chapter focuses on linkages across supply chains rather than on individual operations. This chapter also discusses how to reduce wastages across intra-firm and inter-firm boundaries.

In general, the classification of firms may be done in three stages, based on the framework given in Figure 9.1. In stage 1, the firm is structured on a functional basis and each function or department operates as a silo. In other words, each function is myopic in nature, focusing attention on the narrowly defined local performance measures. Even within manufacturing, there are a number of departments with their respective buffers of inventory.

In stage 2, the internal operations are integrated at the organizational level and there is seamless flow of material and information across all departments and the firm functions as one integrated entity. However, wastage still exists at firm boundaries where it interacts with the external members of the chain. These firms have many buffers and the wastage at organizational boundaries result in information and material flow distortions across the chain.

In stage 3, the firm manages to integrate itself with suppliers as well as customers and works as an integrated chain. Supply chain integration involves a conscious effort on the part of the firm to move from stage 1 to stage 2 and subsequently to stage 3. By working on supply chain integration, it is possible to shift the entire efficiency frontier downward, and hence improve the performance on cost and service fronts simultaneously. To make this possible, organizations have to make corresponding changes in the structure, processes and performance measures. Most firms have by and large understood the need for internal integration while very few have realized the need for external integration. Payoffs through internal integration can be likened to the tip of an iceberg. The benefits of external integration though not immediately visible, are immense.

To illustrate this, we look at the performance of two FMCG firms on the inventory dimension. As can be seen from Table 9.1, both firms have done reasonably well on the WIP front, which indicates that they have managed internal integration within manufacturing to some extent. Interestingly, we find that most Indian manufacturing firms have shown reasonable

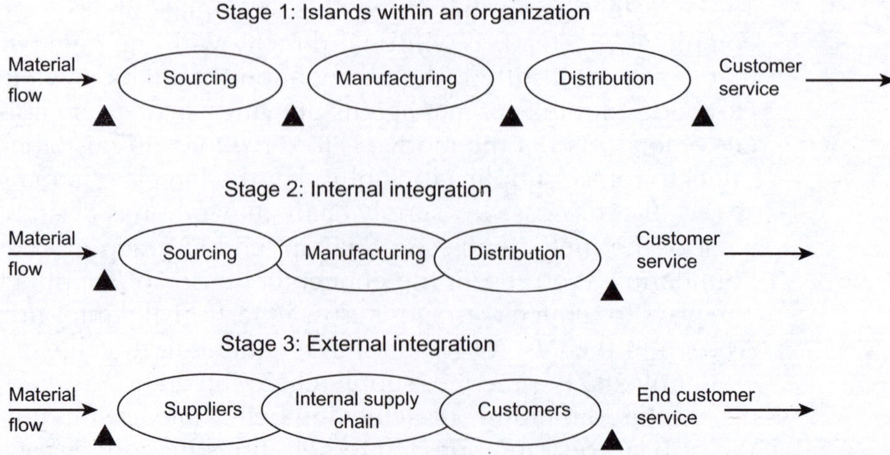


**Figure 9.1**

Achieving an integrated supply chain.

*Table 9.1:* **Inventory in days in supply chain for FMCG companies.**

| | RM inventory* | WIP inventory* | FG inventory* | Channel inventory** |
|---|---|---|---|---|
| HUL | 53 | 2 | 25 | 75 |
| Godrej Soaps | 50 | 16 | 23 | 110 |

*Data Source: Prowess (CMIE).
**Based on limited study carried out by the author in 2001.

improvement on WIP inventory. This essentially reflects the effort on the part of Indian firms in the area of internal integration. For example, HUL has managed to reduce its WIP inventory by about 85 per cent in the last decade. However, even the most progressive of firms have not shown any significant reductions in RM and FG inventory. Further, most firms do not pay enough attention on inventories with channels or suppliers because these inventories do not affect their profit and loss statements or balance sheets directly. In fact, channel inventory data are rarely available with firms and what you see in Table 9.1 is actually estimates. It is not too difficult to figure out that any inefficiency in terms of higher channel inventory will finally come back to focal firms like HUL and Godrej soaps in one form or another. This inefficiency usually shows up as higher accounts receivable (cash does not come back) or higher margins to be paid to the channel or lost sales because the channel is not willing to stock additional material. Further, huge inventory in the channel reduces flexibility in launching any marketing initiatives by FMCG companies.

We start our discussion with internal integration and focus on external integration in the later part of the chapter.

# Internal Integration

A typical firm is functionally organized, and material and information have to go through multiple departments across the internal supply chain. As each function is myopic in nature and is focusing on a narrowly defined local performance, there are many inefficiencies and buffers at departmental boundaries. This is illustrated using two examples.

An electric machinery firm, which has a manufacturing plant in Mumbai, serves the southern market through a stock point in Chennai. The Mumbai plant ships goods to the Chennai stock point once a month because monthly demand amounts to approximately a full truckload. Obviously by shipping goods using full truckloads, the plant is able to minimize transportation costs. As it receives goods only once a month, the Chennai stock point has to keep high safety stocks to ensure a reasonable level of service to its customers. Thus, both the Mumbai plant and the Chennai regional stock point have made so-called locally optimal decisions A detailed analysis shows that it will be optimal (total transportation and inventory cost will be lowest) for the firm to ship goods to Chennai from Mumbai once a week. There is a trade-off between transportation and inventory costs, individual departments chose to ignore this trade-off to make locally optimal decisions, resulting in a substantial increase in the overall cost in the system.

A split pump manufacturer used to offer about 30-odd varieties of pumps in the market place. As per the product design, the pump housing consisted of a top housing and a bottom housing and the exact size of the pump housing varied with each model. The machining of housings was one of the most critical tasks, involving expensive equipment and a significant amount of time. One of the critical operations in the machining of housing involved joint machining of both the housing castings (top and bottom of same model) in one setup. However, the firm found that though it had a huge inventory of housing castings, it rarely had matching pairs of top and bottom housing castings, resulting in serious difficulties in scheduling machining operations, upsetting promised customer delivery schedules. The purchase department had placed orders for top housings with one vendor and bottom housings with another. Since one vendor had quoted lowest for top housing castings and another had quoted lowest for bottom housing castings, the purchase department had placed orders accordingly. While the purchase department had substantially minimized the buying cost at the purchase stage, this kind of ordering resulted in uncoordinated supply by each vendor leading to constant problems for manufacturing. The manufacturing team faces serious problems in scheduling its operations. Even with a huge inventory of individual top and bottom housing castings, operations find it difficult to match pairs for manufacturing. Hence, the company had a typical problem of high inventory and low customer service. A simple solution therefore will be an order of top and bottom housing casting with the same vendor with clear instructions to supply both castings of the same model in one shipment. The purchase department had tried to similarly cut costs by splitting "C" category hardware items' orders to several suppliers and found eventually that many times crucial shipments could not be made because of non-availability of some of these items.

As seen in these cases, each department focuses on local performance measurers and takes independent decisions leading to inefficiencies at the organizational level. Firms therefore have to find ways of coordinating the planning and decision making across the organization.

Firms can achieve this either by centralizing all planning activities or by decentralizing all activities and creating customer supplier links among all members of the internal chain.

## Centralized System

It is obvious that centralizing planning operations eliminate some of the problems arising from decisions based on local myopic performance measures. Thus, centralized planning can ensure that decisions are made from firms' performance point of view and not based on individual department's local performance measures. Clearly, in the centralized scenario optimizing performance at the firm level results in better performance as compared to the decentralization scenario where each entity optimizes its own performance. Although centralized planning has been an appealing concept, necessary technologies hitherto are not in place for most firms. Today, with advances in computing and communication technologies, it is possible to make large complex decisions on a real-time basis. However, centralized systems have their own problems.

In the centralized system, while solving global problems each local constraint is treated as a hard constraint. However, in reality some of these may actually be soft constraints, which means that they can be violated within certain limits. For instance, if X machine breaks down, the component can be shifted to Y machine. Although theoretically it may be possible to codify this knowledge and put it in the centralized system, there are some types of local knowledge that are difficult to codify; for example, if one is not able to deliver an entire lot by the weekend, the marketing manager can phone the customer and convince him to accept the material in smaller lots. Or alternatively he can use his relationship with the customer to request him to accept late delivery of shipments. In the centralized system, one will treat this as a hard constraint and find a way of delivering the entire lot in the time specified. It could be argued, of course, that as in routing flexibility (if machine X is not available use machine Y), one could also build prioritization rules (all export orders get priority over local orders, external customers get a priority over internal customers, etc.) and specify the same in the centralized model. In general, however, all the knowledge available cannot be codified, or even if this were possible the cost of codifying is likely to be prohibitive. A detailed codification exercise will also make the problem extremely difficult to solve as most of these alternatives get modelled as binary variables and large binary problems are very difficult to solve even with today's computing power. Further, some of this knowledge is dynamic in nature. For example, the same customer may not mind late delivery in a lean season but may not accept it in his peak season. Apart from issues related to local knowledge, centralized systems do not encourage innovations at the local level. In summary, although a centralized system provides efficiency it cannot capture the local knowledge and can result in disempowerment of local managers, causing lowered levels of innovations in problem solving.

## Decentralized System

As depicted in Figure 9.1, internal supply chains can be divided into large number of customer supplier linkages. Unlike the stage 1 system where local efficiency gets priority over customer service, the stage 2 decentralized systems works the other way round. This ensures that an assured level of service is provided to internal customers in supplier–customer linkages. One may actually design a system where every customer–supplier link in the firm will have formal service contracts. An example will be an assurance that any order placed by the regional warehouse will be served by the central warehouse within seven days, so that regional markets can make a commitment to a customer without worrying about the detailed plans of the other parts of the system. Each system can manage its operations independently, ensuring that it meets its service agreements. By ensuring that performance measures are aligned, one can coordinate decentralized systems in the internal supply chain. The key issue will be to design these service agreements and to ensure that monitoring and control mechanisms are in place to facilitate smooth functioning of the system. A decentralized system will result in higher innovations in problem-solving situations and more effective use of local knowledge, but this has its inherent disadvantages.

Usually, a decentralized system has higher slack and longer lead times. Customer service is a function of the load on the system. As a result, each link in the system will work out its own lead time based on a worst-case scenario rather than on an average-case scenario. This will result in much longer lead times in decentralized systems compared to centralized systems. In case an internal customer insists on shorter lead times, the supplier unit will have to hold a high buffer capacity to ensure that even in the worst-case scenario performance is within the promised lead time. Further, if the supplier system has multiple customers one will have to find ways of prioritizing internal customers. Higher lead times and slack capacities will obviously increase costs for the firm.

## Hybrid System

A firm may also consider a hybrid approach where it can centralize a few key activities and leave other activities and decisions, which are coordinated using supplier–customer linkages, decentralized. This is similar to the concept of synchronous manufacturing (also known as theory of constraints) proposed by Goldratt. In this approach, schedules/decisions for bottleneck resources are decided centrally while detailed schedules for non-bottleneck resources are left to local decision makers. Buffer inventory is maintained at critical junctures such as bottleneck points and customer serving points. Non-bottleneck machines are not measured on capacity utilization because they have to serve just bottleneck machines and are measured against internal customer service. The hybrid approach may be difficult to apply in cases where the supply chain has multiple products and the product mix keeps varying from time to time. In such a situation, the firm will not have a clearly defined bottleneck; that is, the bottleneck will keep shifting from time to time.

As discussed above, there are no easy solutions apparent and the firm will have to find the best way of using a hybrid approach where the best of the centralization and decentralization approaches can be combined. For example, it may make sense to have a central planner who will handle aggregate planning issues, peak-season demand, new product introductions, special promotions and planning for bottleneck facilities but leaving most other decisions to be handled by decision makers at the local level. In general, having integrated information systems like ERP have helped organizations in ensuring that different sub-systems work with the same information and the same aggregate plan across the organization. Further, integrated systems ensure that any problem in one part of the system is communicated immediately to other parts of systems so that decisions can be changed in real time. Finally, any approach requires corresponding changes in organizational structure and performance measurement schemes. If proper monitoring and control systems are not put in place the firm is likely to gravitate back to stage 1.

## External Integration

In a well-managed supply chain, there should be seamless flow of material/product and information across organizational boundaries. Unfortunately, it is found that information flow gets significantly distorted as we move along the chain and the material/product flow is also correspondingly distorted across the chain. As discussed earlier, in a supply chain all the entities are linked in buyer–supplier chains and have to ultimately serve the end customer. Information is passed on from buyer to supplier in the form of orders, that is, the demand placed by the buyer to the supplier. For example, a garment retailer will place an order with the wholesaler, who in turn will place the order with the garment manufacturer, who passes the order to the fabric manufacturer and so on. It has been found that information in the form of orders gets distorted as we move up the chain. This increased volatility results in increased costs for all the members of the chain. The reason for this increased distortion is that each entity within the supply chain focuses on its short-term performance measures. To understand this issue in greater detail, we first look at demand volatility issues for a typical single buyer–supplier link in the chain and subsequently look at issues related to the overall chain that consists of a larger number of buyer–supplier links.

### *Increase in Demand Volatility While Moving Up the Supply Chain*

In a typical buyer–supplier link, the buyer observes demand in his market and places the order with the supplier so that he gets his material/products when he wants it. This link could be retailer–manufacturer, a garment manufacturer–fabric supplier or an automobile component manufacturer–assembler. In each of these buyer–supplier situations, it has been found that the demand as observed by the supplier has a much higher variability compared to the variability as observed by the buyer at his end.

We illustrate this issue through one specific case of a supplier who manufactures PVC and a buyer who manufactures PVC pipes. We explore all the plausible reasons as to why this kind of behaviour takes place and suggest mechanisms to handle these.

A PVC manufacturer who produces at an even rate throughout the month found that his sales were quite skewed, that is, 70 per cent, took place in the last week of the month. This resulted in an average inventory of about 15–20 days. The manufacturer assumed that this reflected the customer preference and hence could not be changed. Surprisingly, a scrutiny of the manufacturing pattern of PVC pipes revealed an even rate of manufacture. There was an apparent paradox: though the rate of manufacture of PVC pipes was steady over the month, the raw material was purchased only during the last week of the month. On account of this skewed purchasing pattern, both the buyer and the seller ended up carrying 15–20 days of RM and FG inventory, respectively. Further investigations revealed that the PVC manufacturer was actually responsible for the skewed sales behaviour. It was found that the firm was offering bulk quantity discounts, and that this was indiscriminately used by the sales force at the end of the month to meet their monthly targets. The buyer also preferred to purchase in bulk for the coming month to safeguard against any price rise that might be announced. This purchasing pattern ensured maximum discounts and minimum costs for the buyer. Thus, despite the fact that the supplier had very little control over buyer behaviour, the supplier had indirectly altered the purchasing pattern by offering disincentives for purchasing in a uniform manner. The system of incentives offered by the supplier was such that it encouraged the buyer to make decisions, whcih increased the total cost of the supply chain. Improved coordination between the supply chains of both the organizations could significantly reduce the inventory burden on each. In keeping with the production plans of both the buyer and the supplier, the delivery may be made on a just-in-time basis. This collaboration will bring down the inventory from 40 days to merely four days.

As discussed earlier, in a well-managed chain, information flow, in terms of order, should flow smoothly along the chain. In the above case, since the PVC pipe manufacturer uses PVC only to serve his customer, he could ensure that the relevant information is transmitted smoothly in the chain simply by translating PVC pipe demand into PVC material demand. Further, the manufacturer should focus on finding ways of reducing cost at the customer end (total cost of PVC per metre of pipe) rather than reducing cost at his organizational boundary.

In general, we find that demand as seen by the supplier is a much distorted version of demand as seen by the buyer. In Figure 9.2, we present a framework that demonstrates the joint effect of buyer policies and supplier policies on demand distortions within a chain. The demand seen by the supplier has a much higher variability compared to the demand variability observed by the buyer at his end. Demand seen by the supplier is nothing but orders placed by the buyer, which is influenced by both buyer and supplier practices. We discuss supplier and buyer practices in greater detail to understand the cause of this phenomenon.

## Impact of Buyer Practices on Demand Distortions Across the Buyer–Supplier Link

As shown in Figure 9.2, there are two main reasons why a buyer's practices result in information and order distortion across a chain. We discuss both in detail in this section.

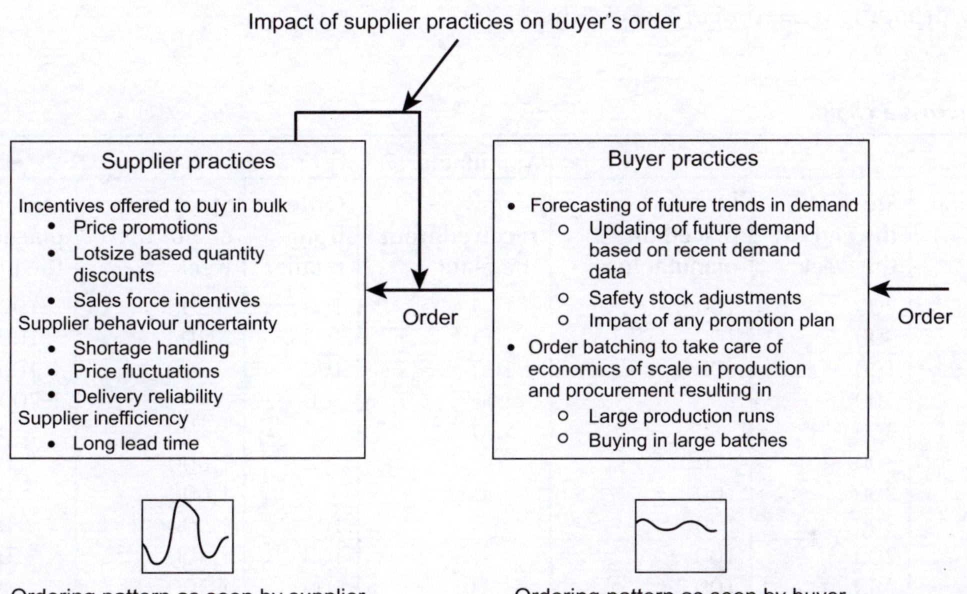


**Figure 9.2**

Demand distortions across the buyer–supplier link.

## Forecast Updating

Every entity in a chain uses order received as an input to the forecasting system and treats that piece of information as a signal for future demand. Using standard forecasting techniques like exponential smoothing, a manager updates forecasts for future demands. Simultaneously, he also makes adjustments in safety stock requirements based on the updated forecast of future demand. Most of the forecasting techniques place substantial weight on recently observed demand realization, and any random increase in demand at the buyer's end is interpreted as a signal for growth. A buyer will increase his order quantity to manage the growth in demand and also to take care of the increase in safety stock requirements to deal with future uncertainty. This increase in the order placed with the supplier is thus much larger than the increase in demand observed at his end. Similarly, a slight decrease in demand at the buyer's end will be interpreted as a decline in demand and will lead to a substantial decrease in the order that is placed with the supplier. Further, a longer supplier lead time will further result in a higher forecast inaccuracy, leading to a higher level of distortion across the chain.

We illustrate the impact of the forecast updating effect using a simple example. Let us take a supply chain with just two links in the chain: retailer and manufacturer. For a retailer, the supply lead time from the manufacturer is two weeks: one week for order transmission and one week for physical delivery. The manufacturer has his own production facility, which also has two weeks of lead time. Every week, based on the customer's demand the retailer places an order that reaches the manufacturer after one week. Similarly, the manufacturer receives the order every week (order placed by retailer in week 1 will reach the manufacturer in week 2) and ships the material from the stock and places an order on internal manufacturing, which will require two weeks to deliver. We will assume that there are no capacity constraints in manufacturing and that the plant can access raw material in unlimited quantity instantaneously. We further assume that to take care of uncertainty both the retailer and the manufacturer keep two weeks of demand as safety stock. We will also assume that both work with a simple forecasting rule that demand for the current week is the forecast for future demand. As can be observed in Table 9.2 (demand data for weeks 1 and 2), the supply chain has been facing a demand of 100 units per week and both the retailer and the manufacturer have a safety stock of 200 units each. If the demand increases to 200 units in week 3 and comes back to 100 units in week 4, it skews the order pattern for many subsequent weeks as shown in Table 9.2. The order placed by the retailer increases by 400 units in week 3 and the order placed by the manufacturer on its plant increases by 1,600 units in week 4, subsequently dropping to zero many weeks thereafter.

***Table 9.2:* Demand distortion across a chain.**

| | **Retailer** | | | | **Manufacturer** | | | |
|---|---|---|---|---|---|---|---|---|
| **Week** | **Shipment received from manufacturer** | **Demand** | **Stock at the end of the week** | **Order placed on manufacturer** | **Supply received from the plant** | **Order from retailer** | **Stock at the end of the week** | **Order placed on the plant** |
| 1 | 100 | 100 | 200 | 100 | 100 | 100 | 200 | 100 |
| 2 | 100 | 100 | 200 | 100 | 100 | 100 | 200 | 100 |
| 3 | 100 | 200 | 100 | 500 | 100 | 100 | 200 | 100 |
| 4 | 100 | 100 | 100 | 0 | 100 | 500 | –200 | 1,700 |
| 5 | 300 | 100 | 300 | 0 | 100 | 0 | –100 | 0 |
| 6 | 100 | 100 | 300 | 0 | 1,700 | 0 | 1,600 | 0 |
| 7 | 100 | 100 | 300 | 100 | 0 | 0 | 1,600 | 0 |
| 8 | 0 | 100 | 200 | 100 | 0 | 100 | 1,500 | 0 |
| 9 | 100 | 100 | 200 | 100 | 0 | 100 | 1,400 | 0 |
| 10 | 100 | 100 | 200 | 100 | 0 | 100 | 1,300 | 0 |

Since the retailer adjusts his forecast update to 200 units per week and correspondingly increases his safety stock to 400 units, he has a resultant increase in demand of 500 units in week 3. Subsequently, in week 4 he updates his forecast back to 100 units and likes to make corrections in his required safety stock. Therefore, he does not place any orders for the next three weeks. The manufacturer updates his forecast to 500 units per week in week 4 and places a demand of 1,700 units on his plant. Subsequently, in week 5, he updates his forecast and does not place any order on the plant for the next 15 weeks. In other words, an increase in 100 per cent demand for 1 week at the retailer level resulted in a 500 per cent increase in demand at the manufacturer's end and translated to 1,700 per cent increase in demand at the plant level.

As a consequence of this extreme fluctuation, the plant manager may assume the market to be highly erratic. In reality, however, distortions have been created by various decision-making units in the chain because everyone has been updating the forecast based on the demand at their end and also the long lead time and safety stock adjustments compound the issue. Obviously, if the plant manager could actually observe the end customer demand at the retailer end, he is likely to make better quality decisions.

While taking decisions on order quantity, apart from regular forecast updating, the retailer may also like to budget for his future promotion plans. In the absence of any specific instructions, this one time planned increase looks like uncertainty in the market demand as far as the supplier is concerned. This further results in increased variation in orders at his end.

### Order Batching for Economies of Scale

The buyer has his own economies of scale in both manufacturing and purchasing. Because of high setup costs he may decide to manufacture the month's entire demand in one setup. He may buy quantities in truckloads so as to take advantage of economies of scale. Similarly, because of certain fixed costs in ordering at his own setup he might order just once a month. So even though demand as seen by the buyer in his market may be uniform he will place orders on suppliers in batches, resulting in distortion in ordering pattern by the buyer.

## Impact of Supplier Practices on Demand Distortions Across the Buyer–Supplier Link

In the earlier section, we looked at demand distortions created by the buyer in the buyer–supplier link. In this section, we show that supplier practices also influence buyer behaviour, which further adds to demand distortions. We examine each factor shown in Figure 9.2 in detail.

### Incentive Offered to Buyers for Large Size Orders

Suppliers usually offer incentives to buyers to buy in bulk. There are mainly three major types of incentives: lot-based discounts, end-of-month discounts and special price promotions.

- *Lot-based discounts.* Most organizations are of the view that their selling and distribution costs are a function of the number of customer orders they serve. Companies therefore offer quantity discounts, which encourage buyers to place a few large-volume orders rather than placing a large number of small-volume orders. With advances in IT, the cost of serving a small-volume order has reduced significantly. Unfortunately, some firms who have been working with traditional costing have not managed yet to capture these effects. Companies need to move to volume-based quantity discount rather than lot-based quantity discount. In the lot-based scheme, discounts are offered based on quantity bought in one lot, while in volume-based discount, they are offered based on volume of purchases made over a period. This encourages the buyer to buy in small lots over a period rather than buying the entire period's requirement in one lot.

- *End-of-period discounts offered because of sales force incentives.* Managers are quite obsessed with monthly and quarterly performance measurers. In most organizations, performance reviews are carried out on a monthly basis or on a quarterly basis and therefore sales force incentives are usually based on quantity sold during the evaluation period of a month or a quarter. This results in the marketing people putting in much more effort during the fag end of the month or the quarter. Usually, the sales force has certain discretion in terms of magnitude of discount and period of credit that they can offer to immediate customers, so they usually offer these extra discounts or longer credit periods at the fag end of the evaluation period to meet their monthly targets or to optimize their monthly or quarterly incentives. Even in a situation where the immediate buyers have sufficient stock, the sales force usually tries and dumps additional stocks to their immediate customer so as to meet their monthly targets. Incentives offered are usually higher discounts or higher credit period or promise of future favours. Obviously, dumping of material results in flow of goods from the supplier to the buyer but does not result in inflow of cash at the supplier's end. The supplier firm observes an increase in sales but is not better off because cash has not come in and the firm just sees conversion of FG inventory to accounts receivables in the account books. Obviously, since products have been dumped and not supplied against actual requirement, no sales take place for the first two weeks of the next month and the organization perpetuates this vicious cycle that, apart from increasing the cost for the overall supply chain, also results in high average inventory and high accounts receivables in the chain.

  This phenomenon, where the bulk of the sales takes place in the last week of a month, is known as the hockey stick phenomenon. Most Indian firms suffer from this skewed sales syndrome, although some progressive firms have tried to encourage their marketing people to achieve linear sales throughout the month. Suppose the organization currently gets 60 per cent of sales in the last week, they provide separate targets for the first and second halves and performance is monitored on a fortnightly basis. Or they may divide the entire market into multiple regions and the entire period, let us say a fortnight, is divided into seven parts and each market/region is served in a phased manner. This phasing of service does not affect retailers but reduces observed demand distortions at the supplier's end.

- *Special price promotions.* In the consumer goods industry, it is quite usual to offer trade promotions in terms of price discounts during certain periods. These deals are usually offered to shift demand from the peak period to the slack period so as to smoothen demand and production throughout the year. Special price promotions are also used in a situation where the company has not met its quarterly or yearly sales targets or has surplus inventory to be disposed. By offering these trade deals, firms either hope to increase their sales in the short term or hope to dispose surplus inventory. In certain industries it has become a rampant practice and marketing has come to believe that without these kinds of deals the firm will never be in a position to meet sales targets. Unfortunately, these deals result in forward buying of sales and the excess quantity bought does not lead to increased consumption at the end customer level. Inventory merely moves from the firm to the channel and the firm experiences an increase in sales during the promotion period but this temporary increase in sales comes at the cost of future sales. It is not uncommon to find that at the end of the trade promotion sales drop considerably for the next couple of weeks because the channel has enough material to take care of its demand for the next couple of periods. Obviously, this kind of incentive system distorts the demand in a significant way. It also perpetuates the firm's belief that without trade deals one cannot induce dealers to buy the firm's products.

  Firms believe that because of these kinds of discounts customers will buy more quantity; however, it is observed that discounts offered at specific points in time result in aggregation of demand by a buyer and results in forward buying rather than an actual increase in the quantity purchased. In recent times, FMCG companies in India have been increasing the spending on sales promotion at the expense of brand building. This is definitely not a healthy trend for the industry.

### Effect of Supplier Behaviour Uncertainty

While deciding on order quantity, the buyer does keep in mind supplier uncertainty on three dimensions and adjusts his order for the current period accordingly.

- *Handling of shortage situations.* There are periods when shortages can happen and how these situations are dealt with affects the future behaviour of buyers under similar situations. For example, most buyers are aware that during a shortage, the supplier resorts to rationing. As the buyer wants a supply matching the actual requirement, he inflates the order so that he gets his required quantity after the rationing by the supplier. An intermediary, if involved in serving the final market, sees the shortage situation as an opportunity to make a lot of money by cornering a significant amount of items in short supply. If rationing is carried out based on the order quantity, each buyer has an incentive to inflate the demand, as it is extremely difficult for the supplier to judge what is actual demand and what is inflated demand. He therefore starts his planning based on this distorted demand and ends up buying a huge quantity of raw materials and sometimes even adds capacity to take care of this inflated demand. After the shortages are overcome, the supplier usually discovers that the actual demand has not really increased and what he saw was a dummy demand.
- *Price fluctuations.* If the supplier changes the prices frequently, at every instance of the purchase situation the buyer starts speculating. Based on this expectation about likely price behaviour in the future, the buyer will change his order for the current period. If he expects that the prices are likely to go down he will reduce his safety stocks and so reduce his demand for the current period. If he expects a price increase in the near future he may buy more so as to make abnormal profits when the actual price increase takes place. In industries where prices are volatile in nature, the buyer keeps increasing or decreasing his stocks so as to optimize his profit performance. In general, if there is price uncertainty, different members of the chain like to either increase their stocks or decrease it. This behaviour results in distortions of information across the chain.
- *Delivery uncertainty.* If supplier delivery reliability is low, the buyer has to keep higher safety stocks at his end. As discussed in the forecasting updating section, higher safety stock results in higher adjustments during situations of change in demand forecast and results in higher distortions in demand placed by buyers.

### Impact of Supplier Inefficiency

If the supplier is inefficient and has a longer delivery lead time, the buyer has to forecast for a longer time horizon, leading to higher forecasting error. This error coupled with a long lead time results in a higher safety stock. So a longer lead time will have implications that are similar to the effect seen in case of delivery uncertainty. As discussed in the forecasting updating section, higher safety stock results in higher degree of adjustments during situations of change in demand forecast and results in higher distortions in demand placed by buyers.

## Bullwhip Effect: Demand Volatility and Information Distortions Across Supply Chains

So far we have looked at the causes of demand volatility and information distortions across the buyer–supplier link. The same logic is also valid when multiple stages are involved in the supply chain. Predictably, as you move away from the end customer, demand volatility keeps increasing. An increase in demand variability as one moves up in the chain is referred to as the bullwhip effect. In a typical supply chain, as we move up in the chain from retailers to wholesalers and to manufacturers, each stage in the chain distorts demand and the variability in demand keeps increasing. Thus, though variability is quite low at the

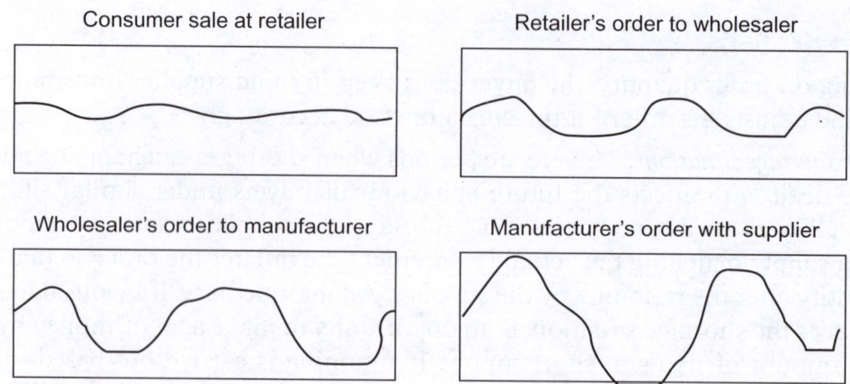


**Figure 9.3** Demand fluctuations at different stages of a supply chain.

final customer end, a manufacturer usually sees a high demand variability at his end. We therefore see the behaviour known as the bullwhip effect or the whiplash effect in supply chain literature.

In Figure 9.3, we show the bullwhip effect in a supply chain consisting of a retailer, a wholesaler, a manufacturer and his supplier. The order to the upstream member in the supply chain exhibits greater distortion (order variance) than the actual variation observed in orders at the retail sale.

The variance of orders increases as one moves upstream. Although it is expected that for functional products like grocery or FMCG products demand at the retail level should be more or less stable, for a typical manufacturer or supplier to the manufacturer, a large variability is seen at their ends as shown in Figure 9.3.

Therefore, it is not uncommon to find 3–6 months of inventory being stuck in distribution. According to one estimate, in the United States of America the total inventory exceeds about 100 days of supply. In India, it is estimated that about 20 weeks of inventory is stuck in the distribution channel in the FMCG industry. In general, this results in higher inventory and lower responsiveness on the part of the FMCG industry. If firms have 20 weeks of inventory in the channel they will never be in a position to plan and coordinate marketing and logistics activities. It is not uncommon to find that a firm has created demand through advertising campaigns but the corresponding product or promotion scheme is not available in the market at the same point in time. Further, high distortions result in very high costs for everyone in the supply chain.

On the basis of this discussion, we identify five prominent causes for the bullwhip effect:

- *Forecast updating.* Multiple forecast updates by each entity in the chain leads to significant distortions. Each member of the chain updates forecast based on orders received at his end and not based on the demand raised by the end customer.
- *Order batching.* Each member of the chain has his own economies of scale in production and transportation resulting in planning practices leading to order batching. Sometimes order bunching also takes place because of the planning practices of the firm. For example, if a firm runs MRP software once a fortnight, obviously all the orders for the fortnight will get bunched.
- *Price fluctuations.* Discounts or price promotions result in forward buying, causing much distortion. Further, frequent price changes affect the ordering pattern of the buyer.
- *Shortage gaming.* In a situation of shortages the supplier usually resorts to rationing, which in turn provides incentives to buyers to inflate orders.
- *Long lead time.* Long lead times increase the planning horizon of other partners in the chain. Further, each partner is forced to keep large amounts of safety stock, resulting in an overall distortion increase in the chain.

Procter & Gamble has understood the drivers of the bullwhip effect and has put in systems in place to tame this in its supply chain operations.

### PROCTER & GAMBLE: TAMING THE BULLWHIP EFFECT[2]

Procter & Gamble (P&G) had estimated the cost of the bullwhip effect and during the 1990s, it started an ambitious programme through which it virtually eliminated this effect in its supply chain. It has entered into a relationship with Wal-Mart (the largest customer accounting for about 17 per cent of business in the US market), wherein Wal-Mart does not place any orders but shares point of sales data with P&G and P&G in turn maintains the required inventory at Wal-Mart shelves. Wal-Mart also shares its future promotion plans with P&G so that there is complete information integration in the chain. To avoid problems associated with price fluctuations, P&G has stopped offering various trade deals that used to encourage retailers to do forward buying. Rather than offering frequent trade promotions (offering hi–low prices), P&G works with the concept called everyday low prices (EDLP). It has reduced its list prices by 12–24 per cent and managed to reduce its inventory by about 25 per cent. P&G maintains similar relationships with suppliers like 3M.

## Remedial Strategies to Counteract Demand Distortions Across Supply Chains

It is possible to design systems in a way that will enable organizations to minimize demand distortions across supply chains. There are broadly three kinds of initiatives through which one can minimize distortions in a supply chain:

- Information sharing across the chain
- Aligning incentives across the chain
- Improving operational efficiencies

### Information Sharing Across the Chain

Normally, the main communication channel in a supply chain is order information. Each entity in a chain gets the order from its immediate customer and tries to forecast future demand based on the order pattern that is received at its end. As discussed earlier, order is a distorted version of demand and as you move up the supply chain every entity adds to the distortion, with a result that if you are at a distance from the actual customer you will see acute distortions in the ordering pattern. Problems of multiple-forecast updating by members of the chain can be handled by information sharing across the chain.

Now, instead of communicating information about just the orders, if the end customer demand is communicated across the chain, one can reduce the distortions in the chain and these can be reduced further if firms can work towards collaborative forecasting as well. Similarly, distortions within a chain can be reduced if the customer can keep the supplier informed about future promotion plans. With advances in IT and communication technologies it is possible to share information in a cost-effective manner across the chain.

### Aligning Incentives Across the Chain

Alignment of interest should make the chain behave as if it is one entity and should create incentives for decision makers to take decisions from the chain perspective. Alignment of interest across the chain ensures that each entity in the chain focuses on global rather than local optimization.

Alignment of the chain will essentially involve removing incentives from the system that encourage distortions in ordering pattern. Specifically, it will remove incentives that encourage buyers to buy in bulk and avoid a shortage gaming situation in the chain.

In general, firms have to eliminate incentives given to their respective managers to improve their short-term local performances. For example, the sales bonus given to the sales force by the manufacturer for achieving monthly targets results in the dumping phenomenon. However, if sales bonuses are tied to sales at the end customer level, sales personnel will not indulge in dumping material to the next partner in the chain. If sales bonus is awarded for sales over a rolling horizon rather than sales for a month, the surge in sales at the end of the month will cease. Similarly, lot-based quantity discounts should be discontinued and instead discounts should be offered for purchases over a longer horizon. Also, firms should resist offering frequent trade promotions, which results in forward-buying behaviour.

Shortage gaming is a natural behaviour on the part of a supply chain member in the absence of any corrective mechanism. An organization can minimize the likelihood of shortage gaming by following transparent allocation policies, where during a shortage situation each buyer gets a quantity that is based on his past demand, that is, demand during normal times. So there is no incentive on the part of the buyer to create artificially inflated demands during shortage situations. In addition to building fair allocation policies which do not provide incentives for inflation of orders, firms have to create credibility in their allocation policies during shortage by bringing in transparency in the process. Companies like GM and HP have been successfully using this kind of system in a shortage environment.

Aligning incentives across the chain, however, is more difficult in a situation of volatile raw material markets and highly uncertain end-market demand conditions. In a situation of volatile raw material prices, distortions can be minimized by introducing transparent price change mechanisms. For example, in the PVC manufacturer's case since prices of crude oil keeps fluctuating the price of PVC will change correspondingly, but a meaningful buyer–supplier integration will take place only if partner firms have worked out fair and transparent processes through which price changes will take place. Similarly, contract manufacturers for electronic assembly offer prices that remain valid for three months at a time but since prices of flash memory are highly volatile, they work with the understanding that prices actually charged by the contract manufacturer in any transaction will be revised upward or downward to accommodate price change in flash memory at some benchmark exchange. Similarly, in the metal industry it is not unusual to work with prices that are benchmarked at prices in the metal exchange in London. In a situation of uncertain demand conditions, one can dampen the bullwhip effect by using contracts that have either buyback or price adjustment clauses in place. Of course, such contracts are likely to work only if there are transparent credible monitoring mechanisms in place. Take the case of the computer industry where prices keep declining with the result that dealers aim to minimize stock holding at their end. But since this will result in major lost sales opportunity which will adversely affect the overall chain performance, the manufacturer must develop a practice where in the event of price reduction he passes on rebates to dealers to compensate for the stocks bought at higher prices and held at his end. Similarly, if a manufacturer is introducing a new product that might cannibalize an existing product the dealer will want to reduce his stock holding of existing products. In such a situation, it will make sense for the manufacturer to offer a buy back scheme, which will reduce the risk for the dealer and at the same time will result in alignment of interest across the chain. Similarly, in the case of products such as movie videos and books, where variable costs are low and demand uncertainty is high, buy back schemes will encourage retailers to increase their stocks of such products resulting in higher profitability at the chain level. We discuss these issues through a simple analytical model in our chapter on supply chain contracts. In general, one can create contracts through which chain alignment can be attempted. Monitoring mechanisms for these kinds of contracts may involve sharing of information across the chain. In normal situations, firms may be reluctant to share information but better alignment of interest along the chain will motivate firms within the chain to share information across the chain.

Suguna Poultry has come up with an innovative franchise framing model that ensures that there is an alignment of interest across the supply chain.

### SUGUNA'S FRANCHISE FARMING MODEL[3]

Suguna Poultry is a leading poultry manufacturer with a business value of Rs 14.01 billion. The fast growth and overall success of Suguna Poultry lies in its unique model of franchise framing where breeding of chicken is managed by 13,000 framers who own broiler farms. By adding more farmers to its network, Suguna is able to ramp up its operations at a rapid pace in 10 different states. The farmer's performance is manifested in the mortality of the birds as well as the average weight of the broilers obtained. Suguna has devised a unique compensation structure for the farmers so as to incentivize them for better performance. The production cost per kilogram of the end product, obtained using the standard costing approach, for the farm is used to determine the appropriate compensation, that is, growing charges per kilogram to the farmer. For any increase or decrease in production cost, 30 per cent of the benefit/cost goes to the farmer while the rest is shared by the company.

### Improving Operational Efficiencies

The bullwhip effect across the chain is created because of long lead time and order batching owing to high transaction costs in the chain and can only be handled by improving operational efficiencies in the chain. By reducing the transaction costs involved in purchasing and reducing the setup time one can reduce the batching effect in the chain. Similarly, the magnitude of duration and uncertainty in lead time can be monitored and partners can work on joint improvement programmes essentially targeting lead time duration and uncertainty. Operational efficiency improvement programmes on this front will create additional value in the chain and help firms in further dampening the bullwhip effect.

The bullwhip effect essentially destroys significant value within the chain. Measures like sharing information and aligning incentives across the chain will essentially help in minimizing the value destructive behaviour of the bullwhip effect.

The ideas discussed in this section have been operationalized in various popular industry-level initiatives and these are discussed in a later part of this chapter.

## Barriers to External Integration

Unlike internal supply chain integration, external supply chain integration is inherently more difficult and quite demanding in nature. While it is relatively easy to impose performance measures (top management has to only ensure internal consistency) in the case of the external supply chain situation, performance measures have to be negotiated so as to make business sense for both parties. In the internal supply chain context, if the decision makes sense from the overall organizational perspective, hierarchy can be invoked. But in the external supply chain context, unless all the concerned parties agree it may not be possible to find ways in which interest can be aligned within the chain.

In popular business press there seems to exist a naive belief that all parties will be interested in working towards supply chain integration since one can show that an integrated supply chain will result in lower costs for the overall chain. Obviously, if one can optimize performance globally the overall costs will come down compared to local optimization. But one finds many instances where two parties in the chain can have genuine differences and so external integration will be difficult in such a situation.

### Differences in Objectives Leading to Conflicts in the Chain

There are genuine differences in several situations of buyer–supply links in supply chains. Some examples are illustrated below:

- *Manufacturer versus multi-brand retailer.* In a competitive market, the manufacturer will want the retailer to work with a high service level so as to ensure availability of his product on the shelf.

However, multi-brand retailers like Shopper's Stop or Foodworld will want to maintain a high product availability at the category level and would not mind a comparatively lower service level at the individual brand level. Since substitutes in terms of competing brands are available for commodities where brand loyalty is not very strong (e.g., in products like butter, chocolates, garments or soft drinks), a multi-brand retailer will want to work with a lower service level so that his overall costs are low. As far as he is concerned, so long as he can serve the customer with any of the competing brands he has fulfilled his obligation. So there is an inherent conflict between the retailer and the manufacturer. In a single sourced item in a business-to-business environment, one does not have a conflict of this kind.

- *Supplier competing in the end-product market.* If a supplier competes with a customer in the end-product market it may not be possible to align the interests of both partners. For example, Cannon supplies printer heads to HP and also competes with HP in the printer market.

- *Excessive focus on quarterly financial performance by member firms.* Listed firms have to present quarterly financial performance report to the investor community. Since all firms believe that their main objective is to improve shareholder value, there is a compulsion to report growth every quarter. Therefore, firms will want to find ways of converting FG inventory into sales. Apart from increased sales they will also report increase in profits, as FG inventory is valued at cost while sales price includes the profit margin. Often this higher sales is carried out by dumping goods to the next partner in the chain by giving higher credit and discounts resulting in higher accounts receivables and lower profit margins in the long run. This trade-off between the lower profitability in short run versus overall higher profitability in the long run is not clearly understood by typical decision makers and decisions are usually made from the short-term performance angle and not necessarily from long-term profitability point of view. Firms similarly offer trade promotions with the intention of solving local problems at either the department level or at the firm level. As discussed earlier, behaviour of this kind results in lowering of performance for all the parties in the chain in the long run. These pressures especially at the firm level have increased because of intense pressure by analysts and business media.

- *Supplier serving multiple industries.* Whenever a supplier serves two different industries, priorities of a supplier to a specific industry and customer will vary based on fluctuations in fortunes of competing industries. For example, computer chip suppliers were serving telecom and electronic products markets in the late 1990s. Growth and profitability in the telecom industry created incentives to chip suppliers to shift their priorities from the electronics sector to the telecom sector.

Companies do not share the same worldview about macroeconomic factors such as industry growth and company market share. During the initial period of downturn in the telecom industry, contract manufacturers and other suppliers did not share Cisco's rosy projections of the future. Cisco therefore entered into rigid contracts and had to buy all the parts and material even though there was no demand for telecom equipments and ended up writing off about $2.2 billion worth of inventory.

## Imbalance in Power Leading to Focus on Value Appropriation

Even in a situation where there is no conflict of interest between two parties, it is possible that firms may be competing for value appropriation within the chain. The focus of discussion in the earlier section has been on creating a bigger pie for the supply chain but at the same time there has been strategy literature where firms are advised to focus more on cornering a greater share of the pie. Consequently, firms tend to focus more on appropriating value from the chain rather than creating value for the chain. Strategy literature takes the view that firms within the supply chain essentially compete with each other to appropriate value from the chain. For example, within the PC industry Intel and Microsoft have appropriated value

## INTERVIEW WITH

S. RAVICHANDRAN

*TVS Logistics, a TVS group company, is a leading logistics provider in the automotive sector. It employs 4,000 people and has an annual turnover of Rs 2.5 billion. Mr S Ravichandran is the president of TVS Logistics.*

*What is the scale and the level of complexity of logistics operations that can be handled by TVS Logistics?*

**S. Ravichandran:** We provide an integrated logistics service to both global and Indian automobile companies. We provide inbound as well as outbound logistics and even handle in-plant logistics activities for some of our clients. We run about 1,600 trips per month on average. Today, TVS Logistics handles over US$1.5 billion worth of parts annually and controls about two million square feet of warehouse space. We also have gone global because a lot of our clients wanted us to service their global operations. We now have presence in several countries across the globe.

*What are the operations challenges that TVS Logistics faces?*

**S. Ravichandran:** Automobile companies are known to work with lean inventories. Given the nature of infrastructure and other bottlenecks in India, it is a challenging task to manage lean logistics operations under infrastructure constraints and volatile demand situations. As the automobile market is highly competitive, our customers are always under cost pressure, and so they in turn pass on their pressure to us and expect us to improve our service and reduce cost on a continuous basis.

*TVS Logistics focuses on supply chain integrations. How is the integration achieved?*

**S. Ravichandran:** Our vision statement itself demonstrates our commitment to supply chain integration: We have first focused on internal integration within the firm. We have put in structured processes and also have internal service agreements between functions. This allows us to function seamlessly within the firm. We are hoping to work the same way with customers so that we can provide end-to-end integration for customers. We create value by operating from within the customer's existing networks and maximizing the potential. By being in the complete management of the solution, we aim to achieve a holistic balance in the complete loop of operation.

*What are the innovations that the company has adopted?*

**S. Ravichandran:** We as a company only work on automobile vertical. This allows us to develop deep domain expertise which in turn allows us to offer best processes and practices.

We proactively keep looking at the way in which we can add value to clients. TVS Logistics' "Logistics Plans" incorporates the principles of JIT, Kanban, scheduling and ensures timely availability of parts and components for production with virtually bare minimum inventory. The collection system from vendors are developed and monitored. The system is supported by the powerful "track and trace" IT system. We also have come up with innovations on the pricing front. For example, with some clients, we have moved to innovative pricing for inbound logistics where we get paid on the number of vehicles shipped by the company. This has helped us and the client in reducing a whole lot of non-value added processes. In general, we have found that in every project we are able to reduce cost by about 5–15 per cent in clients' cost of operation.

We have created knowledge management function at the highest level, which reports directly to me. This allows us to learn from all the client engagements and transfer learning across the firm. Since we focus only on the auto sector we are able to develop a lot of capabilities. There is lot of respect for our capabilities. This has allowed us to develop deep domain level expertise in all the relevant operational areas.

*What are the future challenges for TVS Logistics?*

**S. Ravichandran:** All our customers are demanding higher level service at lower cost. But, we cannot change cost substantially if the client is not willing to change its internal processes. Some clients look at us as infrastructure provider and not solution provider and in such a situation our ability to improve performance is limited. We have to continuously educate our customers so that they are open to ideas through which we can help them in reducing cost and improving services.

within the chain and made huge profits while all other members within the chain have been struggling to make money.

Whenever a new supply chain idea is initiated, it will be interesting to observe whether this initiative will result in value creation for the chain or if it is essentially an attempt by the powerful player in a chain to appropriate value for itself. New initiatives are usually started by a focal firm (also known as steward firm), which provides leadership to the entire value chain

*Table 9.3: Cost impact of supply chain action/initiative.*

| Type of initiative | Supplier costs | Customer costs | Supply chain costs | Action/initiative enabler |
|---|---|---|---|---|
| I | ↓ | ↓ | ↓ | Supply chain partnership |
| II | ↑ | ↓ | ↓ | Power equations |
| III | ↑ | ↓ | ↑ | Power equations |
| IV | ↑ | ↑ | ↑ | Power equations and gaming by two parties |

*Note*: ↑ stands for increased costs.
↓ stands for decreased costs.

and ensures that the chain simultaneously addresses customers' best interest and drives profit for all the chain partners. For example, HUL may start an initiative and expect suppliers and customers to participate in the same.

Based on our discussion on value creation and value appropriation, we can classify all supply chain initiatives into four categories as shown in Table 9.3. Let us take up the case of a supplier–customer relationship where the customer has more power in the chain, and as shown in Table 9.3 we discuss four possible types of initiatives based on the differential cost impact on both partners.

A type I initiative results in cost reduction for both parties and, of course, results in cost reduction at the chain level. Most supply chain initiatives discussed in the literature are of type I. In the type II initiative, even though chain-level costs come down, the supplier will be worse off because of reallocation of activities. Ideally, in a case where a firm starts a type II initiative, it should redistribute costs and benefits in a way that other members are not affected because of the initiative. Type III and type IV initiatives are dysfunctional in nature, where the chain level costs goes up. Type III initiatives are carried by inward looking firms who have enormous power. Type IV initiatives are carried out in supply chain relationships where both parties start playing for opportunistic gain and in the long run such an initiative results in cost increase for everyone in the chain. Most trade promotion types of initiatives are of the type IV category. It is not uncommon for very successful firms to enter into type II or type III initiatives. In Box 9.1, we present a case of a type III initiative by a very successful firm.

Similar analysis can be carried out in a situation where a supplier is more powerful in supply chain relationships.

As discussed earlier, powerful firms tend to work with type II and III initiatives, focusing on their internal performances without worrying about the impact of the same on the performances of the partners in the chain. But it is important to keep in mind that relationships are not permanent in nature: each partner keeps benchmarking value brought in by the other partners in the chain. No firm will like to get tied down to a partner who keeps extracting maximum possible value from the chain. The partner who gets a raw deal in a series of such initiatives will either withdraw from the partnership or start activities that might restore the balance of power. It has been found that retail stores usually introduce private brands so as to increase their bargaining power with branded manufacturers. Foodworld has started offering private branded products like tomato ketchup, which competes directly with companies like HUL and Nestle.

## Building Partnership and Trust in a Supply Chain

Historically, supply chain relationships have been based either on power or on trust. There seems to be differences in approach across cultures: Japanese firms have traditionally focused on trust-based relationships while American firms have focused on contract-based relationships.

**BOX 9.1** Use of Power in the Supply Chain Context

Over the last two decades, HUL has managed to reduce its working capital cycle from 84 days to -13 days. Most firms envy HUL for this achievement and the business media claims that HUL has achieved this by improving its supply chain practices. A scrutiny of the data for the last 20 years reveals the truth behind the popular perception.

As can be seen from the table blow, the bulk of the reduction in WC has been achieved by reduction in inventory (40 days reduction in RM inventory, 11 days in WIP inventory and 20 days in FG inventory) and by extracting greater amount of credit (from 68 to 100 days) from its suppliers. By extracting higher credit from suppliers, HUL has ensured that its operations are financed by suppliers. In a typical FMCG chain, the cost of funds for various entities in the chain is of the following kind:

| Entity | Suppliers | FMCG firm | Stockist | Whole-salers | Retailers |
|---|---|---|---|---|---|
| Cost of funds | 14–16% | 8–10% | 14–16% | 20–22% | 24–36% |

Given the fact that firms like HUL can raise money at the lowest rate in the market, why does HUL use suppler funds to finance its operations? Financing HUL operations using supplier funds results in lower costs for HUL, but the cost for the overall chain is higher because more expensive funds are used in managing the supply chain.

When a firm forces its suppliers, who have higher costs of fund, to offer longer credit period the former is financing its operations using supplier funds, which are more expensive in nature. This behaviour is similar to that shown in a type III initiative. At a firm level, an FMCG firm will feel that it has managed to get the best deal for the firm but actually it has increased the overall costs in the chain. Further, HUL has clout in the market place and so it offers very little credit to its stockist. Obviously, the inventory in the channel (industry average in FMCG is 20 weeks and for HUL this is reported to be about 12 weeks) is financed by various channel partners. If the cost of carrying inventory is not the same for HUL and its channel partners, then financing of the channel using more expensive funds will result in an overall increase in cost for the chain.

***HUL: Working capital performance over the last 20 years.***

| | 1993 | 1995 | 1997 | 1999 | 2001 | 2003 | 2005 | 2007 | 2009 | 2011 | 2013 |
|---|---|---|---|---|---|---|---|---|---|---|---|
| Raw materials and spares days | 74 | 64 | 49 | 53 | 53 | 61 | 64 | 66 | 57 | 47 | 34 |
| Work in progress | 17 | 9 | 4 | 3 | 4 | 4 | 3 | 2 | 11 | 10 | 8 |
| Finished goods days | 46 | 39 | 31 | 31 | 31 | 36 | 29 | 32 | 37 | 33 | 28 |
| Average debtors days | 15 | 15 | 8 | 9 | 13 | 17 | 19 | 14 | 15 | 14 | 11 |
| Average creditors days | 68 | 84 | 68 | 74 | 83 | 96 | 94 | 97 | 108 | 104 | 94 |
| Net working capital cycle days | 84 | 44 | 26 | 23 | 18 | 22 | 20 | 17 | 12 | 2 | –13 |

Data Source: Prowess (CMIE).

In power-based relationships, the stronger party usually exploits the weaker one. In the short run, the stronger party is able to benefit at the expense of weaker one but since this is not sustainable, in the long run either the relationship breaks down or the overall chain performance starts deteriorating.

There have been extensive research studies that have the shown long-term benefits of trust-based relationships. In replacement automotive parts supply chains, retailers with higher trust in the manufacturer's products sell more and are rated higher by the manufacturer.

## *Steps in Building Successful Relationships*

Though importance of trust in the supply chain context is understood, it is very hard to build and sustain a trust-based relationship. Most supply chain relationships have historical baggage so one cannot switch to a trust-based relationship overnight. Even in a new relationship, both sides will look at each other with apprehension, so a process is needed through which trust-based relationships can be built over time. Such relationships are built as a result of a series of interactions between the parties involved.

It has been found that successful relationship building involves the following three elements:

- *Design relationship with cooperation and trust.* At the design stage, one has to ensure that the relationship is win-win in nature and assess the value of the relationship for both partners. There will exist certain grey areas and an attempt should be made to clarify operational roles and decision rights for all parties involved. In the initial stages of the relationship both parties may worry that the other may take advantage of the relationship, so formal contracts must be signed specifying performance measures and design conflict resolution mechanisms. This helps in establishing ground rules for the relationship.
- *Manage and nurture relationships.* Once the relationship is designed, during the operations phase both partners begin to understand the finer details about the environment and the tasks involved. It is possible however that actual payoffs may not be on the lines of what one had expected at the design stage. Similarly, one party may end up committing more resources than planned for. At this stage, both sides are in a better position to evaluate the costs and benefits of the relationship. This helps parties to revise the conditions of partnership so that it is a fair partnership. It is important that the initial contract be designed with sufficient flexibility to facilitate such changes. If both parties work within the spirit of partnership, trust gets built over a period of time and the relationship moves on an upward spiral where each interaction helps in carrying the partnership further. A supply chain partnership moves in a downward spiral if the perceived benefits from the relationship diminishes, or if one party is seen as behaving in an opportunistic manner.
- *Redesign relationship with change in environment.* It should be realized that any relationship operates in a larger economical environment. One cannot expect the environment to remain stable, and with changes in environment, technology and competition, one has to redesign the relationship.

## Effect of Interdependence on Relationships

Trust-based relationships are likely to work very well in a situation where both parties are mutually interdependent. For example, take the case of a relationship between a company like HUL and its dealers: HUL's dependence on the dealer is low because it has a large number of dealers, whereas the dealer's dependence on HUL is high. Similarly, look at the relationship between Foodworld and the supplier of an unbranded item, the dependence of the supplier on Foodworld is high whereas the inverse is not true. But in a relationship between Foodworld and HUL, both are equally dependent on each other. In general, one can classify relationships using the schema shown in Figure 9.4. Relationships that are in the upper most quadrant are more likely to succeed.

In the right lower corner, where the organization is powerful compared to the supplier, it can build a trust-based relationship if it works with long-term interest in mind. The Toyota model is a clear example where a powerful partner plays the role of a hub and ensures that there exists a fair relationship through which it develops a network of suppliers.

We know of a case of a global automobile company that requested its global logistics partner to set up operations in India when the former wanted to start its own operations in India. At the end of four years of operations, the automobile company realized that it had not been able to achieve the kind of volumes that it had projected while deciding the price structure for the logistics company. The automobile major decided to compensate the logistics company for the losses it made in the India operations because of lower volume of business.

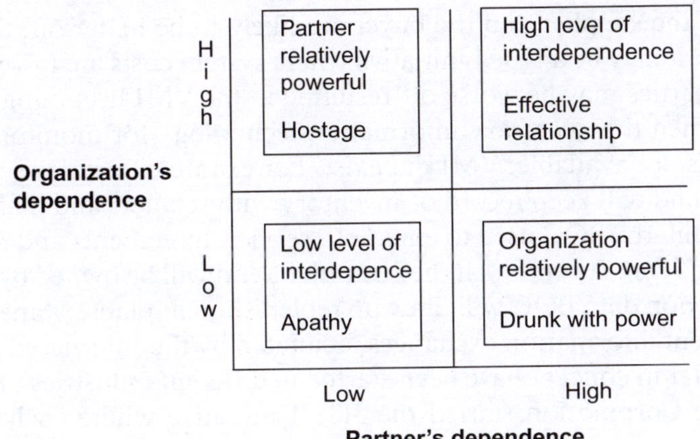


**Figure 9.4**

Classification of relationships.

*Source*: N. Kumar, "The Power of Trust in Manufacturer–Retailer Relationships," *Harvard Business Review* (November–December 1996): 92–106. © 1996 Harvard Business School Publishing Corporation. All right reserved.

## Supply Chain External Integration: Industry-level Initiatives

There have been several popular industry-level initiatives. We describe some of these in this section.

### *Vendor-managed Inventory*

In vendor-managed inventory (VMI), the supplier or vendor monitors and manages the inventory at the customer's warehouse. VMI is an approach to inventory and order fulfilment whereby the rights to decision about when to buy and how much to buy are shifted to the vendor or the supplier. Typically, a buyer makes decision about when to buy and how much to buy and the vendor makes decisions about production and shipping accordingly. Under the VMI system, the vendor tracks sales and inventory data at the buyer end and makes decisions regarding replenishment. The customer withdraws material from the warehouse just at the time when it requires and only at that point in time does the ownership of the inventory shift from the vendor to the customer. There are service-level agreements between buyers and vendors, which ensure that service levels do not go below the level specified. This initiative is quite popular in the electronic assembly and automobile assembly sectors, where suppliers are asked to keep a minimum of 10–15 days of material as inventory in the supply hub, which is a warehouse located very close to the manufacturers' plant. The supplier can monitor inventory and withdrawals by the manufacturer and replenish accordingly. Since the vendor is working with actual consumption (withdrawal from retailer's warehouse or withdrawal from supplier hub) or sales data, the bullwhip effect is likely to be lower and this will reduce the system cost at the supply chain level. Further, the supplier can make coordinated production and transportation decisions for multiple customers so that he can use the same production setup and trucks to manufacture and then ship goods to them, thus saving on fixed cost in setup and transportation. Thus, it is easy to see that the overall system cost as well as the buyer cost goes down. The supplier may or may not be better off because he has to carry this additional inventory at the buyer end. While shifting to the VMI, if the buyer does not share his forecast and information about future plans and price and credit terms do not change, the supplier is likely to be worse off even though the overall costs in the supply chain will be lower in nature. Reduction in cost owing mainly to sharing of fixed cost of setup and production costs may not compensate him for the increase in inventory costs at his end. But in case the supplier agrees to share data about future plans and forecasts and is willing to change price and credit terms, the overall costs will be lower and both the supplier and the buyer are likely to be better off. So depending on the clout of the buyers, it may be a type I initiative where system costs are lower and both are better off, or one of the parties may be worse off resulting in the VMI becoming a type II initiative.

Even earlier when the necessary information technology for monitoring inventory at the customer's end was not available, VMI did exist. For example, Fritolay's salesman will physically visit retailers and will keep record of inventory with retailers and make replenishment-related decisions. Similarly, BOC used to enter into service agreements and manage inventory of gas at the customer's end. Inventory at the customer's end will be owned by BOC, and based on historical consumption data BOC will draw up replenishment plans. Managing a VMI is much simpler with frequent information exchanges facilitated by the Internet.

Initiatives similar in concept have been started in different industries under different labels. For example, Bose Corporation started the JIT II initiative where each major supplier was expected to position one of its employees at the plant of Bose Corporation. This member will have all relevant information available and will coordinate all replenishment-related decisions and ensure that relevant material is supplied to Bose Corporation just in time.

## Efficient Customer Response

Efficient customer response originated in the grocery industry and was designed to integrate supply chain and demand management related operations of retailers and suppliers. It has broader aims and objectives compared to the VMI. According to one estimate, the ECR initiative in the United States of America itself is likely to show savings to the tune of $30 billion or 5 per cent of retail sales.

See Figure 9.5 for a comprehensive conceptual view of the ECR. Under the ECR initiative, various ideas have evolved over time, the major features of which are presented here:

- *Category management.* Traditionally, retailers and manufacturers think about what they sell in terms of how the consumers buy: one brand of one type of item (e.g., Lux for toilet soaps). There is now a realization on the part of retailers and manufacturers that consumers think in terms of product category like hair oil or snack and not as individual brands. So it will make sense for the retailer and manufacturer also to think on similar lines and to group various brands using the logic of categories that seem natural to the customer.

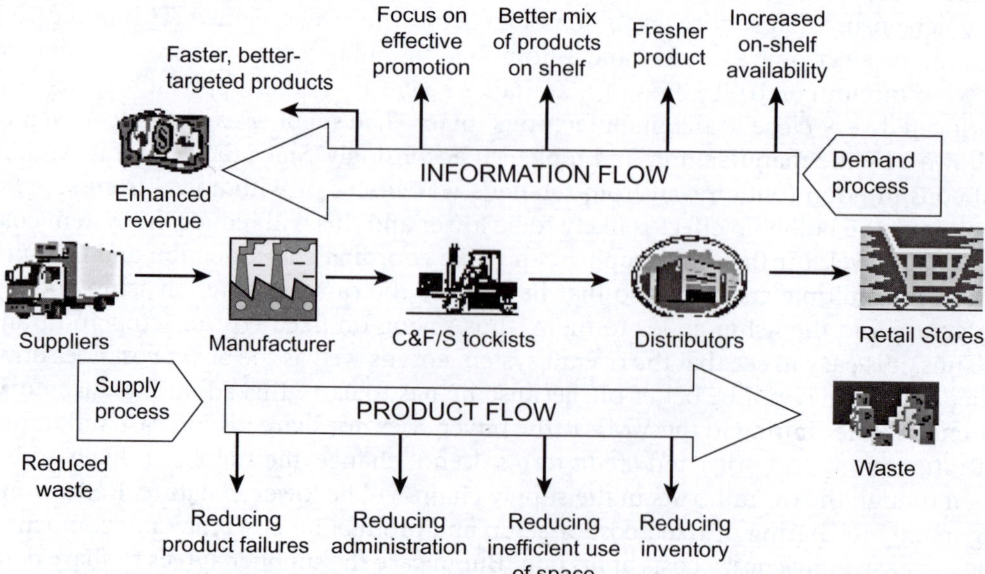


**Figure 9.5** Conceptual view of the ECR.

ECR is promoting ideas of category management where the manufacturer and retailer will work together to understand each category's dynamics as perceived by the customer (from the end customer's point of view). Crucial decisions about shelf space allocation, new product introduction and assortment management are done at the category level rather than at the brand level. P&G claims that in the laundry category they have cut down significant number of SKUs and brands so as to avoid unnecessary variety, which is expensive from the retailer and manufacturer perspective.

- *Continuous replenishment programme (CRP).* Similar to the VMI initiative, the ECR works with continuous replenishment where suppliers will replenish more frequently and as a result retailers work with low inventory. POS data are made available to the supplier who in turn will replenish more frequently, resulting in lower inventory and lower costs in the chain. Information sharing required standardization of codes and methods and implementation of electronic data interchange (EDI). EDI had certain standards-related problems and involved huge investments, which resulted in small and medium-sized firms not using EDI technologies. With the advent of the Internet, many small and medium-sized firms are also participating in this revolution. CRP participants are also trying to automate processes related to replenishment, which will also help in reducing costs in the chain.
- *Efficient promotions.* As observed in the bullwhip discussion, uncoordinated promotions tend to create distortions within the chain, resulting in higher costs for all the partners in the chain. Under ECR, the retailer and the manufacturer jointly work out promotions so as to ensure that it is a win-win proposition for both. Efficient promotions jointly analyse data about consumer behaviour to discover what is selling at what price and to whom, and design appropriate promotion plans. Rather than working with varying prices (high-low prices), ECR promotes the idea of everyday low prices.

Realizing the potential of ECR, several companies have come together to promote the idea in India. See Box 9.2 for details on the ECR India initiative.

### WHIRLPOOL CORPORATION: IMPLEMENTATION OF CPFR[5]

Whirlpool Corporation, with a turnover of $11 billion, is one the world's leading manufacturers of home appliances. In 2000, Whirlpool formally created a supply chain department with the idea of making supply chain its key competitive advantage. Whirlpool decided to focus on two key metrics: forecast accuracy and demand variability. To improve its performance on these two metrics, Whirlpool decided to work on CPFR initiative using the structured process approach. It first ensured that there was internal as well as external buy-in. Recognizing the difficulty involved in implementing a new concept, it started a pilot project with two trade partners. Whirlpool and its trade partners saw a reduction in weekly variability. It also found that forecast accuracy improved significantly. Apart from those tangible benefits, improved relationship helped both partners in developing a better understanding of each others' problems. Based on the success of the pilot project, Whirlpool decided to extend the same to all other major trade partners.

## CPFR

Collaborative planning, forecasting and replenishment (CPFR) is aimed at facilitating and improving collaboration between partners in a chain. As discussed earlier, when partners forecast independently there is the possibility of a bullwhip effect, which results in higher inventory and poor customer service at the end customer level. Even with the same data, partners in the chain are likely to come with different forecasts, so replenishment will not work well if forecasts are not collaborative in nature. CPFR offers a structured approach through which early forecast can be refined and a number arrived at using a collaborative process, which in turn helps in the replenishment process. Since 1998, voluntary interservice commerce solutions

**BOX 9.2** ECR Initiative in India[4]

There are two nightmare scenarios for any FMCG organization. One is when its customers return empty-handed because the product they wanted was not available in the store, and the other is when the customer is compelled to buy goods just a few days before the expiry date. Both these threats emanate from the common problem of supply chain inefficiency. These incidentally are the very problems that the entire FMCG industry in India is facing owing to the overwhelmingly fragmented supply chain, and the large inventories trapped in it.

ECR is about these companies who combat for a share of the Rs 400 billion FMCG market coming together to:

- Monitor and share the stockout data of their own brands
- Benchmark their figures against those of the others
- Share best practices to minimize new product failures
- Tackle problems of excess inventory in the supply chain

This is achieved through sharing resources such as trucks and warehouses, using a common business language in order to meet the ECR objective of fulfilling consumer demand better, faster and at a lower cost by eliminating unnecessary expenses and inefficiencies from the supply chain. ECR expedites flow of products and information on consumer demand. The intermediary margin cost, cost of logistics and cost of holding inventory can be reduced to up to 40 per cent through ECR and this will be passed on as a benefit to the consumer.

The ECR initiative is being implemented through four workgroups comprising representatives from the participating companies.

**The Stockouts Group**

This group measures the actual level of stockouts in the industry and evolves common solutions. This group has established a pilot study to monitor the stockout levels of 85 key SKUs of five companies.

**The Logistics Group**

The group draws up logistics standards and drives possible cost-saving measures through collaboration. This group works out synergies through shared warehouses for non-competing products of different companies and has established a pilot for backhaul arrangements (using the same trucks to carry one company's product in one direction of the route and another company's product during the return journey), which results in 5–10 per cent savings in transport costs.

**The Dataflow Group**

This team is responsible for standardizing data definition and flows between various constituents of the supply chain. The idea is to develop a communication framework that is understood by all players. Thus, a 13-digit code (European Article Number or EAN) has been developed to identify an SKU and plans are afoot to develop codes for all entities like manufacturers, distributors and retailers. EAN will help in ensuring that the bar coding is adopted by participating companies. This will enable an enhanced accuracy of up to 90 per cent in demand estimation and tracking of stocks all along the supply chain, and result in annual savings of up to Rs 10 million for the retailers.

**The FMCG Policy for Organized Retail Group**

This group draws up policy guidelines for FMCG transactions with organized retail. It is responsible for the benchmarking of intermediary margins in India with other comparable countries. They plan a value chain analysis where every activity of every intermediary in the supply chain will be examined to define the margins that each deserves.

Together, these groups intend to launch an unprecedented ECR initiative in the country that will serve as a shining example for others who may join in later so that this becomes an industry-wide practice.

ECR is expected to change the current way of functioning of the intermediaries—from push-based to demand-led pull-based operations where the trading partners lift products based on actual demand. This will also eradicate the biggest evil of excess inventory in the supply chain. The entire FMCG supply chain is estimated to be carrying an inventory worth Rs 150 billion (20 weeks' sales), which amounts to an inventory carrying cost of Rs 16.5 billion every year.

(VICS) has been working on these issues. Software companies have been keen on establishing standards for communication across partners in the chain. This has been tested at a few pilot sites and the results have been encouraging. VICS has suggested a model for reliable data exchange over the Internet for all trading partners in the chain. But this is a relatively new initiative and there are many organizational issues involved that need to be sorted out. Whirlpool Corporation has been one of the early successful implementers of CPFR in India.

## Summary

- In well-managed chains, material, information and finance flow seamlessly across departmental and organizational boundaries.
- By working on supply chain integration, it will be possible to shift the entire efficiency frontier downward, which in turn will allow the firm to improve performance on cost and service fronts simultaneously.
- Firms should work towards internal integration initially and at a later stage should attempt to work towards external integration.
- To make supply chain integration possible, the organization will have to make corresponding changes in organization structure processes and performance measures.
- In a typical supply chain, one observes a phenomenon called the bullwhip effect as we move upstream in the chain from retailers to wholesalers and to manufacturers. Each stage in the chain distorts demand and the variability in demand keeps increasing as we move upstream in the chain.
- Five different causes of the bullwhip effect are as follows: multiple demand forecast update by various supply chain members, order batching at various stages in the chain, price fluctuations within the chain, shortage gaming by partners in the chain and long lead time involved in purchasing and manufacturing.
- Companies can avoid the bullwhip effect by information sharing, aligning incentives and improving operational efficiency in the chain.
- It is not unusual to find supply chains where two parties in the chain have genuine differences and therefore external integration will be difficult to be attempted in such a situation.
- It has been found that successful relationship building involves the following three elements: design relationship with cooperation and trust, manage and nurture relationships and redesign relationships with changes in the environment.
- There have been several successful industry-level initiatives like VMI, ECR and CPFR which have tried to achieve external supply chain integration with the industry.

## Discussion Questions

1. Why is it tougher to achieve external integration compared to internal integration?
2. What are the greatest obstacles to implementing concepts of supply chain integration?
3. What is the bullwhip effect and what are the main causes of the bullwhip effect? What can a firm do to minimize demand distortions across the chain?
4. How can one implement the concept of supply chain integration within the planning systems of a firm?
5. Compare and contrast various supply chain initiatives seen in practice.
6. There is a view that it is important to transfer decision rights so that the supply chain is coordinated.
7. In India, the ECR industry initiative was started with a lot of fanfare but it has not made any meaningful progress. What could be the reasons for it? What can be done to improve the chances of success of any such industry initiative?
8. What is the role of trust in supply chain management?
9. What issues must be considered when designing supply chain relationships to improve the chances of developing cooperation and trust?
10. There is a view that it is impossible to achieve external integration in a chain as each firm is interested in maximizing its own benefits. There is limited amount of pie that different parties in the chain are trying to grab. So is this is a zero-sum game, and would one never be able to implement ideas of supply chain integration?

## Mini Project

The main objective of the project is to understand concepts of the bullwhip effect in particular and supply chain integration in general through experiential learning by playing the supply chain game. This project is designed around the famous beer game developed by MIT in the 1960s. Analysis of game will also allow you to understand the impact of information sharing and supply chain structure on the supply chain performance.

*Description of the Beer Game*

This simplified beer supply chain consists of four entities: a retailer, a wholesaler (supplies to retailer), a distributor (supplies to wholesaler) and a factory (brews beer and supplies to distributor). The retailer faces uncertain customer demand and the factory has unlimited supply of raw material. Each entity in the chain has unlimited storage/production and fixed supply lead time and order delay time in the customer–supplier linkage in the chain. The game is played for 30 weeks. Each week, every entity in the chain has to meet the order placed by its immediate downstream customer. Each entity carries some amount of inventory so that the customer order is filled from the inventory. Any unfulfilled order is recorded as backorder and an attempt is made to fulfil the order as soon as possible. Each entity is expected to minimize two supply chain related costs: inventory carrying cost and backordering cost. Visit http://beergame.mit.edu/guide.htm for a detailed description of the game.

*Playing the Game*

This game is played by a team consisting of four participants (or pairs of participants), each taking the role of one entity. At the start of the game, participants are divided into teams. Multiple teams can play the game independently. Each entity needs an individual terminal with Internet connection for playing this game. The instructor usually acts as the manager of the game. Visit http://beergame.mit.edu/ for playing the Web-based beer game. At the end of game, each entity will get the data of costs and charts plotting inventory, backorder and order pattern over time.

*Analysis of the Game*

Each team is likely to see dramatic fluctuations in order and inventory levels. Each team can try and discuss possible reasons for the dramatic fluctuations observed in the game. A team can also try and relate various concepts discussed in section "External Integration". Apart from observing trends in order and inventory levels, each team should calculate demand amplification and variance amplification for all the entities in the chain.

$$\text{Demand amplification}_i = \text{Peak demand}_i / \text{Average customer demand}$$

$$\text{Varince amplification}_i = \text{Variance of order placed}_i / \text{Variance of customer demand}$$

*where i* is the index for various entities in the chain.

Each team can identify ways in which these fluctuations can be dampened. Teams can specifically examine ways of redesigning the decision processes, physical structure and information channel within the beer supply chain for improving supply chain performance. The team can also discuss and debate on the impact of the scenarios described below on supply chain perfomance.

- *Reducing the number of entities in chain.* What happens if a factory supplies directly to the retailer?
- *Reducing order delay.* What happens if a supplier can place an order on the Web so that there is no ordering delay in the system?
- *Reducing shipment time.* What happens if a supplier uses a faster mode of transport?
- *Sharing POS data with brewery.* What happens if a retailer shares POS data with the factory on a real-time basis?
- *Sharing demand/inventory information across chain.* What happens if every player has access to all the information in the chain?
- *Transfer of decision rights to one part in the chain.* What happens if all the decisions in the chain are made by one party? (This idea is similar to the VMI where all the relevant decisions are transferred to the vendor.)

Estimate the likely value of demand amplification and variance amplification for each of the above scenarios.

## Notes

1. See http://economictimes.indiatimes.com/News/News_By_Industry/Services/Subhiksha_sends_legal_notices_to_drug_wholesalers/rssarticleshow/2747121.cms.
2. H. L. Lee, V. Padmanabhan, and Seungjin Whang, "The Bullwhip Effect in Supply Chains," *Sloan Management Review* (Spring 1997): 93–102.
3. See www.sugunapoultry.com/ for details on Suguna. Discussion on incentives schemes are based on the author's discussion with company officials.
4. V. Doctor, "Rushing into Retail," *Business World* (31 May, 1999).
5. Nikhil Sagar, "CPFR at Whirlpool Corporation: Two Heads and an Exception Engine," *The Journal of Business Forecasting* (Winter 2003–2004): 3–10.

## Further Reading

*Continuous Replenishment: An ECR Best Practices Report* (Washington, DC: Grocery Manufacturer's Association, 1994).

Voluntary Inter-industry Commerce Standards. *CPFR: An overview*, 2004.

Y. L. Doz, "The Evolution of Corporation in Strategic Alliances: Initial Conditions or Learning Process?" *Strategic Management Journal* (1997, Vol 17): 55–83.

# Supply Chain Restructuring

## Learning Objectives

After reading this chapter, you will be able to answer the following questions:

- What is supply chain restructuring?
- How is supply chain restructuring different from supply chain integration and optimization?
- What are the ways in which a supply chain can be restructured so as to improve its performance?
- What is postponement? What are the costs and benefits of postponement?
- How do firms decide optimal placement of inventory in the chain?

Priya is planning to buy her first notebook. She has carried out an extensive research on the best possible deals and has consulted everyone she could think of. Armed with advice from friends and family, Priya logs in to the Website of Dell Computers. Her father has handed her the details of his credit card and set no upper limit on the cost front. Priya was not prepared for the range of options that Dell offered her. Not one to be sidetracked by options that she did not want, Priya customized the configuration of her notebook in 30 minutes. As she keyed in the payment details, she figured that had she visited a store, it will have taken far more time. Dell acquired another customer for life.

Dell is famous for its ability to customize the product as per customer specifications at an optimum price. Every potential customer gets the message "Please proceed below to build your system. The price will automatically update as changes are made. Use the "Learn More" buttons to find out more information about any components. When you have completed your selection, please scroll down to the end of the page and click Continue".

Apart from seven base system choices and a choice of five operating system configurations, Dell allows the customer to choose displays and type of video cards. Dell also offers the customer two options for the warranty. Finally, the customer can choose from over a 1,000 possible configurations. Upon confirmation of the order, the product is delivered to the doorstep of the customer at a price that is lower or comparable to the price of a similar brand available at the local neighbourhood store. How is Dell able to offer such a wide array of choices at competitive prices?

In this chapter, we explore the answer to this question. We look at innovative concepts related to supply chain restructuring and the trade-offs involved therein. Many firms choose to offer high service at low cost using such innovations. We examine these innovations in detail.

# Introduction

In the current era of globalization, firms are under relentless pressure to continuously improve their supply chain performance so as to minimize cost and maintain high levels of customer service. In the last decade, several leading firms have reaped substantial benefits by working on initiatives involving supply chain integration and supply chain optimization. These initiatives have helped these firms in ensuring above-average business performance in their respective industry sectors. But in the last few years, leading firms have realized that initiatives involving supply chain integration and supply chain optimization are not enough for ensuring above-average business performance. These initiatives are necessary for the very survival of a firm. These do not ensure an above-average performance. Supply chain integration and related best practices have received adequate attention in the industry. These practices have percolated down from the best firms to emerge as necessary but insufficient conditions for firms to establish themselves as market leaders. They have realized that if they want to retain their leadership, they will have to go beyond these initiatives and look at ways in which they can restructure supply chain architecture and processes. Supply chain restructuring focuses on these innovative practices that separate leaders from the "also-ran" companies. Unlike supply chain integration and supply chain optimization, supply chain restructuring goes beyond supply chain function and requires integrating product and process engineering with supply chain function. Similarly, it may also involve closer integration between marketing and supply chain function.

Unlike other initiatives, supply chain restructuring focuses on questioning the existing processes and architecture of a chain. It essentially involves supply chain innovation involving one or all of the following measures so as to improve customer service and reduce costs: product redesign, process redesign, network design restructure and value offering to customer.

Before we discuss the restructuring of supply chain processes, we look at ways to map the existing supply chain processes. In the last part of the chapter, we turn our attention to examine and improve supply chain architecture.

# Supply Chain Mapping

Before a firm sets out to restructure its supply chain, it has to find a method to successfully capture and evaluate the existing supply chain processes. The method used to capture current supply chain processes is termed supply chain mapping.

As can be seen in Figure 10.1, existing supply chain processes can be characterized on the basis of the following dimensions:

- Shape of the value-addition curve
- Point of differentiation
- Customer entry point in the supply chain

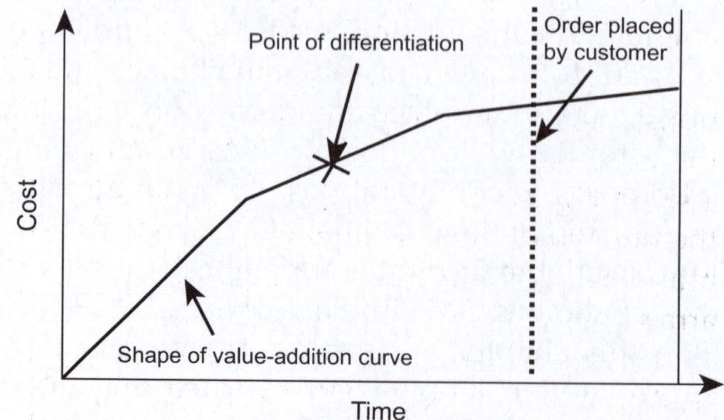


**Figure 10.1**

Supply chain mapping: existing position.

Restructuring of the supply chain process involves altering the supply chain on at least one the three dimensions. It may also involve altering more than one dimension of the supply chain process. We initially take one dimension at a time and later on discuss a specific innovation, which involves altering two dimensions in the process.

## *Value-addition Curve*

The supply chain encompasses all the activities/processes associated with the transformation of goods from the raw material stage to the final stage when the goods and services reach the end customer. A typical supply chain starts with some input material and information, which are transformed into the end product and delivered to the customer. This transformation involves a number of activities, with each activity taking time, incurring cost and adding value. One can debate on whether all activities add value or if there some activities that are non-value-added activities. At this stage, we assume that the firm has removed all non-value-added activities from the supply chain processes. On the $x$-axis we have the total time in a chain or the average flow time in the chain and on the $y$-axis we have the total cost (cumulative) in the chain.

To map this value-addition curve, we work backward from the time at which goods and services are delivered to the end customer and trace back all activities that were carried out to make the finished goods and service available. We map all the activities on two dimensions: time and cost. So the value-addition curve essentially captures the way we add cost over a period of time in supply chain processes. For example, a truck manufacturer receives engine castings from a casting supplier, which then wait till the machining operation is scheduled in the machine shop. After that operation the machined castings go to the intermediate store and later on are taken to the engine assembly stage. Then, the engine is mounted on a chassis in the truck assembly line and the finished truck is dispatched to the dealer. The finished truck will be available at dealer's warehouse till the end customer picks it up. In this simplified version of the process, apart from the conversion and transportation activities, the material in different forms waits at several stages: raw material store, intermediate store, finished good store and dealer warehouse. If we map all the operations (value-added and non-value-added activities), we will get a curve as shown in Figure 10.1. Obviously, since the $y$ axis is capturing cumulative costs, the value-addition curve is increasing with time.

## *Customer Entry Point in the Supply Chain*

The point at which a customer places an order is shown as a dotted line in Figure 10.1. In several industries customers expect material off the shelf in the neighbourhood retail store. In such a case, the customer entry point is at the end of chain and is the same as the delivery time. But in several industries it is not uncommon for customers to give some amount of delivery lead time and in such a case obviously the customer entry point will be ahead of the delivery time. This is similar to build-to-order or configure-to-order supply chain situations. Essentially, the customer entry point captures the order to delivery lead time. This dimension is important because all the operations before the customer order has to be done based on forecast, whereas after the customer order one will be working with actual orders. In other words, before the customer entry point all the activities are carried out based on forecast while subsequent activities are done based on order. As discussed in the chapter on demand forecasting, however good the forecasting process, as per the first law of forecasting, a forecast is always wrong. So if bulk of the activities can be carried out based on order rather than forecast one does not have to worry about the likely forecast error that is inherent in any forecasting exercise.

## Point of Differentiation

The concept of the point of differentiation is valid for any organization that is offering a variety of end products to customers. Products are made in a supply chain consisting of multiple stages. As the product moves in the chain, progressively, the product assumes an identity that is closer to the end product. The point of differentiation is a stage where the product gets identified as a specific variant of the end product. We will illustrate the concept using a toothpaste manufacturing firm. Let us assume that the firm offers variety only in pack sizes. In such a firm, the packing stage is a point of differentiation. At a packing station the same basic material, that is, toothpaste, is packed in sizes of varying dimensions. So till the packing station one has been working with the generic material, but at the packing station the firm has to make an irreversible decision in terms of committing the generic material to a specific product variant. Similarly, at a garment manufacturing firm, at the stitching stage the firm is committing the fabric to different sizes and styles of garment. In automobile manufacturing firms like Tata, where usually large variety is offered in terms of colours, the painting stage becomes the point of differentiation because at that stage the firm makes an irreversible decision about the colour of the car.

In reality, a firm may have multiple points of differentiation. For example, in the case of the garment manufacturer, the fabric dyeing and stitching stages represent two main points of differentiation. At the fabric dyeing stage, the garment firm makes an irreversible decision about colour, and at stitching stage the firm makes an irreversible decision about the style of the garment. Though it is not uncommon to have multiple points of differentiation in a firm, in our conceptual discussion we will focus on the main point of differentiation where significant variety explosion takes place in the firm.

As discussed in Chapter 7, forecasting at the variant level is quite difficult compared to forecasting at the aggregate level. So it is easier to forecast in terms of tons of toothpastes or number of cars or number of garments. But trying to forecast at specific pack size level for toothpastes, specific colour level for automobiles and specific style level for a garment is significantly more difficult.

Before the point of differentiation, one has to forecast at the aggregate level, whereas after the point of differentiation one has to work at the variant level. So the point of differentiation determines the point at which a firm is forced to forecast at the variant level. Further, the longer the time period for which you have to forecast, the higher the forecast error. So if the stage of supply chain at which the point of differentiation takes place is in the early stage of the supply chain one will have to forecast for a longer horizon at the variant level.

# Supply Chain Process Restructuring

Supply chain process restructuring involves playing around with at least one of the three dimensions of the supply chain in the direction as shown below:

- *Postpone the point of differentiation.* By moving the point of differentiation as much as possible, a bulk of the activities can be carried out using the aggregate-level forecast rather than the variant-level forecast.

- *Alter the shape of the value-addition curve.* Shift the bulk of the cost addition as late as possible. This will reduce the inventory in the chain and also help the firm in having some flexibility. If the bulk of the cost addition takes place at a later point in time in the chain, one will be in a position to respond to unforeseen changes with the least cost.

- *Advance the customer ordering point.* Move from an MTS to a CTO supply chain. By moving the customer ordering point as early as possible, one can carry out the bulk of the activities

**INTERVIEW WITH**

**SABYASACHI PATNAIK**

*Asian Paints is India's largest paint company and the third-largest paint company in Asia today, with a turnover of Rs 36.7 billion. Sabyasachi Patnaik is the General Manager, Manufacturing, for the Decorative Paint Business Unit (DBU) at Asian Paints.*

*What is the level of complexity of the supply chain at Asian Paints?*

**Sabyasachi Patnaik:** At DBU, we manage around 500-odd vendors, 5 main manufacturing plants, 13 processing centres, 7 regional distribution centres and 76 depots. We serve about 19,000 dealers who are spread all over the country. On the variety front, we have to manage 750 raw materials and packing materials and 1,500-odd inventoried SKUs at the FG level.

*What are the supply chain challenges that you face?*

**Sabyasachi Patnaik:** Increasingly our customers have become more demanding and as a result we are constantly expected to improve service levels. Further, we add 80–100 new SKUs every year. These new SKUs are more complex products requiring new materials and complex manufacturing processes but usually have lower volumes compared to our existing product lines. It is expected that our business should not only service a larger number of SKUs at higher service levels but also reduce costs related to the supply chain. So, unlike most other businesses, where chains have to be either efficient or responsive, we are expected to be responsive as well as efficient. How to manage this stretch is the most important challenge for supply chain managers at Asian Paints.

*What supply chain innovations have been adopted by Asian Paints?*

**Sabyasachi Patnaik:** We have been known for supply chain innovations in India. We aggressively took up the idea of postponing the tinting operations at the dealer end so that we could offer a large variety to customers without increasing the number of SKUs at the factory. Way back in 1998 we restructured ourselves and created different business units. In the business of decorative paints, we created a position of Vice President supply chain that is responsible for the end-to-end supply chain. We have been early users of information technology in India and we make sure that our information technology initiatives are driven by our business people. Our early investments in information technology has helped us in reducing forecast errors, reduced safety stocks and lowered the freight costs. In past few years, we have focused on improving our capabilities in manufacturing. We have implemented Six Sigma and other lean methodologies to improve quality, reduce cycle times and reduce rework.

To reduce our material costs we have focused on sourcing efficiency as well as on improving formulation efficiency. Hence, our material costs are probably the lowest in the industry. We also have reduced our working capital requirement by exploring ways in which we can get higher credit from suppliers and by reducing the FG and RM inventory levels. Optimal balancing has been done between higher creditors and material costs. I guess our main strength is quality of our execution.

*What are the future supply chain initiatives that the firm is working on?*

**Sabyasachi Patnaik:** With increased variety, we realize that holding stocks close to customers may not be the best option. We are exploring the idea of keeping stocks at central distribution centres (CDC) located close to the plant so that we can apply the idea of delayed differentiation and as a result improve responsiveness and also reduce rerouting, which increase supply chain costs. We also want to focus on extended supply chain where the focus will be on collaborations with our partners.

against an order, which reduces the importance of forecasting. If one were also able to postpone the point of differentiation, one will be able to move from an MTS to a CTO supply chain. In a CTO supply chain, since the point of differentiation takes place after customer order, one does not have to prepare a variant-level forecast.

Before we get into a detailed discussion about supply chain restructuring, it will be important to compare it against supply chain integration and supply chain optimization. As can be seen in Figure 10.2, supply chain integration and supply chain optimization focus on lowering the value-addition curve. This results in overall reduction in cost and time and will result in an absolute shift in the point of differentiation but the relative position of the point of differentiation does not change. Unlike these two approaches, supply chain restructuring affects the shape of the value-addition curve, shifts customer ordering, or shifts the point of differentiation. This

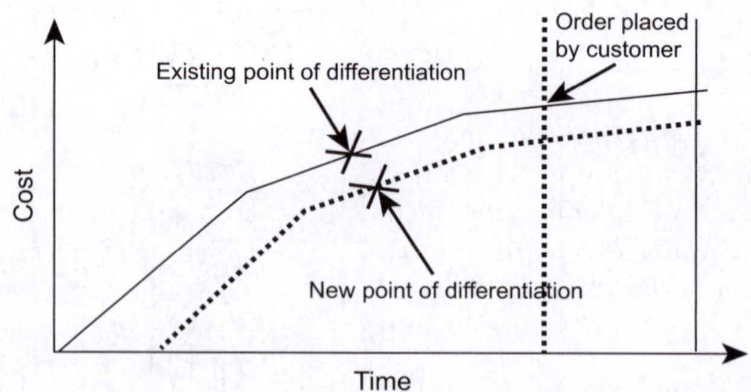


**Figure 10.2**

Impact of supply chain integration/optimization.

will essentially require supply chain process restructuring and may also involve a change in product design or a change in the product service bundle offered to customers. Supply chain restructuring is likely to bring in substantial business benefits in general and in special cases it fundamentally changes the way in which the supply chain is managed by moving from the MTS to the CTO business model.

In next few sections we discuss each of these supply chain process restructuring ideas in greater detail.

# Postpone the Point of Differentiation

Delaying an operational process that results in variety explosion or customization to a later point in the supply chain postpones the point of product differentiation. Delaying the differentiating operations, apart from reducing inventories, also reduces the time period for which one has to carry out forecasting at the variant level and thereby reduces inventory and improves customer service and reduces product obsolescence.

## *Postponement Case Studies*

We illustrate the concept of postponement in this section using several examples. In each of these examples, the firm in question has implemented the postponement strategy in a different way.

### Hewlett-Packard: Postponement of Product Differentiation

A classic case of postponement strategy employment is that of Hewlett-Packard (HP). Late in the 1980s, HP faced inventories mounting into billions of dollars and alarming customer dissatisfaction with its order fulfilment process. The case of a computer peripheral product has been cited extensively in supply chain management literature to show how HP has employed the postponement strategy to reduce inventory and improve order fulfilment. This product is produced in the Vancouver plant in the United States and sells in Europe and North America. Within Europe each country has its own specifications in terms of voltage, plug size and manual requirements. Earlier, under the old design the product differentiation in terms of customization for a given country used to take place within the plant. A product had a dedicated power supply of 110 V or 220 V, which immediately differentiated the product by end customer market as soon as production began. Under the improved design, a universal power supply that works in all countries is built into the product. The product is not differentiated until it is shipped against customer order from DC close to customer destination. The additional benefit of the universal power supply is that HP can easily tranship products from one continent to another when significant imbalance of demand and supply exists between geographical regions.

## Asian Paints: Postponement for Managing Product Variety in the Chain

Asian Paints is an Indian paint manufacturing firm that has employed the postponement strategy successfully in its emulsions product category. Asian Paints offers four emulsion brands. In turn, each brand offers 150–250 shades. Offering a wide variety of colour shades is essential in the emulsions market. An emulsion comprises of a "base" and a combination of "stainers". The base provides the functional aspects while the stainers provide the required shade. The base accounts for 99 per cent of the final emulsion volume. A wide range of shades is developed using just 10 stainers. At Asian Paints, the mixing of the base and the stainers, also known as "tinting", is carried out at the various sales points (SPs) distributed across the country. On an average, there is one SP for every 400 retailers. At the retailer point, the customer chooses from a range of 150–250 shades. The retailer immediately forwards this order to his SP. The effective time for tinting is about 10 minutes. The customer collects the shade of his choice within 1–2 days of placing his order. Except for certain fast-moving shades, the inventory at the SP is mainly bases and stainers. The SPs order these periodically from their designated regional distribution centres (RDCs). The factory warehouses replenish the RDC inventories periodically. The periodicity of ordering depends on the demand volumes. The RDC lead times (factory to RDC) are in the range of 2 weeks to 1 month while the SP lead times (RDC to SP) are in the range of 1–2 days. Thus, the delivery period will have been close to a month had the tinting operation taken place at the factory itself. Tinting is a low-technology operation, due to low capital expenditure and simplicity. The delayed differentiation due to postponement of the tinting operation has reduced the inventory levels drastically. The customer service is high due to the reduced delivery period. Forecasting errors are also reduced considerably. There is no loss of scale economies owing to the postponement of the tinting operation. Being a simple operation, product quality is not diluted due to the transfer of the operation from the factory to the SPs. Asian Paints revolutionized the postponement concept in the Indian paint industry. Asian Paints has been offering substantially higher number of shades and is maintaining its finished goods inventories at about 60 per cent of the industry average. This has helped them to maintain profitability that is consistently higher than the industry average, and has probably contributed to increasing its market share over a period of time. Other firms are also following suit. Jenson & Nicholson (India), through its "Instacolour" scheme, is taking postponement strategy to a higher level by carrying out tinting operation at the retailer points. Of course, you cannot install a mixing machine in every retailer but for large retailers it is economical to shift the tinting operation at the retail level so that mixing can be done after getting an order. We can say that for those retail points where mixing is done after getting an order the retailers have managed to move to the CTO model from the MTS model.

## Benetton: Postponement by Re-sequencing of Processes

Major apparel manufacturer Benetton has employed the postponement strategy by re-sequencing the dyeing and knitting operations. Earlier; the firm used to dye the yarn and then undertake knitting. Being in a fashion business, they found colour was the main fashion element and it was difficult to forecast about the style without too much error. Stitching takes longer and dyeing takes lesser time. Benetton realized that it could reduce inventories and become more responsive by reversing the dyeing–knitting sequence in a single-colour garment case. Presently, for the single-colour garment portfolio Benetton stocks un-dyed garments that are dyed after the start of the selling season when more information on customer preferences is available. Of course, this required technology solution at the dyeing stage that ensured that dyeing of the garment results in same quality of shade as obtained by dyeing of the thread.

## Postponement for Reducing Transportation Cost

Usually, postponing of the assembly process is carried out for shifting the point of differentiation to a later stage. But there have also been cases where firms have used the postponement strategy for delaying an operational process to a later point in the supply chain in order to reduce transportation costs. Transportation cost is reduced in the case of bulky finished products by shifting the assembly operations to the customer end as transporting parts as kits is cheaper than transporting a finished product.

### Postponement in Bicycle Industry

The bicycle industry in India belongs to a category of industries that traditionally practices the postponement strategy. The reasons for this practice are as follows:

- To reduce transport complexities and costs. The bicycle manufacturers limit their activities to production of frames, handle bars and transmission parts. Other suppliers produce the tyres, tubes, seats and many extra fittings. A large number of bicycle dealers stock products of all bicycle manufacturers. The bicycle purchasing process is as follows: when the customer arrives at the bicycle shop, she/he opts for a particular frame size offered by a particular bicycle manufacturer. Similarly, she/he will opt for a particular tyre size, offered by a particular tyre manufacturer and so on. Given this situation, it is imperative that the assembly of the final product is carried out at the dealer point. Additionally, the entire assembly takes just 15–30 minutes.
- Less exposure to damage than when transported as fully assembled bicycles.
- Less need for shop space when material is stocked as components instead of as fully assembled bicycles.
- Low-technology nature of the assembly operation, which ensures there are no inconsistencies in product quality.

Though the bicycle industry has worked on the idea of postponement of assembly so as to primarily reduce transportation cost, they can also take advantage of this strategy and offer higher variety. The bicycle industry can design a modular-level variety and allow customers to choose a combination of modules and the retailer can assemble the bicycle, which is essentially configured to customer requirements. This facilitates the bicycle industry's transition to a mass-customization environment.

## Problems with Implementing the Postponement Strategy

The examples cited above help in understanding the industrial and technological characteristics that make the postponement strategy viable. In general, postponement strategy is likely to be advantageous in the following situations:

- High level of product customization
- Existence of modularity in product design
- High uncertainty in demand
- Long transport lead time
- Short lead time of postponed operation
- Low value addition in transportation
- High value addition in postponed operation
- Difference in tariff rates for components and finished goods in different markets.

From the above list modular product design and high uncertainty deserve special attention. However, the benefits achieved due to quick response to customers, reduction of inventory carrying costs and transportation costs have to be measured against the possible disadvantages:

- Loss in scale economies of the operations postponed.
- In certain cases, the loss of control on the postponed operations may also be highly detrimental to the firm's interests. Transferring critical operations from the central factory to the dealer point may result in dilution of the product quality.

An intangible issue a firm has to consider while evaluating the postponement strategy is the impact on relationships with other members in the supply chain.

Because of globalization, companies are serving large geographical markets and as a result have to carry large amount of FG inventory. Apart from these issues firms also have to grapple with the recent trend towards greater customization. Firms in many industries are introducing new products more regularly than ever before. They are also striving to reduce costs and delivery times and increase flexibility.

# Changing the Shape of the Value-addition Curve

Ideally one will like to alter the shape of the value-addition curve so that the bulk of the cost gets added as late as possible (as shown in Figure 10.3). To understand the difference between the existing value-addition curve and the proposed value-addition curve, we need to classify activities as cost intensive or time intensive. Activities that consume much cost but very little time will be identified as cost-intensive activities, whereas activities that require a long time but incur very little costs will be termed as time-intensive activities This will require us to sequence processes in a way that time-intensive processes are scheduled first and cost-intensive processes are scheduled at a later stage. In other words, one can take cost per unit time as an attribute of activities in the supply chain and arrange activities in ascending order of the same. In general, one works with a belief that technology dictates the sequence of processes within a supply chain. As a result, one assumes that the shape of the value-addition curve cannot be altered, as one cannot change the sequence of operations. This is not strictly true.

In the previous section, we have seen a large number of cases where firms have managed to alter the sequence of activities so that they could postpone the point of differentiation. We also looked at re-sequencing between delivery and assembly process to postpone the point of differentiation. The focus in the earlier section was on the postponement of the point of differentiation, while in this section we examine the cost- and time-related attributes of the process. We illustrate the example of Reliance Infocomm, which managed to come up with an innovative idea through which they could alter the shape of the value-addition curve. All telecom

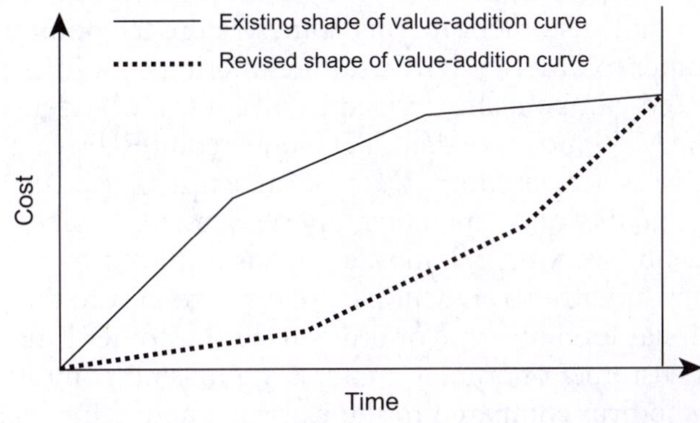


**Figure 10.3**

Impact of the change in the shape of the value-addition curve.

companies have laid fibre optic networks across the country. This usually involves substantial capital expenditure with significant amount of time. The standard process followed by telecom operators like Tata Teleservices and BSNL is as shown below:

| Sequence | Activity | Remark |
|---|---|---|
| 1 | Procuring optical cable | Cost intensive |
| 2 | Obtaining right of way | |
| 3 | Trenching | Time intensive |
| 4 | Laying of cable | |
| 5 | Start the network | |

As we can see from the table given above, a typical telecomm company carries out the cost-intensive process like procuring cable first and carries out the time-intensive process at a later stage. As a result, the bulk of the project cost is incurred at an early stage and the value-addition curve is quite similar to that of existing value-addition curve shown in Figure 10.3. Reliance Infocomm followed a different process in laying the fibre optic cables. Reliance Infocomm has questioned this sequencing of the processes and has re-sequenced activities so that cost-intensive operations are postponed as late as possible. Instead of buying optical cables first, they bought the cables almost at the end. At the time of trenching they do not lay cable but a conduit is laid, which has openings at several places through which cable can be inserted at a later stage. Compared to cable, the cost of conduits is very low and this innovation allows them to postpone buying of cable, which is a cost-intensive process. After completing the time-intensive process of trenching, optical fibre cables are procured and cables are laid and the network is ready for operations.

In general, by questioning activities from time and cost angles, one can examine opportunities for re-sequencing of activities so as to achieve a substantial change in the value-addition curve in the desired direction. In the process, even if costs go up marginally, it may be still worthwhile. For example, in the Reliance Infocomm case they incurred additional costs of conduits but the benefit achieved by changing the shape of the curve outweighed the additional costs involved in the modified process.

## Advance the Customer Ordering Point: Move from MTS to CTO Supply Chain

Moving from the MTS to the CTO supply chain is very attractive to firms because the firm no longer has to forecast at the variant level. As discussed earlier, forecasting at the variant level is quite difficult compared to forecasting at the aggregate level. In a CTO supply chain, variant-level decisions are made based on order rather than forecast. This is appealing to firms because significant inaccuracy in forecast creeps in when firms try to forecast at the variant level.

If the firm wants to move from the MTS to the CTO model, it will have to get the customer to advance his order so that customer ordering comes before the point of differentiation. How does one get the customer to order early? Customer offering by a firm consists of a bundle of product and services and can be characterized by five attributes, delivery time being one of them. Moving from the MTS model to the CTO model requires altering customer offering in a way that the longer delivery time is compensated by an extra offering on any of the four remain attributes: cost, variety, quality and supplementary services. Of course, if a firm wants the customer to accept a longer delivery time, it must compensate the customer by offering something more on the other four dimensions. Essentially, one has to ensure that the revised bundle of offering results in a similar level of value or utility to the customer if not higher than the value offered by the current customer offering. Of course, there is no point in offering a bundle that will increase costs to the firm compared to the existing bundle. Innovative firms have played with customer offering by understanding their own cost structures and customer utility functions. Understanding how different attributes of customer offering affects the value and utility of the customer segment is of crucial importance in this exercise.

## Altering Customer Offering Bundle

Customer offering consists of a bundle of product and services and can be characterized using the following five attributes:

- *Cost.* Cost incurred by the customer to own and experience the product service bundle.
- *Delivery time.* Time taken from customer order to delivery.
- *Product variety.* Range of choices offered to the customer. Customization is the highest form of variety where product and services are tailored as per customer requirements.
- *Quality.* Quality attribute captures product features, performance and reliability.
- *Supplementary services.* Set of supplementary services that surround core product offering to enhance the value to customer.

A firm chooses a bundle of product and service by making appropriate choices on the above five attributes. Depending on the market segment one has to understand the utility functions of the customer set and choose the appropriate bundle. There is a trade-off involved in choices of attributes, and understanding of the relative importance given by customers to the various attributes will help the firm in making appropriate choices.

Each of these attributes has multiple dimensions, and understanding of the customer segment will help in choosing the appropriate dimensions within each attribute. The choice of the attributes set, and within that the choice of the relevant dimensions has implications for supply chain design and operations. We will try and understand this issue through a couple of examples.

- *Customer order delivery time.* In general, one assumes that the lower the delivery time the better the service. At Aravind Eye Care Hospital, the management decided to reduce the time taken from order to delivery, for spectacles. After diagnosis, if the patient wanted to buy the spectacles, Aravind wanted to ensure that they could deliver spectacles with appropriate lenses within 45 minutes from order. At a later stage they realized that faster delivery was not really valued by most of their customers. Bulk of their customers came from towns, and patients prefer to make an extra visit to collect spectacles rather than wait for 45 minutes at the hospital. Similarly, Tanishq, the jewellery manufacturing business unit of Titan, found that for products like rings, where customers make impulse purchases, keeping products on the shelf and offering practically zero delivery time is extremely important to customers. But for customers who are buying necklace worth Rs 50,000, immediate product delivery was not a very important attribute as necklace buying was a planned purchase for some important event like a wedding in the family. So it is possible to explore the possibility of moving from the MTO to the CTO supply chain for necklace category of products. For a pizza company short delivery time is extremely valuable as it cannot expect customers to give them a lead time beyond 20–30 minutes, whereas a company catering to institutional markets can expect orders well in advance. Choosing the right delivery time is a strategic decision, which affects the supply chain design issues in a significant way.

- *Product variety/customization.* In general, customers prefer more variety, but offering higher variety increases production and distribution costs for firms. Managing product variety by understanding the cost and profit implications of variety is an important management decision. For example, an automobile like Mercedes E-class has 3.9 trillion variants while Honda Accord has only 408. It has been found that customers seem to focus only on body style, exterior colour and type of radio as critical input to decision making. Now any attempt at offering a variety on features that are not important to the customer will add manufacturing and distribution complexity without adding any revenue or profit potential. On the same line P&G has in the last decade decided to cut down variety of offering so as to reduce its supply chain related cost.

- *Cost and product/service features.* Cost includes the total cost incurred in procurement as well as consumption over the life cycle of the product. Even the cost of product acquisition involves multiple dimensions. For example, while acquiring a product, a customer may find that prices are lower at Big Bazaar compared to the neighbourhood retail store, but the customer may have to incur additional travel time and cost to reach Big Bazaar. Different customer segments may value disutility involved in travelling to Big Bazaar at different rates. Further, customer segments from the lower-income strata may have tight budget constraints and will buy products of small pack sizes and may be willing to pay a higher cost per unit for the product, whereas customers from the higher-income strata will be willing to buy larger packs so that they have to visit stores less often and in the process may be paying lower prices per unit of consumption. In emerging economies like India, a substantial part of the customer segment is at the bottom of pyramid. These customer segments have tight budget constraints and uncertain income streams. As a result, the Indian market has seen a phenomenon of sachet packaging in several product categories. For example, single-use sachets have dominated the shampoo market. Similarly, in mobile markets the customers want to work with prepaid mobile schemes so that they are able to control their expenses. Further, since their income streams are uncertain they prefer smaller denomination prepaid vouchers for mobile telephone services even if it results in high cost per unit of consumption. Better understanding of customers will help firms in making the right decisions in the supply chain related decisions like location of outlets and appropriate pack mix offering. These decisions have significant impact on the supply chain performance of the firm.

## Illustrative Case Studies

Several firms have moved from the MTS model to the CTO model. We illustrate the approach used by the successful firms with a few examples.

### Dell Computers

A company that practises the CTO strategy in an innovative manner is Dell Computers, a $12 billion company catering largely to the needs of corporate customers. The ingenious process helps Dell Computers in containing the order lead time to one week and inventories to just seven days. Inventory figures are significantly lower than the industry average, providing a formidable competitive advantage. Dell Computers have managed to change customer offering in the computer industry and has managed to work with the CTO model when most of the other firms in the industry work with the MTO model. Competitors like Lenova or HP have traditionally worked with the MTS approach where the manufacturer makes products available on the shelf, while customers of Dell get delivery of their products seven days after placing their orders. Of course, one will like to ask why customers should be willing to give seven days to Dell when it expects immediate delivery from HP or Lenova. It is because Dell is able to offer customization where the customer can configure his PC or notepad and the customer values this offering of customization. As a result he does not mind waiting for seven days even though competitors can offer competing products with practically zero delivery time. This strategy helps Dell in reducing inventory in the supply chain system by significant order of magnitude. Dell gets two levels of benefits, it has to keep inventory at its plants only unlike its competitors who have to provide finished goods at major distribution points in the globe, and it has to keep component inventory while competitors have to keep finished goods inventory, which is more expensive in nature. To understand the impact of centralization of inventory, let us take the case of Dell, which has to keep inventory only at its manufacturing plants: five locations around the world. However, companies like HP and IBM have to keep inventory in at least 100 distribution points so that it can make its products available with very little delivery time. As we had discussed in the inventory management chapter, by centralizing inventory at five places rather than at 100 places as is the case with HP, the company will be able to reduce inventory in the supply chain by $\sqrt{20}$ times, which is about four to five times lower than the competitors. Dell has a modular design, which allows them to respond with lower monetary value tied up in inventory. So it is not unusual that Dell managed with about seven days of inventory whereas the industry works with about 35 days of inventory in the supply chain.

### National Panasonic Bicycle Case

Panasonic bicycle factory is directly linked to the customer via retail outlets. It has the Panasonic Ordering System (POS), wherein the customer can choose from about eight million possible variations based on model types, colour frame sizes and other features. Their production process begins after the arrival of the customer's order and specifications. Once the individualized bicycle order is produced, the bicycle is shipped the same day. The company has invested in computer integrated manufacturing and in robots. Since the assembly process is labour intensive and does not usually require too much set up in changing from one variant to another, it is comparatively easy to offer customization in the assembly process. Most of the component manufacturing processes have larger set up time and also quality control issues, so the firm has invested heavily in manufacturing process technologies. For example, the company has invested in robots for painting and three-dimensional automatic measuring machine to automate the verification task. Each bicycle frame and fork has to be manufactured and tested for the customer's specifications. Advanced manufacturing processes at Panasonic reduces setup time with a result that it can work with a batch of one and also reduce the process time. Custom-made bicycles are priced about 20–30 percent higher than comparable standard bicycles.

## *Moving from MTS to CTO: Alternative Approaches*

So far we have discussed the idea of advancing the customer entry point before the point of differentiation. But firms can simultaneously work on advancing the customer order and postponing the point of differentiation so that the combined effect will help them in getting the desired result. It is possible that both ideas individually may not help the firm in moving from the MTS model to the CTO model, but the combination of both movements, that is, leftward movement of the customer entry point and rightward movement of the point of differentiation, jointly might ensure that the modified customer entry point is ahead of the modified point of differentiation. It is illustrated in diagrammatical form in Figure 10.4. Both Dell Computers and National Panasonic Bicycle have focused on customer entry point as well as on post-differentiation supply chain processes.

Advancing the customer entry point involves changing the product bundle offering to the customer, and postponing the point of differentiation involves change in product and process

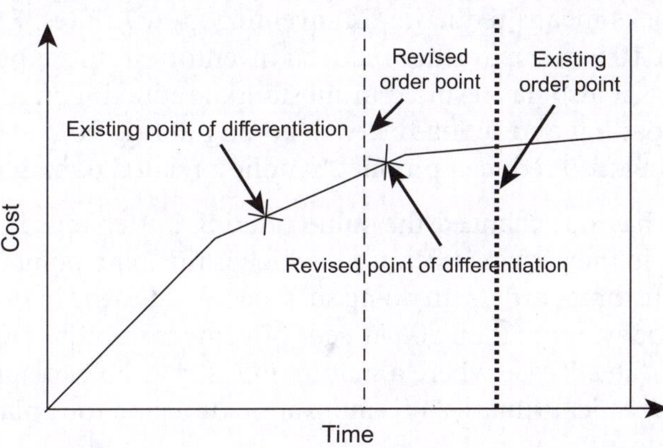


**Figure 10.4**

Move from MTS to CTO.

design. But one can also think of an alternative way in which a firm can move to CTO model without a change in product/process design or change in customer offering. If a firm can manage post-processes in a time-efficient manner one might be able to reduce the time taken in order delivery time by a significant amount and the firm may be able to operate with the CTO supply chain model.

### Cement Industry: Moving from MTS to CTO by Focusing on Post-differentiation Processes

Dalmia cement traditionally used to be in the MTS market where it used to serve its dealers from seven depots that used to maintain stocks for the 10 variants offered by the company. In the cement industry, dealers usually place an order for truckloads of cement bags and expect delivery with 24 hours. Dalmia used to offer three basic types of cement and it used to get packed in different packing media like paper and polythene of different colours, resulting in the company offering 10 different variants in the market place. Since the company has its plant in Trichi and markets its products only in Kerala and Tamil Nadu, it decided to explore the possibility of moving from the MTS model to the pack to order (PTO) business model. Packing in the cement industry is similar to an assembly process where the packaging material and 50 kg of cement gets assembled. This makes PTO similar to CTO in standard engineering industry. Since the transportation time for the farthest dealer was less than 12 hours, managing an order delivery time of 24 hours was a feasible option and so Dalmia wanted to explore this option. A PTO business model will have the following key elements:

- Cement will be stocked only at a centralized place (at the plant) rather than at the seven depots and will be stocked as three variants (three basic types of cement) in silos.
- Cement will get packed in appropriate packing media after getting a firm dealer order and will be dispatched directly to the dealer warehouse using truck as a mode of transport.
- Obviously Dalmia had to tighten the whole lot of processes and change packing schedule. To ensure delivery reliability to its dealers they had to prioritize customer orders based on travel time required in transportation. Orders from the farthest distance will get higher priority at the packing station. Earlier, the company used to focus a lot on labour efficiency at the packing stations, now the focus has shifted to flexibility. The packing schedule has been changed in a dynamic fashion based on actual customer order arrival. Further, as customer orders do not arrive in uniform fashion they need to work with surplus capacity in the packaging system. Earlier packaging and despatching from the plant was delinked from customer orders, whereas now these processes are tightly linked to customer order receipts on a real-time basis. Further, Dalmia does not own its fleet and so has to align transporters' processes with its own processes.
- Centralizing stocks means reduction in inventory by $\sqrt{7}$ times. Further, stocking three varieties against 10 variants further reduced inventory in the supply chain. Apart from inventory savings it also has resulted in substantial reduction in material handling costs because every loading and unloading was adding about Rs 2 to the cost of each bag. Reduced handling also reduced product handling related damages.

Here, the company has not changed the value offering but changed its processes in a way that it is in a position to do the packing operation, which is the main point of differentiation for a company, after getting customer orders. In doing so, it has avoided the intermediate step of stocking cement in depots. Today, more than 50 per cent of cement in India moves through the PTO model. Dalmia demonstrates a case where a mature industry is able to apply very sophisticated processes in less than a decade. Primarily, this innovation diffusion took place because of the cost pressure faced by the industry.

## Moving from the MTS to the CTO Model: The Role of Innovations and Experimentations

In general, it is important to understand that the value addition offered should be appreciated by customers so that they do not mind giving a little more delivery time, but this extra value offering should not result in an excessive cost burden to the company.

For example, in one of our discussions with a heavy commercial vehicle manufacture company, one of the senior executives of the company came up with a brilliant idea of customer offering. In India, the transport industry is in the unorganized sector. Entrepreneurs who individually own less than four trucks own 85 per cent of the trucks. So the typical end customer for this truck manufacturing company is not a large trucking company but an entrepreneur who wants to get into the transport service business or an entrepreneur who has only one or two trucks with him. Now most of the small-time entrepreneurs believe in numerology wherein they will really like to have a vehicle chassis number that matches their own numerology numbers. If this end customer is given the value offering wherein one can promise to match his numerology number with truck chassis number he will be willing to give a longer delivery time to the truck manufacturing firm and the firm can move from the MTS model to the CTO business model. A couple of years back this truck manufacturing firm would not have been in a position to offer this service, but today with ERP in place the company will have no difficulty in offering such a service and such a service will not result in additional cost on the part of the company. It is important to understand consumer behaviour and find out what offerings they value. For example, a company has tried to move into the CTO model by offering higher discounts. The company should do a hard cost–benefit analysis before offering this kind of scheme to customers, but a better approach will be to offer something that does not cost much but is still valued by the customer.

Titan figured out that for customers who are buying necklace worth Rs 50,000, immediate product delivery is not very important as necklace purchase is usually planned for some important event like a wedding in the family. So it is exploring the possibility of moving from the MTS to the CTO market in the necklace category of products. It first toyed with the idea of offering images (photographs) of necklace designs to potential customers. It soon realized that customers wanted to touch and feel the product. Women wanted to wear the product and see for themselves the match between product and personality. So Titan realized that it had to offer a physical product, which does not however have to be a real diamond. So it is experimenting with the idea of prototypes made of gold plated material studded with artificial diamonds, which are kept in retail outlets. This reduces inventory and obsolescence costs for the jewellery manufacturer and at the same time help the firm in offering a larger variety to customers. Retail outlets will stock only prototypes and the customer will get delivery within 1 week. Titan will keep component inventory at a centralized place and will assemble the final product after getting the firm order and courier the same to the respective retail outlet.

It is important that firms encourage experimentation because when one is dealing with customers it is not exactly predictable how they would respond to altered offerings. Like all new products, one has to do a market survey and test out in a few areas. And may be one in five such ideas will work. But given the benefit of the CTO model to a firm which offers higher variety, it is worth encouraging experimentation in the firm.

## Restructuring the Supply Chain Architecture

Architecture in the chain is constituted by the way in which material flow takes place and the position at which the material is placed in the chain. We will discuss specifically two different ways in which architecture gets restructured:

• *Restructure flow in chain.* Differential material flow for different category of goods. Usually, within a firm all products within the same business go through similar flows. But one can restructure a chain so that different materials go through different kinds of flow. Depending on the nature of item one can design differential flow. We illustrate through an example of HUL, wherein the firm has created different material flows for different categories of items such as fast-moving goods and slow-moving goods. Similarly, in the service chain, depending on the priority of customers, stocking policies (where to stock the items) and mode of transport will be different for different categories of customers.

• *Restructure placement of inventory in chain.* A typical supply chain consists of processes and a set of decoupling inventory nodes. Restructuring of placement of inventory questions the existing location of inventory, the given current demand structure, time and cost characteristics of the process and evaluates alternative options.

## Restructure Flow in the Chain: Hindustan Unilever Case[1]

HUL, the largest Indian FMCG company, had until 1997 the typical supply chain and logistics problem as that of an FMCG organization handling several thousand tons of several hundred SKUs and interacting with a large number of third-party intermediaries. It was incurring significant costs in moving its product from its plants to shop shelves without any certainty of delivering the products. This cost included intermediary margins, cost of logistics, cost of inventory holding, and the stockout cost on failing to deliver the products.

This led to the drive to restructure HUL's supply chain into a customer-driven supply chain management in 1997. To start with HUL took stock of the factors in the existing supply chain for its health and personal care (HPC) business (Figure. 10.5).

HUL realized that the HPC business had some high-volume SKUs (A-category packs) and some low-volume SKUs (B-category packs). To ensure transportation cost efficiencies all the products were moved on truckload basis from plants to depots. Now this was okay for fast-moving A-category products but when it came to B-category products, direct shipment from plants to depots resulted in high stocks and stockout situations at the depot level. For example, let us say a depot needs about one truckload of Dove soap once a month. Since slow-moving SKUs were served directly from the plant, the depot will have to keep an average stock of 15 days plus about an additional week's stock as safety stock. Now HUL decided to redesign the system. As shown in Figure 10.6, all the fast-moving items are shipped directly to depots but all slow-moving products are first shipped to a buffer depot, and are consolidated for every depot. In the re-engineered and integrated supply chain, redistribution centres were established which had buffer B-category items to be supplied to the JIT depot on a continuous replenishment basis along with other B-category items supplied from the other factories. The indents for replenishment plans for B-category items were drawn on the basis of data from JIT depots on a daily basis (shown in Figure 10.6).

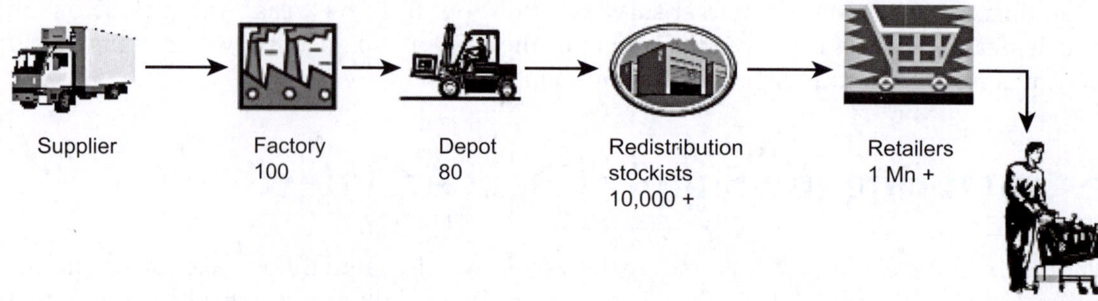


**Figure 10.5**

The supply chain in HUL.

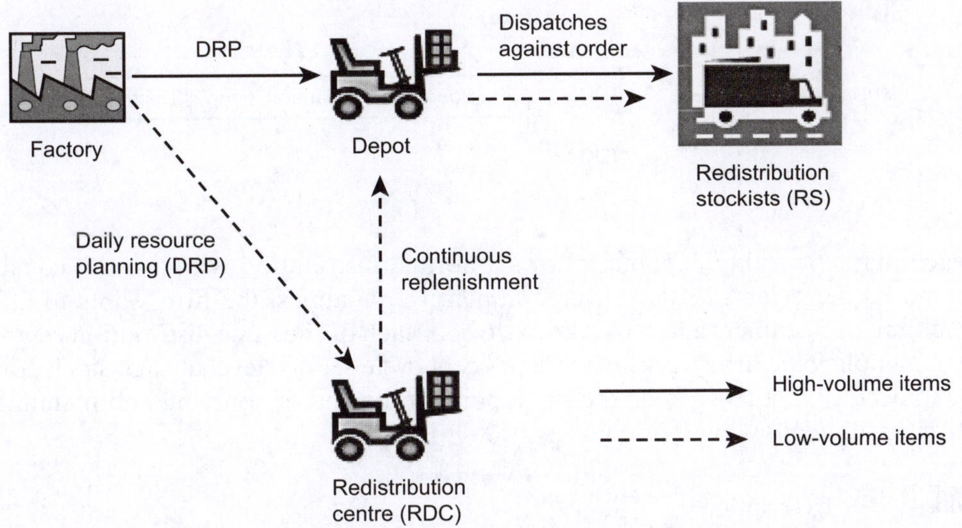


**Figure 10.6**

Re-engineering the supply chain at HUL.

HUL added four buffer depots in Maharashtra, Karnataka, West Bengal and Uttar Pradesh, one for each region, to its existing 50 distribution centres that could continuously replenish low-volume (B category) items to the JIT depots.

Having adopted this restructured supply chain system, the buffer depots keep 4–5 days inventory.

So we go back to Dove case, which now has a lower inventory. In the earlier system HUL used to work with about 15–20 days of inventory. However, now about five days at the buffer depot and an additional two days at the JIT depot are sufficient for the product to reach the dealer. This ensures that the total inventory for such a slow-moving item has dropped from 15–20 days to about seven days, and also increases service levels to the dealers.

## Restructure Placement of Inventory in the Chain

A supply chain network consists of processes and a set of inventory nodes. Usually, the network gets evolved over a period of time and periodically a company should explore the possibility of restructuring the network by re-examining inventory placement in chain.

A decoupling inventory is an inventory that permits the downstream portion of the supply chain to operate independently from the upstream portion. Where to place this decoupling stock is a decision that is strategic in nature. Every stock point has a demand process and a supply process and the network consists of processes and stock point nodes. Processes could be either conversion processes or transportation processes. Each process has a lead time and a corresponding cost associated with the process. For a given set of processes in the supply chain, identifying the optimum number and placement of decoupling nodes is not a trivial decision.

### Illustration

Consider a case of a manufacturing firm with a supply chain consisting one plant and three distribution centres. As shown in Figure 10.7, the firm has three processes: sourcing, conversion and distribution. The lead time and the cost associated with each process are as follows:

| Process | Lead time in weeks | Value addition at process (Rs) | Cumulative value (Rs) |
|---|---|---|---|
| Sourcing | 1 | 50 | 50 |
| Manufacturing | 1 | 25 | 75 |
| Distribution | 1 | 25 | 100 |

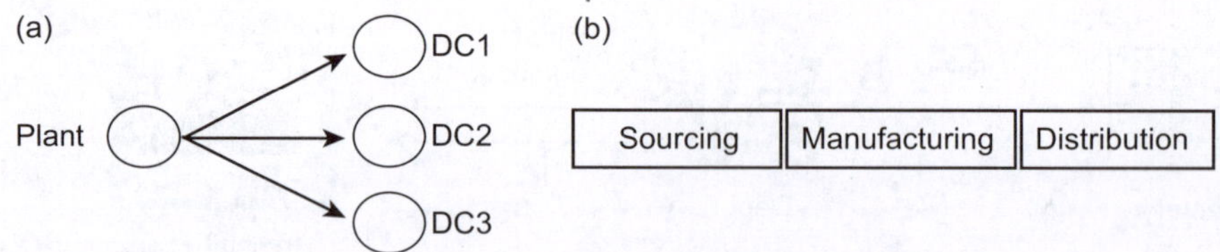


**Figure 10.7**

(a) Supply chain structure. (b) Supply chain process.

In each market, weekly demand follows a normal distribution with a mean equal to 300 and a standard deviation of 100. Given competitive dynamics, the firm wants to offer very short lead time to customers and has to keep stock at each of the three distribution centres. As a management policy the firm works with 98 per cent cycle service level at each stock point. The firm has to decide whether to keep the stock point at the end of sourcing and manufacturing. So the firm has the following four choices:

| Options | Description |
|---|---|
| (0, 0, 1) | No decoupling points |
| (0, 1, 1) | One decoupling point at the end of the manufacturing process |
| (1, 0, 1) | One decoupling point at the end of the sourcing process |
| (1, 1, 1) | Two decoupling points at the end of the sourcing and manufacturing processes |

The end of each process is a potential decoupling stock point and since the firm has three processes each option is captured by a triplet (as shown in the above table). Each element within the triplet denotes the position of the stock points in the system: 0 denotes absence of stock point and 1 denotes presence of stock point.

For a given process, the pipeline inventory will be same in each of the four options but the total value of safety stocks in system will vary in each of the four options.

## Optimum Safety Stock Locations in the Chain

Given the lead time and cost associated with each process one can determine the supply lead time and demand distributions at each of the stock point for each of the four options. The same is presented in the table below.

| Option | Stock point at the end of sourcing | | | Stock point at the end of manufacturing | | | Stock point at the end of distribution (at each market) | | |
|---|---|---|---|---|---|---|---|---|---|
| | Supply LT (L) | Mean demand | SD of demand | Supply LT (L) | Mean demand | SD of demand | Supply LT (L) | Mean demand | SD of demand |
| (0, 0, 1) | | | | | | | 3 | 300 | 100 |
| (0, 1, 1) | | | | 2 | $300 \times 3$ | $100 \times \sqrt{3}$ | 1 | 300 | 100 |
| (1, 0, 1) | 1 | $300 \times 3$ | $100 \times \sqrt{3}$ | — | — | — | 2 | 300 | 100 |
| (1, 1, 1) | 1 | $300 \times 3$ | $100 \times \sqrt{3}$ | 1 | $300 \times 3$ | $100 \times \sqrt{3}$ | 1 | 300 | 100 |

For the stock point at the end of manufacturing under option (0, 1, 1), the lead time will be 2 weeks and the demand will be aggregated across three markets so that it will observe a demand distribution with a mean of 900 and a standard deviation of $100 \times \sqrt{3}$. The coefficient of variation (ratio of standard deviation to mean) at the market is 0.33, while the same at other stock points is 0.19245. Aggregation of demand across markets results in lower coefficient of variation, which in turn results in lower inventory at the plant compared to the market. This is because of the aggregation of demand phenomenon (as discussed in Chapter 4).

As discussed in the inventory chapter, safety stock in units is equal to $K\sqrt{L}\sigma_d$. Taking $K = 2$ for the cycle service level at 98 per cent we can determine safety stock in units for each

*Table 10.1:* ***Safety stock comparisons for four options.***

| Option | | Safety stock at sales point at the end of sourcing | Safety stock at sales point at the end of manufacturing | Safety stock at sales point at the end of distribution | Total | Relative performance ratio* |
|---|---|---|---|---|---|---|
| (0, 0, 1) | Units | 0 | 0 | 1039.23 | 1039.23 | |
| | Value (Rs) | 0 | 0 | 103,923 | 103,923 | 1.07 |
| (0, 1, 1) | Units | 0 | 489.89 | 600 | 1089.89 | |
| | Value (Rs) | 0 | 36741.75 | 60,000 | 96741.75 | 1 |
| (1, 0, 1) | Units | 346.41 | 0 | 848.53 | 1194.94 | |
| | Value (Rs) | 17320.50 | 0 | 84,853 | 102173.50 | 1.06 |
| (1, 1, 1) | Units | 346.41 | 346.41 | 600 | 1292.82 | |
| | Value (Rs) | 17320.50 | 25980.75 | 60,000 | 103301.25 | 1.07 |

*Relative performance ratio = (total safety stock value for the option/minimum possible value of total safety stock across all options).

stock point and the same has been reported in Table 10.1. Safety stock in value is determined by multiplying the safety stock in units with the respective cumulative cost per unit till that stock point. For example, for the (0, 1, 1) option the safety stock at the end of manufacturing will be 489.89 units and the value per unit is Rs 75 at that point in the chain. So the safety stock in value will be Rs 36,742.

## Sensitivity Analysis with Respect to Supply Chain Structure and Demand Variability

In general, there are four variables that affect the performance of various options:

- *Demand variability*. High demand variability versus low demand variability
- *Number of markets*. Large number of markets versus small number of markets
- *Cost distribution in chain*. Distribution of cost addition across all processes
- *Time distribution in chain*. Distribution of lead time addition across all processes

As can be observed from Table 10.2, surprisingly the magnitude of demand variability (high versus low) does not impact the choice of decision regarding the placement of inventory. Because safety stock is a linear function of standard deviation of demand across all stages in all options, the absolute magnitude of inventory will change, but the relative values are not affected. So the decision regarding optimal placement of inventory is insensitive to the magnitude of demand variability. But the rest of the three parameters do affect the relative change in total value of inventory for different options.

The total amount of inventory at the distribution centres is directly proportional to the number of distribution centres in the chain. But inventory at other decoupling points is proportional to the square root of the number of distribution centres. This is because of pooling of variability at the sourcing and manufacturing stages. So the larger the number of regions, pooling makes decoupling at sourcing and manufacturing stages more attractive. As seen in Table 10.2, with a larger number of markets, option (0, 1, 1) is optimal; but with lesser number of markets in the chain, option (0, 0, 1) will be most optimal.

Similarly, relative cost distribution and time distribution in a chain play important roles in the decision regarding optimal placement of the chain. Cost and time intensity in the chain are defined as follows: cost intensive at sourcing stage will mean that the bulk of value addition takes place at the sourcing stage; similarly, time intensive at the distribution stage means that a significant part of lead time in the chain is accounted for by the distribution process. The relative magnitude of safety stock at different stages gets affected by the distribution of time across the chain, and the relative value of safety stock at different stages gets

*Table 10.2:* ***Relative attractiveness of various options* under different scenarios.***

| Option | Demand Variability | | Number of regions (mkts) | | Cost intensity in chain (relative distribution of cost in chain) | | | Time intensity in chain (relative distribution of LT in chain) | | |
|---|---|---|---|---|---|---|---|---|---|---|
| | Low | High | Low | High | Source-int. | Mfg.-int | Dist.-int. | Source-int. | Mfg.-int | Dist.-int. |
| (0, 0, 1) | 1.07 | 1.07 | 1.00 | 1.21 | 1.05 | 1.13 | 1.31 | 1.20 | 1.20 | 1.00 |
| (0, 1, 1) | 1.00 | 1.00 | 1.01 | 1.00 | 1.00 | 1.08 | 1.00 | 1.00 | 1.00 | 1.05 |
| (1, 0, 1) | 1.06 | 1.06 | 1.02 | 1.13 | 1.06 | 1.00 | 1.15 | 1.03 | 1.23 | 1.02 |
| (1, 1, 1) | 1.07 | 1.07 | 1.09 | 1.05 | 1.09 | 1.03 | 1.01 | 1.04 | 1.09 | 1.10 |

*For a given scenario, each cell represents the ratio of total safety stock value for a particular option to the optimal total safety stock value for that scenario.

affected by the cost distribution in the chain. As can be seen in above example, time and cost distribution related characteristics in the chain do impact the relative attractiveness of various options.

In general, one will like to argue that choice of places where one holds decoupling inventory in the chain is not intuitive. Even though it is possible to understand how each of these three variables affects the relative position of various options individually, it is quite difficult to intuitively work out the performance impact of various combinations of the parameter values. Model building and sensitivity analysis by carrying out scenario study can help a firm in choosing the optimal placement of inventory in the chain.

In the above approach, it is assumed that the safety stock will take care of most of the demand realizations. In a few exceptional cases, the safety stock will not be able to handle demand realization. In such a case, the manager might pursue expediting, subcontracting, premium freight transportation or overtime. It is assumed that an organization has such coping mechanisms in place for responding to exceptional circumstances when the safety stock is not able to handle demand realization at any of the decoupling points. The cost of such a response is not explicitly taken into account in the above approach.

## Extending the Approach

The above example is of a three-stage supply chain, but the same approach is valid for a more complex chain. For example, in garment manufacturing, the manufacturing process will consist of two stages: dyeing and stitching. Similarly, in automobile manufacturing, a firm will consist of component manufacturing and assembly. It is possible to keep decoupling stocks at the end of dyeing in garment manufacturing process and at the end of component manufacturing process in automobile firms. Kodak examined 20 possible decoupling points using the above approach before making a final decision about the placement of decoupling inventory in the chain.

So far we have assumed that a firm is just making a decision about the optimal placement of decoupling points, but a firm can also examine alternative choices in processes using a similar approach. For example, in the distribution process a firm can decide to work with air as a mode of transport (LT = 1 week and cost addition in the process = 25 Rs per unit) or can use sea as a mode of transport (LT = 4 weeks and cost addition in the process = 5 Rs per unit). With change in lead time, the pipeline inventory in both options will not be identical, so firms will have to include safety stock as well as pipeline inventory in the analysis. In this specific case, we looked at the transportation process; we can also analyse slow versus fast manufacturing process using a similar approach. In general, restructuring of architecture will result in either change in placement of decoupling points or change in process or a combination of both.

## Summary

- Supply chain restructuring focuses on questioning the existing processes and architecture of the chain.
- Supply chains can be characterized using the following three dimensions: shape of the value-addition curve, point of differentiation and customer entry point. Restructuring of the supply chain process involves altering the supply chain process on at least one of the three dimensions.
- Supply chain restructuring involves supply chain innovations involving either product redesign or process redesign or value offering to customers so as to improve customer service and reduce cost. Using supply chain restructuring firms like Dell Computers and National Panasonic have managed to move from the MTS to the CTO business model.
- Restructuring supply chain architecture involves either altering the way in which material flow takes play in a chain or alteration in inventory placement in a chain.
- Unlike supply chain integration and supply chain optimization, supply chain restructuring goes beyond supply chain function and will require integrating product and process engineering with supply chain function. Similarly, it may also involve closer integration between marketing and supply chain function.
- Business benefits of supply chain restructuring can be quantified with the help of analytical inventory models.

## Discussion Questions

1. What are the key dimensions in a supply chain process?
2. What are the ways in which a firm can move from an MTS model to a CTO Model?
3. Identify industry and technology characteristics that make postponement strategy viable.
4. How do other business functions like product design, process technology and marketing contribute to supply chain restructuring decisions?
5. Why will one want to design different material flow systems for fast- and slow-moving items?
6. Identify variables that affect the inventory placement decisions within a chain?
7. HUL has 100 plants (geographically spread throughout India) where a number of different product lines are manufactured and supplied to 50 odd depots that are geographically spread throughout India. To improve responsiveness and simultaneously to reduce costs, HUL has come up with the concept of regional depots. The company has four regional depots (one in each zone of the country) and all slow-moving items are first brought to regional depots from which the entire basket of slow-moving goods is shipped to 50 odd depots. All fast-moving items are shipped directly from the plants to depots. One of the management trainees has suggested that HUL should redesign its supply chain (for slow-moving items). He has come with the following two options:
   - Have only one central depot at Nagpur (centre of India) and serve the entire 50 depots from one central depot for all slow-moving items.
   - Have four regional depots but each depot should specialize and stock only selected items that gets produced from the plants that are located in that zone. So all depots will get served from four regional depots for slow-moving items (instead of the current arrangement where each depot is served from the closest regional depot for all slow-moving items). Each of the slow-moving items will get stocked at only one of the four regional depots.

   Critically analyse the above two options.

## Mini Project

How will your analysis of the problem discussed in section "Restructure Placement of Inventory in Chain" change if we bring product variety in the analysis: Let us say the company offered three variants and weekly demand for each of the variants in each of the market follows normal distribution with a mean equal to 100 with a standard deviation of 50. The manufacturing company had two sub-stages: manufacturing component and assembly. The manufacturing component accounted for 80 per cent of value addition and lead time.

1. Where should company hold stocks in the system?
2. Determine the optimal level of safety stocks, given the above decision.

3. How will the decision change if:
   a) The number of markets increase (assume that in each market demand distribution is the same, i.e., mean = 300, standard deviation =100)
   b) What is the impact of a different value-addition curve:
      i. RM intensive: distribution: 60:20:20
      ii. Manufacturing intensive: 20:60:20
      iii. Distribution intensive: 20:20:60
   c) What is the impact of differential lead time
      i. RM intensive: (3, 1, 1)
      ii. Manufacturing intensive (1, 3, 1)
      iii. Distribution intensive (1, 1, 3)

## Note

1. See www.etezimandi.com/resreports/companyreports/hll.htm and www.hll.com/HLL/findinformation/archives/photogallery.asp?Category=2.

## Further Reading

S. Bhaumik, A. Shivaram, P. Latha, G. Rajendran, M. Muthukrishnamurthi, and S. R. Ashok, "Titan: Improving the Performance of Supply Chain." In Malini Gupta ed. *Supply Chain Excellence* (Mumbai: SP Jain Institute of Management Research).

J. B. Fuller, J. O'Conor, and R. Rawlinson, "Tailored Logistics: The Next Advantage," *Harvard Business Review* (1993, Vol 71): 87–98.

S. C. Graves and S. P. Willems, "Optimizing Strategic Safety Stock Placement in Supply Chains," *Manufacturing & Service Operations Management* (2000, Vol 2): 68–83.

S. C. Graves and S. P. Willems, "Optimizing the Supply Chain Configuration for New Products," *Management Science* (2005, Vol 51): 1165–1180.

Hau Lee and C. Billington, "The Evolution of Supply-Chain-Management Models and Practice at Hewlett-Packard," *Interfaces* (1995, Vol 25): 42–63.

Hau Lee, C. Billington, and B. Carter, "Hewlett-Packard Gains Control of Inventory through Design for Localization," *Interfaces* (1993, Vol 23): 1–11.

J. Shah and B. Avittathur, "Improving Supply Chain Performance through Postponement Strategy," *IIMB Management Review* (1999, Vol 11): 5–13.

# Supply Chain Contracts

## Learning Objectives

After reading this chapter, you will be able to answer the following questions:

> What are the problems with standard wholesale price contract?

> How effective supply chain contracts improve supply chain performance?

> What are the popular supply chain contracts and how do they help in the coordination of the members within the chain?

> How would one choose appropriate parameters for a given supply chain contract?

Anand and his team members were trying to decide whether they should focus their energy on developing mobile apps for Vodafone and Airtel or on fixed fee IT projects. Anand and few of his friends had developed some mobile apps during their final year of engineering and had decided to take the entrepreneurial route rather than working for large IT firms. Based on the model popularised by Apple, the telecom service industry operated on a 70:30 revenue sharing model. In the sharing model, 70% of all revenue generated through apps download (software applications for mobile handsets downloadable through the internet) by the end users would go to the app developers, while the balance 30% revenue go to Apple, Vodafone or other digital distribution platforms like Appstore. Anand knew a couple of independent developers who focused completely on the revenue generated by the apps. With increasing penetration of smart phones, Anand was confident that app downloads will explode in the future. However, some of his team members wanted to work on the risk-free model of developing applications for clients for a fixed fee.

In app value chain, there are three parties present in the chain, viz. independent developers, digital platform providers, and end users. Like all supply chains, coordination is a challenge in this industry also. Apple had decided to work with a revenue sharing model that created the right incentives and ensured that value chain is coordinated. It was important to design a supply chain contract that was most optimal to the three players and determine the alternatives in which the supply chain can be organised. Further, it was significant to ensure that risk and return were appropriately shared between the three players. About 100 million apps are downloaded each month in India. The most popular mobile apps are games, instant messaging, and music streaming apps. All the major telecom players such as Vodafone and Airtel are trying to develop app supply chain in India on the line similar to Apple, which uses revenue sharing model with its app developers. The purpose of this chapter is to understand the role of supply chain contract in enhancing coordination among members of the chain.

## Introduction

In a theoretical setting, materials, information, and finance flow seamlessly across organizational boundaries and supply chain (SC), and it is the end customer pull and not internal compulsions govern these. However, in a real SC setting, individual firms are more interested in performance at the local level rather than performance at the chain level, resulting in lost opportunities and overall poor SC performance. In Chapter 9, we discussed a broad range of challenges in managing coordination between various partners in the supply chain. We also discussed various coordination mechanisms. Among the various coordination mechanisms, the SC contract is a valuable instrument to coordinate various supply chains. In this chapter, we present an overview of different contracts in practice and discuss few popular contracts such as buyback contract and revenue sharing contract in detail.

First, we show that decentralized chains result in lower performance for the SC. As the players in the SC try to optimize their local performance, overall chain is worse off. As discussed in earlier chapters, the supply chain should focus on the entire chain, but unfortunately, incentives are not aligned, and as a result, we end up with an uncoordinated decentralized chain. In general, one can create innovative SC contracts through which chain alignment can be attempted. We would focus on mechanisms that can create the right incentives through which decentralized chains are coordinated. When performance of a decentralized SC is similar to centralized chain, it is known as a perfectly coordinated decentralized chain. In order to discuss in detail, it is necessary to work with two players in the SC, that is, one manufacturer and one retailer. For this analysis, simple analytical model is used as explained in the chapter on inventory management.

## Incentive Conflicts in Supply Chains

In most SCs in a real life setting, manufacturers usually complain that retailers do not forecast accurately (or do not have required capabilities), the real problem may be with misaligned incentives. Through SC contracts, one can create incentives that are aligned.

We first introduce a few terms that are used throughout the chapter.

- **Centralized supply chains:** Manufacturing and retailing is performed by same organization. For instance, retail firm, Pantaloon, having its own private brands where all the decisions are taken from an integrated chain perspective. Similarly, the watches and jewellery firm, Titan, has its own showrooms, where Titan can take all the SC decisions.
- **Decentralized supply chains:** Multiple parties are involved in chain. Therefore, Pantaloon may retail its own brands but also sell the Arvind brand where garments are supplied by Arvind Limited. Here, Arvind and Pantaloon act as decentralized SC players. Both may act independently and their decisions (manufacturing decisions by Arvind and retailing decisions by Pantaloon) may not be coordinated. Arvind would take manufacturing-related decisions with focus on its performance, and Pantaloons would take retailing decision likewise. Similarly, when Titan works with its own outlets, it would be part of a centralized chain, while when it coordinates with independent retailers, it is part of a decentralized supply chain.
    - **Coordinated decentralized supply chains:** A supply chain is coordinated when the decentralized system behaviour and performance is similar to the centralized SC situation. Even though individual firm in the chain acts independently and focuses on local performance, with the right incentives structure, one can ensure

that different entities in chain do not work at cross purposes. Right incentives can ensure that while focusing on local performance, the individual business entities ensure local optimization, and at the same time, align their actions to maximize the overall SC performance, at a level that is as good as centralized one. In perfectly coordinated decentralized chain system behaviour and performance is identical to the centralized SC.

To discuss this situation, an example of the music CD retailer discussed in Chapter 4 is used.

Let us consider a decentralized chain with two entities in the music CD chain: CD manufacturer and music retailer. Both are independent organizations with focus on maximizing their own individual profits. Apart from deciding the retail price, manufacturer also has to decide the price (we call this wholesale price) at which he sells CDs to the retailer. In practice, the wholesale price is decided based on the power equation in chain. In a situation where the manufacturer has higher power in chain, wholesale price would be closer to retail price (lower margin for retailer), and if retailer is more powerful, wholesale price would be closer to cost (lower margin for manufacturer). For a given wholesale price, retailer has to decide order quantity and the order has to be placed with the manufacturer before the launch of the movie, that is, much before the actual demand is known. Obviously, the retailer takes the ordering decision based on the critical ratio that would optimize profitability.

In this industry, bulk of the demand at the retail place takes place during the first two weeks of a movie release. The retailer is expected to place her order in advance (the number of CDs required) before the release of the movie. During the two weeks (peak demand period), the retailer will not be able to get replenishment from the manufacturer in case the demand exceeds this estimate. However, at the end of two weeks, all the unsold CDs will have hardly any demand, and CDs will have to be sold at throw away prices. For simplicity, we assume that the retailer destroys all the CDs at the end of season. Even though we have assumed that salvage value of leftover CD is zero, we can easily incorporate the positive salvage value in our discussion and insights obtained would be similar in nature. Manufacturer would produce CDs based on order placed by retailer. Hence, manufacturer works with made to order SC, while retailer works with made to stock SC.

The manufacture is defined as the chain's powerful player, who decides the retail price at which retailer would sell the CDs in market. In India, in the packaged goods category, it is mandatory to print the maximum retail price (MRP) and the only key decision made by retailer is the order quantity, that is, how much to order before the movie release.

We work with the same example used in Chapter 4. The retailer buys CDs at Rs. 80 each (wholesale price, $w = 80$) and sells them at Rs. 100 (retail price, $p = 100$) during the first two weeks. After two weeks, the retailer will destroy all the unsold stock. Based on experience, the retailer expects that demand for this kind of CD has a mean demand 100 with standard deviation 30. To arrive at the optimum order level, the following notations would be used (concept of service level and service factor being exactly same as in the safety stock section of inventory management chapter):

$$C_U = \text{cost of understocking} = p - w = 100 - 80 = 20$$
$$C_O = \text{cost of overstocking} = w = 80$$

The cost of understocking is an opportunity loss by the firm for each unit of lost sales. The cost of overstocking is the loss incurred by a firm for each unsold unit at the end of the selling season.

$$\text{Optimal service level} = \text{critical fractile} = (C_U \times 100)/(C_U + C_O) = 20/(20 + 80) = 0.2$$

Optimal service level in this kind of situation is also popularly known as critical fractile.

Optimum order size = mean demand + $k \times$ standard deviation of the demand

$k$ = service factor, $E(k)$ = standard loss function value for a given service factor $k$

For service level of 0.2, from Table 4.3 and 4.4 (refer Chapter 4), respectively, we get values of $k$ and $E(k)$, respectively.
$k = -0.84$ and $E(k) = 0.95$.

Order quantity = 100 – 0.84 × 30= 74.75 ≈ 75

$$\text{Expected stock out} = E(k) \times \text{standard deviation of demand} = 0.95 \times 30 = 28.60$$

$$\text{Expected sales} = \text{mean demand} - \text{expected stock out} = 100 - 28.60 = 71.40$$

$$\text{Expected excess inventory} = \text{order} - \text{expected sales} = 75 - 71.40 = 3.60.$$

$$\text{Expected retailer profit} = \text{expected sales} \times \text{price} - \text{order} \times \text{wholesale price}$$

$$= 71.40 \times 100 - 75 \times 80 = 1140$$

Now, let us try and understand issues from the CD manufacturer perspective.

We start with a case where manufacturer decides the unit wholesale price at Rs. 80 and manufacturing cost is Rs. 20.

$$\text{Manufacture profit} = \text{order} \times (\text{wholesale price} - \text{cost}) = 75 \times (80 - 20) = 4500$$

Unlike in case of the retailer where profit is uncertain (profit depends on the outcome of actual demand), for a manufacturer, profit does not depend on the actual demand, and there is no uncertainty in the profit outcome. SC profit is defined as sum of profits of all players in chain.

$$\text{Expected decentralized SC profit} = \text{manufacturer profit} + \text{expected retailer profit}$$
$$\text{Expected SC profit} = 4500 + 1140 = 5640$$

SC profit is calculated as follows:

$$\text{Expected decentralized SC profit} = \text{expected retail sales} \times \text{retail price} - \text{order} \times \text{cost}$$

From the above-mentioned equation, wholesale price is not directly included in the calculation of SC profit. Wholesale price influences retail order which in turn affects SC profit.

As discussed previously, for a given wholesale price of 80, it would be optimal for the retailer to place an order for 75 CDs. But why should manufacturer choose a wholesale price of Rs. 80 and give about 20% margin (on retail price) to retailer on retail price? It would be interesting to understand how the change in wholesale price that would essentially change the way chain margin is split between two parties – affect retailer order quantity. Before we understand the impact of change in wholesale price, let us consider a setting involving centralized SC or integrated SC. The manufacturing and retailing is done by one entity and this entity faces uncertain demand.

Decision making would be very similar as in the case of the retailer who takes decisions in the face of uncertain demand. The integrated manufacturer is likely to decide the manufacturing quantity based on the cost of understocking and overstocking. Given the high set-up cost involved, we can assume that manufacturer would manufacture once and maintain the entire stock at retail outlet based on actual demand. We would also assume that retail price ($p = 100$) in centralized setting would be same as decentralized SC.

In the centralized case,

$$C_U = \text{price} - \text{cost} = 100 - 20 = 80 \text{ and } C_O = \text{cost} - \text{disposal value} = 20 - 0 = 20$$

Critical ratio = 80/(80 + 20) = 0.8. From Table 4.4, we can obtain corresponding value of $k = 0.84$.

Optimum order quantity = 100 + 0.84 × 30 ≈ 125 units.

For $k = 0.84$, corresponding value of $E(k) = 0.1116$,

expected stock out = 0.1116 × 30 = 3.35, and expected sales = 100 – 3.36 = 96.65

Expected profit = expected sales × retail price + expected excess inventory × disposal price – order × cost

Expected profit for centralized SC = 96.65 × 100 – 125 × 20 = 7165

We get very interesting and counter intuitive result. To manage the same market risk, a decentralized chain orders less quantity (75 in decentralized compared to 125 in centralized case), that is, takes lower risk and with a result has lower expected SC profit (Rs. 5640 in decentralized case compared to Rs. 7165 in the centralized case). As one moves from a centralized SC setting to a decentralized setting, the total chain profit declines by 21%. This would be of serious concern in any business context. As we have discussed earlier, across the world, businesses are moving from vertical integration to outsourcing. But no business can pay this kind of penalty for moving to a decentralized setting. Firms will have to find a way to align interests of all the players in a decentralized setting such that supply chains do not destroy value while outsourcing.

Decentralized chain results in profit reduction by Rs. 1525, and within the chain, the entire market risk is borne by retailer. Manufacturer gets his profit of Rs. 4500 irrespective of the demand outcome. Retailer gets expected profit of Rs. 1140, but the actual profit would depend on demand outcome.

It would be interesting to understand why decentralized chain lowers the profit in chain. The retailer in a decentralized chain has a lower cost of understocking and a higher cost of overstocking; resulting in significant lower critical ratio. This resulted in a lower risk taken by retailer. With the results in the decentralized case, one would observe a stock out in 80% of the time (unlike 20% observed in centralized case) and observe excess stock in 20% of time (unlike 20% observed in centralized case).

In a decentralized chain, the entire chain margin is split between manufacturer and retailer. The retailer gets Rs. 20 of the margin and manufacturer gets Rs. 60 of the margin. This phenomenon is referred to as double marginalization in economics literature. For the same level of market risk, double marginalization (margin being split between two parties) results in reduction in profit for the decentralized chain. This reduction in efficiency is measured by the term called SC efficiency, which is defined as follows:

SC efficiency = Total SC profit in decentralized chain/centralized chain profit

In this case, SC efficiency = 5640/7165 = 0.79

Of course in decentralization chain, both parties also would be interested in their share of profits, and hence, we define manufacturer's share of profits as follows:

Manufacturer's share = manufacture profit/decentralized SC profit; and retailer's share = 1 – manufacturer's share.

In this case, manufacturer's share = 4500/5640.4 = 0.8

Now, let us try and understand how a change in wholesale price – that would essentially change the way chain margin is split between two parties – affect retailer order quantity, SC efficiency, and manufacturer's share in decentralized setting. In Table 11.1, we examine the effect of wholesale price ranging from Rs. 30 to Rs. 90 on various SC performance measures.

*Table 11.1: Impact of wholesale price on supply chain performance for decentralized supply chain.*

| Wholesale price | Critical ratio retailer | Order quantity | Manufacturer profit | Retailer profit | Total supply chain profit | Manufacturer's share | Supply chain efficiency |
|---|---|---|---|---|---|---|---|
| 20 | 0.8 | 125 | 0 | 7165 | 7165 | 0 | 1.00 |
| 30 | 0.7 | 116 | 1160 | 5949 | 7109 | 0.16 | 0.99 |
| 40 | 0.6 | 108 | 2160 | 4825 | 6985 | 0.31 | 0.98 |
| 50 | 0.5 | 100 | 3000 | 3803 | 6803 | 0.44 | 0.95 |
| 60 | 0.4 | 92 | 3680 | 2865 | 6545 | 0.56 | 0.91 |
| 70 | 0.3 | 84 | 4200 | 1976 | 6176 | 0.68 | 0.86 |
| 80 | 0.2 | 75 | 4500 | 1140 | 5640 | 0.80 | 0.79 |
| 90 | 0.1 | 62 | 4340 | 433 | 4773 | 0.91 | 0.67 |

Cost of understocking = $p - w$; cost of overstocking = $w$; and critical ratio = $(p - w)/p$ where $p$ is retail price and $w$ is wholesale price. For a same level of retail price, increasing wholesale price results in decreased value of cost of understocking and increased value of cost of overstocking, translating into a decreased value of critical ratio. Therefore, when we increase wholesale price from 30 to 90, critical ratio decreases from 0.7 to 0.1, and order quantity decreases from 116 to 62. Manufacturer's profit increases from Rs. 1160 to 4500 with the increase in wholesale price from Rs. 30 to Rs. 80. The manufacturer's profit is reduced to Rs. 4340 if wholesale price is raised to Rs. 90. So it would be optimal for manufacture to fix the wholesale price at Rs. 80. But when wholesale price is increased from 30 to 90, retailer orders lower quantity and retailer profit keeps declining with increase in retailer profit. But more importantly SC profit and SC efficiency keeps declining with increase in wholesale price.

As described in the Figure 11.1, overall SC profit and manufacturer profit do not move in same direction. This is not a zero one situation where the manufacturer improves its performance at the cost of retailer. We are dealing with a situation where overall SC is worse off. For example, when the manufacturer increases the wholesale price from Rs. 50 to Rs. 80, his profit increases by Rs. 1500, but retailer profit decreases by Rs. 2644. Hence, overall SC is worse off. Therefore, when the manufacturer decides to charge wholesale price of Rs. 80 so as to optimize his profits, overall SC is worse off. There is destruction in the value of chain. In the above case, it is expected that the movie CD manufacturer would like to keep higher margin in chain because it makes the bulk of the fixed investment. Therefore, we have an interesting dynamics where the manufacturer improves his profit, but in the process destroys value in the chain and overall SC operates at a suboptimal level.

The analysis discussed previously regarding retailer behaviour is only valid under following assumptions:

- **Retailer is rational:** The retailer assesses the costs and benefits while ordering and takes an optimal decision. Mostly, decision makers take decisions based on hunch or certain past practices.

- **Retailer focuses on profit maximization:** Even if the retailer is a rational decision maker, she may have objectives that are different from profit maximization. Many retailers have objectives of revenue maximization or market share maximization. Similarly, some retailers use popular products, such as bread and milk, as loss leaders (offer high discounts resulting in loss) with the hope to attract higher footfalls and hope that

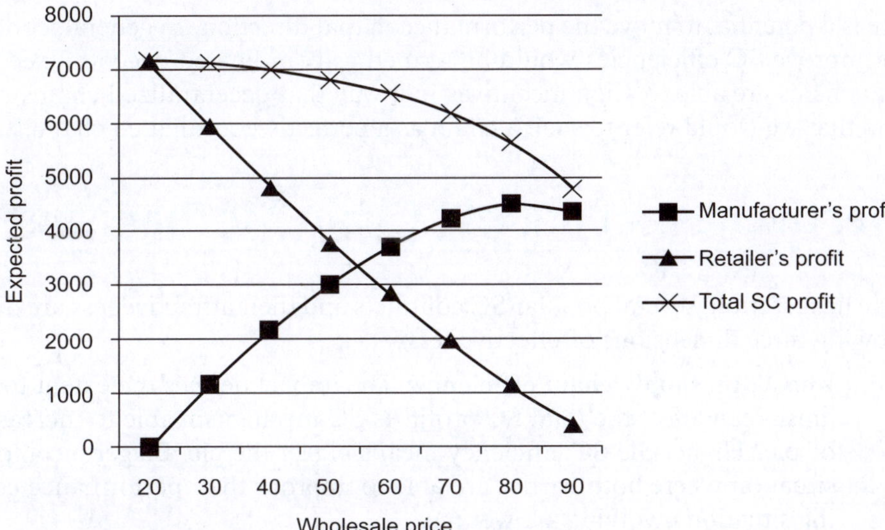


**Figure 11.1**

Impact of wholesale price on expected profit for decentralized supply setting.

when customer visits store to buy highly discounted products that they would also buy high-margin products that are stocked in retail outlets. In such case, the retailer would place order for much high quantity than presented in Table 11.1 and would also offer price at high discount value.

- **World view is same across entities in chain:** We have assumed that both manufacturer and the retailer share similar world view about market demand of Music CDs before launch. It is not uncommon to find situations where both may have different world views. For example, manufacturer might be optimistic and expect the mean demand close to 150, while retailer may be pessimistic and would expect the mean demand closer to 70.
- **Both the entities are risk neutral:** We have assumed that retailer is risk neutral, and as a result, it does not assign different weights to downside risk (i.e., in a situation where the retailer incurs loss when order quantity is 100 and demand turns out to be 40) and upside risk (i.e., in a situation where demand turns out to be 160 resulting in opportunity loss or lo profit potential).

In the following section, we assume that the retailer is rational, risk neutral, and coordination problems arise from double marginalization only. In other words, given lower returns, the retailer ends up ordering a lower quantity from manufacturer. As far as SC profit is concerned, if the retailer can influence the retailer ordering decision, the retailer should order 125, and this would ensure that total SC profit would be 7165.

## Types of Supply Chain Contracts

Contract is an agreement that legally binds two parties: manufacturer and retailer in our case. However, the role of a SC contract between two SC partners goes beyond the terms and conditions of business. Contracts specify who will bear how much of risk and also explicitly define the pay-offs for the parties. With the agreed-upon risk and incentive as per contract, SC entities take their local optimization decisions in decentralized setting. An appropriately designed contract can align the decision of decentralized players and induce actions of individual firms such that performance of overall SC is enhanced. Even if overall SC's optimization is not achieved, there is a potential to move the performance in that direction. In general, contract mechanisms that improve SC efficiencies would be termed as coordinated decentralized SCs. In case, SC mechanisms are able to align incentives in a way that decentralized chains mimic centralized chain that we would refer to such a chain as a perfectly coordinated chain.

## Effectiveness of Supply Chain Mechanisms

In the next section, several popular SC contracts and their attractiveness are discussed based on following three dimensions of effectiveness:

- **Impact on supply chain efficiency:** The impact defines the extent to which SC mechanism can affect the total SC profit. Is SC mechanism able to increase the overall size of pie? Higher the SC efficiency means bigger the pie. Bigger pie allows us to create a situation where both parties are able to improve their performance compared to existing situation involving a lower pie.
- **Flexibility in sharing supply chain profits:** Total SC profit would get shared between two partners based on their power. An ideal SC mechanism should allow us to distribute profit among partners in a flexible manner. The parameters can be chosen to suit the specific condition in the supply chain. This should not affect the size of pie; it should just help us in distributing the pie in desirable way.
- **Ease of implementation:** Mechanisms should be easy to implement and should not increase administrative costs excessively for both partners in chain. As we will discuss later in the chapter, some of the contract mechanisms would expect greater information sharing and firms in chain may have to make substantial investments in technology or may result in increased variable costs of operations. While examining SC mechanisms, we would start with the benchmark contract (the benchmark contract is referred as pure wholesale price contract) with wholesale price of 80 and manufacture profit = 4500 and retailer profit = 1600. We treat the centralized chain as an ideal goal that results in a retail order of 125 units and total SC profit = 7165.

Well-designed mechanisms should not only increase the total SC profit from benchmark case (wholesale price contract with $w = 80$) but also ensure that both manufacturer and retailer are better off with the proposed SC contracts. An ideal contract would deliver a performance equivalent to that in a centralized SC. We focus on those mechanisms that ensure win-win situations, that is, both the manufacturer and the retailer are better off. In the absence of a win-win situation, there is no incentive for individual parties to move from the existing situation, that is, the wholesale price contract.

### *Buyback Contract*

Publishing companies in USA came up with innovative idea of buyback scheme in book industry way back in 1930s. They observed that they can reduce the downside risk for the retailer by offering a buyback scheme. As per buyback contract, all the unsold goods at the end of season can be sold back to publisher at a pre-announced buyback price ($b$). If buyback price is $b$, cost of overstocking would reduce from wholesale price $w$ to $w - b$ and cost of understocking would remain the same, that is, $p - w$. Of course the retailer would be very happy with this arrangement because at any buyback price $b > 0$, she would be able to increase her profits. One might ask – why would the manufacturer be interested in offering this contract? Only if manufacturer is better off, would he offer this arrangement to retailer. Under the buyback contract, relevant profits would get computed as follows:

- Expected retailer profit = expected sales × retail price + expected leftover inventory × buyback price – order × wholesale price
- Expected manufacture profit = order × (wholesale price – cost) – expected leftover inventory × buyback price
- Expected supply chain profit = expected sales × price – order × cost
- Expected sales = mean demand – expected stock out
- Expected leftover inventory = order – expected sales

Now, consider the buyback contract in the context of our music CD example and compare buyback contract with base case involving wholesale price contract with the wholesale price = 80.

Let us consider what happens to SC performance when the manufacturer offers buyback contract with $w = 80$ and $b = 30$. Cost of overstocking for retailer = 80 – 30 = 50 and cost of understocking is = 100 – 80 = 20. Therefore, critical ratio = 20/(20 + 50) = 0.286, and correspondingly $k = -0.565$ and $E(k) = 0.744$.

$$\text{Order quantity} = 100 - 0.565 \times 30 = 83.02 \approx 83$$

Expected stock out = 0.744 × 30 = 22.32; expected sales = 100 – 22.32 = 77.68; and expected leftover inventory = 83 – 77.68 = 5.34

$$\text{Retailer profit} = 77.68 \times 100 + 5.34 \times 30 - 83 \times 80 = 1286$$

$$\text{Manufacturer profit} = 83 \times (80 - 20) - 5.34 \times 30 = 4821$$

Supply chain profit = 1286 + 4821 = 6106 and SC efficiency= 6106/7165 = 0.85 and manufacturer share = 4821/6016 = 0.789

In Table 11.2, the performance of the above buyback contract with two comparable wholesale price contracts involving wholesale prices of Rs. 80 and Rs. 71.4 is compared. Wholesale price of Rs. 80 is most preferred by manufacturer because it gives him the highest profit. It can be observed that a wholesale price of Rs. 71.4 would result in retailer order quantity of 83 and total SC profit of Rs. 6108.

As can be observed from Table, compared to the base case of wholesale price contract, the SC efficiency has improved from 0.79 to 0.85 and both manufacturer and retailer are better off because the profitability of both parties in chain has improved. Interestingly, the manufacturer could have obtained the same SC efficiency by lowering the wholesale price to Rs. 71.4, but his profit would have gone down, obviously this arrangement is unlikely to be acceptable to manufacturer.

Let us see, how SC performance would get affected by changing the buyback price for a given wholesale price of 80. For a wholesale price of Rs. 80, the buyback price can be varied

**Table 11.2: Impact of 'w' and 'b' on supply chain performance for decentralized supply chain under buyback contracts.**

| *w* | *b* | Order quantity | Manufacturer profit | Retailer profit | Total supply chain profit | Manufactuer's share | Supply chain efficiency |
|---|---|---|---|---|---|---|---|
| 80 | 0 | 75 | 4500 | 1140 | 5640 | 0.8 | 0.79 |
| 80 | 30 | 83 | 4820 | 1288 | 6108 | 0.79 | 0.85 |
| 71.4 | 0 | 83 | 4266 | 1842 | 6108 | 0.70 | 0.85 |

from Rs. 0 to 80. Obviously, it would not make sense for manufacturer to offer a buyback price higher than wholesale price. In real life, firms do not offer buyback price that is similar to the wholesale price because there are administrative costs of returns, cost of carrying inventory, and logistics cost of sending excess stock. At a wholesale price of Rs. 80, the retailer would be tempted to place very large order. There is no downside risk for him because cost of overstocking would be zero and the retailer would have no incentive to forecast or estimate demand. He would simply order a large number because the entire downside risk is passed on to manufacturer. Hence, instead of going all the way to Rs. 80, we allow buyback price to go up to Rs. 79 in our analysis. As can be observed in Figure 11.2, the expected retailer profit steadily increases with increase in buyback price but expected manufacturing profit and expected supply chain profit goes up then starts declining.

As can be seen in Table 11.3 at a buyback price of Rs. 70, order size is close to centralized chain and efficiency is 0.99. Overall expected SC goes up and relative share of manufacturer goes down from 80% to 76%. Even though the manufacturer share declines, his absolute profit is higher than benchmark profit of 4500. But if we go overboard and offer buyback price of Rs. 79, retailer is incentivized to order 150 which would result in significantly higher average return quantity which hurts the manufacturer, but retailer is obviously better off because he is able to

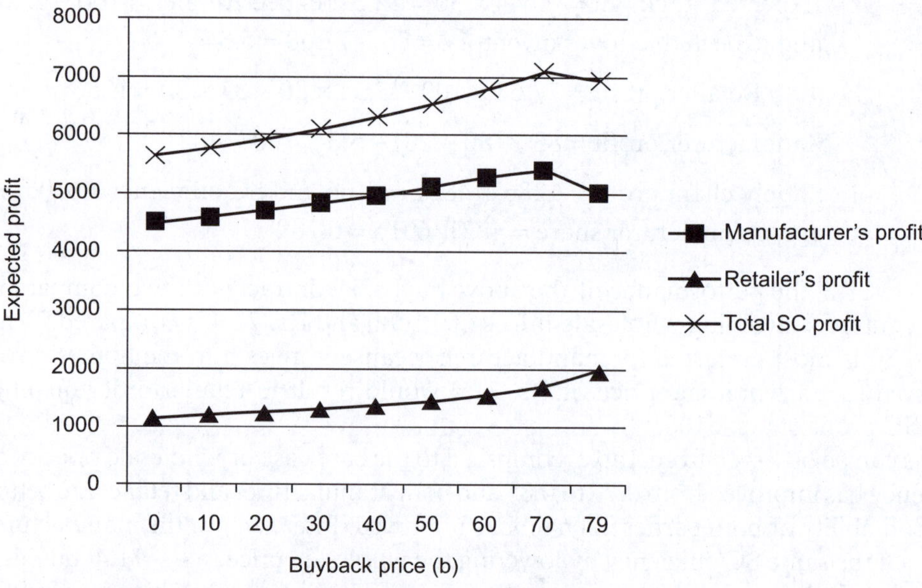


**Figure 11.2**

Impact of '*b*' on expected profit for decentralized supply chain.

***Table 11.3:* Impact of '*b*' on supply chain performance for decentralized supply chain.**

| *b* | Critical ratio retailer | Order | Manufacturing | Retailer | Total | Manufacturers fraction | Efficiency |
|---|---|---|---|---|---|---|---|
| 0 | 0.2 | 75 | 4500 | 1140 | 5640 | 0.80 | 0.79 |
| 10 | 0.222 | 77 | 4582 | 1198 | 5780 | 0.79 | 0.81 |
| 20 | 0.25 | 80 | 4706 | 1224 | 5930 | 0.79 | 0.83 |
| 30 | 0.286 | 83 | 4821 | 1289 | 6110 | 0.79 | 0.85 |
| 40 | 0.333 | 87 | 4960 | 1350 | 6310 | 0.79 | 0.88 |
| 50 | 0.4 | 92 | 5110 | 1430 | 6540 | 0.78 | 0.91 |
| 60 | 0.5 | 100 | 5280 | 1520 | 6800 | 0.78 | 0.95 |
| 70 | 0.667 | 113 | 5408 | 1672 | 7080 | 0.76 | 0.99 |
| 79 | 0.952 | 150 | 5003 | 1937 | 6940 | 0.72 | 0.97 |

take advantage of the upside possibility of higher demand with hardly any downside risk. This reduces the SC profit, and obviously, the manufacturer profit. Hence, it is important to strike a right balance while designing any SC contract. Sound buyback policy would improve the performance of both retailer and manufacturer, and we call the buyback policy a coordinating channel. But it would be interesting to understand whether we can get perfectly coordinated decentralized chain using buyback contract. Perfectly coordinated contracts would have 100% SC efficiency.

As discussed earlier, total SC profit gets dictated by retailer order quantity. If we can ensure that retailer optimal order is 125, we would be able to get a perfectly coordinated chain. We have to make sure that the critical fractile for retailer in a decentralized chain is the same as the critical fractile obtained in centralized chain situation.

$$\text{Critical ratio for centralized chain} = (p - c)/p$$

$$\text{Critical ratio for buyback contract} = (p - w)/(p - b)$$

If we equate above ratios, we get a condition that If $b = p \times (w - c)/(p - c)$, we would have perfectly coordinated chain.

Therefore, we obtain an interesting result that as long as $w$ and $b$ satisfy above equation, SC would be perfectly coordinated.

For $w = 80$, we would get perfectly coordinated chain if $b = 100 \times (80 - 20)/(100 - 20) = 75$.

At $w = 80$ and $b = 75$, we would get critical fractile = 0.8 and retailer would order quantity = 125 and our decentralized chain would behave like a centralized chain.

### Buyback Schemes in Indian Publishing Industry

All magazine publishers offer buyback schemes where distributors can return unsold goods back to the publishers. Magazines have a life of one week to fifteen days. Magazine publishers allow unlimited return quantity, while book publishers do not. In book publishing industry, some of the large publishers put restriction on quantity that can be returned. Usually, they restrict the quantity to be returned to 10% to 20% of the order size. Usually, publishers give time limit within which distribution partners can return the goods but in practice, the entire book is not returned and just cover page and copyright page are returned. This would ensure that extra costs incurred in return are minimized. Most of the time contracts are not formally signed, but everybody is aware of the practices.

Let us check whether we can ensure flexible sharing of profits without reducing the chain profit. In Table 11.4, wholesale price is varied from Rs. 30 to Rs. 90 and we obtain the

**Table 11.4: *Impact of 'w' and 'b' on supply chain performance for perfectly coordinated decentralized supply chain.***

| *p* | *w* | *b* | Order | Manufacturer profit | Retailer profit | Total supply chain profit | Manufacturer's share | Efficiency |
|---|---|---|---|---|---|---|---|---|
| 100 | 30 | 12.5 | 125 | 896 | 6269 | 7165 | 0.13 | 1.00 |
| 100 | 40 | 25 | 125 | 1791 | 5374 | 7165 | 0.25 | 1.00 |
| 100 | 50 | 37.5 | 125 | 2687 | 4478 | 7165 | 0.38 | 1.00 |
| 100 | 60 | 50 | 125 | 3583 | 3583 | 7165 | 0.50 | 1.00 |
| 100 | 70 | 62.5 | 125 | 4478 | 2687 | 7165 | 0.63 | 1.00 |
| 100 | 80 | 75 | 125 | 5374 | 1791 | 7165 | 0.75 | 1.00 |
| 100 | 90 | 87.5 | 125.2 | 6274 | 896 | 7170 | 0.88 | 1.00 |

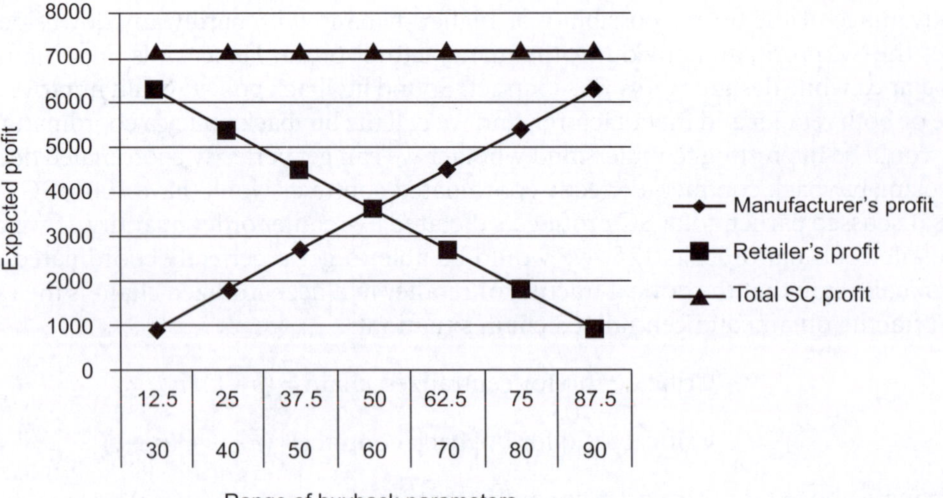


**Figure 11.3**

Impact of '*w*' and '*b*' on expected profit for decentralized supply chain.

corresponding value of buyback price using expression obtained previously. As can be observed in Figure 11.3, expected SC profit remains unchanged with increase in wholesale price, but manufacturer profit increases while retailer profit decreases. Therefore, the buyback contract is a very powerful contract. If one chooses the right set of parameters (wholesale price and buyback price), one can ensure that SC efficiency is 100%. Moreover, one can vary the manufacturer share and retailer share in the desired manner based on power equations in chain. Of course we would have to make sure that manufacturer profit is above the benchmark profit of 4500 (base case involving wholesale price contract of $w = 80$) and benchmark retailer profit of 1140. This would mean that manufacturer share should be a minimum of 62.8% (total SC profit is 7165 and 62.8% share would ensure that manufacture profit is at least 4500) and maximum 84% because beyond that retailer profit would be lower than the base case profit of 1140.

To understand risk sharing under buyback contract, consider a contract with $w = 80$ and $b = 75$ and observe how the performance of manufacturer and retailer would get affected under different demand scenarios. In Table 11.5, we look at five demand scenarios involving actual demand at level as low as mean − 2 × standard deviation and highest demand at a level of mean + 2 × standard deviation. Unlike wholesale price contract where the manufacturer had a guaranteed profit of 4500, we now have an expected profit of 5374. During low demand, the manufacturer profit can go down to 1125, while under high-demand scenario, the profit can go up to 7500. What is interesting is that the share of manufacturer and retailer remains same and as a result, the risk is shared between manufacturer and retailer. Therefore, if we have a risk-averse manufacturer, he might prefer a conservative but risk-free profit of 4500 compared to the expected profit of 5374. In other words, SC contracts also alter the nature of risk shared between parties in the chain. Some people are concerned that as the risk of retailer goes down in buyback contract, and with a result, the retailer may not put in the same kind of effort that would have been put in a wholesale price contract where the entire risk is borne by the retailer.

***Table 11.5:* Manufacturer versus retailer profit under different demand scenario for different buying contracts.**

| Actual demand | Sales | Returned quantity | Manufacturer profit | Retailer profit | Supply chain profit | Manufacturer's share |
|---|---|---|---|---|---|---|
| 40 | 40 | 85 | 1125 | 375 | 1500 | 0.75 |
| 70 | 70 | 55 | 3375 | 1125 | 4500 | 0.75 |
| 100 | 100 | 25 | 5625 | 1875 | 7500 | 0.75 |
| 130 | 125 | 0 | 7500 | 2500 | 10000 | 0.75 |
| 160 | 125 | 0 | 7500 | 2500 | 10000 | 0.75 |

# Revenue-Sharing Contract

Another popular contract is the revenue-sharing contract where the manufacturer offers a lower wholesale price but additionally gets a fractional share of retail revenue. For every rupee earned by retailer, fraction '$f$' is retained by retailer and balance is passed on to manufacturer. Let us examine this arrangement in the context case of music CD case discussed earlier.

The music CD manufacturer can decide to reduce the wholesale price to Rs. 30 and ask for a 40% share in revenue from retailer. Therefore, for every CD sold in the market, the retailer would get a share of Rs. 60 as revenue (60% of retail price, $f = 0.6$), and this would translate into a margin of Rs. 30 for every CD sold. The retailer would lose Rs. 30 for every unsold CD. As compared to a pure wholesale price contact, the cost of overstocking for retailer would reduce from Rs. 80 to Rs. 30, while the cost of understocking would increase from Rs.20 to Rs. 30. In general, cost of overstocking would be lower, but cost of understocking could be higher or lower based on value of $f$ and $w$. For the retailer, unlike in the buyback contract where only the cost of overstocking changes in desirable direction, revenue sharing would affect both cost of overstocking and cost of under stacking.

$$\text{Cost of understocking} = f \times p - w = 0.6 \times 100 - 30 = 30 \text{ and cost of overstocking} = w = 30$$

$$\text{Critical ratio} = (f \times p - w)/(f \times p - w + w) = (f \times p - w)/(f \times p) = 30/(30 + 30)$$

$$= 0.5 \text{ and corresponding } k = 0 \text{ and } E(k) = 0.399$$

$$\text{Order quantity} = \text{mean demand} + k \times \text{standard deviation} = 100 + 0 \times 30 = 100$$

$$\text{Expected stock out} = E(k) \times \text{standard deviation of demand} = 0.399 \times 30 = 11.97$$

$$\text{Expected sales} = \text{mean demand} - \text{expected stock out} = 100 - 11.97 = 88.03$$

$$\text{Expected excess inventory} = \text{order} - \text{expected sales} = 100 - 88.03 = 11.97$$

$$\text{Expected retailer profit} = \text{expected sales} \times \text{price} \times f - \text{order} \times \text{wholesale price}$$

$$= 88.03 \times 0.6 \times 100 - 100 \times 30 = 2282$$

$$\text{Expected manufacture profit} = \text{order} \times (\text{wholesale price} - \text{cost}) + (1 - f) \times \text{expected sales} \times \text{retail price}$$

$$= 100 \times (30 - 20) + 0.4 \times 88.03 \times 100 = 4521$$

$$\text{Supply chain profit} = \text{expected sales} \times \text{price} - \text{order} \times \text{cost} = 88.03 \times 100 - 100 \times 20 = 6803$$

In Table 11.6, we compare the performance of above revenue-sharing contract with two comparable wholesale price contracts involving wholesale price of Rs. 80 and Rs. 50, respectively. Rs. 80 is the benchmark wholesale price preferred by the manufacturer because it gives him the highest profit. On the other hand, a wholesale price of Rs. 50 would result in retailer order quantity of 100 (same as the order quantity obtained by revenue-sharing contract under the discussion) and total SC profit of 6803.

*Table 11.6:* ***Impact of different revenue sharing contracts on supply chain performance for decentralized supply chain.***

| $w$ | $f$ | Order quantity | Manufacturer profit | Retailer profit | Supply chain profit | Manufacturer's share | Supply chain efficiency |
|---|---|---|---|---|---|---|---|
| 80 | 0 | 75 | 4500 | 1140 | 5640 | 0.8 | 0.79 |
| 30 | 0.6 | 100 | 4521 | 2282 | 6803 | 0.62 | 0.95 |
| 50 | 0 | 100 | 3000 | 3803 | 6803 | 0.44 | 0.95 |

As can be seen in Table 11.6, compared to the base case of wholesale price contract, the SC efficiency has improved from 0.79 to 0.95 and both manufacturer and retailer are better off in revenue sharing arrangement. Interestingly, the manufacturer could have obtained same SC efficiency by lowering wholesale price to Rs. 50, but his profit would have gone down, obviously not acceptable to manufacturer.

To study the impact of different revenue-sharing fractions on total SC profit and the way profits get distributed, we vary revenue share retained by retailer from 0.4 to 0.9 in Table 11.7. Obviously, it would not make sense for the retailer to accept any fraction that is lower than or equal to 0.3, because the retailer would pay wholesale price of Rs. 30 and get revenue of Rs. 30 as his share for every CD sold. This would mean that he would make a loss, and therefore, he would expect his share of fraction to be greater than 0.3.

In Table 11.7 and Figure 11.4, fraction varies from 0.4 to 0.9. As expected, with increase in retailer fraction, the retailer profit increases but manufacturer profit keeps declining. As can be observed from Figure 11.4, the fraction kept by retailer increases from 0.4 to 0.9, manufacturing profit declines from 5317 to 2064, while retailer profit increases from 612 to 5016. The SC efficiency increases from 0.83 to 0.99. Of course '*f* vales above 0.6 would not be acceptable to manufacturer because his profit would be below the threshold value of 4500. Similarly, '*f* values below 0.5 would not be acceptable to retailer as expected retailer profit would drop below benchmark profit of Rs. 1140. We have managed to obtain range of revenue sharing policies ('*f* values ranging from 0.4 to 0.6) which would improve the performance of retailer and manufacturer, and therefore, we could call the revenue-sharing policy a coordinating contract. But it would be interesting to understand whether we can get a perfectly coordinated decentralized chain using revenue-sharing contract.

As discussed earlier, the total SC profit gets dictated by retailer order quantity. If we can ensure that retailer optimal order is 125, we would be able to get a perfectly coordinated chain.

**Table 11.7: *Impact of 'f' value on supply chain performance for decentralized supply chain.***

| *w* | *f* | Critical ratio | Order | Manufacturer profit | Retailer profit | Supply chian profit | Manufacturer's share | Supply chain efficiency |
|---|---|---|---|---|---|---|---|---|
| 30 | 0.4 | 0.25 | 80 | 5317 | 612 | 5929 | 0.90 | 0.83 |
| 30 | 0.5 | 0.4 | 92 | 5113 | 1433 | 6545 | 0.78 | 0.91 |
| 30 | 0.6 | 0.5 | 100 | 4521 | 2282 | 6803 | 0.66 | 0.95 |
| 30 | 0.7 | 0.571 | 105 | 3766 | 3188 | 6954 | 0.54 | 0.97 |
| 30 | 0.8 | 0.625 | 110 | 2944 | 4077 | 7021 | 0.42 | 0.98 |
| 30 | 0.9 | 0.667 | 113 | 2064 | 5016 | 7080 | 0.29 | 0.99 |

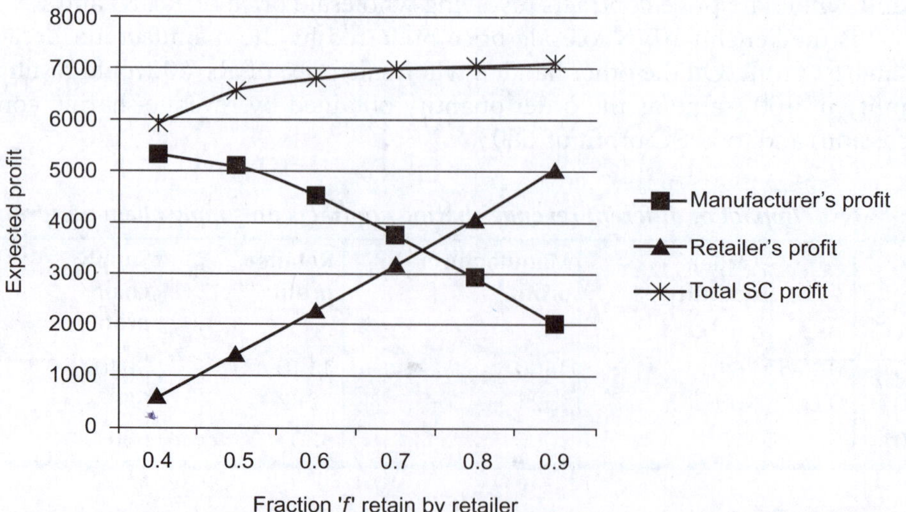


**Figure 11.4**

Impact of range of sharing '*f*' in revenue contracts on expected profit for decentralized supply chain.

We have to make sure that the critical fractile for retailer in a decentralized chain is the same as the critical fractile obtained in centralized chain situation.

- Critical fractile for centralized chain = $(p - c)/p)$
- Critical fractile for revenue-sharing contract = $(f \times p - w)/f \times p$

$$(p - c)/p) = (f \times p - w)/f \times p$$

That is

$$f \times c = w$$

Given that $f$ is less than 1, wholesale price has to be less than cost. This is an unusual result. We need to fix $f$ and $w$ in a way such that $f \times c = w$. Therefore, for $f = 0.6$, the corresponding $w = 12$. As $f \leq 1$, optimum $w \leq c$ in perfectly coordinated chain. Therefore, with a wholesale price less than cost and a value of '$f$' at ratio equal to $w/c$, manufacturer can coordinate the chain. Many manufacturers are not comfortable at fixing wholesale prices at less than cost price.

Let us check whether we can get range of revenue sharing contracts involving flexible sharing of profits without reducing the chain profit. In Table 11.8, the value of $f$ is varied from 0.875 to 0.125 and we obtain the corresponding value of wholesale price $w$ using the abovementioned expression. As can be seen in Figure 11.5, as expected the supply chain profit remains unchanged with a decrease in wholesale price; however, manufacturer profit increases, while retailer profit decreases. Thus, the revenue sharing contract is a very powerful contract. If one chooses the right set of parameters (wholesale price and fractional share retained by the retailer), one can ensure that supply chain efficiency is 100%. Moreover, one can vary the manufacturer share and retailer share in the desired manner based on the power equations in chain. Of course, we would have to make sure that manufacturer profit is above the benchmark profit

**Table 11.8: Impact of 'w' and 'f' on supply chain performance for decentralized supply chain.**

| p | w | f | Order | Manufacturing | Retail | Total | Manufacturer's | Supply chain efficiency |
|---|---|---|---|---|---|---|---|---|
| 100 | 17.5 | 0.875 | 125 | 896 | 6269 | 7165 | 0.13 | 1.00 |
| 100 | 15 | 0.75 | 125 | 1791 | 5374 | 7165 | 0.25 | 1.00 |
| 100 | 12.5 | 0.625 | 125 | 2687 | 4478 | 7165 | 0.38 | 1.00 |
| 100 | 10 | 0.5 | 125 | 3583 | 3583 | 7165 | 0.50 | 1.00 |
| 100 | 7.5 | 0.375 | 125 | 4478 | 2687 | 7165 | 0.63 | 1.00 |
| 100 | 5 | 0.25 | 125 | 5374 | 1791 | 7165 | 0.75 | 1.00 |
| 100 | 2.5 | 0.125 | 125 | 6269 | 896 | 7165 | 0.88 | 1.00 |

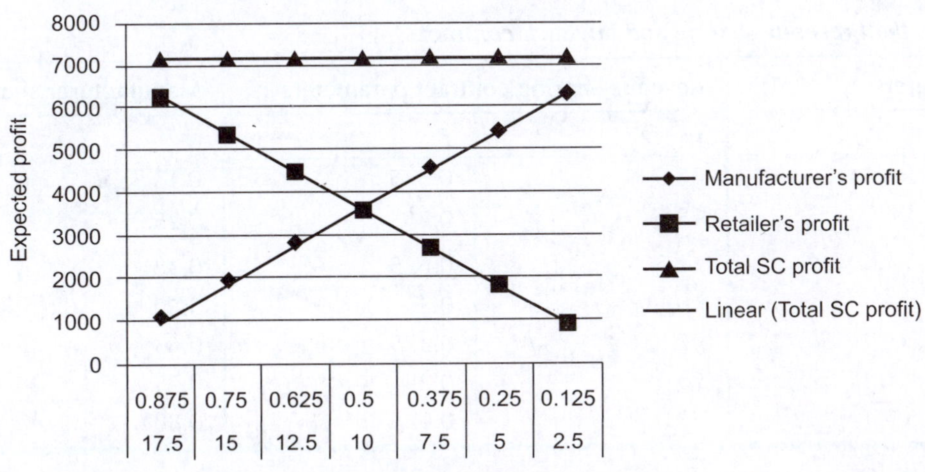


**Figure 11.5**

Impact of 'w' and 'f' on expected profit for decentralized supply chain.

of 4,500 (base case involving wholesale price contract of $w = 80$) and the benchmark of retailer profit is 1,140. This would mean that manufacturer share should be a minimum of 62.8% (total supply chain profit is 7,165 and 62.8% share would ensure that manufacture profit is at least 4,500) and maximum 84%; because beyond that retailer profit would be lower than the base case profit of 1140.

Revenue-sharing contract would require that manufacturer has perfect information about the revenue earned by the retailer. With information technology, it is easy for manufacturer to track information about quantity sold at retailer place. Of course there would be tendency by the retailer to cheat and show lower amount in terms of quantity sold, thus denying the manufacturer the contracted payment. This can be addressed with a third party audit which ensures that the retailer maintains correct record of quantities sold, which can then be accessed by the manufacturer.

In early part of this century, the Government of India had allowed revenue sharing in the telecom sector in place of annual fixed fee which was the case till that date. The telecom players responded by reducing tariff. Given the nature of demand elasticity in the sector, lower tariffs resulted in huge demand in terms of number of users and overall talk time used by telecom customers. As telecom operators were not required to earn a minimum amount and did not have to pay a fixed fee, telecom players experimented with lower tariffs (risk was shared with government) and same resulted in telecom revolution resulting in higher earnings by telecom players and the government.

At this stage, it would be interesting to compare revenue sharing contract and buyback contract. Both allow us to come up with parameters that would perfectly coordinate the chain.

## Equivalence of Revenue Sharing and Buyback Contracts

In this section, we show that revenue sharing and buyback contracts are equivalent. This would mean that for every buyback contract one can design unique revenue-sharing contract which would have exactly same outcome in terms of ordering quantity and expected manufacturer and retailer profit. Critical fractile for buyback policy = $(p - w_b)/(p - b)$

Crtical fractile for revenue sharing = $(f \times p - w_r)/f \times p$

Where $w_r$ = wholesale price in revenue-sharing contract, $w_b$ = whole sale price in buyback contract

Equating same, we get following relationship:

$f = 1 - b/p$ and $w_r = w_b - b$

For example, buyback policy involving $w_b = 30$ and $b = 12.5$

***Table 11.9:*** **Range of equivalent revenue sharing and buyback contracts.**

| **Buyback contract parameters** | | **Revenue-sharing contract parameters** | | **Manufacturer share** |
|---|---|---|---|---|
| $w_b$ | $b$ | $w_r$ | $f$ | |
| 30 | 12.5 | 17.5 | 0.875 | 0.13 |
| 40 | 25 | 15 | 0.75 | 0.25 |
| 50 | 37.5 | 12.5 | 0.625 | 0.38 |
| 60 | 50 | 10 | 0.5 | 0.50 |
| 70 | 62.5 | 7.5 | 0.375 | 0.63 |
| 80 | 75 | 5 | 0.25 | 0.75 |
| 90 | 87.5 | 2.5 | 0.125 | 0.88 |

As can be seen in Table 11.9, one would get identical performance measures in buyback and revenue-sharing contracts. Hence, conceptually, one could argue that the buyback contract and revenue-sharing contract are identical in nature. It allows perfect coordination and also allows a whole range of sharing of profits between two partners in the chain. It is interesting to see that buyback contracts have evolved in the publishing industry, while revenue sharing is more prevalent in service industries, such as entertainment, telecom, and ecommerce. Of course, with revenue-sharing contract, there is extra effort involved in monitoring revenue earned by retailer. Therefore, revenue-sharing contracts are unlikely in situations where the manufacturer has low power and SC efficiency is reasonably high. Revenue sharing is very difficult mechanism to put in place.

Under a revenue-sharing contract, the retailer initially pays the manufacturer a small unit wholesale price for each item acquired and later pays the supplier a fraction of the revenue earned. From the supplier's point of view, the initial wholesale price is usually less than manufacturing cost and so he maintains a negative cash flow until the buyer sells a sufficient number of items and retailer shares the fraction of revenue earned as part of contract. Under a buyback contract, the retailer initially pays a wholesale price to the supplier for each item ordered in advance and receives payment from the manufacturer for the returned items (unsold items). Compared to the revenue-sharing contract, the buyback contract offers the supplier relatively higher cash flow at initial stage but at later stage, part of that is returned to retailer as per buyback agreement. At a conceptual level, the two contracts are equivalent in terms of their resulting profit realizations, yet timing of the financial transactions are quite different.

Let us look at above phenomenon for the following two equivalent contract: buyback contract with ($w$ = 80, $b$ = 75) and revenue-sharing contract ($w$ = 5, $f$ = 0.25) using five scenarios discussed in Table 11.10. As can be seen in Table 11.10, under different scenarios cash flow implications would widely vary between two contracts. In general, in buyback contract, manufacturer gets huge net cash flow (revenue from retailer-manufacturing cost) of Rs. 7500 upfront, and depending on the actual demand scenario, he would have cash outflow at the end of season (at the end of season when one would get an estimate of unsold quantity). In revenue-sharing contract, manufacturers would have fair amount of negative cash flow at the initial stage and would get the relevant quantity of share of revenue once actual sales information is available. As one can observe total net cash flow to manufacturer is same across two contracts, but nature and timings are significantly different.

***Table 11.10:*** ***Impact of equivalent buyback and revenue sharing on timing of cash flow of manufacturing and retailer.***

| | | | | | Buyback contract with $w = 80$, $b = 75$ | | Revenue-sharing contract with $w = 5$ and $f = 0.25$ | |
|---|---|---|---|---|---|---|---|---|
| **Actual demand** | **Sales** | **Unsold quantity at the end of season** | **Manufacturer profit** | **Retailer profit** | **Net cash inflow for manufacture before the launch** | **Net cash inflow for manufacture after the season** | **Net cash inflow for manufacture before the launch** | **Net cash inflow for manufacture after the season** |
| 40 | 40 | 85 | 1125 | 375 | 7500 | −6375 | −1875 | 3000 |
| 70 | 70 | 55 | 3375 | 1125 | 7500 | −4125 | −1875 | 5250 |
| 100 | 100 | 25 | 5625 | 1875 | 7500 | −1875 | −1875 | 7500 |
| 130 | 125 | 0 | 7500 | 2500 | 7500 | 0 | −1875 | 9375 |
| 160 | 125 | 0 | 7500 | 2500 | 7500 | 0 | −1875 | 9375 |

## Other Popular Supply Chain Contracts

There are several other popular types of SC contracts besides buyback contracts and revenue-sharing contracts that are used in practice. In this section, some of the popular SC contracts used in practice are described.

- **Two part tariff contract:** The two-part tariff SC contract coordinates decentralized SC by charging some fixed fee and a variable unit price for the supply quantity. In the music SC example, we know that the manufacturer should find a way of encouraging retailer to place an order of 125 units. This ordering decision would ensure that the decentralized chain would result in SC profits equal to centralized SC profits. Manufacturer is aware of the fact that retailer would place an order of 125 units if wholesale price is fixed at Rs. 20. But no manufacturer would fix such a price because he would not make any money. But in a two-part tariff SC contract, the manufacture can charge a fixed fee of Rs. 4500 and wholesale unit price of Rs. 20 per unit. Stock out costs and overstocking costs are influenced by variable costs and fixed costs do not influence ordering decision. Therefore, two-part tariff can ensure perfect SC coordination (SC efficiency of 1) and by changing the quantum of fixed fee, one also has the flexibility of allowing different share in profitability of different partners in the chain.
- **Quantity flexibility contract:** Quantity flexibility contracts allow retailers to change the quantity ordered after observing the actual demand during the initial part of the season. For example, in the case of music CDs, for pure wholesale contract, the retailer is likely to place order of 75 units that is placed before observing the demand. Under quantity flexibility contract, manufacturer may allow the retailer to change his order (both upward and downward direction) by 20%. Therefore, if the demand is lower than 75, the retailer can reduce his order up to 60, and if the demand turns out to be higher than 75, the retailer can increase his order size up to 90. In practice, the following outcomes may result:

  (i) Manufacturer delivers 60 units of the item before the start of the season and promises to deliver quantity up to 30 units during the season if required by retailer;

  (ii) Manufacture delivers 90 units before the start of the season and retailer has right to return up to 30 units and would be reimbursed at the whole sale price for the returned goods.

  (iii) Manufacturer might either manufacture 90 pieces before the start of the season or produces only 60 units before the season and ensure that he has responsive capacity of 30 units, and items could be produced at short notice during the season.

  It is easy to show that retailer is better off and would have higher profits and would order higher quantity. There is also a variant of above contract known as an option contract, wherein the retailer would buy an option along with firm order. This is similar to the financial option where the retailer has the right to order up to some pre-specified units during the season but no obligation to buy those units. Thus, to buy this option, the retailer would pay option premium per unit and would pay exercise price for every unit of option exercised. This is similar to financial option used in financial markets.
- **Consignment model:** Here, the manufacture decides how much quantity to be stocked at retailer and the inventory is in the books of manufacturer. Only when the items are sold, the manufacture raises invoice on retailer. As a result, the entire risk is borne by the manufacturer. This would also result in channel coordination. The manufacturer would have an expected return and retailer would not end up with excess stock.

For instance, branded jewellery players like Tanishq and Gitanjali offer designs of smaller jewellery suppliers who operate with consignment model. This is prevalent especially in the case of unbranded products where retailer would not like to take any risk associated with the unknown brands. In case where a music artist has produced his own CD, he might be able to convince a music retailer to keep his music CDs on a consignment asis.

Consignment model is very common in the garment industry and is usually offered by new manufacturers. Retailer is protected as there is no loss incurred if the actual demand turns out to be lower than estimated. Of course, the retailer has an opportunity cost of the space used by manufacturer in the consignment model. Therefore, in practice, the retailer would not allow the manufacturer to stock unlimited quantity and would give him some limited space-based on his assessment of likely demand.

Variety of contracts enable risk sharing and with a result increase coordination. Coordination results in the better alignment of interests of the parties. This should increase profit for both parties and create win-win situations. Therefore, we could refer such contracts as ideal SC contracts.

## Summary

- Decentralised chains result in low performance for the supply chain. As the players in the supply chain try to optimise their local performance, overall chain is worse off. In a decentralised chain involving manufacturer and retailer, the entire chain margin is split between the two parties. For the same level of market risk, double marginalisation (margin being split between two parties) results in the reduction of profit for the decentralised chain.
- Effective supply chain contract can ensure that while focusing on local performance, the individual business entities ensure local optimisation, and at the same time, their actions maximise the overall supply chain performance at a level that is as good as centralised one.
- Effectiveness of supply chain contract can be measured using three dimensions: impact on supply chain efficiency, flexibility in sharing supply chain profits and ease of implementation.
- Buyback is a popular contract in publishing industry wherein all the unsold goods lying with retailer at the end of season can be sold back to the publisher at a preannounced buyback price (b). It is possible to construct a buyback contract that would result in perfectly coordinated chain.
- Revenue sharing is a popular contract in entertainment industry where the manufacturer offers not only a low wholesale price but also a share of retail revenue. For every rupee earned by the retailer, a fraction is retained by the retailer and balance is passed on to the manufacturer. It is possible to construct a buyback contract that would result in perfectly coordinated chain.
- For every buyback contract, one can design unique revenue sharing contract that would have exactly same outcome in terms of ordering quantity and expected manufacturer and retailer profit.

## Discussion Questions

1. Explain the concept of double marginalisation in the context of wholesale price contract.
2. In the example discussed in the chapter, we had assumed that manufacturer is the most powerful entity in the chain. How would our analysis change if the retailer was the most powerful entity in the chain? Analyze the supply chain efficiency in the context of balanced chain where both parties have more or less equal power.
3. Different industries seem to prefer different kinds of contracts. For example, the publishing industry prefers buyback contract, while telecom industry seems to prefer revenue sharing contract. Why would one prefer one contract over the other?
4. Revenue sharing and buyback contracts have been shown to be equivalent. Why would one prefer one over the other?
5. Why a revenue sharing contract by retailer is likely to result in lower sales effort when compared to pure wholesale contract?
6. What is the role of information technology in the implementation of revenue sharing contract?

## Exercises

1) For the music CD example discussed in the chapter, under wholesale price contract, let us assume that demand and retail price do not change. Therefore,
   i. What would be optimal wholesales price if manufacturing cost = 50 instead of 25? Further, compute
      - manufacturing profit
      - retailer profit
      - total supply chain profit
      - supply chain efficiency
   ii. How do supply chain dynamics change with ratio of c/p (manufacturing cost as % of retail price)?

2) For the music CD example discussed in the chapter, under wholesale price contract,
   i. Compute the optimal wholesales price and supply chain efficiency if salvage price = 10 instead of 0. Assume that the demand and retail price do not change.
   ii. How do supply chain dynamics change with the change in ratio salvage price/wholesale price?

3) For the buyback contract discussed in the chapter (Table 11.2), determine the supply chain efficiency for $w = 80$ and $b = 40$.

4) For the revenue sharing contract discussed in the chapter (Table 11.6), find the supply chain efficiency for $w = 50$ and $f = 0.3$.

## Further Reading

M. S. Altug and G. van Ryzin, "Is Revenue Sharing Right for Your Supply Chain?" *California Management Review*, (2014, Vol. 56, no. 4): 53–81.

G. P. Cachon and M. A. Lariviere, "Turning the Supply Chain into a Revenue Chain," *Harvard Business Review* (2001): 20–21.

G. P. Cachon and M. A. Lariviere, "Supply chain coordination with revenue-sharing contracts: strengths and limitations," *Management Science*, (2005, Vol. 51, no. 1): 30–44.

J. D. Dana Jr and K. E. Spier, "Revenue sharing and vertical control in the video rental industry," *The Journal of Industrial Economics*, (2001, Vol. 49, no. 3): 223–245.

F. A. Martinez-Jerez and V. G. Narayanan, "Strategic Outsourcing at Bharti Airtel Limited," *Harvard Business Review* (2007): 9–107.

V. I. P. L. Padmanabhan and I. P. Png, "Returns policies: make money by making good," *MIT Sloan Management Review*, (1995, Vol. 37, no. 1), 65.

B. A. Pasternack, "Optimal pricing and return policies for perishable commodities," *Marketing Science*, (2008, Vol. 27, no. 1): 133–140.

# Agile Supply Chains

## Learning Objectives

After reading this chapter, you will be able to answer the following questions:

> How are agile supply chains different from traditional supply chains?
> Under what situations do forecast updating play an important role?
> How does a firm design its supply chain so that it can respond rapidly to forecast updating?
> How do responsive supply chains differ from speculative supply chains?
> What are the sources of supply chain disruptions?
> How can a firm mitigate risks of supply chain disruptions?

Termed as the largest commercial product launch in the history of the electronics industry, the launch of the iPhone created headlines across the world. Serpentine queues could be seen in front of every Apple store. This was the case not only in the United States but also in Europe. The frenzied crowds could barely wait for the stores to throw open their doors.

However, not even the best analysts could actually predict accurately the demand even though Apple has long been known for its demand shaping ability. This time too, Steve Jobs was confident that he had a winner on his hands. He was confident that the phone will sell 10 million units within the first 18 months of launch. While the figures are yet to substantiate this prediction, it is common knowledge that the supply matched the demand. This is no mean accomplishment.

The pertinent question here is when an operation is planned on this massive scale, how can we predict the demand? How does one ensure that the supply chain is equipped to handle variations in demand? This problem is compounded further if we consider the long and complex supply chain that Apple has put in place for the iPhone. To keep costs down and maximize profits, the iPhone is manufactured in Asia. In the face of demand uncertainty, the responsiveness of the supply chain is indeed very difficult to ensure.

In this chapter, we focus on solutions that can help firms deal with demand uncertainty on a large scale. We examine the characteristics of agile and responsive supply chains, using illustrative examples. We also examine the consequences of uncertainty in supply on the supply chain. We conclude the chapter with a brief discussion on possible methods to handle disruptions in the supply chain.

## Introduction

Operating in a global environment has resulted in an increased velocity of change on all parts of business. On the one hand, customers are demanding lower cost and higher service while on the other hand firms have to grapple with higher velocity of change on both demand and supply fronts. Progressive firms ensure that their supply chain design and operations reflect the three factors identified in Figure 12.1. For attaining a high level of supply chain performance, a firm not only has to ensure that the supply chain configuration is aligned with the business strategy but also that its supply chain is robust enough to handle demand as well as supply uncertainty. In this chapter, we focus on the robustness of a chain, and those supply chains that can handle a high level of demand uncertainty and supply uncertainty are termed agile chains.

Low levels of demand and supply uncertainty can be handled using appropriate levels of safety stocks in the system as discussed in Chapter 4. In this chapter, we focus on supply chains that have to deal with high levels of either demand or supply uncertainty or both. Demand uncertainty has received much attention from researchers as well as practitioners. As discussed in Chapter 2, based on the nature of demand uncertainty, products can be classified as functional products or innovative products. In the case of functional products, the focus is on meeting predictable demand in a cost-effective manner, while for innovative products the focus is on creating cost-effective response mechanisms for handling unpredictable demand. Thus, for functional products one needs to design efficient supply chains, while for innovative products one needs a responsive chain. Unlike demand uncertainty, supply uncertainty has not received enough attention. Unlike demand, a firm has a greater control on supply, and the popular view was that supply side uncertainty can be handled by choosing appropriate partners in the chain, and as a consequence the focus had been on supplier selection and supplier development rather than on the management of supply uncertainty. The terrorist attack in September 2001 forced firms to look at their supply chain vulnerabilities, and firms have realized that they need to focus on both demand uncertainty and supply chain disruptions. Managing supply chain disruptions involves managing certain events that have low probability of occurrence but have high impact on supply chain performance.

Firms that have configured their supply chain design and operations to handle high-level demand uncertainty effectively are known as responsive supply chains. Firms that have configured their supply chain design and operations to handle high levels of demand uncertainty and supply chain disruptions effectively are known as agile supply chains.

Agile supply chains combine practices of responsive chains and will have practices in place that can handle supply chain irregularities. To develop a better understanding of the characteristics of agile supply chains, we discuss demand side responsiveness and supply chain disruption in separate sections.

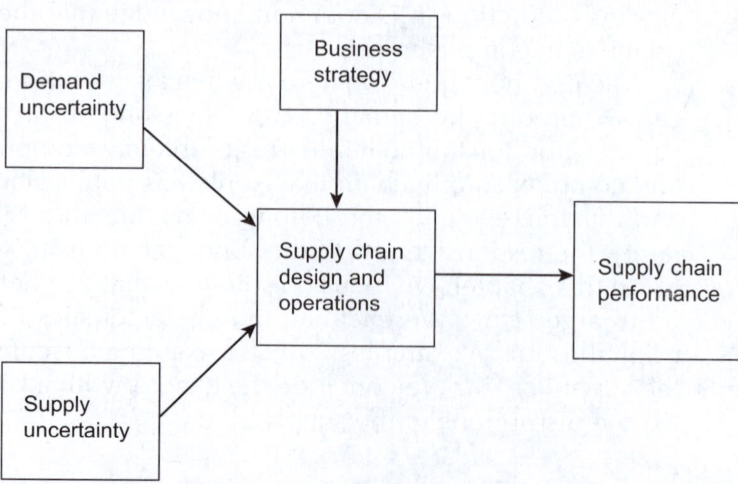


**Figure 12.1**

Supply chain configuration design.

**INTERVIEW WITH**

**SURESH KUMAR**

*Madura Garments, a division of Aditya Birla Nuvo, is a leading Indian apparel company with a turnover of Rs 9 billion. Madura Garments has made its presence felt in lifestyle brands (major brands: Louis Philippe, Van Heusen, Allen Solly) and popular brands (Peter England, Elements). Suresh Kumar heads the supply chain and logistics at Madura Garments.*

*What is the level of supply chain complexity at Madura Garments?*

**Suresh Kumar:** Madura Garments works with a large number of brands and each brand offers a huge variety and, at any point in time, we have more than 100,000 active SKUs of style, colour and size in our portfolio. Another dimension of complexity is the sheer number of channel partners. Our products are sold through a network of more than 200 exclusive franchisees and over 2,000 premier multi-brand outlets.

*What supply chain challenges do you face?*

**Suresh Kumar:** We are in the fashion business. Our product life cycles are short and the market is very volatile. In a typical season, 75 per cent of our offering is new and only about 25 per cent is repeat offering. Further we do not release the entire new offering at one go at the start of the season. We ensure that every month in a season we introduce new offerings so that customers see freshness in our collection throughout the season. With a large variety and 75 per cent new offerings, ideally, we will like agile supply chains with short lead times. Unfortunately, our supply chain lead times are very long. The fabric requires 2–3 months of time and converting the fabric to garments takes another month and warehousing and logistics takes another 15 days, so effectively we are talking of 3–4 months of lead time.

*What supply chain innovations have you adopted at Madura Garments?*

**Suresh Kumar:** We have been working with ideas of supply chain collaborations with a few of our suppliers. We share data as well as fashion trends with them and based on this information, the supplier stocks base materials. This has led to a reduction in the effective lead time required for supplier from 3–4 months to 30–45 days. There is some amount of risk involved but given our long-term relationship with our suppliers and the trust they have put in us helps them in taking certain risky decisions which reduce cycle time and increase agility in chain. We have also worked on increasing our volume flexibility because we have a lot of seasonality in our business. The ability to increase capacity in supply chain at short notices is of great value to us. By having a large number of jobbers in our vendor base, we are able to increase and decrease garment conversion capacity within the chain at short notice. We also have realized that not all our channel partners have the necessary forecasting capabilities. So during trade shows when they place their order with us, we share our data with them and help them in improving their forecast so that they do not end up buying the wrong kind of assortment during the season.

Unlike other parts of the world, significant festival demand is a unique Indian phenomenon. So we have introduced a third season in our planning called the festival season. This has helped us in supply chain planning and operations.

*What are the challenges in supply chain management that you are likely to face in the future?*

**Suresh Kumar:** With robust growth in India and the possibility of a recession in several markets, India is emerging as an important market for a lot of global players. So we are likely to see more intense competition in the future. Further, we are also working with a lot of new fabrics including non-iron, stain-free with 3x dry technology, double stretch, use of milk-protein and soya fibres, as a consequence of which the old data which we use for forecasting become less reliable. We also want to see how we can use new technologies like RFID in supply chains. We have started a pilot project through which we hope to learn ways in which we can use new technologies for improving supply chain performance.

## Supply Chains for High Demand Uncertainty Environment

The demand for several product categories in the fashion industry and in the high-technology industry is inherently unpredictable. Firms usually work with inaccurate forecasts and end up with high obsolescence and lost sales costs. Supply chain restructuring discussed in Chapter 10 suggests several approaches that are likely to be of great help for firms dealing with highly uncertain market places. Supply chain restructuring essentially involves supply chain innovation involving product redesign, process redesign, network design restructure or value offering to customer so as to improve customer service and reduce cost.

In this section, we look at industries that have a high degree of demand uncertainty as well as short life cycles. The garment industry in particular and soft goods industry in general fall into this category. They suffer from poor forecast accuracy as they offer a large variety and usually have product life cycles of a few months. By observing early sales patterns, firms can update their forecasts and respond to the market with the use of quick response manufacturing and high speed transportation such as air shipments so as to reduce obsolescence and lost sales costs. Zara, the Spanish fashion retailer, manages its supply chain effectively and is known for its rapid response capabilities.

### THE ZARA SUPPLY CHAIN[1]

Zara is a chain of fashion stores owned by Inditex, the Spanish fashion retailer with a turnover of 8.2 billion Euros (as in 2006). With 12.2 per cent net profit over sales, Zara is one of the most profitable apparel brands in Europe. Zara's success has been attributed to its focus on rapid response to the market. Unlike its competitors, Zara does not outsource all its production activities. Most of the production capacity (in-house as well as outsourced) is located in Europe so that Zara can work with short lead times. The bulk of the apparel is shipped by air so that Zara can ensure delivery in 72 hours to all its retail outlets located in different parts of the globe. Because of this ability to respond quickly, Zara is able to bring a product on the shelf of its retail stores within 15 days of idea creation. Zara ensures that it always has a fresh line of products at its retails outlet and no product is on the shelf for more than four weeks.

We illustrate the concepts of quick response supply chains through the example of global supply chains from the garment industry.

## Forecast Updating

A global garment supply chain involves three main activities: fabric production, garment manufacturing and transportation. A supply chain for garments has always been quite long and the bulk of the time is taken up at the fabric manufacturing stage. Over a period of time global supply chains in the garment industry have become longer because the bulk of the manufacturing has shifted to China and transporting via sea from China has added to the time required in supply chain operations. In the fashion garment business, product life cycle is of the order of a few months and as a result the bulk of the supply chain decisions are taken before the start of the season. Since the garment industry offers a large variety and the product portfolio is changed every year, usually a firm is not able to predict likely demand for each style offered for the coming season. Unfortunately, as can be seen in Figure 12.2, most of the forecasts are usually off the mark. In Figure 12.2, we present data on forecast accuracy as observed by Sport Obermeyer, a firm operating in the fashion garment industry. It compares forecast versus observed demand for representative items from the product portfolio of the firm. The experience of Indian firms in the fashion garments industry is similar. Firms have to realize that in spite of significant effort, quality of forecast is likely to be poor and extra effort in improving forecasts before the start of the season is not likely to yield meaningful results. As a result, firms end up with lost sales in quite a few items and also end up with excess stock in several other items that have to be salvaged at a loss at the end of the season. Several players in this business believe that they have to live with this gamble and they have focused their energies on reducing cost by moving

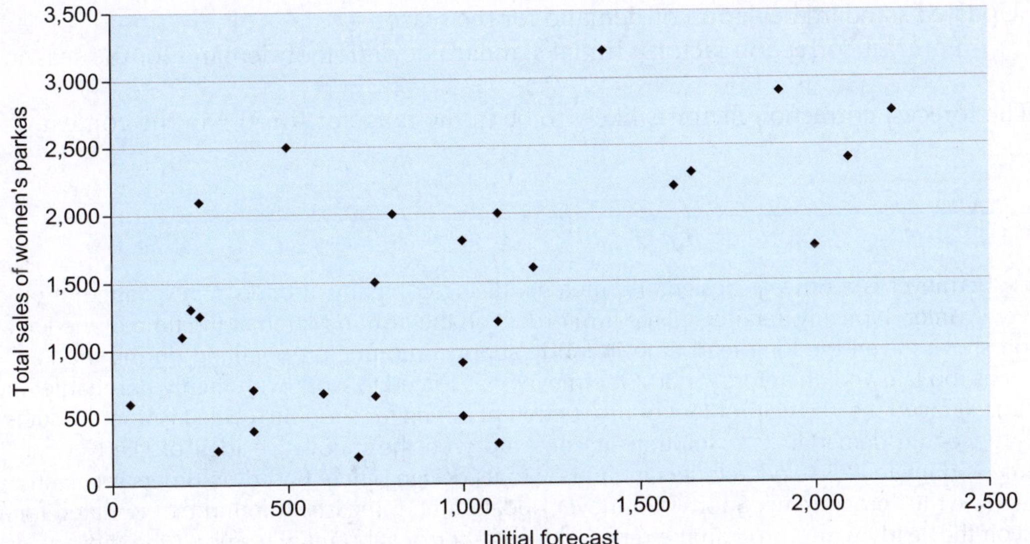


**Figure 12.2**

Initial forecast versus actual demand.

*Source*: Reprinted by permission of *Harvard Business Review.* M. L. Fisher, J. H. Hammond, W. R. Obermeyer, and A. Raman, "Making Supply Meet Demand in an Uncertain World," *Harvard Business Review* (1994, Vol 72): 83–93. 

manufacturing to offshore locations in Asia. We will call this approach the speculative approach. The best a firm can do is to use the inventory model for short life cycle products, discussed in Chapter 4.

In recent times, some firms have realized that even though forecasting before the start of the season is difficult, data obtained from initial sales observed in the early part of the season can help a firm in updating forecasts that are likely to have reasonably high forecast accuracy. Sport Obermeyer Ltd found that if forecast can be revised after observing 20 per cent of the actual demand, as shown in Figure 12.3, the forecast error will drop down by a significant amount. Essentially, one will find that the standard deviation of demand for an updated forecast will be of a much lower magnitude compared to the standard error associated with initial forecasts. That is, if one defines a parameter called forecast correction factor, one will observe the following:

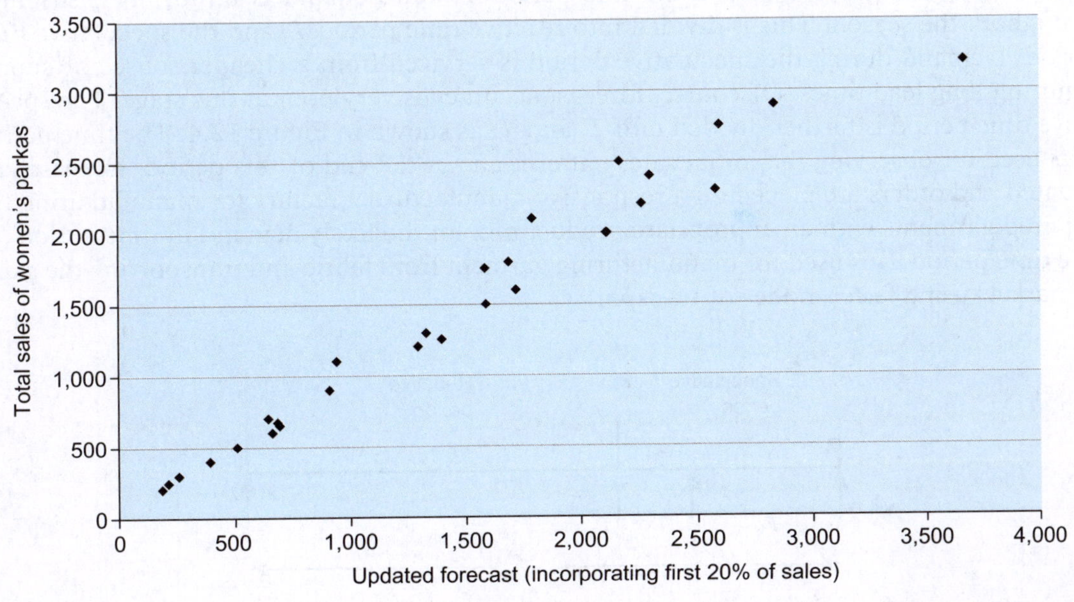


**Figure 12.3**

Updated forecast versus actual sales.

*Source*: Reprinted by permission of *Harvard Business Review.* M. L. Fisher, J. H. Hammond, W. R. Obermeyer, and A. Raman, "Making Supply Meet Demand in an Uncertain World," *Harvard Business Review* (1994, Vol 72): 83–93. 

Updated standard deviation of demand for the season =
Forecast correction factor × Initial standard deviation of demand for the season

The forecast correction factor is likely to be in the range of 0.1–0.4 in the context of new products.

### FORECAST UPDATING AT SPORT OBERMEYER[2]

Sport Obermeyer is a skiwear design and merchandising company. It offers a new range of products for every winter. Typically, retailers place firm orders on the firm in March at the time of the Las Vegas fashion show. Given the long lead time in fabric supply, information obtained during the Las Vegas show was too late and, therefore, Sport Obermeyer was forced to work with highly unreliable internal forecasts. It faced the classic problem of production planning for short life cycle fashion products with highly uncertain demand. As a solution, it came up with the innovative idea of "Early write" programme and invited 25 select retailers in January to its design office. Based on orders received during the "early write" programme, Sport Obermeyer updated the forecasts. It found that updated forecasts based on the "early write" programme reduced forecast error substantially. Sport Obermeyer was able to cut down on the quantum of obsolescence as well as markdowns, which are the usual problems faced by all fashion merchandising firms.

## Responsive Supply Chain: Optimal Use of Dual Sources of Supply

Responsive supply chain approach takes advantage of lower variability of demand observed in the updated forecasts. Given the fact that fabric manufacturing takes a long time, one will have to stock fabric, and based on the revised forecast, the later part of the season can be serviced from responsive garment manufacturing facilities that are located close to the market. Further, firms can use faster modes of transport like air so that the time taken in transportation can be cut down by a significant amount. We call this approach the responsive approach. In a responsive approach the firm divides the season into two components: speculative time and responsive time. The speculative part of season is managed using a long but efficient chain using the speculative forecast available before the start of the season. Demand for the later part of the season is serviced using a responsive supply chain based on updated forecasts derived from observation of initial sales.

Let us say we have a season of time period $T$, and demand is uniformly distributed throughout the season. This is divided into reactive time period $T_3$ and the speculative time period. Demand during the speculative period is serviced from a cheaper source of supply requiring long lead times. Of course, forecast accuracy is very poor at this stage. The speculative time period is further divided into $T_1$ and $T_2$ as shown in Figure 12.4. The time period $T_1$ is used for observing the initial sales pattern, and at the end of this period, forecasts are updated and orders are placed on a responsive manufacturing facility for manufacturing the required garments with an appropriate product mix for the likely demand in time period $T_3$. The time period $T_2$ is used for manufacturing garment from fabric and transporting the same to markets using faster modes of transport.

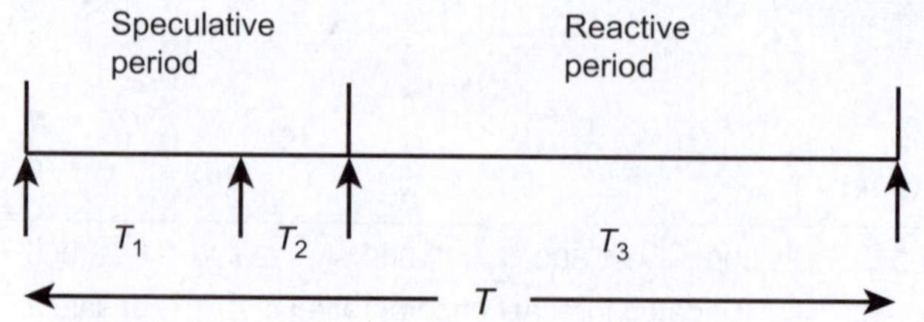


**Figure 12.4**

Responsive approach.

Thus, demand during the speculative period ($T_1 + T_2$) is managed using the speculative approach, and demand during the reactive period ($T_3$) is managed using the responsive supply chain. The responsive chain is more expensive because it usually involves garment manufacturing facilities located close to markets and these facilities generally work with smaller batches. Further, faster modes of transport also results in additional cost. Essentially, expensive manufacturing and transportation will be traded-off against lower lost sales and markdown costs. Much before the start of the season, orders are placed from cheaper sources of supply for garments required for speculative period and for fabrics required for reactive period.

## Illustration of Responsive Supply Chain Approach

We illustrate the idea discussed above with an example of a branded garment company serving the US market. The firm offers two types of shirts for the summer season consisting of 4 months. The two variants are regular shirts and designer shirts. Both variants are made from the same fabric and the only difference is in terms of style of stitching.

The garment firm found it difficult to predict demand before the start of the season mainly because every year they came up with a new set of designs and one could never be certain about the acceptability of the new design by the target consumer segment. Based on the acceptability of design, demand is likely to be high, moderate or low. We will designate these three possible outcomes as high-demand scenario, moderate-demand scenario and low-demand scenario. One could never predict customer reactions in advance. But collection of data in the first few weeks will allow the firm to know with certainty whether one is going to see a high-demand scenario, moderate-demand scenario or low-demand scenario. From their past experience they knew that once they have an idea about perceived design attractiveness based on initial sales, by and large demand uncertainty was low and was of a smaller magnitude in size. That is, for a given scenario, the standard deviation of the demand will be reasonably low for all three possible scenarios. From past experience the firm can estimate the subjective probability of each of the scenarios. For the purpose of illustration, we assume that all three scenarios have equal chances, that is, the probability of occurrence of each scenario is one third. Not knowing which scenario is going to develop is the main source of uncertainty for the garment manufacturer. The estimate of mean and standard deviation of demand for each of the three scenarios for both types of shirts are presented in Table 12.1.

As we can see from Table 12.1, the mean demand will depend on the type of demand scenario observed during the season. In this illustration, just to reduce complexity, it is assumed that once a scenario is observed during the season the standard deviation of demand for a given scenario is the same for all three scenarios. In the standard shirt category, the scope for creativity is on the lower side and as a result design changes from year to year will be minor in nature. In the designer shirt category, the firm experiments quite a lot and as a result designs are likely to be significantly different from year to year. As a result, the relative difference in volume of demand between the high-demand scenario and the low-demand scenario differs considerably across both categories. In the standard category, the mean demand varied from 840 to 1,160 among the three scenarios, but for designer shirts the mean demand varied from as low as 340 to as high as 860.

***Table 12.1:*** ***Possibility of the emergence of the three scenarios for the firm.***

| Category | High | | Moderate | | Low | | Price | Cost | Salvage Value |
|---|---|---|---|---|---|---|---|---|---|
| | Mean | SD | Mean | SD | Mean | SD | | | |
| Designer shirt | 860 | 30 | 600 | 30 | 340 | 30 | 500 | 90 | 30 |
| Standard | 1,160 | 20 | 1,000 | 20 | 840 | 20 | 200 | 85 | 40 |

## Speculative Approach

Demand during the season for shirts is likely to follow a normal distribution, and demand distribution for both categories of shirts is independent of each other. One unit of fabric is required to manufacturer one unit of shirt. Fabric cost is Rs 70 per unit and stitching charges are Rs 20 and 15 for the designer and standard categories, respectively. All the stocks left at the end of the season can be salvaged at Rs 30 per unit for the designer shirt and Rs 40 per unit for the standard shirt.

In the speculative approach, information revealed at the end of the first few weeks of a season is of not much use because all the orders will have been placed before the start of the season, and given the long lead time involved in the supply chain one will not be in a position to place any fresh orders during the season. So as far as the firm is concerned the uncertainty in mean for the three scenarios got translated into uncertainty of demand.

### Optimal Decision in Speculative Approach

Let $j$ = index representing possible scenarios in the season

$MD\_S_j$, $SD\_S_j$ = Mean and standard deviation of demand during the season for a given scenario $j$

$MD\_S$, $SD\_S$ = Mean and standard deviation of demand during the season as per speculative forecast

$p_j$ = Probability of outcome $j$

$$MD\_S = \sum p_j \times MD\_S_j$$

$$SD\_S = \sqrt{\left(\sum_j p_j \times \left[SD\_S_j^2 + (MD\_S_j - MD\_S)^2\right]\right)}$$

Worked out values of mean and standard deviation for the season demand as per the speculative forecast are presented in Table 12.2.

In the speculative approach, the firm can use a single-period model described in Chapter 4. The firm will be working with speculative forecast, that is, forecast made before the start of the season, and the relevant parameters are as shown in Table 12.2. For simplifying our calculations, we will work with normal distribution with the above parameters.

$C_u$, $C_o$ are costs of understocking and overstocking, respectively

$OSL$ = Optimum service level for single period model = $C_u \times 100/(C_u + C_o)$
$k$ = Service factor for a given OSL
Order = $MD\_S + k \times SD\_S$

For a given OSL, based on nature of distribution one can work out the corresponding value of $k$. For a normal distribution, one can determine the value of $k$ from the standard normal distribution table available in Chapter 4.

**Table 12.2: Speculative forecast.**

| | Mean demand | Standard deviation | Coefficient of variation |
|---|---|---|---|
| Designer shirt | 600 | 214 | 0.27 |
| Standard | 1,000 | 132 | 0.17 |
| Aggregate | 1,600 | 251 | 0.15 |

*Table 12.3: Relevant values of OSL and k for speculative approach.*

| Approach | Garment | Price | Cost | Salvage value | Cost of overstocking | Cost of understocking | Optimal service level | k | Remark |
|---|---|---|---|---|---|---|---|---|---|
| Speculative | Designer | 500 | 90 | 30 | 60 | 410 | 0.872 | 1.14 | |
| | Standard | 200 | 85 | 40 | 45 | 115 | 0.719 | 0.58 | |
| Speculative period (fabric) | Designer | | | | 402* | 15 | 0.964 | 1.8 | Fabric to be converted in to designer shirt in reactive period |
| | Standard | | | | 107* | 15 | 0.877 | 1.15 | Fabric to be converted into standard shirt in reactive period |
| Reactive period | Designer | 500 | 98 | 30 | 68 | 402 | 0.855 | 1.06 | |
| | Standard | 200 | 93 | 40 | 53 | 107 | 0.669 | 0.44 | |

*Cost of understocking is arrived at by looking at opportunity cost of not sending bale to manufacturer of designer/standard shirt because of non-availability of fabric.

Relevant values of *OSL* and *k* for the speculative approach are presented in Table 12.3. The optimum order quantity for a speculative approach will be

$$\text{Order (designer)} = 600 + 1.14 \times 214 = 843.96 \approx 844$$

$$\text{Order (standard)} = 1{,}000 + 0.58 \times 132 = 1076.56 \approx 1{,}077$$

## Implication of Speculative Approach on Business Performance

Even though the above approach provides us with optimal order size, since demand is uncertain, the profits obtained will depend on the actual demand observed during the season. Now, given the high demand uncertainty the firm will have stockouts during certain situations and will have to salvage leftover shirts in several situations. In the designer shirt category, one will end up with an excess stock in 87.2 per cent of the situations and one will have stockouts in 12.8 per cent of the situations. Similarly, it is possible to have a scenario of excess standard shirts in 71.9 per cent of the cases. Since we want to compare two different approaches, speculative versus responsive, one will have to work with expected value of profit as a measure of performance. It is not possible to analytically calculate the expected value of profit, but one can carry out simulation and the result of such an exercise will give us the expected value of profit. We can carry out simulation using Excel spreadsheet as discussed in detail in the Appendix. For order value of 844 and 1,077 for standard and designer shirts, respectively, the expected value of profit will be Rs 335,238.

Before we discuss the responsive approach, we will discuss a postponement model (discussed in detail in Chapter 10) where the stitching operation is postponed after the customer makes a decision about the purchase. If the firm can postpone the stitching operation after the customer makes the decision about the style, the firm will have to hold fabric inventory instead of garment inventory at the retail outlet. Of course, the firm will have to have a garment manufacturing capability at the retail outlet (the tailor who can stitch the required garment in 30 minutes). In this business model, the firm does not have to worry about demand distributions for individual variants. As long as the fabric is available, the firm can fulfil demand for designer or standard shirt by stitching the appropriate style from the fabric available at the outlet. In a postponed approach, one is working with aggregated demand with distribution parameters as shown in Table 12.2. Given that demand for designer and standard shirts is independent of each other, the standard deviation of aggregate demand can be worked out as follows:

$$\text{Standard deviation of aggregate demand} = \sqrt{214^2 + 132^2} = 251 \text{ units}$$

In a postponement approach, as far as the firm is concerned, it is going to face demand distribution with a mean of 1,600 units and a standard deviation of 251 units. So for ordering a fabric the firm can apply a short life cycle model with the above parameters of demand distribution. Of course, in this specific context it is quite difficult for a firm to postpone the point of differentiation close to customer buying. But this is an appealing idea in several other contexts as aggregate demand has much lower variability and as a result the firm will have lower lost sales and markdowns.

## Responsive Approach

In the responsive supply chain approach, the firm divides the season wherein the speculative time is one month and the reactive period is three months. That is, $T_1 + T_2 = 1$ month and $T_3 = 3$ months. The firm will observe demand for $T_1$ and based on this information it will know the demand scenario with certainty. Given the scenario, the firm will work with specific distribution of demand for that scenario and decide the optimal order quantity to be manufactured for the reactive period demand. Unlike in the case of the speculative approach, not the entire lot but only the garment needed for the speculative period will be produced in China and the demand for the reactive period will be manufactured in Mexico and a faster mode of transport will be used for transporting the garment from the plant to the retail outlet. Of course, the fabric required for garment production for the reactive period also will be sourced from China and will be held at the Mexican garment factory.

### Optimal Decisions for Speculative Period

First we work out values for optimum garment and fabric quantity, which will be ordered from a cheaper source located in the chain, and at a later stage we work out the optimum order quantity for the reactive stage.

Let $P$ = fraction of season covered by the speculative time period = $(T_1 + T_2)/T$
$MD\_P$, $SD\_P$ = Mean and standard deviation of demand during the speculative period
Since $P = 0.25$, $MD\_P = 0.25 \times MD\_S$ and $SD\_P = (0.25)^{0.5} \times SD\_S$

The optimal value of speculative orders for designer shirts and standard shirts can be worked using the methodology already discussed.

$$\text{Speculative order (designer)} = 0.25 \times 600 + 1.14 \times (0.25)^{0.5} \times 214 = 271.9 \approx 272$$

$$\text{Speculative order (standard)} = 0.25 \times 1{,}000 + 0.58 \times (0.25)^{0.5} \times 132 = 288.2 \approx 288$$

Working out fabric requirement is tricky. First, there is uncertainty regarding how the fabric will be used after updating the forecast. Second, there is a possibility that some amount of stock of designer and standard garments will be left at the end of the season. Based on service level numbers (see Table 12.3), we know that in 87.2 per cent of the cases we will have surplus designer shirts and in 71.9 per cent cases we will have surplus stock of standard shirts at the end of speculative season. Depending on the quantity of surplus shirts available at the end of the speculative season, we have to adjust our orders for the reactive season. To get over the second problem we can first work out the fabric requirement over the season using aggregate garment demand distribution. Fabric demand for the season will follow a normal distribution with a mean of 1,600 units and a standard deviation of 251 units. The total fabric requirement can be worked out using the short life cycle model using appropriate cost parameters. For the speculative period, we have already manufactured some quantity of shirts and the equivalent fabric must be subtracted from the total so as to arrive at the fabric requirement for the reactive period. Now we come to the first issue, that is, we do not know how the fabric will be used after updating the forecast. For applying the short life cycle model, we need to work out the cost of understocking, and as shown in Table 12.3 the cost of understocking a designer shirt is Rs 402 while the cost of understocking a standard shirt is Rs 107 only. It is reasonable to assume that while allocating fabric to both types of garments for the reactive period one will give priority to the designer category and only after fulfilling the requirement of the designer category will the balance fabric be allocated to the standard category. So the relevant optimal service level will be 1.15, which captures trade-offs involved in cost of understocking and overstocking when the fabric will be converted into a standard shirt while planning for the reactive period. The approach discussed above can be operationalized as follows:

Order (fabric) = mean (aggregate) + 1.15 × standard deviation (aggregate) – speculative order (designer) – speculative order (standard)

Order (fabric) = 1,600+ 1.15 × 251 – 272 – 288 = 1328.65 ≃ 1,329

So before the season starts one will have a stock of 272 designer shirts, 288 standard shirts and 1,329 units of fabric.

Of course, this approach is likely to give a reasonably good solution but is not necessarily the optimal solution. So we can carry out simulation with different values or quantity for fabric and choose one that gives the best results.

## Optimal Decisions for Reactive Time Period

Now we need to work out the methodology for decision making during period $T_2$ after the demand has been updated.

$MD\_R_{up}$, $SD\_R_{up}$ = Updated mean and standard deviation of demand during the reactive period of the season

Since $P = 0.25T$ and given that demand is uniform throughout the season, the updated parameters will be as follows:

$$MD\_R_{up} = MD\_S_k \times (1 - P) = MD\_S_k \times 0.75$$

$$SD\_R_{up} = (1 - P)^{0.5} \times SD\_S_k = 0.75^{0.5} \times SD\_S_k$$

where $k$ represents the scenario that has been revealed at the end of $T_1$.

Based on the updated parameters of demand distribution for both types of shirts, ideally we will like to start the reactive period with the following opening inventory:

$$\text{Desired opening inventory for period } T_3 = MD\_R_{up} + k \times SD\_R_{up}$$

The relevant value of $k$ can be obtained from Table 12.3. The desired production order for the reactive period will depend on the closing inventory of the garments at the end of the speculative period. If the closing inventory is more than the desired opening inventory, obviously one will not place any order for garment manufacturing in the period $T_2$.

Desired order in period $T_2$ = Max (Desired opening inventory – Closing inventory at the end of the speculative period, 0)

Of course, the actual order placed will be constrained by the availability of fabric and garment capacity. Since the garment manufacturing capacity booked is of the same size as fabric quantity, we can ignore it in our future discussion.

Reactive production order = Min (Desired order, Available fabric)

As discussed earlier, it is reasonable to assume that while allocating fabric to both types of garments for the reactive period, one will give priority to the designer shirt category as it has higher profitability.

Reactive order (Designer) = Min (Desired order (designer), Fabric inventory)

Fabric (designer) = Fabric allocated to designer shirt = Reactive order (designer)

Reactive order (standard) = Min (Desired order (standard), Fabric inventory – Fabric (designer))

Fabric (standard) = Fabric allocated to shirt = Reactive order (standard)

So at the end of allocation there is a possibility that we will have surplus fabric that will have to be salvaged at the end of the season:

Fabric (salvage) = Quantity of fabric to be salvaged at the end of the season
= Fabric inventory – Fabric (designer) – Fabric (standard)

## Reactive Time Period: Decisions for Alternative Scenarios

We demonstrate the above-mentioned methodology by looking at four different scenarios of demand. For one particular scenario involving high demand for both types of shirts we show the detailed workings, and for the other three scenarios the summary of the results are presented in Table 12.4. Though based on actual demand observed during $T_1$ (3 weeks) there will be some uncertainty involved in forecasting the total demand during the first month of the speculative period. But we will ignore this uncertainty and assume that the projected demand for the speculative period = $\{(T_1 + T_2)/T_1\} \times$ (Demand observed during $T_1$).

In the high–high scenario, the demand observed is as follows:

Observed demand in $T_1$ (designer) = 189; Observed demand in $T_1$ (standard) = 237

Projected demand over $P$ (designer) = 252; Projected demand over $P$ (standard) = 316

Inventory (designer) = Max (272 – 252, 0) = 20; Inventory (standard) = Max (288 – 316, 0) = 0

***Table 12.4:*** ***Summary of results of the speculative approach.***

| Scenario | Speculative order | | Observed demand in speculative period | | Inventory at end of speculative period | | Desired inventory at beginning of reactive period | | Desired order | | Actual order | | Fabric salvage |
|---|---|---|---|---|---|---|---|---|---|---|---|---|---|
| | Des. | Std. | Des. | Std. | Des. | Std. | Des. | Std. | Des. | Std. | Des. | Std. | |
| Low–low | 272 | 288 | 48 | 184 | 224 | 104 | 283 | 637 | 59 | 533 | 59 | 533 | 737 |
| Low–high | 272 | 288 | 48 | 316 | 224 | 0 | 283 | 877 | 59 | 877 | 59 | 877 | 393 |
| High–low | 272 | 288 | 252 | 184 | 20 | 104 | 673 | 637 | 653 | 533 | 653 | 533 | 143 |
| High–high | 272 | 288 | 252 | 316 | 20 | 0 | 673 | 877 | 653 | 877 | 653 | 676 | 0 |

$$MD\_S_k \text{ (designer)} = 860; \; SD\_S_k \text{ (designer)} = 30$$

$$MD\_S_k \text{ (standard)} = 1{,}160; \; SD\_S_k \text{ (standard)} = 20$$

$$MD\_R_{up} \text{ (designer)} = 860 \times 0.75 = 645; \; SD\_R_{up} \text{ (designer)} = 0.75^{0.5} \times 30 = 26$$

$$MD\_R_{up} \text{ (standard)} = 1{,}160 \times 0.75 = 870; \; SD\_R_{up} \text{ (designer)} = 0.75^{0.5} \times 20 = 17$$

$$\text{Desired inventory (designer)} = 645 + 1.06 \times 26 \approx 673$$

$$\text{Desired inventory (standard)} = 870 + 0.44 \times 17 \approx 877$$

$$\text{Desired reactive order} = \text{Desired inventory} - \text{Inventory at the end of the speculative period}$$

$$\text{Desired order (designer)} = \text{Max } (673 - 20, 0) = 653$$

$$\text{Desired order (standard)} = \text{Max } (877 - 0, 0) = 877$$

$$\text{Reactive production order} = \text{Min (Desired order, Available fabric)}$$

$$\text{Reactive production order (designer)} = \text{Min } (653, 1{,}329) = 653$$

$$\text{Reactive order (standard)} = \text{Min } (877, 1329 - 653) = 676$$

$$\text{Fabric (salvage)} = 0$$

In first three scenarios, there is enough fabric so we will have to salvage the fabric, but in the fourth scenario we first allocated fabric to the designer shirt and we do not have enough fabric so as to manufacture the desired amount of standard shirts for the reactive period.

While allocating fabric to different products for the reactive period demand we have assumed that the firm will work with hierarchy of products based on profitability. For example, only after allocating the required quantity for designer shirts will the firm allocate fabric to standard shirts. This will not result in optimal allocation of fabric. Since we have limited quantity of fabric available, one should allocate it based on marginal analysis; as we start allocating fabric to individual products, the value of marginal benefit starts coming down with allocation.

## Performance Comparisons of Different Approaches

We can carry out simulation using Excel spreadsheets for the above decisions approach and the expected value of profit for the responsive approach is equal to Rs 344,526. If we compare the profitability of the responsive approach with the standard approach, we find that the responsive approach increases profit by about 3 per cent. In the days of tight profit margins, a 3 per cent improvement in profit is of great value to fashion retailers. Over a period of time margins in the fashion industry have come down and this kind of improvement will be of great value.

In general, one will expect that the benefit of the responsive approach will increase with the following:

- Higher level of demand uncertainty
- Higher degree of improvement in forecast accuracy
- Larger number of products sharing common material
- Lower incremental cost involved in faster mode of production and transportation

The same ideas can be applied for managing supply chains for new products. While introducing new products at the initial stage, where demand uncertainty is high, one can work with the responsive supply chain approach. Once one has enough historical demand data, one will be able to improve forecast accuracy and one can use a cheaper source of supply and work with the efficient supply chain approach. So at different stages in the life cycle of a product one can use different approaches.

## Impact of Negatively Correlated Demand Structure

So far in our discussion we have assumed that demand for individual products is independent of each other. That is, the demand for designer shirts does not affect the demand for standard shirts. We assumed that the demand for the two kinds of shirts are independent of each other; that is, these are two unrelated business segments.

But in several business situations this may not be true. It is possible that both products are substitutes for each other and in case a customer picks up a designer shirt he will not the buy standard shirt. So demand for designer and standard shirts are negatively correlated; that is, if demand for designer shirts goes up, demand for standard shirts comes down and vice versa. In the case of negatively correlated demand, if demand for designer shirts is high, demand for standard shirts will be low, and vice versa.

While calculating aggregate demand, the correlation coefficient plays an important role.

Let the mean demand for the two types of shirts be $D_1$, $D_2$ with standard deviation equal to $SD_1$, $SD_2$ and a correlation coefficient equal to $\rho_{12}$. The parameters for aggregate demand distribution will be as follows:

$$\text{Mean} = D_1 + D_2; \quad \text{Standard deviation} = \sqrt{SD_1^2 + SD_2^2 + 2\rho_{12} SD_1 SD_2}$$

$\rho_{12}$ takes a value between −1 and +1. The demand for the two products is perfectly positively correlated if $\rho_{12} = 1$, and the demand for the two products is perfectly negatively correlated if $\rho_{12} = -1$. The demand for the two products is independent if $\rho_{12} = 0$.

In general, if we have $n$ products each with demand $D_i$ and standard deviation $SD_i$ for the $i$th product where $i = 1,..., n$ and correlation coefficient across two products $i$ and $j$ being $\rho_{ij}$, the parameters for aggregate demand distribution will be as follows:

$$\text{Mean} = \sum_{i=1}^{n} D_i; \quad \text{Standard deviation} = \sqrt{\sum_{i=1}^{n} SD_i^2 + 2\sum_{i>j} \rho_{ij} SD_i SD_j}$$

If we find that for the garment firm the demand for standard and designer shirts is perfectly negatively correlated, the standard deviation of aggregated demand is as follows:

$$= \sqrt{214^2 + 132^2 + 2 \times (-1) \times 214 \times 132} = 82$$

The fabric required at the initial stage will be

$$= 1{,}600 + 1.15 \times 82 - 272 - 288 = 1134.3 = 1134$$

Unlike the independent case, where the required quantity of fabric is 1,329, in the negatively correlated demand case one will need only 1,134 units. As a result, pooling is going to be of great value for products with a negatively correlated demand structure.

In such a case, benefits from the responsive approach will improve further, because at the aggregate level the uncertainty is very small. So one can manage with much lower value of fabric capacity, and our ability to meet order requirement during the reactive period increases significantly. Of course, using similar logic one can show that if demand is positively correlated, the benefit of pooling will be lower in nature.

The ideas discussed in this section can be applied to all the product categories that have a high degree uncertainty as well as short life cycles. We had assumed that demand is uniform throughout the season, that is, 25 per cent of a season's demand is generated in each month. It is possible that demand may follow different patterns during the season for different category of products. Two other patterns observed commonly are life cycle pattern and decaying demand pattern. In the life cycle pattern, the demand rate is low in initial period, peaks somewhere in the middle of the season and again is low towards the end of the season. Certain goods follow the demand pattern that peaks at the beginning and start decaying with time throughout the season. Music and movie DVDs follow this kind of pattern. The responsive approach discussed here can easily be applied to both these types of demand patterns. In this section, we have assumed that salvaging of surplus garments is done only at the end of the season. In Chapter 12, we discuss the use of markdowns, which will allow us to generate higher revenue from the likely surplus stocks of the garments.

## Sources of Supply Chain Disruptions and Its Impact on Business*

For large companies the world over, global supply chains have become the norm in recent years. In their drive to enter new markets and at the same time cut costs, their supply chains are becoming increasingly long and tenuous. With a substantial increase in the number of companies adopting lean manufacturing techniques, one of the major fallbacks of yesteryears—holding substantial inventory to meet market fluctuations—has fallen out of favour. On the other hand, these very techniques of lean inventory have created chains with longer paths and shorter clock speeds, resulting in more opportunities for disruption and a smaller margin of error for a disruption to take place.

### *Sources of Supply Chain Disruptions*

Lengthy supply chains are increasingly proving to be a source of concern in the face of disruptions in sourcing, production and distribution of goods and services. Such disruptions may be caused by natural disasters such as cyclones and tsunamis, industrial accidents or acts of terrorism. These disasters have created greater demands on companies to keep supply chains flexible and integrate disruption risk management into every facet of supply chain operations.

It has been noticed in several cases pertaining to the latter that an overcompensating knee-jerk government response to such acts generates more losses in the longer term. Delays due to closure of ports and airports, more stringent and time consuming security checks causing longer lead times, a rush to set up duplicative facilities/sources to guard against future attacks, huge insurance premiums and higher costs for emergency sourcing of raw materials are some of the added problems faced by firms. After the 9/11 attack such thinking was seen to directly affect the production of several companies, especially ones working with the JIT processes. Ford Motor Co., for example, was forced to let some of its assembly lines be idle as trucks full of auto components were stuck at the Canadian and Mexican borders, while several others such as Toyota came dangerously close to expending all of their inventories for JIT-sourced components and shutting their assembly lines. In attempts to become lean, several automobile companies in India have reduced raw material inventory significantly. Toyota Kirloskar works with less than 48 hours of inventory for the parts received from different parts of the country. Low inventory levels often put supply chains at a huge risk.

*The sections on "Sources of Supply Chain Disruptions and their Impact on Business" and "Methodologies for Handling Disruptions" have been contributed by Ashish Dhongde, student of MBA, IIM Bangalore, 2006 batch.

Several Indian firms assess the risk of a terrorist attack directly affecting their operations in India as fairly low and thus refrain from investing too much time and effort in countering it. This is very different from the attitude of firms in the United States, where the government is collaborating actively to ensure security at all stages of the supply chain with emphasis on sourcing from South-East Asian or Middle Eastern firms. Several companies have become a part of the US Customs' initiative C-TPAT, allowing for faster border crossing of containers arriving from relatively more secure sources. Suppliers to some US-based companies are now explicitly required, through their contracts, to put in place security enhancing and verification measures. Wal-Mart, for example, has asked its major suppliers to adopt RFID to reduce the possibility of in-transit tampering.

Besides terrorism, Indian companies may face disruptions in their operations due to several other causes—natural (tsunami, floods, etc.) or man made (strikes and riots). The result of all of these disruptions is similar in its end effects—late order compliance and idle production capacity; in the latter case loss of future contracts, as the supplier country is seen as unreliable and risky.

Disruptions in a supplier's operations have caused substantial losses to companies in the past. Consider the losses to Ericsson when its only microchip supplier Philips suffered a fire in its plant in March 2000 and was unable to manufacture chips. Rival Nokia, which also sourced its chips from the same location, came up with a quick response to manage the crisis.

### NOKIA: MANAGING SUPPLY CHAIN DISRUPTIONS[3]

In March 2000, cellular handset giant Nokia faced a major crisis. It discovered that its supply for radiofrequency chips (RFCs) was to be disrupted as the supplier's manufacturing facility in Albuquerque, New Mexico, had been destroyed by fire. In a highly competitive market, any disruption in the supply of key components puts Nokia in a really vulnerable position. The company immediately created an executive-led "strike team" that pressured its supplier, Philips, to dedicate other plants to manufacturing the RFCs that Nokia needed. Nokia engineers also quickly re-designed the RFCs so that the company's other suppliers in Japan and the United States could produce them. Quick action on the part of its supply chain team helped Nokia to meet its production goals, and even boost its market share from 27 to 30 per cent—more than two times that of its nearest rival.

The way the two companies responded has become a textbook case for the dos and don'ts of disruption risk management and a lesson in how the proper approach can turn into a competitive advantage. Unlike Nokia, Ericsson reacted much more slowly. On account of the delayed reaction, Ericsson lost the opportunity to find other ways to meet customer demand. Thanks to the fact that Ericsson relied exclusively on the Albuquerque plant for the RFCs, Ericsson—unlike Nokia—found itself with nowhere else to turn to for these vital components and posted a loss of nearly $1.7 billion for the year and lost market share to Nokia. Even though Indian firms may not face a large direct threat, their integration into global markets requires that they address the sourcing concerns of their customers for whom such problems are very real. As more and more of their global customers insist on having backup operations in place, Indian companies must make such policies as part of their offerings. In effect, an Indian supplier will be better able to service a customer if it is able to take care of supply chain disruptions that may result in a loss to its foreign downstream partner due to delays, loss of opportunity for making a sale or due to security concerns. By taking care of such supply end disruptions, Indian firms can offer a service that will be increasingly valued by foreign customers in the future.

Any policy of introducing redundancies goes against the accepted dogma of reducing inventories and slack at every level of operations. While Indian supplier firms have achieved phenomenal gains by adopting lean methodologies, changes in risk levels over the last five years or so must now force firms to at least perform a cost–benefit analysis for higher inventory reserves or better still redundant capacities, all of which can be utilized to tide over disruptions. The present phase of incorporating lean manufacturing and other techniques should be followed-up by the next one—one where companies should consider the level of flexibility (in terms of scaling up their operations and by holding strategic reserves of inventory) that they can accord to their customers. Such flexibility may soon be a qualifier for placing orders, specifically stated as a requirement by foreign firms in the future.

## *Consequences of Supply Chain Disruptions*

Firms when trying to identify the disruptions that may effect their operations generally focus on the risks that they can see. The supply chain function within that firm will also tend to concentrate on risks that it will be held accountable for. Thus, costs to mitigate a probable natural disaster or a terrorist strike will not typically be factored into risk assessment. Instead of taking this often fallacious approach, supply chain firms need to identify vulnerabilities from critical processes and equipment to manufacturing and warehousing sites, from technology and transportation to distribution and management.

The cause of the disruption is secondary to defining the portion of the operations it affects. In this sense, a flood, a hurricane or a fire may all have the same effect—say a temporary delay in transportation. Disruptions can thus be classified on the basis of their *effect* into six major kinds:

| Failure mode | Description |
|---|---|
| Disruption in supply | Delay or unavailability of materials leading to shortage of inputs |
| Disruption in transportation | Delay or unavailability in transportation infrastructure, leading to restrictions on inbound and outbound movements |
| Disruption at facilities | Delay or unavailability of plants, warehouses or office buildings |
| Freight breaches | Violation of integrity of cargoes and products, leading to loss or adulteration of products |
| Disruption in communication | Delay or unavailability of the information and communication infrastructure |
| Disruption in demand | Delay or disruption downstream can lead to loss of demand affecting upstream companies |

*Source:* Adapted from a study by MIT research group on "Supply Chain Response to Global Terrorism," Sheffi, Rice, Fleck and Caniato (2003).

Indian firms engaged in outsourced manufacturing have to be concerned mainly with the disruptions in transportation and breaches in freight security. Steps to address most of the six kinds of disruptions have been taken, especially in the United States of America, and include adoption of best practices for port security, tracking and monitoring of goods in transit, supply network visibility and greater participation of the vendor in the verification and security process.

# Methodologies for Handling Disruptions*

Handling disruptions in the supply chain requires the combination of two different kinds of actions. The first consists of putting in place physical backup facilities to which production/sourcing can be shifted at times of disruptions. The second consists of being able to map and standardize the knowledge of the processes of a company to enable quick replication when the firm is faced with the loss of its key people or facilities. Let us consider these two actions is greater detail:

- *Physical backup or redundancies.* Several methodologies exist in the industry for handling disruptions, some of them more direct than others. Among the most direct are the holding of slack capacity (a variation of which is the use of multiple sourcing locations) and the holding of excess inventory at a stage immediately after a high-risk segment of the supply chain. This caters to either sourcing and transportation disruptions or large variations in demand. Firms must realize the importance of such "strategic reserves" of inventory instead of considering only the expenses incurred in inventory holding costs.

• *Knowledge backup along with standardization of processes for easy replication.* The effect of large-scale and long-term disruptions, however, cannot be met only by the above-mentioned techniques. To be truly resilient in the face of shocks, the company must be able to store and replicate the knowledge of its processes when the situation demands. Setting up operations in a different location (e.g., a temporary office for a call centre due to problems in its primary facility) should be standardized and simplified into a set of clear cut guidelines, which can be quickly understood and implemented. This requires substantial investment in standardizing knowledge and disseminating it across the staff. The objective of the whole exercise is to introduce redundancy in physical as well as administrative processes. Consider the example of the financial services firm Salmon Smith Barney, which had offices in the World Trade Center. Its employees were saved in time and were able to get the company up and running in 12 hours from backup sites by invoking and following a set of emergency backup processes.

The ability to ensure business continuity was first seen as important by IT companies, which adopted several means of ensuring knowledge availability in the face of disruptions. Enterprises with no tolerance for any data gaps have invested huge sums to put in place replication facilities and high-speed data transfer lines between two geographically separated sites.

Besides replication, other kinds of redundancy may include back up of data at standalone storage locations (often in premises of a third-party insurer), setting up of alternative facilities in the resident city or similar facilities that are able to take on extra inflow of employees in other cities, and ensuring that passports of their key people are updated so that they can work from offices abroad.

## Multi-location Sourcing

Let us consider the option of multi-location (or flexible) sourcing in a little more detail. Though this is not a new concept, with the recent interest in developing redundancies and using real options analysis (for estimating the financial value of a flexibility offered by holding more than one source of production, transportation, sourcing, etc.), companies are now more interested in developing options for all of their crucial processes. The dual-sourcing concept (a simplified form of multi-location sourcing) depends on having two (sets of) suppliers. The first is a main supplier for fixed volumes with higher efficiency and low transaction costs catering to the majority of requirements. The second is for flexible quantities, with lower and higher volume limits and who consequently charges a higher price. The value of this flexibility to choose where to produce/source/transport from, in the face of constant change (change in availability of production facilities, exchange rate fluctuations, demand or a change in raw material costs), has to be matched against negatives such as lowered cost efficiency due to several production locations/vendors, higher transaction and quality control costs and the possible lack of interest on the vendor's side due to the small size of the order.

There is no doubt, however, that flexible sourcing allows a company to get over temporary disruptions. For example, in 2002 during the US east coast longshoremen strike, Dell Computers followed two procedures to maintain its supply to customers. First, as was its usual practice, it changed the price structure of its models so that customers were more inclined to buy those that were easier to produce (due to relatively greater ease in sourcing of components). Second, it flew in components, effectively setting up a parallel transport chain for its sourcing.

ITC, which is a major player in the consumer goods sector, has built up what is essentially a mobile production capability. In the face of disruptions in production in one of its fixed plants, it is possible for the company to pack up and move its mobile factory to another area and tide over the problem.

The requirement of firms is, therefore, to put in place such backup options before they are faced with disruption. This requires the firm to perform a cost–benefit analysis of introducing a redundancy in any of their processes. Doing this includes estimating the probability of the disruption, a process that is extremely difficult. By assuming a value for the probability (preferably erring on the higher side), and using real options to place a value on the flexibility accorded, firms can have a solid financial ground to opt for flexibility in their operations.

## Location of the Secondary Source

The decision to go in for a redundant sourcing/production operation is closely dependent on the location of the secondary source. For example, it may not make much sense for a manufacturer in the United States of America to locate both its sources in a single country or region from the point of view of maintaining steady supplies. In such a case, any disruption in the inbound freight processes (such as closure of borders due to another terrorist strike) will lead to the US firm being cut off from both its sources. Another concern may be the stability of the country where the vendor is located. A third issue is the spreading out of suppliers geographically so that a natural calamity does not have the same debilitating effect on all.

The risk assessment of a supplier from the point of view of its location needs to be carried out in a much more detailed manner. Some of the associated risks that will be included are

- Transport risk (relative ease of disruption in transportation)
- Country risk (risk from internal troubles), which includes economic and political risk
- Risk arising from the location of suppliers further upstream which supply to the immediate suppliers

What firms must look for is *a negative correlation among the parameters* listed above. For this companies must develop a correlation matrix to evaluate the outsourcing location vis-à-vis the domestic location in terms of the above-mentioned parameters. Consider the example of weather or currency fluctuations. Monsoon months in India are sure to play havoc with transportation at least in the southern and western states. This implies that on the basis of the parameter "weather", an alternative location that does not experience such debilitating effects (by virtue of its location in a relatively drier place that is unaffected by monsoons) will be negatively correlated with the original locations in southern and western states. Similarly, for exchange rate fluctuations, setting up facilities in countries whose exchange rates are negatively correlated provides a way of hedging currency risk. Obviously, a much more detailed set of parameters will be required to be looked into, for which firms should refer to country risk assessment documents such as the Political Risk Services' *International Country Risk Guide*.

There is a need for incorporating redundancies into all the segments of supply chain operations in the face of new uncertainties brought about by operating in the global markets. International suppliers such as those in India must adopt policies that concern issues that are very important to foreign markets. Perspectives of suppliers and customers may often be opposite, with customers looking at increasing security, hedging and introducing redundancies into operations (especially sourcing) at every level and suppliers looking at consolidated orders and lowering cost of transportation. A common ground has to be achieved by which incentivized suppliers adopt new practices, incorporating flexibility at the required crucial stages when catering to foreign markets.

## Summary

- While designing supply chain configuration, a firm needs to understand the nature of demand and supply uncertainty in the context of its business. Firms dealing with high uncertainty of demand and/or supply have to ensure that they have agile supply chains.
- Firms facing high uncertain demand have to look at innovations involving product redesign, process redesign, network design restructure or value offering to customer.
- By observing early sales patterns, a firm operating in the fashion industry should update forecasts and respond to the market with the updated, responsive manufacturing and high-speed transportation systems.
- Managing supply chain disruptions involves managing certain events that have a low probability of occurrence, but that which would have high impact on supply chain performance.
- Firms first need to identify vulnerabilities across the entire range of its operations—from critical processes and equipment to manufacturing and warehousing sites, from technology and transportation to distribution and management.
- To handle vulnerabilities, firms have to either create physical redundancies in the chain or develop the necessary capabilities in the system that can manage the supply chain disruption situation in an effective manner.
- Agile supply chains configure their supply chain design and operations for handling high-level demand uncertainty and supply chain disruptions.

## Discussion Questions

1. How can firms offering a high variety of products combine dual sources of supply—a low-cost high lead time source and the other a high-cost but shorter lead time source?
2. Agile firms and efficient firms are likely to differ in the way they manage and measure supply chain performances. Identify a few key areas of differences in these two types of firms.
3. What is role of IT in managing agile supply chains?
4. Traditionally, lean manufacturing has suggested that we should remove all redundancies in the supply chain. In this chapter, it is suggested that firms should create redundancies in supply chains so as to manage supply chain disruptions. How do firms manage these two conflicting ideas?
5. Why are issues related to supply chain resumption becoming more important in today's business context?
6. What are the main sources of supply chain disruptions? How do supply chain disruptions impact business performance?
7. If firms want to shift to dual sources of supply from sole sourcing so as to handle supply disruptions, what are the issues firms should keep in mind while selecting the second supplier?
8. Buyers will insist on redundancies in chain while suppliers will like to remove redundancies so as to reduce cost in the chain. How do firms reconcile differences in objectives between the two sides?

## Notes

1. See www.inditex.com and Hau Lee, "The Triple-A-Supply Chain," *Harvard Business Review* (October 2004).
2. M. L. Fisher, J. H. Hammond, W. R. Obermeyer, and A. Raman, "Making Supply Meets Demand in an Uncertain World," *Harvard Business Review* (1004, Vol 72): 83–93.
3. "Flexibility in the Face of Disaster: Managing the Risk of Supply Chain Disruption," *Knowledge@Wharton* (6 September 2006).

## Further Reading

B. E. Claude, R. H. Campbell, and E. V. Tadas, "Political Risk, Economic Risk, and Financial Risk," Report on International Country Risk Guide, *Financial Analysts Journal* (November/December 1996).

M. A. Cohen and A. Huchzermeier, "Global Supply Chain Network Management Under Price/Exchange Rate Risk and Demand Uncertainty," In M. Muffato and K. S. Pawar, eds. *Logistics in the Information Age* (SGE Ditorali, 1999).

M. L. Fisher, J. H. Hammonmd, W. R. Obermeyer, and A. Raman, "Making Supply Meets Demand in an Uncertain World," *Harvard Business Review* (1994, Vol 72): 83–93.

"Flexibility in the Face of Disaster: Managing the Risk of Supply Chain Disruption," *Knowledge@Wharton* (6 September 2006).

W. H. Hausman, "Lead-time Optimization: The Strategic Link to Learning," INFOSYS White Paper.

M. K. Mantrala and S. Rao, "A Decision Support System that Helps Retailers Decide Order Quantities and Markdown for Fashion Goods," *Interfaces* (2001, Vol 31): 146–165.

J. B. Rice, ed., "Supply Chain Response to Terrorism—Planning for the Unexpected," Report for the MIT Center for Transportation and Logistics under the MIT Industrial Liaison Program (December 2005).

Y. Sheffi, "Supply Chain Management Under the Threat of International Terrorism," *International Journal of Logistics* (2001, Vol 12): 1–11.

L. V. Snyder, "Facility Location Under Uncertainty: A Review," Technical Report #04T-015, Department of Industrial & Systems Engineering, Lehigh University, February 2005.

## Appendix: Simulation Using Excel

Simulation is a powerful tool for modelling complex supply chain problems that are not easy to be handled analytically. Several supply chain problems involving demand and supply uncertainty cannot be tracked analytically and simulation is quite useful in such situations. Simulation also gives the capability to test new ideas before implementation. There are several sophisticated simulation software available, but the bulk of the supply chain simulations can be carried out using Excel. In this appendix, we try and demonstrate the use of Excel for simulation using the example discussed in the main chapter.

In the garment company case, the manager has to decide on the optimal number of designer and standard shirts he must procure from China. From past experience he has some idea about the nature of uncertainty involved but the final outcome in terms of sales and resultant profit will depend on the actual demand. The simulation model generates a large number of instances (season demand) where each instance is drawn from the underlying demand distribution. If the manager who has been working with the speculative approach wants to explore the idea of using the responsive supply chain, he can build relevant simulation model and test alternative policies for a large number of instances of demand situations. This will allow him to choose the option that will give higher expected profit compared to other policies/options.

One of the key requirements of the simulation exercise is that it should allow us to generate random numbers for different demand distributions.

### *Generating Random Numbers Using Excel*

The RAND() function in Excel generates a random number that is uniformly distributed between 0 and 1. This means that with 25 per cent chance numbers generated by the RAND() function will be less than 0.25 and with 75 per cent chance the number generated by the RAND() function will be more than 0.25. This function can be used to generate a random number for a variety of uniform distributions. For example, if demand is going to be distributed uniformly between 0 and 100, one can enter formula 100 * RAND() in Excel. This will ensure that we get demand that is distributed randomly between 0 and 100. If demand is going to be uniform between 50 and 100 one can work with formula 50 + 50 * RAND(). We also can generate a discrete distribution by using the RAND()

function. Let us look at a case where we want to generate distribution where there is 50 per cent chance of demand equal to 100 and 50 per cent chance that demand will be 200. We know that the random number will be less than 0.5 with 50 per cent probability and will be more than 0.5 with 50 per cent probability. We can use the "If" function of Excel where we can specify that if the random generated is less than 0.5, demand will be 100 else demand will be 200.

Excel has also several inverse functions for various distributions like normal, log normal and Gamma, where the function will return the inverse of cumulative distribution for the specified parameters of the distribution. This can be combined with the Rand function to generate random numbers of the distribution of interest. For example, Excel function NORMINV(RAND(), MD, SD) generates a random number that is normally distributed with the mean equal to MD and standard deviation equal to SD. As RAND() generates random numbers uniformly between 0 and 1, it is able to capture the entire range of cumulative probability distribution between 0 and 1.

## Building a Simulation Model

We illustrate the use of Excel for simulation using the example of the garment company. We start with the speculative approach where the manager does not look at the underlying three possible scenarios (high, moderate and low demand) and assumes that demand during the season follows normal distribution.

As can be seen in Figure A12.1, we first enter the base data in Excel in cells B2:F3. In cells G2:G3 we enter decision variables, that is, order quantity for the types of shirts. For generating demand and calculating various variables of interest, we use the formula as shown in Table A12.1. In Table A12.1, we present formulas for cells A7, C7, E7 and G7 for designer shirts, and exactly similar formulas need to be entered in cells B7, D7, F7 and H7 for standard shirts.

Row 7 represents one possible outcome of season demand and we want to simulate large numbers of such outcomes. So we copy A7:I7 to A8:I506. That is, we now have 500 outcomes and in I507 we will get the value of expected profit over 500 possible outcomes, and demand in each row from 7 to 506 represents one outcome. For example, in row 7 we have designer demand, which is less than order quantity, so we will have surplus stock of designer shirts at

E2 fx 600

| | A | B | C | D | E | F | G | H | I | J | K |
|---|---|---|---|---|---|---|---|---|---|---|---|
| 1 | | Price | Cost | Sal Value | Mean Dem | SD of Dem | Ord. Qty. | | | | |
| 2 | Designer | 500 | 90 | 30 | 600 | 160 | 844 | | | | |
| 3 | Standard | 200 | 85 | 40 | 1000 | 170 | 1077 | | | | |
| 4 | | | | | | | | | | | |
| 5 | Demand | | Sales:Units | | End of Sesson Inv. | | Lost Sales: Units | | Profit | | |
| 6 | Designer | Standard | Designer | Standard | Designer | Standard | Designer | Standard | Total | | |
| 7 | 794 | 1236 | 794 | 1077 | 50 | 0 | 0 | 159 | 446521 | | |
| 8 | 649 | 1226 | 649 | 1077 | 195 | 0 | 0 | 149 | 378212 | | |
| 9 | 759 | 941 | 759 | 941 | 85 | 136 | 0 | 0 | 408090 | | |
| 10 | 633 | 1030 | 633 | 1030 | 211 | 47 | 0 | 0 | 363403 | | |
| 11 | 798 | 715 | 798 | 715 | 46 | 362 | 0 | 0 | 390314 | | |
| 12 | 930 | 979 | 844 | 979 | 0 | 98 | 86 | 0 | 454165 | | |
| 13 | 734 | 1161 | 734 | 1077 | 110 | 0 | 0 | 84 | 418173 | | |
| 14 | 734 | 1096 | 734 | 1077 | 110 | 0 | 0 | 19 | 418356 | | |
| 15 | 418 | 781 | 418 | 781 | 426 | 296 | 0 | 0 | 222569 | | |
| 16 | 546 | 1302 | 546 | 1077 | 298 | 0 | 0 | 225 | 329799 | | |
| 17 | 555 | 737 | 555 | 737 | 289 | 340 | 0 | 0 | 279780 | | |
| 18 | 572 | 1073 | 572 | 1073 | 272 | 4 | 0 | 0 | 341169 | | |
| 19 | 482 | 872 | 482 | 872 | 362 | 205 | 0 | 0 | 266813 | | |
| 20 | 510 | 1218 | 510 | 1077 | 334 | 0 | 0 | 141 | 313066 | | |
| 21 | 593 | 884 | 593 | 884 | 251 | 193 | 0 | 0 | 321001 | | |
| 22 | 832 | 1096 | 832 | 1077 | 12 | 0 | 0 | 19 | 464324 | | |
| 23 | 667 | 702 | 667 | 702 | 177 | 375 | 0 | 0 | 326859 | | |
| 24 | 568 | 1155 | 568 | 1077 | 276 | 0 | 0 | 78 | 340180 | | |
| 25 | 628 | 1102 | 628 | 1077 | 216 | 0 | 0 | 25 | 368434 | | |
| 26 | 546 | 1007 | 546 | 1007 | 298 | 70 | 0 | 0 | 318469 | | |
| 27 | 727 | 1124 | 727 | 1077 | 117 | 0 | 0 | 47 | 414724 | | |
| 28 | 766 | 1372 | 766 | 1077 | 78 | 0 | 0 | 295 | 433446 | | |
| 29 | 766 | 906 | 766 | 906 | 78 | 171 | 0 | 0 | 405695 | | |
| 30 | 443 | 901 | 443 | 901 | 401 | 176 | 0 | 0 | 253213 | | |

**Figure A12.1**

Spreadsheet view for normal demand distribution case.

*Table A12.1:* **Relevant spreadsheet formulas for the normal distribution case.**

| Cell | | Cell formula | Remark |
|---|---|---|---|
| A7 | Demand | = NORMINV(RAND(),$E$2,$F$2) | Will generate random number from normal distribution with parameters specified in cells E2 and F2 |
| C7 | Sales in units | = Max(A7,$G$2) | Maximum of demand and stock will determine sale quantity |
| E7 | End of season inventory | = Max($G$2-A7,0) | |
| G7 | Lost sales | = Max(A7-$G$2,0) | |
| H7 | Profit | = C7*$B$2+D7*$B$3+E7*$D$2 + F7*$D$3-$G$2*$C$2-$G$3*$C$3 | Profit = Revenue from sales + Revenue from salvage cost |
| I507 | Expected profit | = AVERGAE(I7..I506) | Expected profit is obtained by taking average over 500 instances of demand |

the end of season, which will have to be salvaged. While in the standard shirts case demand outstrips our order, so we will have a stockout situation resulting in lost sales of 159 shirts. In A7 to A506 we have random numbers that have been generated from normal distribution with mean equal to 600 and standard deviation of 160.

Now we take a little more complex case where we explicitly generate random demand where the mean demand is likely to be high, moderate or low with equal probability. As discussed in the main chapter we assume that the standard deviation of demand is same for all the three possible mean demand scenarios. Base data are entered in cell B2:I3. Demand for low, moderate and high demand scenarios are shown in cells E2:E3, F2:F3 and G2:G3, respectively. As the random number generated in cell A7 will be uniformly distributed between 0 and 1, one-third of the number will be less than 0.3333, one-third will be between 0.333333 and 0.666667 and one-third will be more than 0.666667. Cell C7 will take the value of low mean demand if the random number in cell A7 is less than 0.33333, the value of moderate demand if the random number is between 0.333333 and 0.666667 and the value of high mean demand if the random number is above 0.666667. The formula in E7 will generate demand from normal distribution with a mean value equal to value in cell C7 and a standard deviation specified in H2. In Table A12.2, we present formulas for cells A7, C7, E7 and G7 for designer shirts, and exactly similar formulas need to be entered in cells B7, D7, F7 and H7 for standard shirts.

Now row 7 represents one possible outcome of season demand and we want to simulate large numbers of such outcomes. So we copy A7:I7 to A8:I506. That is, we will now have 500 outcomes, and in I506 we will get the value of expected profit over 500 possible outcomes while the demand in each row from 7 to 506 represents one outcome.

*Table A12.2:* **Relevant spreadsheet formulas for the three mean demand scenarios.**

| | Variable | | Remark |
|---|---|---|---|
| A7 | | RAND() | Will generate random number between 0 and 1 from uniform distribution |
| C7 | Mean demand | If A7 < 1/3,$E$2,(If A7 < 2/3,$F$2,$G$2) | Will generate three possible demand means (L, M, H) with equal probability |
| E7 | Season demand | = NORMINV(RAND(),C7,$H$2) | Will generate random number from normal distribution with mean = C7 and standard deviation equal to H2 |
| G7 | Revenue | = $B$2*MAX(E7,$I$2) + $D$2*Max($I$2–E7,0) | Revenue = Revenue from sales + Revenue from salvaging of end of season inventory |
| I7 | Total profit | = G7+H7–$I$2*$C$2–$I$3*$C$3 | Profit revenue (designer) + Revenue (standard) – Cost (designer) – Cost (standard) |
| I507 | Expected profit | = Average (I7...I506) | |

Let us look at the more complex case of the responsive approach. We will only show modelling of demand generation for the speculative period, decision about garment order for the reactive period and demand generation during the reactive period. Modelling revenue, cost and profit will be more or less similar to the other models discussed. Base data about designer and standard garments are presented in cells B2:L3. In J2:J3 the cost for producing in the reactive period is shown. In K2:K3, data about the ratio of the speculative season to the total season is shown. This is because mean and standard deviation of demand during speculative and reactive periods will get affected by the length of the speculative period.

Let $f$ be a fraction representing the ratio of speculative period to season period. In the specific case of the garment company under discussion, $f$ is equal to ¼ = 0.25.

Mean (speculative) = $f \times$ Mean (season) and SD (speculative) = $f^{0.5} \times$ SD (season)

Mean (reactive) = $(1 - f) \times$ Mean (season) and SD (speculative) = $(1 - f)^{0.5} \times$ SD (season)

Since standard deviation of demand during the reactive period is known in advance one can work out the safety stock required for the reactive period in advance. For specifying safety stock in the reactive period one does not need information about the specific nature of the scenario, which will only be revealed at the end of the speculative period. The required safety stocks quantity has been specified in L2:L3. Since the fabric is also ordered in the speculative period, data regarding cost, salvage value and order quantity for the fabric are entered in cells C4, D4 and I4, respectively.

In Table A12.3, we present formulas for cells A7, C7, E7, G7, I7 and K7 for designer shirts and J7 for standard shirts. Similar relevant formulas for standard shirts can be entered in cells B7, D7, F7, H7 and K7.

Revenue and profit related columns can be entered in the few other columns of the seventh row. Finally, one can copy the relevant column of the seventh row to the eighth row to 506. This will allow us to generate the expected profit over 500 possible outcomes, as demand in each row from 7 to 506 represents one outcome.

As discussed in the main chapter, the suggested order quantity for fabric is based on a heuristic approach, so the manager can benefit by testing various values of fabric order quantity so that he can find a solution that gives a reasonably good value of expected profit. Of course, simulation will not give us the optimal solution, but since we can test our decisions over a large range of values, it can be ensured that the chosen solution will result in reasonably good outcome and in some cases the chosen decision is likely to be close to the optimal solution.

***Table A12.3:* Relevant spreadsheet formulas for the responsive approach case.**

| | Variable | | Remark |
|---|---|---|---|
| A7 | | RAND() | Will generate random number between 0 and 1 from uniform distribution |
| C7 | Mean demand | If A7 < 1/3,$E$2,(If A7 < 2/3,$F$2,$G$2) | Will generate three possible demand means (L, M, H) with equal probability |
| E7 | Demand: Speculative† | = NORMINV(RAND(), C7*$K$2,$H$2*$K$2^0.5) | Will generate random number from normal distribution with mean = C7 * K2 and standard deviation equal to H2*K2^0.5 |
| G7 | Inv(End of speculative period) | = MAX($I$2-E7,0) | |
| I7 | Order(Reactive period): Designer | = Min [Max{C7*(1-$k$2) + $L$2-G7},$I$4] | Order = Min(Desired Order,‡ Fabric Inventory) |
| J7 | Order(Reactive period): Standard | Min[Max{D7*(1-$k$3) + $L$3-H7},$I$4-I7] | Order + Min(Desired Order,‡ Fabric Inventory – Reactive order(designer) |
| K7 | Demand: Reactive† | = NORMINV(RAND(),C7*$(1-$K$2), $H$2*(1-$K$2)^0.5) | Will generate random number from normal distribution with mean = C7 * (1 – K2) and standard deviation equal to H2*(1–K2)^0.5 |

† As discussed mean and standard deviation get corrected by the K2 factor.

‡ Desired order = Desired inventory at the beginning of the reactive period – Inventory at the end of the speculative period.

# Pricing and Revenue Management

## Learning Objectives

After reading this chapter, you will be able to answer the following questions:

> What is revenue management?

> Why do firms offer differential prices to different market segments?

> What are the conditions under which revenue management can be practised in an effective way?

> How do firms make optimal pricing decisions in the context of revenue management?

> Why does the fashion industry offer markdown pricing during the end of the season?

Sanjay Rathore is a busy man. He is responsible for the country-wide operations of the company that employs him. The company has 12 offices in India alone and an equal number in South-East Asia. Consequently, Sanjay lives out of a suitcase, spending most of his waking hours either at an airport or in meetings. Thanks to his erratic schedules, he does not get much time to plan his trips and book tickets in advance. Under the best circumstances, his tickets are reserved 48 hours prior to the flight.

He was to reach the Gurgaon office urgently to deal with transportation issues that the office was facing. A colleague from the finance team was also taking the same flight. Since it is a routine visit, the tickets for Sanjay's colleague were booked a fortnight in advance. To his dismay, Sanjay had discovered the previous evening that the airlines had charged him almost three times of what it had charged his colleague.

Sanjay managed to wrap up a quick breakfast with some colleagues from Singapore and somehow made it to the airport on time. Ten minutes before the scheduled departure, he was told that the airlines could not offer him a seat on that flight. In anticipation of last-minute cancellations or no shows, they had overbooked the flight. However, since there were none in actuality, they were unable to offer him a seat. Furious at the executive at the help-desk and the airline for this mix-up, Sanjay logged on to the Website to file a complaint. While browsing through the site, he realized that not only is this a standard practice for an airlines company but also that it is legal in most countries.

Why do airlines charge different prices for different customers for the same flight? Why do airlines book seats more than the capacity of the aircraft? We examine the reasons that drive airlines and other firms to resort to such measures of differential pricing and overbooking. We discuss the need and utility of these concepts in revenue management to maximize revenue and profits.

## Introduction

So far, we have focused on managing a supply chain so as to service the end customer. But demand is actually influenced by the marketing decisions taken by the firm. We have thus for assumed that a firm works in a hierarchical fashion where marketing decisions, including pricing decisions, are made first and that the supply chain is expected to manage its operation so that the firm can meet the demand at the lowest cost. Instead of working in a hierarchical fashion, a firm can also make joint decisions. However, the benefit of coordinated decision making is likely to be outweighed by the transaction costs involved in the process in most of the supply chain situations. In limited-supply situations, though, the opportunity cost of hierarchical decision making is likely to be significant. Revenue management essentially addresses these situations. Under conditions of limited supply (scheduled flight in airlines, long lead time supply items in the fashion industry, etc.), the bulk of the capacity and supply-related costs have already been incurred and consequently revenue management attempts to make optimal pricing decisions so that the firm can generate the highest possible revenue so as to generate the highest possible profit.

In this chapter, we focus on pricing decisions by a firm in limited-supply situations. We examine two scenarios as part of this discussion:

- *Supply is limited by the available capacity in perishable products or service situations.* Since one cannot store perishable products and services, the capacity of a plane, a hotel or a truck restricts the supply position in these businesses.
- *Supply is limited by available inventory in long lead time supply situations.* The ability to handle demand is constrained by the fact that the supplier needs a long lead time and within that period the firm has to manage with the inventory available at hand.

We begin by introducing a few concepts in pricing and follow it up with a discussion on revenue management for the two situations described above. We also look at the effect of uncertain demand in such cases.

## Pricing

The decision to price a product at a particular value is a marketing decision. Prices are fixed with the ultimate goal of maximizing profits. The law of demand states that as the price of a good or service increases, the demand for the good or service will decrease and vice versa. Therefore, for maximizing profits, an optimal pricing decision is needed.

### Law of Demand and Optimal Pricing Decision

The law of demand is normally depicted as an inverse relation of demand quantity and price. To illustrate this concept, let us take the hypothetical case of Super Airlines, which wants to make a pricing decision for its daily morning flight from Bangalore to Mumbai. Super Airlines caters to business customers, and based on market surveys, it has estimated the following relationship between demand for seats on the said flight and price charged by the airline:

$$\text{Demand} = 160 - 20 \times \text{Price (where price is in thousand rupees)}$$

The above equation is valid only in the price range of Rs 0–8,000. At Rs 8,000, no customer will be willing to book a seat and demand will increase by 20 units with decline in unit price (unit in this case is thousand rupees). At a price close to zero, demand will shoot up to 160. The profit generated from the flight is as follows:

Profit = Revenue – Fixed cost – Variable cost
= Price × Seats booked – Fixed cost – Variable unit cost × Seats booked

The bulk of the cost of operating a flight between Bangalore to Mumbai is fixed. Once the Airline has announced the flight and allocated aircrafts (these decisions are made well in advance), the firm has no choice but to operate the announced flight and hence the fixed cost is like a sunk cost. Let the fixed cost involved in operating a flight from Bangalore to Mumbai be Rs 300,000 and we start with the assumption that the marginal cost of filling one more seat is close to zero. In such a case, optimizing profit is equivalent to optimizing revenue. The revenue function for this airline will be as follows:

$$\text{Revenue} = 160 \times \text{Price} - 20 \times \text{Price}^2$$

As one can see from Figure 13.1, the revenue against price curve will be an inverted U-shaped curve. The revenue will increase initially when the firm increases its price from zero and will peak at a price of Rs 4,000 and will subsequently decline with further increase in price. So it will be optimal for the airlines to price the Bangalore–Mumbai flight at Rs 4,000, which will result in a demand of 80 seats. This will generate a revenue of Rs 320,000 and amount to a profit of Rs 20,000 per flight.

For a general case of the linear demand curve, the formula is as follows:

$$D = a - bp$$

where $D$ is the demand, $p$ is the price and $a$ and $b$ are parameters of the demand curve.

One can easily show that the optimal price denoted as $p^*$ is as follows:

$$p^* = \frac{a}{2b} \text{ and revenue}^* = \frac{a^2}{4b}$$

In the case of Super Airlines,

$$p^* = \frac{160}{2 \times 20} \text{ and revenue}^* = \frac{160^2}{4 \times 20} = 320$$

At a price of Rs 4,000, 80 seats will get booked. So while choosing the aircraft for this flight, the firm should ideally choose an aircraft whose capacity is just higher than the demand

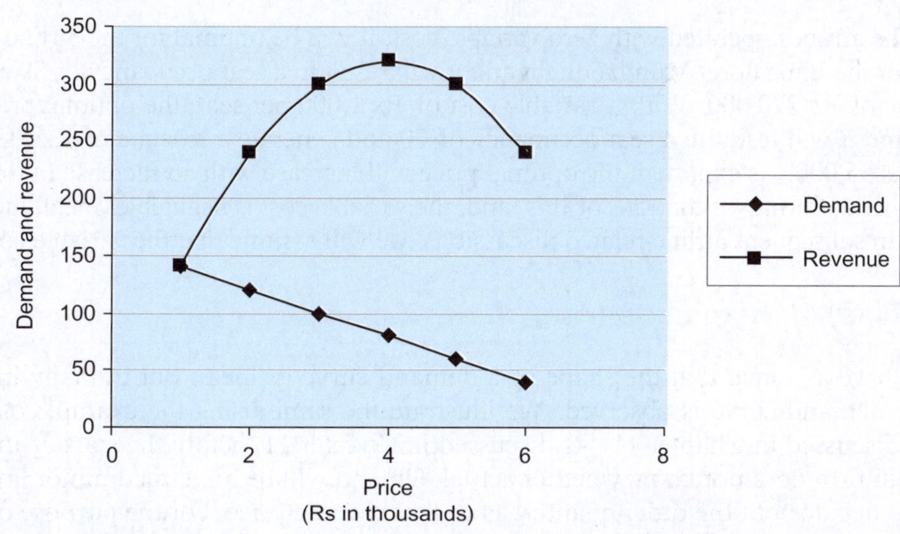


**Figure 13.1**

Demand and revenue curve.

likely to be observed at the optimum price. So if the airline company had to choose between two aircrafts with a seating capacity of 120 and 180, it will make sense to use the 120-seat aircraft for the Bangalore–Mumbai route.

### Pricing Under Capacity Constraints

Now if Super Airlines chose to use an aircraft with a capacity of only 60 seats (because it was operating an ADR, which has a capacity of only 60 seats), it will not make sense to fix the price at Rs 4,000 and decline seats to 20 customers.

So if Capacity > Demand($p^*$), it makes sense to work with a lower capacity utilization rather than to fill up the plane. But if Demand($p^*$) > Capacity, then it will be optimal to fix the price as follows:

$$p^* = \frac{a - \text{capacity}}{b}$$

In Super Airlines, for a capacity of 60, the price = (160 – 60)/20 = 5.

Therefore, it can fix the price at Rs 5,000, which will give the firm a revenue of Rs 300,000. If the firm had fixed the price at Rs 4,000, it might have had to refuse seats to 20 passengers and earn lower revenue (Rs 240,000).

### Pricing in a Situation Involving Significant Variable Cost

So far we have assumed that the variable cost is zero. Let us assume that the variable cost is $c$ per seat. So

$$\text{Profit} = \text{Revenue} - \text{Variable cost} - \text{Fixed cost}$$

$$\text{Profit} = (a - bp)(p - c) - \text{Fixed cost}$$

where $c$ is the variable cost per unit.

So optimal profits will be when

$$p^* = \frac{(a + bc)}{2b}$$

Let us take a case where the variable cost per seat for Super Airline is Rs 1,000:

$$p^* = \frac{(160 + 20 \times 1)}{2 \times 20} = 4.5, \quad \text{demand} = 160 - (20 \times 4.5) = 70$$

$$\text{Revenue} = 70 \times 4.5 = 315, \quad \text{Profit} = 315 - 300 - 70 \times 1 = -55$$

So if the airlines operated with zero variable cost, it will be optimal for the airline to charge Rs 4,000 for the Bangalore–Mumbai flight and it will result in a seat occupancy of 80 and generate revenue of Rs 320,000. With a variable cost of Rs 1,000 per seat, the optimal price will be Rs 4,500 and it will result in a seat occupancy of 70 and generate a revenue of Rs 315,000 and a loss of Rs 55,000. As expected, the optimal price will increase with an increase in the variable cost. In general, for most situations of this kind, the variable cost is negligible (meal, incremental fuel cost). In subsequent airline-related discussions, we will assume that the variable cost is zero.

## Case of Non-linear Demand Curve

So far we have assumed that the shape of a demand curve is linear. But in many instances a non-linear demand curve is observed. We illustrate the same using the example of designer garments discussed in Chapter 11. As discussed in Chapter 11, before the start of the season, the garment firm does not know whether actual demand will be high, medium or low, but the firm has to decide both the order quantity as well as the sale price. For the purpose of pricing, the firm will carry out analysis using average demand numbers. Based on past data and market survey results, the demand for designer shirts is estimated to be as follows:

$$\text{Demand} = 2{,}100 - 4.5p - 0.003p^2 \text{ for } 200 \le p \ge 600$$

$$\text{Revenue} = 2{,}100p - 4.5p^2 + 0.003p^3$$

The demand curve is valid for a price range of Rs 200–600. We assume that the firm has a policy that the price has to be in multiples of hundred, so it is looking at a choice of six possible prices with the minimum being Rs 200 and the maximum being Rs 600. (Most firms prefer to price products with price ending at 99. According to a 1997 study published in the *Marketing Bulletin*,[1] approximately 60 per cent of the prices in advertisements ended in the digit 9. But for simplicity we will work with round figures of prices.)

As can be seen in Table 13.1, the highest profitability is achieved at a price of Rs 500. If there was no demand uncertainty, the firm will have bought 600 shirts and expected to earn a profit of Rs 246,000 over the entire season. On account of uncertainty, the firm will estimate the cost of understocking and overstocking and will eventually end up stocking 844 shirts for which it will incur a cost of Rs 78,690, but the actual demand will be discovered only during the season. As discussed earlier, ordering 844 shirts will provide a service level of about 87 per cent. In other words, there is an 87 per cent chance that they will have surplus stock at the end of the season and a 13 per cent chance that they will have a stockout situation. At the end of the first month, they will have a better understanding of the demand situation (whether demand is high, medium or low). So in case actual demand turns out to be on the lower side, ideas of revenue management help the firm to optimize its revenue (cost incurred in procuring shirts is sunk cost). Later in the chapter, we will use the example of designer shirts to illustrate the application of revenue management ideas for inventory assets.

## Revenue Management for Multiple Customer Segments

So far we have assumed that we are dealing with a homogenous group of customers and hence we have one demand curve and the associated price elasticity. Most situations involve multiple segments of customers, each segment having a different price elasticity with a different demand curve for each submarket. In the case of airlines and the hotel industry, we usually have two clear segments: business travellers and leisure travellers. Both have different price elasticity and hence provide an opportunity for revenue management.

To understand the mechanistics of situations involving multiple customer segments, we consider again the hypothetical case of Super Airlines. We derive the total demand curve where the total demand consists of the demand observed from different submarkets.

**Table 13.1: *Impact of price on demand and revenue*.***

| Price (*P*) | Demand over season (*Q*) | Revenue = $P \times Q$ | Variable cost (VC) = $VC \times Q$ | Profit = Revenue – Variable cost |
|---|---|---|---|---|
| 200 | 1,320 | 264,000 | 118,800 | 145,200 |
| 300 | 1,020 | 306,000 | 91,800 | 214,200 |
| 400 | 780 | 312,000 | 70,200 | 241,800 |
| 500 | 600 | 300,000 | 54,000 | 246,000 |
| 600 | 480 | 288,000 | 43,200 | 244,800 |

**VC* = 90.

Let us say that Super Airlines realizes that it is operating at low capacity and wants to increase demand by attracting leisure travellers on the Bangalore–Mumbai route. Leisure travellers are likely to be more price conscious and, thus, this segment will have a different demand curve. Based on a market survey, the demand curve for leisure travellers has the following relationship:

$$Demand\_LT = 240 - 60p$$

Demand for leisure and business travellers will be denoted by *Demand_LT* and *Demand_BT*, respectively. So at a price of Rs 4,000, no leisure travel will be interested in this service, but with every thousand-rupee reduction in price, the airlines will be able to increase demand by 60 seats. The potential market size for leisure travellers is larger than business travellers but they are quite conscious of the price.

So if we assume that the airlines is attracting only leisure travellers, the optimal price will be

$$\text{Price}^*(LT) = 240/(2 \times 60) = 2; \quad Demand\_LT\,(\text{Price} = 2) = 120$$

If the airlines is offering the service to leisure travellers only, it will be optimal for the airlines to price the Bangalore–Mumbai flight at Rs 2,000, which will result in a demand of 120 seats, and generate a revenue of Rs 240,000. This would amount to a loss of Rs 60,000 per flight.

Now if the airlines estimates the total demand curve (business plus leisure travellers), as shown in Figure 13.2, the demand will be as follows:

$$\text{Demand} = 160 - 20p \text{ if price} > 4$$

$$\text{Demand} = 400 - 80p \text{ if price} \leq 4$$

Demand for submarkets leisure and business are added horizontally to get the total market demand curve. As we can see there is a kink in the total demand curve at a price of 4 (Rs 4,000). At higher prices only business travellers have a positive demand, while at lower prices the demand curve adds up the respective demand for business as well as leisure travellers. It can be easily shown that if the firm has to offer one price to both the segments, it will be optimal for the firm to charge a price of Rs 2,500. At this price, the airline will be able to book 200 seats and generate a revenue of Rs 500,000 and a profit of Rs 200,000.

If the airlines can find a way of distinguishing these two types of customers, the firm could charge different prices to business and leisure customers for the same seat. In such a situation, the airline should charge Rs 4,000 rupees to business travellers and Rs 2,000 to leisure travellers. As can be seen from Table 13.2, this will result in a demand of 200 seats and will yield

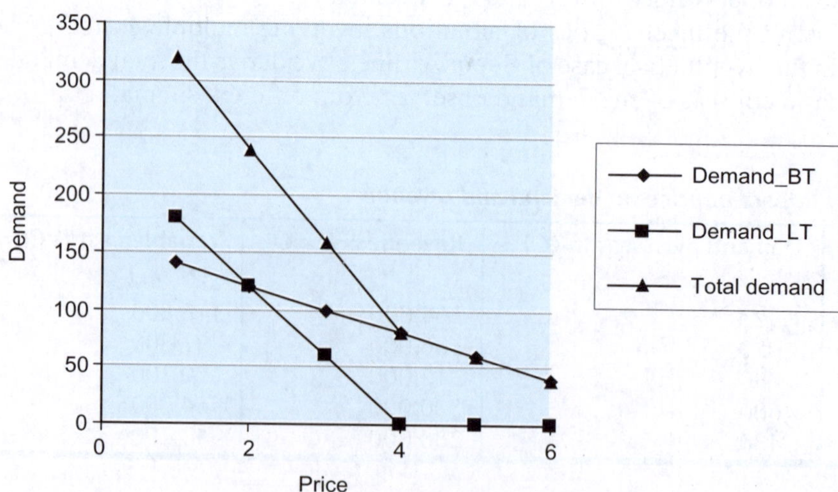


**Figure 13.2** Demand curve for multiple customer segments.

*Table 13.2:* **Impact of price on revenue for multiple segments.**

| Focus | Price (in thousands rupees) | Demand (seats) | Revenue (in thousands) | Remark |
|---|---|---|---|---|
| Business traveller | 4 | 80 | 320 | |
| Leisure traveller | 2 | 120 | 240 | |
| Business + leisure travellers | 2.5 | 200 | 500 | 200 passengers constitute 110 business travellers and 90 leisure travellers |

a revenue of Rs 560,000 and the profit will be Rs 260,000, an increase of 12 and 30 per cent, respectively. The biggest challenge is to ensure that customers in the high-price segment do not buy the low-price service. Also, the firm will not want a situation where customers will buy a service at low prices and sell the same to other customers at a higher price later. To maintain the distinction between the two customer segments, the firm has to introduce booking rules that create barriers or fences between these market segments. This is known as third-degree price discrimination in economics literature where self-segmentation by customers takes place. In Box 13.1, we discuss the case of peak-load pricing where revenue management concepts have been applied in an innovative manner.

In some cases, one can use demographics to separate the two submarkets. For example, Indian Airlines offers a discount to senior citizens and students. In this case, it is possible to verify the identity and hence ensure that price-sensitive customers will not take advantage of the low prices offered to senior citizens and students. So the firm has managed to create a fence between two markets and it can offer differential prices to different segments. But in most business situations, one may not be able to use demographics for separating submarkets. However, a firm can impose a booking condition with an offer of seat, so that based on utility or disutility of these booking conditions customers will get separated into relevant submarkets. It is important that these booking conditions should be able to effectively fence customers within different segments. While designing booking rules, airlines and hotels take advantage of the fact that business travellers cannot plan their travel in advance and that they want the flexibility of cancelling the flight in case of business exigencies. Since the company pays for the travel, the business traveller is less price sensitive compared to leisure travellers. Unlike business travellers, leisure travellers usually plan well in advance and are not interested in liberal cancellation

### BOX 13.1 Peak-load Pricing: Case of Differential Pricing

Peak-load pricing involves charging different prices at different points in time: Peak time and off-peak time. By having differential pricing, one can encourage customers who are price elastic to shift their demand from peak time to non-peak time. Telecom companies used to charge higher rates during the day time and lower rates during night. Persons using telephone service for business purposes cannot move to night time and are willing to pay higher prices during the peak demand time of the day. Customers using telecom service for personal use are highly price sensitive and will not mind using the service during the night. So by offering differential prices a firm is able to shift customers from peak time to non-peak time and as a result the firm will be able to earn higher revenue compared to the pricing practice where the same price is charged during the peak time as well as during the non-peak time.

For restaurants there are two kinds of customers: working professionals and students. If restaurants divide the business day into two parts, afternoon and evening, they find that demand during evenings exceed their capacity. Hence they offer happy hour pricing where afternoon prices are lower compared to evening prices. While working professionals can only use the evenings, students can shift their demand to the afternoons without much difficulty. Thus by offering happy hour pricing, restaurants are able to shift student demand from the evenings (peak time) to the afternoons (non-peak time).

policies. Essentially, leisure travellers have low disutility for booking conditions like no cancellations policy and requirement of early booking. Therefore, these booking rules can be used for separating business and leisure travel submarkets. Marriott Hotel first experimented with different types of booking rules at a couple of sample locations before they launched the firm-wide revenue management practices.

### REVENUE MANAGEMENT AT MARRIOTT HOTEL[2]

Marriott Hotel wanted to understand the appropriateness of ideas of revenue management in its context. It first decided to carry out a few tests at a couple of sample locations with different booking conditions. In December 1990, during the holiday season, it offered a discount rate of $48 with booking conditions like advance reservations (14 days in advance) and no refund on cancellations policy. It sold about 54,000 room-nights over 180 locations. During the market research it found that 70 per cent of the customers who had booked the rooms under this arrangement were not regular users of the Marriott hotels. Based on its initial positive experience, Marriott carried out different tests with different booking conditions before they launched firm-wide revenue management practices. Before launching the revenue management at the firm level, Marriott wanted to make sure that some of theses practices should not result in brand dilution. Since the early 1990s Marriott hotels use revenue management practices extensively.

In most of the revenue management policies where you are allowing customers to do a self-segmentation you will not be able to create a watertight compartment, and some amount of spill over will happen (for example in the student discount scheme in the airline case one will have no spill over because the airline is able to neatly segment the customers using student identity cards) where customers who are less price sensitive would have bought capacity at a higher price end up paying lower prices. As long as this fraction is low, revenue management schemes will increase revenue and profitability for a firm. If a firm is not able to keep this fraction at a low level, the firm might find that revenue and profits might decline. Just imagine if in our airline case if all the passengers end up buying service at Rs 2,000: the firm will end up losing lot of money. Aravind Eye Hospital has come up with an innovative way of segmenting different types of patients and uses revenue management ideas in its eye care operations.

### SEGMENTING PATIENTS AT ARAVIND EYE HOSPITAL[3]

Aravind Eye Hospital offers eye care services to two categories of patients: free and paid patients. Surgeon and operation theatre capacity is shared among both the category of patients. Since they finance their operations from internally generated funds, it is important for them that patients who can afford to pay for the services should ideally use paid services. At the same time, Aravind will not like to humiliate poor patients by asking for proof of income from prospective patients desirous of availing the free services. They have found an ingenious way of segmenting the market. Patients who want free service are expected to stay for a longer time at the hospital and will be provided dormitory accommodation while paid patients will get individual rooms and will spend fewer days at the hospital. This ensures that patients who are less price sensitive and have a higher opportunity cost of time will opt for paid service. Poor patients whose opportunity cost of time is low will not mind the inconvenience of a longer stay at hospital and dormitory accommodation during their hospital stay. This allows them to meet their objective of providing free eye surgery to needy patients without hurting the viability of the hospital.

To sum up, a firm can apply ideas of revenue management under any of the following conditions:

- Capacity is perishable (one cannot store an unused airline seat)

- The same unit of capacity can be used to deliver product or service to different submarkets having their own demand curves with differing price elasticity
- Using appropriate booking rules a firm can create a fence among the relevant submarkets

So far we have assumed that demand can be estimated accurately. In the case of demand uncertainty, there are additional complexities involved when one wants to offer differential pricing schemes and new opportunities open up for enhancing revenue from limited perishable capacity or inventory.

## Pricing Under Capacity Constraint for Multiple Segments

The practice of revenue management is also known as yield management. In airlines typically one is trying to optimize yield per seat. Since we have limited capacity, the revenue maximization problem translates to the yield management problem where you maximize yield per unit of capacity. Of course, as discussed earlier, if a firm has substantial marginal cost it should be focusing on profit maximization and not on revenue maximization alone.

As discussed earlier, the airline may have limited capacity and in such a situation based on price–demand equations of all the relevant customer segments the firm will have to alter its prices. The firm will have to fix prices that will automatically allocate capacity to multiple segments. Let us use index *i* to identify the relevant decision variables and parameters for different classes of customers.

So for each category we will have

$$Demand_i = a_i - b_i P_i \quad \text{and} \quad Revenue_i = (a_i - b_i P_i) \times P_i$$

So the firm will like to solve the following problem:

$$\text{Maximize} \quad \sum_i (a_i - b_i P_i) \times P_i$$

Subject to

$$\sum_i (a_i - b_i P_i) \le \text{Capacity}$$

$$(a_i - b_i P_i) \ge 0 \quad \text{for } i = 1, \ldots, n$$

The same problem can be solved using standard optimization software.

Let us take the example of an airline that, let us say, is flying a Boeing with a capacity 120 seats. As the airline does not have enough capacity to accommodate 200 passengers, it will make sense for airline to change its prices so that it can maximize its revenue. The airline will have to solve the following problem:

$$\text{Maximize} \quad (160 - 20P_{\text{bt}}) \times P_{\text{bt}} + (240 - 60P_{\text{lt}}) \times P_{\text{lt}}$$

Subject to

$$160 - 20P_{\text{bt}} + 240 - 60P_{\text{lt}} \le 120$$

$$160 - 20P_{\text{bt}} \ge 0; \quad 240 - 60P_{\text{lt}} \ge 0$$

This will ensure that we choose appropriate prices for both segments so that we work within the given capacity of 120 seats.

As can be seen from Table 13.3, it will be optimal to price business travellers at Rs 5,000 and leisure travellers at Rs 3,000; thus, each category of customers will be allocated 60 seats.

**Table 13.3: Impact of different price schedules on revenue under capacity constrained case.**

| Price charged for business travellers | Price charged for leisure travellers | Seats allocated to business travellers | Seats allocated to leisure travellers | Total revenue (in thousands) |
|---|---|---|---|---|
| 4 | 3.333333 | 80 | 40 | 453.3333 |
| 5 | 3 | 60 | 60 | 480 |
| 6 | 2.666667 | 40 | 80 | 453.3333 |
| 7 | 2.333333 | 20 | 100 | 373.3333 |

## INTERVIEW WITH RATAN RATNAKAR

*Kingfisher Airlines, a division of UB holdings, is a leading full-service airline in India with a turnover of Rs 60 billion. Ratan Ratnakar is the Vice President of Revenue Optimization at Kingfisher Airlines and Deccan Airlines.*

*What is the scale of operations of Kingfisher Airlines?*

**Ratan Ratnakar:** Currently Kingfisher Airlines serves 41 destinations in India with a fleet of 40 planes and offers 270 daily flights across India. As a group (Kingfisher–Air Deccan combined) we are the largest domestic airline company, both in terms of market share and fleet—77 aircraft including 43 Airbus aircraft and 34 ATR aircraft. This combined King Power offers 540 daily flights covering 72 cities in India. We also plan to start international operations in the near future, operating non-stop services to the United States of America, convenient flights to the United Kingdom and providing seamless connectivity to the Far East and the Gulf. With the ability to offer full service and value under a single brand, Kingfisher is in a strong position to play a key role on the world stage.

*What revenue management strategies does Kingfisher Airlines follow?*

**Ratan Ratnakar:** Over the past two years, we have worked on building the required infrastructure and inculcating effective revenue management practices. We have put a team in place that has both domestic and international experience; and we are continuously providing opportunities for growth. To derive optimum benefits, we have ensured the integration of the four arms, pricing, distribution, yield management and central reservation system, with the technology and tools in place. The KRA of the staff ensures a constant effort by the yield analysts to track revenue performance, both sector- and flight-wise. At the planning stage itself, revenue optimization plays the anchor role in analysing flight profitability based on competition, market demand, connectivity and network benefit. Competitor activity does play a role in pricing and capacity allocation, but on key routes where we are the leaders we ensure that we are the price leaders as well.

*What difficulties does Kingfisher Airlines face in implementing revenue management?*

**Ratan Ratnakar:** When Kingfisher started operations in May 2005, the Indian market was starting to ride the crest of an unprecedented boom in the aviation sector. The key challenge was to gain market as a new entrant without upsetting the price. The market was experiencing, for the first time, the "low-cost carrier" experience. At that same moment, Kingfisher entered the market with a full-service product never before seen in the Indian skies. The data that we were trying to build were extremely erratic at times due to the massive explosion of capacity and frequency in the market. This combined with two mergers, ensured that the data available in the Indian market had to be carefully utilized. Kingfisher adopted a clear revenue focus at this stage, as a focus on the yield will have resulted in a new entrant not having the ability to scale up in a growing market.

The biggest challenge was accurate forecasting. With erratic market conditions and wild swings in the booking curves, the analysts had to be regularly alert to forecast errors due to data inaccuracy that could result in either spillage or spoilage.

*What are the future challenges that you see?*

**Ratan Ratnakar:** We expect the industry to stabilize but with spiralling fuel prices, effective revenue management processes are critical. We are constantly providing opportunities for people to grow into the analyst's role after working in the central reservation, revenue integrity functions. With the ability to scale up to international standards, we have to constantly look for effective solutions that suit our business processes. With the integration of Kingfisher and Deccan there is also a pool of data and talent available, which, if harnessed effectively, can pave the way for future growth without manpower issues.

We intend to use the data pool to realize optimum results from our revenue management systems and look at improved forecast accuracy.

# Revenue Management Under Uncertain Demand and Limited-capacity Situations

While designing differential pricing for perishable capacity, so far we have assumed that demand can be estimated accurately. But in most business situations demand cannot be estimated accurately. This will pose some serious problems in the implementation of a differential pricing scheme so as to meet the goal of revenue optimization. In the airlines case, we segmented the leisure and business travellers by putting early booking requirement conditions for leisure travellers. Since demand for business and leisure travellers cannot be estimated accurately, if we are not careful, we might end up with a situation wherein the capacity of the plane has been filled with leisure travellers and with not enough seats for the high-paying business travellers who are likely to book seats closer to the timing of the scheduled flight. Hence, there has to be some limit on the capacity allocated to leisure travellers. But since the demand is not certain a way of allocating capacity among the different submarkets will have to be found. Similarly, firms also have to be prepared for the cancellation of bookings by customers, which will result in idle seats on the scheduled flight. To avoid potential loss of revenue because of idle seats, airlines will have to overbook. But since the number of cancellations cannot be estimated accurately, firms will need a methodology of determining the optimal quantity of overbooking so as to maximize revenue. Both these problems are analysed in detail in this section.

American Airlines was one of the first major airline companies to use revenue management ideas for countering the threat from low-cost airlines.

### AMERICAN AIRLINES: REVENUE MANAGEMENT FOR SURVIVAL[4]

American Airlines is known to be one of the earliest and the most successful users of revenue management ideas. Deregulation of US airline industry in the 1970s led to the entry of low-cost players like People Express, who offered fares that were significantly lower than the fares offered by full fledged airlines like American Airlines. By the early 1980s, People Express was flying on a number of routes and was operating at around 75 per cent utilization levels. American Airlines used revenue management to counter the threat posed by such low-cost airlines. It started offering differential pricing and as a result could attract a whole lot of customers who otherwise will have opted for low-fare airlines. This innovative practice by American Airlines effectively resulted in low-load factor at People Express and People Express collapsed eventually. American Airlines estimated that within three years of implementing differential pricing, it benefited to the tune of $1.4 billion.

## Capacity Allocation Among Multiple Segments

If an airline just accepts reservations on a first-come first-served basis, it is quite probable that the flight will be full with just leisure travellers, as they generally book in advance and there may not be enough seats for the business travellers who are charged a higher rate. Hence, firms must reserve a minimum number of seats for the high-price category and the same is known as *protection level* in revenue management terminology. Similarly, there is an upper limit on the number seats that are booked under the low-price category:

$$\text{High-price protection level} = \text{Capacity} - \text{Low-price booking limit}$$

Protection level is the lower bound on the capacity available for the high-price segment and booking limit is the upper bound on the seats used for the low-price segment. So an airlines will close booking of customers under the low-price fare once the relevant booking limit has been reached. There is a trade-off involved. If too many seats are reserved for the high-price category, then some seats may remain unused and in such a case the firm will have lost an opportunity to earn revenue from those empty seats. If firms reserve too few seats for the high-price category, they will have lost an opportunity for earning higher revenue from high-price customers who will be denied seats because the same had been already allocated to low-price customers.

This problem is similar to the one-period inventory problem (inventory management for short life cycle products) discussed in Chapter 4, where we estimated the cost of understocking ($C_u$) and the cost of overstocking ($C_o$), and based on the same, the optimum service level was estimated, which allowed us to work out the optimum order quantity.

In the present case, the airlines also has to manage trade-offs between the cost of overstocking and the cost of understocking. We will assume that there is enough demand in the leisure market segment and that the firm can book the entire capacity of the plane in the leisure traveller submarket. Now the airlines has a classic problem in that if it reserves $x$ seats for business travellers and the actual demand turns out to be less than $x$ (situation of overstocking), then the airlines has lost an opportunity for using the unused seats for leisure travellers; and if the actual demand turns out to be more than $x$, the airlines has reserved too little (situation of understocking), and has lost an opportunity of earning high fares from those business travellers who had to be denied seats. Let $P_b$ be a price charged to the business traveller and $P_l$ the price charged to the leisure traveller:

$$\text{Cost of understocking} = P_b - P_l$$

$$\text{Cost of overstocking} = P_l$$

$$\text{Optimal service level} = (C_u \times 100)/(C_u + C_o) = (P_b - P_l) \times 100/(P_b - P_l + P_l)$$
$$= (P_b - P_l) \times 100/P_b$$

Optimum protection level for the high-price segment
= Mean demand for the high-price segment + $K$
× Standard deviation of the demand for high price

where $K$ is the service factor, and for a given service level the corresponding value of $K$ can be obtained from Table 4.3.

Now let us take a case of Super Airlines when demand for business travellers is uncertain and the plane has a capacity of 180 seats. Let us say that Super Airlines decided to charge Rs 2,000 for leisure travellers (who are expected to book 14 days ahead of the scheduled flight day) and Rs 5,000 for business travellers. With a price of Rs 2,000 for leisure travellers, the airlines can fill up the entire plane with leisure travellers, so it has to decide the protection level for business travellers and the booking limit for leisure travellers. At a price of Rs 5,000, based on market survey and past data, the airlines has estimated that demand for business travellers is likely to follow normal distribution, with the mean demand being 60 seats and standard deviation of demand being 20 seats. As discussed earlier, the airlines has a classic problem in that if it reserves 70 seats for business travellers and the actual demand turns out to be 50, then it has lost an opportunity for using these 20 seats for leisure travellers, and if actual demand turns out to be 80 it has reserved too little and it has lost an opportunity of earning high fares for those 10 seats.

$$P_b = 5{,}000; \quad P_l = 2{,}000$$

$$C_u = P_b - P_l = 5{,}000 - 2{,}000 = 3{,}000; \quad C_o = P_l = 2{,}000$$

$$\text{Optimal service level} = 3{,}000 \times 100/(3{,}000 + 2{,}000) = 60 \text{ per cent}$$

From Table 4.3, a service level of 60 per cent means $K \approx 0.25$.

Optimum protection level for high-price segment
= Mean demand for high-price segment + $K$
× Standard deviation of the demand for high-price segment

$$= 60 + 0.25 \times 20 = 65$$

High-price protection level for business travellers = 65 seats

Booking limit for low-price fares = 180 – 65 = 115 seats

So a firm can accept booking for low fare (for travellers who book 14 days ahead) up to a limit of 115 seats.

In this case, 60 per cent of the times the airlines will have idle seats in the flight and about 40 per cent of the time 65 seats reserved for high-price fares will not be enough and the airlines will have to refuse seats to high-fare-paying customers.

Though, so far, we have discussed the issue of allocating capacity among different market segments only for the airlines and the hotel industries, the same idea is applicable in several situations where one set of customers are willing to book the capacity in advance (forward buying) at lower prices while another set of customers will not be able to book in advance and will like to do spot buying and be willing to pay a higher price for the required units of capacity.

## Forward Market Versus Spot Market

In several industries like transport, warehousing and contract manufacturing, firms face a business-to-business market in which perishable capacities are sold either at spot prices or through forward contracts. Forward buying (advanced purchase) is required to be done in advance by customers at reduced prices, whereas spot buying provides flexibility to customers (buying at the last minute) but at premium prices. Offering differential prices in two submarkets allows firms to practice price discrimination and apply ideas of revenue management. In most of these industries, variable costs are negligible and firms have a limited perishable capacity and as a result, the focus is on revenue maximization.

The actual spot market demand for any week/month will be uncertain, but based on past data a firm will have an assessment of demand distribution. Service provider firms will have to reserve capacity for the more lucrative spot market demand; otherwise, they will end up booking the entire capacity in the less lucrative forward market. If a firm reserves too much capacity for the spot market and demand for spot at that specific time period turns out to be on the lower side, it runs the risk of idle capacity, and if it keeps too little capacity for spot demand it runs the risk of losing opportunity. This can be solved using the single-period model because capacity cannot be stored for the future period. So let us assume the forward price is $P_f$ and the spot price is $P_s$; in general, there is enough demand in the forward market so you can always fill up your capacity to 100 per cent in the forward market. We need to estimate the costs of understocking and overstocking for the spot market:

$$\text{Cost of understocking} = P_s - P_f$$

$$\text{Cost of overstocking} = P_f$$

$$\text{Optimal service level} = (C_u \times 100)/(C_u + C_o) = (P_s - P_f) \times 100/(P_s - P_f + P_f)$$

$$= (P_s - P_f) \times 100/P_s$$

Given the optimum service level, firms can estimate the optimum reserve capacity for the spot market.

Let us take a case of a warehousing firm that has a warehouse in Gurgaon and as per industry practice the firm rents out capacity, with month as the unit of time. It has a physical warehousing space for storing 50,000 MT of goods and is trying to decide on how much capacity to reserve for spot market customers for a coming December month. The firm knows that there is enough demand in the forward market and the firm can book the entire capacity of 50,000 MT in the forward market. But forward market price is Rs 150 per MT whereas the spot market price is 200 per MT. Based on past experience the firm has found that demand for warehousing capacity in the spot market in December follows normal distribution, with the mean demand being 10,000 MT and standard deviation of demand being 3,000 MT:

$$P_s = 200; \quad P_f = 150$$

$$\text{Cost of understocking} = P_s - P_f = 50; \quad \text{Cost of overstocking} = P_f = 150$$

$$\text{Optimal service level} = (P_s - P_f) \times 100/P_s$$

$$= 50 \times 100/200 = 25 \text{ per cent}$$

From Table 4.3, a service level of 25 per cent means $K = -0.7$.

$$\text{Optimum reserve capacity} = \text{Mean demand} + K \times \text{Standard deviation of demand}$$

where $K$ is the service factor. So the optimum reserve capacity for the spot market is as follows:

$$10{,}000 - 0.7 \times 3{,}000 = 7{,}900 \text{ MT}$$

So the firm should book 42,100 MT in the forward markets and reserve 7,900 MT for the spot market. On the average, this policy will result in 25 per cent cases where the firm will have idle capacity in the month because the actual demand in the sport market will turn out to be lower than the reserve capacity and 75 per cent of the time it will end up with a situation where it will not be able to supply demanded capacity to the spot market.

So far we have looked at the problem from the point of view of the service provider, but we can look at the same problem from the point of view of the firm that buys these services. Manufacturing firms that need warehousing have to estimate for their warehousing space demand in December and the firms can apply a mixed strategy whereby they can book the capacity in advance at lower prices but are unaware of precisely how much capacity they will need in December. By mid-November it will have a firm operating plan for December and it will know precisely the exact requirement of warehousing space. So the firm can use a mixed strategy and book some capacity at lower price in the forward market prior to November and in mid-November it can procure the required balanced capacity in the spot market.

Broadcasting companies too face similar problems, when they have limited number of advertisement slots for major events (e.g., one-day cricket World Cup finals) and have to determine how many slots to sell in advance and how many to reserve for last minute bookings. Of course, last minute bookings are priced at a higher level but one is not sure of the quantum of demand for last minute bookings (the uncertainty is because of several factors, one of them being whether India enters the final or not). This problem is similar to the forward versus spot problem discussed above.

## Overbooking

Overbooking is the practice of booking seats/rooms in excess of the actual seats available in flights or rooms available in a hotel. Whenever there are chances of cancellations (at the last hour) or no-shows (customer not showing up), if airlines do not do overbook, they will end up with a lot of unused capacity. For example, no-shows in the airlines case will result in empty seats in the aircraft, resulting in lost revenue for the firm. Typically, airlines and hotels maintain historical data on cancellations and no-shows and based on patterns observed in the past, the firms make policy decisions about the extent of overbooking. Of course, the actual number of cancellations and no-shows will be random in nature and firms can either end up with excess overbooking where they will have to deny seat/room to a customer who had booked in advance, or can end up with not enough overbooking and as a result have a couple of units of unused capacity. As per the estimates of American airline companies, on an average on a typical flight, 15 per cent of customers either cancel the ticket at the last hour or simply do not show up. Overbooking is allowed by law and all international airlines and hotels have regular processes in place for handling cases of excess overbooking. In case the airlines is not able to provide a seat to a customer who had booked in advance, the airlines has to compensate that customer.

Let a firm charge price $p$ for the unit of capacity sold and let $b$ be the net cost incurred by the firm (arranging for room at an alternative hotel, arranging for seat in another airlines) in making backup arrangements in case the firm is not able to provide the booked unit of capacity to the customer. We can apply the inventory management of the fashion industry discussed in Chapter 4, and work out the optimal quantity of overbooking. Understocking in the current context represents a case when actual cancellations are larger than the overbooking done by the firm and the cost of understocking is the opportunity cost of idle rooms in a hotel, which is $p$. Overstocking in the current context represents a case when actual cancellations are smaller than overbooking and as a result some customers are denied the room and the cost of overstocking is $b$. Using our standard inventory model, the optimum service level is as follows:

$$\text{Optimal service level} = (C_u \times 100)/(C_u + C_o) = p \times 100/(p + b)$$

$$\text{Optimum order size} = \text{Mean demand} + K \times \text{Standard deviation of the demand}$$

where $K$ is the service factor.

Let us take the case of Bangalore Hotel, which has 100 deluxe rooms and has observed in the past that cancellations at the last minute (including no-shows) follow a normal distribution, with a mean of 15 and a standard deviation of 5. The hotel charges a room rent of Rs 2,600 per day from all its customers. Because of overbooking policy, whenever Bangalore Hotel faces shortage of rooms it accommodates the customers in another hotel in the neighbourhood, which charges Rs 4,000 to Bangalore Hotel for providing rooms at short notice. In such a case:

$$C_u = P = 2{,}600; \quad C_o = b = 4{,}000 - 2{,}600 = 1{,}400$$

The cost of overstocking is only Rs 1,400 and not Rs 4,000 because out of Rs 4,000 Bangalore Hotel will collect Rs 2,600 from the customer and Rs 1,400 is a penalty or marginal cost of the backup arrangement made by Bangalore Hotel. Thus,

$$\text{Optimal service level} = 2{,}600 \times 100/(2{,}600 + 1{,}400) = 65 \text{ per cent}$$

From Table 4.3, a service level of 65 per cent means $K \approx 0.4$.

$$\text{Optimum number of overbookings} = \text{Mean cancellations} + K \times \text{Standard deviation of cancellations}$$

where $K$ is the service factor. So the optimum number of overbookings = $15 + 0.4 \times 5 = 17$.

In this case, 35 per cent of the time the hotel will have an empty room and 65 per cent of the time it will have to deny room for a customer who had booked a room in advance and will have to incur the necessary costs.

Of course, a firm will do a lot of overbooking if the value of $b$ is small (if customers are not demanding, it may put up the customer in a hotel that is inferior in standard compared to Bangalore Hotel) compared to the price charged. But while dealing with very demanding customers it may have to accommodate them in a hotel that is superior in standard, resulting in higher cost of overbooking, which in turn will translate to a reduced level of overbooking.

## Revenue Management for Inventory Assets: Markdown Management

As discussed in Chapter 11, it is common practice in the fashion industry to procure the entire requirement for the season in one lot, especially when one is procuring from long lead suppliers. In this section, we assume that the firm is working with a traditional approach where the entire lot is procured at the start of the season and the quality of forecast is likely to be poor when goods are ordered before the start of the season.

In Chapter 11, we assumed that salvaging of surplus garments is done only at the end of the season. In this section, we look at the use of markdowns so as to generate higher revenue from the likely surplus stocks of the garments. In the speculative approach, in the designer garment case, 82 per cent of the times we are likely to end up with surplus stocks. One will have the information about the likelihood of surplus garments at the end of speculative period when forecast updating takes place. Instead of waiting for the end of the season, one can influence demand during the reactive part of the season by offering markdown. Markdown during the season is likely to fetch much higher value than the salvage value available at the end of season. Even in the responsive approach, it is possible that likely demand for the season is going to be less than the inventory available at the end of the speculative season. In such a case, again the firm can resort to markdowns during the season itself rather than waiting till the end of the season for salvaging the leftover stocks of garment.

In this section, we will just focus on designer shirts and we will also assume that for a given scenario demand during the reactive period, part of the season is known with certainty. Let us look at a situation where a firm has a stock of 694 shirts left at the end of month one, and it knows that demand is going to be 150 shirts per month in the remaining three months of the season. So if the firm does not offer any markdowns, it will have excess stock of 244 shirts at the end of season, which it will have to salvage at the price of Rs 30 per unit only. Given that demand price is elastic, the garment firm can offer markdowns during the remaining three months. Of course, as per industry practice, only markdown is allowed, which means that once you do a markdown, prices in all subsequent months have to be less than or equal to the price offered in the current month. In all subsequent months, the price cannot go up. If the firm offers 20 per cent markdown in month 2, then in all subsequent months during the season it has to offer at least 20 per cent markdown. Let us say the firm has two possible markdown options, that is, 20 and 40 per cent, which results in demand increase by 30 and 70 per cent, respectively. Of course, the firm has an option of 0 per cent markdown, which is no markdown during the season. Altogether the firm has 10 options as shown in Table 13.4.

*Table 13.4:* **Markdown options.**

| Options | Period 2 | Period 3 | Period 4 | Revenue |
|---|---|---|---|---|
| 1 | 0% | 0% | 0% | 232,320 |
| 2 | 0% | 0% | 20% | 233,970 |
| 3 | 0% | 0% | 40% | 230,670 |
| 4 | 0% | 20% | 20% | 235,620 |
| 5 | 0% | 20% | 40% | 232,320 |
| 6 | 0% | 40% | 40% | 229,020 |
| 7 | 20% | 20% | 20% | 237,270 |
| 8 | 20% | 20% | 40% | 233,970 |
| 9 | 20% | 40% | 40% | 227,700 |
| 10 | 40% | 40% | 40% | 208,200 |

The firm has to just optimize revenue as the cost incurred in acquiring shirts is a sunk cost at this stage. We have 10 choices and firms can calculate revenue for each option and choose the option that will result in the highest revenue for the firm. For example, monthly demand for 20 per cent markdown will be 195 units and demand for 40 per cent markdown will be 255 units. At the end of the season, all the leftover stock shirts will be sold at a salvage value of Rs 30 per unit.

For any month $t$, Price($t$), Demand(Price($t$)), Stock($t$), Sales($t$) are price, demand, stock and sales at the end of period $t$, respectively. Revenue for any option can be worked out as follows:

$$\text{Sales}(t) = \text{Min}(\text{Demand}(\text{Price}(t)), \text{Stock}(t-1))$$

$$\text{Stock}(t) = \text{Stock}(t-1) - \text{Sales}(t)$$

$$\text{Revenue} = \text{Price}(2) \times \text{Min}(\text{Demand}(\text{Price}(2)), \text{Stock}(1)) + \text{Price}(3) \times \text{Min}(\text{Demand}(\text{Price}(3)), \text{Stock}(2)) + \text{Price}(4) \times \text{Min}(\text{Demand}(\text{Price}(4), \text{Stock}(3)) + \text{Salvage value} \times \text{Stock}(4)$$

$$\text{Revenue for option 7} = 400 \times 195 + 400 \times 195 + 400 \times 195 + 30 \times 109 = 237{,}270$$

As can be seen from Table 13.4, option 7 is the optimal choice as it results in the highest revenue of Rs 237,270, which is 2.1 per cent higher than option 1, which is no markdown policy. We can also see that indiscriminate markdown policies can hurt the firm. For example, at a first glance option 9 looks attractive because it ensures that all the garments will be sold during the season. Given the fact that the price available at the end of season is Rs 30 only, one will be tempted to offer markdown, which will generate at least revenue of Rs 300 per unit garment. But option 9 will actually result in lower revenue than option 1, which is no markdown policy.

It is common practice for firms to work with standard markdown policies. For example, a firm may have a policy that if it is likely to have surplus garments deep markdowns will be offered in the last month of the season. Instead of a standard markdown policy, as suggested in this section, the firm should decide optimal markdowns based on demand elasticity and estimate of the excess stock.

Markdown management discussed in this section is also known as dynamic pricing. Dynamic pricing involves change in prices over a period of time. Dynamic pricing offers the potential to increase revenues and profits. At the same time, it creates an incentive for consumers to strategize over the timing of their purchases. That is, customers may anticipate the entire price path and try to optimally time their purchases. In such cases, a firm should ideally use its pricing and stocking decisions to try to profitably influence this strategic behaviour. One approach is to create a rationing risk by understocking products. This will ensure that customers cannot take it for granted that the product will be always available at the end of season at lower prices.

## Innovative Pricing

There are several instances where firms have used innovative differential pricing schemes to increase revenue and profits. Firms can offer differential prices to customers even in a situation where there are no capacity constraints. An extreme case of differential pricing will involve customized pricing where each customer is charged different prices based on his utility and willingness to pay.

Marketing firms like P&G have been using rebates or a coupon to enhance the sales of their products. Rebates are usually payment made to the buyer (based on proof of purchase) from the manufacturer after a sale takes place. Coupons are promotions in which a certain fraction of purchase price is deducted at the point of sale. There is a lot of overhead involved in printing coupons, mailing them and handling coupon redemptions and servicing customers in their rebate request. Customers who are low-price-elasticity buyers are likely to use rebates and coupons; so P&G is able to effectively discriminate buyers and offer different prices to different sets of buyers.

It is important that a firm should ensure that innovative pricing schemes are not perceived as unfair practices by customers. Otherwise firms might lose a lot of goodwill from brand-loyal customers. Amazon.com tried to charge more to loyal customers because they felt loyal customers will not search extensively on the Internet for price comparisons compared to casual buyers who are likely to search extensively over the Internet and be more price conscious. A number of loyal customers were shocked to discover that Amazon.com was charging higher prices to the extent of 3–5 per cent from brand-loyal customers. Looking at the customers' reaction, Amazon.com discontinued those experiments and now does not discriminate buyers based on their past buying behaviour and charges a uniform price to all its customers. Coca-Cola had tried out an experiment where prices varied based on season and temperature of the day. It calculated that the value of coke, as perceived by customers, will vary based on temperature. On the basis of this estimate, it designed smart kiosks with the idea of charging higher prices on hotter days. It also decided that Coca-Cola kiosks located close to a football match will have higher prices. These plans did not go down well with the customers and as per some reports,[5] Doug Ivester, the then Chairman of Coca-Cola, had to leave the company due to customer dissatisfaction over the pricing strategy.

Innovative pricing, like customized pricing does alter the demand curve and the firm must make sure that the supply chain function is kept in the decision-making loop so that the supply chain is geared to handle this altered demand curve in a cost-effective way.

## Summary

- In a situation where capacity is perishable, the bulk of the capacity and supply-related costs have already been incurred, and revenue management attempts to make an optimal pricing decision so that a firm can maximize both the revenue, and by extension, the profit.
- Revenue management can be practised where the same unit of capacity can be used to deliver product or service to different submarkets having their own demand curves with differing price elasticity.
- Firms should be able to come up with innovative ways of separating different submarkets, so that they can offer differential pricing schemes. Using different booking conditions, the firms should be able to create a fence between various submarkets.
- As different submarkets book capacity at different points in time, firms have to a priori allocate capacity to various submarkets. In uncertain demand situations, firms face a delicate task of deciding on the capacity to be reserved for high-fare-paying customers who usually book capacity at a later point in time. Given the uncertainty in demand, while reserving capacity for high-fare-paying customers firms have to balance cost of overreserving versus cost underreserving.
- Firms can use ideas of revenue management in any industry (not restricted to the case of perishable capacity context) by applying innovative pricing schemes like customized pricing, so as to increase revenues and profits.

## Notes

1. J. Holdershaw, P. Gendall, and R. Garland, "The Widespread Use of Odd Pricing in the Retail Sector," *Marketing Bulletin* (1997): 8.
2. R. D. Hanks, R. G. Gross, and R. P. Noland, "Discounting in the Hotel Industry," *Cornell Hotel and Restaurant Administration Quarterly* (1992, Vol 33): 1523.
3. J. Shah and L. S. Murty, "Compassionate, High Quality Health Care at Low Cost: The Aravind Model," *IIMB Management Review* (September 2004): 31–43.
4. B. C. Smith, J. F. Leimkuhler, and R. M. Darrow, "Yield Management at American Airlines," *Interfaces* (January–February 1992): 8–31.
5. V. Johnson and S. C. Peppas, "Crisis management in Belgium: The Case of Coca-Cola," *Corporate Communications: An International Journal* (2003, Vol 8): 18–22.

## Discussion Questions

1. Why do firms offer different prices to different customers for the same unit of capacity?
2. Identify the key characteristics of industries where revenue management can be applied.
3. For airline/hotel industry, how will the magnitude of benefit from revenue management change with the following:
   a) Reduction in demand uncertainty of business travellers
   b) Increase in price elasticity of business travellers
   c) Increase in capacity of planes/hotels
4. Explain why dynamic pricing provides higher profits compared to fixed pricing?
5. How important is IT for implementing ideas of revenue management?
6. Why does the fashion industry offer price discounts close to the end of the season?
7. In what ways can the Indian Railways apply the idea of revenue management in its operations?
8. Some hotels have found that the application of revenue management resulted in an increase in capacity utilization but resulted in reduction in total profits. What could be the reason for this?
9. How important is markdown management for firms in short life cycle products?
10. What are the key characteristics of effective markdown management policies?
11. A retailer operates with a standard markdown policy as follows: *In case we are likely to have surplus stocks offer 50 per cent discount in the last month of the season.* How effective is the above markdown policy?

## Exercises

1) A Bangalore-based retail company owns two outlets—one in an upmarket mall and the other a discount store in Chennai. It has procured 2,000 quantities of a new toy at a unit cost of Rs 300 from China for the Christmas season. The retailer plans to sell the toy at Rs 500 at the discount store and at Rs 800 in the upmarket mall during the Christmas season. The retailer knows that at the discount store there is unlimited demand for this new toy but demand at the upmarket mall is likely to be normally distributed with a mean of 600 and a standard deviation of 200. As per company policy, all the leftover toys at the end of the Christmas season will be donated to charity. How many toys should the retailer reserve for the upmarket mall retail outlet?

2) A trucking company owns 50 oil tankers. A large oil company is willing to book the entire fleet in advance at Rs 15,000 per tanker per month. The owner of the trucking company has found that on the spot market customers are willing to pay a price of Rs 25,000 per tanker per month. Demand however is uncertain in the spot market. From the past data the owner has estimated that demand in the spot markets is likely to follow normal distribution with a mean of 25 tankers and a standard deviation of 5. How many tankers should be reserved for the spot market?

3) Super Airlines is working out its overbooking policy during Diwali holidays. It knows that during the Diwali season flights always get fully booked, but several passengers seem to cancel the tickets at the last minute. Revenue from the flight is Rs 2,500 per seat. If the flight is overbooked, the airline incurs an average cost of Rs 5,000 per passenger in making alternative arrangements for those who could not be given seats because of overbooking. From past data the airlines knows that the number of cancellations is likely to follow normal distribution with a mean of 10 and a standard deviation of 5. By how many seats should Super Airlines overbook the flight?

4) Refer to the example of the designer garment case discussed in the section "Revenue Management for Inventory Assets: Markdown Management". The firm has 694 shirts left at the end of month 1 and knows that demand is going to be 150 shirts per month for the remaining three months of the season. Let us look at a scenario where demand elasticity of price is on the lower side. The firm estimates that 20 and 40 per cent reduction in price will result in a demand increase by about 20 and 50 per cent of base price demand, respectively. In this scenario, work out the optimal markdown strategy for the garment firm.

## Further Reading


Robert G. Cross, *Revenue Management* (New York: Bantam Doubleday Dell, 1997).

P. G. Keat and P. K. Y. Young, "*Managerial Economics* (Upper Saddle River, NJ: Prentice-Hall, 1992).

S. Netessine and R. Shumsky, "Introduction to the Theory and Practice of Revenue Management," *INFORMS Transactions on Education* (September 2002, Vol 3): 34–44.

Barry C. Smith, John F. Leimkuhler, and Ross M. Darrow, "Yield Management at American Airlines," *Interfaces* (January–February 1992): 8–31.

Kalyan T. Talluri and Garret Van Ryzin, *The Theory and Practice of Revenue Managements* (Boston: Kluwer Academic, 2004).

# Sustainable Supply Chain Management*

## Learning Objectives

After reading this chapter, you will be able to answer the following questions:

> What does sustainable supply chain entail?
> How do sustainable supply chain initiatives impact firms?
> What are the various metrics to measure environmental performance of a firm?
> What are the costs and benefits of green supply chain initiatives?
> What impact do product returns have on supply chains and firms?
> What are the social aspects of sustainable supply chains?

As Alexis walked into an electronics store in Gurgaon to purchase a long awaited air conditioner to beat the summer heat, he was flocked by the store's salespersons showcasing various air conditioners of different sizes and styles. Flummoxed by the variety of air conditioners being talked about, he decided to go with the single most important criterion that he had decided upon before stepping into the store. He asked the salespersons to showcase 5-star rated energy-efficient air conditioners only. With choices now limited to a few sizes and styles, Alexis was able to purchase the air conditioner he wanted and happily walked out of the store.

Rising energy costs and electricity charges have gradually led Indian customers to demand more energy-efficient and environmentally friendly appliances. The changing consumer demand has important implications for the manufacturers of electrical and electronics appliances. Appliance manufacturers not only have to work towards resolving conventional supply chain issues but also work towards designing and manufacturing environmentally friendly products. The changing consumer demand has also transformed the nature of competition between appliance manufacturers.

Consumer demand is one among several other factors that are forcing firms to go green. In this chapter, we look to explore some of these aspects. We look at what sustainable supply chains encompass and examine factors that drive firms towards green supply chain initiatives. We also look at global firms that have undertaken such initiatives and study the phenomenon of product returns and the associated issues with it. We look at reverse logistics and other remanufacturing processes and study initiatives of firms towards social betterment. We conclude the chapter with a better understanding of sustainable supply chain issues and suggest ways to design and manage solutions benefiting the firm, environment and people.

---

*This chapter has been contributed by Debabrata Ghosh, Assistant Professor, IIM Calcutta with support from Sirish Gouda, Doctoral Student, IIM Bangalore.

## Introduction

Sustainability has emerged as an important area of focus for the United Nations and several governmental and non-governmental organizations in the last few years. The United Nations Environmental Programme for example, has undertaken focussed steps towards climate change, ecosystem management, environmental governance and resource management among other objectives. Sustainability definition and understanding as evolved through several years. The Brundtland Commission in 1987 combined "development and environment" to provide a comprehensive definition of sustainability as "development that meets the needs of the present without compromising the ability of future generations to meet their needs."

In the operations management context, this concept is further understood through the idea of *triple bottom line*. First proposed by John Elkington in 1994, it argues for simultaneous consideration and balancing of *economic, environmental and social* performance of organizations. It is advocated that only through development of the three aspects of operational performance would organizations attain competitive advantage. Complex operations and globally spread supply chains today have exposed organizations to various social and environmental concerns in addition to the economic considerations of cost reduction or profitability increase. To illustrate, clothing, footwear, sportswear and equipment manufacturer, Nike, headquartered in the United States, faced serious accusations from consumers, over a period of several years, who have criticized the organization of practising child labour and allowing tough labour conditions in its factories spread in Pakistan, Vietnam, China, Indonesia, etc. The accusations led to a serious dent in the brand image and reputation of the global manufacturer and it brought about significant reforms to eradicate child labour and improve working conditions among several other changes. Nike also worked closely with its suppliers in the countries of South East Asia and introduced a code of conduct covering workplace conditions, labour treatment and minimum wages to which its suppliers had to adhere to. The spread of production facilities of Nike to South East Asian countries brought about unforeseen risks in social and environmental factors to the company. In another instance, giant retailer Tesco in U.K was accused of selling canned meat in its stores which was sourced from a supplier in Brazil whose operations have led to significant deforestation of Amazon rainforest. The retailer was forced to cut off its ties with the Brazilian supplier and cease its sourcing of canned meat from the supplier. The event led to calls for sustainability evaluation at every stage of the supply chain.

Thus, in today's scenario of global procurement and operations, it becomes important for organizations to responsibly handle their supply chains. The three facets of sustainable operations and supply chains are namely economic development, environmental excellence and social betterment. Refer Figure 14.1.

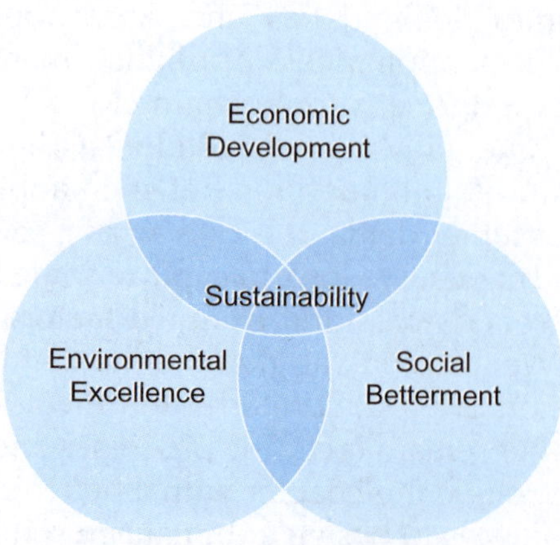


**Figure 14.1**

Facets of Sustainable Supply Chain

- **Economic Development** – This deals with practices of cost reduction, revenue generation, market penetration and profit increase. Economic development has been the primary focus of most companies and firm operations and supply chains are designed and executed to achieve the strategic focus of the company.
- **Environmental Excellence** –This focuses on measuring and reducing the environmental impact of supply chains, incorporating recycling practices, increasing focus on renewable sources of energy and lessening pollution in operations.
- **Social Betterment** – The scope of operations and supply chain include socially responsible operations and products, improving labour standards and community welfare.

Several global organizations have set ambitious targets to align their business and operations strategy based on the above definitions of sustainable supply chains. Consumer goods company Unilever for example, unveiled its *Sustainable Living Plan* in India which includes cutting greenhouse gas emissions of products by 50 percent across the product lifecycle by 2020, reducing water consumption associated with its products by half, source nearly 100% of its agri raw materials sustainably and engage another 500,000 small farm holders in its supply network by 2020.U.S based retailer Walmart over several years has strived hard to reach ambitious goals of sustainable operations: *to be supplied 100 percent by renewable energy, to create zero waste and to sell products that sustain Walmart s resources and the environment.* Some of its initiatives are encouraging sea food procurement only from suppliers who are certified by the Marine Stewardship Council and increased investments in solar and wind energy in Mexico, Canada and the U.S. It has also made a commitment to purchase wind power equal to 15 percent of its total energy load in deregulated markets in Texas. Additionally, Walmart has invested heavily into procurement of organic cotton from its suppliers in order to introduce organic cotton clothing through its stores. Large consumer goods manufacturer P&G, headquartered in U.S. has also entered into the manufacturing and marketing of several environmentally conscious products. Products like Ariel Excel Gel, Pampers, and Gillette Fusion have been innovatively designed such that they not only consume less water and energy during usage but also during their manufacturing. Numerous instances of sustainability initiatives are coming into the light today.

## Factors Influencing Green Supply Chain Initiatives

Before we delve in details of sustainable operations and supply chains in further details, it is important to understand why organizations strive for sustainability, in particular for the *environmental* aspect of sustainability. Research has revealed few factors which are outlined below:

- **Consumer demand driven green initiatives:** Consumer demand for environmental friendly products serves as an opportunity for manufacturers to capture the "green" consumer segment. The demand for energy star appliances, fuel efficient vehicles, green furniture, safer toys, apparels, etc. have increased significantly over the years and firms are under increased pressure to deliver safe products. Demand for environmentally friendly products also necessitate that manufacturers relook at their products and processes and collaborate with supply chain partners to reign in necessary changes.

  Further, it is also suggested that environmentally sound products or services enhance a firm's reputation. Firms want to build goodwill and a green image which further drive the consumer demand. Firms realise the brand value that green products carry and for many industrial sectors greening is turning into an important value proposition for competition. To cite few examples, automotive sector which is often considered to be at the forefront of technological innovation has displayed new product lines of hybrid cars, fuel cell based vehicles, less energy intensive engines and more fuel efficient vehicles. Modern day car manufacturers like Toyota realise that the next step to consumer demand for vehicles is for greener vehicles.

- **Cost reduction through greening:** For several firms greening provides an opportunity to relook at existing practices and improve processes to eliminate waste and reduce costs. Through improvements in product design, manufacturing capabilities, distribution practices firms are able to reduce wastage and save costs. For example, Nike substituted air shipment by ocean container shipment for several of its material procurement from manufacturing facilities in Asia and reported significant reduction in transportation costs as well as carbon emissions. The practice was initiated in 2003. In another example, Walmart worked with Minute Maid to eliminate an additional distribution centre in its supply chain and reduce the lead time of delivery from production centres of Minute Maid to Walmart distribution centres. This practice not only led to reduction of carbon emissions but also improved the shelf life of orange juice.

- **Price Premium Potential through greening:** Contrary to the common understanding that customers would be highly price-sensitive about green products, a major share of customers are willing to pay for eco-friendly products. A recent survey by Nielsen states that 50 percent of global consumers are willing to pay for socially and environmentally responsible products. Products such as Hybrid cars, LED and CFL lighting solutions, energy efficient white goods, organic food and clothing are among the most demanded products by consumers despite their high prices. Even though these products are priced higher, they help the consumer recover these costs through savings during the product-use phase.

  Sresta Foods sells organic food products under the brand name *24 Mantra*. Organic food products demand high price premium from consumers as they are more sustainably produced. For example, 1 Kg of Basmati Rice (of a premier brand called India Gate) is priced at Rs. 120 while *24 Mantra* demands Rs. 180. Having started in Hyderabad, 24 Mantra now has around 1500+ outlets in India, Europe and United States and boast of a double digit growth year-on-year.

  In another example, initiatives by Fab India (an Indian craft based retail chain) to collaborate with Indian artisans to build a profitable business and a well-known brand; have been documented and researched over time. Through an innovative strategy of consolidation of upstream supply chain activities; Fab India focuses on an organic, khadi loving consumer market and garners good margins for its products. Fab India's innovative upstream supply chain consolidation includes setting up of "supplier region companies (SRCs)" involving community of artisans, handloom workers and craftsmen who are responsible from sourcing to producing most of Fab India's product categories.

- **Government regulations driven greening:** In the process of conserving the natural habitat and reducing the negative effects of industrial activities, regulatory authorities have pushed the firms to go the green way. Government and regulatory bodies try to protect the environment through various schemes such as carbon taxes, fuel efficiency regulations, restriction of hazardous materials, subsidies and, cap and trade mechanisms. Since its inception in 2002, Waste Electrical and Electronic Equipment (WEEE) directive along with Restriction of Hazardous materials (RoHS) directive have successfully enforced recycling and recovery targets for various electrical and electronic goods in EU, along with prohibiting the use of hazardous materials in new electronic equipment introduced into the market.

  Automakers in different parts of the world have to comply with different regulations. For example, in USA, automakers are subject to CAFE regulations which assess the fleet level average fuel efficiency. In European Union and other developing countries automakers are subject to assessment of tailpipe emissions under norms such as Euro-6 and Bharat Stage IV, etc. These regulations have driven automakers to make technological advancements that have given consumers highly eco-friendly cars (with high fuel efficiency and low tailpipe emissions).

In USA, Corporate Average Fuel Efficiency (CAFE) regulations were first enacted in the year 1975 to increase the fuel efficiency of the cars. These fuel efficiency levels are calculated for automakers at the fleet level. In 1990, these standards stood at 27.5 mpg while the current target for automakers stand at 54.5 mpg (to be achieved by 2025). These regulations played a major role in motivating automakers to develop new technologies to achieve higher fuel efficiency. Several Automakers such as Ford, BMW, Toyota, Honda and Nissan already have vehicles in their fleet which have achieved these targets.

India has been slow to catch up with such initiatives. Recent changes by the Indian Legislation are gradually directing firms to undertake sustainable initiatives. The National Manufacturing Policy, 2012 issued by the Department of Commerce outlines regulatory and market based incentives to drive firms towards green initiatives. This includes setting emission and discharge standards, suggesting a choice of technologies for cleaner and greener operations, incentivising the indigenous development of green technology through tax concessions and subsidies and setting up a Technology Acquisition and Development Fund (TADF) for the acquisition of appropriate technologies.

In another example, the Security and Exchange Board of India (SEBI) mandated the Top 100 listed entities (based on market capitalization) at Bombay Stock Exchange (BSE) and National Stock Exchange (NSE) to disclose what is called the Business Responsibility Report covering Environmental, Social and Governance perspectives. Further, in 2011, the Ministry of Environment and Forests drafted the E-waste (Management and Handling) Rules which made producers of electrical and electronic equipment manufacturers responsible for the life-cycle of products and for take-back, recycling and disposal. It came into complete effect only in May 2012. India generated around 0.8 million tonnes of e-waste in 2012 and by the year 2018, e-waste generated from India is expected to exceed 2 million tonnes.

## Challenges of Going Green

Inspite of several initiatives by firms in undertaking sustainable initiatives, challenges remain in successful design and deployment of sustainable supply chains. A criticism often levied against sustainable initiatives of organizations is that they are restricted to sustainability reports and on field initiatives may not have been effectively implemented. Secondly, critics of sustainability argue that the cost of such initiatives for firms is high. Most firms can identify and incorporate the easier changes to their operations (considered low hanging fruits); however the costs significantly increase with every marginal increase in greening improvements where large investments are required. Further, sustainability as a practice does not depend exclusively on the firm but also on the partners of its supply chain. For example, Hindustan Unilever finds that committing to ambitious targets for its sustainability agenda requires as much participation from its suppliers, distributors and even consumers in India. Combined with product innovation, the company also intends to work on shifting the consumer behaviour in the country towards more environmental friendly products. With globally spread supply chains, firms find it increasingly difficult to measure and improve the impact of supply chains on environment and society. Additionally, some of the payoffs from large scale investments in sustainable operations may not reap immediate benefits. This often clouds active participation from managers in sustainable practices. Lastly, sustainable supply chains are also about designing and developing environmental and consumer friendly products through research and development. Bringing about technology and product innovation remains a challenge for several firms.

In such a context, it becomes important for managers to measure and analyse the benefits of sustainability programs and deploy them effectively for sustainable competitive advantage. It can also be argued that although all the three facets of supply chains are important from a sustainability stand point, it may not be possible for a firm to simultaneously develop the three aspects. An important reason for this could be attributed to the existence of limited resources and capability of the firm. For example, Tesco, UK's largest retailer, faced significant challenge in marking carbon labels in each of its 70,000 products. Not surprisingly, it had managed to label only 500 of its products by 2010–11 and was considering shelving its plans of carbon labelling all its products. Carbon labelling a product involves tracking back the ingredients of the product through their respective supply chains upto the manufacturing process and calculating their associated emissions. Inspite of the willingness of the retailer to spread consumer awareness through carbon labelling of its products, the complexity of the process and the sheer volumes of the products may not make it a successful venture. It may thus be challenging for firms to dedicate their existing resources in developing all three facets of the supply chain. Instead, decision making in focussing resources in enhancing another aspect of the supply chain in addition to the economic performance may go a long way in benefitting the firm. Hindustan Unilever also faces stringent tasks of achieving its ambitious targets developed under its *Sustainable Living Plan*. The company argues that even for environmental improvements like sustainable sourcing and reduction of greenhouse gas emissions from its products, it requires strong collaboration with its suppliers and rapid product innovation which may be difficult to achieve in-house. In such a case the company has launched an open innovation initiative welcoming individuals and institutions for collaborative work. Also, in several cases, sustainability programs already undertaken by firms may need to be revisited or changed, as the costs or benefits generated out of such programs may be contrary to the goals of the program. For example, Walmart aimed at sourcing its wild caught seafood only from suppliers certified by the Marine Stewardship Council (MSC). The certification aimed at providing complete visibility to Walmart from sourcing to selling of its seafood. However, the MSC certified fish was found to cost higher which was contrary to the strategy of Walmart. The company had to instead pursue procurement of farm-raised seafood using certification standards of Global Aquaculture Alliance which turned out to be quicker and cost effective for Walmart.

It is thus important for managers to assess the benefits of sustainability programs and dedicate resources to specific aspects of their sustainability programs. Out of the three facets, in conjunction with economic focus of supply chains, the environmental focus of supply chains would be the main focus of this chapter.

## Green Supply Chain Management

Green supply chain management is defined as managing the environmental effects of "researching developing, manufacturing, storing, transporting, and using a product, as well as disposing of the product waste." While it has been well proven that effective supply chain design and management hold strategic value for firms; managing environmental impact of supply chains creates additional challenges in terms of product lifecycle management, product pricing, inventory management, reverse logistics design, remanufacturing capabilities and relationships with supply chain partners.

To illustrate further, a simple can of cola has the following stages in a supply chain and each stage has profound impact on the environment through natural resource consumption during the raw material procurement and manufacturing process, energy consumption during the manufacturing, packaging, distribution and consumption process, water and air emissions during the procurement, manufacturing and distribution stage and waste management related to disposal of cans. Figure 14.2 illustrates each stage of the cola can's supply chain.

Green supply chain management for a cola can would entail environmentally friendly usage of raw material for the cola can; redesign of cola can for minimal material usage while incorporating recyclability properties in the can so as to not result in landfills during disposal; energy efficient and clean raw material procurement; energy efficient production and refrigeration techniques; eco-friendly and less polluting distribution practice. Clearly such a requirement for change in cola can design, material and existing processes requires an innovative approach in comparison to the existing supply chain solutions.

The key metrics that are tracked to measure the environmental performance of the supply chain for a single can of cola are:

- Energy Consumption
- Water Consumption
- Greenhouse Gas Emissions (Carbon dioxide in particular)
- Waste Generation

Out of these, the measurement of carbon dioxide emissions generated by the supply chain of a single can of cola (a single product unit) is called **Carbon Footprint** measurement. Carbon footprint also takes into account other greenhouse gas emissions. However, the focus of the metric remains on measuring carbon dioxide emissions.

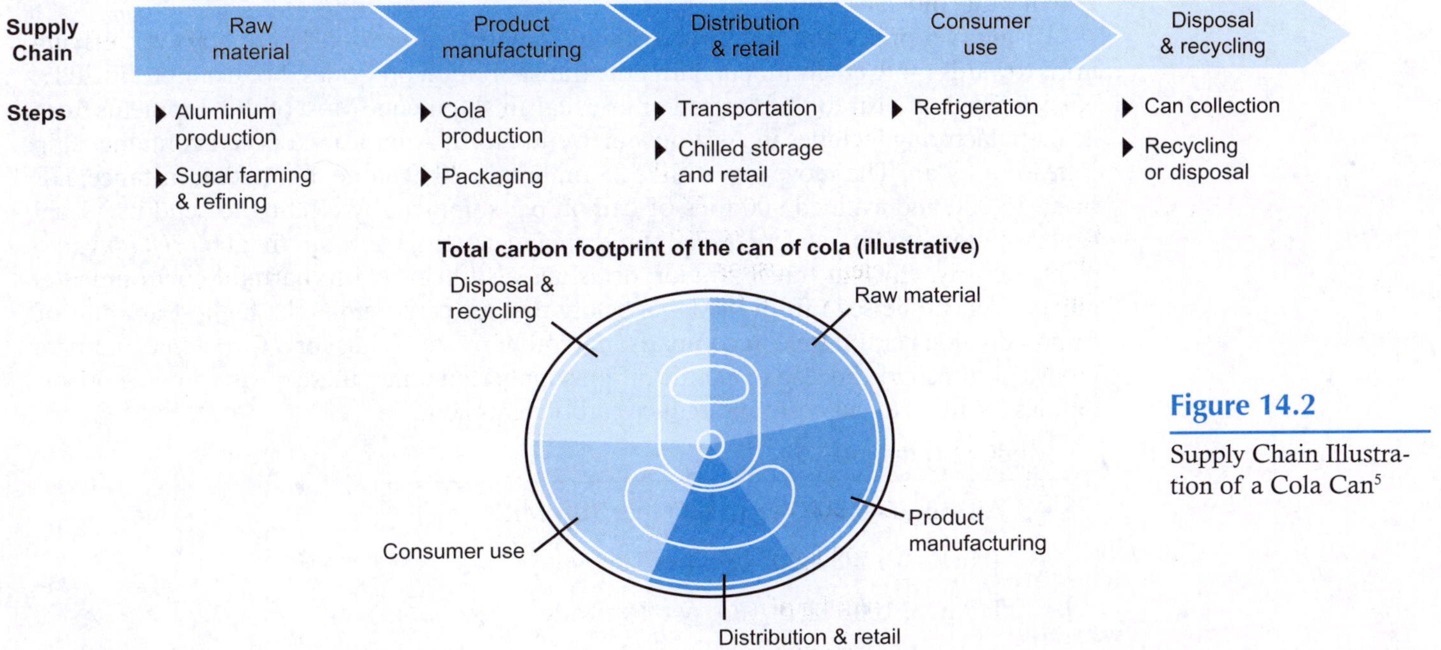


**Figure 14.2**

Supply Chain Illustration of a Cola Can[5]

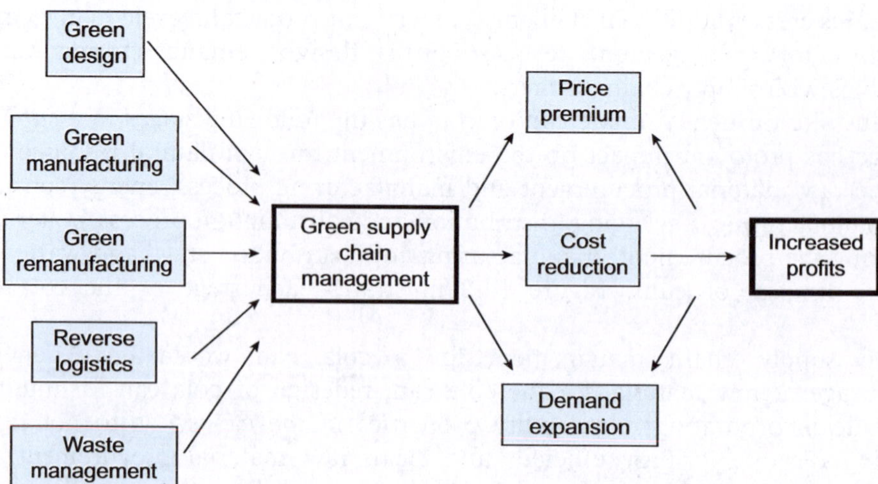


**Figure 14.3**

Green supply chain management framework

In summary, from procurement to consumption, disposal and recycling processes, green supply chain management entails the design and execution of environmentally friendly processes and products. The various components of green supply chain management can be further understood from Figure 14.3. While green design, green manufacturing, green remanufacturing, reverse logistics and waste management are aspects of green supply chain management, it is expected that such improvements would result in benefits to firms in terms of price premium, cost reduction or consumer demand expansion (as discussed previously) which should lead to increased profits.

### Green House Gas (GHG) Emissions: Role of Transport sector[6]

The U.S. Environmental Protection Agency (EPA) estimates that the total GHG emissions over 1990 has increased by 32 percent globally leading to 45000 million metric tonnnes of carbon dioxide equivalent emissions. A primary source of these emissions is the transport industry among others. Importantly, though while the contribution of GHG emission by transport sectors in the U.S. and Europe have increased by a rate of 13% and 35% (over 1990) respectively, India's GHG emissions from the transport sector have grown by as much as 111%.

Rising fuel prices and the various factors mentioned previously are however, driving firms towards more environmental friendly transportation processes. For example, in 2003, Nike decided on a cargo shift instead of its usual air shipments. Most of the shipments from its manufacturing facilities in Asia now arrive in North America via ocean container ship instead of by air. The move saved Nike $8 million in 2009 alone. In another instance, HP saved $7,000 and avoided 900 tons of carbon per shipment by electing to send its Visual Collaboration Studio, a telepresence conferencing system, by ocean freighter over a cargo plane. Clearly, efficient transportation decisions also help reduce harmful environmental impact. As can be seen from the table below that air cargo emits the highest amount of carbon dioxide per ton mile in comparison to other modes. Thus for a firm while alternate modes of transport can lead to a trade off on supply lead times, these means provide opportunities for firms to cut costs and reduce carbon emissions.

Mode of transport

- Air cargo - 0.8063 kg of $CO_2$ per Ton-Mile
- Truck - 0.1693 kg of $CO_2$ per Ton-Mile
- Train - 0.1048 kg of $CO_2$ per Ton-Mile
- Sea freight - 0.0403 kg of $CO_2$ per Ton-Mile

Medical supply company Baxter for example, experimented with intermodal transportation in the U.S where it used trains to carry containers over long distances and trucks took over to deliver goods to the final destination. This change was brought about between 2005 and 2010 which led to the company slashing carbon emissions by 14,000 metric tons.

In a pioneering effort to increase the efficiency of its trucking fleet and reduce carbon dioxide emissions significantly, giant retailer Walmart adopted auxiliary power unit (APU) technology in 2005 which eliminate the need to keep engines on for long haul trucks during driving breaks. The company has estimated that APU's can save $25 million annually in fuel costs. In addition, doubling the efficiency of trucking fleet could eliminate nearly 13 million tonnes of carbon dioxide emissions. In addition to the APU unit, Walmart's use of super single tires, aerodynamic tractor package and trailer side skirts in its model trucks is expected to save the retailer much more in fuel costs.

### Walmart's Green Supply Chain Management Initiatives– A Note[7]

On October 24th, 2005, the then CEO of Walmart, Lee Scott Jr. delivered a strong message addressing the entire 1.6 million workforce and its 60,000 suppliers about Walmart's "business sustainability strategy". Walmart wanted to be supplied 100 percent by renewable energy, to create zero waste, and to sell products that sustain resources and the environment. Thus, this strategy did not just involve using sustainable processes within the firm but also to extend its principles to other players in the supply chain, especially suppliers.

To kick-start this project, the firm identified 14 Sustainable Value Networks (SVN) and reached out to its stakeholders (including suppliers, logistics partners, NGOs, etc.) to embrace this philosophy. These 14 SVNs were mapped with the broader goals of Renewable Energy (Global greenhouse strategy, Alternative Fuels, etc.), Zero Waste (Operations and internal procurement, Packaging) and Sustainable Products (Textiles, Electronics, Seafood, etc.). These SVNs were not only held responsible for long-term goals of environmental and social sustainability, but also had to generate short-term paybacks. The sustainability strategy made business sense as the firm produced savings that were comparable with several super centres.

Over a period of time, Walmart has used various strategies to involve different supply chain partners to achieve these targets. For example, to source sustainable procured seafood, Walmart partnered with Marine Stewardship Council (MSC), which certified suppliers on their processes. By involving Not-for-profit organizations like MSC and incentivizing suppliers to get certifications from them, Walmart not only has increased transparency in its procurement process, but also enjoys higher customer satisfaction.

To minimize the negative impact of electronic waste, Walmart has partnered with suppliers who could source products that comply with Waste Electrical and Electronic Equipment (WEEE) and Restriction on Hazardous Substances (ROHS) directives. Walmart has also worked with Green Electronics Council (GEC) to design a scorecard that indicates how sustainable their suppliers' products are. With the help of these scorecards that measure energy efficiency, durability and end-of-life solutions, the firm is promoting energy efficient products and processes.

Walmart continues to strive to achieve a right balance between promoting sustainable products and processes while keeping a tab on issues such as increased costs, demand and supply and cannibalization of products.

## *The "Re-" process*

One of the primary areas of focus of supply chain research in the past decade under the lens of "green supply chain management" has been on "closed-loop supply chain management"

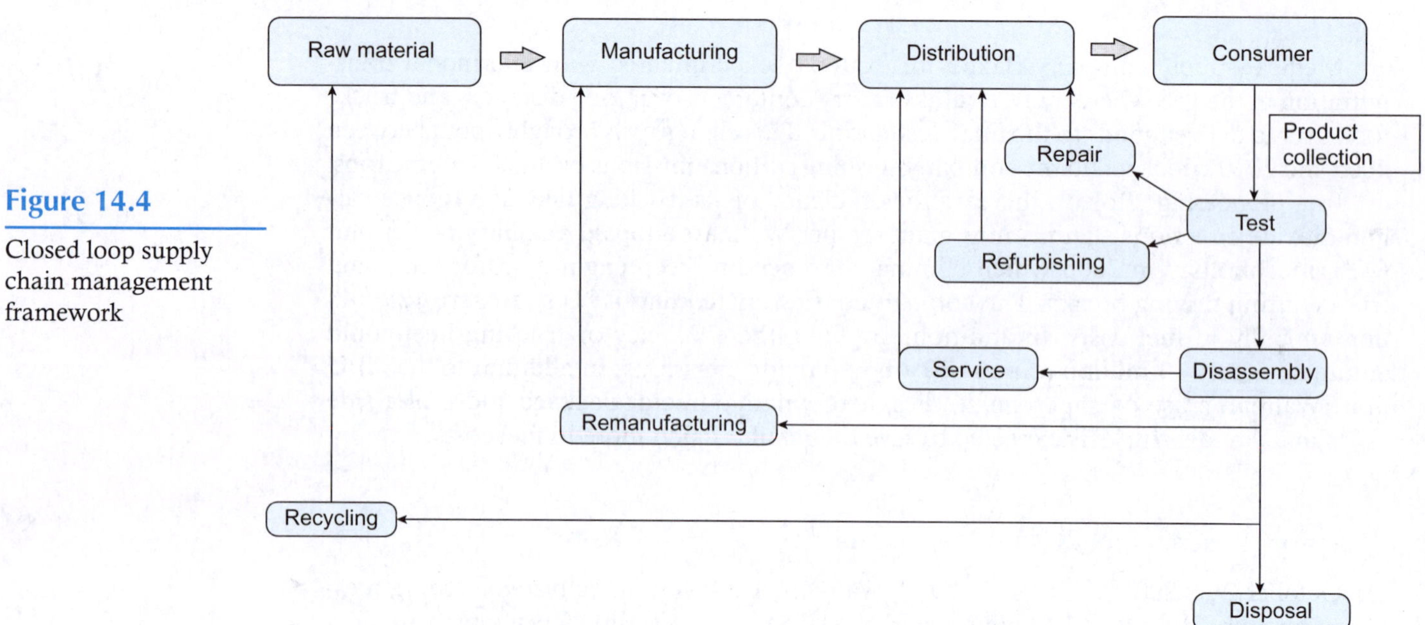


**Figure 14.4**

Closed loop supply chain management framework

(Also Refer Figure 14.4). Over the last decade, firms have been increasingly concerned about product returns and looking seriously at the issue of managing returned products and designing logistics around product collection, testing and handling facilities. In EU, this concern has risen primarily due to the WEEE (Waste Electrical and Electronic Equipment) Legislation and RoHS (Restriction of Hazardous Substances Directive) directive which make the producers of electrical and electronic equipment responsible for collection of their products at their end-of-life, and also working towards reuse, recycling and recovery of these products. In addition, the RoHS directive restricts usage of certain toxic substances in products. In the United States, closed-loop supply chain management initiatives have been undertaken primarily due to increasing realization that product collection, take back and timely reuse can lead to profit realization. In addition, the Environmental Protection Agency in the United States also mandates automotive and electrical and electronic equipment manufacturers to work towards product collection and recovery in several states.

So what do these legislations mean for supply chains? What challenges arise under product collection, reuse and recycling processes? Are they similar to those of forward supply chains? In order to answer some of these questions, let us first understand closed supply chains further. The below framework provides an understanding of various points through which products enter back into the supply chain.

A product can enter back into the supply chain under the following scenarios:

i. Commercial returns - Liberal retail policies and intense competition in the retail sector are leading firms to provide customer friendly return policies. A 30-day, 60-day or 90-day return policy often leads to large scale returns. Guide and Wassenhove (2009) report that retailers such as Home Depot in the U.S. can have return rates as high as 10% of its sales. Products that are returned to the retailer or reseller within these stipulated time periods by customers are called commercial returns.

ii. End-of-use returns – Customers often tend to return their phones in return for technological advanced phones, or under removal of operating system support, several customers return their functional desktops, laptops, tablets, etc. These functional products are considered as End-of-use returns.

iii. End-of-life returns – Products which are past their total life cycle usage and contain no further utility for the customer are often returned back and are considered end-of-life returns. Cathode ray television sets, small utility vehicles which are past their life are considered end-of-life returns.

It can be understood that several of these products enter the supply chain of a firm at different stages. For example – a commercial return at the retailer's end may be handled at the retail store end with minor refurbishing. Similarly, commercial returns which may need minor repairs may be handled at the retail store end. However, an end-of-use return may need remanufacturing at the manufacturer's end depending on the quality of the components in the product. Also, end-of-life product returns would typically need disposal or recycling. The quality of each product return impacts the choice of refurbishing, repair or remanufacturing significantly. Hence, adequate product collection effort and testing facilities need to be established to determine the quality of product returns and subsequently determine the process of product returns management. Thus, the movement of products from sourcing to consumer end and returns from consumer back into the supply chain is called closed loop supply chain management. It entails processes such as product collection, testing, disassembly, reverse logistics, refurbishing, remanufacturing and recycling. The aim of closed loop supply chain management is to reduce harmful effect of products on environment (minimizing product disposals in landfills, etc.) by maximizing product reuse.

### Reverse Supply Chain Management

- A reverse supply chain deals with the reverse flow of material, where the product moves back from the end customer (point of use) to the manufacturer. It can deal with either the entire product or a part of product (e.g., packaging material like the bottles in which Coke is sold). A firm has to manage this process during different phases of the product life cycle.
- There can also arise situations of product return at an intermediate stage of the product life cycle, as observed in the recent case of Mattel, where the company recalled its product because of lead paints in toys (In 2007, the global toy manufacturer and marketer Mattel, Inc. recalled almost 800,000 Chinese-made toys.)

Closed loop supply chain management throws unique challenges in the management of supply chains as firms not only need to work towards designing and managing forward supply chains but also manage product returns and reverse supply chains. To illustrate, product collection entails incentivizing customers to return the products to the collection centres or resellers which can have significant financial impact on the OEM's. Further, while the collection centres and testing facilities may be established by the OEM after undertaking investments, inadequate supply of returns can hamper the capacity utilization of these centres. In addition, enough volume of returns and hence extraction of components would be required to justify investments in remanufacturing facilities. There may not be enough economies of scale in these operations. In addition, the movement of returned products from collection centres to remanufacturing facilities needs to be time efficient and cost effective which requires expertise in reverse logistics design.

Reverse logistics are difficult to manage because of uncertainties in quantity and timing of returns. Further, one may not have the necessary economies of scale in collection and transportation. Most firms have not been able to integrate their forward and return supply chains. In India, reverse supply chain is still in a nascent stage. However, as observed in developed markets, reverse supply chain will become an important issue of concern for most firms in the coming decade.

Guide et al. (2006) report how HP realized that to extract the maximum value from its InkJet printers and to reintroduce them back into the highly competitive printer market with short product lifecycles, HP had to complete product collection and remanufacturing in record time. HP has subsequently worked with its resellers and remanufacturing teams to reduce time between collection, remanufacturing and reintroduction of the Inkjet printers in secondary markets.

While there are challenges in operational decisions, questions also remain on strategic decisions of firms on remanufacturing. Many firms do not invest in remanufacturing as it may result in cannibalization of their new product sales. Further, incentives of sales persons in most organizations today are aligned with sales of new products and not remanufactured products. As a result, remanufactured products do not receive the same attention as sales of new products. In addition, clarity on how to price the remanufactured products and through which channels (offline, online) to sell remanufactured products is not well developed either. Thus, for many OEM's, remanufacturing is not a strategic decision.

However, increasingly companies are looking at remanufacturing as an important decision in closed loop supply chain management. *Why?* The opportunity cost of not remanufacturing can lead to a firm facing costly regulations determining product disposal norms as can be seen with the implementation of RoHS and WEEE regulations. In addition, for several firms remanufacturing is an opportunity to generate savings by extending the life cycle of their products.

Ferguson(2010) reports that Xerox corporation demonstrated savings of $200 million as early as 1991 by remanufacturing copiers returned at the expiration of leased contracts. Further, construction equipment manufacturing company Caterpillar established a remanufacturing division that markets both equipment and parts to contractors and in 2007, the division clocked a $2 billion in sales and was one of the fastest growing divisions in Caterpillar.

Further, not remanufacturing products can leave an opportunity for several third party remanufacturers to enter the market. Emerging economies are littered with various remanufacturers and most of this sector is unorganized. The entry of third party players can lead to a severe price competition between original and remanufactured products.

Ferguson (2010) reports that several OEM printer manufacturers did not realize the potential threat from printer cartridge remanufacturers. As a result, many cartridge remanufacturers are present globally who are alterative suppliers of low priced printer cartridges to consumers. Only lately did the major OEM cartridge manufacturers realized this issue and have spend significant effort in terms of costly litigations, void warranties, etc. to challenge the remanufacturers.

In addition, for many OEM manufacturers, remanufacturing by unorganized third party players in emerging markets can hold potential threat to the quality of the remanufactured products. It can also lead to severe issues in counterfeiting of products. To counter this either OEM's can undertake remanufacturing themselves or extend support to reliable remanufacturers. IBM for example, offers a low-cost certification to remanufactured IBM equipment by third-party firms (Ferguson, 2010).

Remanufacturing as an industry has picked up pace across the world. While estimates on size of this industry vary from $40 billion to $53 billion in the United States, the remanufacturing industry in India poses difficulty in size estimation largely due to its unorganized nature.

However remanufacturing for certain products like automotive parts, cranes and forklifts, furniture, photocopiers, telephones, televisions, tires and toner cartridges has been in existence in India since quite a long time. The need for OEM's is to look at remanufacturing as an integral part of their supply chain strategy.

## The Social Aspect of Sustainable Supply Chain Management

In 2012 and thereafter, several fires raged through the apparel factories at Bangladesh killing several employees. These factories were a part of the multi-tiered supply networks of giant apparel companies located in the U.S. and European regions. Several such incidents brought back the focus on safety and maintenance of standard working environment requirement for workers across global supply chains. It also led to a closer scrutiny of supply chain practices of apparel supply chains by Governments, media, NGO's and consumers. Increased outsourcing has enhanced the risk on the working conditions and health of labour employed and society at large across global supply chains. This is further aggravated by the fact that multi-tiered supply networks also make it increasingly challenging for firms to audit and maintain standard health, safety and quality conditions for labour engaged in remotely located production facilities. However any adverse impact on labour or society at large due to supply chain processes can damage the company reputation severely. Giant footwear and apparel manufacturing company Nike has faced several accusations of child labour in its outsourced factories in South Asia in the past which led to dedicated efforts by the company to conduct stringent audits, review its contracts with third parties and also increase visibility of its supply networks. Several of these efforts have helped reduce the adverse social impact of supply chains of Nike and also improved its image manifolds.

Interestingly, the concept of environmental protection and social impact of supply chains is so closely intertwined that it is difficult to disengage the discussion of one from another. For example – One of the leading soft drink makers of the world had been accused in India of impacting water levels because of its bottling plant operations. This had also impacted the lives of locals as depleting water levels had adverse impact on drinking water availability and agricultural produce. In another instance, clothing company Patagonia in the United States, found out that one of its products – the rain shell jacket contained perfluoro-octanoic acid (PFOA) — a chemical that accumulated in the bloodstream with use. Consumers demanded a more health friendly version of the product and with time, Patagonia had to work with its suppliers to introduce a more eco friendly version of the rain shell jacket.

Positive environmental and social impacts also help businesses in turn. Indian conglomerate ITC works closely with farmers and agri producers, providing them helpful information about agricultural practices, livestock maintenance and upkeep information and training of rural youth to help support rural livelihoods. ITC in turn benefits as several of ITC's agri business products are sourced from local farmers and livestock owners. These efforts of the company go a long way in improving the brand image of the company while placing it aptly on the path towards a sustainable supply chain. Another multinational conglomerate in India, the Tata Group has also established a strong reputation through years of community initiatives in addition to environmental stoicism. Besides ensuring employee health and safe working conditions in many of its businesses, the TATA Group has worked significantly with marginalized communities in the states of Jharkhand, Gujarat, Andhra Pradesh and several others, to support individuals in different spheres be it education, sports, women-children welfare and tribal welfare among several others.

To summarize, in this chapter, we looked at various sustainability initiatives of firms globally. A combination of the factors outlined previously is driving firms to undertake green initiatives. However, the challenges of implementing green initiatives remain. For many firms, forward supply chain issues pose challenges which the firms fret over solving on a regular basis.

As a result, greening initiatives often take a back seat. Under such circumstances, firms which innovate to bring in greener products and practices will stand to significantly benefit. Strict enforcement of environmental legislations will also bring forth a significant competitive advantage to greener, sustainable firms while improving their brand image manifolds. As supply chains spread globally, scrutiny of sourcing, production and distribution practices along with environmental and labour standards will get tougher. Under such circumstances, firms which surge ahead with sustainable practices will stand to benefit.

## Summary

- Sustainable supply chain has emerged as a new field of focus for firms and governments.
- Sustainable supply chain encompasses economic development, environmental performance and social betterment.
- The following factors drive firms towards greening:
  - Consumer demand-driven green initiatives
  - Cost reduction through greening
  - Price premium potential through greening
  - Government regulations-driven greening
- Green supply chain implementation faces challenges in terms of increasing costs of greening and unclear benefits of greening in short term. In addition, most green supply chain initiatives are achieved through collaboration with partner firms, which are difficult to implement.
- The following are the key metrics to measure the environmental performance of a supply chain:
  - Energy consumption
  - Water consumption
  - Greenhouse gas emissions
  - Waste generation
- One of the key focus areas of sustainable supply chain management is "closed loop supply chain management" and it consists of activities that manage the movement of products from consumer back into the supply chain.
- Closed loop supply chain management throws unique challenges in the management of supply chains as firms not only need to work towards designing and managing forward supply chains but also need to manage product returns and reverse supply chains.
- Supply chains also have increasing social impact particularly in the communities that they operate in. It is equally essential that firms work towards social betterment as part of their sustainable practices.

## Discussion Questions

1. Why is it difficult to implement green supply chain initiatives? Discuss with examples from practice.
2. Discuss a carbon footprint measurement initiative of a company. What metrics has the company designed?
3. What could be the potential inventory management problems with respect to returned products? What new challenges does it throw up for the focal firm? Discuss.
4. How can government regulations play an important role in forcing firms to undertake green initiatives?
5. "Societies are demanding more responsible supply chains". Comment on the statement using observations from global supply chains.

## Notes

1. John Elkington is associated with corporate responsibility and sustainable development. He is currently the Founding Partner and Executive Chairman of Volans, a future-focused business working at the intersection of the sustainability, entrepreneurship and innovation movements.
2. http://www.sustainablebrands.com/news_and_views/behavior_change/50-global-consumers-willing-pay-more-socially-responsible-products
3. Prices as seen on 28/04/2015 at www.bigbasket.com
4. J Messelbeck, M Whaley, Greening the health care supply chain: triggers of change, models for success. Corporate Environmental Strategy, 6 (1) (1999), pp. 39–45
5. http://www.carbontrust.com/media/84932/ctc616-carbon-footprints-in-the-supply-chain.pdf
6. http://www.forbes.com/sites/justingerdes/2012/02/24/

how-nike-wal-mart-and-ikea-are-saving-money-and-slashing-carbon-by-shipping-smarter/

7. http://www.ssireview.org/articles/entry/the_greening_of_wal_mart

## Further Reading

Craig R. Carter and Dale S. Rogers, "A Framework of Sustainable Supply Chain Management: Moving Toward New Theory," *International Journal of Physical Distribution and Logistics Management* (2008 Vol 38.5), 360–387.

T. Choi, and T. Linton, "Don't Let your Supply Chain Control Your Business," *Harvard Business Review* (December 2011).

V. Daniel R. Guide Jr., et al., "Time Value of Commercial Product Returns," *Management Science* (2006, Vol 52.8): 1200–1214.

V. Daniel R. Guide Jr., T.P. Harrison, and Luk N. Van Wassenhove, "The Challenge of Closed-loop Supply Chains," *Interfaces* (2003, Vol 33.6): 3–6.

V. Daniel R. Guide Jr. and Luk N. Van Wassenhove, "OR FORUM-the Evolution of Closed-loop Supply Chain Research," *Operations research* (2009, Vol 57.1): 10–18.

K. Das and N.R. Posinasetti, "Addressing Environmental Concerns in Closed Loop Supply Chain Design and Planning," *International Journal of Production Economics* (2015, Vol 163): 34–47.

K. Devika, A. Jafarian, and V. Nourbakhsh, "Designing a Sustainable Closed-loop Supply Chain Network Based on Triple Bottom Line Approach: A Comparison of Metaheuristics Hybridization Techniques," *European Journal of Operational Research*, (2014 Vol 235.3): 594–615.

M. Ferguson, "Strategic and Tactical Aspects of Closed-loop Supply Chains," Now Publishers Inc. (2010, Vol 8).

D. Mahler, "The Sustainable Supply Chain," *Supply Chain Management Review* (2007, Vol 11.8): 59–60.

Q.P. Qiang, "The Closed-loop Supply Chain Network with Competition and Design for Remanufactureability," *Journal of Cleaner Production* (2014).

J. Quariguasi Frota Neto, G. Walther, J. Bloemhof, J.A.E.E. van Nunen, and T. Spengler, "From Closed-loop to Sustainable Supply Chains: The WEEE Case," *International Journal of Production Research* (2010 Vol 48.15), 4463–4481.

S. Schaltegger and R. Burritt, "Measuring and Managing Sustainability Performance of Supply Chains: Review and Sustainability Supply Chain Management Framework," *Supply Chain Management: An International Journal* (2014 Vol 19.3), 232–241.

M. Schenkel, M.C.J. Caniëls, H. Krikke, and E. van der Laan, "Understanding Value Creation in Closed Loop Supply Chains—Past Findings and Future Directions," *Journal of Manufacturing Systems* (2015).

Samir K. Srivastava, "Network Design for Reverse Logistics," *Omega* (2008 Vol 36.4), 535–548.

M. Tseng, M. Lim, and W.P. Wong, "Sustainable Supply Chain Management: A Closed-loop Network Hierarchical Approach," *Industrial Management & Data Systems* (2015, Vol 115.3): 436–461.

# PART V

# Supply Chain Cases



In this part, the focus is on applying the concepts of supply chain management to real-life business situations. The case studies featured in this part bring the real-life supply chain environment to the class room, ensuring that students are faced with the types of decisions and dilemmas supply chain managers confront every day. Collectively, these cases cover all aspects of the rich landscape of issues managers confront in the Indian supply chain context—from sourcing to distribution, from the strategic to the operational, from small companies to large institutions, from consumer products to industrial products and from corporate to non-profit sectors.

Cases like Kurlon, Global Green, Suguna and Marico are comprehensive in nature, dealing with the whole gamut of supply chain issues that affect business, whereas other cases are sharply focused on specific dimensions of supply chains. Cases like the Baroda dairy case and the Suguna case present situations set in the agriculture context and deal with problems that are uniquely Indian. The Dalmia and the APR Ltd case studies present different problems related to logistics. Finally, the Subhiksha case study presents the innovative Indian model of organized retailing and the case describes supply chain challenges in managing low-cost supply chain operations in the retail environment.

Real-life supply chain problems involve analysis and readers are expected to analyse and synthesize conflicting data and points of view, to define and prioritize goals, to persuade and inspire others who think differently and to make tough decisions with uncertain information.

# Kurlon Limited (A)*

It was a sunny April morning in 1998. Narendra Kudva, Joint Managing Director, Kurlon Limited, was reflecting on events of the past month and was worried whether he will be able to come up with some meaningful ideas when he meets the chairman the next day. It was about a month back that K. K. Rao, Chairman of Kurlon, had called Narendra and shared his concerns about supply chain management at Kurlon. K. K. Rao had just returned from Europe and during his visit he had an opportunity to discuss this issue with the president of a leading European mattress-manufacturing firm. He discovered that this European firm was able to manage operations with short lead times and provide good customer service and still limit finished goods inventories to just 3–4 days of sales. Of course, Mr Rao was aware of the fact that unlike Kurlon, the European firm had much fewer sizes in its product portfolio. The chairman was also worried about the increased competition, from other branded and unbranded mattresses, and the challenges of providing higher variety to customers. Rao had asked Narendra to come up with a specific plan of action within a month.

*Janat Shah (Professor, IIM Bangalore) and Balram Avittathur (Assistant Professor, IIM Calcutta) prepared this case in 1999 as a basis for class discussion rather than to illustrate either effective or ineffective handling of an administrative situation. 

## Background

Kurlon Limited is the largest manufacturer of mattresses, pillows and coir mats in India. The mattresses accounts for about 80 per cent of Kurlon's total sales. Its mattress has over the years become the trusted brand leader in India. They are mainly used in hospitals, universities, hotels and homes. Kurlon has approximately 65 per cent share in the branded rubberized coir mattress market. It produces mattresses in 126 different configurations. The mattresses are produced at two manufacturing facilities, Bangalore and Bhubaneswar. The Bangalore plant caters to the demands of southern, western and northern parts of India. The Bhubaneswar plant caters to demands from the eastern part.

Kurlon has pioneered most of the product innovations in mattresses in the Indian market. For example, Kurlon is the first mattress manufacturer to introduce quilting, which improved the aesthetic appeal of mattresses significantly. The firm follows a traditional organizational structure. A Vice President (VP) heads each important functional area. Kurlon employs 500 people, in the executive and worker levels. The organization structure is as shown in Exhibit 1.

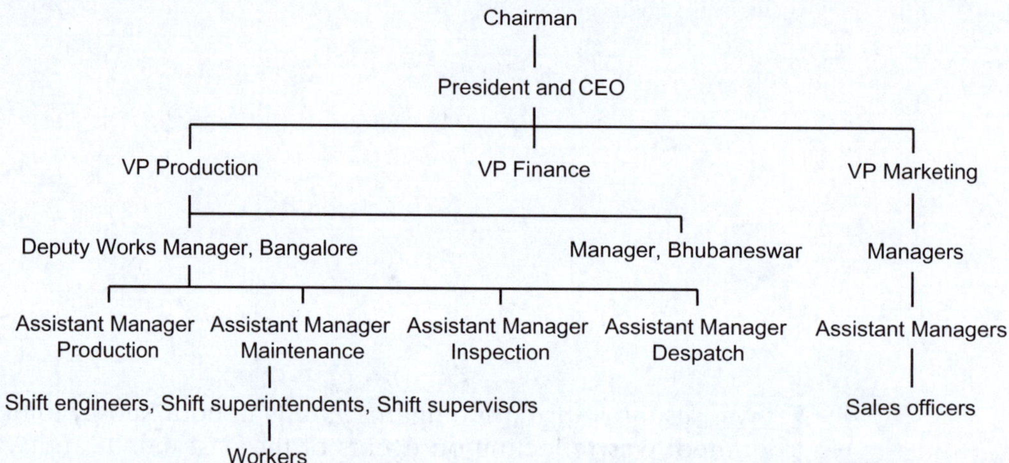


**Exhibit 1**

Organization structure.

Kurlon has witnessed rapid growth in sales and market share in the last couple of years. In the previous year, however, sales and growth in market share had stagnated. The net profit had not increased as expected (see Exhibits 2 and 3 for financial statements of the last two years).

***Exhibit 2:* Balance sheets.**

| | 31-03-97 (Rs million) | 31-03-96 (Rs million) |
|---|---|---|
| Source of funds | | |
| Net worth | | |
| Share capital | 70.9 | 70.9 |
| Reserves and surplus | 110.9 | 90.2 |
| Total borrowings | | |
| Secured loans | 187.7 | 169.3 |
| Unsecured loans | 44.0 | 46.9 |
| Current liabilities and provisions | | |
| Current liabilities | 181.8 | 150.9 |
| Provisions | 29.2 | 13.1 |
| Total | 624.5 | 541.3 |

*(Continued)*

**Exhibit 2: Continued**

| | 31-03-97 (Rs million) | 31-03-96 (Rs million) |
|---|---|---|
| Employment of funds | | |
| Gross fixed assets | | |
| Land and building | 62.6 | 59.1 |
| Plant and machinery | 201.7 | 198 |
| Other fixed assets | 27.3 | 24.2 |
| Capital work-in-progress | 0.5 | 2.7 |
| Less: Cumulative depreciation | 102.8 | 81.4 |
| Net fixed assets | 189.3 | 202.6 |
| Investments | 3.2 | 0.3 |
| Inventories | | |
| Raw materials | 50.1 | 39.0 |
| Stores and spares | 6.6 | 5.3 |
| Finished goods | 86.5 | 61.4 |
| Semi-finished goods | 9.2 | 15.1 |
| Receivables | 238.2 | 184.8 |
| Cash and bank balance | 41.4 | 32.8 |
| Total | 624.5 | 541.3 |

**Exhibit 3: Income–expenditure statements.**

| | 1996–97 (Rs million) | 1995–96 (Rs million) |
|---|---|---|
| Income | | |
| Manufacturing | 950.4 | 871.3 |
| Trading and others | 171.8 | 158.6 |
| Expenditure | | |
| Raw materials | 557.8 | 545.4 |
| Stores and spares | 8.0 | 5.3 |
| Purchase of finished goods | 103.3 | 110.7 |
| Wages and salaries | 36.7 | 30.9 |
| Energy (power and fuel) | 19.5 | 14.2 |
| Other manufacturing expenses | 10.8 | 10.4 |
| Indirect taxes | 7.1 | 8.9 |
| Repairs and maintenance | 8.9 | 7.1 |
| Advertising and marketing | 122.2 | 93.8 |
| Distribution | 89.5 | 79.3 |
| Miscellaneous expenses | 41.1 | 33.0 |
| Interest | 47.4 | 42.0 |
| Depreciation | 21.3 | 18.3 |
| Profit before tax (PBT) | 48.6 | 30.6 |
| Tax provision | 8.5 | 0.5 |
| Profit after tax (PAT) | 40.1 | 30.1 |

## Mattresses Product Range

Kurlon mattresses come in three lengths (72, 75 and 78 inches) and seven widths (30, 35, 36, 42, 48, 60 and 72 inches), under four different brand names. The four brands are Apsara (non-quilted,

*Table 1: Product variety in Kurlon mattresses.*

| Brand | Variety parameters | | | | | Covering |
|---|---|---|---|---|---|---|
| | Quilting | Thickness | | | | Cloth material |
| | | RC pad (inches) | Foam (inches) | Bonded foam (inches) | Total (inches) | |
| Apsara | No | 2.5 | 1 × 0.5 | Nil | 3.0 | Cotton |
| | No | 3.5 | 1 × 0.5 | Nil | 4.0 | Cotton |
| Super Deluxe | Yes | 2.5 | 1 × 0.5 | Nil | 3.0 | Cotton |
| | Yes | 3.5 | 1 × 0.5 | Nil | 4.0 | Cotton |
| Romantique | Yes | 3.5 | 2 × 0.5 | Nil | 4.5 | Plain viscose |
| Klassic | Yes | 2.5 | 2 × 0.5 | 1.5 | 5.0 | Printed viscose |

cotton cloth covering), Super Deluxe (quilted, cotton cloth covering), Romantique (quilted, plain viscose cloth covering) and Klassic (quilted, printed viscose cloth covering). Apsara and Super Deluxe are offered in two thicknesses, 3 and 4 inches. Romantique and Klassic are available in only one thickness, 4.5 and 5 inches, respectively. Thus, Apsara and Super Deluxe are available in 42 configurations each, whereas Romantique and Klassic are available in 21 configurations each. This works out to a total of 126 configurations. The product variety offered by Kurlon is as described in Table 1.

Both rubberized coir (RC) pads and foams are available in three lengths (71, 74 and 77 inches) and seven widths (29, 34, 35, 41, 47, 59 and 71 inches). Additionally, the RC pads are available in two widths, 2.5 and 3.5 inches. Thus, there are 42 configurations of RC pads and 21 configurations of foams. The variety offered by Kurlon are much higher than the variety offered by a typical mattress-manufacturing firm in Europe or the United States. Since furniture manufacturing in India is in the unorganized sector, cots and other furniture get manufactured in a wide variety of sizes, with no standards operating in the industry. Most mattress buyers buy a cot first and then prospect for a mattress of matching size. Hence, Kurlon is forced to offer a wide variety of sizes in its product portfolio.

# Production

The Bangalore plant is the oldest and largest among the production facilities. The Bangalore plant produces almost 65 per cent of Kurlon's total mattress output. The practices at Bhubaneswar plant are similar to that at the Bangalore plant.

## *Bangalore Plant*

A coir mattress produced by Kurlon consists of an RC pad, a foam layer and a covering cloth. The RC pads and foam are made in-house. The cloth is procured from a cloth mill, dedicated to Kurlon's needs. The fabrication of the three modules (RC pad, foam and covering cloth), to get the final mattress, is done in-house. The plant normally operates three shifts a day for 6 days a week. Since the plant deals with inflammable material, there is always the possibility of a fire hazard. Even after adequate precautions, there have been four fires in the last 15 years. The fires normally result in a production loss of 2–3 days. Figure 1 describes the material flow at Kurlon Limited.

## *RC Pad Manufacturing*

Kurlon makes RC Pads by combining coconut fibre (coir) and latex in the ratio of 3:2. The coir fibres are soaked in water to make them flexible and then intertwined into a rope. This operation is carried out at Kurlon's Arsikere plant, which is about 160 km from Bangalore.

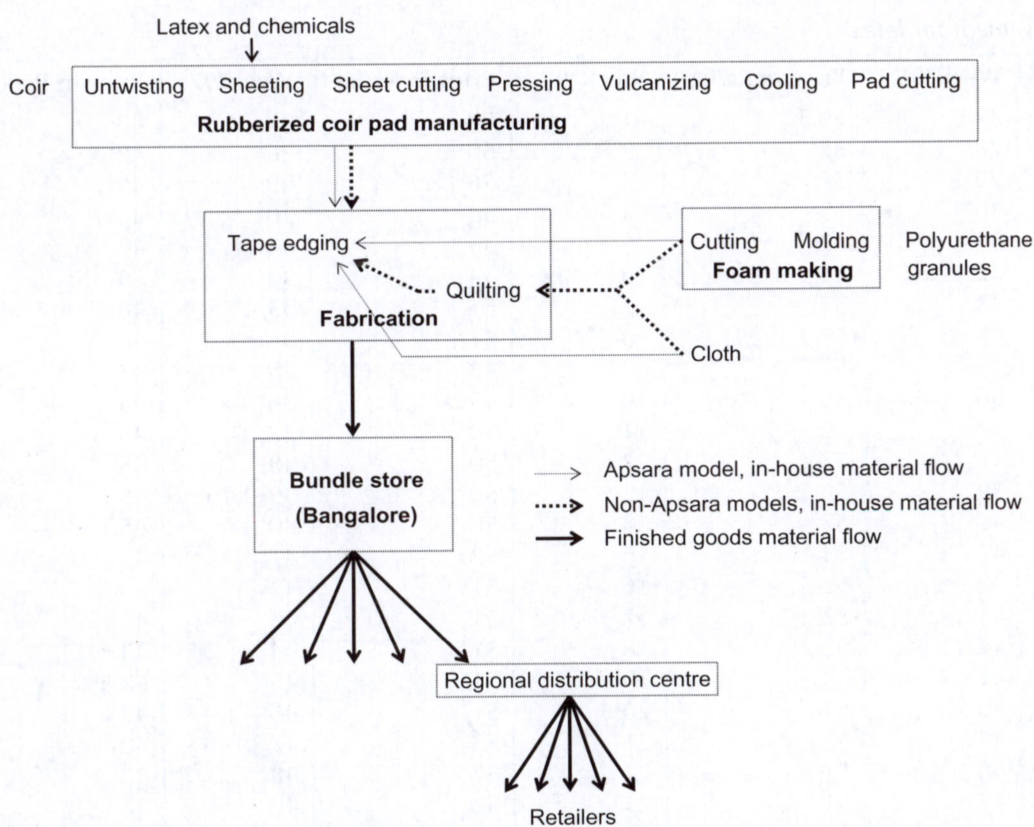


**Figure 1**

Kurlon material flow chart.

Coir fibres are kept in rope form for about 80 days. During this period, the moisture content in the fibre decreased by evaporation and each fibre got the shape of a spring. There is fluctuation in coir production owing to seasonality in coconut husk supply. Also, latex price fluctuations are quite regular; in some instances prices changed by as much as 12 per cent within a month (see Exhibit 4 for price movements of latex). Hence, Kurlon deliberately stocks coir ropes and latex to counter these uncertainties.

The operations in RC pad manufacturing are untwisting, sheeting, sheet cutting, pressing, vulcanizing, cooling and pad cutting. The first three operations are part of a computer-controlled continuous-flow process. This central computer takes care of the input and output rates of these three operations. The operations are as described below.

## Untwisting

The coir ropes procured from the Arsikere plant are stored in the coir room. Before commencing the untwisting operation, the moisture content is checked. Only ropes with moisture content less than 15 per cent are fed to the untwisting machines. There are eight untwisting machines. After untwisting, fibres that are at least six inches are separated and fed to the next operation. The average yield rate in this operation is 85 per cent. As already mentioned, untwisting, sheeting and sheet cutting operations are part of a continuous flow process.

## Sheeting

In the sheeting operation, the coir fibres are continuously fed to a conveyor in a sheet form of specific width (75, 78 or 81 inches) and thickness (constant). This specified width of the sheet translates to the required RC pad length with trim allowance. While in transit, a chemical compound, comprising of latex, clay and bonding chemicals, is sprayed across the entire breadth on the upper and lower surfaces. The sprayed sheet then passes through a chamber that

*Exhibit 4:* **Data on price movement for latex*.**

| Week '96 | Price in Rs/kg | Week '96 | Price in Rs/kg | Week '97 | Price in Rs/kg | Week '97 | Price in Rs/kg |
|---|---|---|---|---|---|---|---|
| 1 | 65 | 27 | 59.5 | 1 | 59 | 27 | 48 |
| 2 | 65 | 28 | 57 | 2 | 60 | 28 | 48 |
| 3 | 63 | 29 | 56 | 3 | 56 | 29 | 48 |
| 4 | 62 | 30 | 59 | 4 | 52 | 30 | 48 |
| 5 | 59 | 31 | 52 | 5 | 53 | 31 | 47 |
| 6 | 63 | 32 | 54 | 6 | 54 | 32 | 53 |
| 7 | 60 | 33 | 57 | 7 | 51 | 33 | 48 |
| 8 | 61 | 34 | 57 | 8 | 51 | 34 | 48 |
| 9 | 60 | 35 | 57 | 9 | 49 | 35 | 48 |
| 10 | 60 | 36 | 56 | 10 | 49 | 36 | 45 |
| 11 | 59 | 37 | 56 | 11 | 50 | 37 | 45 |
| 12 | 57.5 | 38 | 57 | 12 | 50 | 38 | 45 |
| 13 | 58 | 39 | 56.5 | 13 | 50 | 39 | 45 |
| 14 | 58 | 40 | 57 | 14 | 50 | 40 | 45 |
| 15 | 57.5 | 41 | 54 | 15 | 52 | 41 | 45 |
| 16 | 60 | 42 | 52.5 | 16 | 51 | 42 | 43 |
| 17 | 60 | 43 | 52 | 17 | 51 | 43 | 43 |
| 18 | 60 | 44 | 52 | 18 | 51 | 44 | 43 |
| 19 | 58 | 45 | 53 | 19 | 51 | 45 | 42.5 |
| 20 | 57.5 | 46 | 54 | 20 | 51 | 46 | 42 |
| 21 | 61 | 47 | 52 | 21 | 52 | 47 | 40 |
| 22 | 62 | 48 | 51 | 22 | 52 | 48 | 38 |
| 23 | 62.5 | 49 | 51 | 23 | 52 | 49 | 38 |
| 24 | 61.5 | 50 | 50 | 24 | 53 | 50 | 38 |
| 25 | 61 | 51 | 50 | 25 | 51 | 51 | 35 |
| 26 | 61.5 | 52 | 56 | 26 | 48 | 52 | 35 |

*Source*: *Economic Times* Agri-Commodity prices

*Prices reported in the table refer to prices of rubber. Latex is a concentrated form of rubber and prices of latex move with prices of rubber.

is heated to around 100°C. At this temperature, the chemical compound permeates into the interstices of the coir sheet. The sheet is flowed at a speed of about 5.2 inches per second. This temperature also ensures proper bonding of rubber and coir.

## Sheet Cutting

In the sheet cutting operation, the RC sheets are cut to one of 12 specific widths, ranging from 62 to 86 inches (see Table 2). The outputs of the cutting operation are referred to as fleeces. The above-mentioned computer control ensures that the effective output rates of the sheet cutting operation and the effective output rates of the previous two operations are balanced. As these three operations are part of a continuous flow process, there are no in-stage inventories.

The untwisting, sheeting and sheet cutting operations together engage 10 workers in a shift of eight working hours.

## Pressing

In the pressing operation, a specific number of fleeces are pressed, at a temperature of about 120°C and a pressure of 2.5 bar. The output of the pressing operation is referred to as semi-finished composite RC pad. A semi-finished composite RC pad could be of three lengths (75, 78 or 81 inches) and vary in width between 62 and 86 inches. To obtain a 2.5-inch-thick RC pad, five fleeces are pressed. To obtain a 3.5-inch-thick RC pad, seven fleeces are pressed.

*Table 2:* ***Output combinations at the pad cutting operation.***

| Composite RC pad width (inches) | Option | RC pad output | | | | | | | Total RC pads output |
|---|---|---|---|---|---|---|---|---|---|
| | | 29 inches | 34 inches | 35 inches | 41 inches | 47 inches | 59 inches | 71 inches | |
| 62 | 1 | 2 | | | | | | | 2 |
| 63 | 1 | | | | | | 1 | | 1 |
| 67 | 1 | 1 | 1 | | | | | | 2 |
| 68 | 1 | 1 | | 1 | | | | | 2 |
| 72 | 1 | | 2 | | | | | | 2 |
| 73 | 1 | | 1 | 1 | | | | | 2 |
| 74 | 1 | 1 | | | 1 | | | | 2 |
| 74 | 2 | | | 2 | | | | | 2 |
| 75 | 1 | | | | | | | 1 | 1 |
| 79 | 1 | | 1 | | 1 | | | | 2 |
| 80 | 1 | 1 | | | | 1 | | | 2 |
| 80 | 2 | | | 1 | 1 | | | | 2 |
| 85 | 1 | | 1 | | | 1 | | | 2 |
| 86 | 1 | | | 1 | | 1 | | | 2 |
| 86 | 2 | | | | 2 | | | | 2 |

Three presses are available, of which two presses could produce 10 semi-finished composite RC pads in one pressing, whereas the third could produce eight semi-finished composite RC pads in one pressing. The pressing time is 27 minutes for 2.5-inch pads and 31 minutes for 3.5-inch pads. The three presses together requires 10 workers in each shift.

## Vulcanizing

The purpose of the vulcanizing operation is to make the pads elastic and springy. The pads are loaded in a tray, which is then fed to the vulcanizing chamber. A tray can accommodate 18 semi-finished composite RC pads. The vulcanizing operation lasts 30 minutes. There is always a stock of more than 500 semi-finished composite RC pads before the vulcanizing operation. The vulcanizing operation has the least capacity among the different RC pad manufacturing operations.

## Cooling

The vulcanized pads are cooled before being sent to the pad cutting section using overhead fans. This operation consumes minimal time and is never a bottleneck. Hence, there is never an inventory pileup at this stage.

The vulcanizing and cooling operations together engage five workers per shift.

## Pad Cutting

The vulcanized composite RC pads are cut to different pad widths in this operation. Additionally, the trimming of the edges are also done in this operation to make the edges smooth and even. The sheeting and sheet cutting operations are set such that the composite RC pads have 2-inch trim allowance on all four edges. Pad cutting is the final operation in the manufacturing of RC pads. There are two pad-cutting machines. The output combinations at pad cutting are described in Table 2.

Consider a composite RC pad that is 79-inch long and 62-inch wide. On removing 2 inches on the four edges, the length and the width become 75 and 58 inches, respectively. By length-wise cutting, this can be converted to two pads, each 75-inch long and 29-inch wide. Thus, the output of the pad cutting operation is two RC pads. Consider another composite RC pad that

*Exhibit 5:* ***Material cost composition for Super Deluxe 75 × 36 × 4 mattress as on January 1997.***

| Weight of mattress: 13.406 kg | % of total raw material cost |
|---|---|
| Latex (32%) | 47.88 |
| Coir (70%) | 7.33 |
| Chemicals (10%) | 7.48 |
| Rubberized coir pad | 62.69 |
| Foam | 11.09 |
| Satin cloth | 19.16 |
| Miscellaneous | 2.98 |
| Packing | 4.08 |
| Total raw material cost | 100.00 |

is 75-inch long and 63-inch wide. On removing 2 inches on the four edges, the length and the width become 71 and 59 inches, respectively. This is a standard RC pad dimension and there is no further cutting. Thus, the output of the pad cutting operation is 1 RC pad.

There are a few reasons for cutting the fleeces in one of the 12 specific widths mentioned in Table 2. The primary reason is better utilization of capacity in the pressing and vulcanizing operations. The slots in the presses as well as in the vulcanizing tray can accommodate widths of up to 86 inches. Another reason for combining widths is to reduce trim losses. Hence, from the objectives of better capacity utilization in pressing and vulcanizing operations and reduction of trim losses, it is important that production should be scheduled such that fleece widths were as close as possible to 86 inches. The company paid attention to reduction of trim losses, as material cost constituted a significant part of the product cost. See Exhibit 5 for a break-up of the material cost.

At any particular instant, three composite RC pads are loaded, one above the other, and subjected to cutting. The entire cycle of cutting and trimming of three composite RC pads takes 5 minutes. There is excess capacity in this operation and, hence, no inventory pileup. The finished RC pads are shifted to the storing bay in the fabrication shop. The pad cutting section engages 10 workers per shift.

The set-up times in all the above operations are negligible.

## Foam Making

Ordinary foam sheets are 0.5-inch thick whereas bonded foam sheets are 1.5-inch thick. Foam making has just two operations. The raw material is polyurethane granules. These granules are converted to foam in a foam-moulding machine. After 24 hours of curing, foam edges are trimmed to obtain the exact foam dimensions. About 30 workers are engaged in every shift in the foam-making operations. On an average, there are 3 days stocks of raw materials as well as semi-finished foams. Set-up times are minimal in both foam-making operations. Foam making has never been a constraint in the past.

## Fabrication

There are two operations in mattress fabrication, quilting and tape edging. The RC pads and foams are shifted manually to the fabrication shop. At least one day's requirement of RC pads, foams and cloth are stored in the fabrication shop to ensure that production was not affected. On an average, these items are stocked for approximately three days in the fabrication shop. The covering cloth comes in bales, each bale sufficient to fabricate about 150 mattresses. A model is defined by its cloth type (cotton/plain viscose/printed viscose). However, it is not defined by the cloth shade or design. Hence, the bale size is presently not a production planning constraint. Currently, Kurlon uses five shades on the average, each having about 50 designs. The decision about design mix is left to the fabric supplier.

### Quilting

In the quilting operation, the cloth that covers the top surface of the mattress is quilted to foam. This operation is not carried out for Apsara model mattresses. There are two quilting machines, one with a capacity of 750 mattresses per day (three shifts) and the other with a capacity of 250 mattresses per day (three shifts). Both machines require two operators each.

### Tape Edging

In the tape edging operation, the quilted panel is first placed over the RC pad. The side-surface cloth is then inserted and the mattress is taped along the upper edges. It is then turned upside down. The bottom-surface cloth is then placed and the mattress taped along the lower edges. Taping is stitching of the side-surface cloth to the upper-surface cloth or the bottom-surface cloth. There are 10 tape edging machines, each capable of producing 50 mattresses per shift. Operating a tape edging machine requires two operators.

After tape edging, the finished mattresses are inspected and packed in plastic sheets. They are then shifted to the bundle store.

## *Production Planning*

Production planning is at two levels, long term and short term. The long-term production planning, carried out in the last quarter of the financial year, is essentially a capacity planning exercise. Plans for increasing machinery or manpower are made in this exercise. This exercise is also used for planning for the Diwali month, which falls either in October or November. The company has found that demand during the Diwali month (in the year 1997–1998, Diwali was in the month of October) was twice that of the average monthly demand. If required, Kurlon would build inventory before the Diwali month so as to meet the extra demand.

The short-term production planning is done every month and is essentially a production scheduling exercise. At the Bangalore plant this is fully computerized. The dispatch section received indents with configuration-wise break-up, from the regional distribution centres that it served, in the last week of every month. These indents are aggregated to receive the monthly target of each mattress configuration. The monthly targets are then converted to weekly targets. A standard MRP package is then used to generate the weekly production targets of the individual production departments (RC pad manufacturing and foam making). The production-planning department followes a "lot-to-lot" lot-sizing rule with a week as a unit of time. There is a usual practice of budgeting 5 per cent of capacity to take care of machine breakdowns and operator absenteeism.

Though all the 126 configurations are mentioned in the price list, about a third of them are only produced against specific retailer orders. The company takes about one month of time to deliver these non-moving configurations.

# Distribution

The distribution of Kurlon products is through a multi-echelon inventory system. Kurlon has two central warehouses, attached to the Bangalore and Bhubaneswar plants. The finished goods are shifted to the respective central warehouses. On a periodic basis, material is shifted from the central warehouses to the regional distribution centres by road. Material from the regional distribution centre is also shifted periodically to the retailer outlets.

## Bangalore Central Warehouse (Bundle Store)

The bundle store is adjacent to the fabrication shop. Mattresses from the bundle store are transferred to Kurlon's regional warehouses in southern, western and northern parts of India. All transfers to the regional warehouses are in lots of 160 or 320 mattresses. These lot sizes correspond to ordinary and jumbo truckloads, respectively. Kurlon has long-term rate contracts with different transporters. For example, the full-load rate contract for transportation from Bangalore to Delhi by an ordinary truck (160 mattresses) is Rs 14,000 while by jumbo truck (320 mattresses) it is Rs 24,000. To avoid in-transit damages, the firm insists on full truckloads to avoid transportation of its products with other goods.

A given truck transports mattresses ordered by one region only. The material needed for two or more regions are never clubbed in one truckload. Transportation time varies considerably owing to road accidents, truck breakdowns and infrastructural constraints. For instance, the transportation time from the Bangalore central warehouse to the Delhi regional distribution centre varied from 3 to 10 days.

In the beginning of each week, the number of truckloads to each region is determined. If the requirement in a regional warehouse is two or more truckloads, the despatches are spread throughout the week. When a truck arrives at the bundle store, the mattresses are loaded as per the indent raised for the despatch. However, if a particular configuration was not available some other configuration is loaded. Thus, it is not uncommon to find mismatches between indents and despatches.

## Regional Distribution Centres

Kurlon distributes its products to retailers through 42 regional distribution centres, spread across the country. The decision on setting a distribution centre is based on local tariff considerations, geographical distances and management perceptions about the demand in that area. The manager of each regional distribution centre (area sales office) would send a work order (indent) once a month by mail or by fax to the head office in Bangalore, which in turn is forwarded to the despatch section of the plant serving this centre. The work order for a particular month is sent before the 25th day of the previous month. This work order specifies both size and variety of the mattresses that are to be despatched to the regional distribution centre on a weekly basis. The work order is based on demand forecast for the coming month and the stocks available at the regional warehouses. There is no formal forecasting process in place, but the area sales manager uses his experience and his understanding of the market in finalizing the work orders for the coming month.

The area sales offices' performances are presently measured on the basis of total revenues achieved. Kurlon does not have any system in place for measuring its performance in terms of customer service (to what extent orders from retailers were fulfilled).

## Retailers

In India, the concept of exclusive outlets for selling mattresses is at the infancy stage. Most of the Kurlon retailers also stock other branded mattresses. Given this situation, Kurlon has to constantly maintain pressure on the retailers for placing orders. The chances of lost sales are also very high in this situation. Hence, it is very important for Kurlon that its products are well stocked. The problem is compounded by the fact that most of the retailers are constrained by space and credit availability. It is not uncommon to find retailers placing orders for quantity as low as six mattresses. There are about 5,000 retailers, spread all over the country, who stock Kurlon products.

Order placements by retailers are mostly verbal, either by telephone or through a visiting sales representative. The frequency of order placement is on a weekly basis. The average time for replenishing retailer orders is about 1–2 days. Retail outlets are interested in stocking only fast-moving mattresses. On the average retailers hold 1–2 weeks of stock of fast-moving mattresses.

Even though Kurlon offers mattresses in 21 sizes, retailers receive enquires for sizes outside this range. Some of the large retailers have their own facility to cater to the demand for non-standard sizes. The demand for non-standard sizes constitute about 10–30 per cent of the total demand. About a year back, Kurlon also started offering this service for some of the large distribution centres. The customization involves reduction of length, reduction of width or reduction of both from a standard sized mattress. After making the necessary cuts, the covering cloth is restored by manual stitching. Kurlon charges Rs 100 per alteration and takes about a week's time to deliver.

Initially, there was a big debate in the organization because the change in size involved manufacturing work and the regional office or the warehouse did not have the necessary expertise. The firm was concerned about the responsibility and accountability for quality. These issues were not resolved entirely, but because of competitive pressures, marketing took the responsibility to offer these services. Manufacturing was not very happy with this idea; they initially thought that any alteration could be treated as a make-to-order case. Eventually, manufacturing realized that it would increase complexity in manufacturing planning and control. Finally, it was decided that it will be treated as a service that marketing would offer.

## Future Plans of Kurlon

Kurlon has ambitious plans and wanted to introduce two different types of mattresses in the Indian market. It has already started test marketing spring-based mattresses. The Kurlon board has just cleared a proposal of a joint venture company with DUPONT. DUPONT would provide the know-how for manufacturing core pads with imported fibrefill using vertical fold technology and the joint venture company would manufacture these core pads. The core pads are to be finished into mattresses after quilting and tape edging by Kurlon. As per the proposal, the finished mattresses would be marketed by the proposed joint venture company through the distribution network of Kurlon. Kurlon would establish separate manufacturing facilities at Bangalore to handle the manufacture of spring mattresses as well as the finishing of fibrefill mattresses by end of 1998.

With the introduction of these products into the Kurlon product portfolio, the product range is expected to cross 200 configurations. This is bound to increase the complexities in production and distribution significantly.

## Improving Supply Chain Performance at Kurlon

Over the last month, Narendra had spent most of his time in data collection. For the purpose of his analysis he decided to focus only on the Bangalore plant and the markets that were served by the Bangalore plant. Since Kurlon had different platforms and stand-alone systems in different departments, he had a tough time putting all relevant data together for any meaningful analysis. Since data collection was going to involve a lot of effort, he decided to study one area sales office (ASO) in greater detail. He ended up selecting the Delhi ASO as it provided the highest business among all branches. (See Exhibit 6 for SKU-wise break up for 1997–1998 sales for the Delhi ASO. See Exhibit 7 for Delhi ASO weekly sales data on a few selected SKUs.) He collected all the relevant weekly data of indents, inventories and sales for the Delhi ASO for 1997–1998. For the same time period he also collected aggregate data on indents, despatches and inventories at the Bangalore central warehouse (see Exhibit 8 for relevant data for a few selected SKUs on material flow for the Delhi ASO and the Bangalore central warehouse). For the purpose of his analysis he decided to focus only on the Bangalore plant.

**Exhibit 6: SKU-wise data on annual sales at Delhi ASO*.**

| No | Brand | Size | Annual sales quantity | No | Brand | Size | Annual sales quantity |
|---|---|---|---|---|---|---|---|
| 1 | SDL | 72 × 30 × 4 | 866 | 20 | SDL | 78 × 48 × 4 | 46 |
| 2 | SDL | 72 × 35 × 3 | 54 | 21 | SDL | 78 × 72 × 4 | 90 |
| 3 | SDL | 72 × 35 × 4 | 11032 | 22 | SDL | 78 × 60 × 4 | 53 |
| 4 | SDL | 72 × 36 × 4 | 973 | 23 | Apsara | 72 × 35 × 4 | 2438 |
| 5 | SDL | 72 × 42 × 4 | 72 | 24 | Apsara | 72 × 36 × 3 | 38 |
| 6 | SDL | 72 × 48 × 4 | 453 | 25 | Apsara | 72 × 36 × 4 | 549 |
| 7 | SDL | 72 × 60 × 4 | 141 | 26 | Apsara | 75 × 35 × 4 | 571 |
| 8 | SDL | 72 × 72 × 4 | 190 | 27 | Apsara | 75 × 36 × 4 | 189 |
| 9 | SDL | 75 × 30 × 4 | 326 | 28 | Apsara | 72 × 48 × 4 | 134 |
| 10 | SDL | 75 × 35 × 4 | 4563 | 29 | Klassic | 72 × 35 | 1070 |
| 11 | SDL | 75 × 36 × 4 | 1891 | 30 | Klassic | 72 × 36 | 284 |
| 12 | SDL | 75 × 42 × 4 | 61 | 31 | Klassic | 75 × 35 | 882 |
| 13 | SDL | 75 × 48 × 4 | 150 | 32 | Klassic | 75 × 36 | 492 |
| 14 | SDL | 75 × 60 × 4 | 209 | 33 | Klassic | 75 × 72 | 38 |
| 15 | SDL | 75 × 72 × 4 | 250 | 34 | Klassic | 78 × 36 | 72 |
| 16 | SDL | 78 × 30 × 4 | 160 | 35 | Romantique | 72 × 35 | 221 |
| 17 | SDL | 78 × 35 × 4 | 373 | 36 | Romantique | 75 × 35 | 108 |
| 18 | SDL | 78 × 36 × 4 | 531 | 37 | Romantique | 75 × 36 | 53 |
| 19 | SDL | 78 × 42 × 4 | 48 | | | | |

*Fifty-six out of a total of 126 SKUs had non-zero sales during the year. This table reports data on 37 SKUs, which cumulatively accounted 99% of demand for the year 1997–1998.

**Exhibit 7: Weekly sales data for 1997–1998.**

| Period | SDL 72 × 35 × 4 | SDL 75 × 35 × 4 | Apsara 72 × 35 × 4 | Romantique 72 × 35 | Klassic 72 × 35 | Total* |
|---|---|---|---|---|---|---|
| 1 | 0 | 0 | 0 | 0 | 0 | 24 |
| 2 | 68 | 0 | 6 | 0 | 0 | 129 |
| 3 | 180 | 29 | 24 | 6 | 0 | 481 |
| 4 | 402 | 257 | 126 | 6 | 6 | 1,284 |
| 5 | 56 | 12 | 60 | 0 | 8 | 295 |
| 6 | 235 | 102 | 42 | 6 | 36 | 636 |
| 7 | 213 | 64 | 42 | 6 | 8 | 450 |
| 8 | 508 | 321 | 192 | 0 | 81 | 1,653 |
| 9 | 6 | 12 | 0 | 0 | 0 | 95 |
| 10 | 55 | 1 | 18 | 0 | 12 | 145 |
| 11 | 249 | 136 | 60 | 0 | 20 | 666 |
| 12 | 646 | 176 | 66 | 6 | 60 | 1,512 |
| 13 | 24 | 6 | 0 | 0 | 0 | 62 |
| 14 | 73 | 43 | 54 | 12 | 12 | 312 |
| 15 | 140 | 94 | 42 | 0 | 20 | 519 |
| 16 | 569 | 280 | 72 | 0 | 46 | 1,331 |
| 17 | 12 | 6 | 0 | 0 | 4 | 48 |
| 18 | 28 | 22 | 48 | 12 | 12 | 230 |
| 19 | 136 | 38 | 50 | 0 | 48 | 423 |
| 20 | 631 | 223 | 126 | 6 | 144 | 1,630 |
| 21 | 0 | 0 | 0 | 0 | 0 | 18 |
| 22 | 18 | 20 | 12 | 0 | 16 | 169 |
| 23 | 150 | 36 | 36 | 6 | 8 | 405 |
| 24 | 436 | 170 | 196 | 6 | 32 | 1,363 |
| 25 | 0 | 0 | 0 | 0 | 1 | 13 |
| 26 | 294 | 118 | 126 | 24 | 12 | 716 |

*(Continued)*

**Exhibit 7: Continued**

| Period | SDL 72 × 35 × 4 | SDL 75 × 35 × 4 | Apsara 72 × 35 × 4 | Romantique 72 × 35 | Klassic 72 × 35 | Total* |
|---|---|---|---|---|---|---|
| 27 | 544 | 218 | 108 | 1 | 64 | 1,368 |
| 28 | 1198 | 306 | 24 | 46 | 28 | 2,479 |
| 29 | 15 | 7 | 4 | 0 | 5 | 38 |
| 30 | 59 | 19 | 18 | 0 | 14 | 132 |
| 31 | 119 | 51 | 24 | 1 | 12 | 306 |
| 32 | 405 | 187 | 118 | 5 | 75 | 1,445 |
| 33 | 41 | 13 | 5 | 3 | 10 | 78 |
| 34 | 52 | 21 | 31 | 4 | 8 | 191 |
| 35 | 172 | 83 | 43 | 5 | 13 | 484 |
| 36 | 640 | 298 | 136 | 6 | 34 | 1,842 |
| 37 | 25 | 7 | 3 | 3 | 2 | 107 |
| 38 | 24 | 52 | 15 | 0 | 2 | 237 |
| 39 | 77 | 57 | 30 | 3 | 14 | 445 |
| 40 | 847 | 212 | 187 | 12 | 64 | 1,837 |
| 41 | 7 | 5 | 4 | 0 | 5 | 63 |
| 42 | 31 | 33 | 11 | 1 | 0 | 153 |
| 43 | 138 | 45 | 47 | 2 | 6 | 373 |
| 44 | 502 | 160 | 81 | 3 | 44 | 1,388 |
| 45 | 27 | 7 | 1 | 4 | 13 | 90 |
| 46 | 30 | 26 | 34 | 5 | 28 | 281 |
| 47 | 193 | 93 | 62 | 7 | 48 | 451 |
| 48 | 747 | 320 | 178 | 12 | 93 | 1,996 |

*Total weekly sales data for 126 SKUs.

**Exhibit 8a: Sample data of material and order flow at Delhi area office.**

| | Period | SDL 72 × 35 × 4 | | | SDL 75 × 35 × 4 | | | Apsara 72 × 35 × 4 | | | Romantique 72 × 35 | | | Klassic 72 × 35 | | |
|---|---|---|---|---|---|---|---|---|---|---|---|---|---|---|---|---|
| | | I | S | OS | I | S | OS | I | S | OS | I | S | OS | I | S | OS |
| April | 1 | 210 | 0 | 404 | 270 | 0 | 0 | 90 | 0 | 0 | 0 | 0 | 24 | 20 | 0 | 0 |
| | 2 | 90 | 68 | 404 | 30 | 0 | 0 | 60 | 6 | 0 | 0 | 0 | 24 | 20 | 0 | 0 |
| | 3 | 90 | 180 | 666 | 30 | 29 | 180 | 60 | 24 | 108 | 0 | 6 | 24 | 20 | 0 | 0 |
| | 4 | 30 | 402 | 594 | 30 | 257 | 313 | 30 | 126 | 150 | 0 | 6 | 24 | 0 | 6 | 0 |
| May | 5 | 330 | 56 | 270 | 420 | 12 | 206 | 90 | 60 | 84 | 18 | 0 | 18 | 40 | 8 | 74 |
| | 6 | 480 | 235 | 520 | 330 | 102 | 434 | 60 | 42 | 216 | 0 | 6 | 18 | 40 | 36 | 94 |
| | 7 | 300 | 213 | 1,107 | 390 | 64 | 902 | 90 | 42 | 186 | 0 | 6 | 12 | 20 | 8 | 130 |
| | 8 | 150 | 508 | 1,020 | 60 | 321 | 1,090 | 0 | 192 | 234 | 0 | 0 | 6 | 0 | 81 | 138 |
| June | 9 | 150 | 6 | 806 | 0 | 12 | 925 | 30 | 0 | 78 | 0 | 0 | 6 | 0 | | 57 |
| | 10 | 0 | 55 | 950 | 0 | 1 | 913 | 78 | 18 | 204 | 30 | 0 | 6 | 20 | 12 | 57 |
| | 11 | 0 | 249 | 895 | 60 | 136 | 912 | 30 | 60 | 186 | 0 | 0 | 6 | 20 | 20 | 85 |
| | 12 | 0 | 646 | 646 | 60 | 176 | 830 | 60 | 66 | 186 | 0 | 6 | 6 | 20 | 60 | 85 |
| July | 13 | 450 | 24 | 0 | 180 | 6 | 678 | 90 | 0 | 120 | 18 | 0 | 0 | 40 | | 25 |
| | 14 | 300 | 73 | 294 | 90 | 43 | 684 | 30 | 54 | 180 | 12 | 12 | 30 | 20 | 12 | 65 |
| | 15 | 330 | 140 | 551 | 120 | 94 | 929 | 30 | 42 | 210 | 0 | 0 | 18 | 20 | 20 | 73 |
| | 16 | 150 | 569 | 993 | 0 | 280 | 967 | 60 | 72 | 174 | 0 | 0 | 18 | 0 | 46 | 73 |
| August | 17 | 60 | 12 | 424 | 42 | 6 | 687 | 60 | | 162 | 0 | 0 | 18 | 20 | 4 | 27 |
| | 18 | 330 | 28 | 886 | 54 | 22 | 807 | 60 | 48 | 168 | 18 | 12 | 36 | 104 | 12 | 63 |
| | 19 | 300 | 136 | 1,086 | 42 | 38 | 797 | 0 | 50 | 204 | 0 | 0 | 24 | 112 | 48 | 107 |
| | 20 | 0 | 631 | 950 | 0 | 223 | 759 | 90 | 126 | 184 | 24 | 6 | 24 | 20 | 144 | 219 |
| September | 21 | 48 | 0 | 325 | 240 | | 536 | 36 | 0 | 148 | 12 | 0 | 30 | 0 | 0 | 75 |
| | 22 | 480 | 18 | 653 | 210 | 20 | 812 | 120 | 12 | 172 | 18 | 0 | 30 | 20 | 16 | 75 |
| | 23 | 300 | 150 | 845 | 444 | 36 | 996 | 60 | 36 | 316 | 30 | 6 | 36 | 20 | 8 | 99 |
| | 24 | 0 | 436 | 1,079 | 150 | 170 | 1,254 | 60 | 196 | 388 | 0 | 6 | 30 | 0 | 32 | 91 |

(Continued)

***Exhibit 8a:* Continued**

| | Period | SDL 72 × 35 × 4 | | | SDL 75 × 35 × 4 | | | Apsara 72 × 35 × 4 | | | Romantique 72 × 35 | | | Klassic 72 × 35 | | |
|---|---|---|---|---|---|---|---|---|---|---|---|---|---|---|---|---|
| | | I | S | OS | I | S | OS | I | S | OS | I | S | OS | I | S | OS |
| October | 25 | 36 | 0 | 649 | 120 | | 1,384 | 60 | 0 | 192 | 12 | 0 | 24 | 32 | 1 | 59 |
| | 26 | 2,370 | 294 | 889 | 240 | 118 | 1,642 | 252 | 126 | 408 | 30 | 24 | 60 | 76 | 12 | 86 |
| | 27 | 270 | 544 | 1,663 | 310 | 218 | 1,818 | 72 | 108 | 342 | 12 | 1 | 66 | 8 | 64 | 146 |
| | 28 | 270 | 1,198 | 2,781 | 90 | 306 | 1,714 | 42 | 24 | 234 | 12 | 46 | 65 | 8 | 28 | 82 |

I, indent; S, sales; OS, opening stock.

***Exhibit 8b:* Sample data of material and order flow at Bangalore central warehouse.**

| | Period | SDL 72 × 35 × 4 | | | SDL 75 × 35 × 4 | | | Apsara 72 × 35 × 4 | | | Romantique 72 × 35 | | | Klassic 72 × 35 | | |
|---|---|---|---|---|---|---|---|---|---|---|---|---|---|---|---|---|
| | | I | D | OS | I | D | OS | I | D | OS | I | D | OSI | D | OS | |
| April | 1 | 480 | 120 | 1,956 | 540 | 240 | 409 | 150 | 120 | | 6 | 0 | 30 | 6 | 0 | 48 |
| | 2 | 366 | 540 | 1,836 | 60 | 180 | 289 | 90 | 114 | 588 | 12 | 0 | 30 | 28 | 0 | 48 |
| | 3 | 168 | 354 | 1,296 | 120 | 228 | 133 | 80 | 156 | 474 | 12 | 0 | 30 | 24 | 4 | 48 |
| | 4 | 120 | 120 | 942 | 90 | 162 | 13 | 60 | 60 | 318 | 0 | 18 | 12 | 0 | 88 | 44 |
| May | 5 | 402 | 696 | 822 | 474 | 390 | 477 | 102 | 204 | 258 | 18 | 0 | 12 | 40 | 36 | 92 |
| | 6 | 774 | 1,284 | 276 | 432 | 612 | 213 | 102 | 42 | 354 | 12 | 6 | 12 | 56 | 112 | 36 |
| | 7 | 552 | 246 | 30 | 462 | 252 | 39 | 132 | 90 | 312 | 0 | 0 | 6 | 32 | 16 | 44 |
| | 8 | 264 | 372 | 48 | 150 | 216 | 81 | 30 | 96 | 312 | 12 | 0 | 6 | 12 | 0 | 44 |
| June | 9 | 462 | 612 | 1,164 | 204 | 216 | 291 | 216 | 222 | 426 | 42 | 0 | 6 | 20 | 8 | 28 |
| | 10 | 1,050 | 180 | 990 | 252 | 90 | 513 | 108 | 12 | 492 | 30 | 0 | 6 | 32 | 40 | 20 |
| | 11 | 276 | 564 | 1,242 | 150 | 216 | 423 | 90 | 270 | 222 | 0 | 0 | 6 | 20 | 60 | 100 |
| | 12 | 288 | 686 | 1,674 | 240 | 294 | 207 | 168 | 18 | 204 | 6 | 0 | 6 | 48 | 8 | 40 |
| July | 13 | 778 | 396 | 996 | 358 | 30 | 627 | 198 | 60 | 144 | 60 | 72 | 150 | 84 | 44 | 150 |
| | 14 | 498 | 588 | 600 | 168 | 438 | 735 | 78 | 84 | 60 | 12 | 0 | 78 | 32 | 84 | 108 |
| | 15 | 714 | 1,146 | 408 | 192 | 486 | 309 | 186 | 354 | 300 | 0 | 0 | 78 | 32 | 20 | 144 |
| | 16 | 198 | 90 | 900 | 42 | 12 | 501 | 72 | 84 | 60 | 6 | 0 | 78 | 0 | 0 | 124 |
| August | 17 | 180 | 690 | 1,296 | 102 | 126 | 549 | 120 | 30 | 324 | 6 | 18 | 78 | 24 | 40 | 124 |
| | 18 | 570 | 522 | 1,332 | 204 | 402 | 861 | 156 | 252 | 84 | 18 | 30 | 60 | 108 | 56 | 84 |
| | 19 | 564 | 90 | 1,056 | 246 | 84 | 603 | 98 | 60 | 252 | 30 | 6 | 30 | 112 | 164 | 28 |
| | 20 | 78 | 6 | 1,020 | 30 | 12 | 645 | 102 | 90 | 210 | 24 | 12 | 24 | 20 | 0 | 64 |
| September | 21 | 276 | 630 | 1,014 | 156 | 162 | 651 | 24 | 90 | 48 | 30 | 6 | 12 | 8 | 8 | 64 |
| | 22 | 762 | 762 | 498 | 210 | 216 | 207 | 144 | 42 | 312 | 24 | 6 | 6 | 64 | 68 | 56 |
| | 23 | 840 | 636 | 204 | 150 | 171 | 333 | 126 | 240 | 78 | 48 | 0 | 0 | 24 | 40 | 68 |
| | 24 | 228 | 162 | 732 | 90 | 90 | 438 | 132 | 0 | 516 | 6 | 0 | 0 | 8 | 4 | 28 |

I, indent; D, dispatch; OS, opening stock.

For the last two days he had been trying to make some sense out of the data without any breakthrough. He realized he was just getting lost in a maze of data. He had a feeling that the system could have been managed in a much better way but he couldn't put his finger on anything specific.

## Discussion Questions

1. Evaluate the performance of the Kurlon supply chain? What are the causes of the problems faced by Kurlon?
2. Evaluate the performance of the Delhi area office on the supply chain dimension? For your analysis you may like to focus on SDL 72 × 35 × 4.
3. What is your evaluation of the company's planning processes?
4. What specific actions do you recommend to Narendra Kudva to address supply chain performance problems?

# Kurlon Limited (B)*

In May 2015, Narendra Kudva, Chief Operating Officer, Kurlon Limited, reflected on Kurlon's performance in the last 18 years. Kurlon had covered a lot of ground since 1997 and had weathered the challenges faced in the last decade and a half. The company had improved its financial position considerably. The company had managed to maintain its market leadership despite severe competition from local and foreign players. The company had warmed up to the Internet revolution and had developed software to manage its ordering process online.

However, Narendra knew that change was a constant element of consumer markets, and as Kurlon planned for its next phase of growth, new challenges on the horizon were abound. A number of customers purchased through the Internet, and Narendra knew that suitable marketing solutions were needed to address this trend. With the prevalence of the Internet, e-commerce had created new market places, and Kurlon hoped to leverage from this trend. While Narendra knew that the foreign players did not possess the product variety that Kurlon had, developing an efficient distribution solution to meet customer needs for varied products was an immediate challenge facing Kurlon.

---

*This case has been prepared by Mandar Nayak and Professor Janat Shah, IIM Udaipur.

## Kurlon in 2015

As Narendra Kudva went through the operations for Kurlon in the last 18 years, he could note that the company had done well over the years. In comparison with Kurlon's operations in 1997, the company had grown considerably. The company had expanded its reach in the domestic market and increased the number of sales offices, dealers, and warehouses in India. The company had also recently started exports to markets outside India.

In order to bring better efficiency to its operations, Kurlon had also made improvements in its supply chain practices. The company had moved its entire order management system to the Internet, and an online portal facilitated real-time management of the ordering process. The improvements had also manifested favourably on Kurlon's financials, which showed a double digit growth over the last decade and a half.

## Operations

Kurlon's operations had increased considerably. At the end of 2014, the company had improved the number of manufacturing facilities to five factories viz. two at Bangalore, Karnataka, one at Bhubaneshwar, Orissa, one at Gwalior, Madhya Pradesh, and one at Uttaranchal. The number of ASOs (Area Sales Offices) had increased to 72 and the company operated through more than 6,000 dealers. The company had developed three hubs, warehouses at Dabaspet, Peenya, and Yeshwantpur, Karnataka, where the mattresses were stocked before delivery to the ASOs. Kurlon had also implemented changes in its product variety, which included five lengths and eight widths resulting in about 40 varieties of mattresses.

## Supply Chain Practices

One of the most important changes made at Kurlon was the overhaul of its supply chain practices. As Narendra Kudva recounted,

> "We wanted to improve the visibility of the orders as they traversed our operations. We took the big leap when we decided to develop the software to achieve this. As the Internet came along, the software moved to the online domain. Today we can say that developing the software has been our main improvement in the last 15 years".

The online portal, accessible to the head office, ASOs, and manufacturing facilities provided all details to the user for the ordering process. Exhibit 2 provides screen shots of the online ordering portal at Kurlon. Each sales office had a unique login name and password for using the portal. Using the portal, ASOs could indent directly from the plant. The indents could be raised for any of the five plants at Kurlon. A dropdown list was available for easy selection of the plants. The portal facilitated the sales office to select the length, breadth, thickness, and density and also the recommended quantity for indenting. Details of opening stock, average sales, and pending indent for each plant were available on the portal.

As Narendra Kudva recounted,

> "The software has helped the management to check the stock each day in the morning and also if any goods were in transit. Thus, every day, the factory knew what was to be dispatched at the end of the day. The online software has provided us with much needed visibility of our operations, and as a result of which tracking and monitoring of our orders has become so much easier".

The dashboards prepared as a part of the online portal ensured that details of stock of every SKU (Stock Keeping Unit) at the 72 sales offices were available to the senior management at Kurlon. The portal provided a ready reference for the fast moving and slow moving products. Fast moving categories were highlighted in blue and slow moving categories were highlighted in orange. The portal provided details of excess stock and recommended that the sales office to reduce the indent unless there was a specific order. In case the sales office had indented less, the stock was highlighted in yellow and recommended that the sales office review its stock position.

With the use of the portal, Kurlon had managed to streamline its ordering process and achieve efficiency in terms of stocks. Sufficient buffers were maintained for each SKU in the sales office. The online ordering system also helped to reduce manufacturing time, transit time, and the frequency of the truck visits to the sales office.

## Financials

As Narendra Kudva glanced through the unaudited financials for Kurlon in 2015, he could see that they showed improvement over 1997. Exhibit 1 shows Balance Sheet and Income–expenditure of the company in 1997 and 2015 (unaudited). For the year ending March 2015, Kurlon's total income had improved to ₹800.56 crores including ₹2 crores from exports. The company's Profit After Tax (PAT) had also improved to ₹19.29 crores. The company's investment in its distribution had improved considerably, as seen from the fact that distribution expenses was close to 23% of income in 2015.

## Market Share

Kurlon was still the market leader though its market share in 2014 was probably between 25% and 30%, a far distance away from the 65% market share of branded rubberized coir mattress that it had enjoyed 18 years back. A major reason for this was increased competition from local players and entry of foreign players such as Tempur, Snoozer, and King Koil, which had set up manufacturing facilities in India.

## Future Challenges and Concerns

Among the mattresses that were ordered daily, about 25% of the mattresses were odd sizes. While the product variety was favourable to Kurlon's competitive advantage, the proportion of odd sizes worried Narendra. In his words,

> "The fact that we work with a large variety of products is good for us. Most foreign players worked with standardized sizes and the variety of their products in terms of the number of different sizes was low. But managing the distribution and the supply chain in light of the product variety was a logistics challenge because different sizes meant different size of trucks".

Kurlon was envisaging developing cutting centres in different markets in India. Locating the cutting centres close to the consumer meant that Kurlon could optimize on the number of trucks required for delivering the mattresses to the customer. The company was in the process of identifying markets with higher orders and the robustness of the demand in various markets. As Narendra said, "We believe that by developing cutting centres close to the customers, the demand could be significantly increased, and in such markets, developing cutting centres would be a viable option".

Consumer awareness had increased considerably over the years because of the Internet and Narendra knew that Kurlon would have to address this trend as early as possible. The company was aware of the growth in e-commerce in the last decade and was in the process of developing a suitable solution to address and tap the growth. As Narendra Kudva recounted,

> "As more and more people use the Internet, their awareness has improved considerably. Today, customers are aware of our products even before we could reach them. Social media sites and other consumer blog sites discuss product variety and product quality. The Internet has created new marketplaces, and as a market leader in this industry, we need to be present in that space as well. We are in the process of developing marketing solutions in light of the social media. We have also observed that a large number of customers ordered online and developing marketing (sales and distribution) a solution in this regard was a critical challenge for us".

While Narendra was aware that it would take a while before foreign players entrenched themselves in the Indian market, Kurlon still needed to keep a close watch on the competition. Maintaining its market leadership was important to Kurlon, and Narendra Kudva was well aware of the fact that Kurlon could not rest on its achievements so far and strive for continuous improvements.

***Exhibit 1:* *Financials in 2015 vs. 1997.***

| **Balance sheet** | 31-03-97<br>Rs. Crore | 31-03-15<br>Rs. Crore(Unaudited) |
|---|---|---|
| **Source of funds** | | |
| Net worth | | |
| Share capital | 7.09 | 37.43 |
| Reserves & surplus | 11.09 | 15.98 |
| Total borrowings | | |
| Secured loans | 18.77 | 118.46 |
| Unsecured loans | 4.4 | 0.00 |
| Current liabilities & provisions | | |
| Current liabilities | 18.18 | 200.29 |
| Provisions | 2.92 | - |
| Deferred Tax | - | 3.06 |
| **Employment of funds** | | |
| Gross fixed assets | | |
| Land & building | 6.26 | 36.53 |
| Plant & machinery | 20.17 | 65.41 |
| Other fixed assets | 2.73 | 10.11 |
| Capital work-in-progress | 0.05 | 12.59 |
| Less: Cumulative depreciation | 10.28 | 9.17 |
| Net fixed assets | 18.93 | 115.48 |
| Investments | 0.32 | 0.00 |
| Inventories | | |
| Raw materials (including stores and spares) | 5.67 | 21.47 |
| Finished goods | 8.65 | 54.28 |
| Semi-finished goods | 0.92 | 10.73 |
| Receivables | 23.82 | 65.77 |
| Cash and bank balance | 4.14 | 50.83 |
| Loans and Advances | - | 56.66 |

**Exhibit 2:** ***Screenshots of the portal developed at Kurlon***

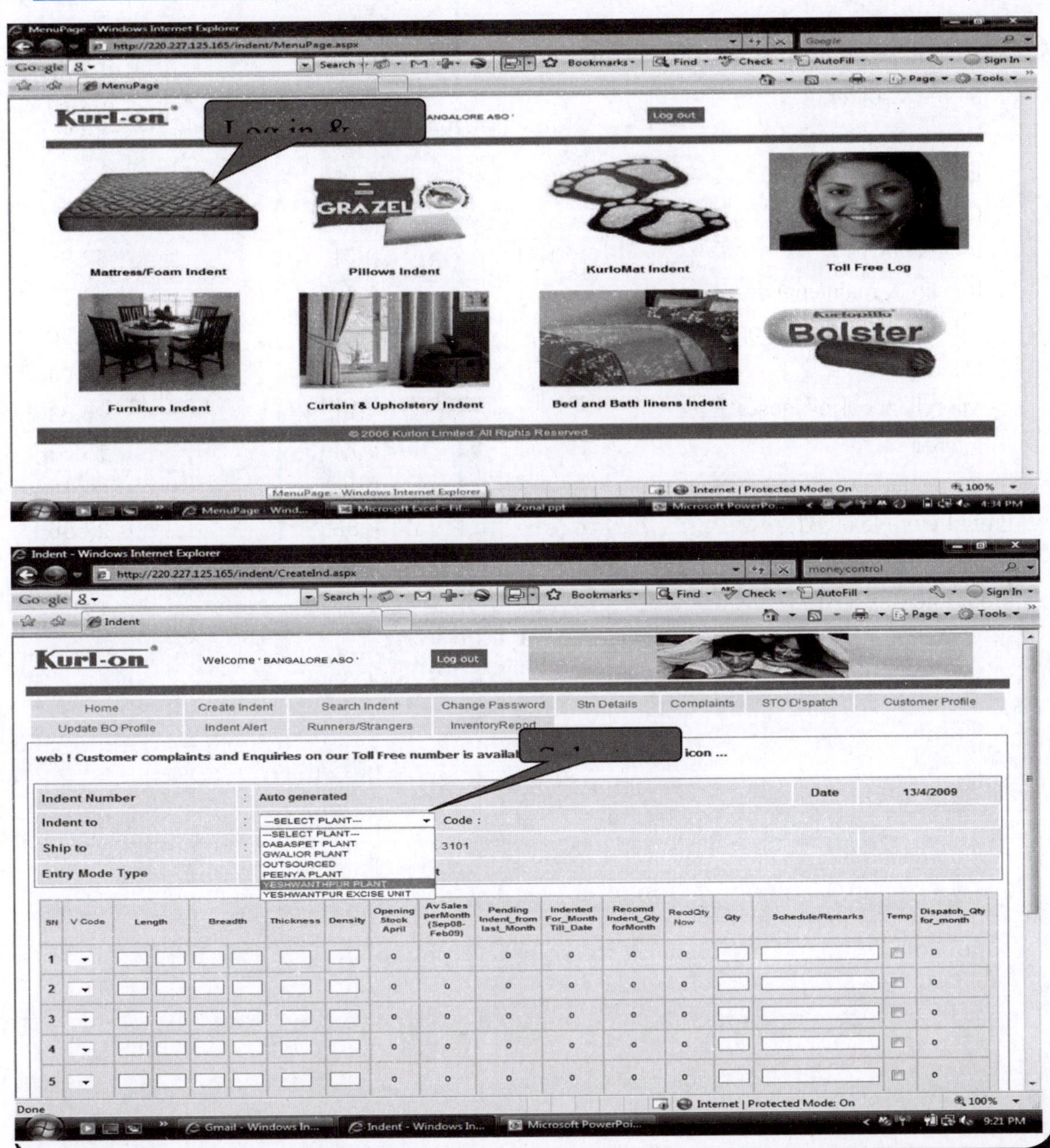


**Source:** Kurlon

**Exhibit 3:** ***Income–expenditure statement.***

| | 1996-97<br>Rs. Crore | 2014-15<br>Rs. Crore (Unaudited) |
|---|---|---|
| Income | | |
| Manufacturing | 95.04 | 759.99 |
| Trading & Others | 17.18 | 38.57 |
| Exports | - | 2.00 |

*(Continued)*

**Exhibit 3: Continued**

| | | |
|---|---|---|
| Expenditure | | |
| Raw materials (incl. purchase of finished goods) | 66.11 | 368.97 |
| Stores & spares | 0.80 | 3.54 |
| Wages & salaries | 3.67 | 37.29 |
| Energy (power & fuel) | 1.95 | 17.77 |
| Other manufacturing expenses | 1.08 | 49.75 |
| Indirect taxes | 0.71 | 52.95 |
| Repairs & maintenance | 0.89 | 2.27 |
| Advertising & Marketing | 12.22 | 19.80 |
| Distribution | 8.95 | 189.04 |
| Miscellaneous expenses | 4.11 | 6.83 |
| Interest | 4.74 | 15.62 |
| Depreciation | 2.13 | 9.17 |
| Profit Before Tax (PBT) | 4.86 | 27.56 |
| Tax provision | 0.85 | 8.27 |
| Profit After Tax (PAT) | 4.01 | 19.29 |

# Vehicle Routing at Baroda Union*

Jagdish Patel looked at the cost figures for the last six months and he knew the meeting with the chairman was not going to be very pleasant. The chairman was once again going to raise the issue of milk prices paid to farmers. Jagdish, General Manager (Procurement) of Baroda District Co-operative Milk Producer's Union Ltd (Baroda Union), had observed that neighbourhood unions like Kheda and Valsad were giving much better milk prices to farmers than what Baroda was paying. As he looked at the cost figures once again, he knew he had to do something about transportation costs for milk procurement, as it was the most significant part of the operating cost under the control of the management. Jagdish was aware that in another two months they will have to start the work on issuing a tender for the next year's transportation contracts. Baroda Union had been working with the same procurement routes for the last couple of years and these routes were evolved historically. Jagdish felt that Baroda Union will not be in a position to reduce the transportation costs unless they could come up with a more scientific way of designing these routes. He was just wondering whether he could apply any of the ideas that he had picked up when he recently attended an executive programme on logistics management.

---

*This case has been prepared by Professor Janat Shah, IIM Bangalore.

## Background

Baroda Co-operative Union was set up in late 1960s with the Anand model in mind. As per the Anand model, each village forms a co-operative society of all farmers who had surplus milk available with them. As each village-level society would not have enough volume to justify setting up a milk processing plant, all the village co-operative societies in a district would form a union, which in turn would collect milk from all societies and process it in a centralized processing plant. The basic philosophy was that as milk was a perishable commodity farmers would not get remunerative prices for their surplus milk unless they own the processing facility. Traditionally, middleman used to exploit farmers by paying them ridiculously low prices. Baroda Union had membership of 700 village-level co-operatives spread all over the district. These 700 societies were covered by 44 truck/tempo routes, wherein milk was collected twice a day and 365 days in a year. Since these 700 societies were geographically spread out, the union had faced a difficulty in getting milk in time from some of the far-flung societies. Given the perishable nature of the product, it was important that the time lag between milking and processing should not exceed seven hours. So Baroda Union had set up one chilling centre at Bodeli so as to take care of this problem of distances. Out of the 700 societies, about 180 societies were connected to the chilling centre through 12 procurement routes. Milk procured from these societies would be brought to the chilling centre where it would be kept in a chilled condition, and from there it would be sent to a centralized processing centre via special tankers. The remaining 580 societies were directly connected to the processing centre at Baroda through 32 truck/tempo routes. Each vehicle route would cover approximately 15 societies depending on the total supply of milk and is given a specified schedule (see Exhibit 3 for a sample route).

The main concern was that because of its perishable nature, milk must either get processed or kept in a chilled condition so as to avoid curdling. If milk gets curdled, the Union could not use that milk in any productive way. During the summer season about 5 per cent of the milk was received in a curdled form.

The main objective of the Union was to minimize total costs so that members (farmers) would get the highest payment per litre of milk. Last year's data showed that transportation costs in milk procurement accounted for 17 per cent of costs (see Exhibit 1 for costs break-up).

## Milk Routes

Since Baroda union was already 30 years old, it had by and large stable routes and every year they floated a tender wherein transport contractors are asked to bid for pre-specified routes. The tender also specified the type of vehicle (truck or tempo) required. In the tender all the details were provided. For various reasons, the price quoted per kilometre varied significantly across routes (see Exhibit 2 for detailed data on the same, for a few of the routes of the Bodeli

***Exhibit 1:* Cost per litre of milk for Baroda Union.**

| Expense component | Percentage of cost |
|---|---|
| Transportation | 17.50 |
| Processing | 15.00 |
| Salary & Wages | 15.60 |
| Packaging | 20.50 |
| Distribution | 13.00 |
| Admn. Expenses | 8.90 |
| Others | 9.50 |
| Total | 100.00 |

***Exhibit 2:*** ***Tender details for sample routes of Bodeli chilling centre.***

| Route number | Type of vehicle | Contractor name | Rate per kilometre |
|---|---|---|---|
| 51 | Tempo | Ghanshyamdas | 3.00 |
| | | Ibrahimkhan | 3.28 |
| 52 | Tempo | Dhanishran | 3.38 |
| | | Rajput | 3.50 |
| 54 | Tempo | Salimbhai | 3.78 |
| | | Galubhai | 4.26 |
| 55 | Tempo | Ghanshyamdas | 2.68 |
| | | Shantilal | 2.72 |
| | | Jugalkishore | 3.36 |
| | | Girdhari | 3.52 |
| 60 | Tempo | Jashwant | 4.60 |
| | | Dhanisharan | 4.66 |
| 62 | Tempo | Gabubhai | 3.34 |

chilling centre). Since milk procurement was quite seasonal in nature, the Union designed routes keeping in mind peak procurement, which took place in the winter. Actually there were two seasons, winter and summer. Procurement in the summer would drop down to about 50 per cent of the winter procurement level.

Milk was collected twice a day, once in the morning and once in the evening. Societies that did not have any motorable approach roads delivered the milk at some nearby point on the road or a nearby co-operative. Milk was collected in cans, which carried the name of the society for identification. The cleaned and empty cans required for the morning procurement were delivered while collecting the evening milk. Similarly, cans required for morning milk were delivered to societies during the evening trip. Each can could hold 40 litres of milk. The milk collected had to be delivered at the processing plant or chilling centre at specified hours. The contractor was given a grace time of one hour to take care of unforeseen circumstances on any particular day. If a contractor delayed delivery by more than an hour he had to pay a penalty. The routes have to be designed such that the truck arrivals are spaced out uniformly to avoid problems at the receiving dock. On reaching the processing centre or the chilling centre, the truck would have to join a queue and would be taken to the receiving centre on a first come first served basis. The truck would unload cans on the receiving dock. At the receiving dock each can is weighed and a sample is collected to check for milk curdling. Each truck took about 20–25 minutes at the receiving dock. If milk was found to be curdled, the respective cans were kept separately. Good milk was emptied into a tank. Societies that supplied curdled milk were paid only nominal rates. If the milk got curdled because of delay on the part of the transport contractor he would end up paying the differential charges to the respective societies.

Jagdish had called Ramesh, who handled designing routes and contractors, to discuss the idea of designing scientific routes. Ramesh was not very enthusiastic about the idea. After a long discussion Ramesh summarized his views as follows:

> I think over a period of time we have come up with routes that are quite optimal. Further, since the contractor bids on a route and not on kilometre basis, there is a chance that the overall distance in terms of kilometres may come down though the actual costs may go up. I know you are thinking of using some scientific way of designing routes. I have a feeling that you will get routes that are petal shaped. Petal-shaped routes are not going to be acceptable to societies that are near the plant but for those at the beginning of such a petal-shaped route. This is because their rate would go up. Also, it would result in substantial alterations in the collection times at the societies. Most of the farmers have worked out their milking times and other schedules around the current truck schedules. Do you think we can force a change in their present working schedule? Finally, they are the owners of this Union.

## A Sample Problem

Jagdish knew that it would be very difficult to try out a new set of routes for the entire range of societies. Also, he was not sure about the applicability of using standard vehicle routing ideas of building scientific routes for a dairy kind of situation. To build his intuition about routing decisions, he decided to look at a smaller version of the problem. Since the Bodeli chilling centre involved only 12 routes, he thought it might be a good starting point for experimentation. He collected all the necessary data that would be required to do the meaningful exercise. From the 12 routes he further decided to narrow his focus to six selected routes (route numbers 51, 52, 54, 55, 60 and 62), which were in close proximity. Even these six routes accounted for 84 villages, which made the problem quite large. To reduce the problem size further, he decided to represent these six routes with modified routes that would have at most six pickup points in any route. All those societies, which were either geographically close to each other or fell by and large on a straight-line road, were combined and treated as one pickup point. These six modified routes with 33 pickup points are as shown in Exhibits 3 and 4. Jagdish calculated the distance matrix showing the values of all the pair-wise (34 × 34) distances for all the possible combinations. See Exhibit 5 for data on the distance matrix.

While designing routes he also had to ensure that the load on any route should not exceed the vehicle capacity and that the route length should be within some limit so as to handle issues related to curdling of milk. The time taken by a vehicle on any route would include travel time and waiting time at societies. Regarding travel times, he knew that road conditions varied and all roads were by and large classified as pakka road (good road) and kachha road (not a good road). To take care of this issue he decided to assume that a vehicle would run at an average

***Exhibit 3:*** ***Route number 51.***

| **Actual route** | | | **Modified route*** |
|---|---|---|---|
| **Society name** | **Milk collection time for morning route** | **Expected maximum quantity of milk in litres** | **Pickup point: representing the concerned society** |
| Khandibara | 6.00 | 70 | 1 |
| Thadgam | 6.25 | 210 | 1 |
| Aathadungari | 6.35 | 30 | 1 |
| Jamba | 6.55 | 130 | 2 |
| Nalwant | 7.05 | 250 | 2 |
| Vadhay | 7.25 | 160 | 2 |
| Sandhaliya | 7.35 | 490 | 3 |
| Palasani | 7.45 | 30 | 3 |
| Kandwa | 8.15 | 700 | 3 |
| Kukawati | 8.25 | 60 | 3 |
| Nawagam | 8.50 | 230 | 4 |
| Vanthada | 9.00 | 70 | 4 |
| Pochamba | 9.10 | 50 | 4 |
| Kandha | 9.20 | 60 | 5 |
| Baroli | 9.40 | 150 | 5 |
| Nannupura | 10.00 | 35 | 6 |
| Haripura | 10.20 | 130 | 6 |
| Sindhikuwa | 10.30 | 240 | 6 |
| Bodeli | 11.15 | – | – |

*Actual route would involve vehicle starting from Bodeli and visiting each of the 18 societies in the route and returning to Bodeli. In the modified route, societies Khndibara, Thadgam and Aathadungri would be represented by one point, which would be located at Thadgam and be called pickup point 1. The waiting time at this pickup point would be assumed to be 15 minutes as it actually represents three societies. So, the modified route 51 would be Bodeli-1-2-3-4-5-6-Bodeli.

*Exhibit 4:* ***Data on modified routes for the remaining five routes.***

| Route number | Pickup point | Milk collection | Number of actual societies represented by the pickup point* |
|---|---|---|---|
| 52 | 7 | 880 | 3 |
| | 8 | 260 | 2 |
| | 9 | 220 | 2 |
| | 10 | 230 | 2 |
| | 11 | 560 | 2 |
| 54 | 12 | 690 | 2 |
| | 13 | 820 | 3 |
| | 14 | 950 | 3 |
| | 15 | 570 | 2 |
| | 16 | 690 | 3 |
| | 17 | 210 | 2 |
| 55 | 18 | 130 | 3 |
| | 19 | 240 | 2 |
| | 20 | 890 | 4 |
| | 21 | 290 | 3 |
| | 22 | 800 | 4 |
| 60 | 23 | 610 | 2 |
| | 24 | 300 | 2 |
| | 25 | 100 | 2 |
| | 26 | 770 | 2 |
| | 27 | 930 | 3 |
| 62 | 28 | 220 | 2 |
| | 29 | 140 | 2 |
| | 30 | 370 | 3 |
| | 31 | 100 | 2 |
| | 32 | 360 | 2 |
| | 33 | 230 | 2 |

*Expected waiting time at the pickup point = 5 × Number of actual societies represented by the respective pickup point.

speed of 30 kilometres per hour. Based on his past experience he also knew that on an average a vehicle would spend about 5 minutes at each society to take care of loading, unloading and other activities like document transfer. Regarding vehicle capacity, he could safely assume that a typical tempo would be able to accommodate about 100 cans. Now that he had all the necessary data in place he hoped that he would be in a position to apply all the ideas that he had learnt during the executive programme on logistics to see if it would result in any substantial savings in transportation costs.

## Discussion Questions

1. Identify the key challenges faced by the Baroda Union. How important is in-bound logistics for Baroda Union?
2. Suggest a suitable approach that Baroda Union can use for designing efficient routes for milk collection. What kind of conflicts are these revised routes likely to create at Baroda dairy? How should Baroda Union handle these issues?
3. In what way will the problem of designing optimal vehicle schedules be affected by the nature of ownership (corporate sector vis-à-vis co-operative dairy like Baroda Union)?
4. If you were Jagdish Patel, what would you do?

***Exhibit 5:* Distance matrix.**

| | 0* | 1 | 2 | 3 | 4 | 5 | 6 | 7 | 8 | 9 | 10 | 11 | 12 | 13 | 14 | 15 | 16 | 17 | 18 | 19 | 20 | 21 | 22 | 23 | 24 | 25 | 26 | 27 | 28 | 29 | 30 | 31 | 32 | 33 |
|---|---|---|---|---|---|---|---|---|---|---|---|---|---|---|---|---|---|---|---|---|---|---|---|---|---|---|---|---|---|---|---|---|---|---|
| 0* | 0 | | | | | | | | | | | | | | | | | | | | | | | | | | | | | | | | | |
| 1 | 48 | 0 | | | | | | | | | | | | | | | | | | | | | | | | | | | | | | | | |
| 2 | 49 | 7 | 0 | | | | | | | | | | | | | | | | | | | | | | | | | | | | | | | |
| 3 | 44 | 12 | 7 | 0 | | | | | | | | | | | | | | | | | | | | | | | | | | | | | | |
| 4 | 51 | 29 | 22 | 18 | 0 | | | | | | | | | | | | | | | | | | | | | | | | | | | | | |
| 5 | 43 | 35 | 30 | 24 | 13 | 0 | | | | | | | | | | | | | | | | | | | | | | | | | | | | |
| 6 | 31 | 23 | 21 | 15 | 22 | 19 | 0 | | | | | | | | | | | | | | | | | | | | | | | | | | | |
| 7 | 40 | 8 | 12 | 12 | 29 | 33 | 18 | 0 | | | | | | | | | | | | | | | | | | | | | | | | | | |
| 8 | 35 | 18 | 16 | 10 | 20 | 20 | 5 | 14 | 0 | | | | | | | | | | | | | | | | | | | | | | | | | |
| 9 | 26 | 40 | 38 | 31 | 29 | 18 | 17 | 34 | 22 | 0 | | | | | | | | | | | | | | | | | | | | | | | | |
| 10 | 21 | 36 | 35 | 28 | 31 | 22 | 13 | 29 | 18 | 7 | 0 | | | | | | | | | | | | | | | | | | | | | | | |
| 11 | 25 | 29 | 28 | 21 | 27 | 21 | 6 | 22 | 11 | 12 | 7 | 0 | | | | | | | | | | | | | | | | | | | | | | |
| 12 | 39 | 12 | 18 | 19 | 36 | 39 | 22 | 7 | 19 | 38 | 32 | 26 | 0 | | | | | | | | | | | | | | | | | | | | | |
| 13 | 34 | 14 | 17 | 14 | 30 | 32 | 15 | 6 | 12 | 30 | 25 | 18 | 8 | 0 | | | | | | | | | | | | | | | | | | | | |
| 14 | 27 | 21 | 24 | 22 | 36 | 35 | 16 | 13 | 16 | 29 | 22 | 17 | 12 | 8 | 0 | | | | | | | | | | | | | | | | | | | |
| 15 | 32 | 17 | 17 | 12 | 26 | 26 | 8 | 10 | 6 | 24 | 19 | 12 | 14 | 6 | 10 | 0 | | | | | | | | | | | | | | | | | | |
| 16 | 22 | 27 | 27 | 22 | 31 | 26 | 9 | 19 | 12 | 17 | 11 | 6 | 21 | 14 | 11 | 10 | 0 | | | | | | | | | | | | | | | | | |
| 17 | 15 | 34 | 36 | 33 | 44 | 39 | 22 | 26 | 25 | 27 | 20 | 19 | 24 | 20 | 13 | 20 | 14 | 0 | | | | | | | | | | | | | | | | |
| 18 | 60 | 21 | 27 | 33 | 49 | 56 | 42 | 25 | 38 | 59 | 53 | 47 | 22 | 29 | 33 | 35 | 43 | 45 | 0 | | | | | | | | | | | | | | | |
| 19 | 56 | 27 | 34 | 38 | 56 | 61 | 44 | 28 | 41 | 60 | 53 | 47 | 22 | 30 | 32 | 36 | 43 | 40 | 12 | 0 | | | | | | | | | | | | | | |
| 20 | 45 | 9 | 16 | 19 | 37 | 42 | 26 | 9 | 23 | 43 | 37 | 31 | 6 | 13 | 18 | 19 | 27 | 30 | 16 | 19 | 0 | | | | | | | | | | | | | |
| 21 | 35 | 22 | 28 | 28 | 45 | 46 | 28 | 17 | 26 | 41 | 34 | 29 | 10 | 15 | 13 | 20 | 24 | 20 | 25 | 20 | 15 | 0 | | | | | | | | | | | | |
| 22 | 22 | 31 | 35 | 32 | 46 | 44 | 25 | 23 | 26 | 33 | 26 | 23 | 20 | 18 | 11 | 21 | 18 | 8 | 39 | 33 | 26 | 13 | 0 | | | | | | | | | | | |
| 23 | 20 | 28 | 29 | 24 | 34 | 29 | 12 | 21 | 15 | 19 | 11 | 8 | 22 | 15 | 11 | 12 | 3 | 11 | 44 | 42 | 28 | 23 | 15 | 0 | | | | | | | | | | |
| 24 | 17 | 31 | 32 | 27 | 37 | 31 | 15 | 24 | 18 | 19 | 12 | 10 | 24 | 18 | 12 | 15 | 6 | 8 | 46 | 44 | 30 | 24 | 14 | 3 | 0 | | | | | | | | | |
| 25 | 21 | 29 | 29 | 23 | 31 | 25 | 9 | 21 | 13 | 16 | 9 | 5 | 23 | 16 | 13 | 12 | 2 | 14 | 45 | 45 | 29 | 26 | 19 | 3 | 6 | 0 | | | | | | | | |
| 26 | 15 | 33 | 35 | 30 | 40 | 35 | 18 | 25 | 21 | 22 | 15 | 14 | 24 | 19 | 12 | 18 | 9 | 5 | 46 | 43 | 31 | 23 | 12 | 6 | 4 | 9 | 0 | | | | | | | |
| 27 | 11 | 37 | 40 | 35 | 45 | 39 | 23 | 30 | 27 | 25 | 18 | 19 | 28 | 24 | 16 | 23 | 15 | 4 | 49 | 45 | 35 | 25 | 12 | 12 | 9 | 14 | 5 | 0 | | | | | | |
| 28 | 23 | 43 | 47 | 45 | 59 | 55 | 38 | 36 | 39 | 43 | 36 | 35 | 31 | 31 | 24 | 34 | 29 | 16 | 47 | 39 | 37 | 22 | 13 | 27 | 24 | 30 | 21 | 18 | 0 | | | | | |
| 29 | 25 | 33 | 37 | 35 | 50 | 48 | 29 | 26 | 30 | 38 | 30 | 28 | 21 | 21 | 14 | 24 | 22 | 12 | 38 | 31 | 26 | 13 | 4 | 20 | 19 | 23 | 16 | 15 | 10 | 0 | | | | |
| 30 | 22 | 27 | 31 | 27 | 40 | 38 | 19 | 20 | 21 | 28 | 21 | 18 | 17 | 14 | 6 | 15 | 12 | 7 | 38 | 35 | 24 | 14 | 6 | 10 | 10 | 13 | 8 | 11 | 18 | 10 | 0 | | | |
| 31 | 18 | 32 | 35 | 31 | 43 | 39 | 21 | 24 | 24 | 28 | 20 | 18 | 22 | 18 | 10 | 19 | 13 | 2 | 42 | 38 | 28 | 18 | 6 | 10 | 8 | 14 | 6 | 7 | 16 | 10 | 4 | 0 | | |
| 32 | 21 | 31 | 35 | 32 | 45 | 42 | 24 | 24 | 25 | 32 | 24 | 22 | 20 | 18 | 10 | 20 | 16 | 6 | 40 | 35 | 26 | 15 | 2 | 14 | 12 | 17 | 10 | 10 | 14 | 6 | 5 | 4 | 0 | |
| 33 | 13 | 39 | 42 | 38 | 50 | 44 | 28 | 31 | 31 | 31 | 24 | 24 | 29 | 26 | 18 | 26 | 19 | 6 | 48 | 43 | 35 | 23 | 10 | 16 | 13 | 19 | 10 | 6 | 12 | 12 | 12 | 8 | 8 | 0 |

* Note: 0 Represents Bodeli chilling centre.

# Supply Chain Initiative at APR Limited*

Saloni once again went through all the printouts that her secretary had prepared for the exercise she had in mind for the day. It was the first Sunday of February 1998; Saloni had come early to ensure that all relevant materials were in place for carrying out a manual simulation exercise. Four of her senior colleagues were going to join her for the exercise and being a Sunday she knew they will not be disturbed during the day. She was desperately hoping that the whole exercise will provide some meaningful insights at the end of a day.

During that early morning walk to the office, she had reflected on the events of last few months. She knew that there was no way the company could have started work on all the issues that the consultant had listed. She was quite clear that she had neither resources nor enough credibility within the organization to initiate all the supply chain initiatives at one go. She had to pick up one area and make sure that her group delivered something concrete. With the idea of making an impact she had decided to pick up the wood logistics area, which was also the most difficult one.

---

*This case has been prepared by Professor Janat Shah.  Adapted with permission.

## Background

APR Limited was a diversified Thapar group company engaged in a number of businesses like pulp, packaging, soyameal and leather footwear.

Rayon grade pulp accounted for 70 per cent of the company turnover. The pulp manufacturing plant was located in the remote area at Kamalapuram, Warangal district of Andhra Pradesh. APR Limited had been doing reasonably well and was confident that it could sell all the quantities of pulp it could produce. In early 1995, the company decided to make substantial investment so as to double its capacity by 1997 end from 150 MT of rayon pulp to about 300 MT per day. The company had further plans to increase the capacity so as to reach to the level of 500 MT per day by 2002.

In the beginning of fiscal year 1997, the government slashed custom duty on rayon pulp from 25 to 10 per cent. Subsequently, international pulp prices dropped by about 40 per cent, putting the company under tremendous pressure. Prices that were ruling at about 35,000 per MT dropped to a level of about 25,000 per MT. So the company not only had to gear up for doubling the production level, it also had to cut its costs substantially.

Sometime in November 1997, Gautam Thapar, Managing Director, had asked Saloni Yashpal, General Manager—Business Systems, to look into the whole range of issues connected with the APR supply chain. Saloni had just joined the company and had no familiarity with the pulp industry. She decided to get some help from an external consultant who had just submitted the report. A brief summary of the report is shown in Appendix 1.

Saloni decided to focus on wood logistics because Gautam Thapar was also worried about the fact that company was holding about 6 months of wood stock at its woodyard. Wood constituted about 33 per cent of the cost of pulp.

## Wood Logistics

The company procured wood from a number of wood contractors who sourced wood from different places. These contractors were paid by weight for their logs. The company was currently using two types of wood—namely, eucalyptus and casuarina—in the respective proportion of 60:40 for producing one ton of pulp; the plant needed about 4.2 tons of wood.

The company purchased wood in the form of logs, which were converted into woodchips before being fed into a digester, which was the starting point of pulp making. The company has two chippers that are used for converting logs into woodchips. The chips are stored in silos. There are separate silos for eucalyptus and casuarina. This separate and temporary storage of chips permitted the controlled mixture of chips in the proportion of 60:40, and optimized the performance of the process. This proportion varied from month to month based on factors like availability of wood. In the last four years the proportion of eucalyptus had never gone below 50 per cent, at the same time there was a month when the company operated with a high proportion of eucalyptus (as high as 70 per cent) (see Exhibit 1 for data on wood consumption).

The process at APR began with receiving woods in the form of logs. From 6 a.m. to 8 p.m., a steady stream of trucks would arrive at the gates of the company, each carrying about 10 MT of logs. Each truck was weighed at the weigh bridge and depending on the chipping schedule and the availability of chipper at that point in time the truck was either sent to the chipper so that logs could be unloaded directly into the chipper or sent to the woodyard for unloading. Quality control personnel would collect a sample from the incoming truck so as

***Exhibit 1:* Wood consumption and pulp production*.**

| Year | Casuarina | | Eucalyptus | | Rayon production | |
|---|---|---|---|---|---|---|
| | Quantity (tons) | Value (Rs million) | Quantity (tons) | Value (Rs million) | Quantity (tons) | Value (Rs million) |
| 93–94 | 84,118 | 130.8 | 111,369 | 154.6 | 46,544 | 807.5 |
| 94–95 | 68,404 | 107.8 | 124,777 | 179.6 | 45,529 | 871.5 |
| 95–96 | 74,127 | 151.9 | 115,361 | 217.2 | 46,245 | 1298.3 |
| 96–97 | 73,729 | 165.1 | 88,463 | 174.4 | 38,721 | 1005.2 |

*Production was lower in the year 96–97 because the plant was under shut down condition for expansion work.

to determine the quality of wood. On the average a truck took about 10 minutes at the weigh bridge. The company would prefer if the truck was unloaded directly at the chipper. Because if a truck unloaded at the woodyard and material was subsequently brought to the chipper, it would result in extra material handling costs of Rs 100 per ton. At each chipper only one truck could be unloaded at a time (because truck unloading required special equipment) and the balance material was brought from the woodyard using tractors that could carry about two tons of material. Unloading of each tractor would take about 10 minutes and one tractor cycle (starting with loading at the woodyard and then unloading at the chipper and subsequently the empty tractor returning to the woodyard) would take about 30 minutes. The quality control group took a sample from each tractor to determine the moisture content of the material coming from the yard. The company had enough number of tractors and since tractors were unloaded manually it could unload multiple numbers of tractors at the chipper. Truck unloading and tractor unloading also can be carried at the same point in time. Unloading of material at the chipper can be carried out only when the chipper is operational, that is, when the chipping process is on. The average time taken by a truck at the chipper for unloading was about 20 minutes.

If a truck was diverted to the woodyard, it would have to wait in the queue for the purpose of unloading. At the woodyard they had capacity to unload a maximum of six trucks at a time. Unloading of a truck required about 1.5–2 hours. For all the material handling activities (except for unloading of a truck at the chipper) the company employed contract labourers who were paid on the piece rate basis.

After unloading wood, the truck would go back to weigh bridge for the purpose of weighing the unloaded truck. On the average an empty truck took about five minutes at the weigh bridge. After weighing, the empty truck could leave the plant premises.

The company usually has two kinds of contracts with the suppliers who supply the wood. In one kind the price of wood is based on its moisture content. The contract price would mention the price for wood having say, 10 per cent moisture. The actual moisture content in wood would vary from one truck to another. Based on the sample collected at the time of receipt, the quality control personnel would estimate the actual moisture content in the incoming wood and the supplier would be paid accordingly. Another kind of contract involved fixed prices per ton of wood irrespective of the moisture content in the incoming wood. The company ideally would have liked to get wood based on the first type of contract, but unfortunately most of the suppliers insisted on the latter type. As there was shortage of wood in the Andhra Pradesh region, the company had no choice but to accept the terms dictated by suppliers. Usually, freshly cut wood would have moisture content in the range of 25–30 per cent. With every month of storage, during the first three months the moisture content would come down at the rate of 4–5 per cent per month. Subsequently, with every month the moisture content would come down at the rate of 1–2 per cent per month. From the pulp making process perspective, varying moisture content in wood poses no specific quality problem. The moisture content is measured at various stages for the purpose of wood accounting.

## Managing Wood Logistics

Managing effective logistics involved coordinating with various departments. Saloni was aware of the fact that unless she got all of them involved, she would not be able to make any headway.

Wood procurement was managed by procurement personnel, the woodyard was managed by stores personnel and the chipper was managed by production personnel. She also had to involve maintenance personnel to replace blunt knives with sharpened knives at the chipper, which affected the daily chipper schedule.

Sometime in January she had called the meeting of all the people concerned. At the end of a long day, during which the group worked with the consultant, the following ideas came up:

- *Invest in one more weigh bridge.* Even if the company decides go for one more weigh bridge, there was no consensus about the way in which the company could use the second weigh bridge more effectively. One of the proposals was to have one weigh bridge dedicated to eucalyptus and other one for casuarina. Another idea was to have one weigh bridge for incoming trucks and use the other weigh bridge for outgoing trucks.
- *Invest in one more chipper.* This would provide more flexibility in matching the chipping schedule with the truck arrival pattern.
- *Invest in one more chipper and also increase silo capacity for chips.* This would provide more flexibility in determining the chipping schedule.
- *Use better quality of knives so as to reduce downtime at chipper.* Better quality of chipper knives would have longer and more reliable life and would reduce the frequency of replacement.
- *Reduce the time required to replace blunt knives.* This would require working with maintenance personnel to find ways of reducing replacement time.
- *Invest in integrated information system.* Each truck driver would have a smart card and he would swipe his card at the weigh bridge. Similarly, at the time of unloading, chipper and woodyard personnel would be expected to update the relevant information. An integrated information system would ensure that each and every entity in the system would have complete knowledge on real-time basis about the status of the system. This would help all departments to take optimal decisions on a real-time basis.

Saloni was not sure whether she actually had real a understanding of the situation. She was also not sure whether senior executives involved in wood logistics had a complete view of the system. She sat with the production manager and worked out the likely chipping schedule the production personnel were likely to follow during a typical April day. See Table 1 for the chipping schedule. She had also collected data for the truck arrival pattern during the previous week and it is as shown in Table 2. She was not sure about the validity of data, as she had observed during her early morning walks that actually many trucks come during the night and wait outside the factory gate. Data collected regarding truck arrival only captured the entry time of a truck at the gate, which in turn was controlled by the woodyard personnel. She tried to check this issue with wood contractors. The discussion with wood contractors was not very helpful because they just kept talking about the number of uncertainties involved. Wood contractors were also concerned about the fact that with increase in production level, trucks were increasingly taking unusually long times at the company in unloading activity. Wood contractors actually asked for increase in rates so as to compensate them for the increase in waiting time at the company.

Currently, the company was still working at a production level of about 200 MT but most of the teething troubles at the plant were likely to be over by March end. From April 1998, the company was expected to work at the full capacity of 300 MT per day. Saloni was aware of the kind of problems they were facing in managing wood logistics at the current production

*Table 1: Likely wood chipping schedule during April 1998.*

| Shift/chipper | Schedule | Type of wood | Expected volume of chipping in MT* |
|---|---|---|---|
| Chipper 1 | 8 a.m. to 1 p.m. | Casuarina | 125 |
| Chipper 2 | 7 a.m. to 1.30 p.m. | Eucalyptus | 230 |
| Chipper 1 | 4 p.m. to 7.30 p.m. | Casuarina | 150 |
| Chipper 2 | 4.30 p.m. to 9.30 p.m. | Eucalyptus | 260 |
| Chipper 1 | 10.30 p.m. to 1.30 a.m. | Casuarina | 105 |
| Chipper 2 | 11.30 p.m. to 5.30 a.m. | Eucalyptus | 185 |

*Chipping rate was not uniform throughout the day. Initially when knives were sharp, the chipping rate would be higher and subsequently it would slow down as knives get blunted over a period of time. Typically, knives had a lifetime of about 6–12 hours. As casuarina was harder, knives working on this wood were likely to get blunt faster compared to the chipper that was working on eucalyptus. Currently, the company followed practices of replacing the knives at the beginning of the second shift.

*Table 2: Expected truck arrival pattern on a typical day.*

| Time | Number of trucks with debarked eucalyptus* | Number of trucks with debarked casuarina* |
|---|---|---|
| 6.00–8.00 | 8 | 5 |
| 8.00–10.00 | 14 | 7 |
| 10.00–12.00 | 18 | 10 |
| 12.00–14.00 | 10 | 6 |
| 14.00–16.00 | 10 | 6 |
| 16.00–18.00 | 6 | 4 |
| 18.00–20.00 | 4 | 2 |

*Casuarina was sourced from various parts of AP; 60% of eucalyptus was sourced from Andhra Pradesh, 20% from Karnataka and the balance from Uttar Pradesh.

level of 200 MT per day. She could not imagine the situation in April when the production rate would go up to 300 MT per day.

While Saloni was sure that the pulp division could manage with lower wood inventory, plant personnel were very uncomfortable with the whole idea since holding six months of inventory was a standard practice followed by the paper and pulp industry. Every one agreed that the cellulose content in the wood did get affected with time and the plant yield usually would be lower if wood was stored for a longer period of time. But Saloni could not find a way of quantifying the same. She also wanted to find ways and means of reducing material handling costs in the management of wood logistics. At that point in time the company was paying about Rs 10 million to the labour contractor for the material handling of wood.

Saloni also wondered whether the proportion of wood mix used by the plant personnel needed re-examination. She was also wondering whether she should also look at the issue of material accounting at the woodyard. Currently, it was not unusual to post shortage of 4–5 per cent because of problems of moisture accounting.

Most of the plant personnel were quite sceptical about the whole exercise as there were many uncertainties that they faced while actually managing wood logistics. Truck arrival pattern would change drastically on a day-to-day basis. Production personnel also changed their chipping schedules frequently during the day and rarely followed the schedule that they would have given to the woodyard personnel at the beginning of a day.

Saloni wanted all the concerned executives to have a system view of entire wood logistics. In the actual pressurized environment of day-to-day operations it was difficult to understand how decisions were taken by the various departments, or how they interacted with each other. To develop this system perspective in the group, she decided to simulate the events for one of the typical days in April when the production would touch 250 MT per day. She decided to involve all the senior managers who were involved in managing day-to-day operations in this simulation exercise. She was hoping that the simulation exercise would also help her in building a consensus about the impact of various policies on wood logistics. Appendix 2 contains the note that Saloni had prepared on the simulation exercise.

## Discussion Questions

1. As Saloni Yashpal, what would you do to address the wood logistics problem? Where would you focus your attention and solution efforts?
2. What options exist? What would you recommend? Why?
3. In what way the simulation exercise suggested by Saloni Yashpal would help APR in attacking the wood logistics problem?

## Appendix 1: Supply Chain Management Initiative at APR Limited

APR Limited has expanded from a capacity of 150 to 300 MT per day. Apart from managing issues arising from increased capacity, the company also has to face pressures on the price front. There is a realization that with the opening of the economy the RG pulp market is quite vulnerable to changes taking place on global markets. The custom duty on rayon pulp has been reduced from 30 to 10 per cent in the last budget and is likely to be further reduced in the future. This has already affected the price realization at the market place. Further, the company would like to expand its capacity to 500 MT per day to get economies of scales (typical RG pulp plants in international markets operate at capacities of 1,500 MT per day). This is going to pose the following significant challenges to APR Limited in the future:

- *Managing logistics of incoming material.* With the increased capacity, the company has to procure more material and manage traffic of about, on the average, 150 trucks on a daily basis. Existing systems and infrastructure at the plant are not geared to handle the increased quantities of material. This problem is going to become quite severe when the company expands capacity further to 500 MT per day.
- *Managing multiple products and multiple grades.* When the company increases its capacity to 500 MT per day, there may not be enough demand in the RG pulp market. So the company will have to look at alternative markets like paper industry and pharmaceutical industry. This is likely to pose conflicting demands on marketing and manufacturing functions.
- *Managing logistics so as to reduce inventory and handling related costs and simultaneously improve customer service.* Currently, the company is holding high amounts of inventory and is incurring significant handling costs.

To face the above-mentioned challenges, the company needs to gear itself up at this point in time. A supply chain management initiative can be an important exercise in this regard. The entire initiative can be divided into two phases. In the first phase, the company should create awareness about the basic issues in supply chain management and acquire capability in-house to prepare itself for the challenges mentioned above. At the end of phase 1, the company would have a set of people who are equipped with capabilities to handle the challenges faced by the company in the area of supply chain management. In the second phase, the company can set up task forces that would analyse the problems and come with ideas/proposals to handle future challenges in the area of supply chain management.

## Phase 1

The first phase of the initiative would consist of following:

- *One day workshop for the senior management of APR Limited.* The main objective of this workshop would be to provide a conceptual understanding of supply chain management. The workshop would also be used to analyse challenges facing APR Limited and an attempt would be made to spell out the detailed goals of overall supply chain initiatives.
- *Two day workshop for middle and junior managers of APR Limited.* The main objective of this workshop would be to equip participants with necessary tools and techniques to handle challenges faced by APR Limited in the area of supply chain management. The target group would consist of middle and junior managers from functions like procurement, manufacturing, marketing and corporate planning.

## Phase 2

In the second phase, the company should form three task forces consisting of executives trained in phase 1. The three task forces can look at the following specific areas:

1. Planning for inbound logistics of wood
    - This would also involve issues in coordinating inward movement of wood with chipping schedule
    - Inventory planning for wood
    - Raw material mix (proportion of eucalyptus and casuarina) related issues
    - Planning for coal and other chemicals
2. Planning for outbound logistics of finished goods
3. Managing manufacturing and marketing interface
    - This would involve examining the range of issues involved in managing multiple products and grades from both manufacturing and marketing angles.

This supply chain management initiative would help APR Limited in preparing for the future challenges. It is also likely to improve customer service and reduce costs simultaneously.

## Appendix 2: Wood logistics—Simulation

Wood logistics simulation exercise would manually simulate a day's activity and would require four participants managing/tracking the following four activities:

- *Truck monitoring in-charge.* Monitor truck arrival and departure activities
- *Weighbridge in charge.* Monitor activities at the weighbridge
- *Chipper operations in-charge.* Monitor activities at both the chippers
- *Woodyard in-charge.* Monitor activities at the woodyard, which includes managing six unloading bays

All the trucks are given unique identity numbers (ID) at the time of arrival so as to track all their activities within the APR premises. The arrival pattern for the trucks would be as shown in Table 2. For example, the first eucalyptus truck arriving in a day would be given the ID E1, the second truck would be given the ID E2 and so on. Similarly, the first casuarina truck arriving in a day would be given the ID C1, the second truck would be given the ID C2 and so on. Typically, a truck would go through the following operations:

- Arrival
- Weighing of loaded truck at weigh bridge
- Get instruction about where to unload (whether at chipper or at woodyard)
- Unloading at the respective place
- Weighing of unloaded truck at the weigh bridge
- Departure

Each truck is likely to wait in a queue during weighing and unloading if the respective resource is busy.

The actual time for a given truck for any of the respective operations is likely to be *T*1, *T*2 or *T*3. Probability distribution and values for *T*1, *T*2 and *T*3 are as shown in Table 3.

During the simulation every participant would be given a dice and the actual time would be generated by throwing dice at each and every operation for each of the truck. The throw of a dice would result in an outcome, that is any number from 1 to 6 with equal probability. If the throw of the dice results in an outcome that is 1 or 2, *T*1 would be taken as the actual time for the operation. Similarly, if the throw of the dice results in an outcome that is 3 or 4, the actual time would be taken as *T*2; if the outcome is 5 or 6, the actual time would be taken as *T*3. Values of *T*1, *T*2 and *T*3 for all operations are as shown in Table 3.

The decision rule about whether to send the truck to the woodyard or chipper would be jointly done by the team consisting of all participants. Based on actual decisions on this issue, the chipper in-charge would calculate the quantity of wood that would be available directly from trucks for each hour of operation. Given the planned chipping schedule (Table 1), the chipper in-charge would be able to calculate the quantity of total wood needed by the chipper for each hour of operation. Based on these data, the chipper in-charge would have to organize the balance material (wood required minus wood available directly from trucks) from the woodyard trough tractors.

Each of the participant would use the following data sheets for tracking their respective activities:

- *Truck monitoring in-charge.* Truck monitoring sheet
- *Weigh bridge in-charge.* Weigh bridge monitoring sheet
- *Chipper operations in-charge.* Chipper operations sheet, chipper wood monitoring sheet
- *Woodyard manager.* Woodyard monitoring sheet

**Table 3: *Value and probability distribution of relevant times (in minutes).***

| | Time at weigh bridge—loaded truck | | Time at weigh bridge—unloaded truck | | Unloading time at chipper | | Unloading time at woodyard | | Time of truck arrival* | |
|---|---|---|---|---|---|---|---|---|---|---|
| | **Time** | **Prob.** | **Time** | **Prob.** | **Time** | **Prob.** | **Time** | **Prob.** | **Time** | **Prob.** |
| *T*1 | 8 | 0.33 | 3 | 0.33 | 15 | 0.33 | 90 | 0.33 | Mean time –5 | 0.33 |
| *T*2 | 10 | 0.33 | 4 | 0.33 | 20 | 0.33 | 105 | 0.33 | Mean time | 0.33 |
| *T*3 | 12 | 0.33 | 5 | 0.33 | 25 | 0.33 | 120 | 0.33 | Mean time + 5 | 0.33 |

*Within 2-hour slots trucks are expected to arrive uniformly at the rate shown in Table 2. For example, in the 2 hour slot between 6.00–8.00 a.m., on the average an eucalyptus truck is expected to arrive every 15 minutes. That is, the mean inter-arrival time between two trucks would be 15 minutes. But the actual arrival could be within +5 or –5 minutes. So the first eucalyptus truck would arrive at 6.00 a.m. and second eucalyptus truck would arrive at 6.10, 6.15 or 6.20 a.m.

The formats for the monitoring sheets are presented in Appendix 3.

At the end of simulation, the team would calculate the distribution of truck waiting time at all the resources (weigh bridge, chipper and woodyard) and calculate the extra loading and unloading costs (all the materials brought from the woodyard by tractors would result in extra loading and unloading costs).

## Appendix 3: Data Sheets for Simulation Exercise

*Truck monitoring sheet.*

| Eucalyptus truck data | | | Casuarina truck data | | |
|---|---|---|---|---|---|
| Truck ID | Arrival time | Departure time | Truck ID | Arrival time | Departure time |
| E1 | | | C1 | | |

*Weighbridge monitoring sheet.*

| Weigh bridge queue | | | | Weigh bridge operations | | | |
|---|---|---|---|---|---|---|---|
| Truck ID | Truck status* | Time of joining | Time of leaving | Truck ID | Truck status | Start of operations | End of operations |
| | | | | | | | |

*To distinguish between loaded and empty truck trucks, truck status attribute is introduced: L for loaded truck and UL for empty truck.

*Chipper operations sheet.*

| Chipper queue | | | Chipper 1 operations | | | Chipper 2 operations | | |
|---|---|---|---|---|---|---|---|---|
| Truck ID | Time of joining | Time of leaving | Truck ID | Start of operations | End of operations | Truck ID | Start of operations | End of operations |
| | | | | | | | | |

*Chipper wood management sheet.*

| Chipper I | | | Chipper 2 | | |
|---|---|---|---|---|---|
| Time Slot | Wood received directly | Wood received from woodyard | Time slot | Wood received directly | Wood received from woodyard |
| 8.00–9.00 | | | 7.00–8.00 | | |

***Woodyard management sheet-I.***

| Woodyard queue | | | Unload-1 operations | | | Unload-2 operations | | |
|---|---|---|---|---|---|---|---|---|
| | | | Truck ID | Start of op. | End of op. | Truck ID | Start of op. | End of op. |
| | | | | | | | | |

***Woodyard management sheet-II.***

| Unload-3 operations | | | Unload-4 operations | | | Unload-5 operations | | | Unload-6 operations | | |
|---|---|---|---|---|---|---|---|---|---|---|---|
| Truck ID | Start of op. | End of op. | Truck ID | Start of op. | End of op. | Truck ID | Start of op. | End of op. | Truck ID | Start of op. | End of op. |
| | | | | | | | | | | | |

# Supply Chain Management at Dalmia Cement Ltd*

Puneet Dalmia had just joined the company three months back and was wondering how to handle his first major assignment. After completing his management studies, Puneet had joined the family business as VP Marketing. The company had asked him to look at the whole range of issues related to finished goods logistics. The immediate concern was that from December 1997 the rail link from Dalmiapuram would not be available for a period of six months. This railway line was going to be converted from metre gauge to broad gauge and the conversion would take about six months. Puneet was looking at the situation in October 1997. There was lot of pressure from his marketing team. They felt that unless the company started building stocks at Trichi, they would have a problem in servicing stockists from January 1998. The GM Marketing was of the view that while examining this short-term issue the company should also seriously re-examine its transportation mode mix and come up with an optimal transport policy after the broad gauge rail link was in place. Puneet knew that issues related to non-availability of rail link had to be resolved fast, but he was more concerned with long-term issues. He was wondering whether they can change their business model completely and start serving the bulk of their demand directly from Dalmiapuram and may be not have depots at all.

*This case was written by Professor Janat Shah, IIM Bangalore.

## Background

Dalmia Cements is a 60-year-old company with the cement division contributing 85 per cent of its revenues. In the last couple of years it had diversified into a number of areas such as electronics and travel services. Its cement manufacturing plant is located at Dalmiapuram, which is about 45 km from Trichi. See Exhibit 1 for the profit and loss data and Exhibit 2 for the balance sheet data of the company. Cement companies in the south had not thus far faced too much price pressures, but surplus capacities in the northern and western regions had resulted in price erosion in those markets. Companies in the south were also likely to face similar pressures in the coming months. In the financial year 1997–1998, with rising power costs and increasing competition, the company was likely to face tremendous pressure in the future on the profitability front.

## Manufacturing Process

The manufacturing process is quite simple and involves two operations: clinker manufacturing and cement manufacturing. For all the types of cements manufactured by company the type

***Exhibit 1:* Balance sheet.**

| | 31-3-1997 (Rs Million) | 31-3-1996 (Rs Million) |
|---|---|---|
| *Source of funds* | | |
| Net worth | | |
| Share capital | 76.5 | 76.5 |
| Reserves and surplus | 1742.2 | 1523.5 |
| Total borrowings | | |
| Secured loans | 1937.1 | 1121.1 |
| Unsecured loans | 222.7 | 76.2 |
| Current liabilities and provisions | | |
| Current liabilities | 243.9 | 211 |
| Provisions | 375.3 | 296 |
| Total | 4597.7 | 3304.3 |
| *Employment of funds* | | |
| Gross fixed assets | | |
| Land and building | 549.3 | 502.6 |
| Plant and machinery | 2352.8 | 2069.4 |
| Other fixed assets | 74.9 | 65 |
| Capital work-in-progress | 642 | 73 |
| Less: cumulative depreciation | 1100 | 972.4 |
| Net fixed assets | 2519 | 1737.6 |
| Investments | 181.3 | 45.7 |
| Inventories | | |
| Raw materials | 44 | 20.7 |
| Stores and spares | 245 | 232.9 |
| Finished goods* | 376.7 | 282.4 |
| Semi-finished goods | 62.7 | 30.7 |
| Receivables** | 825 | 873.2 |
| Cash and bank balance | 344 | 81.1 |
| Total | 4597.7 | 3304.3 |

*Cement business accounted for 40% (value-wise) of finished goods inventory.

**Cement business accounted for 25% of receivables.

***Exhibit 2:* Income and expenditure statement.**

| | 31-3-1997 (Rs Million) | 31-3-1996 (Rs Million) |
|---|---|---|
| Income | | |
| Manufacturing | 2787.4 | 2464.3 |
| Trading and others | 292.2 | 372.8 |
| Expenditure | | |
| Raw materials, stores, etc. | 705.4 | 561.9 |
| Wages and salaries | 199.7 | 168.8 |
| Energy (power and fuel) | 591.1 | 590.1 |
| Other manufacturing expenses | 8.4 | 6.8 |
| Indirect taxes | 366 | 349.5 |
| Repairs and maintenance | 173.8 | 136 |
| Advertising and marketing | 13.8 | 11.4 |
| Distribution | 114.1 | 106.1 |
| Miscellaneous expenses | 150.2 | 129.9 |
| Interest | 240.9 | 175.8 |
| Depreciation | 126.2 | 111 |
| PBT | 390 | 489.8 |
| Tax provision | 99 | 108.8 |
| PAT | 291 | 381 |

of clinkers used is of the same quality and only at the cement manufacturing stage does the product get differentiated. The company manufactures mainly three types of cements: OPC, PPC and PSC. The product composition for these are as follows:

| | OPC | PPC | PSC |
|---|---|---|---|
| Clinker | 95% | 80% | 60% |
| Gypsum | 5% | 5% | 5% |
| Fly ash | | 15% | |
| Slag | | | 35% |

Clinker and cement manufacturing operations are quite de-linked as the company keeps sufficient quantity of clinker as buffer. The company has enough storage capacity to store clinkers and one can store clinkers for a reasonably long period of time without the quality being affected. For storing cement the company has 14 silos (see Exhibit 5 for details on silos). Cement is packed in a standard pack size of 50 kg but using different kinds of packaging material, resulting in effectively 10 SKUs in the market place. Different types of packaging offered by company are as follows:

| Type of packaging | Paper | | | Plastic | |
|---|---|---|---|---|---|
| Colour/type of stitching | Yellow | Brown | | White | Yellow |
| | | Single stitched | Double stitched | | |
| OPC | * | * | * | * | * |
| PPC | | * | * | | * |
| PSC | | * | | | * |

There are preferences for different packaging and colours in different markets.

# Marketing

The company operates only in two states, Tamil Nadu and Kerala. It has divided the entire market into seven zones, which in turn are divided into districts. The company has one marketing executive for each of the zones and all of them in turn report to GM Marketing. The company supplies the product to stockists. Most of the stockists stocked cement of at least two manufacturers. In some of the areas Dalmia was a market leader and historically it had a good image for quality. It maintained seven depots so as to provide prompt service to its stockists. The market was becoming increasingly competitive.

The company used various modes of transport to reach its stockists. There were four options that the company used

| Option | Mode of transport | Material routed through depot | % of Material handled in 1996–97 |
|---|---|---|---|
| 1 | Rail + Truck | Yes | 45 |
| 2 | Rail + Truck | No | 5 |
| 3 | Truck | Yes | 30 |
| 4 | Truck | No | 20 |

Option 4, which involved direct shipping, was the most preferred option by the company from the cost point of view.

Availability of rail wagons was not a problem. With a notice of three days the company could get a wagon from Indian Railways. Usually, the company would send material in a lot of 40 wagons and each wagon had a capacity of 18.6 MT. The company had an excellent relationship with authorities in the Indian Railways. There were times when the company requested wagons with a day's notice and Indian Railways had obliged. Similarly, when authorities in Indian Railways had to meet their monthly targets they would approach Dalmia who would in turn oblige by hiring wagons. Since the company usually asked for 40 wagons at a time, the cement would reach in a day or two to the respective location, from where the material was shipped directly to stockists or to depot. Option 1 was the most expensive and time-consuming option as it would involve lot of material handling and involvement of multiple modes of transport. For every loading and unloading operation the company incurred a cost of Re 1 per bag. Also two truck engagements to reach the same distance would be more expensive than direct shipping using only one truck engagement. Since Dalmia shipped cement for short distances, railway freight used to be more expensive than truck freight.

After the conversion to broad gauge, the company may have to revisit the transport mode decisions. Each wagon would have a capacity of 40 MT and the company was not sure about the lead time required for the wagons.

Rail freight and road charges in Rupees per MT for various destinations are given below;

| | Ernakulam | Trichur | Kollam | Palghat | Madurai | Trichi | Coimbatore |
|---|---|---|---|---|---|---|---|
| Rail freight | 393 | 335 | 401 | 266 | 181 | 107 | 249 |
| Road freight | 385 | 350 | 395 | 320 | 156 | 70 | 235 |

The full transport costs did not figure into profit and loss because the company billed its stockists on ex-factory/depot basis. This was done mainly to avoid sales tax on the freight. A stockist would place an order by phone and the company had to organize transport and deliver the cement to the stockist at his premises, but the actual transport charges were supposed to be paid by the customer. A truck could carry up to 10 MT of cement. See Exhibit 3 for data on distances for all the districts in which the company operated.

## Optimal Transport Mode Mix

Puneet was not sure how he should approach the problem. He found it very difficult to get truck rates that he could use for his calculations. He was given the impression that it was

***Exhibit 3:*** ***District-wise volume and distance data.***

| Dalimapuram | Average distance from plant (in km) | 1996–1997 sales volume in '000 tons | Nearest depot | Distance from nearest depot |
|---|---|---|---|---|
| Madras | 315 | 45 | Trichi | 303 |
| Chenglepet | 315 | 91 | Trichi | 251 |
| Ambedkar | 275 | 7 | Trichi | 240 |
| Sambyvarayar | 220 | 8 | Trichi | 181 |
| Cudda Vallalar | 120 | 24 | Trichi | 156 |
| Villa Ramasamy | 165 | 19 | Trichi | 155 |
| Pondi Karaikal | 175 | 25 | Trichi | 177 |
| Tanjore | 70 | 58 | Trichi | 48 |
| Quaid-E-Millat | 120 | 48 | Trichi | 126 |
| Trichi district | 60 | 86 | Trichi | – |
| Pudukottai | 115 | 21 | Trichi | 50 |
| Dharmapuri | 220 | 0 | Trichi | 158 |
| Coimbatore | 250 | 14 | Coimbatore | – |
| Periyar | 180 | 2 | Coimbatore | 117 |
| Salem | 150 | 20 | Trichi | 111 |
| Madurai district | 190 | 19 | Madurai | – |
| Anna-Dindigul | 160 | 8 | Trichi | 183 |
| Ramnad | 215 | 8 | Madurai | 79 |
| PTT | 180 | 17 | Madurai | 40 |
| Kamarajar | 265 | 5 | Madurai | 18 |
| NKB | 315 | 6 | Madurai | 153 |
| VOC | 325 | 7 | Madurai | 135 |
| Kanyakumari | 415 | 7 | Madurai | 242 |
| Palghat | 300 | 16 | Palghat | – |
| Trichur | 380 | 87 | Trichur | 56 |
| Ernakulam | 440 | 61 | Ernakulam | – |
| Quilon | 445 | 14 | Quilon | – |
| Trivandrum | 454 | 10 | Trivandrum | – |

difficult to get trucks in the monsoon. Similarly, during the season for mangoes truck operators got much better freight from the mango business, so again it was very difficult to get trucks during that season. Puneet was not sure whether it was a supply problem or the price issue. Most of the people whom he talked to gave an impression that the company could get trucks if they were willing to pay rates that were 50 per cent higher than normal rates. The company worked with transport brokers who would organize trucks from the Trichi truck market. The company entered into annual fixed price agreements with brokers. Each broker had the responsibility for one zone. During the mango season and during the monsoon, brokers would inform the company in advance that they should make alternative arrangements as trucks would be difficult to get in the Trichi market.

Puneet was aware of the fact that some other companies managed a fleet of vehicles so that they had a better control over transport operations. Either they owned the trucks or they used to hire trucks on annual contract basis. The marketing team was not very enthusiastic about the whole idea. Trying to manage this fleet would add to the workload and also would be a very expensive way of meeting transport needs. He was told that trucks could be hired on a monthly basis at the rate of Rs 25,000 per month and the company would have to incur an additional cost of two rupees per kilometre as fuel and other variable expenses. But since the pattern of demand was quite random in nature it would very difficult to estimate the number of trucks the company might need on a daily basis (see Exhibit 4 for daily data on sales for the company and for two selected districts).

**Exhibit 4: Day-wise sales for the month of May 1997 (in tons).**

| Date | Chengelpet | | | Kanyakumari | | | Total | | |
|---|---|---|---|---|---|---|---|---|---|
| | OPC | PPC | PSC | OPC | PPC | PSC | OPC | PPC | PSC |
| 1 | 341 | 0 | 0 | 10 | 27 | 0 | 1,374 | 265 | 0 |
| 2 | 443 | 0 | 0 | 0 | 0 | 0 | 1,621 | 212 | 100 |
| 3 | 299 | 0 | 129 | 0 | 0 | 0 | 957 | 125 | 271 |
| 4 | 239 | 0 | 0 | 0 | 0 | 0 | 1,717 | 141 | 0 |
| 5 | 148 | 0 | 0 | 48 | 14 | 0 | 1,381 | 368 | 19 |
| 6 | 96 | 0 | 13 | 0 | 0 | 0 | 858 | 215 | 364 |
| 7 | 250 | 0 | 24 | 0 | 0 | 0 | 1,249 | 205 | 180 |
| 8 | 279 | 0 | 0 | 0 | 0 | 0 | 1,020 | 196 | 202 |
| 9 | 426 | 0 | 10 | 7 | 0 | 0 | 1,507 | 225 | 113 |
| 10 | 598 | 0 | 0 | 10 | 0 | 0 | 1,873 | 108 | 10 |
| 11 | 320 | 0 | 0 | 17 | 0 | 0 | 1,406 | 163 | 0 |
| 12 | 250 | 0 | 0 | 0 | 0 | 0 | 1,384 | 183 | 0 |
| 13 | 256 | 0 | 0 | 0 | 28 | 0 | 1,452 | 486 | 0 |
| 14 | 68 | 0 | 12 | 0 | 49 | 0 | 1,269 | 213 | 56 |
| 15 | 136 | 0 | 330 | 6 | 12 | 0 | 1,092 | 203 | 514 |
| 16 | 296 | 0 | 40 | 0 | 10 | 0 | 1,496 | 201 | 137 |
| 17 | 229 | 0 | 0 | 8 | 0 | 0 | 913 | 164 | 30 |
| 18 | 203 | 0 | 0 | 10 | 22 | 0 | 1,250 | 326 | 5 |
| 19 | 235 | 0 | 0 | 0 | 29 | 0 | 908 | 243 | 11 |
| 20 | 79 | 0 | 0 | 0 | 17 | 0 | 1,156 | 252 | 0 |
| 21 | 429 | 0 | 98 | 0 | 40 | 0 | 1,388 | 519 | 158 |
| 22 | 0 | 0 | 32 | 0 | 22 | 0 | 582 | 350 | 136 |
| 23 | 529 | 0 | 38 | 0 | 58 | 0 | 1,351 | 263 | 135 |
| 24 | 156 | 0 | 36 | 0 | 32 | 0 | 938 | 368 | 234 |
| 25 | 163 | 0 | 120 | 0 | 0 | 0 | 924 | 203 | 295 |
| 26 | 334 | 0 | 0 | 0 | 0 | 0 | 1,275 | 100 | 89 |
| 27 | 182 | 0 | 0 | 0 | 0 | 0 | 979 | 60 | 0 |
| 28 | 172 | 0 | 0 | 0 | 0 | 0 | 1,354 | 124 | 0 |
| 29 | 319 | 0 | 0 | 0 | 0 | 0 | 1,289 | 29 | 19 |
| 30 | 278 | 0 | 0 | 0 | 0 | 0 | 1,606 | 64 | 19 |
| 31 | 447 | 0 | 0 | 0 | 0 | 0 | 2,033 | 238 | 20 |

## Moving from Pack to Stock to Pack to Order

Puneet was wondering whether it would be possible for the company to supply most of the cement directly from the factory. The ideal situation would be that cement would be stocked in silos only and no cement stock would be kept in a packed condition. After the receipt of the order and after arranging for a truck, the cement could be packed in the required package and loaded directly into trucks. This would reduce handling and finished goods inventory costs substantially. Puneet had lot of interactions with stockists and he felt that if the company could service a stockist in 24 hours, then the stockist would not mind if the material was shipped directly from the factory. The entire cycle from receipt of order to delivery of material to stockist should not take more than 24 hours. Obviously, this would put a lot of strain on the transport contractors and packaging people. Though the company had lot of surplus capacity (see Exhibit 5 for data on silo and packing capacity), it may have to re-examine some of the policies followed in the packing section. For example, currently the company employed about 100 loaders who were involved in labour-intensive packing operations. These loaders were paid on a piece rate basis. At the beginning of a day, the packing section would freeze its packing

***Exhibit 5a:*** ***Packing capacity: the company had five packing machines.***

| SN | Machine | Capacity (tons/hour) |
|---|---|---|
| 1 | Haver & Boecker | 60 |
| 2 | Polysius | 45 |
| 3 | Darnley & Taylor | 50 |
| 4 | ROTO 1 | 120 |
| 5 | ROTO 2 | 180 |

***Exhibit 5b:*** ***Silo capacity: the company had 14 silos. Silo number 14 had four compartments (14a,14b,14c,14d).***

| Silo number | Type of silo | Capacity in tons |
|---|---|---|
| 1, 2, 3, 4, 6, 7, 9, 10, 12, 13, 14a, 14b, 14c, 14d | Big silo | 1550 |
| 5, 8, 11 | Small silo | 1285 |

***Exhibit 5c:*** ***Connectivity between silos and packing machines: not all could be connected to all packing machines.***

| Machines | Silos |
|---|---|
| Haver & Boecker, Polysius | 1, 2, 3, 4, 5, 6, 7 |
| Darnley & Taylor, ROTO 1 | 6, 7, 8, 9, 10, 11, 12, 13 |
| ROTO 2 | 14a,14b, 14c, 14d |

schedule and allot a specific packing machine to a loader at the beginning of a shift, and he was not moved to any other packing machine throughout the shift. This practice ensured that the company used loaders efficiently and that loaders got fair wages on a daily basis. If the company wanted to shift to pack to order, it would have to change some of these practices. Similarly, currently not all silos were connected to all the packing stations. With some investment it would be possible to connect all the silos to all the packing machines, but Puneet was not sure about the value of this flexibility. Apart from the difficulty in transportation and packing operations, there was also concern about seasonal demand issues. Some his marketing colleagues were worried that without finished goods inventory the company would not be in

***Exhibit 6*:*** ***Monthly demand (in tons) distribution for the entire Indian cement industry for the year 1996–1997.***

| | |
|---|---|
| April 1996 | 5,818,362 |
| May 1996 | 5,901,055 |
| June 1996 | 5,855,182 |
| July 1996 | 5,961,247 |
| August 1996 | 5,502,600 |
| September 1996 | 4,774,810 |
| October 1996 | 5,198,640 |
| November 1996 | 5,365,270 |
| December 1996 | 5,734,560 |
| January 1997 | 6,334,500 |
| February 1997 | 6,085,380 |
| March 1997 | 7,197,670 |

* *Source*: India Infoline.

a position to handle seasonal variation in demand. See Exhibit 6 for data on monthly demand distribution over the year. From whatever data he had seen, Puneet had not observed any significant seasonality in cement demand. So Puneet was not too worried about this issue.

By and large, Puneet found that his own people were sceptical about the whole idea. The competitors were opening more depots and Puneet was talking about reducing the dependence on depots. He just kept thinking about the reaction of GM Marketing who had said that we might be able to reduce costs but in the process might lose the business.

## Discussion Questions

1. What is the impact of railway gauge conversion (from metre gauge to broad gauge) on Dalmia Cement's distribution operations?
2. What should be the optimal transport mode mix for Dalmia Cement?
3. Suggest ways in which Dalmia can get assured supply of trucks throughout the year.
4. Should Dalmia change its transport policy and manage a fleet of trucks on its own for its distribution function?
5. Why was Dalmia Cement exploring the option of moving from pack to stock to pack to order strategy? What conflicts or barriers internal to Dalmia would the pack to order strategy create? How should Dalmia Cement handle these issues?

# The Global Green Company*

In June 1999, Debashish, Chief Officer, Global Green Company (GGCL), felt a sense of satisfaction looking back at the performance figures of his company. The company had grown at a tremendous pace in the last 3 years and had clocked a turnover of ₹24 crores for 18 months ending December 1998. With a turnover of ₹4.5 cores in 1996 and ₹7.2 crores in 1997, the company was fast approaching break-even levels of operations.

Global Green Company was into the business of exporting preserved vegetables to European and American markets. Their main business was export of gherkins or greens, which gave the company its name. The market was stable but extremely quality conscious and with stringent regulations. GGCL was growing at a tremendous pace and was known for good quality products. The company intended to maintain this heady growth in future.

Debashish was a very ambitious and hard working person. He had managed to bring professionalism and dynamism in his organization. He believed that he could continue and even exceed the past growth rate while at the same time improving the bottom line of his company. He was aware of various issues involved in making his dream come true and believed that these could be tackled with a systematic management of all functions especially the operations of the company.

Looking at the latest order data, Debashish was concerned about the delays in order delivery that had occurred in the past. He knew that he was in a good position as far as new orders were concerned. He did not have to worry about the market. He could easily increase his sales and maintain the ambitious growth targets. However, did Global Green Company have a supply chain capable of meeting these targets? What was nagging at his mind were the various supply chain issues that had been causing a delay in delivery. He also felt that the supply chain costs were on the higher side and was wondering how to control these costs. Debashish had hired a team of internal consultants to take a complete look at the supply chain including procurement, inbound logistics, wastage, and cost, and identify critical issues in supply chain. He wanted this team to suggest solutions to reduce the delays and make the whole process more efficient.

---

**This case was prepared by Professor Janat Shah and Anil Joshi in 1999 as a basis for class discussion rather than to illustrate either effective or ineffective handling of business system.*

# Global Green Company

The Global Green Company Ltd. is a part of the respected Thapar Group in India. The Thapar group is one of the largest conglomerates in India having a turnover of more than US$ 2 billion mainly from chemicals and paper. The Thapars were into business even before the independence of India in 1947 and had contributed to the national economy for more than 80 years. They had recently ventured into agribusiness. In the early 1990s, agriculture was the latest area of corporate intervention in India. Corporate India had directed its attention to this sector considering the tremendous potential for agricultural exports. Thapars were the early entrants in this field through Global Green Company.

The organization structure of GGCL is shown in Exhibit 1. GGCL processes and markets a wide range of fresh and preserved foods like fruits, vegetables, and allied products, conforming to international quality standards. Its main product is preserved gherkins in bulk and bottled packs, constituting more than 90% of the business. The Thapars had identified the climate near Bangalore to be favourable for cultivating greens for 10 months in a year, i.e., almost throughout the year and had decided to make investments in developing local farmers for supplying gherkins. Before GGCL's entry, gherkins were not cultivated in this region due to absence of any market. GGCL made tremendous efforts in educating and helping these farmers at different stages including seed procurement, sowing, cultivation, and harvesting practices.

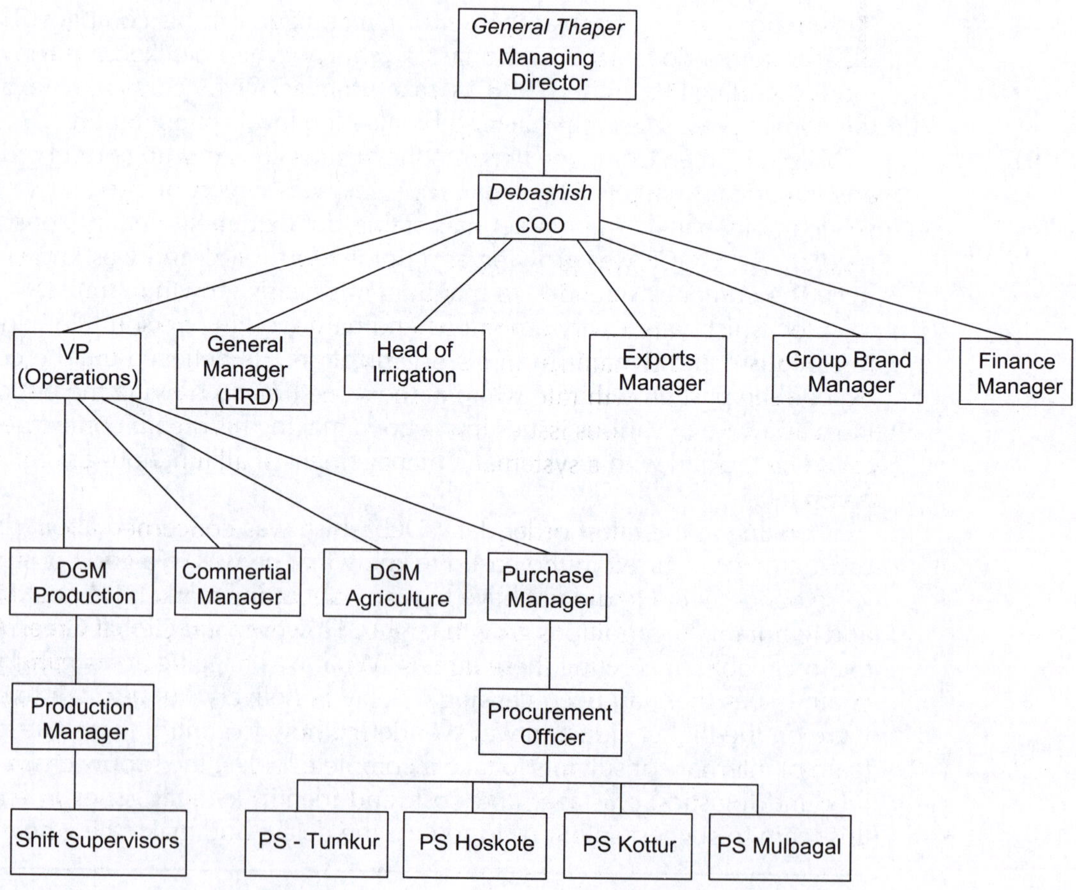


**Exhibit 1:**

Organization structure at Global Green Company Ltd.

*Note:* Sporulina and Saptashri are separated business

## Market

The market for preserved vegetables in American and European countries is large. Gherkins are part of established food habits and hence this market does not face any threat of substitution. The market is expected to grow at a steady rate due to moving towards vegetarianism in these countries. Consumers in these markets are extremely quality conscious and food regulations are strict. Hence, GGCL has to concentrate on achieving high levels of quality to meet the requirements. GGCL is quality conscious in all its operations. It has received ISO 9002 certification from BVQl for processing and marketing preserved foods and vegetables.

Exhibit 2 sums up the sales, raw material, and supply chain costs from December 1997 to November 1998. The customers of GGCL had experienced delays in the past in order delivery. See Exhibit 3 for delayed shipments based on sample data. The key performance figures for GGCL from December 1998 to June 1999 are shown at Exhibit 4.

***Exhibit 2:*** ***Sales, raw material and supply chain costs (₹lakh).***

| **Description** | **Total** |
|---|---|
| Sales (Dec 97 to Nov 98) | 1,489.70 |
| Receivables (As on Nov 98) | 339.90 |
| Payables (As on Nov 98) | 755.90 |
| Raw materials cost (Dec 97 to Nov 98) | 1,108.51 |
| Production Cost (Dec 97 to Nov 98) | 1,368.93 |
| CoGS (Dec 97 to Nov 98) | 1,590.12 |
| Supply Chain Cost (Dec 97 to Nov 98) | 304.42 |

***Exhibit 3:*** ***Delayed shipments.***

**Order executed on time (based on sample data)**

| **Customer** | **Expected** | **Actual** | **% on time** |
|---|---|---|---|
| | **Full container loads** | | |
| A&F | 27 | 22 | 81% |
| A&F | 75 | 34 | 45% |
| JOGREX | 50 | 41 | 82% |
| JOGREX | 38 | 20 | 53% |
| FAWCETT | 27 | 11 | 41% |

***Exhibit 4:*** ***Key performance figures for GGCL (Dec 98–Jun 99).***

| GREENS | | | Dec | Jan | Feb | Mar | Apr | May | Jun |
|---|---|---|---|---|---|---|---|---|---|
| | Reclassified (in kg) | 160+ | 31,502 | 63,387 | 1,40,819 | 3,09,053 | 1,96,702 | 1,77,728 | 3,75,773 |
| | | 60-160 | 20,837 | 50,723 | 1,29,057 | 2,92,957 | 2,04,413 | 1,96,739 | 4,05,254 |
| | | 20-60 | 13,994 | 37,161 | 1,06,447 | 3,09,541 | 2,37,992 | 2,37,130 | 3,39,250 |
| | | C/N | 1,067 | 5,955 | 5,536 | 20,965 | 9,092 | 5,820 | 13,890 |
| | | Biggies | 1,991 | 63,073 | 80,981 | 90,210 | 40,120 | 1,56,655 | 1,52,648 |
| | | | 69,391 | 2,20,299 | 4,62,840 | 10,22,726 | 6,88,319 | 7,74,072 | 12,86,815 |

*(Continued)*

**Exhibit 4: Continued**

| | | | | | | | | |
|---|---|---|---|---|---|---|---|---|
| Processed (in kg) bulk | In Vinegar | 31,528 | 54,453 | 1,43,525 | 2,70,939 | 1,77,881 | 1,92,915 | 3,35,544 |
| | In Acetic Acid | 3,527 | 14,216 | 29,239 | 49,491 | 49,491 | 4,172 | 6,789 |
| | *In Brine* | 1,138 | 374 | 0 | 31,741 | 31,741 | 53,172 | 2,36,912 |
| | Bottling | 25,519 | 1,01,914 | 2,34,975 | 4,65,604 | 465,04.6 | 3,25,977 | 4,75,279 |
| | *No. of Bottles* | 68,060 | 2,64,637 | 5,31,407 | 11,21,480 | 11,21,480 | 6,22,354 | 9,65,976 |
| | Greens Utilization per bottle | 0.37 | 0.38 | 0.44 | 0.41 | 0.041 | 0.52 | 0.49 |
| Packing material | Bottles | | 2,93,049 | 5,37,406 | 11,38,806 | 7,80,898 | 6,36,792 | 9,16,614 |
| | Caps | | 2,93,050 | 5,50,538 | 11,37,516 | 7,76,850 | 6,29,133 | 9,25,588 |
| | Labels | | | 5,09,405 | 11,39,236 | 7,80,252 | 6,18,657 | |
| | Cartons | | | 43,853 | 94,946 | 63,214 | 47,330 | |

## The Order Cycle

The sales order cycle starts with an enquiry from a customer. The inquiry is obtained through various means such as personal visits of the marketing staff to the clients, trade shows, and interaction with the embassies, supermarket chains, packers, and private label manufacturing. Existing customers may ask for increase in quality or recommend the product to other customers. Customers request samples for checking the "taste profile" and details regarding price, minimum order quantity lead-time, etc. GGCL sends these details and requests for the customer's sample in order to duplicate the recipes. Simultaneously, the international marketing department looks at the request from the customer to see if all the information required by GGCL is available. There is a checklist against which this is verified. The missing information if any is asked from the customer. The critical information is about product and packaging specifications, part of delivery, and shipping instructions. After getting this information, GGCL quotes its price per jar/bottle in customer's currency and the packaging specifications, for instance, 12 bottles or carton, etc. There may be a round of price negotiations. The supply schedule in terms of actual months in which supply is required and GGCL's capability are evaluated. The customer may have his supplies in bulk and have it in his own bottles or in GGCL's bottles. In case GGCL's bottles are required, samples are asked and then the quality is tested at the customer's site.

After the price negotiation is done, the orders are finalized and size of order is decided. GGCL then asks for details like pro-forma invoice and the monthly schedule of shipment, port of discharge, etc. The same order may have different lots sent to different ports according to the inbound logistics planning of the customer. GGCL has one price for one country irrespective of the port of shop.

The customer gives purchase order and other additional information about shipping if required. The bottled finished goods have customer's labels on them. A proof of labels is sent for approval and the customer sends any changes if required. Once the labels are approved, the shipping schedule and shipping instructions are finalized.

The production planning is done according to the shipping schedule for the month. Sometimes the orders do not have lead-time sufficient to plan greens production, i.e., growing and harvesting cycle of gherkins is longer than the lead-time for the first shipment. In such cases, a part of the order may be accommodated in the current production plan through reshuffling, and rest being delayed till greens could be grown against the order. The bulk inventory maintained at the warehouse is used for bulk orders but rarely for order for bottles. There may also be some delays due to unavailability of correct grades due to drop in procurement or mismatch in procured grades against the forecasted. Some of these effects get cushioned if the annual operating plan had forecasted the orders.

Materials requirement planning for raw material other than greens is done for the order as per the specifications for bottle, cap, and label as well as the spice and preservatives required. A bill of materials is prepared and the orders are placed. A sample Bill of Materials is shown in Exhibit 5. For bottles, there may be stock in inventory because the sizes are standardized. Labels have to be made for the specific order. Delays in getting the raw material are caused due to shipping delays, port saturation, etc. Air lifting of raw materials is done in the case of emergencies.

***Exhibit 5:* Sample Bill of Materials.**

**Bill of Materials Spec 014 Dill Pickle International Delicacies**

| | |
|---|---|
| **Product** | **Grade 20/60** |
| **Party Name:** | **Jar Size 720 ml** |

| S.No | Ingredients | Unit | Quantity | Rate | Cost |
|---|---|---|---|---|---|
| 1 | Vinegar 14% | kg | 0.047 | 15.91 | 0.75 |
| 2 | Acetic Acid | kg | 0 | 22.7 | 0 |
| 3 | Salt | kg | 0.025 | 2.3 | 0.06 |
| 4 | K M S | kg | 0 | 94 | 0 |
| 5 | Sugar | kg | 0.005 | 15.8 | 0.08 |
| 6 | Flavour Dill | kg | 0 | 3,070 | 0 |
| 7 | Flavour Garlic | kg | 0 | 1,170 | 0 |
| 8 | Colour | kg | 0.0001 | 450 | 0.05 |
| **A** | **Total (Ingredients)** | **kg** | | | **0.94** |
| **S.No.** | **Spices & Herb** | **Unit** | **Quantity** | **Rate** | **Cost** |
| 1 | Dill Weed | kg | 30 | 0.008 | 0.24 |
| 2 | Onion Fresh | Kg | 20 | 0 | 0 |
| 3 | Garlic Fresh | Kg | 70 | 0.003 | 0.21 |
| 4 | Dill Seed | Kg | 45 | 0 | 0 |
| 5 | Capsicum | Kg | 45 | 0.004 | 0.18 |
| 6 | Black Pepper | Kg | 245 | 0.00125 | 0.31 |
| 7 | Mustard | Kg | 43 | 0 | 0 |
| 8 | Celery Seed | Kg | 55 | 0 | 0 |
| 9 | Coriander | kg | 48 | 0 | 0 |
| **B** | **Total (Spices and herb)** | | | | **0.94** |
| **S No.** | **Packing Materials:** | **Unit** | **Quantity** | **Rate** | **Cost** |
| 1 | Jar | Nos | 4.3 | 1 | 4.3 |
| 2 | Cap | Nos | 2.3 | 1 | 2.3 |
| 3 | Labels | Nos | 0.28 | 1 | 0.28 |
| 4 | Glue | kg | 45 | 0.002 | 0.09 |
| 5 | Ink | kg | 4,500 | 0.000031 | 0.14 |
| 6 | Carton Separator | Nos | 2 | 0.083 | 0.17 |
| 7 | Carton | Nos | 10 | 0.083 | 0.83 |

| S.No | Wastage | Unit | Quantity | Rate | Cost |
|---|---|---|---|---|---|
| 1 | Raw Materials | kg | 0.0975 | 4.3 | 0.42 |
| 2 | Ingredients | kg | | | 0.07 |
| 3 | Packaging Materials | Nos | | | 0.16 |
| D | **Total (Wastage)** | | | | **0.65** |
| **S.No** | **Total Cost** | **Unit** | **Quantity** | **Rate** | **Cost** |
| | Cost of Gherkin | | | | 1.68 |
| A | Ingredients | | 0.39 | 4.3 | 0.94 |
| B | Spices and Herbs | | | | 0.94 |
| C | Packing Materials | | | | 8.19 |
| D | Wastage | | | | 0.65 |
| | **Grand Total** | | | | **13.49** |

*(Continued)*

**Exhibit 5: Continued**

| | | | | | |
|---|---|---|---|---|---|
| 8 | BOPP Tape | kg | 0.64 | 0.125 | 0.08 |
| 9 | Tray | Nos | | | 0 |
| 10 | Shrink Film | kg | 125 | | 0 |
| 11 | Stretch Film | kg | 190 | | 0 |
| C | **Total (Packing Mat.)** | | | | **8.19** |

Once the product is ready for shipment, the marketing department sends dispatch instructions to production. The dispatch schedule and payment terms are sent to the customer. The customer confirms the delivery on the receipt of the container. There are two types of shipments possible: CIF (Cost, Insurance, and Freight) and FOB (Free on Board). In CIF, GGCL is responsible for all risks and costs till unloading at the customer's port. In FOB, GGCL is responsible till loading the container on the ship. CIF has additional costs like freight cost, insurance, port demurrage charges, etc. These may vary depending on the circumstances of shipping, etc., and in case of emergencies, GGCL might have to ship from ports such as Mumbai, Cochin, and JNPT instead of Chennai depending on the availability of ships. This increases the transportation cost by 15–30%.

# Supply Chain

## Overview

The supply chain for gherkins begins with procurement of seeds and ends with delivery of the bottled product at the port specified by the customer. The main points of value addition are growing and harvesting of greens by the farmers, grading and selection (carried out at present by both the farmers as well as the company), processing of greens, bulk packing or bottling by the company, and delivery to the customer/market intermediary. Subsequent value addition is in terms of intangibles like the brand name of the company. The movement of material across locations adds to the costs. There is a supplementary chain for the preservation media, e.g., vinegar, acetic acid, and packing material, e.g., bottles, caps, labels, and drums.

There is wastage at different points in the supply chain. The gherkins if not processed within 24 hours of harvesting get damaged. Greens can be kept under refrigeration for up to 48 hours but it is a very costly option. There is also wastage during processing and packaging due to breakage of bottles and caps. Exhibit 6 shows the wastage data during processing for greens as well as the wastage data for bottles and caps.

**Exhibit 6: Wastage's—bottles and caps (nos.).**

| | Processing greens | | | | Bottles | | | | Caps | | | |
|---|---|---|---|---|---|---|---|---|---|---|---|---|
| Month | Receipt | Processed | Wastage | | Consumed | Produced | Wastage | | Consumed | Capped | Wastage | |
| | | | *Nos* | % | | | *Nos* | % | | | *Nos* | % |
| Jan-98 | 70,734 | 64,152 | 6,582 | 9.3 | 36,904 | 35,720 | 1,184 | 3.21 | 37,341 | 35,720 | 1,621 | 4.34 |
| Feb-98 | 2,42,940 | 2,26,543 | 16,397 | 6.7 | 1,50,398 | 1,46,714 | 3,684 | 2.45 | 1,54,793 | 1,54,793 | 8,079 | 5.22 |
| Mar-98 | 10,93,556 | 9,09,455 | 1,84,101 | 16.8 | 8,28,211 | 8,13,555 | 14,656 | 1.77 | 8,52,417 | 8,52,417 | 38,862 | 4.56 |
| Apr-98 | 4,39,075 | 3,10,047 | 1,29,028 | 29.4 | 3,72,192 | 3,62,279 | 9,913 | 2.66 | 3,82,612 | 3,82,612 | 20,333 | 5.31 |
| May- 98 | 1,19,835 | 80,198 | 39,637 | 33.1 | 47,742 | 46,920 | 822 | 1.72 | 49,672 | 49,672 | 2,752 | 5.54 |

(*Continued*)

*Exhibit 6: Continued*

| | Processing greens | | | | Bottles | | | | Caps | | | |
|---|---|---|---|---|---|---|---|---|---|---|---|---|
| **Month** | **Receipt** | **Processed** | **Wastage** | | **Consumed** | **Produced** | **Wastage** | | **Consumed** | **Capped** | **Wastage** | |
| Jun-98 | 3,28,889 | 2,83,082 | 45,807 | 13.9 | 27,884 | 27,391 | 493 | 1.77 | 28,541 | 27,391 | 1,150 | 4.03 |
| Jul-98 | 15,05,590 | 10,87,166 | 4,18,424 | 27.8 | 9,05,938 | 8,72,817 | 33,121 | 3.66 | 9,13,350 | 8,72,817 | 40,533 | 4.44 |
| Aug-98 | 7,65,220 | 6,20,850 | 1,44,370 | 18.9 | 6,82,914 | 6,55,909 | 27,005 | 3.95 | 6,85,747 | 6,55,909 | 29,838 | 4.35 |
| Sep-98 | 5,47,982 | 5,16,826 | 31,156 | 5.7 | 1,45,068 | 1,43,779 | 1,289 | 0.89 | 1,45,065 | 1,43,779 | 1,286 | 0.89 |
| **Total** | **51,13,821** | **40,98,319** | **10,15,502** | **19.9** | **31,97,251** | **31,05,084** | **92,167** | **2.88** | **32,49,538** | **31,75,110** | **1,44,454** | **4.45** |

## Greens Production

Gherkin cultivation is a labour-intensive process. Usually the acreage for gherkin cultivation per farmer is 1 acre or less. Gherkin production starts with the sowing of seeds on the selected sites according to the sales forecast. Global Green Company works with more than 6,000 farmers. These farmers are located around Bangalore in areas like Hoskote, Haveri, Tiptur, Kollegal, etc. The company enters into contract with these farmers for each harvesting cycle. The contract is the smallest unit of identification in the agricultural MIS of the GGCL. The company has various standardized parameters for selection of farmers. The farms are evaluated for soil condition, history of crop failures, availability of water, etc. Once a contract is made, the values for these conditions are noted in the agricultural MIS and used for forecasting of the crop in the agri forecasting system. GGCL has been known to retain around 25% of farmers for more than one cycle. This farmer loyalty has been the result of prompt payment for the gherkins procured and guidance as well as help from the agricultural department of GGCL to the farmers.

The seeds take around 35–40 days for germination followed by the start of harvesting cycle. Harvesting cycle is normally 35 days from start of the harvesting period. The company contracts to buy the entire yield from a farm for one harvesting cycle. The farmer may have 2–3 cycles in a year. The lean season is from August to November during which the yield per acre goes down. The agri forecasting system is provided such as continuous feedback during the growth stage on weather conditions, flowering pattern, general crop conditions in the area, etc. These are used to fine-tune the forecast at the contract level. The grade of gherkins also depends on the harvesting practices followed by the farmer. The farmer is asked to harvest the different grades of gherkins according to the following distribution.

*Table 1: Recommended ratio of gherkin grades for production.*

| S.No. | Grade (Piece per kg) | Recommended Percentage of Total | Procurement Price (₹Per kg) |
|---|---|---|---|
| 1 | 160+ | 40 | ₹10 |
| 2 | 60–160 | 30 | ₹7.50 |
| 3 | 20–60 | 30 | ₹2.50 |

Gherkins are graded on the basis of size and weight. The normal way of grading is based on pieces per kg. Smaller sizes are preferred; hence, larger the number of Gherkins per kg, the better it is. The company usually follows three grades as shown in the Table 1, but sometimes finer grading may be done depending on customer orders where grades are also considered. Biggies are greens that are less than 20 pieces per kg. These may be used for slicing or may be sold as bulk. There are a lot of deformities possible in greens. Common among these are crooked and numboids (C/N). These are not used for bottling.

The ratio as shown in the Table 1 is the ideal ratio if correct harvesting processes are followed. The actual production by farmers has been found to have a high variation from the recommended ratio. The variance in forecasted and actual values is high at farmer level but gets averaged out as the level of aggregation is larger. Thus, in spite of such continuous modifications, the agri forecasting is still far from perfect. Exhibit 7 shows farmer level data for one farmer for one month. It can be seen that there is large variation and it is different for different areas. Exhibit 8 shows the grade-wise forecasted versus purchase data for GGCL for one year.

## Greens Inbound Logistics

The transportation to the processing plant is carried out in the shortest possible time to avoid wastage. From the agri extension officers or buyers, the inbound logistics department gets the information about location of the farms where the crop is being harvested and the quantity of

***Exhibit 7:* Farmer level data for one farmer for one month.**

| | Actual purchase (kg) | | | | Forecast (kg) | | | |
|---|---|---|---|---|---|---|---|---|
| **Date** | **Total** | **160–200** | **60–160** | **20–60** | **Total** | **160–200** | **60–160** | **20–60** |
| 4-Jul | 40 | 24 | 8 | 8 | 74 | 30 | 19 | 22 |
| 5-Jul | 72 | 35 | 24 | 13 | 74 | 30 | 19 | 22 |
| 6-Jul | 104 | 54 | 30 | 20 | 74 | 30 | 19 | 22 |
| 7-Jul | 82 | 46 | 25 | 12 | 74 | 30 | 19 | 22 |
| 8-Jul | 94 | 57 | 26 | 11 | 74 | 30 | 19 | 22 |
| 9-Jul | 116 | 73 | 31 | 12 | 74 | 30 | 19 | 22 |
| 10-Jul | 123 | 77 | 33 | 14 | 74 | 30 | 19 | 22 |
| 11-Jul | 164 | 80 | 56 | 28 | 143 | 57 | 36 | 43 |
| 12-Jul | 202 | 99 | 79 | 24 | 143 | 57 | 36 | 43 |
| 13-Jul | 142 | 86 | 28 | 29 | 143 | 57 | 36 | 43 |
| 14-Jul | 172 | 87 | 65 | 20 | 143 | 57 | 36 | 43 |
| 15-Jul | 126 | 77 | 44 | 15 | 143 | 57 | 36 | 43 |
| 16-Jul | 151 | 84 | 52 | 16 | 143 | 57 | 36 | 43 |
| 17-Jul | 145 | 72 | 54 | 20 | 143 | 57 | 36 | 43 |
| 18-Jul | 159 | 89 | 50 | 20 | 200 | 80 | 50 | 60 |
| 19-Jul | 147 | 75 | 52 | 20 | 200 | 80 | 50 | 60 |
| 20-Jul | 129 | 71 | 38 | 20 | 200 | 80 | 50 | 60 |
| 21-Jul | 149 | 77 | 52 | 20 | 200 | 80 | 50 | 60 |
| 22-Jul | 111 | 59 | 32 | 20 | 200 | 80 | 50 | 60 |
| 23-Jul | 125 | 63 | 42 | 20 | 200 | 80 | 50 | 60 |
| 24-Jul | 116 | 59 | 38 | 19 | 200 | 80 | 50 | 60 |
| 25-Jul | 132 | 64 | 48 | 20 | 97 | 39 | 24 | 29 |
| 26-Jul | 144 | 72 | 53 | 20 | 97 | 39 | 24 | 29 |
| 27-Jul | 102 | 48 | 34 | 20 | 97 | 39 | 24 | 29 |
| 28-Jul | 136 | 50 | 66 | 20 | 97 | 39 | 24 | 29 |
| 29-Jul | 77 | 31 | 27 | 20 | 97 | 39 | 24 | 29 |
| 30-Jul | 99 | 38 | 41 | 20 | 97 | 39 | 24 | 29 |
| 31-Jul | 85 | 28 | 37 | 20 | 97 | 39 | 24 | 29 |
| 1-Aug | 64 | 24 | 22 | 18 | 57 | 23 | 14 | 17 |
| 2-Aug | 52 | 24 | 12 | 17 | 57 | 23 | 14 | 17 |
| 3-Aug | 27 | 10 | 7 | 10 | 57 | 23 | 14 | 17 |
| **Total** | **3,587** | **1,833** | **1,206** | **566** | **3,769** | **1,511** | **945** | **1,129** |

**Exhibit 8: Purchase versus reclassification data for one year.**

| | Quantity in tonnes at the purchase stage | | | | | After reclassification at factory | | | | |
|---|---|---|---|---|---|---|---|---|---|---|
| **Month/Grade** | **160+** | **60–160** | **20–60** | **C/N** | **Biggies** | **160+** | **60–160** | **20–60** | **C/N** | **Biggies** |
| Jan-98 | 60.9 | 19.5 | 36.7 | 2.8 | 0.2 | 55.4 | 17.4 | 32.8 | 6.1 | 0 |
| Feb-98 | 151.3 | 74.8 | 113.5 | 0.6 | 0.1 | 96 | 60.4 | 110.5 | 13.3 | 0 |
| Mar-98 | 424.2 | 198 | 510.6 | 19.4 | 0.5 | 398.8 | 181 | 520.8 | 29.8 | 0 |
| Apr-98 | 126.7 | 63.6 | 273.2 | 34.6 | 0.8 | 125 | 62.1 | 270.7 | 41 | 0.3 |
| May-98 | 35.7 | 19.1 | 85.2 | 6.9 | 0.4 | 22.3 | 15.8 | 69.3 | 9 | 0 |
| Jun-98 | 143.4 | 56.5 | 125.3 | 2.4 | 104 | 138.6 | 57.5 | 128 | 6.9 | 104.7 |
| Jul-98 | 593.4 | 257 | 510.1 | 6.3 | 130 | 511.4 | 225.9 | 515.6 | 11 | 132 |
| Aug-98 | 298.4 | 169.3 | 282.3 | 11.8 | 26.8 | 266.5 | 160.2 | 267.3 | 27.5 | 30.4 |
| Sep-98 | 316.9 | 95.7 | 134.5 | 5.1 | 10.1 | 302.1 | 94.3 | 138 | 9.1 | 10.6 |
| Oct-98 | 295.9 | 80.3 | 121.3 | 10.3 | 44.9 | 266 | 72.1 | 124.2 | 13.8 | 47.4 |
| Nov-98 | 104.7 | 18.3 | 16.8 | 0.5 | 13.2 | 101.2 | 16.6 | 17.1 | 2 | 13.2 |
| Dec-98 | 34.2 | 22.7 | 13.7 | 0.6 | 2 | 32.4 | 21.3 | 14.2 | 1.4 | 1.8 |
| **Total** | 2,585.7 | 1,074.8 | 2,223.2 | 101.3 | 333 | 2,315.7 | 984.6 | 2,208.5 | 170.9 | 340.4 |
| **Average** | 215.47 | 89.57 | 185.26 | 8.442 | 27.75 | 192.97 | 82.05 | 184.04 | 14.24 | 28.36 |

greens that can be expected. This information is based on the estimated grade-wise production from the agri forecasting system. Based on this information, the procurement officer at the factory decides the number of trucks to be utilized and the required capacity. In Haveri and Kottur areas, there are distribution centres. Here, the decision for the vehicle logistics is taken by the Area Extension Officer (AEO), and for procurement, local vehicles are used, which collect crop from different area and bring it to the centre from where the entire greens are shifted to the factory. The vehicles from these two areas start at midnight and reach the factory in the morning. The routes followed by the vehicles are suggested by the AEOs. In other areas, trucks from the factory go directly to the farms and collect the greens harvested. Procurement assistants from the company go along with the trucks and carry out the buying activities at the farms. The farmers are provided with passbooks for noting down the grade-wise procurement. The procurement assistants make entries into the passbooks. This data is used to make payments to the farmer. In the factory, details for the truck like total distance travelled and the greens procured are noted down at the time of unloading. The greens are sent to the production department where reclassification is carried out. The main problem facing GGCL in this area was the large variance of capacity utilization. This was because the scheduling of vehicles for procurement was done on the basis of forecasted harvest for the day as given by the agri forecasting system. The forecasts were often in variance with the actual harvesting. This resulted in problems in truck scheduling and capacity planning. Exhibit 9 shows the transportation data for Hoskote area using 2 ton and 1.5 ton trucks.

## Greens Processing

GGCL has set up state of the art processing facility at Whitefield, Bangalore. The plant is strategically located to ensure shortest possible time between harvest and processing. The facility has multi-product capabilities and produces a variety of preserved foods and vegetables. These include gherkins, coloured bell peppers, hot peppers, cherry, tomatoes, and baby corn. These are produced in a wide range of styles that include slices, diced, spears, stackers, and wholes. A sophisticated bottling and canning plant is used to pack products in containers that conform

***Exhibit 9:* Transportation data for Hoskote area.**

| Date | Q2.0 (kg) | Q1.5(kg) | FC | Date | Q2.0 (kg) | Q1.5(kg) | FC |
|---|---|---|---|---|---|---|---|
| 3-Jan-99 | 104 | | 586.3 | 22-Jan-99 | | 1,020 | 496 |
| 4-Jan-99 | 472 | | 478 | | 3,562 | | 360 |
| 5-Jan-99 | 395 | | 734 | 23-Jan-99 | 1,105 | | 360 |
| 6-Jan-99 | 696.5 | | 1,882.8 | | | 465 | 929 |
| 7-Jan-99 | 2,470 | | 2,592 | | 1,205 | | 719 |
| | 333 | | 712 | 24-Jan-99 | | 794 | 1,000 |
| 8-Jan-99 | 365 | | 396 | | 1,015 | | 619 |
| 9-Jan-99 | 840 | | 410 | | 2,522 | | 360 |
| | 957 | | 579 | 25-Jan-99 | | 1,168 | 964 |
| 11-Jan-99 | 3,555 | | 766 | | | 1,039 | 720 |
| 12-Jan-99 | 304 | | 522 | | 2,210 | | 360 |
| | | | | 26-Jan-99 | | 842 | 662 |
| 13-Jan-99 | 603 | | 579 | | | 933 | 964 |
| | 1,705 | | 428 | | | 765 | 392 |
| | | 1,158 | 399 | 27-Jan-99 | | 2,161 | 396 |
| 14-Jan-99 | 1,402 | 770 | 543 | | | 1,121 | 1,076 |
| 15-Jan-99 | | 263 | 532 | | | 1,470 | 741 |
| | | 1,480 | 367 | 28-Jan-99 | 1,150 | | 1,148 |
| 16-Jan-99 | | 1,125 | 565 | | | 904 | 788 |
| 17-Jan-99 | 780 | | 532 | | | 1,328 | 1,090 |
| | 1,806 | | 504 | | | 837 | 403 |
| 18-Jan-99 | 658 | | 525 | 29-Jan-99 | | 1,545 | 1,072 |
| 19-Jan-99 | 1,061 | | 536 | | | 1,680 | 763 |
| | | 3,600 | 759 | 30-Jan-99 | 3,023 | | 792 |
| 20-Jan-99 | 811 | | 522 | | 1,804 | | 968 |
| 21-Jan-99 | 4,153 | | 435 | 31-Jan-99 | 2,078 | | 1,026 |
| | | | | | | 1,177 | 687 |
| | | 1,269 | 1,180 | | | | |

*Note:* Multiple rows for same date denote use of multiple trucks.

* *2 ton and 1.5 ton trucks are used.* Q2.0: Greens transported by 2 Ton truck. Q1.5: Greens transported by 1.5 Ton truck. FC: Freight Cost in Rupees

to international specifications. An intensive pasteurization process and exhaustive checks at the company's microbiological laboratory ensure complete security for the customer. The packaging involves two dimensions: the size of the container and the preservative used apart from the product forms like sliced, diced, etc. The different combinations of these form different SKUs. Thus, examples of SKUs may include 'Whole Gherkin in Vinegar (Appel and Frenzel) in 720 ml fluted bottle with printed cap', 'Dill Pickle in 720 ml sided bottle with white 82 mm cap', etc. Preservatives include acetic acid, vinegar, and brine; the concentration of these could change according to customer's prescription. Greens are processed and packaged in bottles or as bulks. Every day, the factory produces batches of bottled product that are made to order and bulks that may be made to order or made to stock.

The greens procured from farmers in the night are available for processing in the morning. The greens are brought in trays according to grading done by the buyers on the farm. These are fed into the assembly line in the factory. The first operation on the line is washing. Washed greens are reclassified in the factory. This process is done manually as well as mechanically on the grading line. Thus, each lot of greens goes through three grading cycles: at farm, manual grading at factory, and then machine grading. The greens have to be re-graded at the factory again since the grading done during purchase is not very accurate. (See Exhibit 8 for Purchase versus reclassification data for one year.) The factory has three grading lines; each having a planned capacity of 10 tonnes per shift. The bottling line can fill 26,000 bottles per shift. Sometimes one of these lines may be dedicated to a particular customer's order. The graded greens are fed into the bottling line. The bottling line handles one grade at a time. Greens belonging to other grades are stored as bulk in barrels with preservatives.

Bottling operations are automated but there are workers at different points along the bottling line. Spices are added at the bottom of the bottles. Spices include dill weed, garlic, red pepper, onions, mustard, etc. The recipe is customer specific. The species may be added as whole or after crushing, depending on the requirements. The bottles containing spices are filled with gherkins by the filling machine. Visual inspection of filled bottles is done to ascertain whether the bottle is looking empty or it is underweight. The workers have a weighing machine next to the line and they can stop the line if required. Preservative at high temperature is then added to the bottle. The bottle passes through a metal detector and another round of visual inspection before going to the capping machine. The metal detector automatically places the defective bottles on a separate tray. From the capping machine, the bottle goes to the pasteurization unit. The pasteurized product is ready for labelling and dispatch. Labelling is the next stage on the assembly line. Labelling is automated and is done by the labelling machine. There are two workers at this point to feed labels and make sure that there is no crowding on the assembly line. They can stop the line if required.

The difference between production of bottled product and bulks occurs after grading. For bulking, the greens are put in large barrels with spices and preservatives. There is a stabilization period of 7–8 days required for bulks during which the preservative is expected to enter inside the greens. Bulk stocks are considered as WIP inventory during this period.

## Procurement of Packing Material

The company imports packaging and processing raw material such as bottles, caps, jars, and vinegar as well as seeds. Local vendors are being developed but the process is not complete. GGCL faced serious problems here due to inferior quality. For instance, the bottles cleared by the vendor's quality department would not stand the acceptance testing at GGCL leading to rejection of whole lots and consequent delays.

The company has started procuring 85% of its bottles requirement from Indian suppliers now. Caps are also being procured from local suppliers but have been found to be not satisfying the stringent quality requirement of GGCL. The company has had quality problems from international suppliers of caps too. The procurement is done on the basis of sales forecast, which is done on yearly basis while preparing the operating plan for the year. There is a high lead-time for the procurement of these items (Exhibit 10). The suppliers of bottles and caps have minimum economic order quantities that run in hundreds of thousands (for bottles it is in the range of 5,00,000), and hence, the order from GGCL may not be taken up before completion of the previous runs. In addition, the domestic suppliers prefer to produce soft drink bottles due to larger volumes. Imports may be delayed due to the transportation done by ships, port saturation, etc.

***Exhibit 10:*** ***Lead-time analysis for the suppliers of bottles and caps from key suppliers.***

| Supplier Name | Item Name | STD Name | STD L T | ORD. No | Date (Ord. placed) | Actual L. T | Variance |
|---|---|---|---|---|---|---|---|
| Owens Brockway Ltd. | Bottles | 45 days | 359/93 | 29/1/93 | 24/2/99 | 27 days | |
| Owens Brockway Ltd. | Bottles | 45 days | 166/98 | 7/7/1998 | 7/3/1999 | 236 days | 191 days |
| L&T | Bottles | 45 days | 259/98 | 15/10/1998 | 20/3/1999 | 124 days | 99 days |
| L&T | Bottles | 45 days | 366/99 | 25/1/1999 | 1/2/1999 | 6 days | |
| L&T | Bottles | 45 days | 389/91 | 1/2/1999 | | | |
| L&T | Bottles | 45 days | 266/98 | 22/10/1998 | | | |
| L&T | Bottles | 45 days | 143/98 | 2/7/1998 | | | |
| PLM Glassworks | Bottles | 2 months | 278/98 | 7/11/1998 | 15/2/1999 | | |
| PLM Glassworks | Bottles | 2 months | 274/98 | 13/11/1998 | | 3 months, 7 days | 1 month, 7 days |
| Mahalakshmi Glassworks | Bottles | 44 days | 207/98 | 3/8/1998 | 30/1/1999 | 182 days | 137 days |
| Mahalakshmi Glassworks | Bottles | 45 days | 258/98 | 9/10/1998 | | | |
| L&T | Caps | 60 days | 407 | 10/2/1999 | 13/2/1999 | | |
| L&T | Caps | 60 days | 406 | 10/2/1999 | 10/3/1999 | 28 days 3 days | |

# Inventory

## *Raw Material*

In order to take care of lead-time and uncertainties in the quality of bottles, caps, etc., the company has to build up inventories. The company keeps safety stock of imported bottles to be used in case of large-scale quality rejections of locally procured bottles. The inventory is replenished when it goes below a minimum level. In spite of this, there are some delays due to stock-out of packaging material.

## *Greens*

Greens inventory is in the form of bulks and bottles. Bottled greens are considered as finished goods inventory. Greens inventory is not considered as raw material. This is because the company has a policy of bottling fresh greens as far as possible. Weekly production planning is done on the basis of agricultural forecast for greens procurement. Any mismatch in procurement and forecast in grades is adjusted in the next week's production plan. This is possible because the shipping requirements from the customer are for a month and the exact dates are flexible. In case of shortages, the agri department is notified and the procurement is looked into for increase in acreage, etc. In case of excess, the excess greens may be refrigerated for up to 48 hours and used in the next day's bottling run. However, usually excess greens are bulked. These bulked greens are usually not used for bottling in future except in rare cases of emergency. Attempt is made to sell off the bulked greens as bulk. Sometimes the inventory of bulks has been found to increase, leading to heavy storage costs.

## Outbound Logistics

The outbound logistics process involves procuring containers, loading these, getting certificate of loading, customs clearance, transportation from warehouse to the port loading on the ships, and unloading at the customer's port. Transportation from the factory is usually handled by the freight line. The marketing department at GGCL arranges for the containers after clearance from production. Full container loads are sent and the number of containers is decided according to the shipping schedule agreed with the customer and availability of processed greens. One 20 feet container usually holds 80 barrels of 40 kg capacity or 21,000 bottles of average 350 g. The number of containers dispatched on a day can be as high as 9 for bulks and 4 containers for bottles. The normal lead-time for a delivery to US is between 45–60 days. It can vary depending upon the availability of ship, the route followed by the ship, etc. The shipping line gives a commitment on the date of delivery and it is their responsibility to deliver on that date. Delays may be caused due to inadequate time for fixing the details with shippers. In which case, there may not be space available on ships or it may come at a premium for last minute booking. There is also minimum load prescribed by some liners.

## Planning and Forecasting

Planning is done at two levels: one at the sales and the other is operations. Sales planning involve the preparation of operating plan for the year based on firm orders and forecasted orders based on previous years data. The operation planning involves planning the acreage under cultivation, getting into contacts with farmers, materials planning, and logistics. Materials planning involve requirements for seeds, packaging materials like bottles, jars, and caps, and preservatives like acetic acid, vinegar, and brine. Logistics involves daily truck capacity planning for greens procurement based on forecasted harvest quantity, route scheduling for these trucks, and also the shipping schedules for firm orders.

The sales department prepares the operating plan for the year based on last year's data. Annual operating plan triggered off by the sales forecast is the driver for the planning of other functions including agricultural management. Agricultural management makes a separate operating plan, which is based on the sales plan and the forecasts given by agri forecasting system. This plan is not linked to the sales plan directly. Every month, there is sharing of information on actual performance against the forecasted one. The impact of this variance leads to a change in the operating plans only if the variance is high. In absence of high variance, the sales order booking is still based on forecasts from Agri management department and not on actual performance. Similarly, the acreage sown continues to be based on the forecasted sales unless the variance between actual order booking and forecasted is very high.

## Agri Forecasting System

Agri forecasting system is based on assumptions delivered by the experience of the agri extension personnel. These include the following:

1. **Days to harvest:** Number of days from sowing date to the commencement of harvesting.
2. **Yield per acre:** The total quantity of greens expected per acre of farm.
3. **Yield distribution model:** The percentage of greens expected in each week after the start of harvesting. This is done on the basis of a distribution model. There is no mechanism to modify the forecast on the basis of daily feedback.

4. **Grade Percentage (GPC) model:** The grade mix expected from a farmer. (See Exhibit 7 for farmer level data of forecast versus actual.)

These assumptions form part of the contact with the farmer. From time-to-time, these are modified based on the feedback about the sowing, weather conditions, farm conditions, etc. The GPC model assumes that the grade mix will remain constant throughout the harvesting season. The area extension officer (AEO) sends regular feedback based on the observations during weekly farm visits. The agri forecast system is updated on weekly basis and there is no correction possible in between.

## Agri MIS System

GGCL has developed a sophisticated MIS for the agricultural operations. Data is captured during various stages of the greens production cycle. Inputs from MIS are used as the basis for forecasting. A contract is the smallest unit of the MIS that refers to a unique contract with a farmer for his land for a particular cycle. For a region, the various levels of aggregation are centre, area, subarea, cluster, location, crop source, and agreement (see Exhibit 11 Classification in MIS). The MIS is used for recording transactions and reporting. The various types of reports possible are as follows:

- Budgets and targets
- Consolidated statistics
- Purchase and forecasts
- Reclassification reports
- Freight cost
- Performance appraisal for closed agreements
- Criteria analysis
- Accuracy of assumptions
- Sowing report

Agri MIS also generates checklist for checking data sufficiency, e.g., agreement checklist, crop purchase summary, reclassification report, forecast review, etc.

## The Future

GGCL has a target to achieve a turnover in excess of ₹50 crores by 2000–2001 (from current business, excluding lateral growth from acquisitions and new business). Domestic sales, under the umbrella brand TIFY were targeted to cross ₹10 crores. During this period, the export mix of the company was expected to shift significantly towards high-value added bottled segment. GGCL will be required to enhance its' operations at all points to meet these challenges. The company also had plans to enter the domestic retail market in 10 major cities in India and establish a strong presence in these regions by the year 2000–2001. The major constraint in achieving these expansion plans was the ability of supply chain system in GGCL to cope with the challenge. Establishing a strong information collection and recording system, enhancing forecasting system and establishing integrated planning system with a common goal of achieving cost effective on time deliveries, were some of the challenges in front of the company.

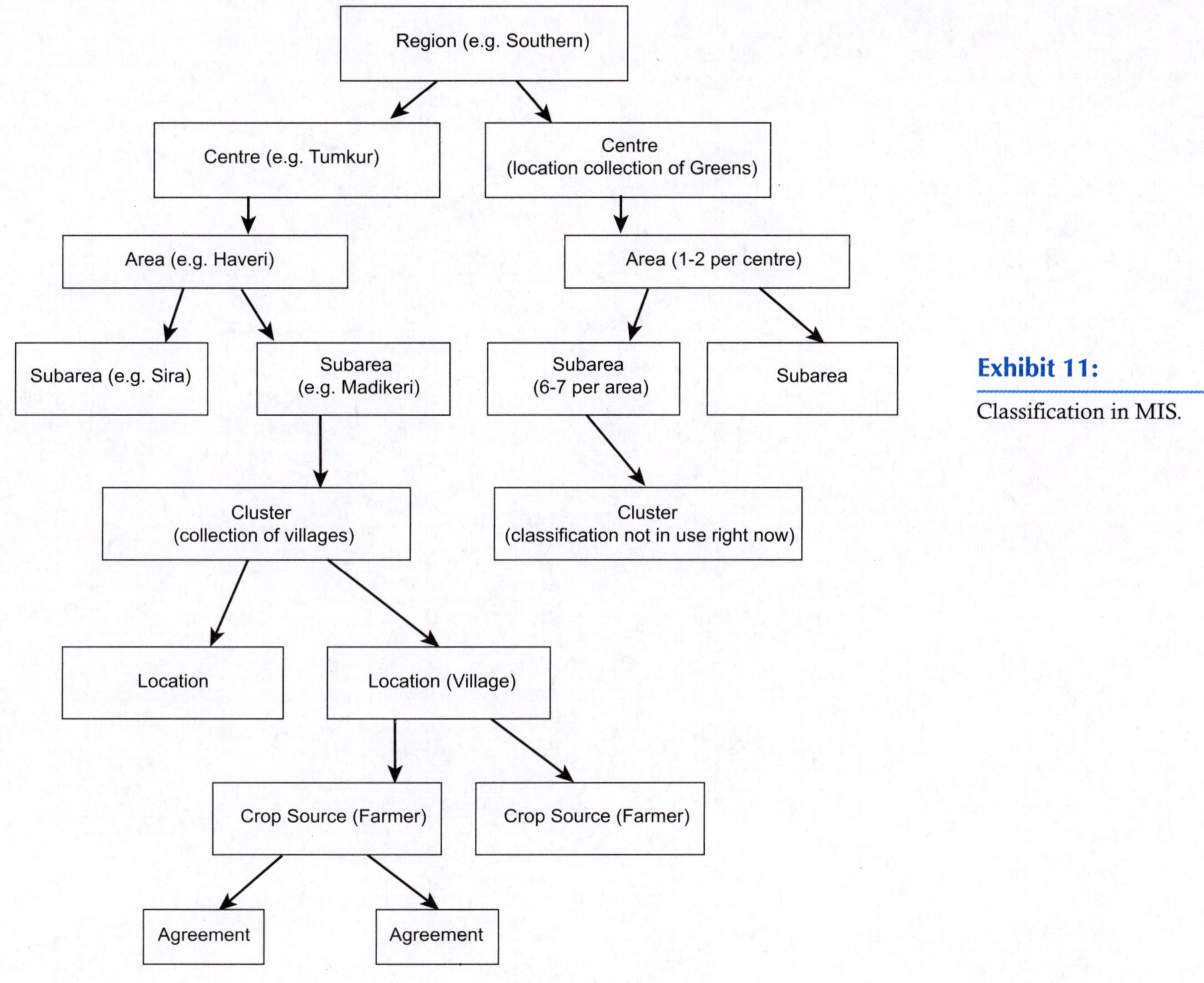


**Exhibit 11:**

Classification in MIS.

## Discussion Questions

1. Identify key challenges faced by Global Green?
2. Evaluate performance of Global Green supply chain? What are the causes of problems faced at Global Green?
3. What is your evaluation of Global Green's planning Processes?
4. What specific actions do you recommend to Debashish to address supply chain performance problems?

# Marico Industries: mySAP™ Supply Chain Management*

## Introduction

During the fluctuating economies of the past 10 years, Marico has maintained steady revenue and profit growth and a leadership position in India's fast-moving consumer goods sector. Most significant is that in the fiscal year ending March 2003, Marico's sales and services had increased 11.4 per cent over 2002 to Rs 7.75 billion (US$169 million) and after-tax profits increased 12 per cent to Rs 562 million (US$12 million).

With the tough economy and growing competition from international giant companies, no other company in its sector achieved double-digit growth.

In Marico's case, success in fiscal 2003 was extremely significant because the company had acted swiftly to reverse the mounting forecasting, supply chain, and image problems created by its ambitious expansion into new brands and markets.

In 2002, the Mumbai-based manufacturer implemented SAP R/3, supply chain planning and management systems throughout the company. These "big bang" initiatives—implemented company-wide within nine months—helped reduce Marico's supply chain costs, improve forecasting and planning and increase funding for advertising, innovation and expansion.

Within the fast-moving consumer goods industry—which includes high-demand, perishable packaged goods—Marico is a major producer of nature care and health care products primarily for India's vast market of one billion people. These products include coconut oils, refined edible oils, hair oils, skin care and fabric care products and food items such as jams and sauces.

---

*This case was written by Janat Shah, Professor at the Indian Institute of Management Bangalore, and Angeline Pantages, President, Pantages Reports Inc, Stamford. This case is to be used as a basis of case discussion rather than to illustrate either effective or ineffective handling of an administrative situation.  Adapted with permission.

As mentioned previously, Marico, incorporated in 1988, began commercial operations in 1990 when it acquired the consumer products division of Bombay Oil Industries. For much of the 1990s, it concentrated on the two consumer goods brands included in the acquisition: Parachute coconut oil and Saffola refined edible oil. With a gradual shift in Indian government policy that has allowed more entry of international consumer goods companies into India, Marico responded with more new brands, and today, the company markets nine brands. Three are India's market leaders; the other six are in the second or third place in their respective categories.

Marico has also entered the service business. During fiscal 2003, the company complemented its skin care product line by entering the world of high-tech skin care clinics, starting with three clinics in Mumbai.

## Branding, Distribution, Cost Management and Innovation

Understanding the impact of this expansion on Marico requires an understanding of its culture, its business strategy and its rigorous approach to creating and sustaining its brands.

The fundamental reason for Marico's success historically has been a culture that emphasizes a customer focus, teamwork and management and product innovation fully supported by funding, resources and methodology.

Early on, Marico's managers determined that its competitive advantage would reside in *superior branding, distribution, cost management* and *innovation.*

Accordingly, its approach to brand development focuses on

- Understanding and anticipating consumer needs
- Developing product and packaging innovations that meet these needs, such as cold-water clothes starch and polyethylene packaging for coconut oils
- Ensuring wide availability of its products on retail shelves
- Creating advertising campaigns to reinforce the value delivered to consumers
- Tracking metrics that support product positioning strategies

Basic to this approach has been Marico's highly regarded nationwide distribution network, which reaches every community of more than 20,000 residents and penetrates many smaller locales. This, in a nation with more than 1 billion people and nearly 3 million square kilometres of land.

The logistics are complex, inasmuch as Marico produces 125 SKUs at its six factories and 15 contract manufacturers, and stores and distributes products from 32 warehouses and sells through 1,000 independent distributors who carry Marico brands exclusively. These distributors provide Marico products to 1.6 million domestic retail outlets.

Beginning in 1995, Marico increased its effort to create new brands and reduce its reliance on its three market leaders (Parachute coconut oil and the Saffola and Sweekar brands of refined edible oil), mainly because of the growing competition from well-capitalized international rivals such as ConAgra Foods and Unilever.

Today the company's new brands are accounting for more and more of company revenues. In fiscal 2003 (ending 31 March 2003), the five new products introduced since 2000 produced 17 per cent of sales, in comparison with 11 per cent in 2002. However, more brands and more products incur costs. Marico's advertising expenditures climbed steadily. The distribution network became more costly and complex, exposing many process inefficiencies. Also, because India's consumer goods producers rely largely on their own "primary data"—that is, their sales to distributors—accurate forecasting and planning for more products became extremely difficult.

The solutions? Clearly, forecast accuracy and the delivery performance of the distribution network had to improve if Marico's products were to remain widely available in the market and sustain the associated positive brand awareness that had become Marico's major strength.

Managers pinpointed initiatives that would be heavily supported and occur in two stages: improvements in major supply chain planning and management and the transformation of distributor relationships into win–win partnerships:

- *Stage 1. Supply chain planning and management.* To lower inventory and supply chain operating costs, Marico had to strengthen the internal supply chain foundation by revamping its supply chain processes—from planning to fulfilment—and providing technological support in the form of highly integrated application systems. Because Marico operated with stand-alone business applications, the technology requirements included not only supply chain planning and management systems but also an integrated ERP system. This, managers decided, would be implemented across the company in a "big bang" rollout in 2001. And it would be done in 9 months.
- *Stage 2. Distributor partnerships and VMI.* To help resolve the forecasting problems and eliminate major inventory and stockout problems throughout the supply chain, Marico needed to create a partner relationship with its distributors. In this effort, the larger distributors would at least be able to provide timely sales and inventory information to Marico and at the same time access Marico's systems for pending orders, stocks-in-transit and other information. Critical to this effort was VMI for major distributors, in which Marico would manage distributor inventory by replenishing stocks on the basis of the distributors' online input of sales to retailers. Implementation would begin in 2002.

For stage 1, after a careful analysis of alternatives, Marico selected SAP's R/3 ERP system, SAP APO, a key component of mySAP SCM, and the mySAP Business Intelligence solution to enable the reengineering of its associated planning and execution processes.

In 2001, Marico completed the implementation of these systems, laying the foundation for the VMI implementation, as well as other major efforts such as electronic procurement.

## Business

Marico Industries Ltd was actually incorporated in 1988 as a sales and marketing spin-off from Bombay Oil Industries. Marico began operations two years later, when it acquired Bombay's consumer products division and two well-established brands: Parachute coconut oil and Saffola safflower oil. These two brands, the most popular in their categories in India, were to remain Marico's flagship lines, the foundation for its future in nature care and health care:

- Nature care encompasses, as Marico advertises, "brands that enhance the appeal and nourishment of hair and skin through distinctive products, largely based on the goodness of coconut and other natural substances". This product line now includes a variety of hair oils and extensions under the Parachute, Oil of Malabar and Hair & Care brands, in addition to a cold-water fabric care product, Revive. In fiscal 2003, Marico added to this stable with the acquisition of Mediker hair-lice shampoo from Procter & Gamble and the purchase of a controlling interest in the US-based Sundari LLC and its line of Ayurvedic skin care products.
- Health care encompasses "branded products needed for healthy living, drawn from agriculture in natural and processed forms". Under the "good for the heart" Saffola umbrella brand are a variety of refined edible safflower oils and blends with rice bran and corn oil, as well as low-sodium salt and cholesterol-reducing wheat flour with soya flour and oats. The Sweekar brand includes refined sunflower oil, mustard oil, soya oil and groundnut oil, and the Sil brand offers a range of jams, squashes and sauces. In 2003, Marico entered the soya foods sector by acquiring Mealmaker.

Hair oils—which in India are a staple of healthy living—represent a market of more than Rs 13 billion, or nearly US$300 million, annually. This market is divided in various ways. Branded companies, such as Marico, Hindustan Lever (a Unilever company) and Dabur India Ltd, account for more than one-third of this market, and the rest is shared among the unorganized regional and local brands and innumerable imitators whose names are often alarmingly close to the word *Parachute*. This imitation occurs for good reason: two-thirds of the hair oil market belongs to coconut oil products, and Parachute has for several years maintained more than a 50 per cent share of this segment.

Although the average Indian consumer has become more aware of the value of consistently high-quality products, price still rules. Also, although the urban trendsetters like quality at a good price, they tend to flock to the latest product from abroad. Thus, differentiation at a reasonable premium (always less than what foreign companies charge) is important, which has led Marico and other companies to offer value-added oils emphasizing health and purity. Witness today's Parachute extensions: Parachute Lite, Parachute Lite with Perfume, Parachute Active Herbs and Parachute Nutra Sheen Cream and Liquid.

Edible oils have many of the same market issues. The majority is sold in loose and unbranded form, but packaged edible oils are gradually capturing a greater share because of the quality and freshness issues. India is one of the largest producers and consumers of edible oils in the world, and the taste preferences vary by region, which is, for example, why the Sweekar brand offers mustard, soya, sunflower and other refined oils.

As in the United States and other nations, the issue of which edible oils are best for health is major in India. Through its advertising and education campaigns, Marico has made the Saffola brand and Sweekar products generally synonymous with the concept of a healthy heart.

Many other factors affect Marico in its markets:

- Nature's sometimes severe impact on crops and the fluctuation in prices, such as copra for coconut oil and safflower for Saffola; both of these crops have suffered in recent years, and in Saffola's case, Marico has compensated for shortages with the introduction of blends of safflower with other oils.
- The Indian government's gradual relaxation of import regulations, albeit with high tariffs, for edible and other oils and the resulting entry of global giants such as ConAgra and other competitors have naturally targeted the largest markets and the brands with the largest shares, such as Marico's Parachute and Saffola.
- The sheer size of the subcontinent, nearly three million square kilometres, and the enormous complexity of the distribution network needed, particularly for rural areas.
- The fact that most of the 1.6 million retailers that handle Marico's products are tiny grocery stores; organized stores—that is, retail chains—represent about 2 per cent of the stores in India, and hence point-of-sale information is not readily available; the organized retailers are not expected to represent 10 per cent of stores in India before 2010.

What makes life somewhat simpler for Marico is that it procures relatively few commodity raw materials, such as vegetable oils and safflower seeds, and it has strong control of its sourcing. The company has no major manufacturing capacity constraints and little sales seasonality is associated with its products. Unlike its American consumer goods counterparts, Marico has minimized artificially induced demand surges by avoiding the use of trade promotions, thus avoiding contractual disagreements, endless paperwork and questionable and unprovable value.

Although Marico may not be able to obtain off-take sales data (retailer sales information) from retailers directly, it does have good sources, the best of which are its own innumerable consumer focus groups and field tests held all over India. It also has the feedback from an ambitious, well-financed advertising program.

Since Marico's inception, its key strength, as noted, has been its ability to build brands and give customers greater value at affordable costs. In its first year of operations, Marico posted Rs 105.8 million (US$2.3 million) in revenues, all from Parachute and Saffola. Parachute had a 50 per cent share of the coconut hair oil market.

In fiscal 1996, with the strategy of increasing brands and extensions just beginning, revenues were Rs 3.5 billion (US$74 million), mostly from Parachute (which had a market share of more than 50 per cent at this point), Saffola and Sweekar.

In 1999, revenues had grown to Rs 5.5 billion (US$116 million), garnered from six brands but still highly dependent on its three leading brands. By 2003, revenues had grown to Rs 7.75 billion (US$169 million), and Marico had nine brands, most occupying first or second position in their categories. Five new products announced since 2000 were contributing 17 per cent of revenues. Parachute and its extensions still held more than 50 per cent of the coconut hair oil market.

At this point, Marico had grown to 1,000 employees, and 125 SKUs. Research and development staffs were working hard creating the value-added varieties of its major brands in ways that would keep the quality high and the costs and retail prices low. Advertising expenditures were climbing. Marico was acting as quickly as it could to grow its business and fend off the international, national, regional and local competition. And it was generally successful.

But the company had long since outgrown its infrastructure. Its core sources of competitive advantage—branding, distribution, cost management and innovation—had fallen out of alignment. Marico's branding and product innovation had become far more efficient and effective than its planning and management of the supply chain. Forecast accuracy was at 70 per cent. Distributors were suffering stock-outs and loss of sales on 30 per cent of Marico SKUs. At the same time, excess inventory at Marico and its channels was growing. The costs of errors in shipments to remote depots were mounting.

The supply chain was in trouble and its poor performance was reducing Marico's cash flow and affecting the strong brand image the company had worked so hard to maintain.

## Supply Chain Challenges: The Vicious Cycle

Like all companies in the fast-moving consumer goods industry, Marico managers fully understand that a well-functioning supply chain provides a huge competitive advantage in India. The logistics involved in dealing with the fragmented nature of India's retail trade and the geographic spread of the market are extremely complex and difficult.

First, as noted, the retail trade for Marico consists of 1.6 million retailers, of which fewer than 2 per cent represent organized retailers in India. Indeed, more than 95 per cent of the retailers are *kiranas* (grocery stores), each occupying less than 300 square metres.

Part of Marico's business strategy is to expand continuously into ever smaller locales until its brands are available to most Indian households. Currently, Marico's distribution network covers every Indian community with a population of 20,000 or more, and the plan is to penetrate more of the rural areas, where 70 per cent of India's people live. Currently, its rural sales and distribution network ranks among the top three in the industry and contributes 24 per cent to the company's sales (see Figure 1 for the different distribution networks used for urban and rural markets).

To reach all areas of the nation, the company's products, bought by 18 million Indian households monthly, are sold to approximately 1,000 distributors. These intermediaries in turn store, sell and deliver Marico products directly to about 1.6 million retailers or indirectly through 2,500 stockists.

These goods, 35 million consumer packs per month, flow into the distribution network from Marico's own physical supply chain, consisting of seven factories 15 contract manufacturers, one redistribution centre to manage logistics activities and 31 depots. (All the fast-moving SKUs are

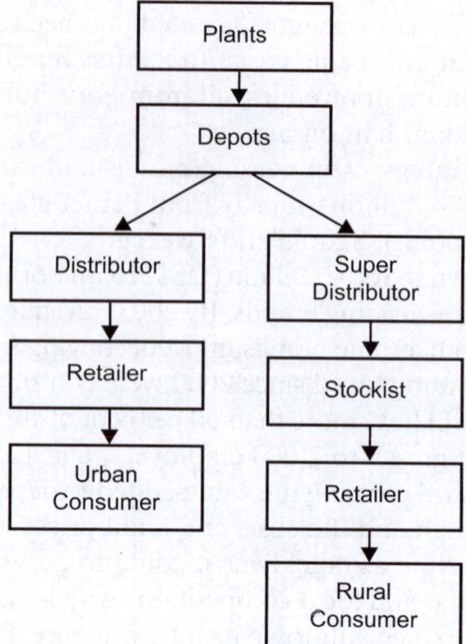


**Figure 1**

Marico supply chain.

shipped directly from the factories to depots, whereas slow-moving SKUs are shipped first to the redistribution centre and subsequently to depots.)

All these elements pose a logistical challenge for even the largest of manufacturers. Added to this mix is Marico's business strategy of growth through new brands and product lines. This entails more sales and markets to track, more forecasts to make, more production to plan, more SKUs to track and more pallets and truckloads to configure and route. The SKU/distribution point combinations run into millions.

With three major brands, some shortcomings in forecasting, planning and supply chain operations can be manageable. When the number increases to nine and the plan is for even more, as is Marico's strategy, critical shortcomings can make the supply chain extremely unstable. This is the position in which Marico found itself in the late 1990s when its forecasts and sales targets became increasingly inaccurate and its costly distribution errors multiplied. (See Figure 2 for an overview of the sequential supply chain transactions that are among the source of these issues). A vicious cycle of ever poorer supply chain performance had begun.

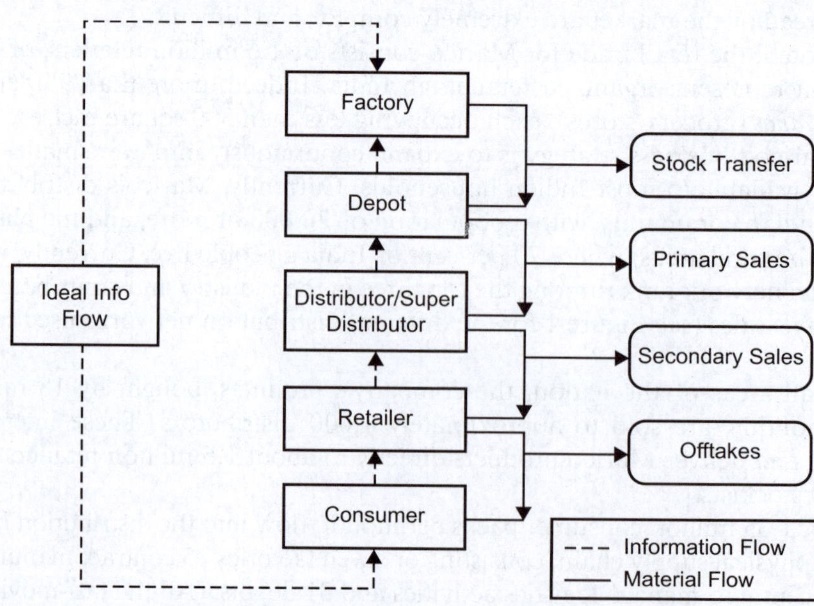


**Figure 2**

Marico supply chain transactions.

## Forecasting and Planning

Several issues contributed to Marico's forecasting and planning problems, primarily poor visibility into internal operations and poor visibility into the marketplace.

### Internal Operations

Poor visibility into internal operations resulted largely from a lack of integration among its transaction systems. For the first few years after its founding, Marico ran its operations largely with paper-based manual systems. In 1995, the company began developing stand-alone application programs for specific processes in several departments. Because the systems were not integrated, departments were often working with conflicting numbers, which resulted in serious coordination problems that affected supply chain planning and execution. The rationalization and consolidation of data for monthly financial statements were of little use for day-to-day supply chain planning.

This situation was aggravated by the fact that Marico had built a planning tool based on the Excel spreadsheet, which has proved inadequate for the needs of an increasingly complex and growing enterprise. Furthermore, only one planner was qualified to run it.

By the time all the data were gathered from sales and marketing, turned by the lone planner into an initial indicative plan, reviewed by the production department and turned into a final production plan, 30 days had passed. If market realities changed during the process, it was nearly impossible to change the production plan. As a result, the sales department often circumvented the system, using their personal relationships to influence actual production and distribution decisions. This in turn compromised the entire integrity of the system and processes in place, leading to further supply chain problems.

### Marketplace Visibility

An equally large obstacle was suboptimal visibility into the marketplace. Traditionally, consumer goods firms in India have relied on primary data, their own sales to distributors, for forecasting and planning. This can severely skew sales. Current off-take is ideal for a fast-moving consumer goods manufacturer, but this is not possible to obtain when most retailers are very small grocery stores, and national consumer research firms produce sales statistics 60–90 days after the event. The next best option is distributor sales to retailers, also not generally available to producers at the time they occur (see Figure 2).

This constraint manifested itself as severe skewing of sales at different periods. Lacking good visibility into the supply chain, Marico operated with a "push" method; that is, supply chain planning was driven by the sales force and the demand they observed within their territories. The company prepared its plans on the basis of its own sales data and sales input, preparing quarterly targets to which sales had to adhere strictly. Hence, when distributor orders fell short in the first 20 days of the month, inventory was often dumped on distributors in the last 10 days. As a result, Marico's distribution levels averaged 15 and 32 per cent for the first and second 10-day periods, respectively, and a hefty 53 per cent for the final 10 days. Marico was passing the production and inventory problems—created by poor forecasts—to its distributors.

Sales across months used to vary significantly because of schemes offered at quarter end to handle quarterly targets. Peak monthly sale to minimum monthly sale ratio used to be 3:1. Adding to this situation was lack of synchronization between manufacturing and distribution; that is, they used different bucketed time horizons for planning: two weeks for production and one week for distribution.

As a result of these shortcomings not only were the distributors unhappy, but there were also high stocks in the channel during certain periods and low service levels at other times.

This in turn affected the freshness of stocks. Certain Marico products have short shelf lives, so products that stay in the chain beyond their expiration dates become obsolete, which results in a loss both financially and in terms of customer satisfaction. (In India, it is mandatory for packaged goods companies to print manufacturing dates on the product.)

## Distribution

Within a distribution network, poor visibility adds other elements to the vicious cycle. For instance, to minimize transportation costs, Marico has always shipped goods in full truckloads. To do this, the distribution group must properly configure the shipments and the routes to meet the demands by the depots scattered across the country.

In Marico's case, its distribution group had to deal with two major obstacles: poor visibility into the depot stocks of the growing numbers of SKUs, and absence of prioritization rules that could help dispatchers make optimal choices in configuring full truckloads.

As a result, they tended to make almost random decisions. Lacking depot stock data, they could not accurately take the depot space constraints into account. The results were costly. When shipments to a depot exceeded the facility's capacity, the managers there would be forced to hire temporary spaces and often had to pay truck demurrages as well. Faulty shipments might also result in excess inventory for some of their SKUs and in stock-outs in others. Depots that did not receive the right shipments in time, of course, would suffer stock-outs. In any case, the maldistribution of goods resulted in a higher delivery cost than necessary. Equally costly was the erosion of sales, customer satisfaction and the distributors' confidence.

Furthermore, Marico found that sales people spent significant time searching for stocks rather than selling and brand-building. Their preoccupation with emergencies in particular, hindered the progress of the small brands, and hence Marico's plan to decrease its dependence on the big three brands. Marico did attempt to build a planning system, but it fell short of the company's intensifying needs.

> The PC-supported legacy system, which was specially developed for Marico through the use of relational database libraries, was struggling to meet increased logistics requirements. We found our sales people were spending significant time in searching for stocks rather than doing the actual job, which is selling and merchandising and following competitor schemes. We realize that we need a reliable and responsive supply chain in place to manage our operations.
>
> —Pradip Mansukhani, CEO – Sales

## Breaking the Vicious Cycle

As mentioned, the company had a planning cycle of 30 days, which hampered its abilities to respond to changes in demand within the planning period and to adjust to the fact that manufacturing and distribution had different bucketed time horizons for planning.

As a result of poor forecasting and planning, distribution levels were uneven during the course of each month, and distributors were not happy with the excess inventory forced on them in the last part of the month.

The mismatch of supply and demand resulted in a mix of inventory build-ups, expired products and stock-outs at Marico and its distributors, all of which ultimately affected the consumer's perception of Marico's brands.

Total delivered costs were increased as a result of storage capacity constraints and the requirement to initiate corrective actions such as inter-warehouse stock transfers, temporary renting of additional storage space and truck demurrage.

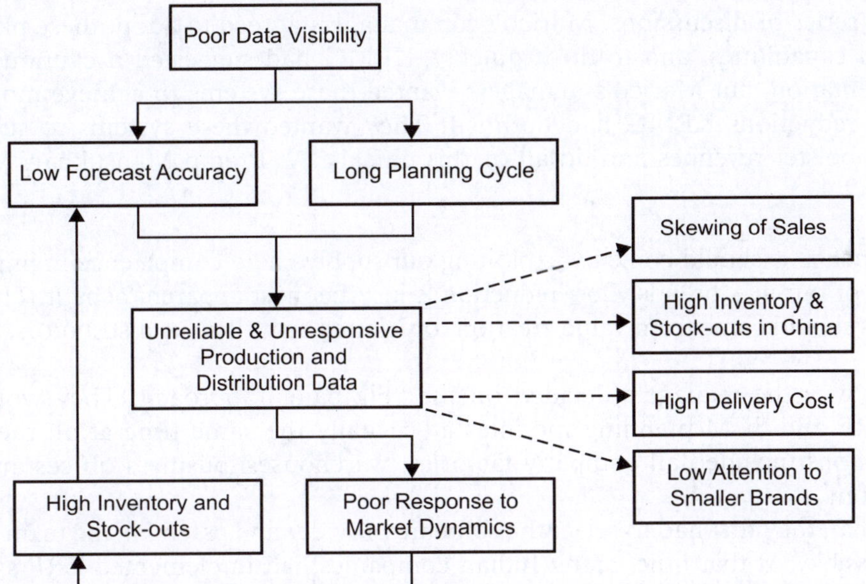


**Figure 3**

Vicious cycle of poor supply chain performance.

Planning process problems were compounded by spreadsheet-based planning methods and multiple, non-integrated transaction systems that inhibited widespread visibility into essential data.

As Figure 3 shows, the "vicious cycle of poor supply chain performance" is an alarming scenario. Marico managers realized the simple facts. To support its strategy of product innovation and affordability, driven by consumer need, the company needed to have a best-in-class operation, effective and efficient. That required superior forecasting accuracy, dynamic planning processes that matched supply and demand, and uniform distribution levels.

Through these means, inventory carrying costs and total supply chain costs would be reduced, freeing cash flow to reinvest in growth-generating activities. Better planning and distribution processes would result in stock-out reductions and accurate, on-time deliveries.

Better and faster sales information was critical to Marico's understanding of retailer and consumer trends. Hence, obtaining secondary data from distributors—their sales to retailers—was critical. In addition to implementing systems, Marico would have to transform relationships and communication with major distributors.

To achieve all its goals, Marico needed a buy-in throughout the enterprise and its supply chain partners, and it needed the systems and tools to support redesigned processes and provide the data visibility so critically needed.

# Implementation

## *Systems Analysis*

Although the benefits of information visibility and supply chain planning were fairly evident to Marico, managers selected KPMG Consulting to carry out a thorough cost–benefit analysis and prepare a blueprint for a detailed plan of action.

KPMG's report stressed that an ERP implementation was vital for the visibility and efficiency of its operations in general. But in view of the complexities of the distribution system and Marico's need to significantly improve its supply chain performance, the consultant urged investment in sophisticated planning tools supported by SCM software.

After a series of discussions, Marico's top managers agreed to adopt these planning and operational capabilities, and to do it quickly. KPMG had suggested a cautious approach in implementation, but Marico's managers wanted these systems to achieve more than the many cost reductions KPMG had outlined. They wanted these systems to support their expansion, bolster revenues and do all of this quickly. As Pradip Mansukhani would later emphasize:

> The benefits ... should come by exploiting our supply chain competence in improving growth of our new brands. Cost reduction is just the most apparent benefit. The main benefits should come from value creation for Marico as well as its distributors.

This is why the managers decided on the "big bang" approach: They would rapidly roll out ERP and SCM planning modules at virtually the same time at all the locations. These locations included all company factories, warehouses, business offices and contract manufacturers.

To do that, they first had to select the software provider and assemble the team that would make it possible. At that time, many Indian companies had implemented ERP systems, but few had implemented SCM software. With the help of KPMG, Marico evaluated several SCM and ERP solutions. These included SAP's R/3 ERP system, mySAP SCM and several other solutions.

The company eventually singled out SAP, the solution being a combination of the following:

- SAP R/3 integrated business systems, including finance, cost accounting, materials management, production planning, quality management, and sales and distribution
- A key component of mySAP SCM, SAP APO, including its demand forecasting and planning, supply network planning (SNP), deployment and supply chain cockpit modules
- mySAP Business Intelligence for supply chain performance management activities, a system that provides data warehousing functionality, business intelligence tools and analytics, best-practice models and administrative resources

> We realized that effective integration of an SCM tool with ERP systems would be a key requirement for overall project success. Among all the options we had looked at, we felt SAP had the best integration capabilities. We were also impressed by SAP's rich functionality, the scalability of its software, and its excellent support services.
>
> —Vinod Kamat, Project Leader

Kamat noted that while deciding on the scope of activities for SAP APO, the company wanted to focus on and use these powerful tools only in the areas in which SAP APO would provide significant benefits. Managers concluded that sourcing and manufacturing were not candidates, being straightforward and relatively simple, because Marico procured only a few commodity raw materials (e.g., vegetable oils, safflower seeds) and had no major manufacturing capacity constraints. Furthermore, the company had no sales seasonality associated with its products, and it minimized artificially induced demand surges by avoiding the use of promotions.

The supply chain network clearly mandated use of SAP APO for demand forecasting and supply chain network planning. This would essentially improve business processes that addressed internal collaborative forecasting between its manufacturing sites and warehouses. It would require what Marico was looking for: clearly defined responsibilities—assigned and accountable ownership—to ensure that distribution from its warehouses to distributors consistently met service level and inventory objectives.

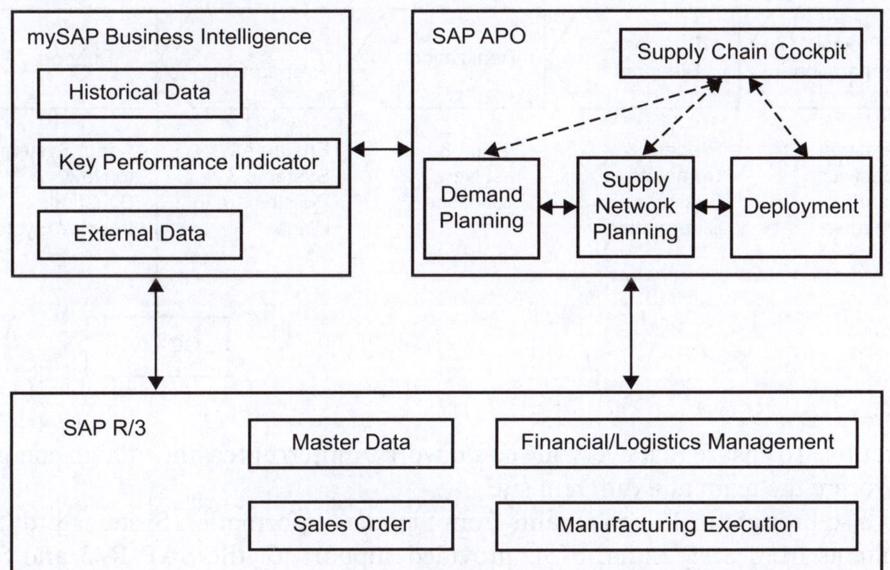


**Figure 4**

Marico supply chain management architecture.

The scope of the SAP R/3 ERP implementation—providing integration of processes and visibility into internal operations and their data—covered finance, cost accounting, materials management, production planning, quality management, and sales and distribution. The information architecture of the proposed solution is depicted in Figure 4.

## Project Planning

As noted, Marico's top managers decided to treat the SAP R/3 and SAP APO implementations as a "big bet, big bang" project. In principle, the managers had decided that they would work only on a few large initiatives at a time, supporting them fully with all the resources needed and complete organizational support. This was the philosophy they applied to brand development and innovation. The "big bang", the rollout to all offices, plants and depots, had to occur within 9 months.

To oversee this project, the company formed a high-power steering committee headed by the Chief Financial Officer. The steering committee consisted of all the department heads who were affected by implementation of the SAP project.

Managers determined that even though the project would involve substantial information technology investment, it would be driven by business perspectives and by business managers. To manage the entire initiative, they selected Vinod Kamat because, as a senior manager, he had been involved with various parts of the supply chain in the organization and, equally important, he had excellent execution skills.

> When I accepted responsibility for the project, I knew that we had all the resources at our disposal and that we would have complete freedom in managing the project. But it also meant that we would have no escape buttons, and the company would expect us to complete the project on time and achieve promised business results.
>
> —Vinod Kamat, Project Leader

To have the project under complete control at all times, Marico formed an 18-member team that represented all relevant functions, including sales, manufacturing, finance and logistics. This team was to work full time on the project, predominantly on the very extensive SAP R/3

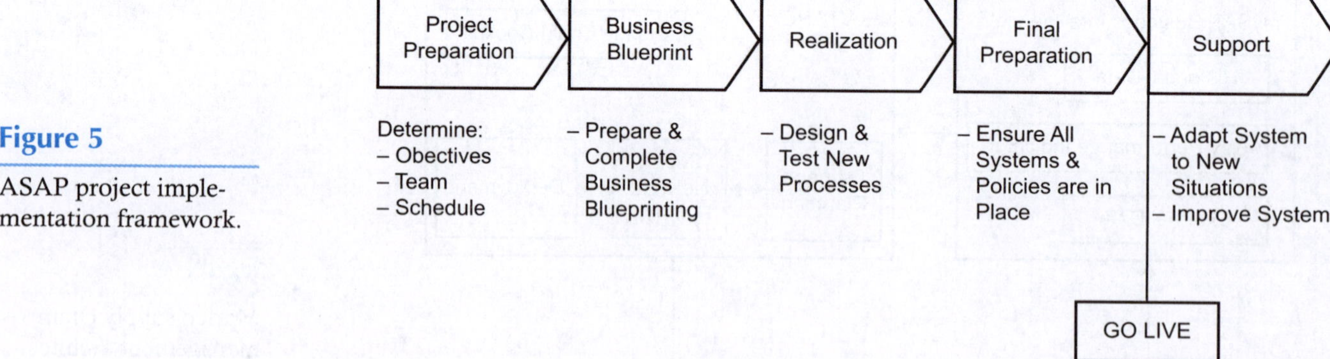


**Figure 5**

ASAP project implementation framework.

implementation. To ensure that everyone could work uninterrupted and at high energy, Marico decided to locate the team at a different site.

Marico also brought in 12 consultants from Siemens Information Systems Ltd (SISL) and four consultants from SAP India. SISL provided support for the SAP R/3 and SAP APO implementation. Since Marico was the first APO project in India, SAP itself was involved in all critical phases.

To implement the project, Marico adopted the basic framework of the Accelerated SAP (ASAP) implementation methodology. ASAP is SAP's comprehensive package for supporting the planning and implementation of SAP solutions. The conceptual roadmap of the implementation, shown in Figure 5, consists of five stages: project preparation, business blueprint, realization, final preparation and support after the go-live.

The entire project team, including SISL and SAP consultants, met every Saturday to discuss all issues thoroughly and ensure that they were resolved by the end of the meeting. In turn, each month the project team reported the project's progress to the steering council. The steering council had established specific milestones, and the project team was expected to meet these milestones both on time and within the project scope.

## Project Execution

Marico was aware that implementation of ERP and SCM software would involve substantial restructuring of processes and buy-in from all the functional managers who would be affected. To achieve this objective, Marico appointed these managers as process owners, making them fully responsible for the revisions of their respective processes. They had to sign off on the revisions at the blueprint stage. Furthermore, to ensure that each manager provided the necessary support to the project, top managers made their work on these initiatives a key measure in their performance appraisals.

To ensure that the project was completed in time and successfully, the team performed a risk analysis, using methodology provided by ASAP. This included a survey of employees about potential obstacles to the success of the new systems. They were asked to rate the risk associated with the following dimensions:

- *Credibility risk.* credibility of the project and the team members
- *Organization risk.* whether the organization would derive benefits
- *Individual risk.* whether the individual was provided the necessary training and felt comfortable with the new processes

This survey was carried out twice: during the pre-implementation phase and during the post-implementation phase. After the first survey, the project team realized that certain departments were seriously concerned about organization and individual risks.

As a result, the project team decided to increase the training component significantly; they ultimately provided 700 person-days of training to 60 power users, several times the original plan. According to the post-implementation risk survey, thorough training increased employee comfort levels with the process changes, improving the individual risk ratings. Furthermore, the project team was able to communicate clearly the benefits of the project, thereby minimizing the perception of organization risk and improving the credibility of the team.

For the purpose of training, users were divided into two categories: ordinary users and power users (the people who would use the system extensively and required more training). The company also adopted the train-the-trainer approach, training first the power users, who in turn trained the ordinary users.

All these measures resulted in very smooth implementations. Implementation of SAP R/3 started in June 2000 and went live as per plan in April 2001. Implementation of the demand planning and SNP capabilities of the SAP APO—along with the mySAP Business Intelligence system—began in August 2000 and went live one month after SAP R/3, May 2001. The SAP APO could not be launched in April along with SAP R/3 because the company required at least one month's data to assess the impact.

In July 2002, with the supply chain foundation in place, Marico began bringing its major distributors online for entry of secondary sales data into the ERP and SAP APO systems and for its VMI program, as discussed later.

## *Strategy-driven Metrics*

During the project implementation, the project team devised metrics to help Marico monitor the performance in the post-implementation phase. After several brainstorming meetings, the team decided that they had to design a small set of metrics that were both simple enough for users to understand and comprehensive enough to capture the supply chain performance data that would help Marico track the progress of the implementation.

The metrics, the team emphasized, had to be viewed in combination. Although individual improvements might have an impact, significant improvements were needed in all areas measured to produce the major supply chain and financial results that Marico expected.

Keeping in mind that managers had expected not only to cut costs but also to bolster revenues, the project team decided to use two types of metrics: pure metric and derived metric (estimates). The following five measures were identified as the main measures of supply chain performance:

- Pure metric
  - Distributor stock-out percentage
  - Excess stocks
  - Forecast accuracy
- Derived metric
  - Estimated secondary loss of sales
  - Estimated primary loss of sales

Apart from these five measures, the project team decided to track total supply chain cost and the freshness index separately; that is, they were not included in the main performance measure. Supply chain cost essentially comprises the costs of maldistribution, which includes truck demurrage, transport involved in inter-warehouse stock transfers and temporary renting of additional storage spaces. The freshness index was expected to capture information about old stocks in the supply chain system.

The mySAP Business Intelligence system was configured so that performance metrics could be obtained on a real-time basis, and users were provided the necessary views to enable them to perform the analysis needed to identify causes of specific performance problems.

## Outcome: The Virtuous Cycle

In the first year of implementation, beginning April 2001, Marico achieved significant operational improvements: reduced planning cycle time, improved forecasting accuracy and improved delivery reliability. In the second year, the improvements continued, aided by the VMI initiative that began in 2002, putting Marico ahead of return-on-investment expectations for the initiatives.

> Marico had invested in the SAP suite of R/3, APO, and Business Intelligence in order to reap business benefits; the investment proposal envisaged that that the project would pay for itself within three or four years. The company has, however, been able to stabilize the suite and realize benefits within a couple of years. Benefits have accrued primarily in supply chain areas through systemic and sustainable improvements: reduction in working capital, reduction of sales lost because of bottlenecks and inaccurate forecasting and reduction in losses resulting from poor controls and lack of data visibility. In addition, the company has realized gains from an overall integrated data processing platform and the attendant visibility and integrity of data.
>
> —Milind Sarwate, Chief Financial Officer

### *Operational Improvements*

The implementation did indeed produce quick results. Within the first year, forecast accuracy had improved from 70 per cent to almost 80 per cent, and the levels of shipment activity through each third of the month had become more even (25, 32 and 43 per cent, respectively). Variation in sales across months came down significantly. Peak mothly sale to minimum monthly sale

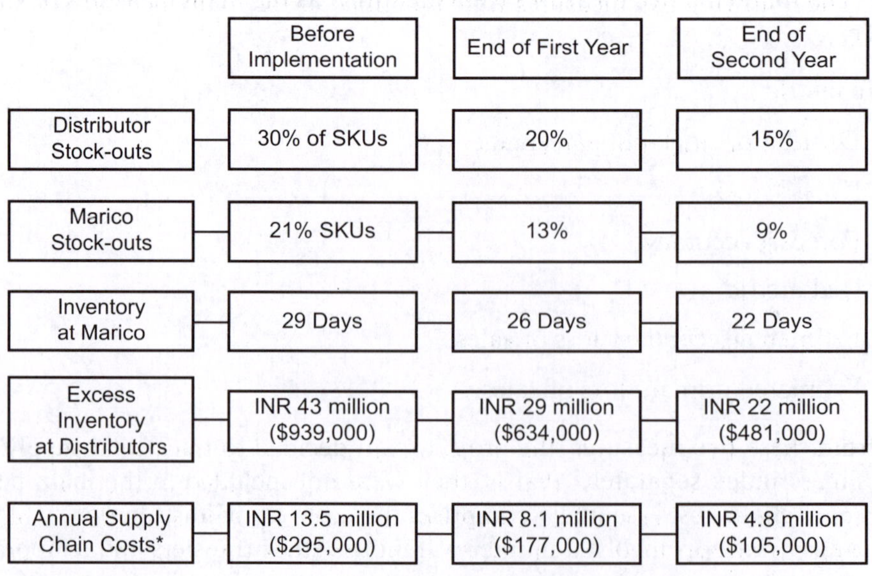


**Figure 6**

Supply chain performance improvements.

ratio which used to be 3:1 came down to 1.3:1. The planning cycle time was reduced from 30 to 15 days, and enhanced reporting facilitated management decision making.

In the second year, forecasting continued to improve, and the supply chain group hopes to achieve an forecast accuracy of 90 per cent at the brand and region levels in the 2004–2005 period. The planning cycle time in the second year dropped again, to a mere 10 days from the initial indicative plan to the final production plan.

The annual performance improvements (based on the key indicators) over two years of implementation have been benchmarked against pre-implementation data, as shown in Figure 6.

These outcomes led to reduced internal and distributor inventory, fewer stock-outs, fewer losses of sales and reduced supply chain exception-handling costs.

The vicious cycle was transformed. The stock-outs associated with distributor sales to retailers decreased by one-third in the first year of implementation, resulting in a reduction in the loss of sales arising out of such stock-outs by 38 per cent. In the second year, an additional 17 per cent reduction in stock-outs (in comparison with pre-implementation performance) resulted in a virtually equal reduction (19 per cent) in lost sales. In short, after two years of operating with its new systems, Marico's distributor stock-outs were cut in half, and losses of sales were reduced by more than half.

Since forecasting had improved and the planning process was reduced to become more responsive to change, the sales department no longer had to force inventory onto distributors in order to meet sales targets. Hence, excess inventory (above the norm) was reduced by 49 per cent after two years.

At the same time, Marico's own average total inventory (raw material plus work in process plus finished goods inventory) was reduced by one-fourth by the end of the second year, from 29 to 22 days.

What happened in the logistics network? The depot managers' problems began to disappear. The incidence of wrong shipments and their attendant trucking and space costs declined. The stock-outs at the depot when shipments did not arrive—and the rush to correct this—declined. In total, Marico reduced the costs associated with supply chain maldistribution by nearly two-thirds; that is, 40 per cent in the first year and an additional 24 per cent in the second year.

## Demand and Supply Planning

How these improvements occurred is another matter. Some of the organizational and cultural issues involved and how process improvements were achieved and confirmed have been described. Two of the key technologies that heavily contributed to these gains were the demand planner and the supply network planner of SAP APO.

### Demand Planning

Using the demand planning module, Marico has put a consensus planning process in place. This process starts in the last week of the month with regional sales managers preparing brand-level sales plans for the coming month. On the basis of preliminary estimates of the primary and secondary sales data of the month, the regional managers prepare the indicative sales plan for the coming period.

After aggregating data received from all regions, the supply chain planning group converts the sales plan into a demand plan by working with the pack-mix heuristic available in SAP APO. On the basis of the actual pack-mix sales of the previous three months, SAP APO works out pack-mix allocation factors and prepares a detailed demand plan at the SKU level.

At this stage, SAP APO checks the production capacity and raw material availability and provides feedback on the feasibility of the plan. This is completed by the beginning of the first week of the month for which the forecasting exercise is being performed. Also, final sales figures, at both the primary and secondary levels, are available for the region; therefore, if necessary, the regional sales team makes minor modifications and releases the final demand plan to the supply chain group at the head office. Before releasing the final plan, the regional sales group also checks the pack-mix allocation to ensure that it reflects actual current trends in the marketplace.

Potential supply problems are highlighted in advance so that the sales department can work out appropriate strategies to handle the situation. This procedure has eliminated any incentive for unorthodox actions on the part of sales department at the time of demand planning. Furthermore, consensus planning ensures that everyone involved agrees with and commits to the plan.

## Supply Network Planning

With the help of the SNP module in SAP APO, Marico has built and put in place reliable, responsive production and distribution planning processes. It has built plant and depot heuristics by using SNP functions to take care of both production- and dispatch-related decisions for the planning period of a month.

For a typical month, to provide a broad feasibility-related feedback to the sales group, the supply chain group at the headquarters first runs unconstrained plant heuristics, using indicative demand plan data. Once the firm demand plan is in place, the supply chain group runs a constrained plant heuristic in SNP and, on the basis of the results, a firm production plan is prepared for factories and contract manufacturing plants. A depot heuristic to create daily dispatch plans is also run.

In depot heuristics, a truck builder module ensures that shipments are sent in full truckloads and that depot inventories simultaneously remain within prescribed inventory norms. The depot heuristic prepares plans in blocks of 10 days in order to manage optimal trade-offs between transportation costs and inventory carrying costs. At any point, the truck builder module has to coordinate multiple SKUs and large numbers of depots.

The supply chain group has built prioritization rules that assign the relative priority of depots and SKUs in the truck builder module. Because actual primary sales are likely to vary from the forecast, depot heuristics are run twice a month, improving Marico's ability to respond more quickly to changes. To further improve responsiveness, Marico plans to run depot heuristics three times a month.

A summary of the virtuous cycle of improved supply chain performance is presented in Figure 7.

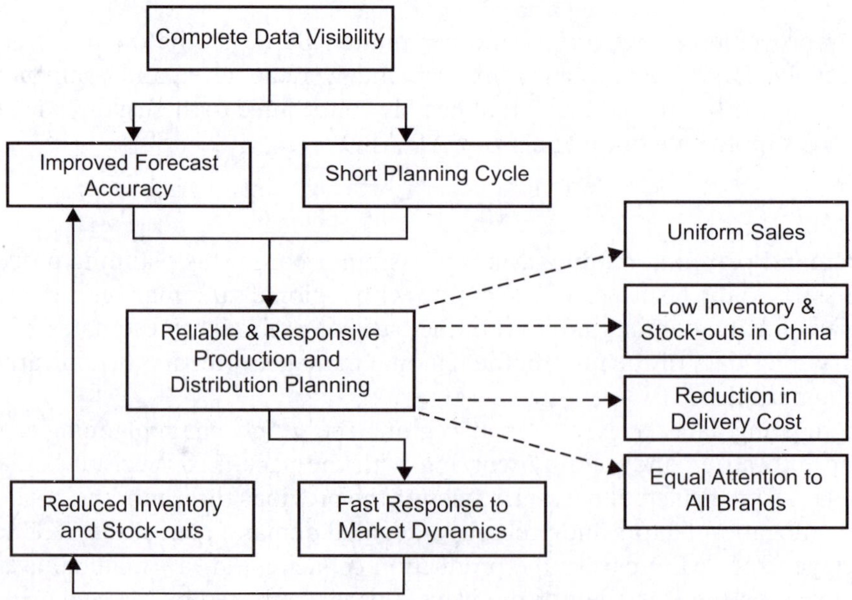


**Figure 7**

Virtuous cycle of improved supply chain performance.

## VMI Implementation

Marico expected short- and long-term positive results for the company from the SCM and ERP implementations in terms of both revenues and profits. But managers also expected a short-term reduction in sales when its improved forecasting and planning reduced stocks at its distributors:

> A reliable and responsible supply chain would result in lower stocks at distributors. Because the company had all along desired to work with lower stocks, we knew that this would temporarily result in lower reported sales. For a company watched closely by the analyst community, this is not an easy decision, but our managing director told us to go ahead. We decided to take the risk and absorb a loss in one quarter's sales so that we could correct the dysfunctions in the system and help distributors reduce their stocks.
>
> —Pradip Mansukhani, CEO – Sales

The change in Marico's relationship with its major distributors went well beyond a reduction in their stocks. After streamlining internal supply chain processes, the company prepared in 2002 for the next logical step by implementing VMI. This would mean that, rather than reacting to distributor orders, Marico would monitor and manage distributor inventory by replenishing stocks on the basis of secondary sales.

In a VMI environment, the supply chain is driven predominantly by the distributors' sales to retailers rather than Marico's primary sales to distributors. This lessens the "bullwhip" effect caused by the many layers of intermediaries between the consumers and Marico: that is, the further up the supply chain from the consumer, the more distorted the demand picture becomes. With VMI in place at the majority of its major distributors, Marico has effectively reduced one layer of distortion and, as a result, observes lower variability in demand.

In addition to reducing supply chain distortions, the company's goal is to improve the distributors' performance, increasing their returns on inventory and generate higher sales for Marico products. Early on in the process, dealers were apprehensive that VMI would again result in either dumping excess inventory on them or creating stock-out situations with certain popular brands. To their surprise, they found that inventory actually was reduced with the VMI implementation.

> With the supply chain foundation in place, we could improve the reliability and responsiveness of our internal supply chain, which in turn gave our distributors confidence in our VMI implementation. We have integrated VMI with our SAP APO, and all dispatch orders for VMI distributors are generated through SAP APO. We hope to roll out VMI for 330 of our top dealers, which account for 75 per cent of value.
>
> —Ram Iyer, Supply Chain Group Leader

The groundwork for this effort had been laid earlier. In parallel with the supply chain initiative, Marico had developed a distribution automation software package called MIDAS (Marico Industries Distribution Automation Software). By March 2001, Marico had installed MIDAS at all its class "A" distributors (turnover greater than Rs 6 million per year) in the urban areas.

Through MIDAS, Marico received distributor stock and sales data in offline mode by means of floppy transfers. However, to implement VMI, Marico needed real-time information about distributor stocks and sales. To that end, Marico envisaged an Internet-based system (MI-NET) in which the distributors could log in and supply the necessary data online.

With MIDAS in place, what Marico needed for MI-NET was an application that would reside on the distributors' PCs and would automatically transfer the data from MIDAS to Marico's central server each time the distributor logged in.

MI-NET was officially launched on 1 July 2002. The plan was to connect 330 of Marico's class "A" distributors, which together account for nearly 75 per cent of its primary sales. By March 2003, 210 distributors were online, with the rest to be linked by the end of the year.

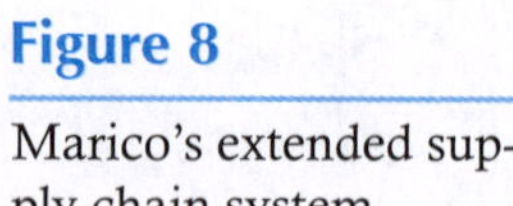

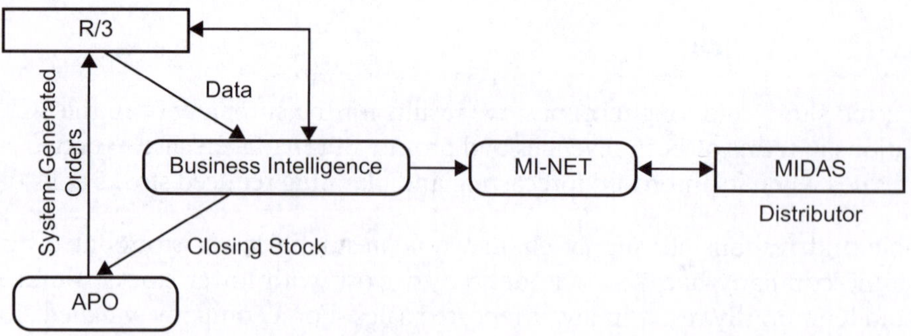


**Figure 8**

Marico's extended supply chain system.

Managers concede that a few of its major distributors feared disintermediation and refused to join MI-NET and the VMI program. Marico severed its ties with them, convinced that partnership with its major distributors was crucial to its own expansion plans and hence to its distributors.

With regard to benefits, MI-NET is mutually efficacious. Through this network, the distributor is directly linked to the SAP R/3 system and has access to such current information as stocks in transit, depot stocks, pending orders, statements of accounts and the various promotion schemes available to distributors. The secondary sales data obtained from MI-NET was expected to help both Marico and its distributors improve their performance through such benefits as fewer losses of sales resulting from stock-outs, lower inventory and better distributor credit management.

The resulting information architecture of Marico's extended supply chain is shown in Figure 8.

## *Sales Benefits of VMI: Productivity, Level Sales*

Sales force productivity has improved significantly as a result of the combination of SAP R/3, mySAP SCM and the MI-NET initiative. Through MI-NET and SAP R/3, field sales personnel have immediate access to current information about Marico's depot stock levels and major distributors, such as order status and distributor performance. This is saving the sales force the hours spent collecting and collating data for sales reports on their territories, freeing them to focus on sales, brand development and distributor relationships.

Providing both sales field force and distributors with information on stock positions at various depots is in fact bolstering trust. Lacking such information in the past, distributors often questioned whether the field salespeople were denying them stock replenishment while supplying the products they needed, to some other distributor.

Another benefit for sales–distributor collaboration is that the dumping of stock to meet sales targets has stopped completely, and the sales skewness in the last month of the quarter has disappeared. That is, sales are more or less even within a quarter. The skewness within a month has not disappeared altogether, but Marico has seen a dramatic reduction.

Because of the complexity of the Indian distribution system, a fast-moving consumer goods manufacturer has to tolerate some skewness at the distributor end. To create an even sales pattern within a month, Marico would have to be able to work directly with retailers, which is not currently feasible.

However, Marico's supply chain monitoring capabilities—and hence, the ability for sales to be more proactive—have been improved through the use of various functionalities in mySAP Business Intelligence. This has helped reduce the artificial sales skewness commonly observed in the pre-mySAP era.

Key in this improvement is Potential Primary, one of the applications Marico developed by using the business information warehouse capabilities of mySAP Business Intelligence. On the basis of the average sales of the previous three months, Potential Primary develops and reports brand and regional sales potential that should be targeted by the sales group. On the basis of cumulative actual sales to date, mySAP Business Intelligence provides daily updates through

Potential Primary allowing everyone to work proactively rather than carry out a post-mortem analysis at the end of each month.

# Outlook

## *Continuous Supply Chain Improvement*

Marico's plan for its new high-technology supply chain network is one of continuous improvement to keep it aligned with the company's planned growth and expansion, as CEO of Sales, Pradip Mansukhani, emphasizes later.

Marico ensured enterprise-wide buy-in for the new processes and systems by making department heads fully responsible for the redesign of processes and by having the staff that would be the primary power users of the systems responsible for the training of other users. The company also created a support group to ensure continuous improvement of all processes. An eight-person team with business management and process skills has been deployed to provide this support at headquarters and in each of the six regions and to help in the distributors' transition to MI-NET and VMI.

> We decided to strengthen supply chain support in all six regional offices. We realized that forecast accuracy improvements and improvements in supply chain reliability and responsiveness are not going to be a single occurrence, but would require continuous improvement in processes over a period of time. Furthermore, we should be in a position to exploit our investments in SAP APO by moving to the VMI implementation once we put our supply chain in order. The supply chain support group was expected to take ownership of new supply chain processes and work on continuous improvement. They would also play an important role in initiatives like VMI.
>
> —Pradip Mansukhani, CEO – Sales

Managers believe that the tools and the people are in place to strengthen the alignment of Marico's supply chain foundation with its business goals. Marico makes its money and resources available, and the results of the "big bet" so far indicate that it has won. In brief, Marico managers have seen proof that they can introduce new brands and value-added extensions without worrying about faulty forecasts, poor planning, poor information, wrong shipments, stock-outs, expired products and inventory-burdened distributors. Now they have turned their full attention back to the business of meeting consumer needs. That means the product laboratory and product acquisitions, the consumer focus groups and field trials, the advertising programs and the sales force. These are the areas on which Marico makes its biggest bets.

> With the VMI implementation, we will be in a position to achieve our dream of becoming a "secondary sales"-driven company, in comparison with the past, in which we were essentially driven by primary sales. We have focused less on cost reduction and more on value creation for Marico as well as its distributors. This does not mean that we have not received benefits from cost reduction, but according to us, cost reduction is just the most apparent benefit. The main benefits of the SAP R/3 and SAP APO implementations should come by exploiting our supply chain competence in improving growth of our new brands. We have managed to reduce our dependence on the big three brands in the past two years. Furthermore, we have introduced new products, and these would not have received supply chain support in the pre-SAP implementation era, in which everybody tended to focus on the three big brands.
>
> —Pradip Mansukhani, CEO – Sales

## Discussion Questions

1. Diagnose the underlying causes of the difficulties that the SAP implementation project was created to solve.
2. How did Marico manage to break the vicious cycle of poor supply chain performance?
3. What conflicts or barriers internal to Marico did the VMI program create? What causes these conflicts? How did Marico handle these issues?
4. Why do you think some of the dealers were reluctant to join VMI programme? How did Marico handle their concerns?
5. Do you believe that other FMCG companies would be able to copy the VMI programme as implemented by Marico? What difficulties are they likely to face and what do they need to do to handle those difficulties?

# Subhiksha: Managing Store Operations (A)*

At 7.30 p.m. on a Saturday evening, Aravindan, President, Karnataka Region, Subhiksha, is getting ready to go home. He has collected the necessary reports that will help him in getting ready for the visit by R. Subramanian (RS as fondly called by everyone in Subhiksha), Managing Director, Subhiksha, on Monday. In the past, a meeting with RS was a gruelling exercise where the bulk of the discussions would take place on the floor of a retail store. He was always amazed at the way RS managed to keep track of every region in the organization, which was growing at breakneck speed. RS somehow seemed to have all the numbers on his finger tips whether it is inventory data, stores data or product availability data. He was looking forward to the meeting because he knew that at the end of day there would be at least two or three fresh ideas that would help improve his operations. A majority of the stores within his region had been operating for more than 18 months and now was the time to focus on getting higher sales from each store in his region.

Once out of his office, on an impulse, Aravindan decided to walk into the Indiranagar store, which was next to his office. It being the first Saturday of the month, the store was crowded and he could see Santosh, the supermarket store manager out in front helping his cashiers. Watching the staff scurrying to and fro to help the customers, Aravindan mused that pharmacy and telecom were relatively simpler to manage. Among the three businesses, the supermarket was the most challenging because of the complexity of the operations arising from the number of SKUs and the typical number of items in a customer basket. As a retailer, Aravindan knew that managing products on the shelf and managing waiting time at the billing counter in the supermarket were at the heart of the store operations at Subhiksha. But as a discount retailer he was also fully conscious of the fact that he had to keep tight control on inventory and operating expenses. So, improving product availability and reducing customer waiting time at the counter with a tighter control on inventory and operating expenses is a never-ending challenge. Of course, this constant pressure to do better than yesterday is what excited Aravindan the most about life at Subhiksha.

---

*Janat Shah, Rahul Patil and Trilochan Sastry prepared this case in 2008 as the basis for class discussion rather than to illustrate either effective or ineffective handling of an administrative situation. Janat Shah and Trilochan Sastry are professors at IIM Bangalore and Rahul Patil is an assistant professor at IIT Mumbai. Data in the case have been disguised. The authors would like to acknowledge the extensive support provided by Mr Mohit Khattar, President, Marketing, Subhiksha. 

## Background

Founded in 1997 by Mr R. Subramanian, an IIT and IIM alumnus, and derived from the Sanskrit word, Subhiksham (giver of all things good), Subhiksha had grown from one store in 1997 to more than 1,000 retail outlets in 2008. It sells FMCG, grocery, pharmacy, mobile products and fruits and vegetables (F&V). It is the largest supermarket and mobile retail chain in India, with presence in 90 cities. It is the only Indian retail chain to feature in the World's top 50 local dynamos list that comprise of 11 Indian firms according to a study conducted by global consultancy firm, Boston Consultancy Group.

In March 1997, Subhiksha opened its first store at Thiruvanmiyur in Chennai with an investment of Rs 0.4–0.5 million and with a clear idea that it would be a part of a larger system. In the first year, it opened 10 stores in Chennai. Subhiksha also started selling medicines at a discount. By 2000, it had expanded to 50 stores in Chennai. In the next two years, it had 120–130 stores across Tamil Nadu. Till 2004, it focused on consolidation in Tamil Nadu. Subhiksha then looked at every part of India that is literate and also a significant consumption market in 2004–2005. It decided to open 420 stores in Gujarat, Delhi, Andhra Pradesh and Karnataka by 2006. Now, it has more than 1,000 stores in India. In its supermarkets, Subhiksha started offering F&V. The logic was that since F&V are bought more frequently by customers, stocking these would increase footfalls to Subhiksha stores. Somewhere in 2005, looking at the tremendous growth in mobile business, Subhiksha started offering mobile telephones at its stores. By 2005, Nokia had become bigger in size compared to HUL, and Subhiksha saw mobiles as a natural extension to its product line. In all its offering it tries to ensure that it provides the highest possible value to customers by offering deepest possible discounts.

In 2008, a typical Subhiksha store has supermarket, pharmacy and telecom store operations, with pharmacy and telecom operating as sub-stores within the main store.

According to Subramanian:

> The success of Subhiksha lies in its Indian retail model. I wanted to do the things the Indian way. Subhiksha targets the middle and lower classes and not the high-end customer. To do so, it operates with an everyday low pricing model and locates several smaller stores to move closer to the customer. At an operational level, it constantly plans to increase supply chain process efficiency to deliver goods at low prices.

## The Indiranagar Supermarket

The Indiranagar supermarket is located on the sixth cross road in Indiranagar 1st stage, Bangalore (Figure 1). It started operations in August 2006. The store is 50 metres from the main street (known as 100 feet road), which is a busy commercial road with departmental stores, supermarkets, restaurants, banks, fast food chains and gas stations.

It operates on a 15-year lease contract that can be renewed. Subhiksha has remodelled the property according to its requirements. It has a 2,000 square feet area, which does not have any fancy fittings, flooring and air conditioning. Out of the 2,000 square feet, 150 square feet each is allocated to telecom and pharmacy, 200 square feet is allocated to backroom store and office and the balance is available for the supermarket.

The pharmacy has sales of Rs 0.3 million per month, whereas the mobile store, operating with wafer thin margins, resulting in high volume, has sales of Rs 6–8 million per month. Grocery and F&V categories have relatively high margins, FMCG and pharmacy work with low margins, and the mobile business works with very low margins.

**Figure 1**

The Indiranagar, Bangalore, Subhiksha store.

The pharmacy business operated by Subhiksha is focused on customers who are on continuous therapy such as cardiac diseases and diabetes and who have a regular consumption pattern and incur significantly large expenditure on medicines. The pharmacy maintains a list of customers and tracks their buying. Usually, either the customer informs Subhiksha before running out of medicines or Subhiksha checks with the customer periodically because it knows the consumption pattern of the customer. Thus, it practically runs with very little stock, and based on the requirements of regular customers, it buys the required medicines from drug wholesalers and passes on the standard discount of 10 per cent to its customers. Most of the customers are old people and a 10 per cent discount translates into huge savings for the customers. Subhiksha sees the pharmacy business as community service. The pharmacy store can be managed with just two people (to take care of two shifts) per store.

In the telecom business, Subhiksha offers handsets, accessories and charge cards from leading brands including Nokia, Motorola, Sony Ericsson, LG and Samsung. Since the number of SKUs offered is less than 100, managing store operations for the telecom business is relatively simpler than the supermarket business. The telecom store can be managed with just two people (to take care of two shifts) per store.

The Indiranagar supermarket sells both branded and private label FMCGs and grocery products in addition to F&V. Within the supermarket 30 per cent space is allocated to F&V and the balance 70 per cent is kept for FMCG and grocery products. Sixth cross road, where it is located, is mainly a residential area with a few commercial properties. Unlike other supermarkets where customers are expected to drive down to the store, the store focuses on customers in the neighbourhood so that they do not have to worry about parking space. Also, locating the store on a side street allows Subhiksha to manage the store at much lower rental costs compared to other organized retail players.

Other supermarkets, for example, Food World, More and MK retail, also operate within a 1-kilometre radius of many *kirana* stores. See Exhibit 1 for the location of the store. *Kirana* stores are typical mom and pop stores. Nilgiris, a supermarket chain, has recently opened an outlet that is close to the store. Hypermarket Big Bazaar is also close by. Despite the increase in competition, Aravindan feels that "the store business has continued to grow in sales because of the unique selling proposition—offering value to the customer through lower price and convenience".

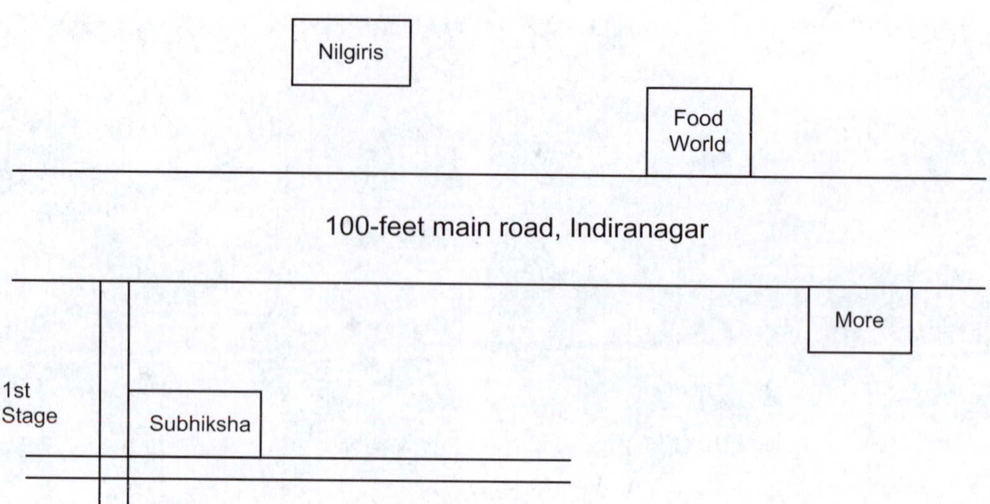


**Exhibit 1**

Location of the Indiranagar store.

The number of households within the 1-kilometre catchment area is 2,000. A typical household (with three consumption units) spends on average Rs 4,000 a month groceries and F&V (excluding non-vegetarian products and clothing).[1] Generally, sales per month are Rs 1–1.2 million in the FMCG and grocery units and Rs 0.3 million in F&V.

Supermarket retail outlet manager (ROM) Santosh grew up in Bangalore. He then worked in a retail outlet in Dubai for a few years. A few months ago, he joined Subhiksha as ROM. Describing the retail business (see Exhibits 2 and 3 for details), he said the following:

> During a day, there is a predictable peak between 5.30 and 9 p.m. In a month, the peak occurs in the first 10 days. Also, in general, business on the weekends is higher. It also depends upon factors such as weather and festivals—one day we would be heading for a record sales, when sudden heavy rains ruin the business for the remaining part of the day.

***Exhibit 2:*** ***Distribution of the FMCG and grocery sales at the Indiranagar supermarket for a peak day and a non-peak day.***

| Peak day (3 February 2008) | | | Non-peak day (20 February 2008) | | |
|---|---|---|---|---|---|
| **Time** | **Number of bills** | **Sales (Rs)** | **Time** | **Number of bills** | **Sales (Rs)** |
| 9–10 a.m. | 9 | 1,134 | 9–10 a.m. | 4 | 95 |
| 10–11 a.m. | 7 | 3,748 | 10–11 a.m. | 10 | 1,330 |
| 11–12 a.m. | 17 | 8,415 | 11–12 a.m. | 9 | 965 |
| 12–1 p.m. | 10 | 1,654 | 12–1 p.m. | 16 | 1,313 |
| 1–2 p.m. | 9 | 4,270 | 1–2 p.m. | 11 | 791 |
| 2–3 p.m. | 20 | 2,833 | 2–3 p.m. | 3 | 848 |
| 3–4 p.m. | 7 | 3,081 | 3–4 p.m. | 3 | 277 |
| 4–5 p.m. | 16 | 8,350 | 4–5 p.m. | 7 | 426 |
| 5–6 p.m. | 15 | 7,802 | 5–6 p.m. | 16 | 4,640 |
| 6–7 p.m. | 28 | 4,430 | 6–7 p.m. | 17 | 2,939 |
| 7–8 p.m. | 22 | 3,509 | 7–8 p.m. | 19 | 3,827 |
| 8–9 p.m. | 25 | 11,717 | 8–9 p.m. | 14 | 1,854 |
| 9–10 p.m. | 9 | 4,631 | 9–10 p.m. | 4 | 917 |
| Total | 194 | 65,574 | Total | 133 | 20,222 |

***Exhibit 3:* Distribution of FMCG, grocery and F&V sales in the Indiranagar supermarket for a month (February 2008).**

| FMCG and grocery | | | Fruits and vegetables | | |
|---|---|---|---|---|---|
| **Day** | **Number of bills** | **Sales (Rs)** | **Day** | **Number of bills** | **Sales (Rs)** |
| 1 | 145 | 32,522 | 1 | 190 | 10,060 |
| 2 | 180 | 52,249 | 2 | 216 | 11,375 |
| 3 | 194 | 65,575 | 3 | 230 | 12,625 |
| 4 | 160 | 52,309 | 4 | 216 | 10,254 |
| 5 | 159 | 29,411 | 5 | 205 | 9,388 |
| 6 | 155 | 32,759 | 6 | 217 | 10,650 |
| 7 | 163 | 36,688 | 7 | 199 | 10,242 |
| 8 | 155 | 29,410 | 8 | 186 | 9,438 |
| 9 | 164 | 37,328 | 9 | 235 | 13,968 |
| 10 | 153 | 33,245 | 10 | 198 | 11,764 |
| 11 | 119 | 16,741 | 11 | 177 | 8,511 |
| 12 | 88 | 17,444 | 12 | 178 | 8,134 |
| 13 | 136 | 21,811 | 13 | 216 | 9,050 |
| 14 | 134 | 25,030 | 14 | 190 | 7,793 |
| 15 | 137 | 25,242 | 15 | 206 | 10,434 |
| 16 | 181 | 38,133 | 16 | 246 | 14,203 |
| 17 | 123 | 22,161 | 17 | 205 | 11,917 |
| 18 | 115 | 24,042 | 18 | 206 | 9,744 |
| 19 | 128 | 32,296 | 19 | 207 | 9,834 |
| 20 | 133 | 20,222 | 20 | 215 | 9,458 |
| 21 | 142 | 25,725 | 21 | 208 | 8,513 |
| 22 | 152 | 23,549 | 22 | 197 | 7,271 |
| 23 | 187 | 40,498 | 23 | 228 | 12,758 |
| 24 | 153 | 30,112 | 24 | 203 | 11,933 |
| 25 | 151 | 26,598 | 25 | 217 | 9,665 |
| 26 | 119 | 28,615 | 26 | 129 | 7,105 |
| 27 | 119 | 23,340 | 27 | 177 | 6,741 |
| 28 | 152 | 28,073 | 28 | 178 | 7,746 |
| 29 | 149 | 29,553 | 29 | 182 | 7,315 |

## Category Management

The supermarket stocks around 1,200 SKUs that can take care of approximately 90 per cent of the customer's value requirements. Typically, the store would stock only products from the top three brands in each product category (sunflower oil, detergent powder – 1-kg packs, etc.). This conscious choice allows the store to manage its operations at much lower inventories, which in turn allows it to offer 8–10 per cent discounts to its customers. To satisfy complete customer requirement would require a bigger store space and explosion in the inventory costs with additional SKUs. In general, stocked SKUs move fast and generate consistent and considerable volume (Figure 2).

Since the store stocks only 1,200 SKUs in the supermarket, it monitors its assortment very carefully so that it really captures the average 90 per cent value requirements of customers. Arvindan commented:

> When we start a new store we make lot of effort to understand the requirement of the target customers in the catchment area. Usually, by end of 6 months we have good idea about the ideal assortment for the store. If a customer finds that we can provide only 50–60 per cent of his requirement he may not visit us again. For 10 per cent of his requirement that is not served by the store he does not mind visiting other stores in the neighbourhood.

**Figure 2**

Supermarket and fruits and vegetables areas.

In FMCGs, 950 branded merchandise and private label SKUs were stocked, while in grocery 150 branded and private label SKUs were sold. From a consumer perspective, brands reduce the uncertainty while choosing products and also give a guarantee of quality.[2] As a result, consumers in general like them.

Private labels provide Subhiksha control over the design and quality of its products. Tatwa, Aaharam and Subhiksha are some examples of private labels kept in the outlet. Subramanian explains, "Besides offering more margins, private labels give the store an opportunity to attract and retain customers due to their low prices". The store sells the private label wheat flour with a maximum retail price of Rs 140 for a 5-kg pack at a Subhiksha price of Rs 102 (Figure 3).

## *Marketing*

The "every day low pricing" model is always followed at the store. In the supermarket, it usually offers an average discount of 8–10 per cent on all the products irrespective of the quantity purchased with reference to the maximum retail price (MRP). The discounts do not change frequently. *Kirana* stores sell their products at the MRP.

The display for each SKU shows both MRP and Subhiksha store price so that consumers can do price comparisons while shopping (Figure 3). Also, the customer bill shows the total discount received so that consumers can estimate the savings realized after the store visit (see

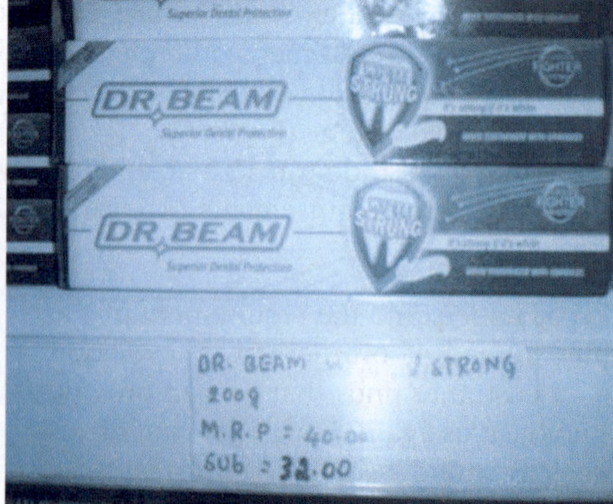

**Figure 3**

Price comparison display (on a shelf and on an SKU).

Exhibit 4). Exhibit 5 shows the price comparison chart for select FMCG and grocery SKUs. Aravindan adds, "the store offers deep discounts on rice and lentils in Bangalore and Mysore stores".

The individual outlet cannot vary the prices; the regional unit sets the price and sends the price list to the store to follow. Given that the terms of trade with all the FMCG companies are fixed centrally, it is mainly grocery items where there is great flexibility in pricing at the regional level. But within a region prices are identical across all stores. On the other hand, some discount retailers such as Wal-Mart allow its managers to vary the prices to handle local competition.[3]

The highest sales occur in the first 10 days of each month. The store always runs some promotional schemes in this time period to increase the footfalls. One of the promotional schemes is as follows: "For purchases above 500, 750, 1,000 rupees, get 25, 50, 75 rupees off, respectively". Sometimes, gift-based promotional schemes are also offered.

Subhiksha periodically advertises through a local radio channel *Radio Mirchi*. It does not advertise through local newspapers and catalogue mailings. TV advertisements are minimal for

SUBHIKSHA TRADING SERVICES LTD.,
#259, 6TH CROSS, 1ST STAGE, INDIRA NAGAR.

TIN: 29030386569 DL NO. KA/BNG.20/21/877

------------------------------CASH BILL----------------------------

Bill No. : INV\16345\till
Date : 13/04/2008 12:22
User ID : BM

KA 100021506

| SNo | Pro. Name | MRP | Rate | Qty | Amt | Del |
|---|---|---|---|---|---|---|
| 1 | TOOR DAL REGULAR 1KG | 60.00 | 45.45 | 1 | 45.45 | |
| 2 | MOONG WHOLE 200 GM | 16.00 | 10.45 | 1 | 10.45 | |
| 3 | RAJMA WHILE 500 GM | 34.00 | 28.45 | 1 | 28.45 | |
| 4 | SUBHIKSHA WHOLE WHEAT ATTA – 5 KG | 140.00 | 102.00 | 1 | 102.00 | |
| 5 | SURF EXCEL MATIC | 80.00 | 74.00 | 1 | 74.00 | |
| 6 | COLGATE TOTAL 500 GM | 59.00 | 57.65 | 1 | 57.65 | |
| 7 | RED LABEL TEA | 108 | 102 | 1 | 102.00 | |
| 8 | SPRITE-600 ML | 20.00 | 18.50 | 1 | 18.50 | |
| 9 | VIM BAR | 17.00 | 15.60 | 1 | 15.60 | |
| 10 | BRITANIA ORANGE-100GM | 12.00 | 10.00 | 1 | 10.00 | |

-----------------Items 10-----------------------Tot. Qty 15.00

Total: 464.10
Serv. Chg: .00
Round Off: .00
Net Amt: 464.10

Indian rupees Four Hundred Sixty Four and Ten Paisa Only

Today's savings for you 81.90

ALL CREDIT/DEBIT CARDS ACCEPTED
FOR FREE HOME DELIVERY CALL:
INCLUSIVE OF ALL TAXES: THANK YOU VISIT AGAIN

**Exhibit 4**

Indiranagar store Subhiksha bill.

***Exhibit 5:* Price comparison chart for select FMCG and grocery products in Indiranagar store (13 April 2008).**

| Private label SKU | Subhiksha | More | Nilgiris | *Kirana* |
|---|---|---|---|---|
| Sprite (600 ml) | 18.5 | 20.00 | * | 20.00 |
| Vim bar | 15.6 | 17.00 | 17.00 | 17.00 |
| Red label tea (500 g) | 102.00 | 111.00 | * | 111.00 |
| Colgate Total toothpaste (150 g) | 57.65 | 59.00 | 59.00 | 59.00 |
| Surf Excelmatic (500 g) | 74.00 | 80.00 | 80.00 | 80.00 |
| Britannia Orange Cream (100 g) | 10.00 | 12.00 | 12.00 | 12.00 |
| *Rajma* (500 g) | 28.45 (SP) | 33.00 (MP) | 25.00 (NP) | 26.00 |
| *Toor dal* (1 kg) | 45.45 (SP) | 51.00 (MP) | 55.50 (NP) | 50.00 |
| Whole wheat *atta* (5 kg) | 102 (SP) | 115 (MP) | 98 (NP) | 140 (AA) |
| *Moong dal* (200 g) | 10.45 (SP) | 14.00 (MP) | 8.50 (NP) | 11.00 |

SP, Subhiksha private label; MP, More private label; NP, Nilgiris private label; AA, Ashirwad whole wheat *Atta* (5 kg).
*Either not stocked or out of stock.

the supermarket. Whenever Subhiksha starts operations in any city it does carry out newspaper or local TV advertisements to create awareness. It mainly depends on word of mouth as a primary medium of reaching people within the catchment area. So, unlike other organized retail players, advertisement expenses for Subhiksha are at a relatively lower level.

## The Crew

The store is open between 9 a.m. and 10 p.m. and is operated by a staff of 13 people (scheduled in two shifts) in the supermarket. In the supermarket, two cashiers, two customer sales representatives (CSRs) and two sales assistants are present in one shift. Some employees work in the split shift (morning and evening slots). One person is assigned for the home delivery. Cashiers handle billing and payment transactions. CSRs are mainly responsible for store cleaning and hygiene, merchandizing and stock arrangements. They also assist customers when sales assistants are busy. Sales assistants mainly interact with customers and assist them in the shopping process. During the peak period, the main focus is on the sales and checkout counters, whereas during the lean period, the focus shifts to cleanliness, inventory check up, stock arrangements and so on. During the first 10 days, almost all the staff members are present in the store and avoid being absent at work.

An ROM and an assistant ROM manage the store in two shifts.

Most of the staff are young men and women, and new to the retail business. Continuous on-the-job training is provided to them. The cashier is the most "sought after" position. Staff members are motivated and promoted to this position based on performance. Also, from the monetary perspective, if a store achieves the sales target, all the staff members in the shop are rewarded by coupons through which they can buy materials from the store. The staff members are trained at the cashier counter during the lean period. Staff requirement at the cashier counter depends upon the business volume. Trained staff members are used at the cashier counter during the peak period. There are two checkout counters for the FMCG and grocery units and one checkout counter for the F&V unit. During the lean period, the FMCG and grocery units and the F&V section have one cashier each who do all the operations—billing, weighing and packaging items. The F&V unit has its own billing counter in addition to two counters allocated for FMCG and grocery products. During peak periods, as the number of customers increase, the number of shopping baskets increase and the queue at the checkout counters increase, more staff members are shifted to the three counters. Santosh remembers the following: "Once, a shopping basket bill was Rs 3,315 against an average bill of Rs 212, and that increased the queue". The additional staff members work at the third checkout counter, the weighing unit in the F&V section and the billed items packaging unit. The average time taken for a customer with a bill of about Rs 250 is about two minutes at the billing counter. But a customer with a large basket will need to spend about five minutes at the checkout counter.

Attrition is one of the main problems faced by the store. Santosh explains, "Subhiksha employees are in huge demand in the retail market, which currently lacks skilled manpower—there is a separate queue for them during recruitments".

It affects the performance of the store. At checkout counters, it takes time for new cashiers to pick up speed. Also, staff members personally know most of the regular customers and their requirements. The ROM addresses the problem of attrition by trying to mitigate the grievances of employees it if it is a small salary or relocation issue.

## Management

An ROM and an assistant ROM manage the store in two shifts. The responsibilities of the managers include managing category-wise sales, increasing customer interactions (the business volume on a daily basis), maintaining store hygiene, managing personnel, F&V wastage and adhering to planogram (identification placards that indicate where each category of product is kept) and they are evaluated based on these parameters.

Since investment in terms of inventory and operating costs in terms of rent, wages, electricity and security are governed centrally the ROM can increase the profitability of the store mainly by increasing category-wise sales and reducing F&V wastages and shrinkage. The Indiranagar supermarket would have a fixed cost of Rs 120 thousand per month, whereas rent, wages, electricity and security account for 40,000, 60,000, 10,000 and 1,000, respectively. A typical store would have Rs 600 thousand in supermarket inventory. For discounts stores, gross margins are much lower compared to other retail players, so generating high sales per store is of highest importance.

The organization has an SBU structure wherein each SBU in the region has the responsibility for operations, which includes the stores and warehouses in the region. The ROM reports to the business development manager (BDM). See Exhibit 6 for the organizational structure. For a cluster of six to seven stores, there is one BDM who in turn reports to the AVP. The BDM monitors the stores on category-wise sales and F&V wastage. He/she also visits the competitor's stores in the region. The AVP would visit each store once in 10 days.

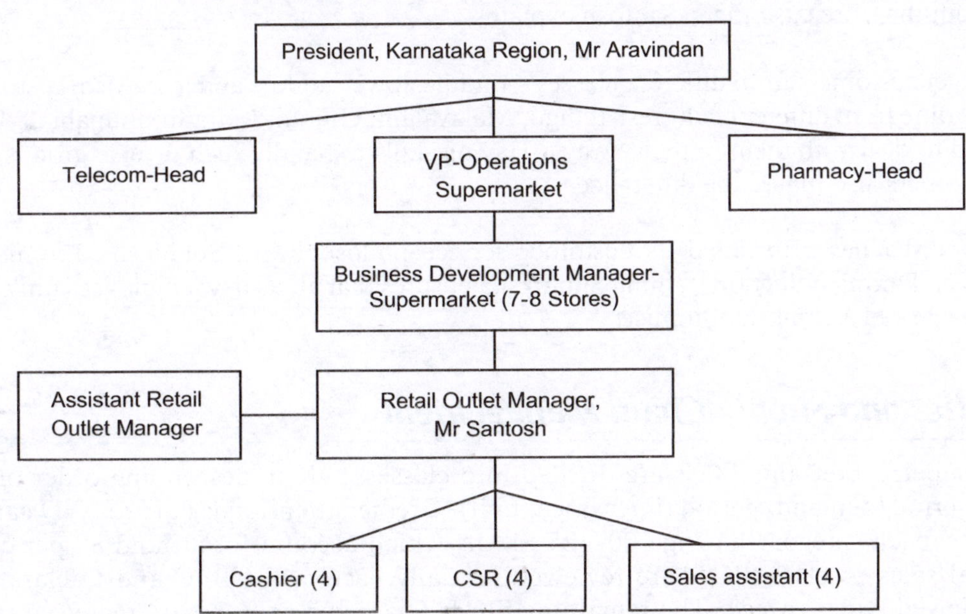


**Exhibit 6**

Organizational structure for the Karnataka region supermarket operations.

Sourcing is a centralized function. For local sourcing of F&V and for a few local brands, a few sourcing personnel would operate from the region, but they report to centralized sourcing. This allows Subhiksha to take advantage of economies of scale. For example, with each major FMCG companies, it negotiates annual terms of trade as it can get significant discounts because of the sheer scale of operations. Central sourcing allows them to develop an in-depth understanding in sourcing food grains and fruits and vegetables across the country.

## Customer Service

Industrial engineering techniques are used to standardize and reduce the time required to process a bill. Barcode technology is used for branded FMCG and grocery products. Private labels provide the product and pricing information. In F&V, some SKUs such as onions are pre-packed in bags. The goal is to speed up the checkout process and to reduce paperwork. Subhiksha has fixed an internal target, that is, once a customer has selected items in the supermarket she or he should be able to leave the Subhiksha premise in five minutes. This does pose a challenge on peak days when many customers visit the store and are also likely to have large number of items in the shopping list.

In Chennai and a few other locations, Subhiksha has put in place a two-stage checkout process wherein billing is done at stage 1 and the payment is received at stage 2. This is an outcome of a detailed time and motion study carried out by Subhiksha.

A customer can place an order on phone. The store staff takes the customer order and informs the customer about the expected delivery time. The order is packed and billed at the store and is kept in the storage area. Also, the customer can do shopping in the store and can ask for a home delivery if the basket is large. A person (dedicated to home delivery) delivers the order to the customer in an autorickshaw. Around 15 per cent of the business is through the home delivery channel. Billing for such orders is done when there is low load at the checkout counters. Though the store expects atleast Rs 1,000 worth of goods to be purchased per shopping basket for home delivery, the ROM adds, "the store did a home delivery for a basket of Rs 250 for a 'regular' customer who was pregnant". Some of the home delivery customers are located at a distance of 2–3 km. The store transport cost for home delivery works out to be 1–1.5 per cent of home delivery sales value. Though the main catchment of the store is households located within 1–1.5 km, home delivery allows the store to extend its reach to households that are located at distances of 2–3 km.

About the store customers, Santosh explains,

> We get customers from different classes—middle, lower-middle and low. Also, customers come from different cultures: Telugu, Malayalam, Gujrati, Marathi, Punjabi ... We need to deal with them in their "way". Having skills to handle such diverse groups of customers also makes the difference.

Subhiksha has articulated its customer service philosophy in Subhiksha Promise (see Exhibit 7). During induction training Subhiksha ensures that all its new employees understand the true spirit of Subhiksha Promise.

## Logistics and Supply Chain Management

In the supermarket, the SKUs are divided into classes A–K in descending order of sales value/period (demand/period times price/unit). Greater attention is paid to A–D category products, each category having 100–125 SKUs, which account for around 80 per cent of the total sales. A-class SKUs are reviewed on daily basis while B, C and D class SKUs are reviewed twice a week. The remaining SKUs (classified as E–K) are reviewed twice a

### The Subhiksha Promise

**Lowest Prices & Great Savings Everyday!**

Subhiksha offers all goods at sharply discounted prices so that consumers can genuinely save in every transaction. Unlike other stores, the low prices at Subhiksha are not limited to a few goods or to a few specific days. Customers can get the same discounted prices on all items, on all days and irrespective of whether they make a small or a big purchase. In fact, the discounts and customer savings at Subhiksha are 4-5 times that offered by other small and big retailers.

**Wide Selection of Goods**

Subhiksha offers consumers a wide selection to choose from:

**Supermarket**
Quality groceries, packaged foods, cosmetics and toiletries, household provisions etc., sourced from the best brands in India - all available at the lowest prices.

**Fruits and vegetables**
A large range of fresh fruits and vegetables is sourced directly from farms on city outskirts and made available to consumers at very reasonable prices. Consumers get the freshest produce at the best prices.

**Pharmacy**
All medicines are made available to consumers at a flat 10% discount. This is especially helpful for elderly consumers and those who are on continuous medication.

**Telecom**
Subhiksha is now India's largest mobile retailer and offers handsets, accessories and charge cards from all leading brands including Nokia, Motorola, Sony Ericsson, LG, Samsung, etc., at the lowest prices. You do not just get genuine company warranty but also amazing exchange offers on old phones, spot finance offers and much more.

**Guaranteed Delivery**

Subhiksha guarantees to deliver the exact product you have selected. In case you have received a different product, or if the product was damaged in transit, please contact us within the stipulated time period and we will ensure that we replace it or refund you for it. Please note, we will deliver goods within the committed time period, but there could be occasional delays. We will contact you, in case deliveries are expected to get delayed.

**Our Simple Return Policy**

If you have purchased something at Subhiksha and are not satisfied with its quality, then you can return the same to us; no questions asked, as long as it is in its original packaging and accompanied by its invoice. We will even make the return process simple for you - just contact our call centre number or nearest Subhiksha outlet from where the stock was delivered to you and we'll arrange to pick up the product from your home. Alternatively, you could drop it off at the nearest Subhiksha store.

**Real Customer Support**

For any information that you require you could contact our call centre at 60607777. Be assured that when you call us, you can talk to someone who will be able to help resolve your problems.

**Exhibit 7**

The Subhiksha promise.

month. Also, the savings benefits to the customers depend upon the class and are decreasing in A–K order. Based on the category of item, maximum batch quantity (MBQ) levels are fixed for each SKU. For example, the MBQ for an A-category item would be fixed at three days of demand while the same for B–D categories would be fixed at 6 days of demand. The MBQ level for E–K categories is fixed at 15 days of demand. Since demand varies across months, the MBQ is usually fixed keeping in mind the peak demand observed during the last three months. Since the peak demand observed for Maggi masala noodle was 10 units, the MBQ for the same is fixed at 30 units. Of course, it is possible that a few stores in the region, which are called hub stores (Indiranagar is a hub store), may have stock that is higher than the MBQ levels. As a philosophy, Subhiksha believes that if there is excess inventory in the system it should be kept in the store rather than in the warehouse subject to availability of storage space. So if there is excess stock it is kept in the hub store because the lead time of supply from the hub store to any other store is half a day compared to two days from the warehouse.

Over a week, every day, a subset of SKUs is scheduled for a review (e.g., on Monday, 100 A and 125 B class SKUs are scheduled for review) such that the review norms are met for each SKU. Except for Sunday this process is carried out all days in week. Store staff physically checks and records the opening stocks of the SKUs (scheduled for review) in the morning. The store compiles and sends electronically this information in the early afternoon to the MIS department located in the area head office. Similarly, all the stores in Bangalore send the information electronically to the MIS department. In the afternoon, the MIS department, using the Manual Indenting module, compares the closing stocks with MBQs to compute the store-wise requirements for each SKU under review. The review schedule is the same across all stores. MIS raises indents for each store and electronically sends them to the Hoskote warehouse in the late evening. Microsoft Excel is used for the computations. Exhibit 8 shows the opening stocks, receipts and sales of three SKUs in February 2008 for the Indiranagar supermarket store. Usually, the required supply for a store is made from the warehouse but it is not unusual to carry out inter-store transfer based on demand and inventory situations at relevant stores. On an average, the store inventory is around Rs 600 thousand. Inventory levels are very tightly controlled at the store. Unlike other firms, Subhiksha manages to operate with inventory turns close to about 20–25.

***Exhibit 8:*** ***Opening stocks and sales of three SKUs (February 2008).***

| Date | Maggi Noodle Masala (400 g; MBQ-30) | | Pepsodent 2-in-1 (MBQ-15) | | Gemini Sunflower Oil (1 litre; MBQ-70) | |
|---|---|---|---|---|---|---|
| | **Sales** | **OS** | **Sales** | **OS** | **Sales** | **OS** |
| 1 | 9 | 19 | 1 | 21 | 10 | 19 |
| 2 | 10 | 10 | 2 | 15 | 17 | 410 |
| 3 | 5 | 0 | 3 | 13 | 14 | 393 |
| 4 | 9 | 2 | 1 | 10 | 21 | 86 |
| 5 | 5 | 5 | 1 | 9 | 14 | 65 |
| 6 | 0 | 0 | 0 | 8 | 15 | 51 |
| 7 | 0 | 0 | 1 | 7 | 18 | 207 |
| 8 | 0 | 5 | 1 | 7 | 10 | 188 |
| 9 | 3 | 5 | 0 | 6 | 18 | 178 |
| 10 | 4 | 2 | 1 | 6 | 10 | 160 |
| 11 | 0 | 0 | 1 | 5 | 12 | 150 |
| 12 | 0 | 0 | 2 | 4 | 14 | 138 |
| 13 | 0 | 0 | 1 | 2 | 7 | 124 |
| 14 | 10 | 15 | 0 | 1 | 13 | 117 |
| 15 | 5 | 5 | 2 | 6 | 11 | 104 |
| 16 | 0 | 0 | 2 | 4 | 14 | 93 |
| 17 | 0 | 0 | 2 | 2 | 14 | 79 |
| 18 | 0 | 0 | 2 | 0 | 15 | 65 |
| 19 | 0 | 0 | 0 | 11 | 26 | 50 |
| 20 | 9 | 9 | 0 | 11 | 1 | 1 |
| 21 | 9 | 12 | 0 | 11 | 4 | 12 |
| 22 | 5 | 10 | 0 | 17 | 1 | 140 |
| 23 | 8 | 0 | 4 | 17 | 11 | 72 |
| 24 | 9 | 21 | 0 | 13 | 13 | 61 |
| 25 | 5 | 12 | 2 | 13 | 2 | 48 |
| 26 | 5 | 32 | 0 | 11 | 10 | 41 |
| 27 | 7 | 22 | 2 | 21 | 8 | 39 |
| 28 | 1 | 19 | 0 | 19 | 7 | 31 |
| 29 | 0 | 27 | 0 | 19 | 5 | 24 |

OS, opening stock (physically checked).
Opening stock = Opening stock (yesterday) + receipts* (yesterday) – sales (yesterday).
*Negative receipt means transfer of Indiranagar store stock to other stores.

On fixing MBQ levels, an employee explains,

> Sometimes one cannot depend on past data. For example, when sunflower oil prices increased by 40 per cent, one would expect that people would substitute the same with cooking oil of lower price range. Such information is used while deciding inventory levels (e.g., Gemini Sunflower Oil in February changed from 150 to 70). Similarly, there are some items with special schemes. But one has to be careful, because one can have too many variables and too many manual changes which will result in a loss of control. So we resist making too many changes. Once in a month, we seriously look at MBQ levels.

The store works with static MBQ levels, that is, the MBQ does not change within a month. But in Chennai stores, Subhiksha is experimenting with dynamic MBQ levels wherein reviewing forecast is carried for relevant days in a time horizon and MBQ levels keep changing during a month. For example, in the initial part of the month demand is expected to be on the higher side so one should carry high inventory, whereas during rest of month the demand is on the lower side and one can work with lower inventory. Dynamic MBQ levels also capture day of the month, day of the week and the effect of festivals in the forecasting horizon. By implementing dynamic MBQ, the average inventory in the system is further reduced.

Losses due to pilferage or breakages, known as "shrinkage ratio", in Indian retail are around 1.5 per cent of the total sales and erode the bottom line. Because of the small size of the store, the store can closely monitor the shopping process. Also, while unloading of the goods (shipped by the warehouse) from the locked vehicle, the store manager and an external security person are present. The manager thoroughly checks the quantity shipped with the dispatch list sent by the warehouse with the security person. The unloaded stock is then kept in the storage area. Ten per cent of space in the store is allocated for storage. Also, the store carries out an audit of the store inventory every month. Training is provided to the staff regarding the handling methods for different kinds of goods. Shrinkage costs at Subhiksha are 0.25 per cent of the total sales.

F&V has its own challenges. In the past, it was difficult to ensure that F&V would reach early in the morning. Now, the delivery schedule is such that they reach the store before 7.30 a.m. Unlike other products, some of the F&V SKUs require special handling because of the fragile nature of the products. Further, it is necessary to keep them shuffling to ensure that the offering looks fresh.

The warehouse delivers goods to the store two times a day (F&V in morning and supermarket in the afternoon). The order fulfilment lead time of the warehouse is two days after receiving the store indents.

## The Hoskote Warehouse

### *Background*

The Hoskote warehouse is located close to Hoskote town, which is near Bangalore (25 km). It is connected to Bangalore via a national highway (Old Madras road). The warehouse serves Bangalore (55 stores) and Mysore (4 stores). Firms such as Amway and ITC have set up their warehouses in the neighbourhood and the warehouse enjoys synergies associated with the "warehouse atmosphere". For example, obtaining good Internet connectivity at comparatively lower cost is because of the existing infrastructure.

The total area of the warehouse is 66,000 square feet. The warehouse has the capacity to serve around 80 stores. Around 200 people work in the warehouse, which does not have any fancy fittings, flooring or air-conditioning.

It operates on a lease contract for 15 years (which is renewable) and is open 24 hours a day (backend). The average business volume per year is Rs 800 million, with Rs 10 million investment in the inventory at the warehouse. The total cost of managing the warehouse is Rs 24 million per year. Transport costs are significant (Rs 10 million per year) whereas rental cost is not high (Rs 2.5 million). Security is managed by an external agency.

The warehouse is divided into different parts according to storage and operations performed. Mobile, pharmacy, grocery, FMCG, retail, F&V bins and store belts are storage locations. There are separate areas for segregation and batch making, private label processing and loading and unloading operations. A small section of the warehouse is allocated for office work. Products are assigned to the bins based on similarity. For example, all "cleaning"-related products are assigned to the same bin.

## Warehouse Operations

Indents raised by the manual indenting module are electronically dispatched to the warehouse in the late evening. The next day, both total and store-wise requirements for each SKU (FMCG and grocery products except rice and wheat) list is given to the segregation and batch making unit. The required number of units for each SKU is withdrawn from the FMCG and grocery bins. The remaining units from open boxes are immediately transferred to the retail bins where the products are more closely watched. A store-wise dispatch list is used for batch making. The withdrawn units of each SKU are divided into different batch making groups which allocate and subsequently put them into the boxes for the respective stores. If an SKU is not available in sufficient quantities, demand is met in the order of A-B-C stores such that each store gets at least five units. The store classification is done based on the sales performance. The boxes are packed and sealed and then shifted to the area allocated for the corresponding store in its belt. A small sheet, which displays the name of the store, is stapled to each box. The SKUs are ready for dispatch to the store in the late evening and is dispatched the next day. Loading, unloading, internal product movements, sorting and batch making operations are manual in nature.

In the F&V section, in the evening and night shifts, the SKUs are made ready for dispatch to the stores as per the dispatch list.

## Transportation Management

Stores are combined into belts such that the transportation distance is minimized.

A typical vehicle serves the demand of 3–4 stores (called as belt). The belt area layout, loading and unloading processes are sequenced to increase speed and to reduce interference and hence possibilities of damage. The first unload–last load rule is followed. The F&V SKUs are dispatched to the stores early in the morning (6 a.m.). The truck returns back to the warehouse at 11 a.m. Around 14 vehicles (both 407 and 709 trucks) are used for transport. In the afternoon at 1 p.m., the FMCG and grocery boxes waiting in the belt area are dispatched to the stores. A few additional vehicles are needed for FMCG dispatch.

The transportation is managed by a third party that can make available additional vehicles at short notice. The transport agreement consists of minimum commitment plus additional rupees per kilometre clause. Vehicle shutters are locked before it leaves the warehouse and are opened when it reaches the store unloading area in the presence of a security person and the ROM. The keys are not with the transport agency.

## Grocery Processing

The warehouse purchases some grocery as raw material (e.g., rice from mills) and processes it to produce private label products. Some private label processes are manual while some operations are done using machines. For example, a worker puts lentils in a private

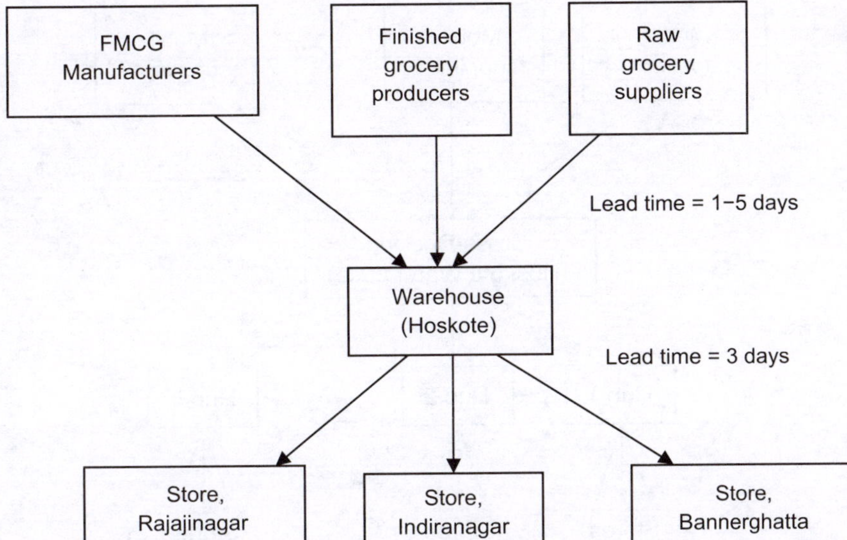


**Exhibit 9**

Subhiksha supermarket supply chain.

label bag, weighs it and then seals the bag. Raw materials are checked for quality at the warehouse as per the set standards. Further, a few samples are sent to Chennai for quality checks. These finished products are kept in the private label bins. Barcode technology is not used for the private labels; instead, the price and the product information are printed on the bag at the warehouse. Since grocery items are procured in bulk, it does contribute to some amount of inventory.

## Supply Management

Around 40 suppliers (10 are major suppliers) feed the warehouse as per the supply norms. For example, Hindustan Lever Limited supplies each day. Most of the suppliers supply products from their depots in Karnataka. As a result, the warehouse does not incur sales tax. Some suppliers expect a minimum order quantity. Nestle supplies once in a week (from its Chennai depot) to manage the transportation costs. The average supplier lead time varies from one to five days. Exhibit 9 shows the supermarket supply chain. Similar to store operations, at the warehouse, SKU review schedules are followed as per review norms. Closing stocks at the warehouse are reported and are compared with the MBQ (of the warehouse) to raise indents from the warehouse to suppliers. Fill rate is a major problem that affects the warehouse operations. Warehouse manager, Rajendra adds,

> Unfortunately, the service levels of most of the FMCG suppliers are in the range of 70–85 per cent and we do not know which items would not be supplied, and lack of supply from FMCG players can directly translate into stock-outs at our stores because we work with lean stores. Though FMCG players have started reserving stock for organized retail, we feel that some of these players have still not geared themselves to handle organized retail like us who would like to run tight ships.

## Mobile Retail Logistics Management

The warehouse does not stock mobile products and instead acts as a cross-docking point as shown in Exhibit 10. Five hubs have been set up in Bangalore to store the products and to feed the different regions of the city. The hubs raise indents and suppliers deliver the

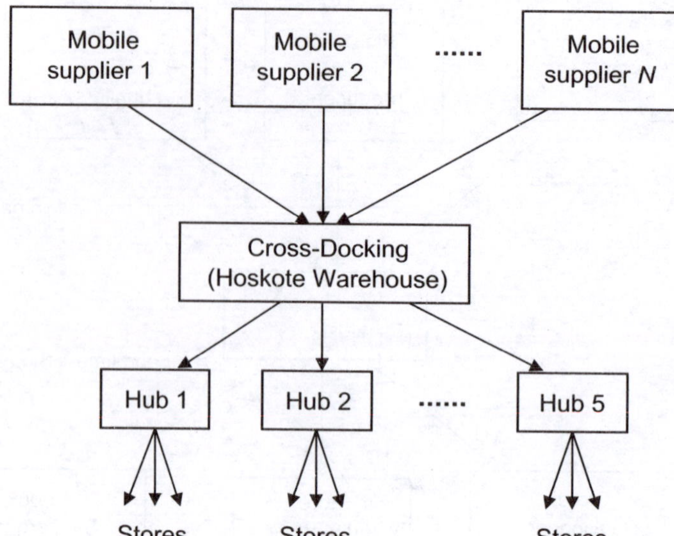


**Exhibit 10**

Subhiksha mobile retail supply chain.

products to the warehouse where the receipts are recorded. The products are segregated as per the hub requirements and are immediately delivered to the hubs. Hubs deliver the products to the stores mainly using motorcycles. Because the hubs are located in the city, the transportation time and cost to the store is small.

## Human Resource Management

The workers at the warehouses are supplied by a contractor based in Delhi. It can make available additional workers at short notice. Most of the workers are not familiar with the retail business. Training is provided to them on a continuous basis to increase their understanding of the warehouse processes. Some important training areas include product handling methods, batch making and segregation process information and product quality check methods.

## Inventory Management

As per Subhiksha philosophy, the warehouse should operate as a cross-docking point and should not keep much inventory. Its warehouse inventory in the mobile and F&V product lines is close to zero. In grocery, since it buys material in bulk and also has some processing lead time, it does maintain some amount of inventory. Given that service levels offered by FMCG suppliers are not at the desirable level, the warehouse ends up maintaining some amount of stock for FMCG products. Within FMCG products, it maintains stocks for items in the A–D categories. For other categories it acts as a cross-docking point.

The total inventory in a region (inventory at stores within a region and inventory at the warehouse) is very tightly controlled. There is a hard limit within which a region is supposed to operate. Category-wise inventory levels are monitored by RS himself.

## Information Technology

MIS and the warehouse currently use an existing backend IT system (Microsoft Office). The top management feels that these tools take a lot of time for routine operations and manual report generations. Stress levels also increase considerably. Subhiksha plans to implement SAP R3 system to manage the backend operations, and store indenting and purchasing operations.

The store will continue to use and further develop the existing and internally developed 3V2 software. This software is continuously improved to build customer intelligence. Loyalty cards are used to understand individual customer shopping behaviour and preferences. The backend system would however be made compatible with the store system. Also, a 1-MBPS line would be used to connect both front and backend operations.

## Future

On his way home, Aravindan was reflecting on the kind of question that RS is likely to raise on Monday:

> Competition in the organized retail in Bangalore has been increasing. Reliance, Birla and Tata groups are adding stores. As a result, retaining existing customers will become even more important. In addition, we must increase the number of footfalls and the average bill size. After all, being a discount retailer, we need to increase the business volume. Are our marketing, category management and business planning activities heading in the right direction? It is good that our business in Bangalore has been growing. But are our SCMs really efficient? Can we further improve them? Are we scheduling and planning our staff in a right manner?

## Notes

1. See http://india.gov.in/govt/studies/report/2.pdf.
2. Note on the retailing industry, Harvard Business School Note, May 1998 (9-598-148).
3. Wal-Mart Stores, Inc, Harvard Business School Case (9-794-024).

## Discussion Questions

1. Examine the various decisions made by Subhiksha and how they match (fit or align) with the business model of Subhiksha?
2. Identify the key challenges faced by Subhiksha. How important is assortment planning and inventory management for Subhiksha?
3. Evaluate the performance of the Indiranagar store on forecasting and inventory management. For your analysis you may like to focus on the three items listed in Exhibit 8.
4. Examine the supply chain practices followed by Subhiksha for different categories.
5. How does Subhiksha manage variation in demand within a month and variation within a day?

# Subhiksha: Managing Store Operations (B)*

In January 2009, Subhiksha, a chain of retail stores across India, announced that it would close down all of its stores by May 2009. What was startling to many, including its investors, was the rapid pace at which the retail chain was forced to shut down its operations.

Started by R. Subramanian, an IIM A and IIT Chennai alumnus, Subhiksha opened its first store at Chennai in 1997. It started out as a discount store offering products at prices which were much lower than other retail outlets. Gaining popularity over the years, Subhiksha expanded rapidly and became known as the company that had found the secret to organized retailing in India. By the year 2007, Subhiksha was a retail store chain, employing close to 15,000. It had stores in most towns in India and sales of close to ₹2,300 crores.

Subhiksha's troubles began to surface in late 2008. By September 2008, Subhiksha had defaulted on its payments and had trouble keeping pace with its operations. With no payments, Subhiksha's vendors stopped supplying products to Subhiksha's stores, resulting in empty shelves at its stores. The employees at Subhiksha were the next to be hit. The employees either received lesser salaries or cheques which were not honoured because there wasn't enough money in the Subhiksha's bank accounts. In the words of a manager at Subhiksha, "We had no money, no work, nothing". As fear and panic spread among the employees, Subhiksha decided to close down its operations.

One of the major reasons attributed to Subhiksha's failure was its ability to cope with the rapid expansion it had followed in previous three years. The retail sector in India had become competitive, and many private players had entered the space including large business groups in India, i.e., Reliance and Aditya Birla group. In response to the competitive trends, Subhiksha had decided to expand rapidly, opening many stores in a short span of time. Subhiksha wanted to be the first store in many towns in India and quickly moved to new locations in India. It had also diversified into medical, grocery, IT, and mobile stores. The capital investments for stores were high and Subhiksha's finances were in disarray, failing to keep pace and maintain a steady cash flow for its expanding operations.

With thin margins, poor cash flow, Subhiksha's supply chain management started to show signs of failure as well. With payments to vendors not made on time, Subhiksha's stores were not adequately stocked with products. Unhappy customers started to desert Subhiksha's stores as well. Poor employee morale also led to discontent among the employees, and Subhiksha's retail operations became financially unsustainable.

---

*This case has been prepared by Mandar Nayak and Professor Janat Shah, IIM Udaipur.

An important reason that added to Subhiksha's troubles was the global slowdown that accompanied Subhiksha's woes. In September 2008, following the closure of Lehmann Brothers, a century old investment bank, the world's financial industry was in the middle of one of the worst crisis since 1930. The foreign banks, such as HSBC and Standard Chartered, with which Subhiksha had bank accounts, were not interested to help Subhiksha out, given the financial crisis. Most of the banks refused to undertake restructuring Subhiksha's loans, and raising capital to tide over the crisis became impossible for Subhiksha.

***Source:*** Adapted from news and articles available on the internet;

1. http://articles.economictimes.indiatimes.com/2011-08-25/news/29926869_1_r-subramanian-subhiksha-renu-ka-ramnath accessed 9th May, 2015.
2. http://trak.in/tags/business/2010/08/07/indian-retail-industry-subhiksha-vishal-retail-fall/ accessed 9th May, 2015.
3. http://www.icmrindia.org/casestudies/catalogue/Business%20Strategy/BSTR333.htm accessed 9th May, 2015.

# Suguna Poultry Farm Ltd.*

It was a typical spring evening in March, when Ashok Tyagi, Regional Manager Karnataka, Suguna Poultry Farm Ltd., was wading through the busy Bangalore traffic after a hard day's work at office. He and his team had just finished finalizing the budget draft for the coming financial year 2007–2008. As he waited in his car endlessly at the next traffic signal, he had ample time to reflect on the recent performance of the company. The Karnataka region had just achieved a 30% increase in sales over the previous year, raising Suguna's market share in the region close to 32%.

Although he was satisfied with the previous year's sales, he was determined to improve the company performance in the following year. Ashok was confident of achieving a sales growth of 35% as projected in the draft; yet, he had an uneasy feeling. The bottom-line of Suguna depended critically on the prevailing market price of poultry and the forecasts always seemed shaky. He wondered if it was possible for the company to figure out a way to handle the vagaries of the poultry industry and sustain the existing growth rate.

---

*Priyanshu Gupta, Prasanna Natekar and Janat Shah prepared this case for class discussion. This case is not intended to serve as an endorsement, source of primary data, or to show effective or inefficient handling of decision or business processes.

# Suguna Poultry

Started in 1984 at Coimbatore, Tamil Nadu, Suguna Poultry was a leading poultry company in India. It spread to 10 states across the country with a business value of ₹14.01 billion[1] in the year 2006–2007. The organizational structure and financial data for the company is given in Exhibits 1 and 2, respectively.

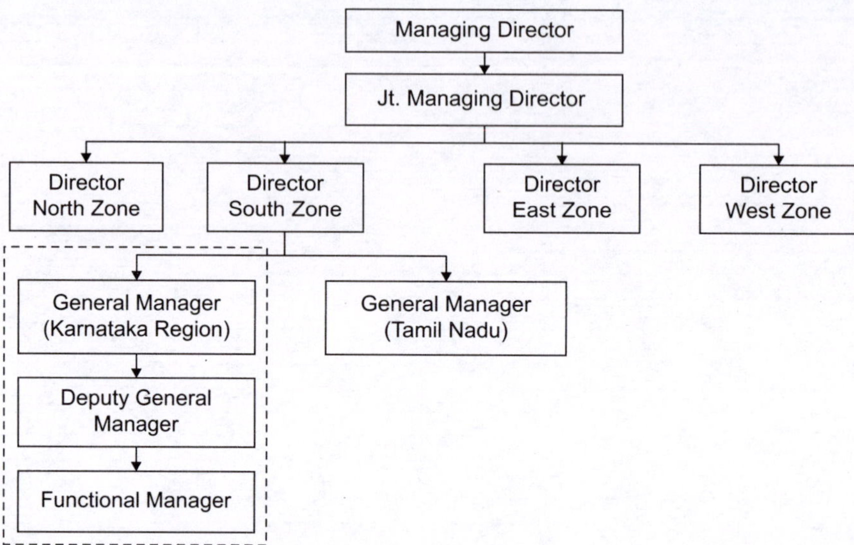


**Exhibit 1**

Organization structure.

***Exhibit 2: Suguna financials.***[6]

| Suguna Financials (in Rs. Cr)[7] | March 2006 | March 2005 | March 2004 | March 2003 | March 2002 |
|---|---|---|---|---|---|
| Equity paid up | 15 | 15 | 15 | 5 | 5 |
| Net worth | 126.47 | 69.75 | 49.1 | 24.28 | 18.65 |
| Capital employed | 418.89 | 271.32 | 170.08 | 56.36 | 38.35 |
| Gross block | 160.65 | 119.65 | 101.03 | 46.31 | 32.16 |
| Net working capital (incl. def. tax) | 255.87 | 163.92 | 84.58 | 16.12 | 10.07 |
| Current assets (incl. def. tax) | 364.47 | 232.9 | 141.09 | 39.99 | 30.86 |
| Current liabilities and provisions | 108.6 | 68.98 | 56.51 | 23.87 | 20.79 |
| Total assets/liabilities (excl reval) | 526.92 | 339.68 | 226.3 | 80.08 | 59.14 |
| Gross sales | 1,075.76 | 819.05 | 557.34 | 198.33 | 145.92 |
| Net sales | 1,075.76 | 819.05 | 557.34 | 198.33 | 145.92 |
| Other income | 25.29 | 2.89 | 1.98 | 0.4 | 0.22 |
| Value of output | 1,075.76 | 824.22 | 546.91 | 196.41 | 157.13 |
| Cost of production | 774.72 | 751.79 | 494.16 | 178.29 | 145.19 |
| Selling cost | 0 | 12.54 | 10.37 | 1.29 | 0.47 |
| PAT | 61.85 | 26.89 | 11.18 | 6.73 | 5.55 |

The company followed a unique model of contract farming to raise poultry and was in touch with more than 13,000 farmers. This model provided a good source of income for farmers and at the same time benefited the company. Suguna had been investing in R&D and technology to manage its rapid expansion and improve the quality of its products. It had an excellent R&D facility where it conducted extensive research in developing optimum feed variety and improving the quality of the broiler. It had partnerships with some leading companies in the business such as Aviagen from UK and Lohmann Tierzucht Gmbh from Germany. These companies supplied high quality poultry breeds to Suguna, which were used for breeding purposes. Suguna also managed to procure funds from The International Finance Corporation, the private sector arm of the World Bank Group and the largest multilateral provider of finance for private enterprises in developing countries.[2]

With its unique business model and strong emphasis on quality, Suguna emerged as the fastest growing company in the poultry industry and had plans to capture 20% of the national poultry market and a sales turnover of ₹30 billion by 2010.[3]

Suguna divided the organization geographically into four zones, each headed by a Director. A zone comprised major regional markets. Typically, a region comprised a major state (such as Karnataka), 2–3 smaller states, or part of a state with well-developed market. Each region was a profit centre. While most regions were managed independently, in times of crisis, e.g., excess or shortfall in demand, broilers were transported across regions. The Karnataka region was managed from the regional office at Bangalore, which was one of the major markets for Suguna in the region. Each region was further subdivided into branches comprising major production centres. Coordination was achieved between adjoining branches through regular interactions. Sometimes, traders were encouraged to source their supplies from adjoining branches to meet any shortfall in demand. Every quarter, the senior management team assembled at the corporate headquarters to take stock of the situation and devise future strategies.

## The Poultry Industry

The Indian poultry industry employed about 2 million people, and contributed 1.1% to the national income.[4] Among all the meat categories, poultry meat experienced the highest growth rate, at over 15% per annum, compared to the overall meat industry growth rate of 5% per annum. In 2010, poultry meat constituted approximately 25% of the total meat production in the country. The industry was dominated by the private sector and majority of the poultry producers still belonged to the unorganized sector. Only a few large players in the industry such as Suguna have been able to flourish. No single player was large enough to be able to influence the price decisively. Typically, in India, most chicken were sold live at various small retail shops. Only 2–3% of the total meat produced was sold in processed and branded form.

The nature of poultry meat introduced some unique challenges to the industry. Poultry meat is perishable and ensuring that there is adequate supply of chicken to meet variable customer demand requires a fine balancing act. The chicks are sensitive and perishable products that need to be handled carefully. The broilers have a certain optimum growth period after which diminishing returns set in if the bird life is prolonged. Hence, timely sale decisions need to be taken to optimize on costs.

The broiler birds were reared in a large number of distinct farms, which means the production was decentralized unlike most other industries. The overall demand for poultry was highly variable. Since poultry is typically a commodity, this demand uncertainty was typically manifested in price uncertainty. The perishable nature of the chicken forced suppliers to make distress sales. This coupled with low margins (10–15%) in the industry could have a major impact on profitability.

Breeding growth cycle of broilers typically lasted about 6 weeks. However, the value chain started much before through the life of parent and grandparent birds which had a 65–70 week lifecycles. Hence, there was a significant lead-time from the time the grandparents were set into production until the broilers were ready for sale. Moreover, the breeding cycle could not be altered easily; hence, the producers had to reduce their lead-times.[5]

## Value Chain

The value chain in the poultry industry started with the grandparent stage where high-yielding varieties of chicken were imported. They gave rise to parents which are further bred. The parent hens then laid eggs which would be used for broiler chicken. Exhibit 3 gives a diagrammatic representation of the value chain.

**Exhibit 3**

Poultry value chain.[8]

## Grandparent

The typical cost of a grandparent was around ₹3,500. The company set up a specialized farm at Hosur (near Bangalore) for housing the grandparent chicks. Extreme quality standards were followed which included specialized feed, medication, temperature control, and even specific norms for the attending veterinarians.

The grandparents followed nearly a 1.5-year lifecycle. Suguna Poultry imported grandparent chicks in batches every 13 weeks. The male–female ratio was generally maintained at about 1:10 in all the farms. The grandparent hen would start laying eggs from nearly the 25th week and continue to do so until almost the 68th week of its lifecycle. Subsequently, it was culled. In its lifetime, a hen laid around 180 eggs. Owing to the high standards followed by Suguna, not all eggs were selected for hatching, and by the time the hatching process was complete, only about 90 day-old-chicks (DOCs) were found to be of good quality.

## Parent

The eggs laid by the grandparents were taken to the hatcheries. Typically, it took around 3 weeks, that is, around 21 days for the eggs to hatch. The hatching efficiency at Suguna was close to 80%. To ensure good quality parent birds, all chicks up to the 16th week were reared at the company-owned farms. Strict quality standards were enforced at all farms, a minimum of 3 sq. feet area per chick was allotted.

Subsequently, the chicks were transferred to various parent farms which were owned by Suguna, franchise-owned, or leased. The parent lifecycle mirrored the lifecycle of the grandparents. However, parents were generally cross-bred to ensure a high yield and good quality broiler eggs. The parent laid around 180 eggs in its lifetime out of which only around 90% eggs were selected for subsequent stages of production.

Through modification of feed, the egg-laying period of the parent bird could be delayed by a few weeks, a phenomenon known as force moulting. However, beyond 4–5 weeks, it was difficult to control egg production by the bird and had adverse consequences on the lifecycle of the bird. Moreover, egg production by the bird subsequent to force moulting was lower. Therefore, owing to the adverse consequences on the biological lifecycle of parent bird, Suguna seldom used this approach for managing its production. The broiler eggs laid by the parent bird were kept in a cold room for about 1 week to delay hatching if the company expected a fall in its demand. If the fall in demand was likely to persist, the company could destroy the broiler eggs to cut down on its subsequent feed and other production costs.

## Broiler Chicken

The broiler eggs were hatched in various hatcheries, subsequent to which, one-day-old chicks were transported to various broiler farms. The broiler farms were managed by a number of farmers on a contract basis. Suguna took care of transporting the broiler chicks to the broiler farms, regular supply of feed to the chicks, administering veterinary care, and supervising the quality and other functions, whereas the farmers were responsible for providing shed, water, labour, etc. Standard operating procedures including the daily feeding charts were provided to each farmer, indicating their responsibilities, and periodic inspections were done to ensure the same. The farm size ensured that the available area per chick was 1 sq. ft. For every 15,000 chicks reared per week in 20 broiler farms, a supervisor was appointed to conduct periodic checks inspecting the body weight of chicks on a weekly basis.

A broiler attained its maximum weight (1.8–2 kg) around the 40th to 42nd day. These chickens were then sold in the market. After the 42nd day, the diminishing marginal returns on the feed became significant. Hence, it was difficult to defer the sale of broiler after this day and beyond the 45th day, even the efficacy of vaccine decreased and mortality increased substantially. The body weight of the chicks could be modified by around 10% by varying the quality of feed given to the chicks. As a result, the chicks could gain their optimal body weight between 38 and 42 days depending on the feed given to them.

The replacement cycle of a broiler farm was typically 9 weeks including 2–3 weeks to take care of the hygiene and sanitation. As a result, almost 30–35% farms were empty at any point of time. Exhibit 4 gives the time line of the entire value chain. The total production cost averaged close to ₹29 per kg of broiler for Karnataka region in the year 2005–2006. With escalation in costs, it was expected to be close to ₹31 per kg in 2007–2008. Suguna incurred fixed costs of close to ₹3 million per month in Karnataka. The average breakup of the costs involved from the hatched egg to the final broiler is given in Exhibit 5.

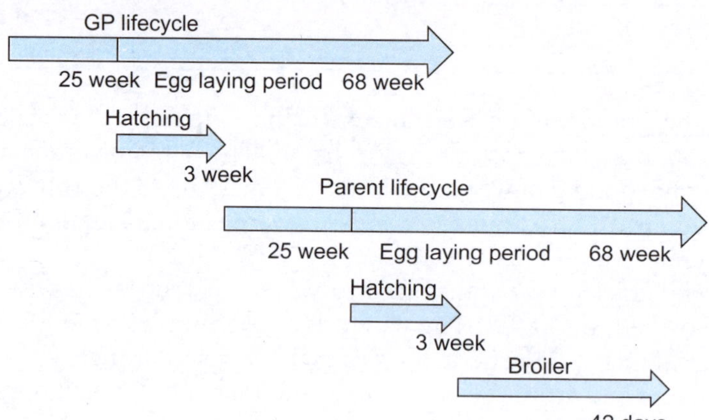


**Exhibit 4**

Time line from GP to broiler chick.

***Exhibit 5:* Average cost breakup in value chain of live broiler produced (Rs. per kg)**

| | |
|---|---|
| **Purchase of hatchable eggs by the hatcheries** | **3.12** |
| Hatch efficiency | 0.83 |
| So, effective cost of hatched eggs | 3.75 |
| Medicine cost of DOC | 0.02 |
| Manufacturing Expenses | 0.42 |
| Repairs & Maintenance | 0.06 |
| Administrative Expenses | 0.01 |
| **Total cost of DOC** | **4.27** |
| Feed cost of broiler | 22.66 |
| Medicine cost | 0.48 |
| Growing charges to farmers | 2.35 |
| Delivery charges feed | 0.53 |
| Chick Delivery Charges | 0.33 |
| Production staff salary | 0.18 |
| Other Direct Expenditure | 0.23 |
| **Total production cost** | **31.04** |

## Distribution

The broiler chickens were sold to large traders who further sold them to retailers. The traders were allocated to a particular branch of Suguna. Subsequently, they picked up the broilers from the various farms in that branch at the daily price announced by Suguna. If the supply was not available, the traders were asked to collect their broilers from nearby branches. They were, however, compensated for the additional transportation costs. The traders sold the broilers to retailers or stocked them at their own retail outlets. Most of these shops were filthy and had unhygienic conditions. To overcome this and to ensure adequate quality standards, Suguna planned to forward integrate into starting its own brand of retail outlets. It planned to start its own culling centre and cold chain to sell processed and branded meat in the near future.

Suguna also considered venturing into selling frozen chicken. The chicken was frozen to the bone at –20°C so as to retain a certain amount of freshness. This would help increase the shelf life of chicken and bring about a positive change to the dynamics of the industry by giving poultry producers certain time to adjust to any market fluctuations. However, the success of this would depend a lot on the consumer preferences which so far had been averse to frozen/chilled chicken owing to two main reasons. First, the social mind block that butchered chicken was fresher and tastier. Second, the branded and packed frozen or chilled chicken had cost of infrastructure added to it making it costlier as compared to fresh chicken. Yet, noticeably a major Indian poultry producer had tried venturing into chilled chicken wherein the dressed chicken was immersed in ice or cold water at a given temperature for a specified period. This could increase the shelf life to a maximum of only 72 hours. After culling, the broiler was chilled to a lower temperature and then brought back to room temperature. Once this was done, the culled broiler could last for a longer period before it was sold. Another technique followed by some companies in India was to sell frozen broilers. Suguna was not keen on this technique as consumers' preferred fresh chicken to frozen ones. The chilling technique had the potential to provide the company more flexibility when responding to short-term price fluctuations.

## Feed

Suguna owned and operated feed mills to supply feed to its various farms, which included the broiler farms as well as the parent/grandparent farms. The feed generally comprised corn (60%), maize, and soya bean de-oiled cake (20%). This was further mixed with various medicines, nutrition supplements, etc. to ensure a balanced diet to the broiler. Among the ingredients, corn showed a high volatility in prices, whereas soya prices were more stable. Moreover, corn harvest was mainly obtained only once a year. Therefore, the company followed the policy of stocking the raw materials for the feed during harvest time. It bought the feed from either large traders or directly from farmers' cooperatives, or then, stocked it in its own warehouses. To supplement any shortfall in any ingredient, Suguna purchased it from the market. Typically, mineral supplements and feed additives were imported.

Different types of feed were provided to the birds at various stages of their lifecycle. For example, for the broiler, "pre-broiler starter" (PBS) was provided during the early stages, "broiler starter" (BS) during the growth stage, whereas "broiler finisher" (BF) was provided before the broiler chicken were ready for sale and culling. On an average, Suguna sent feed supply to a farm every week or as demanded by the particular farm. It used its own vehicles for the purpose.

Typically, the Feed Conversion Ratio (FCR) was around 1.8 for Suguna Poultry, that is, to increase the weight of a broiler by 1 kg, it had to be administered 1.8 kg of feed. Generally, the broiler gained a maximum weight of around 2 kg with an input feed of 3.6 kg. The feed quality had an immediate reflection in the broiler's health. Sometimes, the oil and fat content in the feed could be enhanced by a small amount during the 5th to 6th week of the broiler lifecycle so as to enable it to gain more weight. Thus, the day gain (weight increase during a day) was a function of the quality and quantity of the feed input. Typically, diminishing returns set into the broiler lifecycle around the 42nd day. Subsequently, it was unprofitable to keep the bird any longer. Exhibit 6 describes a typical relationship between day gain and feed input from 36th to 45th day of the broiler lifecycle.

## Price

Suguna followed a policy of announcing its daily prices in local newspapers and other media, which was based on the overall price prevailing in the market. The traders then picked up the broiler stock from the farms as per the agreement reached with the company based on the announced price. Usually, there was a significant differential in prices prevailing in different regions although the various adjoining branches within a region followed similar price trends. Suguna products commanded a premium owing to the greater meat to live weight ratio and better quality of meat.

One of the main challenges of the poultry industry was that the demand tended to be variable. However, the broilers had to be sold within a short span of 4–5 days. Hence, frequently there was a mismatch between supply and demand, which influenced the price drastically. This was further complicated by the fact that the broilers underwent batch production in various farms. It might happen that a farm with a large quantity of birds might make the broiler available in the market and because the broiler is a perishable product, large quantities will be sold within a span of 3–4 days regardless of the price. Exhibit 7 shows the average daily prices witnessed by Suguna in Karnataka region for a particular month. Suguna's field staff was typically able to predict probable prices for the coming week with a reasonable accuracy but grappled on its effective usage.

The price shot up considerably during Diwali, New Year, and other festivities when demand for poultry products was high. However, during the Shravana month, many people fasted and

***Exhibit 6:* Day gain and feed details.**

| | |
|---|---|
| Body weight after 35 days (kg) | 1.60 |
| Feed consumed till 35th day (kg) | 2.82 |
| Production cost excluding last week feed (Rs. per bird) | 51.11 |

| **Feed variety regular** | **Day 36** | **Day 37** | **Day 38** | **Day 39** | **Day 40** | **Day 41** | **Day 42** | **Day 43** | **Day 44** |
|---|---|---|---|---|---|---|---|---|---|
| Day gain/feed consumed | 0.42 | 0.46 | 0.49 | 0.49 | 0.45 | 0.37 | 0.26 | 0.18 | 0.07 |
| Feed consumed (g) | 150 | 150 | 150 | 150 | 150 | 150 | 150 | 150 | 150 |
| Cost of feed (Rs/tonne) | 11,200 | | | | | | | | |
| **Feed variety A (better)** | **Day 36** | **Day 37** | **Day 38** | **Day 39** | **Day 40** | **Day 41** | **Day 42** | **Day 43** | **Day 44** |
| Day gain/feed consumed | 0.52 | 0.51 | 0.45 | 0.31 | 0.27 | 0.18 | 0.10 | 0.08 | 0.02 |
| Feed consumed (g) | 150 | 150 | 150 | 150 | 150 | 150 | 150 | 150 | 150 |
| Cost of feed (Rs/tonne) | 11,700 | | | | | | | | |
| **Feed variety B (worse)** | **Day 36** | **Day 37** | **Day 38** | **Day 39** | **Day 40** | **Day 41** | **Day 42** | **Day 43** | **Day 44** |
| Day gain/feed consumed | 0.34 | 0.37 | 0.40 | 0.43 | 0.43 | 0.43 | 0.38 | 0.35 | 0.28 |
| Feed consumed (g) | 150 | 150 | 150 | 150 | 150 | 150 | 150 | 150 | 150 |
| Cost of feed (Rs/tonne) | 10,700 | | | | | | | | |

***Exhibit 7:* Daily sales information for August 2006 for Bangalore market.**

| Sales data | Quantity in kg | Average Rate (Rs./kg) | Sales Value (Rs.) |
|---|---|---|---|
| 1-Aug-06 | 32,686.2 | 23.83 | 7,78,999.1 |
| 2-Aug-06 | 11,405.8 | 23.9 | 2,72,589.5 |
| 3-Aug-06 | 19,867.9 | 24 | 4,76,778.4 |
| 4-Aug-06 | 12,897.2 | 23.79 | 3,06,809.8 |
| 5-Aug-06 | 12,506.65 | 23.6 | 2,95,177.7 |
| 6-Aug-06 | 13,033 | 25.72 | 3,35,181.5 |
| 7-Aug-06 | 23,670.8 | 26.66 | 6,30,988.9 |
| 8-Aug-06 | 40,108.6 | 29.81 | 11,95,731 |
| 9-Aug-06 | 7,310.1 | 31.98 | 2,33,783.2 |
| 10-Aug-06 | 13,359.9 | 31.99 | 4,27,402.3 |
| 11-Aug-06 | 7,580.8 | 31.93 | 2,42,042.9 |
| 12-Aug-06 | 9,128.5 | 31.78 | 2,90,095.2 |
| 13-Aug-06 | 9,107.8 | 28.66 | 2,60,992.5 |
| 14-Aug-06 | 12,352.9 | 26.67 | 3,29,492 |
| 15-Aug-06 | 85,786.8 | 26.69 | 22,89,939 |
| 16-Aug-06 | 10,479.5 | 26.86 | 2,81,468 |
| 17-Aug-06 | 20,884.1 | 26.79 | 5,59,579.5 |
| 18-Aug-06 | 14,349 | 27 | 3,87,423 |
| 19-Aug-06 | 22,027.1 | 25.69 | 5,65,915.2 |
| 20-Aug-06 | 9,292.7 | 24.97 | 2,32,018.5 |
| 21-Aug-06 | 18,811.3 | 24.89 | 4,68,189.6 |
| 22-Aug-06 | 37,898.4 | 24.79 | 9,39,457.1 |
| 23-Aug-06 | 22,102.3 | 25.73 | 5,68,623.2 |
| 24-Aug-06 | 56,641 | 26.61 | 15,07,489 |
| 25-Aug-06 | 31,673.5 | 28.59 | 9,05,692.6 |
| 26-Aug-06 | 26,531.3 | 29.83 | 7,91,537.1 |
| 27-Aug-06 | 15,552.9 | 31.78 | 4,94,247.3 |
| 28-Aug-06 | 23,148 | 32.81 | 7,59,471.7 |
| 29-Aug-06 | 27,038.5 | 32.75 | 8,85,472.3 |
| 30-Aug-06 | 7,168.1 | 33 | 2,36,547.3 |
| 31-Aug-06 | 11,346.2 | 31.84 | 3,61,274 |
| 1-Sep-06 | 12,415.7 | 30 | 3,72,471 |

consumed vegetarian food, drastically bringing down the prices. At the same time, incidents such as bird flu, which had occurred twice in the past three years, tended to entirely cripple the poultry industry by bringing down demand by almost 80%. Exhibit 8 indicates the monthly data for price and quantity sold by the Karnataka region over the past three years. For data on margins, please refer Exhibit 9 and Exhibit 10 for details on Suguna's budget for Karnataka for the year 2007–2008.

***Exhibit 8:*** ***Monthly price data for past years (Rs./kg).***

| Month | 2004–2005 | 2005–2006 | 2006–2007 |
|---|---|---|---|
| Apr | 30.32 | 27.21 | 28.90 |
| May | 36.06 | 33.55 | 36.94 |
| Jun | 33.42 | 35.21 | 35.89 |
| Jul | 32.12 | 33.87 | 32.20 |
| Aug | 24.50 | 27.67 | 26.61 |
| Sep | 26.79 | 29.64 | 29.57 |
| Oct | 29.74 | 28.83 | 30.72 |
| Nov | 34.31 | 28.83 | 31.52 |
| Dec | 29.25 | 27.00 | 27.75 |
| Jan | 37.55 | 37.60 | 35.87 |
| Feb | 31.57 | 30.52 | 28.51 |
| Mar | 26.65 | 17.47 | 21.92 |

***Exhibit 9:*** ***Karnataka regional broiler budget for 2007–2008.***

| **Budget (Rs. lakh)[9]** | **Apr-07** | **May-07** | **Jun-07** | **Jul-07** | **Aug-07** | **Sep-07** | **Oct-07** | **Nov-07** | **Dec-07** | **Jan-08** | **Feb-08** | **Mar-08** | **2007-08** |
|---|---|---|---|---|---|---|---|---|---|---|---|---|---|
| **Sold quantity (kg lakh)** | **51.88** | **50.53** | **53.46** | **55.25** | **58.55** | **74.65** | **74.99** | **78.97** | **75.44** | **60.72** | **61.53** | **76.02** | **771.99** |
| **Gross turnover** | **1581.00** | **1711.96** | **1855.63** | **1952.15** | **1676.15** | **2122.68** | **2269.45** | **2344.05** | **2435.58** | **2418.23** | **2429.30** | **2704.86** | **25501.03** |
| Less: discounts | 14.52 | 17.48 | 17.21 | 18.36 | 15.75 | 17.67 | 22.90 | 23.51 | 23.12 | 26.85 | 17.96 | 16.72 | 232.06 |
| Production cost | 1696.06 | 1662.01 | 1782.00 | 1830.97 | 2003.19 | 2603.35 | 2335.70 | 2240.23 | 2171.72 | 1763.91 | 1746.09 | 2307.24 | 24142.48 |
| **Gross profit** | **-129.58** | **32.47** | **56.42** | **102.81** | **-342.79** | **-498.34** | **-89.16** | **80.31** | **240.74** | **627.46** | **665.25** | **380.90** | **1126.49** |
| *Gross profit (% )* | *-8.20* | *1.90* | *3.04* | *5.27* | *-20.45* | *-23.48* | *-3.93* | *3.43* | *9.88* | *25.95* | *27.38* | *14.08* | *4.42* |
| Less: fixed Overheads | 12.93 | 12.94 | 12.44 | 12.43 | 12.43 | 14.05 | 16.90 | 12.43 | 14.11 | 14.04 | 12.45 | 12.45 | 159.61 |
| Net profit before royalty | -142.51 | 19.53 | 43.98 | 90.38 | -355.22 | -512.39 | -106.06 | 67.88 | 226.63 | 613.42 | 652.80 | 368.45 | 966.88 |
| Less : royalty | 12.97 | 12.63 | 13.36 | 13.81 | 14.64 | 18.66 | 18.75 | 19.74 | 18.86 | 15.18 | 15.38 | 19.00 | 193.00 |
| **Net profit after royalty** | **-155.48** | **6.90** | **30.61** | **76.57** | **-369.86** | **-531.05** | **-124.81** | **48.13** | **207.76** | **598.24** | **637.42** | **349.44** | **773.89** |
| *Net profit (%)* | *-9.83* | *0.40* | *1.65* | *3.92* | *-22.07* | *-25.02* | *-5.50* | *2.05* | *8.53* | *24.74* | *26.24* | *12.92* | *3.03* |

***Exhibit 10:*** ***Performance of select farms in Karnataka region for October 2007.***

| Farm Name | Chicks Housed | Mort % | FCR | Avg Wt | Mean Age | DGain | Chick Cost | Feed Cost | Medic Cost | Admin Cost | Growing Charges | Prod Cost | Sold Kg |
|---|---|---|---|---|---|---|---|---|---|---|---|---|---|
| Ambuja, Bennikal | 8,634 | 5.36 | 2.146 | 2.204 | 47 | 46.89 | 4.33 | 24.27 | 0.42 | 0.39 | 2.01 | 31.43 | 18,006 |
| Arogya P/F, Koralur | 23,323 | 5.78 | 1.984 | 2.028 | 44 | 46.09 | 4.70 | 22.44 | 0.50 | 0.43 | 2.36 | 30.42 | 44,822 |
| C.B.K, Chinnabelagondapalli | 13,890 | 3.21 | 1.962 | 2.381 | 45 | 52.91 | 3.93 | 22.20 | 0.35 | 0.35 | 2.77 | 29.59 | 32,025 |
| C.S P/F Bettadasanapura | 4,200 | 5.74 | 1.787 | 2.324 | 40 | 58.1 | 4.13 | 20.21 | 0.46 | 0.38 | 3.50 | 28.68 | 9,200 |
| Chowdeswara, Agra | 1,600 | 5.25 | 1.973 | 2.113 | 41 | 51.54 | 4.52 | 22.32 | 0.53 | 0.41 | 2.44 | 30.22 | 3,203 |
| Dharsan P/F | 10,760 | 6.09 | 2.094 | 1.998 | 43 | 46.47 | 4.82 | 23.69 | 0.42 | 0.43 | 1.89 | 31.25 | 20,188 |
| Jayanthi P/F, Chandapura | 30,505 | 9.12 | 2.308 | 1.873 | 44 | 42.57 | 5.29 | 26.10 | 0.70 | 0.48 | 1.78 | 34.36 | 52,100 |
| Jyothi P/F, Jekkeri | 11,410 | 3.66 | 1.956 | 2.303 | 43 | 53.56 | 4.07 | 22.13 | 0.32 | 0.37 | 2.78 | 29.67 | 25,320 |
| Sanjeev P/F, Belekere | 9,054 | 3.4 | 1.836 | 1.939 | 39 | 49.72 | 4.83 | 20.77 | 0.39 | 0.43 | 3.03 | 29.45 | 16,955 |

## Bird Flu

There was widespread bird flu epidemic during 2004 (in SE Asian countries) and February–March 2006 (in India). As a result, the demand for chicken fell substantially, making any production unprofitable. Hence, Suguna poultry had to resort to extreme measures to cut down on its resultant losses. Owing to the criticality to the production process, the grandparent and the parent stages were not disturbed. However, all the broiler eggs were destroyed. The feed supply to the existing broilers was reduced in both quantity as well as quality such that the feed cost to an existing bird was brought down. Despite these measures, Suguna suffered a huge decline in profits.

The sudden dip in prices in March 2006 could be attributed to bird flu, which struck the country in early 2006, resulting in an estimated loss of INR 3,000 Cr for the poultry industry. While incidences of bird flu were reported in subsequent years as well, they were minor in scale and spread out in comparison.

## Contracts with Farmers

As the broiler farms were owned by farmers, which was extremely critical for scaling up at a rapid pace, the relationship between the farmers and the company assumed great significance. This had a tremendous impact on the supply stability and production growth for Suguna. A contract farming model was adopted by Suguna wherein elaborate responsibilities of both parties were communicated. Standard operating procedures were made available to the farmers prescribing each and every minute detail. Regular monitoring by supervisors ensured adherence to the contract. Typically, a supervisor was allocated to 7–8 farms where he conducted a weekly inspection of the health of the birds so as to get certain early warning signals and ensure corrective action if necessary. This was especially critical during the 6th week of the broiler lifecycle, wherein the bird weight and culling day could be varied by changing the type of feed.

Suguna took responsibility for the feed supply to the farms since it believed that the feed was crucial to the quality of broiler produced. The cost to Suguna for the feed supplied to the farms was typically around ₹11.2/kg. However, there were some reports that farmers had sold part of the feed in the market. Ashok feels that as managing farmers is an important aspect of the contract farming model, it is critical to overcome such issues by tracking the performance of different farmers and using it to devise an appropriate incentive structure.

Suguna made extensive efforts to track the performance of its farmers. The production cost per kg of saleable broiler obtained from the broiler farm was used as a metric for measuring performance by the farmer. The farmer's performance manifested in the mortality of the birds as well as the average weight of broilers. Hence, by tracking the production cost and the FCR, it was possible to monitor the farmers. Typically, the FCR for a farm was expected to vary from 1.7 to 2.0 with an average of 1.8. The farmers were graded as A, B, C, D, and E depending on the production cost obtained from the farm. If the performance warranted a grade D or E, investigation was done to ascertain the cause of this poor performance. If, the fault was Suguna's, the farmer was suitably compensated. If the farmer continued to secure a grade D or E for three batches of production, all contracts with the farmer were terminated. Exhibit 11 displays the performance of farmers in Bangalore during October 2007. Suguna had seen a high variability in performance among the farmers, which significantly limited its capacity to control production costs. It was widely believed that there was an urgent need to reduce variability in performance in order to have greater control over the supply chain.

Suguna devised a unique compensation structure for the farmers so as to incentivize them for better performance. The production cost per kg, obtained using the standard costing approach, for the farm was used for determining the appropriate compensation, i.e., growing charges per kg to the farmer. The standard production cost used for devising this incentive

***Exhibit 11: Farmer incentive data.***

| Farmer Incentives Data—Standard Costing | |
|---|---|
| Average (most likely) FCR | 1.8 |
| Average body weight per bird (kg) | 2 |
| Cost of feed (Rs./kg) | 11 |
| Standard compensation (Rs./kg) | 2.5 |
| Incentive share of farmer | 30% |
| Share of company | 70% |

was ₹29/kg; the farmer was compensated ₹2.50/kg. Any increase in feed cost per kg at a farm directly increased the average production cost for the farm. For any increase or decrease in production cost, 30% of the benefit/cost was received by the farmer while the rest was shared by the company. However, the minimum growing charges were pegged at ₹2/kg. Please refer to Exhibit 11 for data on a typical contract between the farmers and Suguna.

# Improving Supply Chain Performance at Suguna

By the time Ashok reached home, he was convinced that an improvement in the supply chain was essential to maintain the company's steady growth. He made up his mind to take a relook at the sales and price data and other aspects of the supply chain and see if he could find anything that he might have missed earlier. He pondered if there was a way to handle short-term and long-term variabilities in prices in order to preserve margins. Further, was there a pattern to monthly prices that could be exploited to improve profitability? Ashok also decided to look into this whole aspect of farmers' contracts and incentive structure to ensure sustainable relationships with the farmers. He wanted to institute mechanisms for transfer of best practices across farmers in order to reduce variability in production performance. As the Bangalore market functioned more or less as an autonomous unit, he decided to concentrate on the data from this market first being quite sure that any improvement here could be easily replicated in other markets in which the company operated.

## Note

1. USD = ₹45
2. http://www.sugunapoultry.com/index.asp
3. "Suguna Poultry set to clock ₹1,100-cr sales",

   http://www.thehindubusinessline.com/2006/03/07/stories/2006030702151200.htm
4. http://www. ciionline. org/news/newsMain.asp?news_id=1262004125333PM
5. Supply Chain and Technology in the Poultry Industry, 'Maximize Profit through Optimizing the Supply Chain', USC Consulting Group
6. www.capitaline.com
7. 1 Crore = 10 million
8. www. sugunapoultry.com
9. 1 Lakh = 1,00,000

## Discussion Questions

1. Identify key challenges faced by Suguna?
2. Identify the levers available to Suguna to manage the short term price variability.
3. Is there any pattern in the monthly prices? Can Suguna exploit seasonality in prices and altering the import of grandparents to make use of the changes in monthly prices?
4. How do you explain the large differences in the performance of the different broiler farms are under the contract farming model? Examine the efficacy of existing contract structure for farmers:
   a. Is the current incentive system for farmers good enough to discourage farmers from selling feed outside?
   b. Is the contract structure the best for effective sharing of best practices across the farmers?
5. How can the logistics costs be reduced through placement of poultry in the various farms?

# BRAND AND COMPANY INDEX

# SUBJECT INDEX

## D

**X**



**Z**